Modern
Philosophies
of Education

Modern Philosophies

CONSULTING EDITOR: PAUL NASH, BOSTON UNIVERSITY

# of Education

John Paul Strain

COLLEGE OF EDUCATION

TEXAS TECH UNIVERSITY

RANDOM HOUSE, NEW YORK

Library of Congress Catalog Card Number: 72–108921

Standard Book Number: 394–30837–9
Manufactured in the United States of America

Designed by Ronald Farber

First Edition
987654

This book is dedicated to my mother and father

Acknowledgme...

Fifteen years in its conception, this book is a product of intensiv study on the nature of philosophy of education. It is a result of wide communication with philosophers and philosophers of education, especially as provided by the Philosophy of Education Society, where every point of view presented here has been defended and discussed. The Philosophy of Education Society and its regional affiliates (the author has had the privilege of belonging to the Southeastern, New England, Middle Atlantic, and Southwestern groups) are the sounding boards for the discipline. Their meetings—forums for the exchange of ideas among philosophers of education—have been an important source of data for the author. To this society and to all his colleagues in philosophy of education, he wishes to express his thanks.

Special gratitude must be given to those who have assisted with particular phases of the present work. The author is grateful to Harold Benjamin for portraying in his classes the importance of Colonel Francis Parker to progressive education, to Clifton Hall for directing the author to Karl Rosenkranz's Hegelian philosophy of education, to Charles Hartshorne and Gene Reeves for major insights into the philosophy of Alfred North Whitehead, to New England analytical philosophers and students of Israel Scheffler for views on Ordinary Language Philosophy, to Richard Morris for insight into the philosophies of Henry Margenau and F. S. C. Northrop, to Lyle Eddy for some personal facts about the life and thinking of John Dewey, to the literary scholars of Trinity College for explanations of the views of Northrop Frye, to Vincent Lin and James Donaldson for aid in clarifying the system of Natural Law Philosophy, to Ulrich Boehnke for personal information on the Tuebingen University philosophers and educators, to Mrs. Ellen Jones for checking the German translation of the Otto Bollnow reading, and to Philip Phenix for criticizing and commenting upon the book's introduction.

The author also wishes to extend his thanks to his graduate students at Emory University, Tufts University, Trinity College in Hartford, and Texas Tech University for the responses and appraisals they have made to the teaching of philosophy of education, and to his wife for the aid she has provided in putting the book together. Finally, to Paul Nash, friend and adviser, the author owes his deepest appreciation for the encouragement given him in the creation of this work.

Contents

THREE Emphasis Upon Values (Perennialism)

Modern
Philosophies
of Education

Introduction

Philosophers and philosophers of education alike have come to the conclusion that the technique of using the "deductive principle" to derive philosophies of education from philosophy is not feasible. Deducing educational system from metaphysical, epistemological, and value structures has no basis in either experience or logic.[1] Many scholars in the field of philosophy of education have taken this to mean that there are no grounds or rationales for identifying the various philosophies of education. A few of these scholars now disclaim the position approach in educational theory altogether.

The recognition of the falseness of the deductive format, however, does not mean that there are no differences between points of view in the field. On the contrary, there are strong indications that distinctions in general outlooks and methods do exist. Every philosopher of education knows that there are major differences in orientations in the field. The most vivid evidence for this is that scholars following a definite approach and method feel more akin to colleagues of similar leanings than to those with different frames of reference. Thus, those who avoid discussing orientations in philosophy of education neglect dimensions of the discipline that are necessary for clarifying the field and for understanding what intellectuals have to say about the basis of education. The purpose of this book, then, is to describe this aspect of philosophy of education, to illustrate the different positions in the field through selected readings, and to provide a useful nomenclature for understanding them.

The Function of Philosophy of Education

Essentially, the function of philosophy of education is to identify and clarify the justifications for education that come from a host of fields. In the main these justifications can be divided into three areas: theoretical,

---

[1] "If we seek the causes of the more prominent intellectual atrocities that have been committed in recent years in the name of philosophy of education, the chief source of offense is not difficult to identify. To play on the language of some of the worst offenders, it can be called the 'metaphysical-epistemological-axiological deductively formulated pedagogical theory principle', a name which should delight even the most fastidious practitioner of contemporary educanto. I refer, of course, to the questionable technique of deducing, or more often seeming to deduce educational theories from speculative theses on the nature of reality, knowledge, and the structure of value. This practice, which fortunately enjoys less respect today than a decade ago, determined the character of far too much of the literature and teaching of educational philosophy in the recent past." Sterling M. McMurrin, "On the Meaning of the Philosophy of Education," *The Monist*, 52 (January 1968), 60.

psychological, social. Philosophers of education include in the theoretical area all justifications for education that are derived from philosophy or theory. Clarification becomes an analysis of basic philosophical and theoretical ideas in relation to educational practices. The psychological dimension pertains to clarification of the justifications made from the nature of man or the nature of mind. Social justifications which the philosopher of education analyzes relate to man as a social being. These justifications recognize that man is educated in and for society, and, therefore, that social views must be a central consideration in matters of educational judgment. Philosophy of education can either make a creative contribution in any of these areas, or provide an analysis of the field as a whole with recognition given to contributions and contributors. The work of philosophy of education is difficult because educational activity is worldwide in scope and because the rationales proposed to justify it are so numerous. But the initial steps of naming the main areas of justification, gathering information about them, and relating them to educational practice have already been taken.

The preceding discussion raises a number of important points. The first is the recognition that philosophy of education has significant relationships with other areas of study. The field cannot rely on its own internal or inherent sources; it is not self-perpetuating. Philosophers of education must rely on other disciplines for the materials of educational justification. Philosophy, sociology, and psychology are the most important of these disciplines but philosophy of education is also concerned with other fields that are relevant to education. Philosophers of education have publicly recognized this aspect of their study in the statement of purpose of their major journal, *Educational Theory*:

> The journal will be devoted to publishing scholarly articles and studies in the foundations of education, and in related disciplines outside the field of education, which contribute to the advancement of educational theory.

The second major point is the necessity for dealing with the different orientations in education. Since there are so many fields with which philosophers of education must deal, each with its own orientations and perspectives, the different educational frames of reference must be accounted for, even though this may strike many as a frustrating task. These plural orientations, what William Frankena has termed "families of dispositions,"[2] cannot be nullified or overlooked. Approaches that suggest avoiding them—the problem-centered or syntopticon methods— abandon important data, and cannot satisfy specialists who seek to identify the main conditions of educational justification.

[2] William K. Frankena, "Educational Values and Goals: Some Dispositions to Be Fostered," *The Monist*, 52 (January 1968), 1–10.

The recognition that different frames of reference are pertinent to the philosophy of education is not a recent idea. For example, the statement of the Committee on the Nature and Function of the Discipline of the Philosophy of Education, which was adopted by the Philosophy of Education Society in 1953, reads, in part, as follows:

> The criteria guiding educational choices and policies may be consistent with the theories and concepts of one philosophical position (e.g., idealism, realism or experimentalism), or with some combination from the alternative positions. Therefore, in order that educational choices and policies be *philosophically* critical they must be made in view of the delineation and examination of alternative philosophical criteria: and anyone, thus oriented, is working within an area that is included in the subject matter of the discipline of the philosophy of education.[3]

The third major point relates to the place of practice in educational theory. Any theory of education is meaningless without some connection with, or suggestion of, its use in practice. Education as a profession is a practice, and any philosophy pertaining to it must reflect this. Some scholars speak as if practice were irrelevant to philosophy of education. However, education itself implies practice, and philosophy of education cannot exist unless it is based on educational justification relevant to practice.

Philosophy of Education as Distinguished from Dialogical Philosophy

The relationship of philosophy to philosophy of education must be defined in order to understand the function and performance of the latter. Because the title of the discipline includes the word "philosophy," it is often suggested that philosophy of education is simply a subdivision of philosophy proper just as aesthetic philosophy or philosophy of science is. However, although philosophy of education utilizes philosophy, it is not the same kind of discipline and does not follow the same procedures and aims. A scholar trained only in philosophy is not automatically an authority in philosophy of education. Conversely, a trained authority in philosophy of education is not by necessity automatically a philosopher. The two disciplines endeavor to do different sorts of scholarly work even though, as we shall see later, there may be much interaction. Philosophy of education can be distinguished from philosophy proper because its intentions are different and because its subject matter is unique. An explanation of dialogical philosophy will indicate the distinctiveness and requirements that must go into philosophy of education.

[3] "The Distinctive Nature of the Discipline of the Philosophy of Education," *Educational Theory*, 4 (January 1954), 2,3.

Philosophy proper, in its purest mode, is a dialogical tradition of philosophical topics that are dictated by the method of logical organization. As a philosopher arrives at a solution to a problem in metaphysics, epistemology, or value theory, his answers raise new issues and reveal logical weaknesses that must be criticized and analyzed by other philosophers. Philosophy is such a program of proposals and counterproposals, which has evolved into a historical tradition. The tradition began with Thales' metaphysical proposal of a concrete substance as the basic elementary thing in existence, followed by Anaximander's counterproposal of a heterogeneous mass of indefinite something. The remaining Greek philosophers continued the logical organization by providing their own suggestions and indicating new problems and new answers. The tradition continued with Plato, Aristotle, and other later ancient philosophers, in the medieval scholastics, and in the modern philosophers Descartes, Spinoza, Leibniz, Locke, Berkeley, Hume, Kant, and more recent philosophers. The enterprise is a search for a rational explanation of basic philosophical questions revealed in the discourse of the historical-critical tradition.

Viewed from this perspective, philosophy is a highly specialized subject that uses one fundamental tool, the tool of philosophical reasoning. The use of this tool distinguishes philosophy from all other disciplines. But the use of philosophical reasoning also makes dialogical philosophy an intellectual study that can be pursued by only a few intellectually gifted individuals. Of course, a larger number can discuss philosophy's history and development, but only a very small minority have the ability to contribute to its tradition.

Because philosophy is so specialized and uses reason in a highly unique way, its actual effect on society and its relevance to social problems has been questioned. In one sense, philosophy appears to have very little affect on society. A philosopher, in his spare time, may teach citizens and students the use of reason in general, and this may well have practical benefits. But such an activity is outside the specialized function of philosophical reasoning, unless one takes into account the slight chance that a talented member of the group may eventually acquire the insights to be able to add to the tradition. This chance is not great, however, and besides, even if the individual does ultimately make a contribution, it must be understood as a contribution primarily to the specialty of the dialogical tradition, rather than to society directly.

When philosophers digress from the dialogical tradition into matters of social practice, they are quite often discontented with the great separation between philosophical thinking and practical results. A vivid example of this disenchantment is the recent recognition that philosophy proper appears to have no effect on educational practice. As we have already indicated, educational practices are not deduced from philosophy. A practitioner seems to devise his practices by deciding which methods he instinctively feels are better than others. There appears to be no direct relation between philosophy and educational practice, a fact confirmed by a number of contemporary scholars in both philosophy and philosophy of education.

If philosophy does indeed have little influence in matters of practice, then we must again ask the crucial question: On what theoretical foundation is practice based? This question is central to the work and purpose of philosophy of education. We cannot answer simply that practice lacks any foundation, but rather seek to discover what is so fundamental to the wholeness of human experience that practice evolves from it. Some philosophers indicate that this component should not be dealt with by their specialty. If they are correct, then philosophy of education must look for another type of foundation, something broader, more inclusive than dialogical philosophy, and something that determines practice and the mode of education.

First of all, this something must be an involvement with society. It cannot be a program so abstract that it bears no useful relation to culture and to the way people live. Second, it must be related to knowledge because man's endeavors have to contain this cognitive component. Knowledge, on the other hand, is dependent on discoveries made about the world. This has to mean that the foundation must be one dependent upon history and historical circumstances. And third, since we know that practice is not deduced from philosophy, the foundation for practice must be found in the feelings, attitudes, and emotions of individuals. Those who devise practices will do so on the basis of their intuitive attractions to certain manners of proceeding rather than from logical deductions.

Such a foundation exists in human experience, but it has never been given a designation. We chose to apply the name "thought pattern" to such a foundation, not because the term reveals the central role of feeling and its structure as related to the experience of the individual, but because manifestations of cognitive and behavioral patterns can be identified in human activity and communication. A thought pattern is basically an internalized order within an individual for his behavior and thought, and it is this order that has relevancy to culture and society, is dependent on historical knowledge, and is the source upon which decisions of practice are made.

Philosophy of Education and "More General" Philosophy

The philosopher of education grants that dialogical philosophy is a highly specialized discipline that has very definite goals and distinctive manners of proceeding. He would not wish to interfere with the assumptions of this kind, nor to reduce philosophical inquiry to dealing strictly with practical concerns for the sake of philosophy of education. There is, however, evidence that certain philosophical presentations are related to definite thought patterns. Not every philosophy, of course, can be identified according to such a pattern, nor is it proper to say that every thought pattern has some one philosopher who represents it. It is true, however, that there are many thought patterns that find their most vivid manifestations in the work of some philosopher.

Does the fact that thought patterns are related to philosophy contradict what philosophy in general stands for? The answer is no, if we conceive philosophy in a less specialized way. We are already familiar with the narrow interpretation as reflected in the manners of dialogical philosophy. At the same time, however, we note that many cultural and temporal insights have entered into philosophy. Those who contributed to philosophical dialogue acquired insights and suggestions from their own cultural backgrounds. Is it possible, for example, to understand Plato without reference to the culture of Athens, or Thomas Aquinas apart from the religious patterns of the later Middle Ages, or John Locke and David Hume distinct from the seventeenth and eighteenth centuries in England? Indeed not, for while these philosophers followed the program of reason in dialogical philosophy, they were influenced by their times and gained philosophical insights from their particular cultures.

The cultural component of philosophical contributions suggests that more is involved in philosophical statements than philosophical reasoning, and this additional factor is the central interest of philosophers of education. We will accept the fact that dialogical philosophy in the opinion of most of its devotees has very little involvement in such matters. But some discipline should have the function of bringing these facts to bear on certain intellectual and practical concerns. Such a discipline must be related to the general rather than the dialogical program of philosophy, and it should be able to tie intellectual, cultural, and practical matters together and construct some kind of workable arrangement or scheme. I am suggesting that philosophy of education is such a discipline, although I do not attempt to exclude other disciplines from pursuing similar interests. But philosophy of education has reached the point where it can no longer fulfill its role without making use of the phenomenon of feeling as a dimension of man's intellectual life.

Thought Patterns and Generality

What is the nature of these thought patterns, which appear so central to the work of philosophy of education? Two characteristics can be inferred from the preceding discussion. First, thought patterns are temporal, occurring within the context of particular social circumstances that give them identity, data, and meaning. Second, thought patterns are psychological; they exist in the feeling-conceptual level of human experience. The feeling-conceptual level is an internalized order in terms of which specific cognitions are organized and data accepted or rejected. These two phases—the historical and psychological—function as the experiential conditions of thought patterns. On the other hand, thought patterns, if they are to be used in a discipline, must have a conceptually constructed meaning, a meaning that can show their relationships to various types of practices and ideas. This conceptually constructed meaning is important to philosophy of education because its aim is to clarify justifications for education by envisioning the influence of concepts on educational practice.

A valid framework for the conceptually constructed meaning is generality. Generality refers to conceptual classes and identities as units of thought. There are grades in the level of generalities, and these grades interact and are no doubt hierarchical. Each kind of generality provides a type of order that is necessary and important in experience and human thought. Generalities, thus, are not all the same—either in kind, relationships, or the functions performed. Though it is possible to identify a number of generalities involved in human thinking, three in particular keynote the work of philosophy of education: the generalities of thought patterns, generic notions, and ideas of specificity.

The generality called thought pattern is the wholistic feeling of intellectual pattern. Its basic function is systematization of cognitive processes. Primarily, this generality is a feeling scheme, a form of mental organization serving three intellectual functions. First, it coordinates in a coherent manner the ideas contained within the system. In this role, it provides an arrangement for the ideas already present to the beholder. In this way, it serves to coordinate the relationship between ideas. Second, this generality evaluates and controls the input data from experience and human communication. Data from the environment have to be processed and organized. It is the function of a thought pattern to accept and evaluate relevant data for the existing system, while eliminating extraneous material. Third, the generality of thought pattern functions in the construction of output. Expression demands order, and a unified system of cognitive regularity provides this order. To be coherent for others, one must not only use language correctly, but also have a theme or consistent conceptual system for relating statements.

The second important generality is that of generic notions. Generic notions are the key concepts that are the central pivots of a thought pattern. A thought pattern is a system and thus more general and more inclusive than generic notions. But generic notions are necessary in order to provide foci for the thought pattern. Generic notions are pivotal centers for the direction of thought and for the stimulation of specific ideas. They are key ideas around which the thought pattern develops, ideas that function for the feeling of importance. Generic notions function internally within the individual as do thought patterns; but unlike thought patterns, they are at root social rather than private. That is, these ideas are public generalities. They arise in the experiences, discoveries, and expositions of man in society. Because of this social element, generic notions are communicable. Individuals who possess the same thought pattern do so because they share common and public generic notions. Examples of generic notions are the struggle for survival from the doctrine of evolution, relativity of events from relativity theory, the dignity of man from Greek philosophy and literature, and the test of evidence from empirical science.

The third generality of special significance for philosophy of education is that of formal ideas expressed by words. These formal ideas are the communicative expressions of argument and claims that derive from a thought pattern, and are most noticeable in explanations of research and rational discourse. These ideas are most often products of careful thinking and experimental work. They are not complete entities in themselves, however. They stem from a thought pattern that gives them direction and order. Philosophy of education is very interested in this phase of expression because formal ideas expressed in words are the formal means of justification for education. Educational documents and treatises are at face value generalities of specific words and ideas.

In summary, philosophy of education utilizes three types of generalities: thought patterns as generality systems, generic notions as foci for the feeling of importance, and specific facts and ideas of research and reason. All of these generalities interact so that a discussion and use of one must involve a reference to information and data from the others. These three and their interactions are the main concern of philosophy of education.

Thought Patterns and General Philosophy

In the preceding discussion, we found that thought patterns are of primary importance to philosophy of education because they are the generalities of structure and system. Thought patterns, however, are private and are therefore not easy to identify. However, thought patterns do have relationships to practices, pivotal centers of importance, and systems of proofs and arguments and these *can* be recognized. Thus, thought patterns do not completely elude intellectual study. It is possible through diligent work to identify them, and the evidence of "anticipation and consequences" can be used to confirm the identification. If a scholar can predict the arguments of another with reference to a thought pattern and find that these arguments do in fact occur with regularity, then it can be said that he has made an identification.

Thought patterns can also be identified because of their relationship with philosophical systems. Since philosophical systems are themselves schemes developed from the mind, there is a relationship they must have with thought patterns. Unsurprisingly, philosophical systems also have generic notions and are closely aligned with the specific ideas of reason and research. Hence, thought patterns and philosophical systems are similar on the grounds of systematization, common pivotal centers of importance, and arguments from reason and research.

On the other hand, the two schemes are different in terms of arrangement. Whereas thought patterns are feeling-conceptual orders that function schematically to evaluate data and produce practices, philosophical systems are explicitly verbal structures, geared to the logic and order of language. The thought pattern is an internalized order that assists the individual in various cognitive and practical endeavors. The philosophical system, in contrast, provides an order for others. Its structure is communicable, and it aims for consistency of abstract and formal statements. Language is the important medium of this system, not only for its ability for communication, but also for its inherent and grammatical order.

The similar themes and general ideas that any particular thought pattern and philosophical system share is the ground for their interaction. Each system feeds data to the other, and they assist each other in creating structure. The order and vocabulary of language add emphases to the dimensions of the thought pattern. This strengthens commitment and makes certain aspects of the scheme more definite. In turn, the feeling structure of the thought pattern, plus the consequences and activities of practice, feed back into the philosophical system to give greater influence and insight into philosophical issues. To an extent, the interaction and feedback make the systems complementary, and allow them to become a unified whole that an individual can integrate into a life-style.

Even though it is possible, although difficult, to identify a thought pattern by its manifestations in practices and cultural activity, it can be discovered most easily by studying the particular philosophy espoused by an individual. In cases where there is little consequential action, this may be the only way of discovering and identifying it. Since, in the majority of cases, a philosophy is related to a particular thought pattern, the researcher can work through the philosophy to the pattern. However, confirmation from behavorial phenomena is still necessary, because, while most individuals who espouse a philosophy integrate that philosophy into a life-style, some do not. Because such exceptions are few, however, it is usually possible to utilize· philosophy to understand a thought pattern. This also implies that a philosopher might comment and make suggestions about education and have these consistent with his philosophical treatises.

Philosophers of education thus find philosophy a most valuable resource for identifying thought patterns. However, other fields can also provide aids to identification. These fields can be divided into two groups. The first group includes fields that, like philosophy, construct rational systems, verbal expositions that can be identified with thought patterns. Scientific treatises and expositions of literary criticism provide excellent examples of this type of rational system. The second group encompasses those fields that are merely influenced by thought patterns. It has been suggested that thought patterns affect many fields of cultural activity. A philosopher of education can study such fields as art, music, drama and literature to discover, not rational order of thought, but the leading generic notions of a pattern in its experiential manifestations. Since they reflect senses of importance, they are valid sources of information. To make a concluding remark: the use of many sources, not just philosophy, is another example of the difference between philosophy and philosophy of education.

Thought Pattern Nomenclature

Philosophy of education has been required to develop a structure peculiar to its own unique endeavors. At the center of this structure are thought patterns, the basic generality of system. But thought patterns must be classified in some way in order to point up their contrasts and likenesses. Only by discriminating among these systems is it possible to relate their differences to differences in practices. Thus, the field must be structured along lines of thought pattern differences in order to reflect the variations that occur in systems of theory and practice.

We have indicated that thought patterns are most easily considered in relation to philosophy. When there is a strong connection between a particular philosophy and a thought pattern, it is obviously appropriate to name the thought pattern after that philosophy. This is done with the full realization that the use of the same name is merely a convenient way of suggesting the relationship, and that all data that go into such a thought pattern category are not explicitly philosophical or even of like material. Since philosophical titles are familiar intellectual headings, since they connote theoretical implications, and since they represent thought patterns in the most accessible way, they are the best available designations for certain categories of thought patterns. There are instances, however, when it is not feasible to make this connection, and philosophers of education must then select a name appropriate to the theme of the thought pattern.

Today, there are nine basic thought patterns that are used to justify educational practice. Although there are less important thought patterns that may someday rise to prominence, only nine appear to play a major role in contemporary education. These thought systems are best named: Naturalism, Experimentalism, Idealism, Process-Structure Philosophy, Logical-Science Philosophy, Ordinary Language Philosophy, Humanism, Natural Law Philosophy, and Existential Phenomenology.

Philosophy of Education Categories

We have shown that the subject matter of philosophy of education is unique. In addition, the special categories the discipline provides for this subject matter also make it distinctive. These categories have evolved as the discipline has attempted to classify various positions in the field. In earlier decades, the discipline conceived special names for three philosophies of education. Recently, it has become evident that these names do not designate philosophical positions in themselves, but instead are simply ways of grouping philosophical orientations.

The three categories initially conceived by the discipline were Progressivism, Essentialism, and Perennialism. Progressivism referred to the progressive education movement in America, which sought to create a better world through an experience-centered education. Essentialism was a reaction against progressive education. It emphasized instead the essentials of basic subject matter; that is, reading, writing, and arithmetic for elementary school pupils, and geography, grammar, history, science, foreign languages, and mathematics for secondary school students. Perennialism, in contrast to Progressivism, which looked to the future, and of Essentialism, which emphasized the present, concentrated on the benefits deriving from the past, and insisted that education should conserve the perennial values of Western culture.

These three classifications, however, were not valid philosophical positions. Although they were graphic terms that were distinctive to education, they were too vague and too limiting to be used for any scholarly study of the actual systems of education. First of all, progressive education took two quite distinctive forms. The first, the child-centered movement of early progressive education, emphasized the natural development of children. The second, the social-centered movement of later progressive education, was critical of its predecessor's permissiveness and sought to construct a better world by controlling human experience by means of the community of the sciences and the scientific method. The other two categories displayed similar inadequacies. Essentialism, for example, was simply a form of Idealism, yet it failed to either consider Idealism as a philosophy or other positions that emphasized knowledge and subject matter. Perennialism was based on a vague theme of

Humanism and Natural Law Philosophy. The three categories were thus neither systems of philosophy nor thought patterns, but rather categories related to special areas of educational interest.

However, these three categories have evolved and now provide a structure for organizing philosophies of education. Every philosophy of education has an educational commitment to three goals—experience, knowledge, and values. However, the degree to which each goal is emphasized is a major point of difference. The three categories can thus be used to distinguish philosophies of education on the basis of their major emphasis. Progressivism, for example, stresses experience. Progressivists feel that knowledge and values can be attained only after experience has become primary in education. Essentialism, on the other hand, emphasizes the priority of knowledge. Attainment of values and adequate experience is achieved through the processes of acquiring knowledge. Perennialism, in contrast to both, lays ultimate stress on values. In Perennialism, values, whether absolute or relative, whether external and transcendental or intrinsic in man's nature, are the key to human existence. Values are prior to the knowledge and experiences we have, and thus to instill, allow, or provide values is the primary function in education.

The value of these three terms as titles for different emphases may well have been destroyed by the connotations they have had in the past. Alternatively, of course, the three categories might be simply the emphasis on experience, the emphasis on knowledge, and the emphasis on values. Whatever designation is given, however, the nine major thought patterns can easily be categorized in these terms. Progressivism encompasses Naturalism (early progressive education) and Experimentalism (later progressive education); Essentialism includes Idealism, Process-Structure Philosophy, Logical-Science Philosophy, and Ordinary Language Philosophy; and Perennialism includes Humanism, Natural Law Philosophy, and Existential Phenomenology. These three groupings are thus very important aids in the clarification of educational justification.

These major categories can also be differentiated in terms of the types of evidence and areas of acknowledged support a proponent most often utilizes for the final confirmation of his stand. Progressivists, for example, usually rely upon evidence from the social sciences; most often, genetic and experimental psychology, sociology, aspects of anthropology, and evolutionary biology. Special stress is placed on the topics of human development, conditioning and learning in experimental psychology, and statistical studies of population behavior.

The areas of confirming evidence for Essentialists, on the other hand, are the natural science fields, those aspects of biology and psychology that are related to physics and chemistry, logical philosophy, and mathematics. Perennialists most often draw their confirming evidence from the philosophy of history, from literature, and from religion. For them, key evidence comes from literature, whether it is sacred writings, the classics of antiquity, or interpretive portrayals of historical events and philosophies of history. The themes of existentialism, for example, are more aptly presented in literature than in philosophical treatises. We are not suggesting that each group draws exclusively upon the area mentioned, but rather that, when a proponent of an educational stand is forced to defend his ultimate source of proof and confirmation, he most often depends upon one of these fields.

The three categories of Progressivism, Essentialism, and Perennialism are thus clearly important to the understanding of positions in philosophy of education. They not only provide a way of classifying different thought patterns, but also a means of viewing the relationships between various points of view. The likenesses and similarities between the various positions must be identified. The categories "emphasis upon experience," "emphasis upon knowledge," and "emphasis upon values" assist the philosopher of education in this endeavor.

The Educational Dimensions Within a Thought Pattern

One last aspect of the nomenclature of philosophy of education deserves discussion. I refer to the arrangement of the data within particular thought patterns. There are several areas of justification in education, and these must be marked and categorized. In the past the discipline has made use of the findings of philosophy, psychology, and sociology for clarifying educational justification. Today, these areas are still significant, but they must be studied more carefully and understood in the light of the subject matter of thought patterns.

The areas of justification in philosophy of education are not difficult to identify. One area, however, which was previously termed philosophical, requires reinterpretation. We have already shown that philosophy is not directly related to education. Therefore, it is not appropriate to indicate that the first subdivision is explicitly philosophical, at least from the philosophical purist's point of view. Since the material included in this first area is related to thought patterns in their relation to education, it must reflect such a connection. Any term describing it must have an educational and theoretical reference rather than a philosophical one. The best term, therefore, is "pedagogical orientation." This term refers to materials involving the underlying conceptual basis of education with roots in a thought pattern and with implications and suggestions of educational practice.

The two other subdivisions of philosophy of education are also derived from thought patterns. These are the "psychological dimension" and the "social concepts dimension." As the title indicates, the primary concern of the former is the individual, that is, the person who is being educated. The psychological dimension seeks to explain the nature of the individual or student, how he behaves and thinks, what endowments he possesses, even the achievements he can attain. The evidence can be empirical, rational, or moral. The social concepts dimension, in contrast, relates to social aims and goals, the nature and purpose of society, and the place of education within society. The category may reflect concern with social needs or with the role and function of the school as an institution in society. Justification for certain social aims and suggested means for attaining them are also topics within this area.

The contents of each of these three areas of interest are derived from thought patterns, but their importance stems from the fact that they focus on key aspects of education: the grounds for educational practice, social circumstances and ends, and the nature of the human individual. There cannot be an adequate understanding of education without the knowledge of these aspects.

Conclusion

The special nomenclature of philosophy of education is indicative of the distinctiveness of the discipline whose ultimate aim is to understand and clarify the justifications for education. A philosopher of education may write on matters of education as others do, may even suggest prescriptions, aims, and endeavors. Much of the time, however, his teaching and research concentrates on the suggestions of others. Moreover, writing on the subject of educational justification is not restricted to trained educators. Any intelligent man can write on the subject. The role of the philosopher of education is not so much the formulation of a philosophy of education as it is the interpretation and understanding of that which has already been written.

Thus it is a peculiar fact that most of the outstanding materials in the discipline are not written by trained philosophers of education, but by brilliant men from innumerable fields who have gained insight into educational matters. Philosophers of education would not wish to deprive humanity of these gifts of educational wisdom. The discipline has to define its aims relative to the invaluable service of others, to use its special system of analyses and knowledge to help clarify the outstanding educational writings. To this end, it uses its peculiar nomenclature and the subject matter of thought patterns. The function of this text is to present the outstanding contemporary authors on philosophy of education, and to provide a framework by which their thought can be understood.

ONE Emphasis Upon Experience (Progressivism)

Naturalism

Naturalism is the thought pattern of what is usually termed "child-centered education" or "early progressive education." Its first generic notion is the emphasis upon the individual child as a self-learner who possesses inherent abilities and an individual natural development plan that progresses through distinct stages. Parents, teachers, and society must therefore coordinate their endeavors with nature's developmental requirements for childhood.

Naturalism's second generic notion is optimism—toward life, nature, society, and childhood. War must be waged against those who perceive in such things anything ugly, dark, or gloomy. Nature is not evil, children are not depraved, the senses are not malign, and science is not oppressive. Naturalists display their optimism by describing education and childhood in aesthetic terms. They attempt to convey to all men and societies that the optimistic belief in nature and God's goodness is the key to the good life. Naturalists feel that the ultimate strength in human beings lies in the power of positive thinking. If everyone would only think positively about life, the world would become a heaven on earth. Educators with this outlook attempt to persuade parents and those preparing for teaching to think positively about the characteristics of children.

These two generic notions indicate a trust in childhood and nature. Since children are the highest and last creation of nature, in the words of Franklin Parker, the two must be intrinsically united and good. From a practical point of view, these beliefs imply that education must focus on what is natural for children and what aspect of nature assists them in their natural development. Two major intellectual forces provide support for the trust in nature and in childhood. They are the philosophy of American Transcendentalism of the nineteenth century and the conceptions of the social sciences commencing at the turn of the twentieth century.

Transcendentalism, which was expounded in the thought of Ralph Waldo Emerson, Henry Thoreau, Margaret Fuller, Theodore Parker, Bronson Alcott, Elizabeth Peabody, and others, was the most important intellectual movement from which child-centered and natural education drew support. Although it is best known as a literary school, Transcendentalism was primarily a prophetic movement that proposed new ways and new directions for living. Emerson, for example, was a noted literary figure. But, with the exception of his poems, all his literary pieces were

19

first delivered in the form of lectures and speeches. Emerson did not conceive of himself as an artist, but as a prophet, a proclaimer of the truths of humanity, nature, and even childhood.

The message of Transcendentalism revolved around three basic principles: trust in nature, faith in man, and the access to truth through intuition and example. Nature, first of all, must always be glorified and respected. If man is to discover beauty and truth, he must turn to nature and lift up his soul in the elevation of nature's gifts. The senses are necessary for making contact with nature, for experiencing its beauty, for finding the anchor for moral goodness. Since nature is the source of man's wisdom and morality, it should form the base of education. Right education, Emerson concluded, is that which is in agreement with nature. The second principal tenet of Transcendentalism is faith in man. Man is a spiritual creature, an embryo of God, an immortal soul of living experience. Every individual has a sacred constitution that is his alone, and this must never be tampered with. Let everyone be himself is the cry of the Transcendentalists. Let each person fulfill what is preordained for him through the unfolding of his own nature. Progressive education's theme of individualized differences derives directly from this aspect of Transcendentalist philosophy. The third major Transcendentalist principle states that intuition and example are the primary modes of knowing truth. Words are finite and abstract. They break up thought and impoverish it. Man must reject the sayings of sages and instead turn to intuition and action as the sources and origin of truth. The application to education is clear. Teachers must not verbalize, but show; they must not demand, but coordinate their activities with those of the children. Nondirective teaching is the most beneficial. Direction in learning must come from the children's own spontaneous activities.

Developments in social science thinking at the turn of the twentieth century provided the second intellectual influence on the thought pattern of Naturalism. The social scientists attacked the same intellectual traditions as the Transcendentalists. They sought to dispel the notion that human nature is evil and weak and to dismiss the idea that mind is an entity separate from nature. They based their conclusions on those aspects of Charles Darwin's theory of evolution that stressed man's connection with nature and animals.

Three topics in the social sciences were integrated with the themes of Transcendentalism in the thought pattern of Naturalism. First, evolution became the scientific key to understanding the natural unfoldings of childhood. Human development progresses through distinct evolutionary stages. From one cell, to animal, to prehistoric and ancient man, to civilized man, each child relives the history of his ancestors. This is the theory of recapitulation, which was popularized by G. Stanley Hall and expressed in the more recent work of Arnold Gesell. A second aspect of

evolutionary theory was applied to transcendentalist concepts to produce
a Naturalist thought pattern. Fixed, inherited qualities were to be considered in discovering the individual constitution of each child. These
qualities are acquired from ancestors and provide the child with certain
abilities and capacities that are his alone. Educators can adjust the
educational environment to their students' native intelligence and abilities. Alfred Binet and Theodore Simon pioneered research in this area.
Finally, the scientific explanation of instincts becomes the means for
understanding children's spontaneous activities. Man is as rich in instincts as animals. These instincts are the appropriate and natural ways
of behaving; they are the unlearned tendencies that cause individuals to
perform in certain ways. Children should follow their instincts because
they are nature's guidelines for success and development. Thus, through
the themes of recapitulation, inheritance, and instincts, the materials
from early twentieth-century social science become evidence for the
support of Naturalism.

Naturalism as a thought pattern forms the basis for child-centered
education, which stresses freedom, initiative, spontaneity, and self-expression. Direction is provided by the child's own level of development,
by the maturation processes of inheritance, and the aim for well-rounded
personality. Since the controls and goals of nature are built into each
child, education must cooperate by giving the child free reign in his
growth. He must not be restrained or coerced by adult traditions and
manners. The child must learn to be himself by following his own
natural rules, and he can follow them only in an environment of freedom
and self-initiative. A child is good, not evil. He becomes a tyrant or a
misfit only through adult interference. A teacher or parent is like a
husbandman whose task is to cultivate the environment and destroy the
weeds in order that the organism can unfold according to its own
internalized developmental plan.

The school must see the child rather than subject matter as the central
focus of education. The school must revolve around the child—his needs,
his development, his activities. A child is naturally active and busy. He
needs only a proper environment to put these qualities to work for
definite ends. The traditional subjects will still be acquired, but only as
the desire to acquire them arises from the child's own inherent interests.
A child naturally seeks the things necessary for his growth. Traditional
schools erred because they imposed unnatural constraints, the adult-
dominated traditions of forms and rules. Activity predominates in a
child's life; therefore, it must be the spring from which interest and
self-expression flow. A school must be a center for activities rather than a
place of formal studies and lessons. It must provide a continuing stream
of divergent experiences unbroken by the partitions represented by
formal subjects. A school must be a place for childhood, a place where

young life is expressed in talking, playing, working, and creating.

The most familiar maxims of Naturalism are: "education never ends, growth is continuous," "one learns by doing," and "education should aim to educate the whole man." Naturalists contradict the teaching of rational philosophy which suggests that the experienced world consists of rationalized opposites. Instead, Naturalists contend that work and play, labor and leisure, and teaching and learning must be seen as interrelated. "I learn from children," says teacher Caroline Pratt, and G. Stanley Hall insists that play is actually a form of effort and education because it is through play the child relives ancestral ways and habits. It is not to reason, therefore, that the educator must turn for information on his subject, but to the experiences of childhood and the natural processes of development. Greater insight can come from the experienced suggestions of educational reformers who perceived these facts (Rousseau, Pestalozzi, Froebel, and Herbart) than from the reasoning of university philosophers.

PEDAGOGICAL ORIENTATION

The Child   /   COLONEL FRANCIS W. PARKER

I propose . . . to present a general exposition of the theory of CONCEN-TRATION.

The least that can be said for this theory is that it presents to some extent an outline of a rounded educational doctrine for the study and criticism of teachers.

In the beginning of these discussions, the question of all questions, and indeed the everlasting question, is: what is the being to be educated? What is the child? What is this little lump of flesh, breathing life and singing the song of immortality? The wisdom and philosophy of ages upon ages have asked this question, and still it remains unanswered. It is the central problem of the universe. The child is the climax and culmination of all God's creations, and to answer the question, "What is the child?" is to approach nearer the still greater question, What is the Creator and Giver of Life?

I can answer the question tentatively. It is a question for you and for me, and for the teachers of the present and the future, to answer; and still it will ever remain the unanswered question. We should study the child, as we study all phenomena, by its actions, and by its tendencies to

"The Child" is reprinted from Col. Francis W. Parker, "The Child", *Talks on Pedagogics: An Outline of the Theory of Concentration,* E. L. Kellog & Co., 1894.

act. The child is born, we are told by scientists, deaf, dumb, and blind, yet, in design, possessing marvellous possibilities for development. It is well for us to stand by the cradle of a little child who has drawn his first breath, and is ready to be acted upon by the external energies which surround him.

One hypothesis we can accept as true: the inherited organism of bone, muscle and brain determines exactly the limits or boundaries of the baby's development. Each nerve-fibre or convolution of the brain says: "Thus far shalt thou go and no farther;" and it is well to say in the same breath that no human being ever had the external conditions for growth by which the full possibilities, predetermined and fixed by the organism, have been realized. The organism itself determines the external conditions for development. Every muscle, every nerve, every fibre, every convolution of the brain, their nature and power, are in themselves possibilities for the reception of those external energies which act upon the body of the child, and make their way to the brain through the sensorium. The child itself is a central energy, or complex of energies, upon which and through which certain external energies act. No simple energy can enter a child's brain except by first touching the child's body (the end-organs), and countless energies touch the child's body which do not enter the brain at all; others enter, but lie below the plane of consciousness.

Forms or waves of light touch the eye and create elementary ideas of color in the brain, but just what colors there shall be in the brain is determined by the passive power and delicacy of the organism itself. Vibrations of air touch and enter the brain through the ear. Strongest and most effective of all is the contact and resistance of the body to objects more dense than waves of air or waves of ether. The great giant sense of touch begins its creative power in the brain at the birth of the child, and even before birth. It is well for us to understand thoroughly that the child, an organic complex of energies, is acted upon and through by external energies, and, whatever matter may be in itself, the mind is conscious of nothing but pure energy, and is primarily developed by external energies which, we infer, act through forms and qualities of matter. Stimuli come from all the surroundings of the child. The products of the stimuli create in the child's mind concepts corresponding to external objects. These concepts are activities in themselves, or phases of differentiated energy. Units of elementary ideas, individual concepts, enable the mind to react upon externality. The child begins to move under the stimulus created by external activities, to smile, to laugh, to stretch out its hands, to see, to hear, to touch, to taste, and to smell.

It is not possible for me to state the exact order of the succession of the arousing to action of the different senses. Our questions here are: What are the spontaneous activities of the child? In other words, what must the child do from the nature of its being, the nature of the stimulus acting through its body and in its mind, and the potentialities of the ego? What are the tendencies of these spontaneous activities? The child's consciousness begins in obscurity, weakness, and vagueness, and still in this very obscurity and vagueness there is great activity. The very few weak and obscure ideas of color and sound and form set the whole being into motion. Before there is any consciousness, before the child has the most obscure feeling of itself, music affects it in a wonderful way. Lullaby songs will soothe it to sleep, changing vague pain into vague pleasure. The whole being is sensitive to the rhythm of music. Not only can it be soothed and lulled to sleep with music, but its first dawning consciousness of life is marked by a smile aroused by a song. The first spiritual breath of external life comes with musical cadences. One of the first sounds that it makes is an imitation of rhythm. What is this marvellous gift that makes the child so sensitive to musical cadence? The whole universe moves in rhythm: the avalanche thunders from the mountain side in deep cadences; the ocean surf roars in musical cadence. The rippling of the brook and the soughing of the breeze in the foliage are the simple music of nature. The little child is the centre of all this rhythm, and the feeling of this rhythm is the truth of the universe whispering its sweet songs to the child's soul.

Perhaps the most marked mental action of the little child is the fanciful creation of new ideas and images. A little vague color and sound, and a few percepts of touch, are sufficient to set the little being into most vigorous action. External objects act upon the child and produce their correspondences, individual concepts, in its mind. As I have already said, these concepts are very vague, obscure, and indistinct. Notwithstanding all this, creation is the moving, central power and delight of the child. The baby creates out of its meagre store of ideas a new world, its own world, in which it lives and moves and has its being. Let us pause a moment, and look at the marvellous meaning of this wonderful power of the child in the creations of fancy. If the little human being were limited to actuality, that is, to the vague reflex of external objects, if it were bound by its own meagre store of so-called facts, it would indeed live in a dark and dismal prison; but it bursts the bands of reality and goes out into a higher world to the invisible life. It lives over again the childhood of the race in the myth. It revels in fanciful forms of its own weak but vivid creations; it spontaneously seeks the invisible.

Next to the cradle song is the cradle story. You know very well how eager a child is for stories that arouse its love for rhythm and excite its fancy. The child most delights in fairy tales, the mythical treasures of the ages. The cruel bonds of stern reality are broken, and it enters a beautiful and invisible world, peopled by creations of its own fancy. If a child were limited in its early stages to the world of reality, if it could not go out into the unknown world, the invisible world, it would lead the life of a brute. The human animal differs from the brute in its faith in an invisible world. The self-created, invisible world, to the child, is the fire-mist heaven; it is the chaos that precedes the spiritual life. Banish myth from the child, and you take away that beauty which is the essence of truth. Parents who forbid the myth because they conceive, forsooth, it is not the truth, limit the child to the baldest materialism, or prepare the way for fancy to run riot to ruin.

What is the myth? The record of the human race is full of myths. Myth comes from the imperfect answer which nature gives to the childish soul of man. The answers are not false, but they are imperfect and partial, and are, to childish souls, the solution of their great problems. Every answer given to a spontaneous and innocent question contains a golden kernel of intrinsic truth. It is that truth which a child can bear in its early years. It cannot grasp precepts and logic, but it can understand the truth, like those who crowded around the Saviour,—in parables. The myth is common to all tribes and nations on the face of the earth. All myths have a wonderful similarity, proving that the human spirit in every stage of growth, and in every clime, and under all environments, has the same strong everlasting tendency upward. Every myth contains a lesson to man. Out of the ignorance of the nature of the child, and from the spirit of dogmatism and bigotry, there has come the falsehood that says the myth does not contain the whole truth, and therefore must be rejected. Who knows the whole truth? Shall the child be robbed of that which delights its soul and lays the foundation of true religious life? No greater mistake can be made in regard to the spontaneous activities of the child, for the myth is the true fire-mist of character, it contains golden symbols that point upward to God and to heaven. The myth is the foundation of faith in the future life, the foundation of all spiritual growth. The fairies and trolls change, as the soul changes, to real folks and real life.

The myth is the beginning of history. The creatures of fancy fore-shadow the real people with whom the child must live. It is, indeed, the child seeing through a glass darkly, but that obscurity of truth and tendency towards it are absolutely essential to its growth. Myth, I say, is the beginning of history. The myths presented to the child should contain in themselves the guiding stars of life and immortality.

The myth is the beginning of science. The human race began, we are told, with a firm belief that every object in the universe was animated, life-like, human-like. This was the childish study of science, but it sustained a great truth. The stone and the mountain are not organisms for life, it is true, but there breathes through them an irresistible energy, which comes from the Giver of all Life. The myth of the early ages points towards the marvellous revelations of the scientific truth of the present. The myth is an imperfect and partial apprehension of truth. The myth clears away under the steady light of the ever-moving mind; it is essential to the weak state of the child. "The night veileth the morning."

Just as the human race arose in its development from the myths of antiquity, so the child must rise from the myths of childhood. The lack of ideality, the failure in spiritual growth, in true religious life, are caused more by the failure of the parents to recognize the true nature of the child and his inborn love for myth than any other cause whatever. The rankest materialism in its worst form has never struck harder blows at true spiritual life than the ignorance of misguided parents, who keep their child from fairy life and fairy land. Fairy land is over the border of the present, into the future, and the truest tendency of the human life is to live in the ideal of the future, to reach forward towards the invisible and the unknown. Slowly the human beings have arisen—guided by a glimmering light—and have climbed spiritually from the earth and the clod, from the shrub and tree up the broad walls of the arched sky, to stars, and moon, and sun, and then beyond the sun, for the divinity seeking and striving imagination stretches away to the invisible, all-powerful, all-controlling, all-loving, One who permeates the universe, lives in it, and breathes His life through it, the eternal life to be taken into the human soul. The myth is the obscure image, in the child's soul, of God Himself. There are many parents who shudder at the myth of Santa Claus, an invisible being that brings the child gifts; but that invisible being, to the child's weak apprehension, is the foreshadowing of the All-Giver, the forerunner of the One who came to man on the blessed Christmas night. No rough voice and no ignorant soul should ever tell the little child that Santa Claus does not exist, for Santa Claus is the foreshadowing of the All-Giver, All-Lover, the One who gives because He loves.

It is impossible to take a child into history, science, ethics, and religion without the continued exercise of these spontaneous fanciful tendencies. You may reply that a child may live in myth and fancy all its life. I admit that this is possible. Many people do live in myth all their lives just because myth is not put into the crucible of highest reason; just because the conditions are not presented for myth to change to history, to science, to ethics, and to religion. This is no proof that the strongest spontaneous tendency of the child is wrong; it is only a proof of neglect to build upon it. I think we can take it for granted that, as God, the loving Creator of the child, made the child His highest creation, He put into that child Himself, His divinity, and that this divinity manifests itself in the seeking for truth through the visible and tangible.

The child is brought into direct contact with its mother, its father, and the whole family, and who will dare to say that the child is not, above all, a student of human nature? Who will say that its eyes, when they touch one's face, cannot read the soul better than older people? The child looks at you with the innocence and purity of childhood, and no hypocrisy, no dissimulation, though it may veil the truth from older eyes, can keep it from the little ones. It studies the relation of being to being, father to mother, parents to children. It may be that I use too strong a word when I say it "studies," but still it is something very like study. The study of family life is the child's beginning of the study of anthropology and of history. The child is not only a student of individual life, but of community life, the life of the family, the life of the neighbors, of the children he meets at play, in the house, in the yard, in the street; and the measure of the child's judgment of community life is the measure in its after study of history. It may study history in school or the university, but in all life the judgments formed at home, in the nursery, in the parlor, in the kitchen, in the street, are the strongest, ever-enduring measures in all his after-judgments of the record of the human life taught by experience and in history. Every human being with whom he comes in contact is a new study to him. The looks, the manners, the dress, the attitude, and the facial expression lead him to make his childish inferences. Then comes the kindergarten and the school, the first step in a broader community life than that which home furnishes. Here, the study, not only of history, but of civics, begins. The true foundation of civics is community life. The child's home measure of life, the government of his home, give him democratic, monarchical, or socialistic principles. Whatever the rule of the home or school may be, that rule is ever afterwards either loved or hated by the child. Thus the child spontaneously begins the study of anthropology, ethnology, and history, and in these studies he has a profound, abiding interest, in these studies he forms habits of judgment which to a great extent are fixed and permanent.

It needs no argument to prove that the child studies or, at least, is exceedingly interested in zoology. Few beings, except, perhaps, the father and mother, can interest a child more deeply than the brute life which surrounds him. The cat is "a thing of beauty and a joy forever"; the dog is its particular friend. It stretches out its little hands before it can speak, and its first utterances follow the attempts of its original ancestors in imitating the voice of the dog. The child delights in birds, butterflies, and bees. Place any moving, living thing before the child, and it moves towards it with an excited interest. It wants to touch it, to stroke it, to know more about it. Endowed with the original idea of animism, it no doubt believes every brute that it sees to have a mind like its own. It will imitate the dog, the cat, and the birds, and will talk to them as to its own companions. He studies zoology in that he becomes acquainted with the animals he meets: every insect, every animal, wild or tame, the grasshopper, the locust, bugs that scurry away when he lifts a stone, the fish-worms which he digs for bait, are objects of intense interest. He knows the difference between the white grub and the common earth-worm. The animals in the woods are his friends. The birds, their habits, their nests, their little ones, and their songs fill him with joy. He can take a lesson from the timid partridge, who is ever ready to give her life for her children. He knows the sly habits of the crows, studies the psychol-ogy of their reasoning. The horses, and oxen, and sheep are all his friends. What farm-boy has not cried over the loss of a favorite sheep, taken away by the cruel butcher?

The child has a great love for vegetable life. There never was a child that lived who did not worship flowers, reach out for them, desire to hold them in its hands, gaze at them, and smell them. Of course, the sponta-neous activities of the child are governed to a great degree by its environment. Take a little boy with the environment of a farm,—such an instance comes to me,—a boy upon a rocky farm in New England. He studies spontaneously his entire environment. It is safe to say that he knows every plant upon the farm, every kind of grass, every weed. He comes in direct contact with worm-wood, sorrel, rag-weed. He can tell all the kinds of grass from the graceful silver grass to the stately timothy. He knows the mosses and lichens that cling to the rocks and carpet the marshy land. He knows the shrubs and bushes; the huckleberry-bush is his delight. The strawberry in the rich meadow he watches from blossom to fruit with a keen sense of the joy which is to follow. Every tree he knows—the magnificent pine, the stately maple, the spreading chestnut in the pasture. He can tell you the shape of the tree; its trunk, its foliage: its fruit he spontaneously classifies. Thus, every child is an earnest, indefatigable lover of botany. In his future life, the farm-boy carries his botany of the farm with him wherever he goes. He compares all other plants and classifies them according to the spontaneous classifications made on the farm. He says: "This was on the old farm; this was not." "This is something new." "This is like something I've seen before." "This bush is like the lilac; this rose is like the rose in the old garden."

Not only is the boy on the farm a student of life, but he extends his study to the forces of earth, and air, and water. The earth touches him, heaven bends down to him and asks him questions. The clouds he knows, from the rounded thunderhead to the mackerel sky. He knows also the winds; he can foretell the weather. He looks with intense joy to the next rainy day; that will bring him rest, or, something better, fishing. He watches the sun with a deep interest. It will be a very stupid boy who cannot tell exactly the noon hour by the sun, aided by that internal monitor, his stomach. Winds, clouds, air, and heat, everything that influences vegetation, come within the mental range of the farm-boy.

Mineralogy, especially upon a rocky farm, comes very close to the boy in clearing the ground, in picking stones, in building stone walls, in quarrying ledges. Watch a crowd of children upon the beach gathering pebbles and curious stones. They are interested in the color and form of the pebbles, and may be made exceedingly interested in the origin of the different forms, if some kind, observant friend is there to continue the questions which the stones themselves ask. Children naturally take to playing in the dirt as ducks to water. The different kinds of soils attract their attention—sand, gravel, and clay. They never tire of playing in the sand, or expressing crude fancies by modelling in the clay. The changes which natural forces bring about on the earth's surface are of deep interest to children, especially the changes brought about by running water, after a rain, or the wind swirling the sand into piles. They never tire of damming up a temporary stream or changing its current, and of watching its effects when it spreads out silt, or the cuts it makes in the soft earth. The brooks and rivers are never-ceasing sources of delight to children; they watch them at flood-time, when the water spreads out over the meadows; they notice the caving in of banks, the carrying of earth by water and its deposition on the shelving shores.

Real geography, or the appearance of the earth's surface, is a subject of intense, though unconscious, interest on the part of the child. Let a boy hunt stray cows or sheep over a large farm; he soon learns to know every crook, every turn and corner in the whole farm, every hiding-place. He knows the hills, valleys, springs, and meadows. Of all the mental pictures that remain vivid through life and are recalled with ever-renewed pleasure, are the pictures of the country surrounding the birth-place, or the house in which we lived when children. The house itself, the fireplace, paper on the wall, furniture,—everything is distinct in our minds when other pictures fade or are blurred by time. The country round about, every hillock, every depression, brook, and rivulet are never-fading images in the brain.

To sum up, the subjects of the child's spontaneous study and persistent interest include all the central subjects of study—geography, geology, mineralogy, botany, zoology, anthropology, etc. In fact, the child begins every subject spontaneously and unconsciously. He must begin these subjects, because he lives, and because his environment acts upon him and educates him. Of course, the difference in environment makes a great difference in the child's mental action, the child's individual concepts; still, in all children there are the same spontaneous tendencies. The boy, for instance, on a farm may have a large range of vegetation to study, and the poor little child in the dark city may worship with his whole soul some potted plant and from it draw lessons of inspiration and love. The child studies the clouds, the sky, the stars, the earth, vegetation, animal life, history, every hour of the day. To be sure, he may have more interest in one subject than another, but to him all these subjects are related one to the other, as the cloud is related to rain, and the rain is related to vegetation and soil. It is the tendency of pedantry to search in the far distance for facts and mysteries, but the truth is that the marvellous is close to us, that miracles are of the most common occurrence.

I wish to call your attention to the wonderful powers acquired by the child in the first three years of its life, and the wonderful persistence there is in such acquirement. Take, for instance, the art of locomotion, the creeping and walking. Watch the face of the child standing for the first time upon its little legs, attracted by the outstretched arms of its mother, who stands across the room; look at the mingled courage and fear in the baby's face. He has a great ambition to move, as he has seen others move, upon his two feet. He stretches out his arms, he fears, he takes courage, he moves one foot and is successful, and then the other; he looks at his mother's encouraging smile, takes another step, and then another, until the great feat of walking across the room is accomplished. From the time he first stands upon his feet to the time he runs around with perfect unconsciousness of his power of movement, there takes place a succession of experiments, of trials, and of failures and successes, all guided and controlled by his desire to walk.

More wonderful than learning to walk is the learning to hear language and to talk. In the beginning the child creates his own language of gesture by means of his own body. He hears language, words that are in themselves complex. Oral words act upon his consciousness and are associated by a fixed and everlasting law of the mind. Idioms are acquired by hearing and association, and with it all comes an intense desire to express thought. With his voice he creates at first his own language, which consists of crudely articulate sounds, and then follows the acquisition of the vernacular which he hears. It is well for us to consider carefully the processes of learning to talk. The child must learn to hear first; that is, the words must act upon consciousness and their correspondences must be associated with the appropriate activities in consciousness. The idioms must act in the same way and be associated with their appropriate activities or relations of ideas. Then follows the making of oral words. He learns enunciation, or the utterance of single sounds. He learns articulation, or the unity of sounds in words. He learns accent, pronunciation, and syntax, all by hearing language and under the one controlling motive of expressing his own thought. He begins, it is true, with crude utterances, but these utterances are to him the best possible expression of his thought. He learns any language and every language that he hears. If we could understand the psychological mechanical processes by which a child learns his own vernacular from the first step of hearing to the last step by which the sentence is in his power, we should understand the whole theory of learning any language. Those who have tried to speak a foreign language will readily understand something of the struggle the child goes through in order to master one single phonic element. You see that he does all this unconsciously, that all these efforts are natural and to a great degree automatic. He never for a moment thinks of a single sound by itself unless that sound is a whole word. He knows nothing at all of the complex elements of a language, nothing of slow pronunciation, nothing of syntax, still he masters the language by a natural process. This word natural is variously interpreted. It is exceedingly ambiguous, almost as ambiguous as the word "abstract." Still I believe that we can find a scientific definition of the word natural. If the word natural means anything, it means strict conformity to God's laws. That is, a child learns every oral word by the same law under which every oral or written word in any and every language must be learned. The child does not know the law, but he obeys the law by instinct. If the child makes these marvellous acquisitions naturally, in conformity to law, why not have him continue that conformity to law in all his after-acquisitions?

Learning to write is far easier in itself, if we follow the law, than learning to hear language or learning to speak. The great lesson to teachers is, find the law, follow the law; give the child conditions in learning to write like those he has had in learning to speak. Indeed, the conditions can be made far better, for learning to speak is left very much to accident and to desultory instruction, while learning to write may be under the most careful guidance.

It goes without saying that the child is a student of form and color. Everything that enters his brain, as I have already said, must touch the end-organs, and these attributes or objects which touch the end-organs are forms of matter. Froebel, who had such divine insight, understood the great value of the tactual sense. Color is representative in its power. It brings into consciousness the correspondences to forms of external objects.

Not only does the child study form, but he makes intuitively a systematic preparation for the study of number. The child begins with no idea of distance. He grasps for the moon with the same confidence as he does for an object near at hand. The ideas of distance, size, weight, are preparations for number. The child first learns to measure by constantly reaching out his hands, creeping and walking, and after that it measures distance by sight. Not only does it begin to measure and estimate distances, but it judges area and bulk, and compares different sizes, areas, weights, and bulks. The study of weight to him also has its charms, the difference of pressure upon his hand, his own weight in the effort of other children to lift him. He measures force and time in the same unconscious way, the time of sleeping, the time between a promised pleasure and its anticipated realization, and soon he learns to look at the clock to help him out in his judgment. He estimates very carefully the value of a cent and a stick of candy. All these spontaneous activities are in the direction of number study, are mingled with all his activities and are absolutely necessary to his mental and physical action. It is true these measures are very inadequate and imperfect, but they are the beginnings of the power of accurate measuring, that mode of judgment which will end, if he continues to have the right conditions, in exact measuring and weighing, and in accurate knowledge of values.

There is at first a perfect unity of thought and action. Hear the voice and watch the movements of a little child! No dancing teacher, no teacher of elocution, no actor, can ever successfully imitate the voice of the child, or the perfectly unconscious beauty and grace of its movements. Indeed it is the highest aim of artists in acting and elocution to acquire the unconscious grace and power of a child. Listen to the voice of the child,—melodious, harmonious, perfect in emphasis, it is the immediate pulsations of his soul, the instantaneous reflex of his consciousness, with unconsciousness of his body, his organs of expression, his forms of speech. The child, until education intervenes, is a unit of action and expression, and that unity is acquired and maintained by action under a motive with no overpowering consciousness of the means or forms of expression. Must that beautiful unity be broken? Can it be perpetuated and strengthened?

There never was such a thing as a lazy child born on earth. Childhood is full of activities of every kind, stimulated by external energies and shaped by internal power. The child experiments continually until it gains its ends. It will reach hundreds of times for an object, and at last succeed. What modes of expression, excepting speech, does a child acquire in the first years of its life? I should say that all children love music, though there is a vast difference in individual organisms in this as in all other modes of expression. Most children strive to imitate that which they hear in rhythm. Making, or manual work, is really the natural element of the child. I think I can say, without fear of dispute, that a child tries to make everything that he sees made. The little girl wishes to use the scissors, needle and thread. In the kitchen, unless repressed by the mother, she makes cakes and bread. In fact, the whole round of housekeeping in the beginning furnishes countless objects for activity and a desire to imitate. Boys in the shop, or on the farm, strive to do what they see done. They harness each other in teams, they drive the dog and the goat, they make mill-wheels and dams. The tendency to imitate, the desire to make the objects they see made, is intensely strong in every child.

Every child has the artist element born in him; he loves to model objects out of sand and clay. Paint is a perfect delight to children, bright colors charm them. Give the child a paint-brush, and though his expression of thought will be exceedingly crude, it will be very satisfactory to him; he will paint any object with the greatest confidence. It is very interesting to watch the crowd of little children near Lake Chautauqua, as busy as bees and as happy as angels. Let us look at the forms the children make out of the pliable sand. Here are caves where the fairies dwell, mountains, volcanoes, houses where the giants live. All these fantastic forms spring from the brain of the child and are expressed by means of this plastic material. See that little three-year-old girl with the model of a house in her brain: she is now wheeling a wheelbarrow, assisted by a little companion; in the barrow is the wood, and in her brain is the house. Energetic, persistent, happy,—in what direction? In the direction of true growth! The little girl in the kitchen is not happy until she can mould and change the flour into dough, and dough into forms for baking; and here begin her first lessons in chemistry, the wonderful changes which heat brings about. She will dress her doll, working patiently for hours. Inexpert beholders may not know what the crude forms mean, but the child knows and is satisfied,—nay, delighted. Give a child a piece of chalk, and its fancy runs riot: people, horses, houses, sheep, trees, birds, spring up in the brave confidence of childhood. In fact, all the modes of expression are spontaneously and persistently exercised by the child from the beginning except writing. It sings, it makes, it moulds, it paints, it draws, it expresses thought in all the forms of thought expression, with the one exception.

I have very imperfectly presented, in this brief outline, some of the spontaneous activities of the little child. The more I strive to present them, the more imperfect seems the result, so much lies beyond in the interpretation of the child's instinctive activities, so much seems to exceed all present discovery. The question, my fellow-teachers, is, what should these lessons teach us? The child instinctively begins all subjects known in the curriculum of the university. He begins them because he cannot help it; his very nature impels him. These tendencies, these spontaneous activities of the child spring from the depths of its being, spring from all the past, for the child is the fruit of all the past, and the seed of all the future. These quiet, persistent, powerful tendencies we must examine and continue with the greatest care. The child overcomes great obstacles by persistent energy, always acting with great confidence of himself and his powers. He overcomes these obstacles because his whole being is a unit of action, controlled by one motive. The spontaneous tendencies of the child are the records of inborn divinity; we are here, my fellow-teachers, for one purpose, and that purpose is to understand these tendencies and continue them in all these directions, following nature. First of all, we should recognize the great dignity of the child, the child's divine power and divine possibilities, and then we are to present the conditions for their complete outworking. We are here that the child may take one step higher; we are here to find and present the conditions adapted to the divine nature of the child.

I have tried to show that the whole round of knowledge is begun by the child, and begun because it breathes, because it lives. If the child loves science and history, and studies or attends to them instinctively, then he should go on, and we must know the conditions or subjects and means which should be presented to him for each new demand or need.

I grant that in the past of education attention has been directed too much to dead forms of thought, and for one good reason at least: the sciences are a modern creation of man and have not yet reached the child. Now we have these marvellous subjects presented to us, worked out by great thinkers of the present, and we are to choose whether we will continue the dead formalism that too often leads to pedantry and bigotry, or whether we are to lead the child's soul in that direction which God designed in His creation of the human being.

In conclusion I commend to you, in the words of our greatest American philosopher [Ralph Waldo Emerson, ed.]:

> A babe by its mother lies, bathed in joy;
> Glide the hours uncounted; the sun is its toy;
> Shines the peace of all being without cloud in its eyes,
> And the sum of the world in soft miniature lies.

I commend to you the "sum of the world" for your study, for in this direction lies all the future progress of humanity.

PSYCHOLOGICAL DIMENSION

Child Study / G. STANLEY HALL

Child study represents four or five lines of work which are quite distinct the one from the other. In the first place there is anthropology, this study of the human species from infancy to old age, and which now, within perhaps three or four years, has begun with great zest to study the civilized child in several countries, so that we have a large body of literature which a friend of mine is to take six lectures to describe.

We have also the pathological side. A distinguished German has looked over the writings of thirty of the chief writers upon education, and noted down in the dictionary every word designating faults of childhood. How many fault words do you think he has found in this pedagogic library of

"Child Study" is reprinted from G. Stanley Hall, "Child Study." Article in *Addresses and Proceedings, 1894*. Washington, D.C.: National Education Association, 1894. Pp. 174–179.

"Some of the Methods and Results of Child Study Work at Clark University" is an abstract of an article by G. Stanley Hall reprinted from *Addresses and Proceedings, 1896*. Washington, D.C.: National Education Association, 1896. Pp. 860–864.

thirty writers? He has found 927 words which designate a distinct fault.

Third, in every civilized country, children are tested by the scores and hundreds, with reference to sight, and they find that it decreases in acuteness as we go up in the school grades, until in some countries it reaches forty to fifty, or sixty-three per cent in the high school senior class. The ear has been tested, and the sensibility of the muscles, etc., and a large body of literature seems to suggest that the modern school may be making the child a little sickly and arresting its development. At any rate, the percentage and number of school-bred diseases was never so large; nor is it strange when we reflect that the child in nature plays freely, and uses all its muscles, and lives in the free air, while the school shuts him up in an artificial atmosphere, sets the child down on a seat, and at a desk, perhaps, which does not fit him. Physiologically it throws the whole strain of school work upon the tiny muscles of fingers and tongue and leaves about ninety per cent of the muscles idle, not in use in the exercise of the school-room. That fact may bring home to us the importance of what we have called pedagogical pathology, which now constitutes an important study in education, and is now claiming our attention in perhaps half a dozen shapes.

Then we have another great department which is devoted to the study of the child's mind; and a very strange and anomalous thing is the great amount of ignorance that has been discovered. The number of things which children ought to know, and do not know, would make a vast body of literature. The direction in which most of these defects of ignorance lie is known to us, and we must go forward and direct the forces of enlightenment toward the real enemies of our civilization.

Thus we have from many sources a great body of truths, that have come, as it were, to the rescue of the child. It seems as though science were dealing with life and history, and that everything must be understood through right conceptions of the right side of man's soul. This is the fact which lies behind and out of sight of the movement which has caused the creation of this new section, and which I ask you to guard as the very apple of your eye. It is this department alone that can make education a science, if it ever can be made a science.

This philosophy is almost new, for the adult psychology is quite a different thing, as different as is the child from the adult. Some have even gone so far as to say that those of us who have spent our lives in teaching the old philosophy could never enter into this new kingdom of child psychology.

It certainly will require an educated insight to enable us so to do, but enough has already been done to prove to my mind a satisfactory augury of the future. The little child now standing in our midst is, I believe, again to be the regeneration of education, to moralize it, to make it religious, to bring the child (because it brings the school) home to the hearts of the men and women, where children should always find a warm place.

I propose to speak briefly of three chief points in this course of study, where they seem to me to have their practical focus.

If I was to address you from the standpoint that I hope to be the motto of this section, it would be, child study is first and foremost for the benefit of the teacher. It educates and stimulates, and keeps the teacher young as nothing else does. By contact with children in their years of growth anybody ought to keep on growing to the very end of life. I believe that by contact with the child, in sympathy and interest, there is a growth for the teacher that no device in all education, no kind of extension movement, can equal in efficiency. So I say that the first chief good to be sought and expected is stimulating an interest, a renewed professional spirit, a scientific spirit, for the best science. The most progressive science of the day is behind the teacher in this movement and it does refresh and invigorate the teacher.

Child study is, secondly, for the sake of the child. To enable us to adapt our methods to the child, so the young teacher shall not merely run the school machinery and keep order, but shall give out an influence which shall go straight from his heart to the heart of every child in the room. Teachers should know that every child they touch has somewhere a secret spring, and it unfolds wonders, while not reducing the general efficiency for the room.

Thirdly and lastly, the value of this study is its advantage for science. Teachers can do great things for science here, and they have done so. Part of this is technical and part scientific; but part of it any teacher can do perhaps better than scientific men. It involves a new contact between the best science of the day and the best teaching of the time, and that is the standpoint for which I appeal for it.

The three practical advantages, which I desire to refer to, are, first, that of health. It does much for health, because the beginning of child study ought to be a great interest for the health of the child, and in that way you can interest the parent. This movement has resulted in Paris in the appointment of about thirty young doctors, before they have established their practice, who about twice a year fill out a little "health book" for each and every child in the schools where this system has been adopted.

If a child on examination has bad eyes, *e.g.*, they write in this book to "send him home at 3 o'clock." The child goes home, and they see that he has excellent medical care. That pleases the parents. This has been one of the best results of child study advocated by the government there.

The fact is we are coming to realize what health means. The sign of health is exuberance. He rejoices in play, the superfluous euphoria, the joy of being alive, and it is a greater joy than any other. The form of greeting among all civilized people, as they shake hands with each other is, "How do you feel"—how is your heart, your euphoria,—have you any extra life in you, over and above that necessary to keep your heart beating and lungs going and just to keep alive? This superfluity of life, over and above sufficient to support the more vital processes, is the raw material of culture. Every discovery, every great work that man has done, has been made out of this spontaneous material. Every great original creative work of man has been done out of this euphoria. Some men have done something when they were sick perhaps, but it is because the dear Lord has not quite denied euphoria even to the sick room. I think, then, it was not without considerable wisdom that the English physician, who lately died, said, that if he could only have the selection of the future queens of Great Britain, or Germany, or the other countries of Europe, he would ask two questions: "First, has she a good normal appetite for wholesome well-cooked food? and, second, does she sleep well? and being satisfied on these two points, for all the rest," he said, "I would trust God." I do not think it is irreverent, therefore, to ask, with all seriousness: "What shall it profit a child or a teacher, if they gain the whole world of knowledge and lose their own health, or what shall we give in exchange for health?" It is not without significance that, in the last three years, hygiene has come to take a prominent part in our education.

My second point is as old as health, and yet new, for the feature of child study is that, like the Gospel, it makes old things new. The first requisite of the good teacher for young children might perhaps be said to be: "Does that teacher succeed in opening the senses of the child?" Many children, it is said, are color blind. A great many people have no ear for music, but experts agree that it is absolutely unnecessary—that everybody might have a good musical ear. The object of the teacher should be to get the child in a condition of responsive sensitiveness to every aspect of nature. It all makes life larger, this contact with nature. There is a school of literature now devoted to the discovery of new sensations, that they may experience a new thrill; and all education should be directed to the unfolding of the senses and the widest possible development of the mind. So what we want to-day is to get as many sensations and as many different views of life as possible. As a boy I was brought up on the farm, or my father very wisely let me spend summer vacations on my grandfather's farm, where old-fashioned industries were seen, and I count the time spent there as the most educative of my life, because I had a natural ambition to do everything. Let me tell you some of the things I learned how to do and can do to-day, and am proud of it, although you may think me egotistical. I can mow; I can milk a cow, and know the right side, which many an artist does not; I can whet my own scythe; I know how to make a garden; I have woven a piece of cloth, or helped to do it, all myself; I have made palmleaf hats as a boy, from the very straw, finished them, and got five cents apiece for them; I can plant, chop, butcher, team it, cut ice, etc.; make cider, maple sugar, fences and stone walls, and all these things have stood me in useful stead in the laboratory, where a man must know and do a little of everything. My laboratory discipline is helped out by the farm work more than anything else. It is the impulse I got there that made it necessary afterwards for me in Germany to go and take a dozen lessons of a bookbinder, and another half dozen of a glass blower; and finally, when two or three years ago, I went into Boston I found a goldbeater, who gave me some lessons in the fine points of gold beating. In this way you open up to the eye of the soul the avenues of impression and expression; you get the soul in harmony with the life without, and there is an exchange between the soul within and the external life without. You thus multiply life, and you increase it two, or three, or four fold.

See what our psychologists are doing—spending their vacations in asylums, among the idiots and insane, and in prisons. We have to visit all kinds of institutions, because it is indispensable that we may know human nature; know it as it is. If you wish to study and understand life in any adequate way, you must look at it through these many different sources. Look at the microscope, and see what new worlds come before you. The man who has studied the microscope, knows many times as much of the world as he who looks at nature with the natural unaided eye, because he sees so many other things. It increases two or three times his capacity to enjoy the world and understand its problems; to know nature and know life. It helps to follow that principle which we have heard stated: "Necessity of taking the whole child into school." That is the second point.

Now the third and last is this: If you were to stop here it would be a very strange kind of a being you would develop. It would lack the very root of personality; namely, unity. Therefore we must have unity, and we must have all these various elements of our nature so compact and incorporated that they will not be easily broken up. You have all read, no doubt, stories of hypnotism and dual personality; but the essential quality in child training and in all education is unity of all the faculties. The eye and the ear, and all the senses, must not only be opened up and developed, but must be brought into their relative relations one with the other, and they grow together by association, and so unity, so far as we can study it, is growth. The pieces of the child's mind are made separately, and then they are put together. It is very important that their combination should be thorough, so that the personality will not be decomposable. One phase of this is seen at adolescence, when many natures almost break up as they pass through adolescent years with such great difficulty. I plead for this unity. I believe it is a question of the greatest seriousness which we have discovered here in the study of adolescence. We must get at the personalities of the child. That unity which accompanies old age, and which is fundamental for moral and ethical training, should be the cardinal aim and end of our endeavor. Therefore I say, children will be selfish before adolescence. It is nature to be selfish. Let them be selfish. Do not impose upon them any artificial conformity to your standard. Do not watch them always while they play, imposing limitations of adult standards upon them. A little child is a bundle of sentiment. It has all the tender feelings of the adult, almost; it can sympathize with your soul, your heart, and it can sympathize with your individuality. Not the intellect, but the heart of the adult and child are almost alike; therefore appeal to the heart, which is the strength and source of life. The mind is hardly able to think in childhood along other than selfish lines, but it should be developed, and the child sent out of the school-room, not selfish at the end, but altruistic and devoted to others, and if the school does not do that I believe it does very little for moral civilization.

Let us remember, then, that while selfishness has its own place in childhood, that religion and civilization show that fundamentally all morality is the instinct or discipline of service and doing good for others, and that view alone, I believe, will elevate education to the plane which it ought to occupy. It has already saved us in the past, and is to do much in the future for this country if it survives from the standpoint of the new enlarging educational philosophy—larger far than any philosophy we have had—the first glimpses of which appear in the study of the child; a philosophy so large that all science and evolution shall have its place in teaching, in order that the very best in the child may be inspired and roused and developed, and thus give to teaching a new consecration.

Some of the Methods and Results of Child Study Work at Clark University

Let me first tell you the method we have been using. We have issued syllabi on the different topics, and propose tabulating the answers collected from a large number of individuals. We have issued thirty-two of these syllabi and have sent them sometimes to nearly 1,000 observers each. We have had them reprinted and shall be glad to send them to all who will drop me a postal-card request.

The first investigation undertook the study of anger, on which some thousands of returns have been digested.

The second study was on dolls. Dolls are historically closely connected with idols. The penates, or household gods, shade over into idols. Dolls serve the tremendous purpose of reducing the world to a very petite form, just the size for children to understand. In Russia there has been a doll congress, and official recommendations for the use of dolls. We have found that the doll passion culminates at the age of eight or nine. It begins with rude things, and passes through all the stages of development to the perfect paper or wax creations.

We next studied crying and laughing, two of the most important phenomena of the race. These are the oldest residual phenomena. The noise and laugh of the child take us back to the beginnings of the race. Just as when we laugh and shake we drop back for an instant toward bliss itself and catch a glimpse of paradise lost, so the laughter of children shows us a real paradise set in the midst of civilization. The child repeats and illustrates the history of the race.

Then comes the study of fears. Just think what a chapter that opens. Out of 4,000 people only three were found who had no fears. Thunder and lightning lead all the rest, though less than one-fourth of 1 per cent die of lightning or of thunder either. Aristotle says "Education is to teach us to fear aright." Surely we have not advanced far on the road to wisdom. Fear cramps and arrests more than anything else all influence to good. Perhaps the chief end of education is to banish fear.

We then made a study of common traits and habits. We find that we each have characteristic movements, and these movements which we find in children beginning to write seem to show traces of residual movements going back to an earlier form of life. Just as fear of what has big eyes, fur and teeth, takes us back to the time when man feared animals more than now; so these automatic movements take us back to primitive times. We have thus traces of automatism, just as we have traces of gills, for example, in every human neck.

In the child's attitude toward nature we find something very akin to man's religious development. Every child is born a pagan, a fetish worshipper. Shall we try to stifle this phenomenon? Just as absurd to cut off a tadpole's tail and expect its legs to grow faster. It never falls off but is absorbed. To cut it off dwarfs its hind legs and ties it to an aquatic life. Just so with fetishism. This is the rudimentary organ—the tadpole's tail; cut it off and you dwarf human religion.

Another study was on children's food. We found all the appetites of all the animals. From the time that everything the child gets goes to its mouth, its arms are only tentacles.

Then we grew bold. We issued a year ago last spring two more syllabi, one upon love, the other upon religion.

We then made a special study of the dull child, and of the effect of different environments. We made here twenty-eight classifications. Then we studied old age; then music; then religious phenomena from another standpoint. Then we took up the "only child" and traced the effects of solitude. We even touched upon habit and instinct among the lower animals.

Some of the observers have organized themselves into societies. There are now several societies for studying children in Great Britain; one among the girls at Newnham College; one at Edinburg; one at Dublin.

Now for a few very general remarks about the future of child study. In the first place I believe it will show us the value of individuality. Children are different. As the Irishman said about the ladies, "They are all alike in being different." We must not forget that success in life depends upon the development of each individual in the particular line in which he excels. Every child should be thus developed enough to make a career. Not only because we live under a republican government, but because it is most economical.

In this connection let me say that child study is only one phase of this new movement in psychology; the front that is toward the teacher.

It also goes into physiology and has built up a small literature there; so also into insanity. It takes up the study of mental life in lower animals. Perez studied two cats. I know a friend who is studying a fly. That is a most fascinating study. Another studied the daily life of an amœba. These are all parts of one great movement.

The child repeats the race. This is a great biological view. We find numerous traces of this in the seventy-two organs of the body, and in many more rudimentary organs. This knowledge has developed since that eventful day when Fitz Müller began his studies on the relations of ontogony and philogomy. Today we take up the literature of the race and use all the traces of archæology to fill in the gap. Alongside of this we can use the child as embodying at different stages the successive changes of the race. We get evidence of this development in the fossils. We find certain fishes like the fossils. We find the mastodon bearing certain relations to the elephant. We find the series so complete in the batrachian group that we can trace all the stages, including the gradual absorption of gills as it crept out of water.

All of these changes are implanted in the germ-cell by which we repeat in a few days or hours the history of untold ages. It is simply a means of economy. Not that we must pass through all these stages, but it is the *shortest* way to reach this stage of development. Sometimes we find in the course of development rapid leaps. Wherever there have been these rapid leaps there is greatest danger of arrest.

A word or two before I sit down about the two views with regard to acceleration. Should the process of development in the individual child be forced or should it be retarded? Le Conte seems to think the child must be forced. Certainly wherever nutrition can take the place of external force it should be allowed to do so. Another method has been to retard development as much as possible. So we have the school of savagery, so that they will leave the children open to natural development. We can trace the stages of the race in the child-life. The mind doesn't follow uniform laws of growth but develops now in this direction, now in that. If you could really succeed in developing the child according to any method ever written you would make him a hopeless idiot. Everybody is a Jack-at-all-trades at some time. As Russell says, he is a little homunculus in whom all traits are generalized. To dwarf any of these elements before the shades of the prison house begin to close in on him is to stunt him.

All of these different lines of work are gradually developing. You know you never find all the geologic stages represented at one place. But the science of geology must study many places, so we are slowly finding our way, despite all doubtful criticisms, toward the real norm. Then, not till then, shall we have a real philosophy of education.

Now let me say a word about treatment. The way to treat the young child is not by fixed method. Jean Paul Richter warns us against letting the clapper rest heavily against the bell if you want a clear note. What the child soul needs is the light touch of the hand to guide the fancy which the children are so ready to take up. The child must be left to freedom. Interest is the main thing. If I had to choose between my child leading in some branch of study without interest, and his having no knowledge, but an interest in knowledge, I should infinitely prefer the latter.

Let me apply some of the results of our work. We are not in a position to apply all the results. We are too bound up in planting and digging about the roots to be ready to pluck the flowers. I rather deprecate haste for results. Though some facts I believe have been established which we may take into the schools. For example, I am convinced that drawing should never begin with copying straight lines. The natural child never makes straight lines or angles. It begins where most drawing ends, with the human figure.

So, too, with writing. I believe stress on writing should come two or three years later. Muscles are not developed so early. The fact of bad writing is against the present system. If we could put off writing two or three years and have it done within two years, we would make a saving and have better writers than now. So too with reading. I believe we could just as well begin with it later. A series of tests on memory powers might be given. Verbal memory of children is nearly as perfect as with the university student. Pestalozzi was right when he said give the memory something to do.

Then with modern languages. These should certainly be learned by the ear. The ear-method develops early. Think how short a time since writing began. How long before that all knowledge was transmitted from ear to ear.

In music there is a chance for a very radical change. Some of our music teachers are in a very bad way. The quality of music is miserable, and not the plan and methods by which it is hypertrophied beyond all sense and petty differences magnified.

So with regard to science, we are trying to make the child undertake college work with the microscope, or at least with technical terms. Science languishes because the child is not brought face to face with nature.

So with religion, we have got to go back to nature to understand what that really means, and begin with natural religion.

There is nothing more needed at present than a system of philosophy. There was a time when we had a system of philosophy. Now we have many systems which are equivalent almost to none. Like the man who describes the driving in a foreign city: He hired a hack and got in to drive to his stopping place. The bottom fell out, he had to run hard all the way and then pay for the hack. Our philosophy has left us in that condition I fear. We need to get a method, to find out the true order of mind and let it express itself. I believe profoundly in this movement, humble though it is, a movement in which every teacher can help; where the kindergarten and college work together. This thorough study of the human soul must result in a radical reconstruction of all theories of morals, and give us a true ideal of the aims of home, school and church, and the true order of their development. It will give us vision, and without vision, the people perish. We must expect a slow radical transformation of almost all subjects taught from the kindergarten to the university. The work is rooted in the strongest human instincts. Love of nature and of children is the glory of manhood and womanhood, and the test of civilization.

SOCIAL CONCEPTS DIMENSION

Infant and Child in the Culture of Today /
ARNOLD GESELL AND FRANCES L. ILG

The Household as a Cultural Workshop

The family remains the most fundamental unit of modern culture. It has been basic throughout the long history of man. The family is both a biological and a cultural group. It is biologic in the sense that it is the best arrangement for begetting children and protecting them while they are dependent. It is a cultural group because it brings into intimate association persons of different age and sex who renew and reshape the

"Infant and Child in the Culture of Today" is reprinted from Arnold Gesell and Frances L. Ilg, pp. 9–11, 40–41, 53–55, 55–58, 271–275, 288–290, in *Infant and Child in the Culture of Today*. Copyright 1943, by Arnold Gesell and Frances L. Ilg. Reprinted by permission of Harper & Row, Publishers.

folkways of the society into which they are born. The household serves as a "cultural workshop" for the transmission of old traditions and for the creation of new social values.

The spirit and organization of the family therefore reflect the historic culture. A totalitarian "Kultur" subordinates the family completely to the state, fosters autocratic parent-child relationships, favors despotic discipline, and relaxes the tradition of monogamy. It is not concerned with the individual as a person. A democratic culture, on the contrary, affirms the dignity of the individual person. It exalts the status of the family as a social group, favors reciprocity in parent-child relationships, and encourages humane discipline of the child through guidance and understanding.

In a very profound way the democratic ideal is also bound up with the spirit of liberty. Liberty is the life principle of democracy, in the home as well as in the community. The home, like the state, has its problems of government and must give controlled scope to the spirit of liberty which animates the growing child. Every living organism strives to attain a maximum of maturity. The spirit of liberty has its deepmost roots in the biological impulse toward optimal growth. Babies as well as adults are endowed with this inalienable impulsion.

The concept of democracy, therefore, has far-reaching consequences in the rearing of children. Even in early life the child must be given an opportunity to develop purposes and responsibilities which will strengthen his own personality. Considerate regard for his individual characteristics is the first essential.

Considerateness, it has been well said, is in itself a social system. The very word conveys the idea of respect for the dignity of the individual. If parents and teachers begin with the assumption that they can make over and mold a child into a preconceived pattern, they are bound to become autocratic. If, on the contrary, parents begin with the assumption that every baby comes into the world with a unique individuality, their task will be to interpret the child's individuality and to give it the best possible chance to grow and find itself.

Considerateness, as we use the term here, is not merely a social grace. It is something of an art, a combination of perceptiveness and imaginativeness which enables one person to appreciate the psychology of other persons. It is an alert liberalism which is sensitive to distinctive characteristics in other individuals. It is a kind of courtesy to which infants are entitled.

Infants are individuals,—individuals in the making as well as by birthright. To understand their individuality it is necessary to sense the underlying processes of development which are at work.

The child's personality is a product of slow and gradual growth. His nervous system matures by stages and natural sequences. He sits before he stands; he babbles before he talks; he fabricates before he tells the truth; he draws a circle before he draws a square; he is selfish before he is altruistic; he is dependent on others before he achieves dependence on self. All of his abilities, including his morals, are subject to laws of growth. The task of child care is not to force him into a predetermined pattern but to guide his growth.

This developmental point of view does not mean indulgence. It means a constructive deference to the limitations of immaturity. It obliges us to accord more courtesy even to the infant, who is often unwittingly handled in an arbitrary manner simply because we have failed to understand the processes of development.

Only in a democratic climate of opinion is it possible to give full respect to the psychology of child development. Indeed the further evolution of democracy demands a much more refined understanding of infants and preschool children than our civilization has yet attained. Should science ever arrive at the happy juncture where it can focus its full force upon the interpretation of life, it will enable us to do more complete and timely justice to the individual personality in the very young. And this in turn will have far-reaching effects upon the adult population.

Maturation and Acculturation

Such classifications are much too simple to do justice to the infinite diversity of human individualities; but they serve to remind us that there are primary individual differences more basic than the differences acquired through acculturation. In the hey-day of Behaviorism there was a popular impression that all babies are very much alike at birth, and that the differences which become apparent as they mature are due to conditioned reflexes. The child's mind was said to consist of a complex bundle of conditioned reflexes, derived from environmental stimuli. According to this point of view, children resemble each other most while they are infants—the younger, the more alike.

There is no evidence, however, that infants are not individuals to the same degree that adults are individuals. Long range studies made in our clinic have demonstrated that such traits as social responsiveness, readiness of smiling, self-dependence and motor agility tend to manifest themselves early and to persist under varying environmental conditions. Every child is born with a *naturel* which colors and structures his experiences. The infant, to be sure, has great plasticity, great powers of learning; but there are lawful limits to his conditionability. He has constitutonal traits and tendencies, largely inborn, which determine *how, what,* and to some extent even *when* he will learn.

These traits are both racial and familial. The racial traits are those which are common to the whole human species. The familial traits are the distinctive endowment which he inherited from his parents and a long line of grandparents. The child comes into this double inheritance through an innate process of growth which we call *maturation*. He comes into the social "heritage" of culture, through a process of *acculturation*. These two processes interact and interfuse, but the process of maturation is most fundamental,—so fundamental that acculturation can never transcend maturation.

Infants are individuals, because the intrinsic forces of maturation operate to keep them from being the mere pawns of culture. The impacts of culture are incessant and often they tend to produce uniformity, but even the tender infant preserves an individuality, through the inherent mechanisms of maturation. We may be duly thankful for this degree of determinism. Did it not exist, the infant would be a victim of the malleability which behaviorists once ascribed to him. He is durable as well as docile. In a boundlessly complex world he says, in effect, "Lo, I too am here!"

Self-Regulation Through Cultural Control

The principle of self-regulatory fluctuations is so fundamental in child development that it has vast cultural implications. The principle applies not only to such "simple" functions as sleeping, eating, and infant play; it applies to the higher forms of learning and of mental organization. The organism during the entire period of active growth is in a state of formative instability combined with a progressive movement toward stability. The so-called growth gains represent consolidations of stability. The opposition between two apparently opposing tendencies results in seesaw fluctuations. Stability and variability co-exist not as contradictory opposites, but as mutual complements. Therefore we must look upon many fluctuations as positive thrusts or efforts toward higher maturity. They may be construed as self-demands, which if adequately satisfied by the culture result in optimal growth of personality organization.

Such is the underlying theory stated in broad terms. This volume conceives cultural guidance in terms of the optimal needs of the individual organism. The cultural pattern must be adapted to the growth pattern, because in final analysis all individual development depends upon intrinsic self-regulation. There is no adjustment to culture other than self-adjustment.

But self-demand is only the beginning of the story of fostering the infant's healthy development. We have seen only too often within recent decades how self-demands may lead to excess. The bewildered parent is shocked when a 4 year old child tells her to "shut up." She has tried hard to have him live by his inner laws; but she comes to realize that he does not live by inner laws alone, for these are of no use to him unless they have come into equilibrium with the laws of the world in which he moves. She may have seen that her child made a good start, but she did not know how to help him finish, how to help him round out his patterns of behavior.

This is why it is so important for the parent to learn the mechanisms of innate and cultural regulation within the first year of the child's life when the patterns are relatively simple. She hears the urgency of the hunger cries of the 4 week old child which can only be controlled with food. She realizes that at 16 to 28 weeks this cry is less frequent and that the child can wait for his feeding. His hunger pains are now less intense, his gastro-intestinal tract is subordinating itself at times to other demands. For now the infant's overflow energy is diverted into active discovery of his own body, his hands, his feet, and also the persons who people his environment. His own inner growth is a controlling and organizing factor.

But this inner ability to wait is specific rather than general. It fails to show itself at the age of 18 months when it is time for juice and crackers. There is a developmental reason for this behavior. The child is acquiring a new control, namely that of demanding food when he sees the table at which the juice and crackers last were served. *Now* is all he knows at this stage of maturity. His mother, realizing the significance of this passing stage of maturity, manages accordingly. She has his mid-morning juice and crackers ready before he sees the table at the expected time. She also knows that she can help him to wait when he is 2½ years old by saying, "Pretty soon." By three years he understands, "When it's time", and by four, he wishes to help in the preparation of a meal. Thus culture in its greater wisdom has led the child steadily onward in relation to his innate readiness to make new adjustments and to curb himself. This is the wisdom of growth guidance as opposed to absolute discipline.

The old and pithy word "curb" harks back to a control that was used in earlier days. The word lives with us in our curbstones. These ancient stones help us in the control of behavior quite as much as do modern traffic lights. But the young child grows only slowly into the realization of what a curbstone means as a limit of safety. His culture having put him in a world of swiftly moving cars, must protect him from dashing out into the street at 18 months. He needs to be harnessed. At two, he not only sees curbstones but has the motor capacity and balance to walk on them endlessly as long as he has a helping and protecting hand available. It is not until two and a half years that he visually sees and is aware of the danger of a car backing up toward him. At three, he continues to accept his mother's hand as he is crossing a street. At four he is more watchful, more conscious of objects coming from both directions, and longs for the independence of crossing a street absolutely alone. The culture knows that he often overstates his abilities at this age, but responds to his eagerness by allowing him to cross narrow, safe, streets (though not thoroughfares) without holding of hands. By five he is less eager and more self-regulated and accepts the new and helpful control of traffic lights, with his ever watchful eyes. It is now that he is capable of greater independence. Culture recognizes the cue.

If he cannot adjust in this orderly fashion, there may be two possible causes. He may be holding on to earlier modes of adjustment (C-type growth pattern). The culture must then wait and watch knowing that the time will come when his behavior equipment will be ready. Often, however, the child cannot make the final step alone, but needs a lift from the environment at the moment when he is ready to accept the help. The custodians of the culture need to realize that sometimes life becomes too complex and must be greatly simplified in behalf of the child.

Through such mutual accommodations between culture and child, human relationships are improved at all age levels. The "culture" teaches the child, but the child also teaches the "culture",—makes it more intelligently aware of the laws, the frailties, and the potentialities of human nature.

The Cultural Significance of Self-Regulation

Does this philosophy of self-regulation imply overindulgence or excessive individualism? By no means; for we always conceive of our individual as growing in a democratic culture which makes demands on individual responsibility. The danger of overindulgence is fictitious, for the goal of self-regulatory guidance is to increase the tensions and the fullness of growth. In the infant the self-demand type of management builds up body stamina and a corresponding organic sense of secureness. The most vital cravings of the infant have to do with food and sleep. These cravings have an individual, organic pattern. They cannot be transformed nor transgressed. Only by individualizing the schedules can we meet these cravings promptly and generously. By meeting them with certainty, we multiply those experiences of satisfied expectation which create a sense of security, a confidence in the lawfulness of the universe.

It is too easy to forget that the infant has a psychology, and that our methods of care affect his mental as well as physical welfare. The individualization of food-sleep-activity schedules is a basic approach to the mental hygiene of infancy. The education of the baby begins with his behavior day.

The mother's specialized education with respect to this particular baby also begins with the selfsame behavior day. The first year of life offers her a golden opportunity to become acquainted with the individual psychology of her child. And what she learns during that first year will be of permanent value, for throughout childhood and adolescence this child is likely to display the same dynamic characteristics which come into transparent view in early life.

The adoption of a self-demand schedule policy creates a favorable atmosphere for the kind of observation which will enable the mother to really learn the basic characteristics of her infant. She escapes the vexation which comes from forcing unwanted food and from waiting for long spells of hunger crying to come to an end. Instead of looking at the clock on the wall, she shifts her interest to the total behavior day of the baby as it records itself on the daily chart. She also notes in what manner and in what direction these days transform as the infant himself transforms. This is a challenge to intelligent perception. Thus she satisfies her instinctive interest in the child's growth and gains increasing insight into the growth process and the growth pattern. It simply comes to this: She has made the baby (with all his inborn wisdom) a working partner. He helps her to work out an optimal and a flexible schedule suited to his changing needs.

Although this seems very simple, it has profound consequences in the mother's attitudes. Instead of striving for executive efficiency, she aims first of all to be perceptive of and sensitive to the child's behavior. Thus she becomes a true complement to him; alertly responsive to his needs. The child is more than a detached individual who must be taken care of at stated clock intervals. And he is more than a treasured possession. He is a living, growing organism, an individual in his own right to whom the culture must attune itself if his potentialities are to be fully realized.

The first year of life is by no means all-determining, but it is the most favorable of all periods for acquiring the right orientation toward the child's individuality. During this first year one does not use sharp emotional methods of discipline. One comes to understand in what way the child's immaturity must be met and helped. We expect the child to creep before he walks. We do not punish him for creeping. We do not prod him unduly into walking. Growth has its seasons and sequences.

The child must do his own growing. For this reason we should create the most favorable conditions for self-regulation and self-adjustment. But this means neither self-indulgence nor laissez faire. The culture intervenes, assists, directs, postpones, encourages and discourages at many turns; but always in relation to the child's behavior equipment and maturity status. When the baby is young we meet his hunger needs promptly. As he grows older he is gradually accustomed to waiting a little longer before his hunger is gratified. He thus acquires increasing hardihood by slow degrees as he is able to bear it. But this method of gradual induction is not possible unless we take fundamental notice of his self-demand cues and shape our guidance on a self-regulatory developmental basis.

This philosophy of child development and of child guidance assumes a democratic type of culture. A totalitarian type of culture would place the first and last premium upon the extrinsic cultural pattern; it would mould the child to this pattern; it would have little patience with self-demands. Cultural guidance, as outlined in the present volume, is essentially individualized. It begins in earliest infancy. It remains individualized not only in the home, but in the nursery school group and in the larger social world.

Absolute Versus Relative Concepts

There are three major brands of philosophy which deal with the principles and practices of child care: 1) authoritarian; 2) laissez-faire; 3) developmental.

The authoritarian approach takes its point of departure from the culture. It assumes that the adult culture knows what the rising generation needs to know. The culture proceeds accordingly to impose its imprint. In its extreme form this philosophy holds that children are habit forming creatures, who can be moulded to the patterns of the culture through the process of learning and of the conditioned-reflex. Behaviorism as a social theory concedes little to the child's heredity, and has great confidence in the power and the authority invested in the environment. It is not inconsistent with totalitarian trends of thought.

Laissez-faire doctrine applies to the child as it does to economic forces. The underlying theory is that "the world goes of itself." Constrain neither child nor culture. Things will work out for the best. For the child will know and select what is best for him if you do not confuse and restrict him. It is the policy of non-interference. It encourages almost complete freedom of action for the child, and requires little effort at intelligent guidance on the part of the adult.

A *developmental philosophy* in temper and in principle lies intermediate between the two foregoing extremes. In matters of child care this outlook is suspicious of absolutes and does not favor license. It is sensitive to the relativities of growth and maturity. It takes its point of departure from the child's nature and needs. It acknowledges the profound forces of racial and familial inheritance which determine the growth sequences and the distinctive growth pattern of each individual child. It envisages the problem of acculturation in terms of growth; but this increases rather than relaxes the responsibility of cultural guidance. Developmental guidance at a conscious level demands an active use of intelligence to understand the laws and the mechanisms of the growth process.

It is easy to see how these three contrasted points of view affect all human relations, including those between adult and child. Discipline under authoritarian auspices tends to be severe, even cruel. The flogging of sailors, corporal punishment, and regimentation are autocratic in temper. Indulgence, excessive freedom, and egocentric self-direction replace severity at the other lackadaisical extreme. The developmental approach does not admit such self-direction. It holds for cultural guidance controls; but it believes in self-regulation and self-adjustment within these controls. It has such confidence in the wisdom of Nature (as opposed to authoritarian cultural goals) that it takes its cues from the child. It aims to conserve all the best potentialities of the child in the broad framework but not in the narrow and rigid compartments of culture.

This requires an intimate knowledge of the growth process; the same kind of knowledge which the present day mechanic has with respect to the operations of an internal combustion engine. Our culture has arrived at that stage of sophistication and discernment that it can no longer carry on satisfactorily in the field of child care without the aids of modern science. There is a type of native intelligence which appreciates the import of growth factors, without formal instruction. But we can scarcely rely on intuition and improvisation in the rearing of children. We must make it our business to better comprehend how their minds grow, how their personalities are formed. Their psychological care needs an informed developmental philosophy, based upon a sympathetic familiarity with the detailed operations of growth.

In other words we must learn to think of growth as a living reality, rather than merely the label of an intricate process. Growth (or development) is not an empty abstraction; it is a series of events governed by laws and forces just as real as those which apply to an internal combustion engine. The psychological growth of the child is a marvellous series of patterned events, outwardly manifested in behavior. The nervous system is the vital part of the machinery which makes the events possible. It weaves within itself a complicated continuous fabric as it matures, a fabric which comes to light in the actions, the attitudes, the personality of the child. Growth ceases to be merely an abstract or rather useless label, if we think of development as a weaving process which gives shape and structure to the mind.

A Science of Child Development as a Cultural Force

Socialized conservation will need all the resources of the life sciences, as well as new visions of cultural welfare. It will be the task of science to define more clearly the limitations of culture as a determinant of human behavior. The anthropologist sees in living cultures, in spite of their apparent diversity, a pervading sameness, arising out of common traits of human nature. This quality of sameness denotes underlying psychological laws which should enable us better to understand ourselves and our cultures, including religion, morals, mores, child care, and government. Thus also we may arrive at more insight into the diseases of culture as manifested in poverty, economic crises, crime and war. It is not strange that cultural anthropology claims to be the very basis of social science. But scientific anthropology, no less than psychology, is inextricably bound up with physics, chemistry, physiology and biology. Culture began with a very primitive man whose descendants have not lost all his primitiveness.

The culture of tomorrow will begin and always rebegin with the development of individual infants and children; for, as Malinowski aptly said, culture is nothing but the organized behavior of man,—"a large-scale molding matrix, a gigantic conditioning apparatus. In each generation it produces its type of individual. In each generation it is in turn reshaped by its carriers."

Now, however, more than ever before, it is necessary to understand realistically the limiting factors in this conditioning mechanism. They are growth factors. They are the laws of child development. Indeed, it might be well to reserve the term matrix for the maturational mechanisms which literally establish the basic patterns of behavior and of growth career. A matrix is that which gives form and foundation to something which is incorporated, in this instance, through growth. By growth we do not mean a mystical essence, but a physiological process of organization which is registered in the structural and functional unity of the individual. In this sense the maturational matrix is the primary determinant of child behavior.

This process of organization, is a life process, is infinitely older than human culture. It is so ancient that man shares it with plants and animals. Darwin grasped the unity of a world web of life. His passionate genius reduced the vast reaches of the evolution of the human race to a comprehensible order; but he left unsolved the great problem of man's capacity to carry the cultures which he creates.

This brings us back to the basic problem of environmental conditioning,—the relationships between maturation and acculturation. In the heyday of behaviorism it was seriously suggested that "almost nothing is given in heredity" and that practically the whole psychology of the child is built in by the mechanisms of habit formation and the conditioned reflex. Such an extreme theory of human development explains too much. It explains, of course, how totalitarian systems of education and government can mold their subjects to a pre-conceived model. But it does not sufficiently explain how this molding process also fails, and why an inexorable spirit of liberty defies it. Surely it has now been demonstrated that any culture which has an overweening confidence in its own authority over the individual endangers the collective sanity. Even the most highly technological civilization cannot survive unless it is compatible with laws of human behavior and organic growth.

For these reasons, the culture of tomorrow will be dependent in no small measure upon adequate sciences of child development and of human behavior. There will also be profounder spiritual insights, but even these must reckon with the laws and limitations of human nature, as embodied in infants and children. Symbolic concepts which oversimplify the intricate problems of good and evil can, alone, no longer suffice as goals and guides. We need a much more penetrating knowledge of the mechanisms of mental development and motivation. Our present-day knowledge of the personality of infant and child is extremely meager and fragmentary. Science can and will in time supply a fuller understanding. And this understanding will have a refining and humanizing effect upon the culture itself. Or shall we say that such science generously expended is an expression of an improving culture?

SPECIAL READING

The Child / MARIA MONTESSORI

Errors of the Past

Hitherto the only aim of the educator, the aim towards which all his efforts were directed, was that of preparing the pupil for that social life in which he would later on be forced to live. Therefore, as what was aimed at principally was that he should know how to imitate the adult, he was forced to suffocate the creative forces of the spirit under the cloak of the instinct of imitation. Preferably he was taught that which was considered indispensable to know in order to be able to live in a civilized community. This forced an absolute assimilation of a form of social life which is not natural to children, and should become natural to them only when they would be adults. In such conditions the real nature of the children could not be appreciated either in the old type of school or in the form of old-fashioned family education. The child was only "a future being." He was not envisaged except as one "who is to become," and therefore he was of no account until he had reached the stage in which he had become a man.

Yet the child, like all other human beings, has a personality of his own. He carries within him the beauty and the dignity of the creative spirit, and these can never be erased, so that his soul which is pure and very sensitive requires our most delicate care. We must not only preoccupy ourselves with his body which is so tiny and so fragile. We must not think only of nourishing and washing and dressing him with great care. Man does not live by bread alone even in his infancy. Material needs are on a step which is lower and can be degrading at any age. Slavery fosters in children, as well as in adults, inferior sentiments and generates an absolute lack of dignity.

The social environment which we have created for ourselves is not suited to the child. He does not understand it and therefore he is kept busy away from it, and as he cannot adapt himself to our society he is excluded from it, and is given into the care of the school which often becomes his prison. Today we can at last see very clearly how fatal are the consequences of a school where the children are taught by old methods. They suffer on this account not only organically but also morally. It is this fundamental problem of education, the education of character, that has been up to now neglected by the school. Also in the family circle there is the same error of principle. There also, it is always the tomorrow of the child, his future existence, which is the constant preoccupation. The present is never taken seriously into account. By the present I mean what the child needs in order to be able to live fully according to the psychic needs of his age. At the most, when things have been going well in families which have more modern ideas, it is the physical life of the child that has begun to be taken into account in these last years. Rational alimentation, hygienic dressing, life in the open air constitute the latest progress that science has brought, during this century, into the life of the child.

But the most human of all the needs of the child is neglected—the exigencies of his spirit, of his soul. The human being who lives within the child remains stifled therein. To us are known only the efforts and the energy that are necessary for the child to defend itself against us. What we know is the weeping, the shouting, the tantrums, the timidity, the possessiveness, the fibs, the selfishness and spirit of destruction. We commit an error which is even more serious and has more serious consequences. That is, to consider these means of defence as if they were the essential traits of the infant character, and to subdue them, as we consider is our strict duty, to try and eliminate them with the greatest severity, with a sternness which carries us even to the extremes of corporal punishment. These reactions of the child are often the symptoms of a moral illness, and very frequently they precede a real nervous disease which makes its consequences felt for the rest of the individual's life.

We all know that the age of development is the most important period of the whole life. Moral malnutrition and intoxication of the spirit are as fatal for the soul of man as physical malnutrition is for the health of his body. Therefore child-education is the most important problem of humanity.

The Remedy

It is for us a question of conscience to try to understand even the faintest shades of the soul of the child, and to take extreme care in our relations with the world of the small ones. Previously we were almost complacent in performing the part of pitiless judges in front of the children. They appeared to us full of defects when compared with adults, and we set ourselves in front of them as examples of beings overflowing with every virtue. We must now be content with a much more modest role, that required by the interpretation that Emerson gave of the message of Jesus Christ:

> Infancy is the eternal Messiah, which continuously comes back to the arms of degraded humanity in order to entice it back to heaven.

If we consider the child in this light, we shall be forced to recognize, as an absolute and urgent necessity, that care must be given to childhood, creating for it a suitable world and a suitable environment. We shall have accomplished a great task in favour of man by doing this. The child cannot lead a natural life in the complicated world of adults; also it is clear that the adult by his continuous supervision, by his uninterrupted advice, by his dictatorial attitude, disturbs and thwarts the development of the child. All the good forces which are sprouting in its soul are suffocated in this fashion, and nothing is left in the child but a subconscious impulse to free himself as soon as possible from everything and every one.

Let us therefore discard our role of prison warden, and let us instead preoccupy ourselves with preparing an environment in which as far as possible we shall try not to harass him by our supervision and by our teaching. We must become persuaded that the more the environment corresponds to the needs of the child, the more limited becomes the activity of the teacher. But here a very important principle must not be forgotten—giving freedom to the child does not mean to abandon him to his own resources and perhaps to neglect him. The help that we give to the soul of the child must not be passive indifference to all the difficulties of its development. Rather we must second it with prudence and affectionate care. However, even by merely preparing with great care the environment of the children, we shall have already done a great task, because the creation of a new world, a world of the children, is no easy accomplishment. As soon as small furniture is prepared, of which children stand in as much need as adult people (perhaps even more, for to them it is not merely a piece of furniture but a means of development) we see that their movements and activity become incredibly ordered. Before, their limbs seemed to be without any master to direct them; they ran about knocking everything down, jumping here, crashing there. Now their movements seem to be directed by a conscious will. They can be left alone without any danger because they know what they want.

The need for activity is almost stronger than the need for food. This has not been recognized heretofore because a suitable field of activity was not there for the child to manifest his needs. If we give him this we shall see the small tormentors who could never be satisfied convert themselves into cheerful workers. The proverbial destroyer becomes the most zealous custodian of the objects that surround him. The noisy and boisterous child, disorderly in its movements and in its actions, is transformed into a being full of spiritual calm and very orderly. But if the child lacks suitable external means, he will never be able to make use of the great energies with which nature has endowed him. He will feel the instinctive impulse towards an activity such as may engage all his energy, because this is the way nature has given him of making perfect the acquisitions of his faculties. But if there is nothing there to satisfy this impulse, what can the child do but what he does—develop his activity without any aim in disorderly boisterousness?

In the preparation of an environment everything depends upon this.

The House of Children

By now almost every one knows of the House of Children. Small furniture and small simple objects whose aim is to serve the intellectual development of the child are being built in all civilized nations: small furniture brilliant in colour, and so light that when knocked against it falls easily, and that therefore the child can easily move about. The lightness of the colour places in evidence the spots and the dust, and in this fashion any disorder or lack of attention on the part of the child is revealed. But as it is revealed easily it can be as easily corrected with the aid of a little soap and a little water. In our House of Children the furniture is like that. Every child chooses the place which he likes best, and places everything to suit his taste, but he must beware of any disorderly action because, as the furniture is light, every disorderly movement is betrayed by the furniture that scrapes upon the floor. So the child is surrounded by admonishing friends whose voices are not the voices of the adults, and he learns to be careful, to be conscious and to direct the movements of his body. It is for this reason that we place in the environment of the child beautiful fragile little objects of glass or of china, because if the child lets them fall they will break, and he will lose forever those beloved little objects that gave him so much joy and that attracted his eyes and hands every time he came into the room. Gone, lost forever, just because he had not taken enough care in the way he held them, just because he left them slip between his fingers! They are now broken into pieces, dead, no longer there to call him and to smile at him. What greater punishment could the child have than that of losing his beloved objects, that nowhere else was he allowed to touch, except in the small house which had been built for him to suit his size, and his mental development! What stronger voice can there be than that which admonishes the child: "Be careful of your movements! Every disorderly movement of yours is a danger of death for one of your beloved friends who surround you?" What great pain the loss of a dear object is for a child; we who have been with him know. And who would not feel the urge of consoling one of these tiny beings who, all red in the face, stands crying before a beautiful little porcelain vase that he has let fall? And if you could see him later! From that time on how concentrated his face is when he carries frail objects, how visible the effort of will to command all his movements in order to achieve their correctness.

So you see it is the environment itself which helps to make the children continuously better, because every error, no matter how small, becomes so evident that it is useless for the teacher to interfere. She can remain a quiet spectator of all the little mistakes that occur around her, and little by little it will seem as if the child heard the voices of the objects that, in their silent language, speak and admonish, revealing to him his small errors, "Be careful. Don't you see I am your beautiful little table? I am all shiny and polished and varnished. Don't scratch me. Don't spot me. Don't soil me!" The aesthetic quality in the objects and in the environment is a great spur to the activity of the child, so that it makes him redouble his efforts. That is why in our House of Children all the objects are attractive. The dusters are gaily colored, the broom-handles are hand-painted in bright tints, and the small brushes are as attractive as the small pieces of soap which, round or rectangular, are there in pink and blue and yellow calling to the eyes of the child, asking to be used. From all the objects that voice must spring forth which says to the child: "Come and touch me, make use of me. Don't you see me? I am the beautiful duster all pink and red. Come, let us go and take the dust off the top of the table." And from the other side: "Here I am, the small broom. Take me in your little hands and let us clean the floor." And still another voice calls to say: "Come, beautiful little hands. Dive into the water and take the soap." From everywhere the bright objects call to the child; they almost begin to form part of its mood, of its being, of its very nature, and there is no longer need for the teacher to say: "Charles, clean the room"; and: "John, wash your hands."

Every child who has been freed, who knows how to care for himself, how to put his shoes on, to dress and undress without help, mirrors in his joy, in his merriment, the reflection of human dignity; because human dignity is born of the sentiment of one's independence.

The joy that the small ones feel in their work makes them accomplish everything with an enthusiasm that is almost excessive. If they are shining the brass handle of a door they do it for such a long time that it becomes as shining as a mirror. Even the most simple things, such as dusting and sweeping, are done with an amount of exaggeration.

Marvellous Results

It is evident that it is not the attainment of an external aim which spurs them to activity, but rather the possibility of being able to valorize and to exercise their latent energies. It is this valorization which decides the duration of the activity and asks for continuous repetition. The repetition of an action, while making the child happy, makes him also accomplish real feats. We see, for instance, children of a very young age dressing and undressing alone, hooking buttons, making bows, laying a table to perfection, cleaning the dishes. But this is not enough; the super-abundance of its energy is revealed in the fact that the child uses what he has just learned to the advantage of those who as yet have not acquired an equal degree of perfection. So we see a child buttoning the clothes of his younger fellow, tying his shoe-strings or quickly cleaning the ground if someone happens to upset the soup. If he washes the dishes he cleans those which others have soiled, and when he lays the table he works for the benefit of many others who have not partaken the work with him. And in spite of this he does not consider this work done in service of others as a supplementary effort deserving praise. No, it is the effort itself which is for him the most sought after prize. I have seen once a little girl sit very sad before a steaming dish of soup without even tasting it. Why? Because they had promised to let her lay the table and then had forgotten about it. And the disillusion was so great that even the clamour of the body's needs had been silenced. Her little heart cried louder than her stomach.

In this way the part of the exterior activity of the child which is aimed towards social purposes is developed. The child has an aim which he understands very well and which he can accept with ease. His intelligence seeks for this aim, and we in placing it within the frame of its environment give to the child the freedom of attaining it. Certainly his real nature, his real interest, has much deeper roots, and the child acts as he does, not merely to finish a duty which he has chosen, but to satisfy his desire for activity and to slacken a thirst which obeys the laws of development. An exterior aim, simple and clear, is necessary in order to bring about the satisfaction of this desire. We shall see him wash his hands God knows how many times, not because they are dirty but because he is compelled by a need which requires of him the progressive development of the necessary secondary actions, such as to bring and to pour water, to make use of the soap and of the towel, etc. The continued and accurate use of all these things, how much work does it all entail? To sweep the room, to change water for the flowers, to place the furniture in the room, to roll the carpets, to lay the table. All these are reasonable activities which are joined to physical exercise. Whoever is in life forced to do this manual work and whoever experiences the fatigue which it causes, he knows how much movement is necessary to accomplish this series of tasks.

Lately much has been spoken of the need of physical exercise. Well, here is an exercise and not of the useless and mechanical kind, but of the type that can be accomplished with clarity of mind and with a purpose behind it. In spite of this, the exercises of practical life that the small ones carry out with so much joy, and that surprise so pleasantly all the visitors to the House of Children, do not as yet represent the essential part. They are but a beginning, an initiation, and form the least important side of the child's activity. It is a well-known fact that scientists give the impression of deep concentration which makes them indifferent to worldy things. All know the anecdote of Newton who forgets to take his food, of Archimedes who does not even notice the furious sounds of the battle for the conquest of Syracuse, and allows himself to be surprised by the enemy intently immersed in geometrical calculations. Well, it is just this sort of anecdote which shows the opposite side, the other phase of this deep concentration. The great discoveries that bring progress for all humanity are not due so much to the culture of the scientists, or to their knowledge, as to this capacity of complete concentration, to the power on the part of their intellect to bury itself in the task that fascinates them, that makes them no longer feel the need of society which they shun, retiring into their house or into some solitary spot.

When the child finds a field of accomplishment which corresponds to the intimate needs of its soul, he will reveal also what else he needs for the development of his existence. He is seeking, for the moment, his relations with the rest of humanity that surrounds him, and he is finding them. There are, however, inner exigencies which, while leading him into his mysterious task, require complete solitude, the separation from all and from every one. No one can help us to reach this intimate isolation which makes accessible to us our most hidden world, our deepest nature, so very mysterious, so very rich and full. If anyone comes to us in such a moment and interferes, he interrupts and destroys this intimate work of the soul. This concentration which is obtained by freeing oneself from the external world must arise in our very soul, and what surrounds us cannot procure its growth, its order and its peace. The state of complete concentration can be found only in great men, and even in them it is exceptional. It is the origin of an inner force, of an inner strength which makes them stand out from among the others. From this concentration springs forth the faculty that the great have of influencing the masses with meditated tranquillity and infinite benevolence. They are men who, after a prolonged separation from the world, feel themselves capable of solving the great problems of humanity while with infinite patience they bear the weaknesses and imperfections of their fellows, even if these rise to the extremity of hate and persecution.

Studying the phenomenon we see that there is a close link between the manual work which is accomplished in common life and the profound concentration of the spirit. Although at first it seems that these two things are opposed, in reality they are deeply united, because the one is but the source of the other. The life of the spirit prepares in solitude the strength which is necessary for ordinary life, and, in its turn, daily life fixes the concentration through orderly work. The wastage of energy is continually replaced from the sources of the concentration of the spirit. The man who sees clearly in himself feels the need of an inner life, just as the body feels the needs of the material life such as hunger and sleep. The soul which no longer feels its spiritual needs is in the same dangerous position as the body which is no longer capable of feeling the pangs of hunger or the need of rest.

But if we find this concentration and this burying of the soul within itself in the child, it becomes evident that the phenomenon does not represent an exceptional state of persons who are especially endowed with spiritual gifts; but it is a universal quality of the human soul which, on account of circumstances, survives in only a few people who have reached adult age. Now if we consider in the children these single glimmers of concentration, a picture is unfolded which is completely different from the one when we spoke of utilitarian tasks that the children performed. An object from which no possible usefulness can be derived suddenly attracts the attention of the child, who begins to fuss around it and move it in all directions. Often they are but small movements, uniform and almost mechanical. Often the hand destroys that which it had constructed but a moment before, in order to start building again. These movements will be repeated so many times that one is forced to think that here is an activity which is not carried out with the special enthusiasm we saw to be the characteristic of the Exercises of Practical Life. It opens a shutter that allows us to glimpse a special phenomenon.

When for the first time I discovered the existence of this aspect of the character of the children, I was surprised and I asked myself if I was not in front of an extraordinary happening; if I was not witnessing a new and marvellous mystery; because I saw being destroyed before my eyes many of the theories that the most renowned psychologists had made us believe. I also had believed that the children were incapable of fixing their attention for a long time upon any task. And here in front of me was a little girl of three years who, with the evident signs of the most intense attention, was placing certain wooden cylinders differing in size within cavities which exactly corresponded to them. She was introducing them with the utmost care, and when they had all been placed she took them out again, to put them back immediately. She did it again and again, taking them out, putting them back, always with the same deep concentration, so that one could not foresee when this would finish. I begin to count. When she had repeated this more than forty times I went to the piano and started playing, while I asked the other children to sing. But she, the little one, continued in her useless task without budging from her table, without lifting her eyes, as if she were completely abstracted from what surrounded her. Then she suddenly ceased, and smiling and glad she lifted her limpid eyes. She appeared as though a weight had been lifted from her shoulders, as if she had undergone a period of rest: she smiled as children do when they wake from a beneficial sleep. Since then I have observed this same manifestation hundreds of times. After any task done with this type of concentration, they appear always rested and intimately strengthened. It seems almost that in their soul a path has been opened for the radiant forces revealing in this fashion the best side of their character. They become then kind to everybody. They give themselves to do in order to be useful to other people and they are full of the desire to be good.

The Key to All Pedagogy

It has happened sometimes that one of the children has come near to the teacher, to whisper in her ear as if revealing a secret: "Teacher, I am good." These observations have been valorized by others, but they have been specially made use of by me. I saw a law in what was taking place in those souls, and I understood it; and this law gave me the vision of the possibility of solving completely the problem of education. I understood that which the child had revealed. Clear before me arose the idea that order, mental development, intellectual and sentimental life must have their origin from this mysterious and hidden fount; and since then I have done all I could in order to find experimentally objects that would make this concentration possible. And I studied with great care how to produce that environment which would include the most favourable external conditions to arouse this concentration, and it was in this fashion that I began to create my method.

Certainly here is the key to all pedagogy: to know how to recognize the precious instinct of concentration in order to make use of it in the teaching of reading, writing and counting and, later on, of grammar, arithmetic, foreign languages, science, etc. After all, every psychologist is of the opinion that there is only one way of teaching, that of arousing in the student the deepest interest and at the same time a constant and vivacious attention. So the whole thing resolves itself in this, to make use of those intimate and hidden forces of the child for his education.

Is this possible? Not only is it possible but necessary. *Attention, in order to be able to concentrate itself, needs graded stimuli.* In the beginning these will be objects which are easily recognized by the senses and these will interest the smaller child—cylinders of different sizes, colours to place in gradation of intensity, different sounds to be distinguished one from the other, surfaces differing in degree of roughness to be recognized only by touch; but later we shall have the alphabet, the numbers, writing, reading, grammar, drawing, more difficult arithmetical sums, natural science; and thus at different ages by different stimuli the culture of the child will be built.

The New Teacher

Consequently the task of the new teacher has become much more delicate than that of the old one, and much more serious. Upon her rests the responsibility, upon her depends whether the child will find its way towards culture and towards perfection, or whether everything will be destroyed. The most difficult thing is to make the teacher understand that if the child is to progress she must eliminate herself and give up those prerogatives that hitherto were considered to be the sacred rights of the teacher. She must clearly understand that she cannot have any immediate influence either upon the formation or upon the inner discipline of the students, and that her confidence must be placed and must rest in their hidden and latent energies. Certainly there is something that compels the teacher to continually advise the small children, to correct them or encourage them, showing them that she is superior on account of her experience and her culture. But until she is able to resign herself, to silence the voice of all vanity, she will not be able to attain any result. However, if she on one side must refrain from interfering directly, her indirect action must be assiduous, and she must prepare the environment with full knowledge of every detail, and she must know how and where to dispose the didactic material and introduce very carefully the children to exercise.

It is she who must be able to distinguish the activity of the child who is seeking the correct way, from that of him who is on the wrong path. She must be always calm, always ready to run when she is called to show her love and her sympathy. To be always ready, this is all that is required. The teacher must consecrate herself to the formation of a better humanity. As were the vestals to whom it had been given to keep pure and clean from ashes the sacred fire that others had lit, so must be the teacher to whose care has been consigned the flame of inner life in all its purity. If this flame is neglected it will be extinguished, and no one will be able to light it again.

THE AUTHORS

Colonel Francis W. Parker (1837–1902). Referred to by John Dewey as the father of progressive education; educational leader and reformer in later nineteenth-century America; strongly influenced by Ralph Waldo Emerson and New England transcendentalism and applied that philosophy to education; famous for the Quincy method as a school program and for placing the child in the center of the educational process. Born in New Hampshire; twenty years teacher and principal in New England; from private to colonel in the Civil War (1861–1865); studied psychology and education at the University of Berlin; superintendent of schools, Quincy, Massachusetts (1875–1880); associate superintendent, Boston (1880–1883); principal of Cook County Normal School (1883–1901); director of School of Education at the University of Chicago (1901–1902). Major publications: *Talks on Teaching* (1883); *The Practical Teacher* (1884); *Course in Arithmetic* (1884); *How to Teach Geography* (1885); *How to Study Geography* (1889); and *Talks on Pedagogics* (1894), one of the first American treatises on pedagogy to gain international recognition.

G. Stanley Hall (1846–1924). Foremost American pioneer in genetic psychology (human development); emphasized natural development in children according to the recapitulation theory of human growth; founder of the first child-study clinic in America; one of the most influential leaders in early American psychology. Born in Ashfield, Mass.; graduated from Williams College (1867); professor of psychology at Antioch College (1872–1876); earned Harvard's first doctorate in psychology (1878); studied at Berlin, Bonn, Heidelberg, and Leipzig (1878–1881); professor of psychology and pedagogics at Johns Hopkins University (1881–1888); president and professor of psychology of the newly founded Clark University (1889–1924). In 1891 he became the first president of the American Psychological Association;

founded and edited the *American Journal of Psychology*. Major Publications: *Contents of Children's Minds* (1883); *Adolescence* (1904); *Youth, Its Education, Regimen, and Hygiene* (1907); *Educational Problems* (1911); *Morals, the Supreme Standard of Life and Conduct* (1920); and *Life and Confessions of a Psychologist* (1923).

Arnold L. Gesell (1880–1961). The most noted recent authority on child development in the tradition of Naturalism; student of G. Stanley Hall in genetic psychology; established the Gesell Institute of Child Development; with the aid of motion pictures, Gesell and his associates analyzed the behavior of some 12,000 subjects to establish patterns of orderly stages of child development. Born in Alma, Wisconsin; graduate of the University of Wisconsin (1903); Ph.D. in psychology, Clark University (1906); M.D., Yale School of Medicine (1915). Instructor in psychology, Los Angeles State Normal School (1909–1911); assistant professor of education, Yale University (1911–1915); founder and director of the Clinic of Child Development, Yale University (1911–1948); professor of child hygiene, Yale School of Medicine (1915–1948); research consultant of the Gesell Institute of Child Development (1950–1958). Major publications: *The Preschool Child from the Standpoint of Public Hygiene and Education* (1923); *Mental Growth of the Preschool Child* (1925); *Feeding Behavior of Infants* (1937); co-authored with B. Gesell *The Normal Child and Primary Education* (1912); F. L. Ilg *Infant and Child in the Culture of Today* (1943); *The Child from Five to Ten* (1946); *Youth: The Years from Ten to Sixteen* (1956).

Maria Montessori (1870–1952). Famous for the Montessori schools that she established throughout the world; emphasized freedom and natural unfolding of the child, self-correct devices (Montessori materials) and children's furniture for the school; conceived her system as a science of education, the teacher functioning as a scientist observing children's activities. Born in Chiaravalle, Italy. First woman in Italy to receive the degree of Doctor of Medicine (1896); assistant doctor, Psychiatric Clinic, University of Rome (1896–1899); director, orthophrenic school, Rome (1899–1901); chair of hygiene, Magistero Femminile, Rome (1896–1906); professor of anthropology, University of Rome (1904–1908); established Casa dei Bambini in Rome, the first Montessori school for normal children (1907); international traveler and lecturer. Major publications: *Pedagogical Anthropology* (1913); *The Montessori Method* (1912); *Dr. Montessori's Own Handbook* (1914); *Spontaneous Activity in Education* (1917); *The Montessori Elementary Material* (1917); *The Secret of Childhood* (1939); *Education for a New World* (1948); *To Educate the Human Potential* (1950).

Experimentalism

Experimentalism as a thought pattern has roots in Naturalism. Both oppose traditional education and the dichotomies of ideal and real, knowing and doing, subject matter and child, school and society, and others. But the Experimentalists reject the laissez-faire individualism, permissiveness, and religious connotations that appeared in early progressive education programs. Experimentalists accept a naturalistic point of view, but one that allows for the control and utilization of nature, not human submission to nature. The central difference between the two thought patterns revolves around antithetical approaches to the theory of evolution. Whereas Naturalists derive the concepts heredity, recapitulation, and instinct from the theory, the Experimentalists derive the notions learning, environment, and behavior from it.

Charles Darwin's *The Origin of Species By Means of Natural Selection or the Preservation of Favoured Races in the Struggle for Life* is the key to Experimentalism and the source of its generic notions and specific ideas. First is the acceptance of the fact that the world is in constant change. As the environment and situations change, the species is challenged and must adjust to these challenges in order to survive. All life is in a state of struggle for survival because there is only so much food to go around. Nature is completely neutral in this struggle. It cares not whether any one thing lives or dies. The weak perish, and those who are able to adjust survive.

Evolution occurs because occasional inaccuracies in the hereditary constitution of offspring produce biological improvements that prove advantageous in meeting challenges of the environment. Man is at the top of the evolutionary ladder because he has acquired by a series of accidents a larger and more complex nervous system, a highly developed vocal mechanism, and physical equipment such as hands and thumbs that enable him to use tools. The basic challenges to man are to solve the problems that arise in the environment, to use his intelligence and physical equipment to meet his essential needs, and to innovate for a better life.

The Experimentalist perspective of evolution is also shared by the discipline of experimental psychology. Darwin's theory is the basis of psychology as a separate field of study without religious or philosophical explanations. Psychology can be constructed on a purely biological foundation utilizing drives, pleasure and pain, and responses to environmental stimuli as the cause and effect materials of its discoveries. Similarly, mental processes can be considered in terms of the organism's task of adjusting to the world. A partnership thus grows between experimental psychology and Experimentalist educators. This partnership establishes an important generic notion of the movement, the compatibility of educational reform and innovation with psychological research and results. This means that curriculum and teaching methods utilized in the schools must be rooted in psychological data rather than in anything resembling philosophical logic.

The place of psychology in Experimentalism centers on the research done on learning. The primary principle discovered and utilized by Edward Thorndike, John B. Watson, Clark Hull, and B. F. Skinner is that a bond or connection can be made or strengthened between a situation (or stimulus) and a response. This means that by controlling a stimulus or by rewarding an action, a response can be manifested or strengthened in an organism by planned human engineering. Educators can use such a program to produce desired responses from students in subject content and in attitudes. A second principle follows from the first and becomes a basic thesis in the programs of Experimental education. The process of education is a step by step movement that goes from the simple to the complex. Learning must begin at a simple level and progress uniformly according to small, sequential steps. This principle is so basic that it is the key to such Experimentalist approaches to growth as Robert Havighurst's theory of developmental tasks, the curriculum and teaching methods of the basic elementary education readers, and the program texts and teaching machines of advanced study.

Although psychology has laid down the guidelines for learning and has become the discipline associated with a society based on progress, adjustment, and a better life, it is to sociology that the Experimentalists turn for understanding such a society. The sociology that Experimentalists accept consists of those hypotheses that reflect the same basic ideas about evolution that are found in psychology. Of the many ideas derived from sociology, the four most important ones for Experimentalism are the following. First, man is a product of his environment. Whatever man attains is a result of learning. Man learns to walk, talk, and eat; he learns to manipulate with words and numbers; he learns how to be a mature adult, a male or female, and a member of society. In the controversy over innateness versus environment, the Experimentalists strictly favor the latter position; they are its leading exponents.

The second important sociological idea is that man is a social being. He requires the assistance of his fellowman in all his endeavors. The sruggle for survival is a group struggle. The problems of man are group problems requiring group solutions. The Experimentalists utilize this idea to emphasize the social character of education. The third idea is the relativity of culture. Since learning depends on the environment, and the environment is different from place to place, different cultures must manifest different customs, languages, and social routines. Experimentalists ask peoples of the world to appreciate and respect one another, to recognize that differences merely reflect environmental circumstances. The third significant sociological idea is the place of technology in social development. Man is a tool-using creature. As he advances in the development and use of tools, he makes progress in his living standards. Experimentalists make much of modern technology and emphasize its importance to education and contemporary life. Technology means progress and social advance. It should become the goal of education to encourage greater technological development.

A major generic notion in both psychology and sociology, which is discussed philosophically by Experimentalist educators, is the "economic and well-being" motive for psychological and social behavior. The goal of man is not only to survive but to live the good life; this means living in harmony with one's fellows and having enough material means to ensure health and comfort. Material abundance and economic welfare for all members of the human species is a fundamental tenet of Experimentalism. It is on this ground that the Experimentalists become involved with the philosophy of democracy. It is not the democracy of laissez-faire individualism and political decentralization which Experimentalists believe in, but the democracy of social cooperation, centralization of functions, and majority rule. It is in democracy that the Experimentalists find hope for solving social problems and providing for universal health and welfare. This point is so important to Experimentalist philosophers of education that many give the name "democratic philosophy of education" to their position.

The educational programs of Experimentalism reflect the basic ideas of the movement. The concept of democracy is perhaps the one notion that is clearly in focus in the consciousness of Experimentalist educators. But the movement consists of a coordination of this vivid concept with the ideas stemming from evolution. Three educational points characterize this thought pattern and keynote this fact.

First is the emphasis on the scientific method, often referred to as "the method of intelligence." The connection Experimentalism has had with experimental psychology and sociology has been noted. A strong connection with the scientific approach is the attempt on the part of educators to emulate the methods of the social sciences in acquiring information and to instill in youth the attitudes and routines of this approach. Basic to the scientific method is the fact that thinking or research begins with a perceived difficulty, a problem to be solved. The problem stems from some circumstance in the environment and requires either adjustment to it by the organism or a solution. Such an adjustment or solution must be

based on evidence and this is derived from the observation of consequences. In the theory of evolution this method relates to problem
solving for survival.

The second point is the emphasis on group processes in education. The
school is a social institution, functioning in part to create cooperative
habits in people. The age has passed when men could live in isolation,
growing their own food and supporting themselves. Modern technology
brings man together under circumstances that require cooperation for
common social aims. Hence, education must train children for social
integration related to endeavors that are purposeful and useful to all.
Lawrence Kilpatrick's "project method" is such a program, constructed
not only from Thorndike's laws of learning, but for the purpose of
developing intelligent cooperation in group activity. Kilpatrick insisted
that the method of education must be consistent with the character of a
democratic social system. The "core curriculum" and "unit method" are
more recent educational programs for teaching group processes. They
emphasize not only student group activities, but student-teacher planning of the curriculum and decisionmaking on relevant problems.

The third point characterizing Experimentalism in education is the
strong belief that the school is an integral part of society at large and
that this society is changing. The school is not an institution that can
function properly if segregated from the general affairs of men and the
changing circumstances of contemporary life. Although there is unanim-
ity among the Experimentalists on this belief, there is some difference of
opinion as to the degree of involvement the school should have with
social change. Two approaches stand out. The first holds that society is
changing and that educators must prepare the children to meet change.
Instead of teaching children static ideas and imposed standards, the
schools should teach children how to think and deal with circumstances
and issues relative to their times. Knowledge quickly becomes out-of-
date. Therefore, children should learn where to get information when it
is needed and how to solve problems, rather than be encouraged to
memorize facts and obey outdated rules. The second view holds that the
school must not merely accept social change, but should be a force
directing it. Since George Counts' famous speech "Dare the Schools
Build a New Social Order," it has been the strong contention of many
Experimentalists that the school should be an agent for forcing social
change. There are inherent injustices in modern society that are inconsistent with the philosophy of modern democracy. Therefore, it must be the
function of the school to work for needed changes through the education
of the young.

PEDAGOGICAL ORIENTATION —
INSTRUMENTALISM

Experience and Education / JOHN DEWEY

The Need of a Theory of Experience

The point I am making is that rejection of the philosophy and practice of traditional education sets a new type of difficult educational problem for those who believe in the new type of education. We shall operate blindly and in confusion until we recognize this fact; until we thoroughly appreciate that departure from the old solves no problems. What is said in the following pages is, accordingly, intended to indicate some of the main problems with which the newer education is confronted and to suggest the main lines along which their solution is to be sought. I assume that amid all uncertainties there is one permanent frame of reference: namely, the organic connection between education and personal experience; or, that the new philosophy of education is committed to some kind of empirical and experimental philosophy. But experience and experiment are not self-explanatory ideas. Rather, their meaning is part of the problem to be explored. To know the meaning of empiricism we need to understand what experience is.

The belief that all genuine education comes about through experience does not mean that all experiences are genuinely or equally educative. Experience and education cannot be directly equated to each other. For some experiences are mis-educative. Any experience is mis-educative that has the effect of arresting or distorting the growth of further experience. An experience may be such as to engender callousness; it may produce lack of sensitivity and of responsiveness. Then the possibilities of having richer experience in the future are restricted. Again, a given experience may increase a person's automatic skill in a particular direction and yet tend to land him in a groove or rut; the effect again is to narrow the field of further experience. An experience may be immediately enjoyable and yet promote the formation of a slack and careless attitude; this attitude then operates to modify the quality of subsequent experiences so as to prevent a person from getting out of them what they have to give. Again, experiences may be so disconnected from one another that, while each is agreeable or even exciting in itself, they are not linked cumulatively to one another. Energy is then dissipated and a person becomes scatter-brained. Each experience may be lively, vidid, and "interesting," and yet their disconnectedness may artificially generate dispersive, disintegrated, centrifugal habits. The consequence of formation of such habits is inability to control future experiences. They are then taken, either by way of enjoyment or of discontent and revolt, just as they come. Under such circumstances, it is idle to talk of self-control.

Traditional education offers a plethora of examples of experiences of the kinds just mentioned. It is a great mistake to suppose, even tacitly, that the traditional schoolroom was not a place in which pupils had experiences. Yet this is tacitly assumed when progressive education as a plan of learning by experience is placed in sharp opposition to the old. The proper line of attack is that the experiences which were had, by pupils and teachers alike, were largely of a wrong kind. How many students, for example, were rendered callous to ideas, and how many lost the impetus to learn because of the way in which learning was experienced by them? How many acquired special skills by means of automatic drill so that their power of judgment and capacity to act intelligently in new situations was limited? How many came to associate the learning process with ennui and boredom? How many found what they did learn so foreign to the situations of life outside the school as to give them no power of control over the latter? How many came to associate books with dull drudgery, so that they were "conditioned" to all but flashy reading matter?

If I ask these questions, it is not for the sake of wholesale condemnation of the old education. It is for quite another purpose. It is to emphasize the fact, first, that young people in traditional schools do have experiences; and, secondly, that the trouble is not the absence of experiences, but their defective and wrong character—wrong and defective from the standpoint of connection with further experience. The positive side of this point is even more important in connection with progressive education. It is not enough to insist upon the necessity of experience, nor even of activity in experience. Everything depends upon the *quality* of the experience which is had. The quality of any experience has two aspects. There is an immediate aspect of agreeableness or disagreeableness, and there is its influence upon later experiences. The first is obvious and easy to judge. The *effect* of an experience is not borne on its face. It sets a problem to the educator. It is his business to arrange for the kind of experiences which, while they do not repel the student, but rather engage his activities are, nevertheless, more than immediately enjoyable since they promote having desirable future experiences. Just as no man lives or dies to himself, so no experience lives and dies to itself. Wholly independent of desire or intent, every experience lives on in further experiences. Hence the central problem of an education based upon experience is to select the kind of present experiences that live fruitfully and creatively in subsequent experiences.

Later, I shall discuss in more detail the principle of the continuity of experience or what may be called the experiential continuum. Here I wish simply to emphasize the importance of this principle for the philosophy of educative experience. A philosophy of education, like any theory, has to be stated in words, in symbols. But so far as it is more than verbal it is a plan for conducting education. Like any plan, it must be framed with reference to what is to be done and how it is to be done. The more definitely and sincerely it is held that education is a development within, by, and for experience, the more important it is that there shall be clear conceptions of what experience is. Unless experience is so conceived that the result is a plan for deciding upon subject-matter, upon methods of instruction and discipline, and upon material equipment and social organization of the school, it is wholly in the air. It is reduced to a form of words which may be emotionally stirring but for which any other set of words might equally well be substituted unless they indicate operations to be initiated and executed. Just because traditional education was a matter of routine in which the plans and programs were handed down from the past, it does not follow that progressive education is a matter of planless improvisation.

The traditional school could get along without any consistently developed philosophy of education. About all it required in that line was a set of abstract words like culture, discipline, our great cultural heritage, etc., actual guidance being derived not from them but from custom and established routines. Just because progressive schools cannot rely upon established traditions and institutional habits, they must either proceed more or less haphazardly or be directed by ideas which, when they are made articulate and coherent, form a philosophy of education. Revolt against the kind of organization characteristic of the traditional school constitutes a demand for a kind of organization based upon ideas. I think that only slight acquaintance with the history of education is needed to prove that educational reformers and innovators alone have felt the need for a philosophy of education. Those who adhered to the established system needed merely a few fine-sounding words to justify existing practices. The real work was done by habits which were so fixed as to be institutional. The lesson for progressive education is that it requires in an urgent degree, a degree more pressing than was incumbent upon former innovators, a philosophy of education based upon a philosophy of experience.

I remarked incidentally that the philosophy in question is, to paraphrase the saying of Lincoln about democracy, one of education of, by, and for experience. No one of these words, *of*, *by*, or *for*, names anything which is self-evident. Each of them is a challenge to discover and put into operation a principle of order and organization which follows from understanding what educative experience signifies.

It is, accordingly, a much more difficult task to work out the kinds of materials, of methods, and of social relationships that are appropriate to the new education than is the case with traditional education. I think many of the difficulties experienced in the conduct of progressive schools and many of the criticisms leveled against them arise from this source. The difficulties are aggravated and the criticisms are increased when it is supposed that the new education is somehow easier than the old. This belief is, I imagine, more or less current. Perhaps it illustrates again the *Either-Or* philosophy, springing from the idea that about all which is required is *not* to do what is done in traditional schools.

I admit gladly that the new education is *simpler* in principle than the old. It is in harmony with principles of growth, while there is very much which is artificial in the old selection and arrangement of subjects and methods, and artificiality always leads to unnecessary complexity. But the easy and the simple are not identical. To discover what is really simple and to act upon the discovery is an exceedingly difficult task. After the artificial and complex is once institutionally established and ingrained in custom and routine, it is easier to walk in the paths that have been beaten than it is, after taking a new point of view, to work out what is practically involved in the new point of view. The old Ptolemaic astronomical system was more complicated with its cycles and epicycles than the Copernican system. But until organization of actual astronomical phenomena on the ground of the latter principle had been effected the easiest course was to follow the line of least resistance provided by the old intellectual habit. So we come back to the idea that a coherent *theory* of experience, affording positive direction to selection and organization of appropriate educational methods and materials, is required by the attempt to give new direction to the work of the schools. The process is a slow and arduous one. It is a matter of growth, and there are many obstacles which tend to obstruct growth and to deflect it into wrong lines.

I shall have something to say later about organization. All that is needed, perhaps, at this point is to say that we must escape from the tendency to think of organization in terms of the *kind* of organization, whether of content (or subject-matter), or of methods and social relations, that mark traditional education. I think that a good deal of the current opposition to the idea of organization is due to the fact that it is so hard to get away from the picture of the studies of the old school. The moment "organization" is mentioned imagination goes almost automatically to the kind of organization that is familiar, and in revolting against that we are led to shrink from the very idea of any organization. On the other hand, educational reactionaries, who are now gathering force, use the absence of adequate intellectual and moral organization in the newer type of school as proof not only of the need of organization, but to identify any and every kind of organization with that instituted before the rise of experimental science. Failure to develop a conception of organization upon the empirical and experimental basis gives reactionaries a too easy victory. But the fact that the empirical sciences now offer the best type of intellectual organization which can be found in any field shows that there is no reason why we, who call ourselves empiricists, should be "pushovers" in the matter of order and organization.

Criteria of Experience

If there is any truth in what has been said about the need of forming a theory of experience in order that education may be intelligently conducted upon the basis of experience, it is clear that the next thing in order in this discussion is to present the principles that are most significant in framing this theory. I shall not, therefore, apologize for engaging in a certain amount of philosophical analysis, which otherwise might be out of place. I may, however, reassure you to some degree by saying that this analysis is not an end in itself but is engaged in for the sake of obtaining criteria to be applied later in discussion of a number of concrete and, to most persons, more interesting issues.

I have already mentioned what I called the category of continuity, or the experiential continuum. This principle is involved, as I pointed out, in every attempt to discriminate between experiences that are worth while educationally and those that are not. It may seem superfluous to argue that this discrimination is necessary not only in criticizing the traditional type of education but also in initiating and conducting a different type. Nevertheless, it is advisable to pursue for a little while the idea that it is necessary. One may safely assume, I suppose, that one thing which has recommended the progressive movement is that it seems more in accord with the democratic ideal to which our people is committed than do the procedures of the traditional school, since the latter have so much of the autocratic about them. Another thing which has contributed to its favorable reception is that its methods are humane in comparison with the harshness so often attending the policies of the traditional school.

The question I would raise concerns why we prefer democratic and humane arrangements to those which are autocratic and harsh. And by "why," I mean the *reason* for preferring them, not just the *causes* which lead us to the preference. One *cause* may be that we have been taught not only in the schools but by the press, the pulpit, the platform, and our laws and law-making bodies that democracy is the best of all social institutions. We may have so assimilated this idea from our surroundings that it has become an habitual part of our mental and moral make-up. But similar causes have led other persons in different surroundings to widely varying conclusions—to prefer fascism, for example. The cause for our preference is not the same thing as the reason why we *should* prefer it.

It is not my purpose here to go in detail into the reason. But I would ask a single question: Can we find any reason that does not ultimately come down to the belief that democratic social arrangements promote a better quality of human experience, one which is more widely accessible and enjoyed, than do non-democratic and anti-democratic forms of social life? Does not the principle of regard for individual freedom and for decency and kindliness of human relations come back in the end to the conviction that these things are tributary to a higher quality of experience on the part of a greater number than are methods of repression and coercion or force? Is it not the reason for our preference that we believe that mutual consultation and convictions reached through persuasion, make possible a better quality of experience than can otherwise be provided on any wide scale?

If the answer to these questions is in the affirmative (and personally I do not see how we can justify our preference for democracy and humanity on any other ground), the ultimate reason for hospitality to progressive education, because of its reliance upon and use of humane methods and its kinship to democracy, goes back to the fact that discrimination is made between the inherent values of different experiences. So I come back to the principle of continuity of experience as a criterion of discrimination.

At bottom, this principle rests upon the fact of habit, when *habit* is interpreted biologically. The basic characteristic of habit is that every experience enacted and undergone modifies the one who acts and undergoes, while this modification affects, whether we wish it or not, the quality of subsequent experiences. For it is a somewhat different person who enters into them. The principle of habit so understood obviously goes deeper than the ordinary conception of *a* habit as a more or less fixed way of doing things, although it includes the latter as one of its special cases. It covers the formation of attitudes, attitudes that are emotional and intellectual; it covers our basic sensitivities and ways of meeting and responding to all the conditions which we meet in living. From this point of view, the principle of continuity of experience means that every experience both takes up something from those which have gone before and modifies in some way the quality of those which come after. As the poet states it,

> . . . all experience is an arch wherethro'
> Gleams that untraveled world, whose margin fades
> For ever and for ever when I move.

So far, however, we have no ground for discrimination among experiences. For the principle is of universal application. There is *some* kind of continuity in every case. It is when we note the different forms in which continuity of experience operates that we get the basis of discriminating among experiences. I may illustrate what is meant by an objection which has been brought against an idea which I once put forth—namely, that the educative process can be identified with growth when that is understood in terms of the active participle, *growing*.

Growth, or growing as developing, not only physically but intellectually and morally, is one exemplification of the principle of continuity. The objection made is that growth might take many different directions: a man, for example, who starts out on a career of burglary may grow in that direction, and by practice may grow into a highly expert burglar. Hence it is argued that "growth" is not enough; we must also specify the direction in which growth takes place, the end towards which it tends. Before, however, we decide that the objection is conclusive we must analyze the case a little further.

That a man may grow in efficiency as a burglar, as a gangster, or as a corrupt politician, cannot be doubted. But from the standpoint of growth as education and education as growth the question is whether growth in this direction promotes or retards growth in general. Does this form of growth create conditions for further growth, or does it set up conditions that shut off the person who has grown in this particular direction from the occasions, stimuli, and opportunities for continuing growth in new directions? What is the effect of growth in a special direction upon the attitudes and habits which alone open up avenues for development in other lines? I shall leave you to answer these questions, saying simply that when and *only* when development in a particular line conduces to continuing growth does it answer to the criterion of education as growing. For the conception is one that must find universal and not specialized limited application.

I return now to the question of continuity as a criterion by which to discriminate between experiences which are educative and those which are mis-educative. As we have seen, there is some kind of continuity in any case since every experience affects for better or worse the attitudes which help decide the quality of further experiences, by setting up certain preference and aversion, and making it easier or harder to act for this or that end. Moreover, every experience influences in some degree the objective conditions under which further experiences are had. For example, a child who learns to speak has a new facility and new desire. But he has also widened the external conditions of subsequent learning. When he learns to read, he similarly opens up a new environment. If a person decides to become a teacher, lawyer, physician, or stockbroker, when he executes his intention he thereby necessarily determines to some extent the environment in which he will act in the future. He has rendered himself more sensitive and responsive to certain conditions, and relatively immune to those things about him that would have been stimuli if he had made another choice.

But, while the principle of continuity applies in some way in every case, the quality of the present experience influences the *way* in which the principle applies. We speak of spoiling a child and of the spoilt child. The effect of over-indulging a child is a continuing one. It sets up an attitude which operates as an automatic demand that persons and objects cater to his desires and caprices in the future. It makes him seek the kind of situation that will enable him to do what he feels like doing at the time. It renders him averse to and comparatively incompetent in situations which require effort and perseverance in overcoming obstacles. There is no paradox in the fact that the principle of the continuity of experience may operate so as to leave a person arrested on a low plane of development, in a way which limits later capacity for growth.

On the other hand, if an experience arouses curiosity, strengthens initiative, and sets up desires and purposes that are sufficiently intense to carry a person over dead places in the future, continuity works in a very different way. Every experience is a moving force. Its value can be judged only on the ground of what it moves toward and into. The greater maturity of experience which should belong to the adult as educator puts him in a position to evaluate each experience of the young in a way in which the one having the less mature experience cannot do. It is then the business of the educator to see in what direction an experience is heading. There is no point in his being more mature if, instead of using his greater insight to help organize the conditions of the experience of the immature, he throws away his insight. Failure to take the moving force of an experience into account so as to judge and direct it on the ground of what it is moving into means disloyalty to the principle of experience itself. The disloyalty operates in two directions. The educator is false to the understanding that he should have obtained from his own past experience. He is also unfaithful to the fact that all human experience is ultimately social: that it involves contact and communication. The mature person, to put it in moral terms, has no right to withhold from the young on given occasions whatever capacity for sympathetic understanding his own experience has given him.

No sooner, however, are such things said than there is a tendency to react to the other extreme and take what has been said as a plea for some sort of disguised imposition from outside. It is worth while, accordingly, to say something about the way in which the adult can exercise the wisdom his own wider experience gives him without imposing a merely external control. On one side, it is his business to be on the alert to see what attitudes and habitual tendencies are being created. In this direction he must, if he is an educator, be able to judge what attitudes are actually conducive to continued growth and what are detrimental. He must, in addition, have that sympathetic understanding of individuals as individuals which gives him an idea of what is actually going on in the minds of those who are learning. It is, among other things, the need for these abilities on the part of the parent and teacher which makes a system of education based upon living experience a more difficult affair to conduct successfully than it is to follow the patterns of traditional education.

But there is another aspect of the matter. Experience does not go on simply inside a person. It does go on there, for it influences the formation of attitudes of desire and purpose. But this is not the whole of the story. Every genuine experience has an active side which changes in some degree the objective conditions under which experiences are had. The difference between civilization and savagery, to take an example on a large scale, is found in the degree in which previous experiences have changed the objective conditions under which subsequent experiences take place. The existence of roads, of means of rapid movement and transportation, tools, implements, furniture, electric light and power, are illustrations. Destroy the external conditions of present civilized experience, and for a time our experience would relapse into that of barbaric peoples.

In a word, we live from birth to death in a world of persons and things which in large measure is what it is because of what has been done and transmitted from previous human activities. When this fact is ignored, experience is treated as if it were something which goes on exclusively inside an individual's body and mind. It ought not to be necessary to say that experience does not occur in a vacuum. There are sources outside an individual which give rise to experience. It is constantly fed from these springs. No one would question that a child in a slum tenement has a different experience from that of a child in a cultured home; that the country lad has a different kind of experience from the city boy, or a boy on the seashore one different from the lad who is brought up on inland prairies. Ordinarily we take such facts for granted as too commonplace to record. But when their educational import is recognized, they indicate the second way in which the educator can direct the experience of the young without engaging in imposition. A primary responsibility of educators is that they not only be aware of the general principle of the shaping of actual experience by environing conditions, but that they also recognize in the concrete what surroundings are conducive to having experiences that lead to growth. Above all, they should know how to utilize the surroundings, physical and social, that exist so as to extract from them all that they have to contribute to building up experiences that are worth while.

Traditional education did not have to face this problem; it could systematically dodge this responsibility. The school environment of desks, blackboards, a small school yard, was supposed to suffice. There was no demand that the teacher should become intimately acquainted with the conditions of the local community, physical, historical, economic, occupational, etc., in order to utilize them as educational resources. A system of education based upon the necessary connection of education with experience must, on the contrary, if faithful to its principle, take these things constantly into account. This tax upon the educator is another reason why progressive education is more difficult to carry on than was ever the traditional system.

It is possible to frame schemes of education that pretty systematically subordinate objective conditions to those which reside in the individuals being educated. This happens whenever the place and function of the teacher, of books, of apparatus and equipment, of everything which represents the products of the more mature experience of elders, is systematically subordinated to the immediate inclinations and feelings of the young. Every theory which assumes that importance can be attached to these objective factors only at the expense of imposing external control and of limiting the freedom of individuals rests finally upon the notion that experience is truly experience only when objective conditions are subordinated to what goes on within the individuals having the experience.

I do not mean that it is supposed that objective conditions can be shut out. It is recognized that they must enter in: so much concession is made to the inescapable fact that we live in a world of things and persons. But I think that observation of what goes on in some families and some schools would disclose that some parents and some teachers are acting upon the idea of *subordinating* objective conditions to internal ones. In that case, it is assumed not only that the latter are primary, which in one sense they are, but that just as they temporarily exist they fix the whole educational process.

Let me illustrate from the case of an infant. The needs of a baby for food, rest, and activity are certainly primary and decisive in one respect. Nourishment must be provided; provision must be made for comfortable sleep, and so on. But these facts do not mean that a parent shall feed the baby at any time when the baby is cross or irritable, that there shall not be a program of regular hours of feeding and sleeping, etc. The wise mother takes account of the needs of the infant but not in a way which dispenses with her own responsibility for regulating the objective conditions under which the needs are satisfied. And if she is a wise mother in this respect, she draws upon past experiences of experts as well as her own for the light that these shed upon what experiences are in general most conducive to the normal development of infants. Instead of these conditions being subordinated to the immediate internal condition of the baby, they are definitely ordered so that a particular kind of *interaction* with these immediate internal states may be brought about.

The word "interaction," which has just been used, expresses the second chief principle for interpreting an experience in its educational function and force. It assigns equal rights to both factors in experience—objective and internal conditions. Any normal experience is an interplay of these two sets of conditions. Taken together, or in their interaction, they form what we call a *situation*. The trouble with traditional education was not that it emphasized the external conditions that enter into the control of the experiences but that it paid so little attention to the internal factors which also decide what kind of experience is had. It violated the principle of interaction from one side. But this violation is no reason why the new education should violate the principle from the other side—except upon the basis of the extreme *Either-Or* educational philosophy which has been mentioned.

The illustration drawn from the need for regulation of the objective conditions of a baby's development indicates, first, that the parent has responsibility for arranging the conditions under which an infant's experience of food, sleep, etc., occurs, and secondly, that the responsibility is fulfilled by utilizing the funded experience of the past, as this is represented, say, by the advice of competent physicians and others who have made a special study of normal physical growth. Does it limit the freedom of the mother when she uses the body of knowledge thus provided to regulate the objective conditions of nourishment and sleep? Or does the enlargement of her intelligence in fulfilling her parental function widen her freedom? Doubtless if a fetish were made of the advice and directions so that they came to be inflexible dictates to be followed under every possible condition, then restriction of freedom of both parent and child would occur. But this restriction would also be a limitation of the intelligence that is exercised in personal judgment.

In what respect does regulation of objective conditions limit the freedom of the baby? Some limitation is certainly placed upon its immediate movements and inclinations when it is put in its crib, at a time when it wants to continue playing, or does not get food at the moment it would like it, or when it isn't picked up and dandled when it cries for attention. Restriction also occurs when mother or nurse snatches a child away from an open fire into which it is about to fall. I shall have more to say later about freedom. Here it is enough to ask whether freedom is to be thought of and adjudged on the basis of relatively momentary incidents or whether its meaning is found in the continuity of developing experience.

The statement that individuals live in a world means, in the concrete, that they live in a series of situations. And when it is said that they live *in* these situations, the meaning of the word "in" is different from its meaning when it is said that pennies are "in" a pocket or paint is "in" a can. It means, once more, that interaction is going on between an individual and objects and other persons. The conceptions of *situation* and of *interaction* are inseparable from each other. An experience is always what it is because of a transaction taking place between an individual and what, at the time, constitutes his environment, whether the latter consists of persons with whom he is talking about some topic or event, the subject talked about being also a part of the situation; or the toys with which he is playing; the book he is reading (in which his environing conditions at the time may be England or ancient Greece or an imaginary region); or the materials of an experiment he is performing. The environment, in other words, is whatever conditions interact with personal needs, desires, purposes, and capacities to create the experience which is had. Even when a person builds a castle in the air he is interacting with the objects which he constructs in fancy.

The two principles of continuity and interaction are not separate from each other. They intercept and unite. They are, so to speak, the longitudinal and lateral aspects of experience. Different situations succeed one another. But because of the principle of continuity something is carried over from the earlier to the later ones. As an individual passes from one situation to another, his world, his environment, expands or contracts. He does not find himself living in another world but in a different part or aspect of one and the same world. What he has learned in the way of knowledge and skill in one situation becomes an instrument of understanding and dealing effectively with the situations which follow. The process goes on as long as life and learning continue. Otherwise the course of experience is disorderly, since the individual factor that enters into making an experience is split. A divided world, a world whose parts and aspects do not hang together, is at once a sign and a cause of a divided personality. When the splitting-up reaches a certain point we call the person insane. A fully integrated personality, on the other hand, exists only when successive experiences are integrated with one another. It can be built up only as a world of related objects is constructed.

Continuity and interaction in their active union with each other provide the measure of the educative significance and value of an experience. The immediate and direct concern of an educator is then with the situations in which interaction takes place. The individual, who enters as a factor into it, is what he is at a given time. It is the other factor, that of objective conditions, which lies to some extent within the possibility of regulation by the educator. As has already been noted, the phrase "objective conditions" covers a wide range. It includes what is done by the educator and the way in which it is done, not only words spoken but the tone of voice in which they are spoken. It includes the materials with which an individual interacts, and, most important of all, the total *social* set-up of the situations in which a person is engaged.

When it is said that the objective conditions are those which are within the power of the educator to regulate, it is meant, of course, that his ability to influence directly the experience of others and thereby the education they obtain places upon him the duty of determining that environment which will interact with the existing capacities and needs of those taught to create a worth-while experience. The trouble with traditional education was not that educators took upon themselves the responsibility for providing an environment. The trouble was that they did not consider the other factor in creating an experience; namely, the powers and purposes of those taught. It was assumed that a certain set of conditions was intrinsically desirable, apart from its ability to evoke a certain quality of response in individuals. This lack of mutual adaptation made the process of teaching and learning accidental. Those to whom the provided conditions were suitable managed to learn. Others got on as best they could. Responsibility for selecting objective conditions carries with it, then, the responsibility for understanding the needs and capacities of the individuals who are learning at a given time. It is not enough that certain materials and methods have proved effective with other individuals at other times. There must be a reason for thinking that they will function in generating an experience that has educative quality with particular individuals at a particular time.

It is no reflection upon the nutritive quality of beefsteak that it is not fed to infants. It is not an invidious reflection upon trigonometry that we do not teach it in the first or fifth grade of school. It is not the subject *per se* that is educative or that is conducive to growth. There is no subject that is in and of itself, or without regard to the stage of growth attained by the learner, such that inherent educational value can be attributed to it. Failure to take into account adaptation to the needs and capacities of individuals was the source of the idea that certain subjects and certain methods are intrinsically cultural or intrinsically good for mental discipline. There is no such thing as educational value in the abstract. The notion that some subjects and methods and that acquaintance with certain facts and truths possess educational value in and of themselves is the reason why traditional education reduced the material of education so largely to a diet of predigested materials. According to this notion, it was enough to regulate the quantity and difficulty of the material provided, in a scheme of quantitative grading, from month to month and from year to year. Otherwise a pupil was expected to take it in the doses that were prescribed from without. If the pupil left it instead of taking it, if he engaged in physical truancy, or in the mental truancy of mind-wandering and finally built up an emotional revulsion against the subject, he was held to be at fault. No question was raised as to whether the trouble might not lie in the subject-matter or in the way in which it was offered. The principle of interaction makes it clear that failure of adaptation of material to needs and capacities of individuals may cause an experience to be non-educative quite as much as failure of an individual to adapt himself to the material.

The principle of continuity in its educational application means, nevertheless, that the future has to be taken into account at every stage of the educational process. This idea is easily misunderstood and is badly distorted in traditional education. Its assumption is, that by acquiring certain skills and by learning certain subjects which would be needed later (perhaps in college or perhaps in adult life) pupils are as a matter of course made ready for the needs and circumstances of the future. Now "preparation" is a treacherous idea. In a certain sense every experience should do something to prepare a person for later experiences of a deeper and more expansive quality. That is the very meaning of growth, continuity, reconstruction of experience. But it is a mistake to suppose that the mere acquisition of a certain amount of arithmetic, geography, history, etc., which is taught and studied because it may be useful at some time in the future, has this effect, and it is a mistake to suppose that acquisition of skills in reading and figuring will automatically constitute preparation for their right and effective use under conditions very unlike those in which they were acquired.

Almost everyone has had occasion to look back upon his school days and wonder what has become of the knowledge he was supposed to have amassed during his years of schooling, and why it is that the technical skills he acquired have to be learned over again in changed form in order to stand him in good stead. Indeed, he is lucky who does not find that in order to make progress, in order to go ahead intellectually, he does not have to unlearn much of what he learned in school. These questions cannot be disposed of by saying that the subjects were not actually learned, for they were learned at least sufficiently to enable a pupil to pass examinations in them. One trouble is that the subject-matter in question was learned in isolation; it was put, as it were, in a water-tight compartment. When the question is asked, then, what has become of it, where has it gone to, the right answer is that it is still there in the special compartment in which it was originally stowed away. If exactly the same conditions recurred as those under which it was acquired, it would also recur and be available. But it was segregated when it was acquired and hence is so disconnected from the rest of experience that it is not available under the actual conditions of life. It is contrary to the laws of experience that learning of this kind, no matter how thoroughly engrained at the time, should give genuine preparation.

Nor does failure in preparation end at this point. Perhaps the greatest of all pedagogical fallacies is the notion that a person learns only the particular thing he is studying at the time. Collateral learning in the way of formation of enduring attitudes, of likes and dislikes, may be and often is much more important than the spelling lesson or lesson in geography or history that is learned. For these attitudes are fundamentally what count in the future. The most important attitude that can be formed is that of desire to go on learning. If impetus in this direction is weakened instead of being intensified, something much more than mere lack of preparation takes place. The pupil is actually robbed of native capacities which otherwise would enable him to cope with the circumstances that he meets in the course of his life. We often see persons who have had little schooling and in whose case the absence of set schooling proves to be a positive asset. They have at least retained their native common sense and power of judgment, and its exercise in the actual conditions of living has given them the precious gift of ability to learn from the experiences they have. What avail is it to win prescribed amounts of information about geography and history, to win ability to read and write, if in the process the individual loses his own soul: loses his appreciation of things worth while, of the values to which these things are relative; if he loses desire to apply what he has learned and, above all, loses the ability to extract meaning from his future experiences as they occur?

What, then, is the true meaning of preparation in the educational scheme? In the first place, it means that a person, young or old, gets out of his present experience all that there is in it for him at the time in which he has it. When preparation is made the controlling end, then the potentialities of the present are sacrificed to a supposititious future. When this happens, the actual preparation for the future is missed or distorted. The ideal of using the present simply to get ready for the future contradicts itself. It omits, and even shuts out, the very conditions by which a person can be prepared for his future. We always live at the time we live and not at some other time, and only by extracting at each present time the full meaning of each present experience are we prepared for doing the same thing in the future. This is the only preparation which in the long run amounts to anything.

All this means that attentive care must be devoted to the conditions which give each present experience a worthwhile meaning. Instead of inferring that it doesn't make much difference what the present experience is as long as it is enjoyed, the conclusion is the exact opposite. Here is another matter where it is easy to react from one extreme to the other. Because traditional schools tended to sacrifice the present to a remote and more or less unknown future, therefore it comes to be believed that the educator has little responsibility for the kind of present experiences the young undergo. But the relation of the present and the future is not an *Either-Or* affair. The present affects the future anyway. The persons who should have some idea of the connection between the two are those who have achieved maturity. Accordingly, upon them devolves the responsibility for instituting the conditions for the kind of present experience which has a favorable effect upon the future. Education as growth or maturity should be an ever-present process.

PEDAGOGICAL ORIENTATION — OPERATIONISM

New Vistas for Intelligence / PERCY W. BRIDGMAN

We are all agreed that the invention of the atomic bomb has presented us with problems which must be solved within the next few decades if the survival of civilization is to be more than a matter of good luck. Nevertheless, in spite of the urgency of these problems, I venture to invite your attention to certain longer range considerations which are equally fundamental and which have an equal claim to the attention of some of us now, for the solution of the longer range difficulties requires a longer period of preparation and must also be initiated in the present. It seems to me evident enough that many of our present social difficulties have their origin in our previous failure to begin thinking about the problems far enough ahead.

The opening of the atomic age may well mark the end of the first chapter of the physical sciences and our partial mastery of our physical environment. It is conventional to ascribe this mastery to the development of scientific method, and there has been much discussion of what the essence of the scientific method is. It appears to me, however, that it is easy to take too narrow a view in this matter. I like to say that there is no scientific method as such, but that the most vital feature of the scientist's procedure has been merely to do his utmost with his mind, *no holds barred*. This means in particular that no special privileges are accorded to authority or to tradition, that personal prejudices and predilections are carefully guarded against, that one makes continued check to assure oneself that one is not making mistakes, and that any line of

"New Vistas for Intelligence" is reprinted from "New Vistas for Intelligence," by P. W. Bridgman in *Physical Science and Human Values*, edited by E. P. Wigner (copyright 1947 by Princeton University Press). Reprinted by permission of Princeton University Press.

inquiry will be followed that appears at all promising. All of these rules are applicable to any situation in which one has to obtain the right answer and all of them are only manifestations of intelligence. The so-called scientific method is merely a special case of the method of intelligence, and any apparently unique characteristics are to be explained by the nature of the subject matter rather than ascribed to the nature of the method itself. For example, the universal and profitable use of mathematics in the physical sciences is a consequence of the possibility of using a system of precise numerical measurements in describing the systems which are the subject matter of physical science. The subject matter of other disciplines is not so often adapted to description in numerical terms, so that mathematics plays a smaller role in such disciplines.

The second chapter in the application of intelligence may well deal with the application of intelligence to the problems of human relationships. There are many people, perhaps the majority, who are convinced that these problems cannot be solved by intelligence. Their attitudes may range from the downright belligerency of those who maintain that the only solution is to be found by some supernatural method to the apathetic despair of those who plead that intelligence has never got us anywhere in the past. I shall not attempt to argue with either of these groups, but I address myself without apology to that minority who have the intellectual morale to believe that a serious application of intelligence to the solution of social problems is worth attempting. I shall pause only long enough to remark that I would challenge the validity of the evidence on which the bellicose base their confidence in the efficacy of supernatural methods, and to point out to the apathetic despairers that the method of intelligence has never had a fair trial.

If we grant that science is merely a special case of the application of intelligence, we may reasonably anticipate that our experience with scientific problems can suggest profitable lines for the attack by intelligence on the infinitely more complex and difficult problems of human relationships. Let us consider some of the suggestions from this experience.

Perhaps most important of all, we have acquired by this experience some insight into the nature of the process of intelligence itself. The revisions of scientific concepts made necessary during this century by relativity theory and quantum mechanics have shown that a certain self-conscious sophistication is necessary about being intelligent. Intelligence has its techniques, and we must be intelligent about being intelligent.

In popular estimate, perhaps the most important characteristic of science is its impersonality or "objectivity". The necessity for impersonality arises not from prejudice against people as such but because of the irrelevance of personal reactions to the commonest enterprises of science, which are concerned mainly with our external environment. In addition there is the consideration that our emotions are too likely to distort our report of factual situations. The "objectivity" of science is usually considered to be a guarantee of its truth. There is much of importance in this point of view to which we might devote our discussion with profit. The connotation here is often that science is objective because it is "public", independent of the idiosyncracies of any particular individual. This aspect of the use of intelligence which constitutes science must not be pushed too far, however, nor allowed to obscure the essential role played by the individual in scientific activity. Science is not truly objective unless it recognizes its own subjective or individual aspects. For example, scientific proof, or the conviction of truth or correctness, is something which each individual has to experience for himself. A proof vicariously accepted is dead. This is generally recognized. No editor of a reputable scientific journal will accept an article unless it is so presented that the reader may repeat the experiment and check the conclusions for himself.

The participation of the individual is necessary in every process of intelligence, not merely in the processes of science. Intelligence can be given a meaning only in terms of the individual. It seems to me that this has a far-reaching significance not usually appreciated, for I believe that here is to be found perhaps the most compelling justification for democracy. Intelligence is based on the individual. An authoritarian society in which the individual is suppressed cannot, by the nature of intelligence, be characterized by *general* intelligence.

There is another and much wider sense in which an objective science must recognize subjective aspects. However objective a science may be, it is still subjective from the point of view of the human race as a whole. Every activity of science and intelligence is a human activity, which necessarily involves the cooperation of the human nervous system. This characteristic of all that we do is so universal that it is not usual for us to recognize its existence. Even worse, we may deny its existence and elaborate its denial into a scheme of philosophy. There is a tendency to do this even in physics. As an example, I mention the philosophy of general relativity theory as distinguished from its mathematical formulation which (it seems to me) is based on an attempt to transcend the inescapable human reference point. Or, in another direction, there is perhaps danger that the spectacular success of the theoretical physicist in contributing to the atomic bomb will make him forget the limitations of the processes which he has used and give him so much confidence that he may even feel that experimental check has become superfluous.

From the wider point of view, the history of most philosophy and religion and much of politics has been the history of an attempt to repudiate the inescapability of the human reference point by the erection of absolutes and transcendentals. Our whole social structure has been built on the widespread acceptance of such absolutes and transcendentals. The intellectual basis for this acceptance goes back far into the past and acquired perhaps its most self-conscious expression with the Greek philosophers. The urge to invent absolutes seems to be an artifact of the human intellectual structure. It doubtless has its pragmatic justification and at a certain stage of evolution may have been as necessary for survival as that other indispensable invention, the external world. But whatever the origin or the pragmatic justification for this urge, there are aspects of it which will not survive intelligent scrutiny, and once the scrutiny is made and doubt begins to spread, the foundations of our social structure begin to crumble. This very process is going on at present. To put it crudely, men no longer believe in hell, and without the belief they will not respond to the same arguments to action which were potent while they believed. This decay of vividness of the old absolutes and transcendentals has been mainly an intellectual affair, due to a growing recognition that the absolutes simply are not "true". The movement has been gaining momentum for perhaps several hundred years, at first underground and only now breaking into the open and threatening social revolution. This is truly a chain reaction; what initiated the reaction would be difficult to say, perhaps the Protestant Reformation or the formulation of positivistic philosophies. The relative time scale of the explosion may not be so different from that of the atomic bomb when the different size of the fundamental units is considered, a human being and a lifetime corresponding to an atom and the duration of an excited state.

One consequence of this chain reaction is of special importance in present society and may be at the bottom of the growing tendency to fascist ideals all over the world. The old philosophical arguments for the necessity of the freedom of the individual rested importantly on the nature of God and other absolutes. If the thesis is to be now maintained new arguments must be found; they may well be based on the relation of the individual to intelligence.

Until now repudiation of the old absolutes and transcendentals has been almost entirely of a negative character. They are no longer accepted, and people are no longer moved by motives which presume their acceptance; but the repudiation is a repudiation in a vacuum, for there are no new motives to take the place of the old ones and no new insights to take the place of the ones we thought we had. Our first task is to convert this repudiation into something more positive and constructive. This reconstruction is the task before us now. It will be a long slow process to which we must devote nothing less than our maximum intellectual capacity.

Such a reconstruction may well begin with an attempt to acquire understanding of the immediate situation by painstaking analysis, without any definite visualization of all the steps by which this analysis may prepare for the final solution. We might perhaps begin by asking what was the precise meaning of the absolutes and transcendentals by which we formerly sought to guide our conduct. In searching for these meanings we may take over the technique by which modern physics discovered the meaning of its concepts.

This technique is to examine exactly what we do when we apply a concept in any concrete situation. For example, an examination of the concept of simultaneity by Einstein by an analysis of the process used to determine whether two events are simultaneous showed the concept to be relative in nature instead of absolute as had been uncritically supposed before the analysis was made. Such a method of analysis will show the predominantly verbal character of most of our absolutes. For instance, analysis will often disclose that we can check in only one way on the propriety of using in a complex situation some word with an absolute connotation—to wit, asking our colleagues whether they would use the same word. There is usually no other method which I alone could apply in a laboratory remote from any social contact. Furthermore, the situation itself to which the word is applied is only too often a purely verbal situation, arising because my colleagues and I would use the same language. Consistent analysis by this method will disclose the exceedingly complex nature of the verbal structure which human beings have erected. Man has always been the builder, not only of pyramids and Chinese walls, but of intellectual and verbal systems as well. These come to absorb his complete attention; within them he may live an entirely self-contained existence, forgetful of the natural world about him and content with the companionship of his fellows. It seems to me that no education should be considered complete until a vivid consciousness has been acquired of this situation. How seldom is this recognized as one of the ends of education!

The analysis of meanings should be extended to all the important terms of daily life. Because there is such a large verbal element in these terms, it will be found that people with different linguistic backgrounds give different meanings to ostensibly the same words. All students of language recognize that it is very seldom that an abstract word in one language has an exact equivalent in another. To attempt to clarify this situation by getting more precise correspondence in different languages may well lead to the next step in the systematic development of a program of intelligence.

This next step might be to find how far the common assumption is justified that men are fundamentally alike intellectually and can come to agreement. This has never been established by direct experiment, but is nevertheless basic to all social thinking. To what extent are different people capable of responding in the same way to the same situation?

After a certain age do people lose their ability to make certain intellectual discriminations as they lose the ability to make certain speech sounds? It is obvious that people of different backgrounds will at first almost certainly respond differently to many situations. But to what extent is this incidental? To what extent may people of different cultural backgrounds be made to see each others' points of view and make the same responses? The answer is not at all obvious, because there are certainly intellectual differences and limitations which are deep-seated and real. For example, it is probable that only a small fraction of the human race is intellectually capable of reacting to the subtleties of logic of the *Principia Mathematica*, and it may well be that there are analogous intrinsic differences in other lines of intellectual activity. It is important to know what the limitations are and at what level it is safe to set the minimum that may be presupposed in social institutions.

I think we have been too complacent in the past in assuming that our diversities of opinion are not of fundamental significance. Diversities are symptomatic of something, and we do not know what. It is time that we analyzed our disagreements and found their significance. Have we a right to our bland assumption that the human race is intellectually all alike, or may there be truly irreconcilable points of view? It is a crying disgrace that after twenty-five hundred years of philosophy the philosophers cannot agree in their description of what it is that they disagree about. I think our campaign of intellectual rehabilitation might well begin by collecting small groups of about five people, with different intellectual interests, and shutting them up until they emerged with statements as to what they could agree on in matters of ordinary social concern. In cases of disagreement they would be required to find the focus of disagreement, and agree in their formulation of the nature of the disagreement.

A prerequisite to the functioning of such groups would be a declaration of freedom from mental reservations by all the members. There must obviously be willingness to ask any question whatever with regard to any topic and to answer that question as honestly and completely as intellectually possible to the individual. That is, no holds are barred. A claim that certain types of topics must be exempt from analysis would automatically disqualify the maker of such a claim from participation, and at the same time would afford a pretty clear presumption as to the character of any opinions which he might hold on such topics.

The group having been properly constituted, its deliberations might well begin by assuring themselves that all are really using language in the same sense. The very minimum of agreement that should be exacted is agreement on description of what happens or of what is done when social situations are verbalized. Physical science could not have started before physical situations could be significantly described in such terms that they could be reproduced. Social science might well set for itself the same prerequisite of significant description. I believe that it is not now known to what extent significant description of social or economic phenomena is even possible. Significant description in the physical sciences is closely correlated with successful prediction. How few social or economic situations there are in which prediction is at present possible! An example of the present confusion is the recent break in the stock market —there were as many attempts at significant description of what caused the break as there were commentators. Although we may never achieve sufficient mastery to predict in social or economic situations as we do in physical situations, I believe that we have the right to demand that we be able to predict at least the words which we use to *describe* such situations.

The ultimate result of such a campaign of analysis would be the removal of misunderstandings as to meanings from the causes of human disagreements. I think that most of us would admit that plain misunderstanding of meaning is one of the most common and potent causes of conflict, and that with its removal our problems would be far on their way to solution.

The people who would be excluded from such a clarification of meanings would be those who have disqualified themselves from making the analysis by their claim that certain holds are barred. It may be that right here will be found an unreconcilable cleavage between human beings, namely between those who bar no holds and those who bar some. If so, this method of attack will at least bring the situation out into the open where it can be better dealt with. The greatest difficulty here is that those who bar certain holds do not like to admit it openly. Part of the problem before us is to generate such a climate of public opinion that those who bar certain holds will feel themselves under pressure to admit it openly. They would certainly also try to justify themselves, and this would be all to the good in the way of clarification.

When the misunderstandings which arise from ambiguous meanings have been removed as a source of human friction, the next task for intelligence is an analysis of the implications and presuppositions of various social systems, in particular the social sytems of the present. One of the lessons made vivid by the war was that in this country there is almost no self-conscious recognition of the necessary conditions of existence of a democracy like that of our ostensible ideal. There is great haziness in our ideas of the relation of the individual to his fellows. What are the minimum codes of conduct, which if universally accepted, would lead to a stable society in which conditions of living would be sufficiently tolerable? No systematic discussion is given of this question. The solution is usually attempted by some method more specialized than the minimum, as, for example, by exhorting everyone to live with complete unselfishness, putting the good of the whole in all cases unquestioningly above his own good. Universal acceptance of this exhortation would doubtless lead to a society appearing harmonious to a visitor from Mars. It is, however, a lazy man's solution, which begs the main questions at issue. Such a lazy man's solution is likely to conceal a metaphysical conception of society, ascribing to it an existence of its own apart from the individuals who compose it, and ascribing a meaning to the good of this superthing. Such a view of the nature of society as a whole may be eliminated by an analysis of what one would have to do to prove the existence of such a superthing. The solution and the justification must be found in the individuals.

The importance of finding a minimum solution is obvious, for any solution more specialized than the minimum involves the imposition by force of the views of certain pressure groups of individuals on other groups of individuals incapable of exerting as strong a pressure. Since a pressure group is itself composed of individuals and functions only through the functioning of its members, the discussion will involve norms of conduct and the ethics of the behavior of individuals in their capacity as members of groups. It seems to me that it is perhaps here that our general social consciousness is in its most primitive state of development. It is seldom indeed that an individual realizes that when he functions as a member of a pressure group his conduct demands special scrutiny, but he is nearly always willing to accept blithely the maximum that the group can obtain by the exercise of naked brute force.

Any discussion of the conditions basic to living together in society will lead inevitably to considerations of norms of conduct, ethics, purposes, and values. Now these are precisely topics which the popular view holds are outside the scope of the methods of science. In so far as the methods of science are methods of intelligence, a corollary would be that questions of value are also not to be answered by the general processes of intelligence. There is a sense in which this contention may be maintained, for the task of intelligence may be regarded as merely to find methods of realizing the values which are presented to it from some external source. This view, while perhaps justified from the point of view of a narrow methodology, certainly overlooks features in the total situations in which values present themselves. For values are not static, but are subject to evolution and to education. The value which we ascribe to a course of action depends on the consequences of the action, and a more vivid realization of the consequences may lead to an alteration in the value ascribed to it. But a vivid appraisal of consequences demands intelligence. Rather than admit impotence in the field of values, it seems to me that just here is one of the most important arenas for the exercise of intelligence, in purging and educating our values.

It will perhaps be not too difficult for anyone to yield formal assent to the justifiability of much of what I have been saying. It will not, however, be easy for him to have a living quickening sense of all that is involved, of the shortness of the path that the human race has trod already, of the magnitude of the reformations necessary, and of the enormous potentialities in the future. Practically all conventional human thinking which deals with abstractions is cluttered with the debris from the past of absolutes and realities and essences. These abstractions are ingrained in all conventional thinking about human institutions, and all must be revised. It seems to me that no scheme of education is adequate to our modern needs which does not instill as its most important ingredient a realization of this situation. I for one am not willing to admit that a man has been liberally educated for a free society who has not learned to view instinctively the doings of men against the background of the potentialities of the future rather than of the incoherencies of the past.

PSYCHOLOGICAL DIMENSION

The Motivation of the Student / BURRHUS F. SKINNER

The word *student* means one who studies. If the Latin root is to be trusted, it also means one who is eager and diligent. This is sometimes hard to believe, yet many students do study and some of them eagerly and diligently. If this were true of all students, education would be vastly more efficient. There is little point in building more schools, training more teachers, and designing better instructional materials if students will not study. The truant and dropout are conspicuous problems, but it is the underachiever, the careless and inattentive student, and the student who does just enough to get by who explain why our grade schools, high schools, colleges, and graduate schools are all running far below capacity.

We can easily invent explanations—we can say that some students study because they have a desire to learn, an inner urge to know, an inquisitive appetite, a love of wisdom, a natural curiosity, or some other trait of character. We thus allay *our* natural curiosity and satisfy *our* urge to know, but we do not improve teaching, for nothing about a trait tells us how to alter it or even keep it alive. William James advised teachers to fill their students with "devouring curiosity," but he did not explain how to do so. Only by turning to the behavior which is said to show the pos-

"The Motivation of the Student" is reprinted from *The Technology of Teaching*, by B. F. Skinner. Copyright © 1968, Meredith Corporation. Reprinted by permission of Appleton-Century-Crofts.

session of these traits can we search effectively for conditions which we may change so that students will study more effectively.

Among the observable things which seem relevant are the consequences of studying or, roughly speaking, what the student "gets out of" studying. At one time we should have spoken of his reasons for studying or his purpose; but reasons and purposes are simply aspects of the field of operant conditioning,[1] and our question really comes down to this: What reinforces the student when he studies?

We might look first at the ultimate advantages of an education—at its utility or value. We point to consequences of this sort to induce young people to go to school or college, or to continue to go, or to return when they have dropped out. One conspicuous example is money—the "dollar value of an education"—and we try to persuade our students by comparing the incomes of educated and uneducated people. Less mercenary advantages are the opportunities to do things which are reinforcing but which the student cannot do until he knows how, such as being a scientist, writer, musician, artist, or craftsman. The advantages of a liberal education are less explicit, but the liberally educated student enjoys things otherwise out of reach. Sheer knowing may be worthwhile in freeing one from puzzlement, insecurity, or the anxieties of not knowing. (These advantages fade as technological advances make what a man has learned less important. Manual skills lose their value under automation. Knowing how to read is less valuable when pictures and recorded speech replace texts. Verbal knowledge loses some of its importance when it is no longer presupposed; a news magazine which refers to "the English novelist Charles Dickens" or "Darwin's Theory—of evolution through natural selection" deprives the reader of some of what he gained from his education if he would have responded just as well to "Dickens" or "Darwin's Theory.") Another ultimate gain is in prestige. The student joins the company of educated men and women with its honors and cabalistic practices; he understands its allusions, enjoys its privileges, shares its *esprit de corps*.

These are, indeed, some of the things a student ultimately derives from an education, and he will probably mention them if we ask him why he is studying, but they do not help in solving our problem. The trouble with ultimate advantages is that they are ultimate. They come at the end of an education—or of some substantial part of it—and cannot be used during it as reinforcers. Their weakness is legendary. The premedical student who badly "wants to be a doctor" gets little if any help from that fact as he sits in his room on a given evening studying a page of biochemistry. The higher wages of the craftsman do not make the

---

[1] B. F. Skinner, "Operant Conditioning," *American Psychologist* 18 (1963), 503–515.

apprentice diligent. The would-be pianist practicing his scales is not encouraged by the applause of the concert hall. When other reinforcers are lacking, the classical result is a profound abulia. The student is not only not diligent or eager, he cannot make himself study at all.

We may try to make ultimate advantages effective by talking about them or by letting the student observe others who are enjoying them. We tell him what is in store for him (and that is probably why he can tell us why he is studying). But this is a rather crude use of conditioned reinforcers which, being derived from remote ultimate consequences, are unfortunately weak.

We often try to rescue something from ultimate advantages by emphasizing progress toward them. In American usage, in particular, a surprising number of words in education come from the Latin *gradus*. The student receives a *grade*, he is in a *grade*, he *graduates* with a *degree*, and enters *graduate* school. His pro*gress* is marked by numbers (from 1 to 8), by two sets of ordinal terms (freshman, sophomore, junior, and senior), and again by numbers (first-year graduate student, second-year graduate student, and so on). But these signs of progress toward the ultimate advantages of an education also function, if at all, only as conditioned reinforcers and also ineffectively.

Contrived Proximate Reinforcers

To arrange good instructional contingencies, the teacher needs on-the-spot consequences. Negative reinforcers were probably the first to be used and they are still certainly the commonest. The rod or cane and the stripping of privileges are naturally aversive; criticism and ridicule are borrowed from the culture; and failing grades and (ironically) extra schoolwork are contrived by the teacher. They can be used in contingencies of reinforcement which "make the student study"—in which, to be specific, he escapes from or avoids these kinds of aversive stimulation. Such contingencies often work, and the result may be superficially reinforcing to teachers, administrators, parents, and even to students. The practice has a long history, and even today educators often look with envy on the disciplined classroom which continues to operate primarily under aversive control.

Serious by-products must be taken into account. We can avoid some of them by moderating the aversive stimulation—by abandoning "corporal" punishment, for example, in favor of slight but constant threats, verbal or otherwise—but even so our students will be studying mainly to avoid the consequences of not studying. Under aversive control they force themselves to study; they work. Indeed, one of the ultimate advantages of an education is simply coming to the end of it.

Quite apart from unwanted by-products, contingencies of this sort are defective. Some results are to be expected when desired forms of behavior directly reduce aversive stimuli, but the usual practice is to punish behavior which is not desired. The pattern is derived from ethical control in which behavior is actually suppressed. Here we want to *generate* behavior, and it is not enough to "suppress not-behaving." Thus, we do not strengthen good pronunciation by punishing bad, or skillful movements by punishing awkward. We do not make a student industrious by punishing idleness, or brave by punishing cowardice, or interested in his work by punishing indifference. We do not teach him to learn quickly by punishing him when he learns slowly, or to recall what he has learned by punishing him when he forgets, or to think logically by punishing him when he is illogical. Under such conditions he may occasionally discover for himself how to pay attention, be industrious, and learn and remember, but he has not been taught. Moreover, he often satisfies the contingencies in the most superficial way; he "attends" only by looking at the teacher or keeping his eyes on a page, he is "industrious" only in the sense of keeping busy. The contingencies encourage superstitious behavior, including many maladaptive or neurotic ways of escaping from or avoiding aversive treatment. The culture starts this, but aversive education carries it on.

From time to time positive alternatives have been suggested. "Avoid compulsion," said Plato in *The Republic*, "and let your children's lessons take the form of play." Horace, among others, recommended rewarding a child with cakes. Erasmus tells of an English gentleman who tried to teach his son Greek and Latin without punishment. He taught the boy to use a bow and arrow and set up targets in the shape of Greek and Latin letters, rewarding each hit with a cherry. He also fed the boy letters cut from delicious biscuits. Privileges and favors are often suggested, and the teacher may be personally reinforcing as friend or entertainer. In industrial education students are paid for learning. Certain explicitly contrived reinforcers, such as marks, grades, and diplomas, are characteristic of education as an institution. (These suggest progress, but like progress they must be made reinforcing for other reasons.) Prizes are intrinsically reinforcing. Honors and medals derive their power from prestige or esteem. This varies between cultures and epochs. In 1876 Oscar Wilde, then 22 years old and halfway toward his B. A. at Oxford, got a "first in Mods." He wrote to a friend[2]: ". . . I did not know what I had got till the next morning at 12 o'clock, breakfasting at the Mitre, I read it in the *Times*. Altogether I swaggered horribly but am really pleased with myself. My poor mother is in great delight, and I was overwhelmed with telegrams on Thursday from everyone I knew." The contemporary student graduating *summa cum laude* is less widely acclaimed.

---

[2] Oscar Wilde, *Letters* (New York: Harcourt, Brace & World, 1962).

Although free of some of the by-products of aversive control, positive reinforcers of this sort are not without their problems. Many are effective only in certain states of deprivation which are not always easily arranged. Making a student hungry in order to reinforce him with food would raise personal issues which are not entirely avoided with other kinds of reinforcers. We cannot all get prizes, and if some students are to get high grades, others must get low.

But the main problem again is the contingencies. Much of what the child is to do in school does not have the form of play, with its naturally reinforcing consequences, nor is there any natural connection with food or a passing grade or a medal. Such contingencies must be arranged by the teacher, and the arrangement is often defective. The boy mentioned by Erasmus may have salivated slightly upon seeing a Greek or Latin text and he was probably a better archer, but his knowledge of Greek and Latin could not have been appreciably improved. Grades are almost always given long after the student has stopped behaving as a student. We must know that such contingencies are weak because we would never use them to shape skilled behavior. In industrial education pay is usually by the hour—in other words, contingent mainly on being present. Scholarships are contingent on a general level of performance. All these contingencies could no doubt be improved, but there is probably good reason why they remain defective.

Personal reinforcers, both positive and negative, raise special problems. When we speak of attention, approval, friendship, or affection, we mean more specifically the behavior of the teacher as he looks at the student, calls on him, talks to him, smiles at him, says "Right" or "Good," eases his lot, caresses him, and so on. On the negative side, we mean ignoring the student, frowning at him, saying "Wrong" or "Bad," making things hard for him, punishing him, and so on. Events of this sort are positively or negatively reinforcing quite apart from any connection they may have with promotion or prestige. They are no doubt highly important. When students suggest ways of improving education, they frequently ask for more personal contact with their teachers. A common objection to teaching machines is that they lack the personal touch— even when, as one computer is said to do, they speak to the child in a "friendly recorded voice."

The very power of personal reinforcers causes trouble. Personal involvements may be serious. In the masculine culture of the Greek Academy, the problem was pederasty. As Marrou has put it, Socrates attracted the "flower of Athenian youth and bound them to him with the ties of amorous passion." Relations between teacher and student show a greater variety today, but they are possibly just as troublesome. The sadistic teacher is equally celebrated. Even the milder versions of personal contact raise problems. The student's need for approval must be appreciable but not desperate; censure must build just the right shade of guilt. Personal reinforcers are readily available, and it is tempting to overuse them. As in the neo-Freudian design of the family, the social and personal environment is enlarged beyond all reason, and unnecessary problems are created. There is nothing personal about mathematics or about learning to read, even though one always reads what a person has written. To add personal reinforcers in an effort to facilitate teaching can be a dangerous strategy. Dr. George D. Stoddard [3] is quoted as saying that "Perhaps a live teacher who infuriates a student is better than a machine that leaves him stuffed with information but cold as a mackerel." Fortunately, these are not the only alternatives.

Personal involvements apart, the contingencies are bad. Many things attract a teacher's attention, and the careless teacher will reinforce the attention-getter and the show-off. Many things please a teacher, from a polished apple to fulsome footnotes in a thesis, and the careless teacher will reinforce fawners and flatterers. Identification with the teacher is often held to be essential, but imitation and emulation may yield undesirable mannerisms and traits. It is not easy for the teacher to evaluate the effects of contingencies and thus guard against shortcomings. Personal contingencies are unstable; the teacher may withhold approval to spur the student on to greater efforts but then approve too quickly when he shows extinction ("discouragement"). He may withhold help in order to give the student as much credit as possible but then give too much help to avoid embarrassing him. Students commonly complain of favoritism and hostility, and not always without justification. As Ben Jonson said, "Princes learn no art truly, but the art of horsemanship. The reason is, the brave beast is no flatterer. He will throw a prince as soon as his groom." A horse maintains the same contingencies for all men.

Natural Reinforcers

The difficulties inherent in contrived contingencies have drawn attention to natural reinforcers. Rousseau explained in detail how they might be used. Away with man-made punishment and—and this was Rousseau's special contribution—away with man-made rewards! Man is naturally happy and good; it is society which corrupts and makes him miserable; let him therefore be taught by nature. Make the student independent of men; teach him dependence on things. Use only those forms of coercion or punishment which arise naturally from his behavior; if he breaks a window, do not repair it, but let him experience a cold room. Use only natural rewards. Social reinforcers cannot be neglected, alas, but they can at least be genuine.

[3] George D. Stoddard, "Report," *Scottish Education Journal* (July 1965).

Rousseau soon had disciples, but a century and a half were to pass before John Dewey put similar ideas into widespread practice. Dewey showed how the child can be brought into contact with the world he is to learn about—a world which he will explore, discover, observe, and remember because it is attractive, intriguing, and naturally rewarding and punishing. Let him learn in school as he learns in his daily life.

Not all natural reinforcers are useful. Most of those having obvious biological significance, like food and injury, are not naturally contingent on the behavior in a standard curriculum. Fortunately, however, the human organism seems to be reinforced by other kinds of effects. A baby shakes a rattle, a child runs with a pinwheel, a scientist operates a cyclotron—and all are reinforced by the results. We are reinforced when a piece of string becomes untangled, when a strange object is identified, when a sentence we are reading makes sense. It is well for the human race that this should be so and fortunate for the teacher. Nevertheless, there are problems. The teacher who uses natural contingencies of reinforcement really abandons his role as teacher. He has only to expose the student to an environment; the environment will do the teaching. It was not for nothing that Rousseau spoke of negative education.

In practice, much remains for the teacher to do. The sheer logistics of natural reinforcers is a problem. The real world is too big to be brought into the classroom, and the teacher must exercise selection. Moreover, as we have repeatedly seen, the student does not learn just from being brought into contact with things. Experience, in the sense of contact, is not only not the best teacher, it is no teacher at all. The joyous, rapid, and seemingly permanent learning in daily life which teachers view so enviously depends upon deprivations and aversive stimuli which are greatly attenuated or lacking in a classroom. Very little real life goes on in the real world of the school. Heroic measures on the part of the teacher are needed to make that world important.

Natural contingencies of reinforcement, moreover, are not actually very good. They are more likely to generate idleness than industry. Trivial, useless, exhausting, and harmful behaviors are learned in the real world. The human organism pays for its great speed in learning by being susceptible to accidental contingencies which breed superstitions. Many natural reinforcers are too long deferred to be effective. No child really learns to plant seed because he is reinforced by the resulting harvest, or to read because he then enjoys interesting books, or to write because he then passes notes to his neighbor, or not to break windows because the room would then grow cold. The behavior which satisfies these terminal contingencies is not taught by the contingencies themselves, and programs are by no means always naturally available. The deferred consequences of precurrent responses of self-management are particularly unlikely to shape the behavior they eventually sustain. For example, natural consequences seldom if ever induce a student to study, either in nature or in school.

The human race has been exposed to the real world for hundreds of thousands of years; only very slowly has it acquired a repertoire which is effective in dealing with that world. Every step in that slow advance must have been the result of fortunate contingencies, accidentally programmed. Education is designed to make such accidents unnecessary. It is quite unlikely that anyone alive today has discovered agriculture or the controlled use of fire for himself. He has learned these things through instructional contingencies in which natural reinforcers play only a minor role. The natural contingencies used in education must almost always be rigged.

Improving Contingencies

In practice, a commitment to real life has sometimes led to improvements. As we have seen, verbal behavior is frequently overemphasized because it is easily imported into the classroom, and a shift to nonverbal knowledge, where natural contingencies are more effective, has been worthwhile. But verbal instruction is not wrong because it is not real (or because it is not naturally interesting, for it may be fascinating, as any mathematician knows). The important distinction is not between nature and artificiality. The teacher is free to use any available reinforcer provided there are no harmful by-products and provided the resulting behavior can eventually be taken over by reinforcers the student will encounter in his daily life. Compared with governmental and economic agencies, the teacher does not have a wide choice. Like the psychotherapist, he usually works with weak variables. But it is not the reinforcers which count, so much as their relation to behavior. In improving teaching it is less important to find new reinforcers than to design better contingencies using those already available.

Immediate and consistent reinforcement is, of course, desirable, but this is not to deny the importance of intermittent or remote reinforcers. Men sometimes work toward distant goals. In a very real sense they plant in the spring because of the harvest in the autumn and study for years for the sake of a professional career. But they do all this not because they are affected by distant and future events but because their culture has constructed mediating devices in the form of conditioned reinforcers: the student studies because he is admired for doing so, because immediate changes in his behavior mark progress toward later reinforcement, because being educated is "a good thing," because he is released from the aversive condition of not-knowing. Cultures are never particularly successful in building reinforcers of this sort; hence the importance of a direct attack on the problem in a technology of teaching.

The student who knows how to study knows how to amplify immediate consequences so that they prove reinforcing. He not only knows, he knows that he knows and is reinforced accordingly. The transition from external reinforcement to the self-generated reinforcement of knowing one knows is often badly handled. In a small class the precurrent behavior of listening, reading, solving problems, and composing sentences is reinforced frequently and almost immediately, but in a large lecture course the consequences are infrequent and deferred. If mediating devices have not been set up, if the student is not automatically reinforced for knowing that he knows, he then stops working, and the aversive by-products of not-knowing pile up.

Programmed instruction is primarily a scheme for making an effective use of reinforcers, not only in shaping new kinds of behavior but in maintaining behavior in strength. A program does not specify a particular kind of reinforcer (the student may work under aversive control or for money, food, prestige, or love), but it is designed to make weak reinforcers or small measures of strong ones effective.

Being right is an example. The teacher's "Right!" derives its reinforcing power from positive or negative reinforcers under the teacher's control. Being right in responding to a program may be reinforcing for similar reasons, but it is likely to share some of the automatic reinforcing effects of "coming out right." A person working a crossword puzzle is reinforced when a response completes a part of the puzzle or supplies material which makes it possible to complete other parts. When we recall a poem, we are reinforced when a word scans or rhymes, even when we have not recalled the right word. A child who is learning to read is reinforced when his vocal responses to a text compose familiar verbal stimuli. The student who is paying attention to a lecture or a text is reinforced when the words he hears or sees correspond to responses he has anticipated— an important ingredient in listening or reading with "understanding." [4] Being right also means progress, and the physical structure of a program usually makes progress conspicuous. In working through a program, a student knows where he stands; in working through a standard text, he must wait to have his achievement evaluated by an impending test.

Some familiar features which are often cited in characterizing a program are really concerned with maximizing the effects of reinforcers. Steps are small—so that reinforcement is immediate. When a sustained passage must be read before a response is made and found to be right, the reinforcement is not sharply contingent upon stimuli provided by the early parts of the passage, and responses to early parts are not strongly reinforced. Errors are minimized—and the number of responses which are automatically reinforced as right is maximized. It is sometimes said

[4] B. F. Skinner, *Verbal Behavior* (New York: Appleton-Century-Crofts, 1957).

that it is reinforcing to be right only when one is often wrong, but that depends on the source of reinforcing power. If being right derives its effectiveness from an unconditioned reinforcer which is subject to satiation, satiation may occur. Intermittent reinforcement, as we shall see in a moment, can sometimes solve that problem. If being right is reinforcing as a release from threat, occasional instances of being wrong may be needed to sustain the threat. But the reinforcements inherent in coming out right and in moving on to later stages in a program are not likely to satiate. On the contrary, progress may be even more reinforcing as the end of a program approaches. Being right may not be very reinforcing if the writer, in an effort to maximize correct responses, has made items too easy. Such programs are often called boring, but only if other contingencies are in force. When a program is not reinforcing, the student simply stops responding. If he continues working because other contingencies, probably aversive, are in force, he may justly complain of being bored.

Frequent reinforcement raises another problem if it reduces the teacher's reinforcing power. Money, food, grades, and honors must be husbanded carefully, but the automatic reinforcements of being right and moving forward are inexhaustible.

"Stretching the Ratio"

Other issues are raised by the size of steps to be taken by the student. In shaping the behavior of a pigeon, success depends on how the requirements for reinforcement are set. If you do not demand much change at each step, you will reinforce often, but your subject will progress slowly. If you demand too much, no response may satisfy, and the behavior generated up to that point will be extinguished. In deciding what behavior to reinforce at any given time, the basic rule is "Don't lose your pigeon!" How much change in behavior is demanded of the student at each step in a program must also be weighed against the need to maintain the behavior in strength.

It is easy to "lose your pigeon" in a kind of programming. The student will be less dependent on immediate and consistent reinforcement if he is brought under the control of intermittent reinforcement. If the proportion of responses reinforced (on a fixed or variable ratio schedule) is steadily reduced, a stage may be reached at which behavior is maintained indefinitely by an astonishingly small number of reinforcements. The teacher's assignment is to make relatively infrequent reinforcements effective. One technique is to "stretch the ratio"—that is, to increase the number of responses per reinforcement as rapidly as the behavior of the student permits.

In setting up new forms of behavior every change in topography or stimulus control requires reinforcement, and intermittent reinforcement is not appropriate. But much of the behavior of the student, particularly the precurrent behaviors of self-management, is repeated many times without substantial change and is normally maintained by intermittent reinforcement. A very simple example of precurrent behavior is going to school. It is intermittently reinforced, as we have seen, by many things— attractive architecture, personal contacts, enjoyable activities, interesting books and materials, pleasant teachers, and successful achievements. (A small reinforcer can sometimes make a great difference. In an experiment designed to see whether orange juice given to grade-school students improved their health, it was found that students receiving orange juice every day were less often absent. Absence was to be taken as an indication of ill health, but a closer analysis showed that the difference was accounted for by students who returned for Friday afternoon classes. They were returning because of the orange juice). Once in school students will be more inclined to start working and continue working if instructional materials are reinforcing. Audio-visual devices may have this effect quite apart from whether they teach in other ways. The effect is often intermittent.

Other precurrent behaviors of self-management are almost always intermittently reinforced. Careful attention to detail does not guarantee successful behavior but is occasionally reinforced when behavior is successful. Memorizing material is occasionally reinforced by successful recall. Techniques of exploration, discovery (including the discovery of what one has to say), and problem solving are reinforced only infrequently, a fact which may explain the popularity of the concept of trial-and-error.

Reinforcers which require a teacher may be used more effectively by making them intermittent. Comments on a paper in composition are poorly contingent on the behavior of writing the paper. As reinforcers they are likely to be weak and imprecise, particularly when a large number of papers must be read. The important reinforcers are largely automatic: a sentence comes out right, it says something interesting, it fits another sentence. If these automatic reinforcers are powerful enough, the student may continue to write and improve his writing even though he receives few if any comments. But comments by the teacher can also reinforce, and the reinforcement can be intermittent. Lindsley [5] has worked out a technique for the intermittent grading of compositions.

The Hard-Working Student

The diligent and eager student comes to class, studies for long periods of time, enters into discussions with his teachers and other students, and

[5] O. R. Lindsley, "Intermittent Grading," *The Clearing House* 32 (1958), 451–454.

is not distracted by extraneous reinforcers. He does all this, not because he possesses the trait of industry or has a positive attitude toward his education, but because he has been exposed to effective contingencies of reinforcement. Almost inevitably he will be called hard-working and said to be doing only what all students *ought* to do. The implication is that he is under aversive control. Since a threat of aversive treatment makes a student diligent, students who are diligent must be working under a threat.

It is true that studying often has aversive consequences. Prolonged attention is a strain, sustained effort is tiring and even punishing, and the dedicated student forgoes other reinforcers. It is easy to believe that these aversive consequences are taken in order to avoid the greater punishment of failure. But under a favorable program of intermittent reinforcement, the student will continue to work hard even though his behavior generates aversive stimuli. A pigeon reinforced on a high ratio will stop the experiment if it can—for example, by pecking a second key which turns the apparatus off—but when properly programmed it will not stop the experiment *by stopping work*. Nor will a student.

If by "work" we mean behavior which has aversive consequences, then the diligent student works, but if we mean behavior under aversive control, then he is not necessarily working at all. The distinction is not easily made by opposing "work" to "play," because play also has two meanings: it may be behavior which does not generate punishing consequences (the dilettante plays at being a scientist) or behavior primarily under the control of positive reinforcement (football players play hard and dangerously). Even a distinction between "hard" and "easy" is misleading. A. N. Whitehead [6] said that "an easy book ought to be burned for it cannot be educational." But did he mean a book so well written or programmed that a student reads it without being forced to do so or a book which can be read without strain or fatigue?

The behavior generated by an effective program of intermittent reinforcement is hard to characterize in traditional terms. The central theme of a project on teaching arithmetic has been expressed as follows: "The study of mathematics should be an adventure, requiring and deserving hard work." [7] The project is designed to generate a high level of activity without recourse to aversive contingencies. The appearance of terms like "requiring," "deserving," "hard," and "work" is an illuminating commentary on the history of education.

Well-designed contingencies of reinforcement will keep the student busily at work, free of the by-products of aversive control. Even more

[6] A. N. Whitehead, *The Aims of Education* (New York: Macmillan, 1929).
[7] D. A. Page, "General Information," the University of Illinois Arithmetic Project (May, 1962).

dramatic achievements are possible with respect to behavior which would traditionally be said to show (1) interest or enthusiasm, (2) the appreciation and enjoyment of works of art, literature, and music, and (3) dedication. Programmed schedules in which the ratio has been stretched are again involved.

The issue is important both while the student is being educated and afterwards. The teacher may count himself successful when his students become engrossed in his field, study conscientiously, and do more than is required of them, but the important thing is what they do when they are no longer being taught. We take this into account when we insist that what the student learns should be appropriate to day-to-day living, but a student who learns to behave in given ways under aversive control may stop behaving as soon as the aversive control ceases, no matter how appropriate the topography of the behavior may be. The student who has been made to practice may never touch the piano again when aversive contingencies come to an end, in spite of the fact that there are good reasons for playing the piano. Natural reinforcers may not automatically replace the contrived positive reinforcers of the classroom. The teacher's approval and praise and even the intellectual excitement of the class-room may have no real life counterparts. Former students often return to an instructional environment when the contingencies in their daily lives do not support behavior formerly exhibited in school or college.

The teacher can make it more probable that the behavior he sets up will continue in strength if he carefully stretches the ratio. Consider, for example, teaching enjoyment and appreciation. We want students to like books, art, and music—that is to say, we want them to read, look, and listen, and continue to do so, and enable themselves to do so by buying or borrowing books, going to museums and concerts, and so on. In particular, we want them to do all this with respect to *good* books, *good* music, and *good* art. This is a particularly important educational assignment in a culture which provides more and more leisure time.

Topography of behavior is not at issue. The student already knows how to read, look, or listen; he is to do so for particular reasons. We therefore arrange for him to be reinforced as he reads books, looks at pictures, or listens to music. This is not easy. It is not enough to expose him to books, pictures, and music if little or no reinforcement takes place. The exposure is often indirect: the student is studying the history of a field, or its technical problems, or the reasons why objects in the field are or should be enjoyed. The instructor often tries to make things reinforcing by exhibiting his own enthusiasm for them. Again, the problem is not to find more powerful reinforcers but to arrange better contingencies. Intermittent reinforcement and programs which stretch the ratio are important.

How, for example, can we produce a student who "reads good books"? It is the schedule rather than the absolute magnitude of reinforcement which must be considered. People read and continue to read cartoons, comics, and short items where the reinforcement, though not great, is contingent on very little actual reading. Primers and early textbooks follow the same principle; something happens as each sentence is read. The variable ratio is of modest size. This is light reading, and many readers never go beyond it.

In "good" books, almost by definition, reinforcers are dispersed. Students usually read such books only because they are required to do so. They "work" at them, and that is scarcely the goal in teaching appreciation. They can be induced to read for pleasure even though reinforcement is infrequent if the change in schedule is properly programmed. A student who has access to a variety of materials will to some extent automatically program a stretching ratio. He will continue to read only those books he is able to sustain. Courses in literature usually make little provision for this natural adjustment. On the contrary, under aversive control the student reads books which do not reinforce him often enough to build up behavior which will be sustained by large ratios.

It is hard to design a sequence of materials in which the student advances to higher ratios only when he can sustain them. With or without aversive contingencies, it is easy to "lose our pigeon," and the student never becomes a reader. The true devoté is usually an accident; a fortunate sequence of contingencies builds up a strong disposition to continue to read even when reinforcers are rare. Many forces oppose the explicit design of such contingencies. On the one hand, it is tempting to use a reinforcer as soon as it becomes available (to give the student at once something he may find reinforcing) rather than withhold it for intermittent scheduling. On the other hand, parents, accrediting agencies, teachers, and others, judge a school or college by the difficulty of the books students are reading, and teachers are therefore reinforced for advancing too rapidly to large ratios.

Books which are good because they are only intermittently reinforcing are a natural product of the art of literature. A great moment is effective only if the reader has been prepared for it. One cannot enjoy a book by skipping from one great passage to another. The necessary intervening material, however, is usually not strongly reinforcing. Thus, the resolution of suspense or puzzlement is reinforcing only if the suspense or puzzlement has prevailed for some time (when it may well have been slightly aversive). Few students ever acquire the sustained behavior which brings the occasional great reinforcements of literature within reach. Similarly, in the appreciation of art and music, students soon learn to enjoy things which are consistently reinforcing, but they may never go beyond that point. The rare and particularly powerful reinforcers await those whose behavior has been built up by, and sustained by, a special schedule.

Possibly even more important than the things students enjoy reading, looking at, or listening to are the things they enjoy doing. We teach them to paint, conduct research, raise orchids, and make friends; but if instruction is to be successful, these repertoires must continue in strength. We may try to build dedicated behavior by clarifying reinforcers, by setting the example of an enthusiastic and dedicated person, by describing our own satisfactions and thrills, or by commending the student's industry, but if we do not take scheduling into account, we may still "lose our pigeon."

A dedicated person is one who remains active for long periods of time without reinforcement. He does so because, either in the hands of a skillful teacher or by accident, he has been exposed to a gradually lengthening variable-ratio schedule. At first, what he did "paid off" quickly, but he then moved on to things less readily reinforced. It is perhaps presumptuous to compare a Faraday, Mozart, Rembrandt, or Tolstoy with a pigeon pecking a key or with a pathological gambler, but variable-ratio schedules are nevertheless conspicuous features of the biographies of scientists, composers, artists, and writers.

Programs which stretch the ratio are most often accidental. A scientist does an experiment which, because of its nature or the scientist's earlier history, quickly turns up interesting results. In following it up, he moves into a more difficult area, builds more complex apparatus, and works longer before the next reinforcement. Eventually he works for months or years between discoveries. Perhaps in the last decade of his life nothing reinforces him, but he dies a dedicated man. Accidental programs having such effects are no doubt rare, but so are the dedicated people whose behavior they are needed to explain.

A dedicated scientist is more than one who knows his field or how to use apparatus. To love to make music is more than knowing how to sing or play an instrument. But education is seldom concerned with the something more. Effective programs depend upon rather unpredictable reinforcers, and it is hard to evaluate the strength of the student's behavior and hence to know when to enlarge the ratio. Perhaps an optimal program is always to some extent an accident, but the general principle of moving from frequent to rare reinforcers is, nevertheless, important. "Standards" are again troublesome. The teacher finds it hard to permit the beginning scientist to be reinforced by fortuitous or irrelevant results, or the beginning artist by cheap or hackneyed effects, or the young musician by a noisy and inaccurate performance, but those who move too quickly to rigorous and valid research or flawless technique and taste may not be on their way to a dedicated life.

As we have seen, the techniques of self-management used in thinking are very similar to those which another person would use to bring about the same changes in the thinker's behavior. Teacher and student manipulate the same kinds of variables to induce the student to pay attention, solve problems, have ideas. They may also take the same steps in solving the problem of motivation. Techniques of self-control are available in heightening one's own industry, enjoyment, and dedication.

Strictly speaking, the student cannot reinforce or punish himself by withholding positive or negative reinforcers until he has behaved in a given way, but he can seek out or arrange conditions under which his behavior is reinforced or punished. Thus, he can choose hobbies or companions because of the contingencies they provide. He can create reinforcing events, as by checking an answer to a problem. He can stop emitting unreinforced responses in an unfavorable situation so that extinction will not generalize to other situations—for example, he can learn not to read books which are too hard for him so that his inclination to read other books will not suffer. He can learn subtle discriminations which improve the contingencies of reinforcement when he listens to his own accent in a foreign language. He can clarify reinforcing consequences—for example, he can mechanically amplify small movements while learning a response of subtle topography or make a record of his behavior, as a writer does in counting the number of words or pages written in a session. If his behavior is strongly competitive, he can sharpen the contingencies by frequently looking at the achievements of his rivals. He can manipulate daily routines involving such things as sleep, diet, and exercise in ways which affect the strength of the behavior at issue.

He will do all those things only if he has learned to do them. Specific instruction is particularly important because self-management is often covert and models are therefore not generally available for imitation. We do not often see people controlling themselves in these ways. Moreover, the natural reinforcing consequences are almost always long deferred. Education has never taught the self-management of motivation very effectively. It has seldom tried. But techniques become available as soon as the problem is understood.

The abulia of those who have nothing to do, who are not interested in anything, is one of the great tragedies of modern life. It is sometimes attributed to alienation, anomie, anhedonia, rootlessness, or lack of values. These are not the causes of anything; at best they are other products of the defective contingencies which are the source of the trouble attributed to them. Through a proper understanding of contingencies of reinforcement, we should be able to make students eager and diligent and be reasonably sure that they will continue to enjoy the things we teach them for the rest of their lives.

Democracy and Educational Administration /

JOHN DEWEY

I shall begin . . . with some remarks on the broad theme of democratic aims and methods. Much of what I shall say on this subject is necessarily old and familiar. But it seems necessary to rehearse some old ideas in order to have a criterion for dealing with the special subject.

In the first place, democracy is much broader than a special political form, a method of conducting government, of making laws and carrying on governmental administration by means of popular suffrage and elected officers. It is that, of course. But it is something broader and deeper than that. The political and governmental phase of democracy is a means, the best means so far found, for realizing ends that lie in the wide domain of human relationships and the development of human personality. It is, as we often say, though perhaps without appreciating all that is involved in the saying, a way of life, social and individual. The keynote of democracy as a way of life may be expressed, it seems to me, as the necessity for the participation of every mature human being in formation of the values that regulate the living of men together: which is necessary from the standpoint of both the general social welfare and the full development of human beings as individuals.

Universal suffrage, recurring elections, responsibility of those who are in political power to the voters, and the other factors of democratic government are means that have been found expedient for realizing democracy as the truly human way of living. They are not a final end and a final value. They are to be judged on the basis of their contribution to end. It is a form of idolatry to erect means into the end which they serve. Democratic political forms are simply the best means that human wit has devised up to a special time in history. But they rest back upon the idea that no man or limited set of men is wise enough or good enough to rule others without their consent; the positive meaning of this statement is that all those who are affected by social institutions must have a share in producing and managing them. The two facts that each one is influenced in what he does and enjoys and in what he becomes by the institutions under which he lives, and that therefore he shall have, in a democracy, a voice in shaping them, are the passive and active sides of the same fact.

"Democracy and Educational Administration" is reprinted from John Dewey, "Democracy and Educational Administration", *School and Society*, April 3, 1937. Reprinted by permission of the Society for the Advancement of Education, Inc.

The development of political democracy came about through substitution of the method of mutual consultation and voluntary agreement for the method of subordination of the many to the few enforced from above. Social arrangements which involve fixed subordination are maintained by coercion. The coercion need not be physical. There have existed, for short periods, benevolent despotisms. But coercion of some sort there has been; perhaps economic, certainly psychological and moral. The very fact of exclusion from participation is a subtle form of suppression. It gives individuals no opportunity to reflect and decide upon what is good for them. Others who are supposed to be wiser and who in any case have more power decide the question for them and also decide the methods and means by which subjects may arrive at the enjoyment of what is good for them. This form of coercion and suppression is more subtle and more effective than is overt intimidation and restraint. When it is habitual and embodied in social institutions, it seems the normal and natural state of affairs. The mass usually become unaware that they have a claim to a development of their own powers. Their experience is so restricted that they are not conscious of restriction. It is part of the democratic conception that they as individuals are not the only sufferers, but that the whole social body is deprived of the potential resources that should be at its service. The individuals of the submerged mass may not be very wise. But there is one thing they are wiser about than anybody else can be, and that is where the shoe pinches, the troubles they suffer from.

The foundation of democracy is faith in the capacities of human nature; faith in human intelligence and in the power of pooled and cooperative experience. It is not belief that these things are complete but that, if given a show, they will grow and be able to generate progressively the knowledge and wisdom needed to guide collective action. Every autocratic and authoritarian scheme of social action rests on a belief that the needed intelligence is confined to a superior few, who because of inherent natural gifts are endowed with the ability and the right to control the conduct of others; laying down principles and rules and directing the ways in which they are carried out. It would be foolish to deny that much can be said for this point of view. It is that which controlled human relations in social groups for much the greater part of human history. The democratic faith has emerged very, very recently in the history of mankind. Even where democracies now exist, men's minds and feelings are still permeated with ideas about leadership imposed from above, ideas that developed in the long early history of mankind. After democratic political institutions were nominally established, beliefs and ways of looking at life and of acting that originated when men and women were externally controlled and subjected to arbitrary power, persisted in the family, the church, business, and the school; and experience shows that as long as they persist there, political democracy is not secure.

Belief in equality is an element of the democratic credo. It is not, however, belief in equality of natural endowments. Those who proclaimed the idea of equality did not suppose they were enunciating a psychological doctrine, but a legal and political one. All individuals are entitled to equality of treatment by law and in its administration. Each one is affected equally in quality if not in quantity by the institutions under which he lives and has an equal right to express his judgment, although the weight of his judgment may not be equal in amount when it enters into the pooled result to that of others. In short, each one is equally an individual and entitled to equal opportunity of development of his own capacities, be they large or small in range. Moreover, each has needs of his own, as significant to him as those of others are to them. The very fact of natural and psychological inequality is all the more reason for establishment by law of equality of opportunity, since otherwise the former becomes a means of oppression of the less gifted.

While what we call intelligence be distributed in unequal amounts, it is the democratic faith that it is sufficiently general so that each individual has something to contribute, whose value can be assessed only as it enters into the final pooled intelligence constituted by the contributions of all. Every authoritarian scheme, on the contrary, assumes that its value may be assessed by some *prior* principle, if not of family and birth or race and color or possession of material wealth, then by the position and rank a person occupies in the existing social scheme. The democratic faith in equality is the faith that each individual shall have the chance and opportunity to contribute whatever he is capable of contributing and that the value of his contribution be decided by its place and function in the organized total of similar contributions, not on the basis of prior status of any kind whatever.

I have emphasized in what precedes the importance of the effective release of intelligence in connection with personal experience in the democratic way of living. I have done so purposely because democracy is so often and so naturally associated in our minds with freedom of *action*, forgetting the importance of freed intelligence which is necessary to direct and to warrant freedom of action. Unless freedom of individual action has intelligence and informed conviction back of it, its manifestation is almost sure to result in confusion and disorder. The democratic idea of freedom is not the right of each individual to *do* as he pleases, even if it be qualified by adding "provided he does not interfere with the same freedom on the part of others." While the idea is not always, not often enough, expressed in words, the basic freedom is that of freedom of *mind* and of whatever degree of freedom of action and experience is necessary to produce freedom of intelligence. The modes of freedom guaranteed in the Bill of Rights are all of this nature: Freedom of belief and conscience, of expression of opinion, of assembly for discussion and conference, of the press as an organ of communication. They are guaranteed because without them individuals are not free to develop and society is deprived of what they might contribute.

What, it may be asked, have these things to do with school administration? There is some kind of government, of control, wherever affairs that concern a number of persons who act together are engaged in. It is a superficial view that holds government is located in Washington and Albany. There is government in the family, in business, in the church, in every social group. There are regulations, due to custom if not to enactment, that settle how individuals in a group act in connection with one another.

It is a disputed question of theory and practice just how far a democratic political government should go in control of the conditions of action within special groups. At the present time, for example, there are those who think the federal and state governments leave too much freedom of independent action to industrial and financial groups, and there are others who think the government is going altogether too far at the present time. I do not need to discuss this phase of the problem, much less to try to settle it. But it must be pointed out that if the methods of regulation and administration in vogue in the conduct of secondary social groups are non-democratic, whether directly or indirectly, or both, there is bound to be an unfavorable reaction back into the habits of feeling, thought and action of citizenship in the broadest sense of that word. The way in which any organized social interest is controlled necessarily plays an important part in forming the dispositions and tastes, the attitudes, interests, purposes and desires, of those engaged in carrying on the activities of the group. For illustration, I do not need to do more than point to the moral, emotional and intellectual effect upon both employers and laborers of the existing industrial system. Just what the effects specifically are is a matter about which we know very little. But I suppose that everyone who reflects upon the subject admits that it is impossible that the ways in which activities are carried on for the greater part of the waking hours of the day, and the way in which the shares of individuals are involved in the management of affairs in such a matter as gaining a livelihood and attaining material and social security, can only be a highly important factor in shaping personal dispositions; in short, forming character and intelligence.

In the broad and final sense all institutions are educational in the sense that they operate to form the attitudes, dispositions, abilities and disabilities that constitute a concrete personality. The principle applies with special force to the school. For it is the main business of the family and the school to influence directly the formation and growth of attitudes and dispositions, emotional, intellectual and moral. Whether this educative process is carried on in a predominantly democratic or nondemocratic way becomes, therefore, a question of transcendent importance not only for education itself but for its final effect upon all the interests and activities of a society that is committed to the democratic way of life. Hence, if the general tenor of what I have said about the democratic ideal and method is anywhere near the truth, it must be said that the democratic principle requires that every teacher should have some regular and organic way in which he can, directly or through representatives democratically chosen, participate in the formation of the controlling aims, methods and materials of the school of which he is a part. Something over thirty years ago, I wrote: "If there is a single public-school system in the United States where there is official and constitutional provision made for submitting questions of methods of discipline and teaching, and the questions of the curriculum, text-books, etc., to the discussion and decision of those actually engaged in the work of teaching, that fact has escaped my notice." I could not make that statement today. There has been in some places a great advance in the democratic direction. As I noted in my earlier article there were always in actual fact school systems where the practice was much better than the theory of external control from above: for even if there were no authorized regular way in which the intelligence and experience of the teaching corps was consulted and utilized, administrative officers accomplished that end in informal ways. We may hope this extension of democratic methods has not only endured but has expanded. Nevertheless, the issue of authoritarian versus democratic methods in administration remains with us and demands serious recognition.

It is my impression that even up to the present democratic methods of dealing with pupils have made more progress than have similar methods of dealing with members of the teaching staff of the classroom. At all events, there has been an organized and vital movement in the first matter while that in the second is still in its early stage. All schools that pride themselves upon being up-to-date utilize methods of instruction that draw upon and utilize the life-experience of students and strive to individualize treatment of pupils. Whatever reasons hold for adopting this course with respect to the young certainly more strongly hold for teachers, since the latter are more mature and have more experience. Hence the question is in place: What are the ways by which can be secured more organic participation of teachers in the formation of the educational policies of the school?

Since, as I have already said, it is the problem I wish to present rather than to lay down the express ways in which it is to be solved, I might stop at this point. But there are certain corollaries which clarify the meaning of the issue. Absence of participation tends to produce lack of interest and concern on the part of those shut out. The result is a corresponding lack of effective responsibility. Automatically and unconsciously, if not consciously, the feeling develops, "This is none of our affair; it is the business of those at the top; let that particular set of Georges do what needs to be done." The countries in which autocratic government prevails are just those in which there is least public spirit and the greatest indifference to matters of general as distinct from personal concern. Can we expect a different kind of psychology to actuate teachers? Where there is little power, there is correspondingly little sense of positive responsibility. It is enough to do what one is told to do sufficiently well to escape flagrant unfavorable notice. About larger matters, a spirit of passivity is engendered. In some cases, indifference passes into evasion of duties when not directly under the eye of a supervisor; in other cases, a carping, rebellious spirit is engendered. A sort of game is instituted between teacher and supervisor like that which went on in the old-fashioned schools between teacher and pupil. Other teachers pass on, perhaps unconsciously, what they feel to be arbitrary treatment received by them to their pupils.

The argument that teachers are not prepared to assume the responsibility of participation deserves attention, with its accompanying belief that natural selection has operated to put those best prepared to carry the load in the positions of authority. Whatever the truth in this contention, it still is also true that incapacity to assume the responsibilities involved in having a voice in shaping policies is bred and increased by conditions in which that responsibility is denied. I suppose there has never been an autocrat, big or little, who did not justify his conduct on the ground of the unfitness of his subjects to take part in government. I would not compare administrators to political autocrats. On the whole, what exists in the schools is more a matter of habit and custom than it is of any deliberate autocracy. But, as was said earlier, habitual exclusion has the effect of reducing a sense of responsibility for what is done and its consequences. What the argument for democracy implies is that the best way to produce initiative and constructive power is to exercise it. Power, as well as interest, comes by use and practice. Moreover, the argument from incapacity proves too much. If it is so great as to be a permanent bar, then teachers cannot be expected to have the intelligence and skill that are necessary to execute the directions given them. The delicate and difficult task of developing character and good judgment in the young needs every stimulus and inspiration possible. It is impossible that the work should not be better done when teachers have that understanding of what they are doing that comes from having shared in forming its guiding ideas.

Classroom teachers are those who are in continuous direct contact with those taught. The position of administrators is at best indirect by comparison. If there is any work in the world that requires the conservation of what is good in experience so that it may become an integral part of further experience, it is that of teaching. I often wonder how much waste there is in the traditional system. There is some loss even at the best of the potential capital acquired by successful teachers. It does not get freely transmitted to other teachers who might profit by it. Is not the waste very considerably increased when teachers are not called upon to communicate their successful methods and results in a form in which it could have organic effect upon general school policies? Add to this waste that results when teachers are called upon to give effect in the classroom to courses of study they do not understand the reasons for, and the total loss mounts up so that it is a fair estimate that the absence of democratic methods is the greatest single cause of educational waste.

The present subject is one of peculiar importance at the present time. The fundamental beliefs and practices of democracy are now challenged as they never have been before. In some nations they are more than challenged. They are ruthlessly and systematically destroyed. Everywhere there are waves of criticism and doubt as to whether democracy can meet pressing problems of order and security. The causes for the destruction of political democracy in countries where it was nominally established are complex. But of one thing I think we may be sure. Wherever it has fallen it was too exclusively political in nature. It had not become part of the bone and blood of the people in daily conduct of its life. Democratic forms were limited to Parliament, elections and combats between parties. What is happening proves conclusively, I think, that unless democratic habits of thought and action are part of the fiber of a people, political democracy is insecure. It cannot stand in isolation. It must be buttressed by the presence of democratic methods in all social relationships. The relations that exist in educational institutions are second only in importance in this respect to those which exist in industry and business, perhaps not even to them.

I recur then to the idea that the particular question discussed is one phase of a wide and deep problem. I can think of nothing so important in this country at present as a rethinking of the whole problem of democracy and its implications. Neither the rethinking nor the action it should produce can be brought into being in a day or year. The democratic idea itself demands that the thinking and activity proceed cooperatively. My utmost hope will be fulfilled if anything I have said plays any part, however small, in promoting cooperative inquiry and experimentation in this field of democratic administration of our schools.

Imperatives for a Reconstructed Philosophy of Education / THEODORE BRAMELD

Recently an invitation came to me, as it did to others, that was unusual not only in itself but because of its signers. I was asked to comment for the impending 10th Anniversary Conference of the New Lincoln School on this kind of question: "What should American education become in the next ten years?" The signers were: William H. Kilpatrick, Jerrold Zacharias, Arthur Bestor, and Robert M. Hutchins. Almost anyone would be intrigued by such an invitation: could it mean that leaders representing such extremely diverse educational views as Kilpatrick and Hutchins were actually going to listen carefully to one another? My reply provides the framework for this article.

Addressing myself to Dr. Kilpatrick, I wrote as follows:

> Your desire to include the views of people of very different educational outlooks is most commendable and surely much needed in a time of extraordinary concern. . . . As you know, my own philosophic position in education is quite unorthodox and differs at rather crucial points not only from your own but particularly from that of Dr. Bestor and Dr. Hutchins whose names accompany your own. . . . I assume that, since you have written me, you wish to have my viewpoint heard along with others.
>
> . . . The challenge of the sputnik has not only aroused the American people from their educational lethargy as few if any events have done, but it has since demonstrated the appalling confusion among us as to the functions and purposes of education in our democracy. Even more appalling, if that is possible, is the evidence that exceedingly powerful voices in America—exemplified by *Life* and *Time*—oversimplify and prejudge the issues. The editorial in the March 31st [1958] issue of *Life*, reprinted in *Time, The New York Times*, and elsewhere, so outrageously falsified these issues that the Philosophy of Education Society in its annual meeting, Indianapolis, April 2, 1958, unanimously went on record in condemnation of such "irresponsible" journalism. The President of the Society, incidentally, was Father R. J. Henle, S.J., and many members are in disagreement with the philosophy of John Dewey, which was especially under attack in the editorial.
>
> And yet, in one respect, the thesis of the *Life* editorial represents the attitudes of millions of so-called, self-appointed "authorities" on American

"Imperatives for a Reconstructed Philosophy of Education" is reprinted from Theodore Brameld, "Imperatives for a Reconstructed Philosophy of Education," *School and Society*, January 17, 1959. Reprinted by permission of the Society for the Advancement of Education, Inc.

education. This thesis is, of course, that education must ultimately choose between two points of view—the one, represented by the progressivism of Dewey and his disciples; the other, represented by the kind of neo-conservatism which *Life* itself espouses and which, typified by the writings of such earnest persons as Professor Bestor, has the support of all those forces in the culture that identify education with traditional forms of learning and classical subject matters.

. . . This kind of either-or choice is quite as false as is the kind of pseudo-syntheses and patchwork proposals exemplified in the equally earnest writings of Professor Paul Woodring. There is, I submit, a radically different approach to the problem which we shall have to give consideration if we are not to be deluded indefinitely by oversimplifications and fuzzy or nostalgic thinking. This approach is based upon at least two fundamental premises.

The first premise is that we live today in one of the greatest periods of crisis in human history. Granting that all history consists of recurrent crises, this one is unprecedented in several ways, the most monstrous of which is the fact that man has achieved the capacity to destroy civilization over night. America, living as it does in an aura of deceptive prosperity and complacency, refuses thus far to admit this fact with any real conviction. In many other parts of the world, however, the masses of people are very deeply concerned—so deeply that, as anyone knows who follows world events, our own country is looked upon with more and more skepticism, less and less as the great democratic vanguard which it once was.

The second premise is that, just as the physical sciences have recently passed through a revolution which was, indeed, partly responsible for the crisis itself, so today the behavioral sciences . . . are rapidly entering upon a revolution of their own. This revolution is already awakening those familiar with it to the realization that mankind is now approaching the opportunity to achieve a world civilization of abundance, health, and humane capacity that is as life-affirming and promising as the crisis symbolized by sputniks and hydrogen bombs is life-denying and dreadful.

The kind of education needed in America must, I submit, be reconstructed upon these two premises. It can become an education that inspires young people to adventure and creation and yet is at diametrically opposite poles from its one real opponent—the totalitarian education of the communist orbit. Instead of being based upon outmoded conceptions of learning and discipline, such as are at bottom endorsed by the neo-conservative forces, it can utilize the richest resources of the behavioral sciences and a theory of unified man which those resources elucidate. The superficial arguments of the pro-science versus the pro-humanities groups are overarched in the same way as are those between the so-called educationists and academicians.

Teacher training, for example, would of course be reorganized once such a conception took hold. Of course it is cluttered with busy work, with over-emphasis upon method, and with all sorts of absurdities. But so, too, would the liberal-arts program of the typical high school and college require reorganization—characterized as it often is with a chaos of unrelated courses, bad teaching, and unmotivated learning. Neither teacher training nor liberal arts can be called satisfactory because neither is governed by a philosophy of education and culture suitable to a world in crisis. And neither is satisfactory because neither is aware (except vaguely at most) that a revolution in the behavioral sciences, which is breaking down old classifications and opening new vistas of human potentiality, is already well under way.

I cannot now indicate in any detail what this conception would mean for the curriculum, for standards of scholarship, for school administration, or for the profession of teaching; I can only suggest that it does mean a completely new look at all of them. The question of how to move from the high level of generalization to the concrete level of practice is, however, answerable in one way here. There is pressing need for new forms of educational experimentation—new designs in the form of testable hypotheses. . . . The time has come to initiate audacious, imaginative pilot projects based upon the conception I have tried to indicate. Teachers and students alike would enter into them with an excitement that could be contagious, and that could affect education not only throughout America but throughout other countries that are attuned to the crisis of our time and await our leadership again.

The remaining paragraphs spell out a little further the implications of the above statement.

The first premise—that we live in an age of crisis—is supportable in a great many ways besides the one selected for mention. Granting that destruction by nuclear war is the most horrifying fear of our time, only a little less horrifying are the insidious disintegrations threatened by radioactive fallouts. Add to these the record of two bloody intercontinental wars within a quarter-century, the rise of a mighty totalitarian system that already jeopardizes America's position as the foremost industrial power, and now the looming conquest of space with its portents of evil as well as good. For any educational system not to give these events priority, for it not to provide every possible opportunity to diagnose their causes and to consider how the growing generation may cope with them while time remains, is for that system to shirk its most urgent responsibility.

Although certain other viewpoints besides the one I support would agree on the fact of major crisis, no other derives from it similar educational imperatives. The most crucial of these rest upon the second major premise—the revolution occurring in the behavioral sciences. This revolution requires education to re-examine its whole conventional structure and to consider new ways of (1) ordering its subject matters, (2) engaging in the processes by which they are taught and learned, and (3) formulating the purposes of school and society.

None of these imperatives would have been practicably realizable before the emergence of such young sciences as cultural anthropology and psychiatry, or the interrelating of these with such older ones as economics, sociology, and history. None of them depends upon metaphysical or otherwise speculative doctrines of the classical philosophies. All of them, while open to a great deal of further clarification and verification, are potentially demonstrable and defensible in the same way that all science is demonstrable and defensible.

Let me try now to illustrate each of the three imperatives in educational terms.

1. Up to this time, the structure of the typical school and college curriculum has been largely a jumble of discrete subject matters that, for the average student, have little or no meaningful relations to one another —languages, mathematics, social science, natural science, and others— each of which is often again subdivided into further discrete units. The behavioral sciences are now demonstrating that, as far at least as all the areas having to do with biopsychological experience are concerned, these divisions and subdivisions are less and less tenable. Concepts such as organism, connoting relationships between parts as much as the parts related, are replacing the older atomistic concepts. Human life, individually and culturally, is increasingly seen in terms of patterns and configurations.

Programs of general or integrated education, recognizing that something must be done to give meaningful unity to the curriculum structure, have sometimes been tangentially affected by this interdisciplinary view of human behavior. Unfortunately, however, they also have been plagued by the same confusions in theory and practice that are chronic to other educational programs. Some general educationists, for example, take their cue from the physical sciences; others, from neo-scholasticism or like doctrines. Few as yet regard the tasks and goals of human beings as the first and most important concern of vital education in an age such as ours, or, for that matter, in any age.

This is not to say that the physical sciences, any more than the humanities, should be neglected by the needed new framework. It does mean that they are encompassed by it. A theory of unified man, both derived from and contributing to our experimental knowledge of human behavior in its multiple perspectives, not only should integrate all other fields of knowledge; it should provide them with a fresh and potent significance.

2. The required rebuilding of teaching and learning processes is heralded by a great body of recent behavioral research, only a fraction of which has begun to permeate educational practice. Perhaps the one point where permeation has occurred at all fruitfully thus far is in the methodology of "group dynamics." Yet, even here, as so commonly happens in educational circles, it has acquired more often the earmarks

of a superficial fad than of a profound process dependent upon a widening range of discoveries about the "fields of forces" that constitute the interactions of human beings in their multiple roles.

Even more promising is the "culture-and-personality" frontier. Here anthropologists and psychologists are joining hands. And they are demonstrating that learning, for example, involves polaristic dimensions of inner and outer experience, some of it quite unconscious, that have been almost totally neglected by the orthodox formulations still underlying classroom routines.

Again, the problem of how to enlist education in the processes of institutional change so that it functions, not merely to transmit but to modify and reconstruct outmoded arrangements, can now be attacked with the aid of substantial knowledge. The concept of crisis itself exemplifies this opportunity. Citing outstanding authorities in the behavioral sciences, I have pointed out elsewhere that

> There is no good reason, except timidity or irresponsibility, that prevents high schools and colleges from encouraging young people to analyze both the meaning of crisis theoretically and its manifestations overtly. Leaders ought accordingly to clarify their orientation here: they ought to face the issue of whether education is to be regarded as capable of sharing importantly in the control and resolution of crises, or as a pawn of overpowering material or spiritual forces beyond control and resolution.

3. The shaping of new purposes for education and culture is also becoming feasible in a way that could hardly have been conceived even three or four decades ago. In other words, the behavioral sciences are beginning to prove, really for the first time in history, that it is possible to formulate human goals not for sentimental, romantic, mystical, or similarly arbitrary reasons, but on the basis of what we are learning about cross-cultural and even universal values. Though studies in this difficult field have moved only a little way, they have moved far enough so that it is already becoming plausible both to describe these values objectively and to demonstrate that most human beings prefer them to alternative values.

Freedom is an example. By analyzing drives and motivations, by determining what human beings in many different cultures most deeply need and want, freedom both as fact and norm undergoes something of a metamorphosis of meaning. Yet it preserves the rich kernel of significance intuited by Jefferson and other geniuses of a pre-scientific age.

This way of constructing educational purposes rests, too, upon an expanding inventory of research evidence. Human resources for a happy life on earth are infinitely greater than we have ever dreamed possible—resources that we have hardly begun to tap because we are so often blinded by conflict, ignorance, and fear. A truly goal-centered education could contribute more than any other agency to displacing these destructive forces by scientifically ascertainable and testable hopes for the future of mankind.

To what extent is educational theory presently concerned with the kind of imperatives that I have indicated? I regret to say: very little, indeed. The only recent books that, in my judgment, help (each in a different way) are three: "The Ideal and the Community—A Philosophy of Education," by I. B. Berkson; "Philosophy of Education for Our Time," by Frederick Mayer; and "Philosophy and Education," edited by Israel Scheffler.

It is difficult, however, to feel that the dominant neo-conservative mood of the moment is anything more than passing. The single most encouraging fact about the behavioral sciences as they are now swiftly developing (I have been able, of course, to reveal only a few glimpses) is that they offer so little comfort to those of such a timid if not defeatist mood and so much support to those who continue deeply to believe in the need of a philosophy and program appropriate to our revolutionary age.

THE AUTHORS

John Dewey (1859–1952). Famous American philosopher of human experience; influenced by the psychology of William James, the philosophy of synthesis of Hegelianism, and the biological conception of the organism's relation to the environment of Charles Darwin; experience is a process of adjustment and reconstruction to a changing environment that calls for intelligent and reflective behavior toward purposes that are worthwhile for the growing individual as a learner. Born on a farm near Burlington, Vermont; graduated from the University of Vermont (1879); teacher of Latin, algebra, and natural science at South Oil City High School, Pennsylvania (1879–1881); Ph.D. from Johns Hopkins University (1884); instructor and assistant professor of philosophy, University of Michigan (1884–1888); professor of philosophy, University of Minnesota (1888–1889); chairman, department of philosophy, University of Michigan (1889–1894); chairman, department of philosophy, psychology, and pedagogy, University of Chicago (1894–1904); administrator, The Laboratory School of the University of Chicago (1896–1903); professor of philosophy, Columbia University (1904–1930); professor emeritus of philosophy in residence, Columbia University (1930–1939); president, American Psychological Association; president, American Philosophical Society. Noted publications: *My Pedagogic Creed* (1897); *The School and Society* (1899); *The Child and the Curriculum,* (1902); *Moral Principles in Education* (1909); *Interest and Effort in Education* (1913); *Democracy and Education* (1916); *Reconstruction in Philosophy*

(1920); *Human Nature and Conduct* (1922); *Experience and Nature* (1925); *Individualism Old and New* (1930); *Philosophy and Civilization* (1931); *How We Think* (1933); *Art as Experience* (1934); *A Common Faith* (1934); *Liberalism and Social Action* (1935); *Logic: The Theory of Inquiry* (1938); *Experience and Education* (1938); *Problems of Men* (1946).

Percy W. Bridgman (1882–1961). One of the most distinguished modern physicists; Nobel prize winner in physics; modernized the philosophy of pragmatism to meet the evidences from the new physics; developed the philosophy of science called operationism in which concepts are understood in terms of operations performed rather than properties of the objects; emphasized the place of human intelligence in human action. Born in Cambridge, Massachusetts, educated in the public schools of Newton, Massachusetts; graduated from Harvard University (1904); M.A. from Harvard (1905); Ph.D. from Harvard (1908); Harvard fellow for research (1908–1910); instructor in physics at Harvard (1919–1926); Hollis Professor of Mathematics and Natural Philosophy at Harvard (1926–1950); Higgins University Professor at Harvard (1950–1954). Rumford Medal of the American Academy of Arts and Sciences (1917); the Cresson Medal of the Franklin Institute (1932); the Roozeboom Medal of the Royal Netherlands Academy of Sciences (1933); Nobel prize in physics (1946); Comstock Prize of the National Academy of Sciences (1953). Major publications: *The Logic of Modern Physics* (1927); *The Nature of Physical Theory* (1936); *The Intelligent Individual and Society* (1938); *Reflections of a Physicist* (1950); *The Nature of Some of Our Physical Concepts* (1952).

Burrhus F. Skinner (1904–   ). Most noted Neo-Behaviorist; has written and lectured extensively on education; inventor of the Skinner box and other instruments for experimental research; promoter of reinforcement as the stimulant for learning; emphasized programmed material and teaching machines as the primary means for educational reinforcement. Born in Susquehanna, Pennsylvania; graduated from Hamilton College, New York (1929); M.A. from Harvard University (1930); Ph.D. from Harvard University (1931). Instructor in psychology, University of Minnesota (1936–1937); assistant professor of psychology, University of Minnesota (1937–1939); associate professor of psychology, University of Minnesota (1939–1945); professor of psychology and department chairman, Indiana University (1945–1948); Edgar Pierce Professor of Psychology, Harvard University (1958–   ). National Research Council Fellow of Harvard University (1931–1932); Howard Crosby Warren Medal (1942); American Psychological Association Award (1958). Major publications: *Behavior of Organisms* (1938); *Walden Two* (1948); *Science and Human Behavior* (1953); *Schedules of Reinforcement* (1957); *Verbal Behavior* (1957); *The Analysis of Behavior* (1961); *The Technology of Teaching* (1968).

Theodore B. H. Brameld (1904–   ). Educational philosopher of reconstructionism; upholder of the scientific method as the means for improving society, with anthropology the social science to perform this reconstruction on a worldwide cultural basis; promoter of long-range goals in education rather than education for short and immediate purposes. Born in Neillsville, Wisconsin; graduated from Ripon College (1926); Ph.D. from the University of Chicago (1931); instructor in philosophy, Long Island University (1931–(1935); instructor in philosophy of education at University of Minnesota (1939–1944); professor at University of Minnesota (1944–1947); professor of educational philosophy at New York University (1947–1958); professor of educational philosophy at Boston University (1958–   ). Visiting professor at Dartmouth College, University of Wisconsin, University of Puerto Rico, Columbia University. Wenner-Gren Foundation Grants (1953–1956); Fulbright research scholar to Japan (1964); president of the Philosophy of Education Society. Major writings: *A Philosophic Approach to Communism*, (1933); *Workers' Education in the United States* (1941); *Design for America* (1945); *Patterns of Educational Philosophy* (1950); *Philosophies of Education in Cultural Perspective* (1955); *Towards a Reconstruction of Philosophy of Education* (1957); *Cultural Foundations of Education* (1957); *Education for the Emerging Age* (1961); *Education as Power* (1965); *The Use of Explosive Ideas in Education* (1965).

TWO

Emphasis Upon Knowledge (Essentialism)

Idealism

GENERIC NOTIONS AND BASIC THEMES

Idealism in education can be explained on two levels—an emphasis on intellectual training and a belief in the distinctiveness of the human being. The first, a nonreflective level, is the one most often espoused today. Exponents of this level are concerned with education in the traditional sense only; they suggest a return to the educational methods and programs of the past, the period just prior to the advent of early progressive education, when the three R's for elementary education and certain basic subjects for secondary education were emphasized. Intellectual training and mental discipline are stressed by these modern exponents probably because they experienced such an educational approach themselves, either indirectly, through their parents' attitudes toward discipline and schooling or directly, through their own experiences in school. They also find support for their beliefs in the example of many European systems of education. Admiral Rickover has discussed many of these.

As a rule, contemporary supporters of this approach to education provide few scholarly or philosophical rationales for their beliefs. This does not mean that there are none, but rather that modern exponents of this approach either do not know them or choose not to discuss them. Their beliefs do follow an intellectual pattern, however. It is the thought pattern of Idealism, the heritage of an earlier period, the epoch of Hegelian Idealism. However, since these contemporaries never refer to this intellectual background, they can at most be called noncognizant Idealists. The organization that best represents them is the Council for Basic Education, which uses most of the clichés and themes of the Idealism of grandfather's day: for example, children are lazy and must be disciplined; work and play are opposites and should not be confused; the mind must be sharpened like a knife by confronting it with some kind of outside resistance. Many examples of such proposals can be found in the earlier period, but nowhere is the relationship more obvious than in a contemporary text titled *The Case For Basic Education* [1] which aims to be a facsimile to the famous 1893 work of the Committee of Ten.

If philosophy of education is to get at the root of this contemporary movement, it must necessarily become involved in a deeper level of explanation and attempt to explain the philosophy of Idealism of the

[1] James D. Koerner, executive secretary, Council for Basic Education, ed., *The Case for Basic Education: A Program of Aims for Public Schools* (Boston: Little, Brown, 1959).

earlier period. This Idealism was primarily Hegelian, although it was based not so much on Hegel's own philosophy in all its difficult subtleties, as on the nineteenth-century interpretation of that philosophy. Indeed, in the last half of the nineteenth century a special interpretation of Hegelian philosophy gained prominence, and it is this interpretation that evolved into a thought pattern that has influenced education from that time to the present.

To understand this Idealist thought pattern, it is essential to recognize certain basic assumptions. The first and most important assumption is that this pattern grew out of the Newtonian mechanistic view of nature. The Newtonian view holds that the world is an absolute order of physical objects and is based on natural laws that are eternal and unchanging. Emphasis can be placed on either the objects by studying cause and effect relationships, or upon the laws themselves. Idealism emphasizes the latter. The world is a logical consequence of an absolute order. Reason is prior to everything else in the universe; physical laws merely obey this reason. Nature is simply the outward manifestation of an inherent logical order that is expressed in the laws of Euclidean geometry, the laws of gravitation and force, and temporal succession in the schemes of absolute time and space.

The second major assumption of the thought pattern relates to the distinctiveness of the human being. Man is different from all other creatures because he alone can envision the existence of logic and order. This vision comes from the power of mind. Man's possession of a mind indicates that he is a rational being, wholly unlike other creatures, who are guided by an unreflected inherent order. While other creatures are slaves of their instincts and immediate circumstances, man is a free creature because he alone has the power to recall the past and foresee the future. Man can act freely in accord with absolute reason because he is aware of more than the immediate environment and his own passions. Man shapes himself in line with his own potentials to become truly human and rational. The purpose of education is to make actual what in the beginning was only potential.

Reason does not change and nature does not change. The only change in the world derives from man when he exercises his own power of self-determination. Man discards his first and animal nature by means of self-estrangement and disciplined habits and attains a second or human nature of self-reflection and reason. This transformation is accomplished through the nurture and external discipline provided by the family and the school. The process is called education because it involves the effort of the mind. It is quite distinct from training, which is the limit of animal accomplishment. You educate man, you train animals. Animal study cannot help us to understand the educational processes of man because it provides no data on the strictly human faculties of perception, reflection, and reason.

Man also changes by means of historical evolution; he attains progressively higher civilized standards that better conform to truth and absolute reason. The successive stages of advancing civilization bear witness to the rational achievements of humanity's growth, achievements that have been preserved by customs (the disciplined habits of social life) and by the objective records of written laws and civilized accomplishments. Social habits condition formally all progress of rational development. If supported by the institutions of state and church, such habits gain strength and are more easily preserved. The school is an institution that is created to teach the social habits and customs that preserve the gains of civilization. Written laws and records are also rational achievements that must be preserved. Writing is the great preserver of truth and accomplishment, hence, the written word must be accorded a certain sanctity. Written law is the basis of the state's functioning; written documents and records explain the state's hardships and history. Education must not only teach respect for patriotic heritage and law, but respect for written language itself. The school must teach the mastery of grammar, reading, figuring, spelling, and written translations from foreign languages. The basic tool is the written textbook. William T. Harris, famous nineteenth-century American educator, says that the textbook, which the pupil can return to again and again, is the best educational tool ever developed. Put in good old-fashioned terms, one goes to school to get "book learning." [2]

Because education deals with the mind, logical order must determine content. In the process of instruction, two minds interact, and the immature mind voluntarily submits to the thinking of the mature mind. The psychological processes are the same in both. But whereas the order is introduced for the first time in the pupil's mind, it has been repeated many times in that of the teacher. The question of who is to be educated enters into the question of instruction. The dullard cannot be educated because he lacks intelligence; therefore, he must be trained for some labor job or manual task. The mediocre student can be educated, but he is usually interested and talented only in one direction. Such a pupil must work to become a specialist. The genius, on the other hand, has a thirst for general culture rather than specialization. He seeks to use his

[2] The Council for Basic Education explains these goals in modern guise: "The CBE believes that the school has many subsidiary purposes, but that its primary purpose is fourfold: (1) to transmit the facts about the heritage and culture of the race; (2) to teach young people to read and write and figure; (3) in the process of (1) and (2) to train the intelligence and to stimulate the pleasures of thought; and (4) to provide that atmosphere of moral affirmation without which education is merely animal training." *CBE Bulletin,* 2 (September 1957).

reason to discover general truth and the nature of things, and he must pursue a course of higher education geared toward general culture and philosophical understanding.

In America there were a number of compromises with the essential thought pattern of Idealism when its proponents attempted to coordinate its generic ideas with Darwin's analysis of evolution and the pre-World War I view of American individualism. These attempts at synthesis led to a hybrid outlook that attempted to incorporate the best ideas and practices of two different perspectives, but contributed nothing of its own. The compromise reshuffled practices that had existed prior to the synthesis, but gave no adequate foundation for their coordination. As a result, the use of the term Idealism to designate a philosophy of education has produced untold confusion. The only way to clear up this confusion is to point out the difference between Idealism as a thought pattern, affecting important practices of education, which is essentially Hegelian, and the later hybrid forms, which are interesting cognitive phenomena, as attempts at synthesis but have little other significance.

PEDAGOGICAL ORIENTATION

Pedagogy as a System / J. K. F. ROSENKRANZ

The General Idea of Education

In the system of the sciences, the science of education belongs to the philosophy of spirit—and in this, to the department of practical philosophy, the problem of which is the comprehension of the essence of freedom; for education is the conscious influence of one will upon another, so as to produce in it a conformity to an ideal which it sets before it. The idea of subjective spirit, as well as that of art, science, and religion, forms an essential presupposition for the science of education, but does not contain its principle. In a complete exposition of practical philosophy (ethics), the science of education may be distributed under each of its several heads. But the point at which the science of education branches off in practical philosophy is the idea of the family, inasmuch as here the distinctions of age and degrees of maturity are taken account of as arising from nature, and the claim of children upon their parents for education makes itself manifest. All other phases of education, in order to succeed, must presuppose a true family life. They may extend

"Pedagogy as a System" is an abridgment of Johann Karl Friedrich Rosenkranz, *The Philosophy of Education*, D. Appleton & Co., translated originally from *The Journal of Speculative Philosophy*, Vol VI, VII, VIII, 1872, 73, 74 from the German *Paedagogik Als System*, translated by Anna C. Brackett, commentary by William T. Harris.

and complement the school, but can not be its original foundation.

Much confusion also arises from the fact that many do not clearly enough draw the distinction between education as a science and education as an art. As a science, it busies itself with developing *a priori* the idea of education in the universality and necessity of that idea, but as an art it is the concrete special realization of this abstract idea in any given case. And, in any such given case, the peculiarities of the person who is to be educated and, in fact, all the existing circumstances necessitate an adaptation of the universal aims and ends, that can not be provided for beforehand, but must rather test the ready tact of the educator who knows how to take advantage of the existing conditions to fulfill his desired end. Just here it is that the educator may show himself inventive and creative, and that pedagogic talent can distinguish itself. The word "art" is here used in the same way as it is used when we say, the art of war, the art of government, etc.; and rightly, for we are talking about the possibility of the realization of the idea or theory.

The science of education must (1) unfold the general idea of education; (2) must exhibit the particular phases into which the general work of education is divided; and (3) must describe the particular standpoint upon which the general idea realizes or will realize itself in its special processes at any particular time.

[I] *The Nature of Education*

The nature of education is determined by the nature of mind—that it can develop what it is in itself only by its own activity. Mind is in itself free; but, if it does not actualize this possibility, it is in no true sense free, either for itself or for another. Education is the influencing of man by man, and it has for its end to lead him to actualize himself through his own efforts. The attainment of perfect manhood as the actualization of the freedom essential to mind constitutes the nature of education in general.

Man, therefore, is the only fit subject for education. We often speak, it is true, of the education of plants and animals; but, even when we do so, we apply other expressions, as "raising," "breaking," "breeding" and "training," in order to distinguish it from the education of man. "Training" consists in producing in an animal, either by pain or pleasure of the senses, an activity of which, it is true, he is capable, but which he never would have developed if left to himself. On the other hand, it is the nature of education only to assist in the producing of that which the subject would strive most earnestly to develop for himself if he had a clear idea of himself. We speak of raising trees and animals, but not of raising men; and it is only a planter who looks to his slaves for an increase in their number.

The idea of education may be more or less comprehensive. We use it in the widest sense when we speak of the education of the race, for we understand by this expression the connection which the situations and undertakings of different nations have to each other, as steps toward self-conscious freedom. In this the world-spirit is the teacher.

In a more restricted sense we mean by education the shaping of the individual life by the laws of nature, the rhythm of national customs, and the might of destiny; since, in these, each one finds limits set to his arbitrary will. These mold him into a man often without his knowledge. For he can not act in opposition to nature, nor offend the ethical sense of the people among whom he dwells, nor despise the leading of destiny without discovering through experience that upon the Nemesis of these substantial elements his subjective power can dash itself only to be shattered. If he perversely and persistently rejects all our admonitions, we leave him, as a last resort, to destiny, whose iron rule must educate him, and reveal to him the God whom he has ignored.

In the narrowest sense, which, however, is the usual one, we mean by education the influence which one individual exerts on another in order to develop the latter in some conscious and methodical way, either generally or with reference to some special aim. The teacher must, therefore, be relatively finished in his own education, and the pupil must possess complete confidence in him. If authority be wanting on the one side, or respect and obedience on the other, this ethical basis of development will be lacking, and it can not be replaced by talent, knowledge, skill, or prudence.

The general problem of education is the development of the theoretical and practical reason in the individual. If we say that to educate one means to fashion him into morality, we do not make our definition sufficiently comprehensive, because we say nothing of intelligence, and thus confound education and ethics. A man is not merely a human being in general, but, as a rational, conscious subject, he is a peculiar individual, and different from all others of the race.

Education must lead the pupil, by a connected series of efforts previously foreseen and arranged by the teacher, to a definite end; but the particular form which this shall take must be determined by the individuality of the pupil and the other conditions. Intermittent effort, sudden and violent influences, may accomplish much, but only *systematic* work can advance and fashion him in conformity with his nature; and, if this is lacking, it does not belong to education, for this includes in itself the idea of an end, and that of the technical means for its attainment.

But as culture comes to mean more and more, there becomes necessary a division of labor in teaching on account of technical qualifications and special information demanded, because as the arts and sciences are continually increasing in number one can become learned in any one branch only by devoting himself exclusively to it, and hence becoming a specialist. A difficulty hence arises, which is also one for the pupil, of preserving, in spite of this unavoidable one-sidedness, the unity and wholeness which are necessary to humanity.

As it becomes necessary to divide the work of instruction, a difference between general and special schools arises, also, from the needs of growing culture. The former give to the pupil with various degrees of completeness all the sciences and arts reckoned as belonging to "general education," and which were included by the Greeks under the general name of Encyclopædia. The latter are known as special schools, suited to particular needs or talents.

For any person, his actual education compared with its infinite possibilities remains only an approximation, and it can be considered as only relatively finished in particular directions. Education is impossible to him who is born an idiot, since the want of the power of generalizing and of ideality of conscious personality leaves to such an unfortunate only the possibility of a mechanical training.

[II] The Form of Education

The general form of education is determined by the nature of the mind: mind has reality only in so far as it produces it for itself. The mind is (1) immediate (or potential); but (2) it must estrange itself from itself, as it were, so that it may place itself over against itself as a special object of attention; (3) this estrangement is finally removed through a further acquaintance with the object—it feels itself at home in that on which it looks, and returns again enriched to the form of immediateness (to unity with itself). That which at first appeared to be another than itself is now seen to be itself.

All culture, whatever may be its special purport, must pass through these two stages—of estrangement, and its removal. Culture must intensify the distinction between the subject and the object, or that of immediateness, though it has again to absorb this distinction into itself; in this way the union of the two may be more complete and lasting. The subject recognizes, then, all the more certainly that what at first appeared to it as a foreign existence belongs to it potentially as its own possession, and that it comes into actual possession of it by means of culture.

> This process of self-estrangement and its removal belongs to all culture. The mind must fix its attention upon what is foreign to it, and penetrate its disguise. It will discover its own substance under the seeming alien being. That is to say, it will discover the rational laws that underlie the strange and foreign being, and thereby come to recognize reason or itself. Wonder is the accompaniment of this stage of estrangement. The love of travel and

adventure arises from this basis. Culture endeavors first to develop the contrast of the strange to the familiar, but it does this in order to annul it and make the alien into the well-known. Thus it enlarges the individual by making him more inclusive, by making him contain his environment. [W. T. Harris]

This activity of the mind in concentrating itself consciously upon an object with the purpose of making it one's own, or of producing it, is *work*. But when the mind gives itself up to its objects as chance may present them, or through arbitrariness, careless as to whether they have any result, such activity is *play*. Work is laid out for the pupil by his teacher authoritatively, but in his play he is left to himself.

Thus work and play must be sharply distinguished from each other. If one does not insist on respect for work as an important and substantial activity, he not only spoils play for his pupil (for this loses all its attraction when deprived of the antithesis of an earnest, set task), but he undermines his respect for real existence. On the other hand, if he does not give him space, time, and opportunity, for play, he prevents the peculiarities of his pupil from developing freely through the exercise of his creative ingenuity. Play sends the pupil back refreshed to his work, since in play he forgets himself in his own way, while in work he is required to forget himself in a manner prescribed for him by another.

Work should never be treated as if it were play, nor play as if it were work. In general, the practice of the arts and the study of the sciences stand in this relation to each other: the accumulation of stores of knowledge is the recreation of the mind which is engaged in independent creation, and the practice of arts fills the same office to those whose work is to collect knowledge.

Education seeks to transform every particular condition so that it shall no longer seem strange to the mind or in any wise foreign to its own nature. This identity of the feeling of self with the special character of anything done or endured by it, we call habit (Gewohnheit = customary activity, habitual conduct or behavior. Character is a "bundle of habits"). It conditions formally all progress; for that which is not yet become habit, but which we perform with design and an exercise of our will, is not yet a part of ourselves.

Habit (i.e., fixed principles of behavior, active and passive) is the general form which culture (or the outcome of education) takes. For, since it reduces a condition or an activity within ourselves to an instinctive use and wont (to a second nature), it is necessary for any thorough education. But as, according to its content (or subject-matter to which it relates), it may be either proper or improper, advantageous or disadvantageous, good or bad, and according to its form may be the assimilation of the external by the internal, or the impress of the internal upon the external, education must procure for the pupil the power of being able to free himself from one habit and to adopt another. Through his freedom he must be able not only to renounce any habit formed, but to form a new one; and he must so govern his system of habits that it shall exhibit a constant progress of development into greater freedom. We must discipline ourselves constantly to form and to break habits, as a means toward the ever-developing realization of the good in us.

Education comprehends, therefore, the reciprocal action of the opposites: authority and obedience; rationality and individuality; work and play; habit and spontaneity. If these are reconciled in a normal manner, the youth is now free from the tension of these opposites. But a failure in education in this particular is very possible through the freedom of the pupil, through special circumstances, or through the errors of the educator himself. And for this very reason any theory of education must take into account in the beginning this negative possibility. It must consider beforehand the dangers which threaten the pupil, in all possible ways even before they surround him, and fortify him against them.

Only when all other efforts have failed is punishment, which is the real negation of the error, the transgression, or the vice, justifiable. Punishment intentionally inflicts pain on the pupil, and its object is, by means of this sensation, to bring him to reason, a result which neither our simple prohibition, our explanation, nor our threat of punishment, has been able to reach. But the punishment, as such, must not refer to the subjective totality of the youth, i.e., to his disposition in general, but only to the act which, as result, is a manifestation of that disposition. It nevertheless acts on the disposition, but mediately through pain; it does not touch directly the inner being; and this (return of the deed upon the doer) is not only demanded by justice, but is even rendered necessary on account of the sophistry that is inherent in human nature, which assigns to a deed many motives (and takes refuge against blame by alleging good motives).

[III] The Limits of Education

The first limit of education is a subjective one, a limit found in the individuality of the youth. This is a definitive (insurmountable) limit. Whatever does not exist in this individuality as a possibility can not be developed from it. Education can only lead and assist; it can not create. What Nature has denied to a man, education can not give him any more than it is able, on the other hand, to annihilate entirely his original gifts, although it is true that his talents may be suppressed, distorted, and measurably destroyed. But the decision of the question in what the real essence of any one's individuality consists can never be made with certainty till he has left behind him his years of development, because it is then only that he first arrives at the consciousness of his entire self;

besides, at this time, many superficial acquirements will drop off; and on the other hand, talents, long slumbering and unsuspected, may first make their appearance. Whatever has been forced upon a child in opposition to his individuality, whatever has been only driven into him and has lacked receptivity on his part or a demand for cultivation, remains attached to his being only as an external ornament, a parasitical outgrowth which enfeebles his own proper character.

The second or objective limit of education lies in the means which can be appropriated for it. That the talent for a certain culture shall be present is certainly the first thing; but the cultivation of this talent is the second, and no less necessary. But how much cultivation can be given to it extensively and intensively depends upon the means used, and these again are conditioned by the material resources of the family to which one belongs. The greater and more valuable the means of culture which are found in a family, the greater is the immediate advantage which the culture of each one has at the start. With regard to many of the arts and sciences this limit of education is of great significance. But the means alone are of no avail. The finest educational apparatus will produce no fruit where corresponding talent is wanting, while on the other hand talent often accomplishes incredible feats with very limited means, and, if the way is only once open, makes of itself a center of attraction which draws to itself with magnetic power the necessary means. The moral culture of each one is, however, fortunately from its very nature, out of the reach of such dependence.

Finally, the absolute limit of education is the time when the youth has apprehended the problem which he has to solve, has learned to know the means at his disposal, and has acquired a certain facility in using them. The end and aim of education is the emancipation of the youth. It strives to make him self-dependent, and as soon as he has become so it wishes to retire and leave to him the sole responsibility for his actions. To treat the youth after he has passed this point of time still as a youth, contradicts the very idea of education, which idea finds its fulfillment in the attainment of this state of maturity by the pupil. Since the completion of education cancels the original inequality between the educator and the pupil, nothing is more oppressing, nay, revolting to the latter than to be excluded by a continued state of dependence from the enjoyment of the freedom which he has earned.

The Special Elements of Education

Education in general consists in the development in man of his inborn theoretical and practical rationality; it takes on the form of labor, which changes that state or condition, which appears at first only as a mere thought, into a fixed habit, and transfigures individuality into a worthy humanity. Education ends in that emancipation of the youth which places him on his own feet. The special elements which form the concrete content of all education in general are the life, cognition, and will of man. Without life mind has no phenomenal reality; without cognition, no genuine—i.e., conscious—will; and without will, no self-confirmation of life and of cognition. It is true that these three elements are in real existence inseparable, and continually exhibit their interdependence. But none the less on this account do they themselves prescribe their own succession, and they have a relative and periodical ascendency over each other. In infancy, up to the fifth or sixth year, the purely physical development takes the precedence; childhood is the time of learning, in a proper sense, an act by which the child gains for himself the picture of the world, such as mature minds, through experience and insight, have painted it; and, finally, youth is the transition period to practical activity, to which the self-determination of the will must give the first impulse.

The classification of the special elements of education is hence very simple: (1) the physical, (2) the intellectual, (3) the practical (in the sense of will-education). We sometimes apply to these the words orthobiotics, didactics, and pragmatics.

[I] Physical Education

The art of living rightly is based upon a comprehension of the process of life. Life is the restless dialectic process which ceaselessly transforms the inorganic into the organic, and at the same time produces the inorganic, and separates from itself whatever part of its food has not been assimilated, and that which has become dead and burned out. The organism is healthy when it corresponds to this idea of the dialectic process of a life which moves up and down, inward and outward; of formation and reformation; of organizing and disorganizing. All the rules for physical education, or of hygiene, are derived from this conception.

[II] Intellectual Education

The development of intelligence presupposes physical health. Here we are to speak of the science of the art of teaching, technically called "didactics." This had its presupposition on the side of Nature, as was before seen, in physical education, but in the sphere of mind it presupposes psychology and logic. Instruction implies considerations of psychology as well as of logical method.

In a complete system of philosophy, didactics could refer to the conception of mind which would have there been unfolded in psychology; and it must appear as a defect in scientific method if psychology, or at least the conception of the theoretical mind, has to be treated again within the science of education. We must take something for granted. Psychology, then, will here be consulted no further than is requisite to place on a sure basis the educational function which relates to it.

Sense-perception, as the beginning of intellectual culture, is the free grasping of an object immediately present to the mind. Education can do nothing directly toward the performance of this act; it can only assist in making it easy: (1) it can isolate the object of consideration; (2) it can give facility in the transition to another; (3) it can promote the many-sidedness of the interest, by which means the return to a perception already obtained has always a fresh charm.

The activity of perception results in the formation of an internal picture or image which intelligence can call up at any time at pleasure, and imagine it as occupying an ideal space, although the object is absent, in fact, and thus this image or picture becomes a sort of general schema (or pattern applicable to a class of objects), and hence an image-concept. The mental image may (1) be compared with the perception from which it sprang, or (2) it may be arbitrarily altered and combined with other images, or (3) it may be held fast in the form of abstract signs or symbols which intelligence invents for it. Thus originate the functions (1) of the verification of conceptions, (2) of creative imagination, and (3) of memory. For their full treatment, we must refer to psychology.

In representation by means of mental images there is attained a general idea or a notion in so far as the empirical details are referred to a *schema,* as Kant called it. But the *necessity* of the connection of the particular details with the general schema is wanting to it. To develop this idea of necessity is the task of the thinking activity, which frees itself from all mental pictures, and with its clearly defined determinations transcends image-concepts. The thinking activity, therefore, is emancipated from dependence on the senses, to a higher degree than the processes of conception and perception. The notion, judgment, and syllogism, develop forms which, as such, have no power of being perceived by the senses. But it does not follow from this that he who thinks can not return out of the thinking activity and carry it with him into the sphere of image-concepts and perception. The true thinking activity deprives itself of no content. The form of abstraction affecting a logical purism which looks down upon conception and perception as forms of intelligence quite inferior to itself is a pseudo-thinking, a morbid and scholastic error. Education will be the better on its guard against this the more it has led the pupil by the legitimate road of perception and conception to thinking. Memorizing especially is an excellent preparatory school for the thinking activity, because it gives practice to the intelligence in exercising itself in abstract ideas.

The logical presupposition of instruction is the order in which the subject-matter develops for the consciousness. The subject, the consciousness of the pupil, and the activity of the instructor, interpenetrate each other in instruction, and constitute in actuality one whole.

First of all, the subject which is to be learned has a specific determinateness which demands in its exposition a certain fixed order of sequence. However arbitrary we may be, the subject has a certain determination of its own which no mistreatment can wholly crush out, and this inherent immortal rationality is the general foundation of instruction.

But the subject must be adapted to the consciousness of the pupil, and here the order of procedure and the exposition depend upon the stage which he has reached intellectually, for the special manner of the instruction must be conditioned by this. If he is in the stage of sense-perception, we must use the illustrative method; if in the stage of image-conception, that of combination; and if in the stage of thinking, that of demonstration. The first exhibits the object directly, or some representation of it; the second considers it according to the different possibilities which exist in it, and turns it around on all sides (and examines its relations to other things); the third demonstrates the necessity of the relations in which it stands either with itself or with others.

All instruction starts from the inequality between those who possess knowledge and ability and those who have not yet obtained them. The former are qualified to teach, the latter to learn. Instruction is the act which gradually cancels the original inequality of teacher and pupil, in that it converts what was' at first the property of the former into the property of the latter by means of his own activity.

The pupil is the apprentice, the teacher the master, whether in the practice of any craft or art, or in the exposition of any systematic knowledge. The pupil passes from the state of the apprentice to that of the master through that of the journeyman. The apprentice has to appropriate to himself the elements; journeymanship begins, by means of their possession, to become independent; the master combines with his technical skill the freedom of production. His authority over his pupil consists only in his knowledge and ability. If he has not these, no external support, no trick of false appearances which he may put on, will serve to create it for him.

These stages—(1) apprenticeship, (2) journeymanship, (3) mastership—are fixed limitations in the didactic process; but they are relative in the concrete. The standard of special excellence varies with the different grades of culture, and must be varied that it may have validity for each period of time. The master is complete only in relation to the journeyman and apprentice; to them he is superior. But, on the other hand, in relation to the infinity of the problems of his art or science, he is by no means complete; to himself he must appear as one who begins ever anew, one who is ever striving, one to whom a new problem ever rises from every achieved result. He can not discharge himself from work, he must never desire to rest on his laurels. He is the truest master whose finished performances only force him on to never-resting progress.

The possibility of culture is found in general, it is true, in every human being; nevertheless, as a practical matter, there are distinguished: (1) incapacity, as the want of all gifts; (2) mediocrity; (3) talent and genius. It is the part of psychology to give an account of all these. Mediocrity characterizes the great mass of intelligences that are merely mechanical, and that wait for external impulse as to what direction their endeavors shall take. Not without truth, perhaps, may we hypothetically presuppose a special talent in each individual, but this special talent in many men never makes its appearance, because under the circumstances in which it finds itself placed it fails to find the exciting occasion which shall give them the knowledge of its existence. The majority of mankind are contented with the mechanical impulse which makes them into something, and impresses upon them certain characteristics. Talent shows itself by means of the confidence in its own especial productive possibility, which manifests itself as an inclination, or as a strong impulse, to occupy itself with the special object which constitutes the object of its ability. Education has no difficulty in dealing with mechanical natures, because their passivity is only too ready to follow prescribed patterns. It is more difficult to manage talent, because it lies between mediocrity and genius, and is therefore uncertain, and not only unequal to itself, but also is tossed now too low, now too high, is by turns despondent and over-excited. The general maxim for dealing with it is to spare it no difficulty that lies in the subject to which its efforts are directed. Genius must be treated much in the same way as talent. The difference consists only in this, that genius, with a premonition of its creative power, usually manifests its decision with less doubt for a special province of activity, and, with a more intense thirst for culture, subjects itself more willingly to the demands of instruction. Genius is in its nature the purest self-determination, in that it feels, in its own inner existence, the necessity which exists in the object to which it devotes itself; it lives, as it were, in its object. But it can create no valid place for the new idea, which is in it already immediately and subjectively, if it has not united itself to the already existing culture as its objective presupposition; on this ground it thankfully receives instruction.

In the process of instruction the interaction between pupil and teacher must be so managed that the exposition by the teacher shall excite in the pupil the impulse to reproduction. The teacher must not treat his exposition as if it were a work of art which is its own end and aim, but he must always bear in mind the need of the pupil. The artistic exposition, as such, will, by its completeness, produce admiration; but the didactic, on the contrary, will, through its perfect adaptation, call out the imitative instinct, the power of new creation.

In the act of learning there appears (*a*) a mechanical element, (*b*) a dynamic element, and (*c*) one in which the dynamic again mechanically strengthens itself.

The mechanical element consists in this, that the right time be chosen for each lesson, an exact arrangement observed, and the suitable apparatus, which is necessary, procured. It is in the arrangement that especially consists the educational power of the lesson. The spirit of scrupulousness, of accuracy, of neatness, is developed by the external technique, which, however, should be subordinated to the interests of the subject studied. The teacher must, therefore, insist upon it that work shall cease at the exact time, that the work be well done, etc., for on these little things many greater things, in an ethical sense, depend.

The dynamical element (i.e., the self-activity of the pupil) consists of the previously developed power of attention, without which all the exposition made by the teacher to the pupil remains entirely foreign to him. All apparatus is dead, all arrangement of no avail, all teaching fruitless, if the pupil does not by his free self-activity receive into his inner self what one teaches him, and thus make it his own property.

The careful, persistent, living activity of the pupil in these acts we call industry. Its negative opposite is laziness, which is deserving of punishment inasmuch as it proceeds from a want of self-determination. Man is by nature lazy. But mind, which is only what it does, must resolve upon activity. This connection of industry with human freedom, with the very essence of mind, makes laziness appear blameworthy.

Now that we have learned something of the relation of the teacher to the taught, and of the process of learning itself, we must note the mode and manner of instruction. This may have (*1*) the character of contingency: the way in which our immediate existence in the world, our life, teaches us; or it may be given (*2*) by the printed page; or (*3*) it may take the shape of formal oral instruction.

And, finally, the school must, by examinations and reports, aid the pupil in the acquirement of a knowledge of his real standing. The examination lets him know what he has really learned, and what he is able to do: the report shows him a history of his culture, exhibits to him in what he has made improvement and in what he has fallen behind, what defects he has shown, what talents he has displayed, what errors committed, and in what relation stands his theoretical development to his ethical status.

[III] *Education of the Will*

Both physical and intellectual education are in the highest degree practical. The first reduces the merely natural (i.e., the body) to a tool which mind shall use for its own ends; the second guides the intelligence, by ways conformable to its nature, to the necessary method of the art of teaching and learning, which finally branches out in the nation into a system of mutually dependent school organizations. But in a narrower sense we mean by practical education the methodical development of the will. This phrase more clearly expresses the topic to be considered in this division than another sometimes used in the science of education (*Bestrebungsvermögen*, conative power). The will is already the subject of a science of its own, i.e., of ethics; and if the science of education would proceed in anywise scientifically, it must recognize and presuppose the idea and the existence of this science. It should not restate in full the doctrines of freedom, of duty, of virtue, and of conscience, although we have often seen this done in works on education. Education has to deal with the ideas of freedom and morality only so far as to fix the technique of their process, and at the same time to confess itself weakest just here, where nothing is of any worth without pure self-determination.

The pupil must (1) become civilized; i.e., he must learn to govern, as a thing external to him, his natural egotism, and to make the forms which civilized society has adopted his own. (2) He must become imbued with morality; i.e., he must learn to determine his actions, not only with reference to what is agreeable and useful, but according to the principle of the good; he must become internally free, form a character, and must habitually look upon the necessity of freedom as the absolute measure of his actions. (3) He must become religious; i.e., he must discern that the world, with all its changes, himself included, is only phenomenal; the affirmative side of this insight into the emptiness of the finite and transitory (which man would so willingly make everlasting) is the consciousness of the *Absolute* existing in and for itself. The Absolute, without change and entirely unaffected by the process of manifestation, constitutes no factor of its changes, but, while it actually makes them its object, permeates them all, and freely distinguishes itself from them. In so far as man relates himself to God, he cancels all finitude and transitoriness, and by this feeling frees himself from the externality of phenomena. Virtue on the side of civilization is politeness; on that of morality, conscientiousness; and on that of religion, humility.

The social development of man constitutes the beginning of practical education. It is not necessary to suppose a special social instinct. The inclination of man to the society of men does not arise from the identity of their nature alone, but is also in each special instance affected by particular relations. The natural starting-point of social culture is the family. But this in turn educates the child for society, and by means of society the individual enters into relation with the world at large. Thus natural sympathy changes to polite behavior, and the latter again to the thrifty and circumspect deportment, whose proper ideal nevertheless is before all the ethical purity which combines with the wisdom of the serpent the harmlessness of the dove.

The essential element of social culture is found in moral character. Without this latter, every graceful device of behavior remains worthless, and can never attain that purity of humility and dignity which are possible to it in its unity with morality. For the detailed treatment of this idea the science of education must refer to ethics itself, and can here give the part of its content which relates to education only in the form of educational maxims. The principal categories of ethics in the domain of morality are the ideas of duty, virtue, and conscience. Education must lay stress on the truth that nothing in the world has any absolute value except will guided by the right.

Thence follows the maxim relating to the idea of duty, that we must accustom the pupil to unconditional obedience to it, so that he shall perform it for no other reason than that it is duty. The performance of a duty may bring with it externally a result agreeable or disagreeable, useful or harmful; but the consideration of such consequences ought never to determine us. This moral demand, though it may appear to be excessive severity, is the absolute foundation of all genuine ethical practice. All "highest happiness" theories, however finely spun they may be, when taken as a guide for life, lead at last to sophistry, and to contradictions ruinous to life.

Virtue must make actual what duty commands, or, rather, the actualizing of duty is virtue. And here we may mention, by way of caption, that the principal things to be considered under virtue are (*a*) the dialectic of particular virtues, (*b*) moral discipline, and (*c*) character.

The consideration of the culture of character leads to the subject of conscience. This is the comparison which the moral agent makes between himself as he is and his ideal self. He compares himself, in his past or future, with his nature, and judges himself accordingly as good or bad. This independence which belongs to the ethical judgment is the true soul of all morality, the negation of all self-illusion and of all deception through another. The educational maxim is: Be conscientious. Depend in your final decision entirely on your conception of what is right.

Social culture contains the formal phase, moral culture the real phase, of the practical mind. Conscience forms the transition to religious culture. In its universal and necessary nature, it reveals the absolute authority of spirit. The individual discerns in the depths of his own consciousness commands possessing universality and necessity to which he has to subject himself. They appear to him as the voice of God. Religion makes its appearance as soon as the individual distinguishes the Absolute from himself, as a personal Subject existing for and by Himself, and therefore for him.

The child comes in contact with definite forms of religion, and will naturally, through the mediation of the family, be introduced to some one of them. His religious feeling takes now a particular direction, and he accepts religion in one of its historical forms. This special realization of religion meets the precise want of the child, because it brings into his consciousness, by means of teaching and forms of worship, the principal elements which are found in the nature of religion.

In contradistinction to the natural basis of religious feeling, all historical religions rest on the authoritative basis of revelation from God to man. They address themselves to the imagination, and offer a system of objective forms of worship and ceremonies. But spirit, as eternal, as self-identical, can not forbear as thinking activity to subject the traditional religion to criticism and to compare it as a phenomenal existence with its perfect ideal. From this criticism arises a religion which satisfies the demands of the reason, and which, by means of insight into the necessity of the historical process, leads to the exercise of a genuine toleration toward its many-sided forms. This religion reconciles the unity of the thinking consciousness with the religious dogmas and ceremonies, which, in the history of religious feeling, appear theoretically as dogma, and practically as the command of an absolute and incomprehensible authority. The religion of reason is just as simple as the unsophisticated natural religious feeling, but its simplicity is at the same time master of itself. It is just as specific in its determinations as any historical form of religion, but its determinateness is at the same time universal, since it is worked out by the thinking reason.

Education must superintend the development of the religious consciousness toward an insight into the necessary sequence of its different stages. Nothing is more absurd than for the educator to desire to avoid the introduction of a particular form of religion, or a definite creed, as a middle stage between the natural beginning of religious feeling and its end in philosophical culture. Only when a man has lived through the entire range of a one-sided phase—through the crudeness of such a concrete individualizing of religion, and has come to recognize the universal nature of religion in a special form of it which excludes other forms—only when the spirit of a church has taken him into its number, is he ripe to criticise religion in a conciliatory spirit, because he has then gained a religious character through that historical experience. The self-comprehending universality must have such a solid basis as this in the career of the man; it can never form the beginning of one's culture, but it may constitute the end which turns back again to the beginning. Most men remain at the historical standpoint. The religion of reason, as that of the minority, constitutes in the different religions the invisible church, which seeks by progressive reform to purify these religions from superstition and unbelief. It is the duty of the state, by making all churches equal in the sight of the law, to guard religion from the temptation of impure motives, and, through the granting of such freedom to religious individuality, to help forward the unity of a rational insight into religion which is distinct from the religious feeling only in its form, not in its content. Not a philosopher, but Jesus of Nazareth, freed the world from all selfishness and all bondage.

With this highest theoretical and practical emancipation, the general work of education ends. It remains now to be shown how the general idea of education shapes its special elements into their appropriate forms. From the nature of education, which concerns itself with man in his entirety, this exposition belongs partly to the history of culture in general, partly to the history of religion, partly to the philosophy of history. The pedagogical element in it always lies in the ideal which the spirit of a nation or of an age creates for itself, and which it seeks to realize in its youth.

PSYCHOLOGICAL DIMENSION

Psychology in Education   /   RURIC N. ROARK

Psychology is the science of mind—mind in whatever manifested. Psychology sustains the same relation to the science of education that anatomy, physiology, and pharmacy sustain to the practice of medicine. It is as necessary that the teacher should know something of the mind's activities as it is that the physician should know the bodily organs and their functions, their normal and their abnormal conditions.

Man gained his first knowledge of the material world through observation of it. So, when man first began to study himself, he turned the mind in upon itself, and observed its phenomena. This observation of self by self is called *introspection.* Introspection is a valid and valuable method of investigation, for the mind presents phenomena which the mind can as truly observe as it can observe the changes going on in the material world. The mind can watch itself reasoning, or enjoying, or desiring, as well as it can watch a laboratory experiment or can an eclipse of the moon. Its interpretations of what it observes are just as trustworthy in the one case as in the other, and the mental phenomena are almost as classifiable as the material phenomena.

The habit of introspection—of observing one's own mental states and acts—is hard to form, and requires effort and practice. The same may be said, however, of the habit of correct observation of any class of phenom-

"Psychology in Education" is an abridgment of Ruric N. Roark, *Psychology in Education,* copyright 1895 by American Book Company.

ena. But once formed, the habit becomes one of the safest and most helpful guides in the study of psychology.

Teaching is consciously doing three things—instructing, developing, training. Education is the broader term, and may, in its unlimited sense, be taken to mean the sum of all influences, direct or indirect, that make the individual what he is. A distinction may properly be made between education in its unlimited sense, and formal education. The five great engines of formal education are (1) the home, (2) the school, (3) the press, (4) the pulpit, (5) the platform. Teaching is more restricted in its meaning, and implies that an intelligent agent is selecting, directing, modifying, and combining right influences to produce a desired effect.

Instructing is directly giving information—knowledge of facts, new ideas, and words—to the pupil. The result of right instruction is knowledge. *Developing* is increasing, through use, the natural power of an organ or faculty; bringing out latent energies and capacities. We may develop—increase the strength of—a muscle, memory, conscience, will. The result of development is power. *Training* is causing an organ or faculty, by constant and carefully directed practice, to function rapidly and well, with the least expenditure of time and energy. We may train the senses, the hands, the judgment. The result of training is skill.

Conditions of Mental Activity

To accomplish a given task in the shortest time, with the least waste of energy, and with the best results, the mind must be *conscious, attentive,* and *habituated* to the kind of activity demanded by the work to be done. It is not forgotten that we may do many things semiconsciously, or even unconsciously; and that we may do many things well which we have not done before, and so could not be in the habit of doing; but it is none the less true that we must do a thing many times consciously and attentively, before we can do that or similar things unconsciously and automatically.

Attention is that condition of the mind in which the energy of one or more faculties is directed upon an object of sense or of thought. The word is also used to name the act of attending. Attention is often miscalled a faculty; but it is plain that it is not, since attention does nothing, but is only a quickened or energized state of one or more faculties.

Habit is that condition of the mind or body which is manifested in the tendency to unconscious repetition of acts or states. Habits are physical, intellectual, and moral. The more work consciousness can hand over to habit, the greater opportunity to rise into new and higher modes of thought and activity. The more we can do automatically through the lower nerve centers, the more power we have left to use in the struggle up to higher levels of thinking, feeling, and willing.

Back of the school stands the greatest factor in forming habits—the home. The things a child learns to do first, the way he learns of doing them; the words he learns to speak first, and the ways in which he learns to speak them; the intellectual and moral surroundings of his first six years—these tend to become fixed in his consciousness; and to remove them is often more than the most helpful teacher can do, after the child comes under his care. The unseen, unfelt nerve paths for impressions and impulses seem harder to change than the courses of rivers. Hundreds of cultured men and women whose early surroundings were not helpful in the formation of correct habits are forced to be constantly on guard against lapses of pronunciation or syntax, or some of the many conventions of polite society. No matter how thoroughly one may think he has put early provincialisms out of his vocabulary, he will almost certainly revert to their use when he is excited, and consciousness is off guard. These are illustrations, merely, of an important and deep-lying fact, whose value to the teacher is evident. In the school the child must form as many right habits as possible, and reform such as may stand in the way of his progress.

But the teacher can do much, and should spare no wise effort to drill his pupils into habits of *cleanliness, neatness, orderliness, punctuality, courtesy, quickness, accuracy, obedience,* and *veracity.* It is better to send forth a pupil with these, and without much knowledge of arithmetic or formal grammar, than to fill him with knowledge and have him lacking in *right tendencies.*

Cleanliness is next to godliness, and probably stands first, for surely no unclean face can reflect the image of God. Soap and water are powerful missionaries. *Neatness* is simply an extension of cleanliness from the skin outward, to the clothes, the desk, the bedroom, the kitchen, the workshop. Pupils should be required to come into the schoolroom with their hair brushed; and they should be held responsible, while in the room, for the condition of the floor and of their desks, for the appearance of the blackboard and the papers upon which any kind of written work is done. Neatness and orderliness are among the chief elements in correct deportment.

Orderliness is closely akin to neatness, and the one cannot be cultivated without the other. No pupil should be permitted to sit, stand, or walk, slouchily and lazily. The teacher must unceasingly insist upon the erect position in sitting or standing, and must allow no shuffling in walking. Carried into the work of the school, orderliness means that the books and papers on the desks shall be kept in proper arrangement; that all written work—solutions, diagrams, maps, essays, etc.—shall be done according to some definite, standard form.

Punctuality is one of the cardinal virtues. The tardy man or woman steals time—the time of those who wait. The child should be taught to come in from play upon the stroke of the bell, to be in his place at the opening of school or class, and to return directly home without delay. It is as easy to be three minutes early as ten minutes late. In the home and in the school everything should go by the clock.

Courtesy is, of course, as much a matter of *heart* as a matter of *habit*, springing as much from a desire to please or help as from practice in forms of politeness; but both heart and habit can be cultivated. The boy should be so habituated, for example, to removing his hat upon entering a house or meeting a lady, that he will do so unconsciously. Children of both sexes should be habituated to silence in the presence of their elders, to giving them precedence through doors or gates, to the "thank you" and "if you please" that mark the well-bred person. In addition to its value as one of the minor morals, unfailing courtesy is of the highest value in winning success in any field of labor. The young man or young woman in whom it is not a habit is heavily handicapped.

Quickness, though a valuable habit, should never be sought at the expense of neatness, orderliness, or *accuracy*. It comes only from persistent practice, combined with more or less of natural aptitude for rapid action of mind or body. The child must be trained to do all work, and all play too, quickly but neatly, and, above all, *accurately*. Many exercises should be set in school, involving the doing of something in a given brief time. Drills in quick addition, subtraction, and all other arithmetical operations; in reading, spelling, especially in pronouncing, writing; in running, catching, climbing, etc.—should be a fixed part of the teacher's daily work.

But *accuracy* is the *chiefest intellectual virtue*. To know *exactly*, to remember *correctly*, to state *colorlessly*, the precise facts—these are rare accomplishments, and no effort should be spared to attain them for one's self, or to cultivate them in those for whose training and character we are responsible. A teacher cannot be too particular about the "little things" in a school exercise. Children must be taught to respect *details;* and *not quite right but near enough, about the required amount, nearly the correct answer*, are expressions of inaccuracy and careless work, that should never be used by either pupils or teacher.

Obedience to lawful authority, in home and state, is the corner stone of the social fabric. The child that forms the habit of intelligent obedience in home and school will grow into a law-abiding citizenhood. The one who is permitted to fix habits of disobedience to parent or teacher will in very many cases learn obedience in reformatories and prisons. There seems now to be a grave weakening of respect and regard for authority in state and nation—a growing contempt for law. There can be no doubt that this condition is directly traceable, in large measure, to the greatly increased *freedom* from *authority*, from which children suffer at home and in school. This decay of home authority has become almost a national characteristic, and it is undoubtedly responsible for much of the lawlessness that exists within our borders. Parents and teachers must enforce an intelligent obedience to rational commands, that shall be as prompt as it should be invariable.

Veracity is accuracy carried forward into the moral sphere. There is an intimate but not necessary connection between intellectual accuracy, and veracity. A boy may be habitually accurate in arithmetic or outdoor observation, and yet be an habitual moral liar. *Truth-telling* must be cultivated as a distinct habit in morals. In many respects it is of the first importance. Every teacher is ready to testify that teaching and managing a school would be infinitely easier than it is now, if pupils had a fixed habit of telling the absolute truth.

The *how* of forming habits in school may be summed up in two words —*drill* and *imitation*. The teacher must *drill* the pupils every day, patiently, persistently, sympathetically, until the nerve tracks of thought and action are fixed in young brains and bodies. Pupils must be drilled in walking, sitting, standing, until correct posture becomes fixed habit; they must be drilled in spelling until the sound of a word will excite the almost automatic action of the muscles by which its letters are uttered or written; they must be drilled in the fundamentals of arithmetic until sum, product, difference, or quotient, of the quantities used, will be presented to consciousness with machine-like precision. The *mechanics* of composition must be drilled into the learner until capitalization, punctuation, and paragraphing will take care of themselves, and leave the brain free to produce ideas. But drilling comes to naught if the teacher does not show in himself the habits he would have his pupils grow into. In these matters the pupils will do as the teacher *does*, rather than as he *tells* them to do. A teacher sitting behind a disordered desk cannot chide a pupil for lack of neatness; the lazy teacher cannot have a punctual school; the deceitful teacher will send out ready liars.

Character, the supreme end of all home training and all school work, is but another name for *habit*—habit that possesses the very fiber of body and mind. As we sow habits in muscle and nerve and brain, so shall we, and those who come after us, reap in aptitude, in skill, in character.

Cultivation of Acquisitive Faculties

Acquisition is the operation of gaining and storing facts, ideas, words, so that memory shall retain and recall them. It is the process of taking in mental food. But as, in the bodily economy, food is of value only when it is properly digested and assimilated, so, in the mental economy, no fact or bit of knowledge is of value unless it is correlated with other facts, and interpreted by things already known. Facts are valueless unless comprehended in their relations to the known. They must be assimilated (made like) to the body of our knowledge and thought already formed in consciousness. To *assimilate* is to *understand*.

Acquisition involves the activity of the perceptives, of judgment, and of memory. The processes of acquisition are *perception, conception, retention*. Perception is the process of gaining primary ideas through the senses and the intuition. The products of perception are called *precepts*. Conception is the act of acquiring general ideas by the combination of percepts or other concepts, or of percepts and concepts. The products of conception are *concepts* (general notions). The faculty by which conception is effected is *judgment*. *Definition*, the last step in conception, is not strictly speaking, a process in the formation of a concept; but a concept is not clearly fixed, not wholly possessed, until it can be accurately defined. *Outlining* is to a series of related concepts what defining is to the single concept: it serves to fix their order and comparative importance in mind, and to make clear their mutual relations. As a definition shows the essential marks or attributes of a concept, so an outline shows the order and relation of the objects forming a class, or the sequence and connections of thoughts in a subject. Retention is the last step in acquisition, since without it no acquisition would be permanent. The faculty is memory whose functions are to *retain* and to *reproduce*.

Since acquisition supplies the mind with all its materials for thought, all its elements for imaginative creation, all its data for intelligent action in everyday affairs, the schools (since they are supposed to give a preparation for actual life) should carefully develop and train the faculties engaged in the accumulation and storing of knowledge-material. There are several studies which are in the list of "required branches" that are especially suited to the cultivation of the acquisitive powers. These are reading, spelling, geography. Of course, the beginnings of any subject furnish more material for acquisition than for any other operation of the mind; but those just named do so, throughout both the primary and advanced work in them, in a greater degree than the other branches.

Reading, properly taught, may be made to cultivate almost every faculty of the human mind. It is more important than any other branch, or—it might not be too much to say—than all other branches taught in the common schools. *It is the key to all stored knowledge.* It cultivates the powers of acquisition from the first word the child reads, through a lifetime of mental growth. The child beginning to read puts forth acquisitive effort upon each new word met with; and the form of the word, its pronunciation, and its meaning, become objects of perception, conception, and retention. When word forms are sufficiently well mastered to enable the pupil to give his thought to the meanings of words rather than to their forms, then reading is a means to the limitless acquisition of new concepts.

Spelling is a memory study, and affords exercise for the visual, auditory, and muscular senses. The child learns to spell best through the *eye*, by observing the relative positions of the letters in words as he sees them. But by writing words often, the muscular effort, associated with the eye impressions, helps to fix the form in memory. There should be much *written* spelling in every school. Each lesson should be made a spelling lesson, the pupil understanding that he may be called on to spell any word in any lesson. This training will quicken and sharpen observation and retention of word forms. Oral spelling is useful mainly in training the ear to correct sounds of letters. It should be used with that purpose constantly in view. Oral spelling has but little use except to aid the pupil in acquiring correct enunciation and pronunciation. If oral spelling exercises are not directed to these ends, they are of little use.

Geography, if taught solely from a text-book (as it almost universally is, even in primary schools), is almost wholly a memory study, affording material mainly for the retentive faculty. As usually taught, it affords cultivation only incidentally for imagination, almost not at all for observation. But since, in the case of children, ready-made concepts are worth little or nothing, it will be found that geography is best taught objectively. In geography, observation should be trained by use of a globe or ball; in political geography, by use of maps and by map drawing; in economic and physical geography, by making relief maps, with actual products placed upon them.

Formal teaching in school should not begin in the case of children, as a rule, until they are seven years old. This is true because formal teaching should not begin until there is a large store of precepts and concepts ready in the child's mind to be used by the teacher. The child enters school with the elements of all knowledge already acquired: it remains for the teacher to ascertain, in each individual case, how extensive this stock of knowledge is, and to use it as a basis for all further acquisition. The concepts the child has already acquired before coming to school are quite different from those he is expected to acquire during his first days at school.

A new subject or a new lesson should be introduced by a sound drill upon the meanings and uses of the unfamiliar terms involved. Attention is to be directed to new words in the next reading lesson; to *plus, add, sum*, etc., when addition is begun; to *nouns* as names with which the pupil is already familiar, etc. General definitions and rules should be ventured upon only when the teacher is sure, from many and varied tests, that the pupil knows the thing to be defined, or the process to be described. Each study has its own terms, more or less technical, its own principles, and its own peculiar set of new ideas. Such of these as are fundamental must be mastered by the pupil. He must acquire them, form the proper concepts, and hold them in memory ready for prompt recall when needed.

What? When? Where?—these three are preëminently the "questions of acquisition," and should be used to exercise the pupil's power to perceive, to form concepts, to define, and to remember. *What* is it, *where* is it, *whence* is it, in nature study and object drills; *what* is it, in reading and spelling; *what* is it and *when* was it, in history—this will serve as a hint of how such questions may be constantly and profitably used in acquisition exercises and studies.

Cultivating the Power to Reason

Reason can be formally defined as that process by which we reach conclusions. The faculty concerned in the essential act of reasoning is *judgment,* but it makes use of all that the other faculties can supply. Through perception and conception the "raw materials" of our conclusions are collected. Imagination frames other possible concepts and relations; and judgment selects, compares, discriminates, combines, and concludes. Since our business, our politics, our religion, our daily conduct in all lines of activity in which we may be engaged, are based on our conclusions, it is evident that the habit of reasoning rapidly and accurately should be formed early and thoroughly.

The natural tendency of the mind, in child or adult, is first in the direction of *affirmative* and *universal* judgments; that is, the mind naturally first seeks resemblances, and affirmative judgments are based upon these. And although the child must for some time make individual judgments, yet, as experience widens, he is, by natural tendency, prone to make affirmations that are widely general. The mind is always desirous of reaching conclusions of the widest possible applicability.

Correct reasoning (correct judging) depends upon careful and accurate observation and accumulation of all facts that may have a bearing upon the matter in hand, and upon the power to perceive quickly and correctly the true relations of the facts. Teachers should train their pupils to observe intelligently, and with interest wide awake, all facts that come in their way. Then with the questions *Why?* and *How?* (preëminently assimilation questions, as *What? When? Where?* are acquisition questions) young minds may be led to discern relations accurately and to draw conclusions correctly. Nothing is more needed in the practical life of to-day than the power to face facts, and *reason upon them.*

The text-book branches specially adapted to cultivating the reflective power are *arithmetic, grammar, advanced history,* and *civics. Arithmetic* cultivates the power to reason from certainties to certainties. But the study of arithmetic may all too easily become a memory-cramming, answer-getting mechanism. No training for judgment can be found in arithmetic unless a careful distinction be made, in the statement of every problem, between the quantities *given* and those *required;* and unless every step in the solution is logically based on a previous step, or on one more of the given conditions: hence the necessity for much oral work in arithmetic, and for requiring pupils to follow a *logical form* in their written solutions. At every step in arithmetic, "Why is this true?" and "How was that obtained?" should be asked by the teacher, until telling the why and how becomes a fixed habit in the pupil.

Grammar is especially adapted to the cultivation of the reflective faculty in pupils old enough to use a text-book in the study of that subject. Technical grammar is *elementary logic.* Diagraming and parsing, which are coming again into favor as school exercises, and which should never have gone out, cannot be done correctly unless the meaning of the sentence be grasped; and this cannot be done unless the true *relations* of the words and phrases to the concepts they name, and to one another, be clearly seen. There is more valuable discipline for the relational faculty in thorough drill in diagraming and analyzing the English sentence than in arithmetic analysis.

History and *civics,* from the time they may be profitably taught from text-books, are of the highest practical value in the education of judgment. They afford ever-recurring occasions for asking questions that stimulate the reflective power of the pupils. To teach history without training the judgment of the pupil is merely to stuff his memory with valueless facts—valueless, because their relations are not perceived, their causes are not understood. The facts of human civilization, of the origin and growth of those things that we call government and religion and liberty and science and art—these are the facts of supremest value to every citizen, whether young or old; but they are valuable only as they are *related* to one another and to our own institutions. It will not do to merely *instruct* boys and girls in the facts of history, on the supposition that they will learn of themselves to correlate and explain these facts as judgment grows more mature. The pupil must be taught to *think* from the start, if he is to do much good thinking later in life. The facts imparted must be, in number and kind, suited to the advancement of the pupil; and he should be led to seek for and find, with the teacher's aid, the *causes* of events.

If the man or woman is expected to be independent and self-reliant, to think clearly and decide wisely, the boy or girl must be trained to accurate observation of facts, and to judicial reflection upon their relations and bearings.

Moral Education in the Common Schools /
WILLIAM T. HARRIS

The separation of church and state is an acknowledged principle in our National Government, and its interpretation from generation to generation eliminates with more and more of strictness whatever ceremonies and observances of a religious character still remain attached to secular customs and usages.

Inasmuch as religion, in its definition of what is to be regarded as divine, at the same time furnishes the ultimate and supreme ground of all obligations, it stands in the closest relations to morality, which we may define as the system of duties or obligations that govern the relation of man to himself as individual and as race or social whole.

To the thinking observer nothing can be more obvious than the fact that the institutions of society are created and sustained by the moral activity of man.

The moral training of the young is essential to the preservation of civilization. The so called fabric of society is woven out of moral distinctions and observances. The net-work of habits and usages which makes social combination possible—which enables men to live together as a community—constitutes an ethical system. In that ethical system only is spiritual life possible. Without such a system even the lowest stage of society—that of the mere savage even—could not exist. In proportion to the completeness of development of its ethical system a community rises above barbarism.

It is quite clear that so deep a change in the principle of human government as the separation of church and state involves the most important consequences to the ethical life of our people.

All thoughtful persons look with solicitude on institutions of an educational character in order to discover what means, if any, can remain for moral education after its ecclesiastical foundation has been removed.

It happens quite naturally that some of the best people in the community struggle to retain the ecclesiastical forms and ceremonies in the secular. They find themselves unable to discriminate between the provinces of morality and religion. With them education in morality means education in performing religious rites. But this view certainly does not

"Moral Education in the Common Schools" is reprinted from W. T. Harris, *Moral Education in the Common Schools,* United States Bureau of Education, Circular of Information, No. 4, 1888, pp. 81–91.

harmonize with the political conviction of our people. From year to year we see the religious rites and ceremonies set aside in the legislature, the town-meeting, the public assembly, the school. If retained they become empty forms with no appreciable effect.

In this state of affairs we might profitably inquire into the principle which permits institutions to be emancipated from the direct control of the church.

Without entering into this question in its details at the present time, we may remark that the history of Christian civilization shows us a continuous spectacle of the development of institutions into independence. It is a sort of training or nurture of institutions by the church into a degree of maturity in which they come to be able to live and thrive without the support of mere ecclesiastical authority.

But an institution attains its majority only when it has become thoroughly grounded on some fundamental divine principle. The state, for instance, is organized on the principle of justice—the return of each man's deed to himself. On such principle the state may be conducted without fear of collision with the church or other institutions.

The school, too, has certain divine principles which it has borrowed from the church through long centuries of tutelage and perhaps can be conducted by itself without church authority and yet be a positive auxiliary to the church and cause of religion.

The school proposes at first this object, to teach the pupil a knowledge of man and nature—in short, to initiate him into the realm of truth.

Certainly truth is divine, and religion itself is chiefly busied with discovering and interpreting the Divine First Principle of the Universe and his personal relations to men. In so far as truth—real truth, in harmony with the personality of God, and not spurious truth—is taught in the school, it is a positive auxiliary to the church and to religion.

But the intellectual pursuit of truth in the school is conditioned upon a deeper principle. Order is the first law, even of Heaven. The government of human beings in a community is a training for them in the forms of social life. The school must strictly enforce a code of laws. The so-called "discipline" of the school is its primordial condition, and is itself a training in habits essential to life in a social whole, and hence is itself moral training. Let us study the relation of school discipline to the development of moral character, and compare its code of duties with the ethical code as a whole.

First let us take an ideal survey of the whole field and see what is desirable before we examine the results of school as actually furnished. One may distinguish moral duties or habits which ought to be taught to youth into three classes:

(*a*) Mechanical virtues, in which the youth exercises a minimum of moral choice and obeys an external rule prescribed for him. In this, the lowest species of moral discipline, the youth learns self-denial and self-control, and not much besides.

(*b*) Social duties, those which govern the relation of man to man, and which are the properly called "moral" duties. In this form of moral discipline the youth learns to obey principle rather than the immediate will of another.

(*c*) Religious duties, or those based on the relation to God as revealed in religion. In these the youth learns the ultimate grounds of obligation and gains both a practical principle for the conduct of life and a theoretic principle on which to base his view of the world. In his religous doctrine man formulates his theory of the origin and destiny of nature and the human race, and at the same time defines his eternal vocation, his fundamental duties. The mere statement of this obvious fact is sufficient to indicate the rank and importance of the religious part of the moral duties.

Turning now to the school, let us take an inventory of its means and appliances for moral education in the line of these several divisions. Let us remember, too, that morality consists in practice rather than in theory and that the school can teach morality only when it trains the will into ethical habits and not when it stops short with inculcating a correct theoretical view of right and wrong, useful as such a view may be.

In the school we note, first, the moral effect of the requirement of implicit obedience; a requirement necessary within the school for its successful administration. The discipline in obedience in its strict form, such as is found in the school-room, has four other applications, which remain valid under all conditions of society:

(*a*) Obedience towards parents; (*b*) towards employers, overseers, and supervisors, as regards the details of work; (*c*) towards the government in its legally constituted authority, civil or military; (*d*) towards the divine will, howsoever revealed.

In each of these four forms there is and always remains a sphere of greater or less extent, within which implicit obedience is one's duty. In the three first-named this duty is not absolute, but limited; the sphere continually growing narrower with the growth of the individual in wisdom and self-directive power. In the fourth form of obedience to the divine will the individual comes more and more to a personal insight into the necessity of the divine law as revealed in Scripture, in nature, and especially in human life, and through this he is emancipated from the direct personal control of men, even of the wisest and best, and becomes rather a law unto himself. He outgrows mere mechanical obedience, and arrives at a truly moral will in which the law is written on the heart.

Obedience to what is prescribed by authority is obviously a training that fits one for religion, even if religion has no direct part in such training. Hence the school in securing implicit obedience is an auxiliary of the church even when perfectly secular.

The pillars on which school education rest are behavior and scholarship. Deportment, or behavior, comes first as the *sine qua non*. The first requisite of the school is order; each pupil must be taught to conform his behavior to the general standard and repress all that interferes with the function of the school. In the outset, therefore, a whole family of virtues are taught the pupil, and taught him so thoroughly that they become fixed in his character. In the mechanical duties habit is everything, and theory little or nothing. The pupil is taught (*a*) punctuality; he must be at school in time. Sleep, business, play, indisposition—all must give way to the duty of obedience to this external requirement—to observe the particular moment of time and conform to it.

Punctuality does not end with getting to school, but while in school, it is of equal importance. Combination can not be achieved without it. The pupil must have his lessons ready at the appointed time, must rise from his seat at the tap of the bell, move to line, return; in short, he must go through all the evolutions with this observance of rhythm.

(b) Regularity is the next discipline. Regularity is punctuality reduced to a system. Conformity to the requirements of time in a particular instance is punctuality; made general it becomes regularity.

Combination in school rests on these two virtues. They are the most elementary of the moral code—its alphabet, in short.

This age is often called the age of productive industry—the era of emancipation of man from the drudgery of slavery to his natural wants of food, clothing, and shelter. This emancipation is effected by machinery. Machinery has quadrupled the efficiency of human industry within the past half century. There is one general training especially needed to prepare the generations of men who are to act as directors of machinery and managers of the business that depends upon it—this training is in the habits of punctuality and regularity.

Only by obedience to these abstract external laws of time and place may we achieve a social combination complete enough to free us from thraldom to our physical wants and necessities.

(c) Silence is the third of these semi-mechanical duties. It is the basis for the culture of internality or reflection—the soil in which thought grows. The pupil is therefore taught habits of silence; he learns to restrain his natural animal impulse to prate and chatter. All ascent above his animal nature arises through this ability to hold back the mind from utterance of the immediate impulse. The first impression must be corrected by the second. Combination and generalization are required to reach deep and wide truths, and these depend upon this habit of silence.

This silence in the school-room has a twofold significance—it is necessary in order that there may be no distraction of the attention of others from their work; secondly, it is a direct discipline in the art of combining the diffused and feeble efforts of the pupil himself.

These mechanical duties constitute an elementary training in morals without which it is exceedingly difficult to build any superstructure of moral character whatever.

Moral education, therefore, must begin in merely mechanical obedience and develop gradually out of this stage towards that of individual responsibility.

The higher orders of moral duties fall into two classes—those that relate to the individual himself and those that relate to his fellows.

(a) *Duties to self.*—These are (1) physical, and concern cleanliness, neatness in person and clothing, temperance and moderation in the gratification of the animal appetites and passions.

The school can and does teach cleanliness and neatness, but it has less power over the pupil in regard to temperance. It can teach him self-control and self-sacrifice in the three disciplines already named, punctuality, regularity, and science, and in so far it may free him from thraldom to the body in other respects. It can and does labor efficiently against obscenity and profanity; that is, immorality in language.

(2) Self-culture. This duty belongs especially to the school. All of its lessons contribute to the pupil's self-culture. By its discipline it gives him control over himself, and ability to combine with his fellow-men; by its instruction it gives him knowledge of the world of nature and man. This duty corresponds nearly to the one named Prudence in ancient ethical systems. The Christian Fathers discuss four cardinal virtues—temperance, prudence, fortitude, and justice. Prudence places the individual above and beyond his present moment, as it were, letting him stand over himself, watching and directing himself. Man is a twofold being, having a particular, special self and a general nature; his ideal self the possibility of perfection. Self-culture stands for the theoretical or intellectual side of this cardinal virtue of prudence, while industry is its practical side.

(3) Industry. This virtue means devotion to one's calling or business. Each one owes it to himself to have some business and to be industrious.

The good school does not tolerate idleness. It has the most efficient means of securing industry from its pupils. Each one has a definite task scrupulously adjusted to his capacity, and he will be held responsible for its performance. Is there any better training yet devised to educate youth into industry and its concomitants of sincerity, earnestness, simplicity, perseverance, patience, faithfulness, and reliability, than the school method of requiring work in definite amounts, at definite times, and of an approved quality?

The pupil has provided for him a business or vocation. By industry and self-sacrifice the pupil is initiated into a third of the cardinal virtues—fortitude.

(b) *Duties to others.*—Duties to self rest on the consciousness of a higher nature in the individual and of the obligation of bringing out and realizing this higher nature. Duties to others recognize this higher ideal nature as something general, and hence as also the true inward self of our fellow-men. This ideal of man we are conscious that we realize only very imperfectly, and yet it is this fact, that we have the possibility of realizing a higher ideal in ourselves, that gives us our value above animals and plants. In our fellow-men we see revelations of this ideal nature that we have not yet realized in ourselves. Each one possesses some special gift or quality that helps us know ourselves. The experience of each man is a contribution towards our own self-knowledge and vicariously aids us without our being obliged to pay for it in the pain and suffering that the original experience cost. Inasmuch as our ideal can be realized only through this aid from our fellow-men, the virtues that enable us to combine with others and form institutions precede in importance the mechanical virtues.

There are three classes of duties toward others:

(1) Courtesy, including all forms of politeness, good breeding, urbanity, decorum, modesty, respect for public opinion, liberality, magnanimity, etc., described under various names by Aristotle and others after him. The essence of this virtue consists in the resolution to see in others only the ideal of humanity and to ignore any and all defects that may be apparent.

Courtesy in many of its forms is readily taught in school. Its teaching is often marred by the manner of the teacher, which may be sour and surly, or petulant and fault-finding. The importance of this virtue both to its possessor and to all his fellows demands careful attention on the part of school managers with a view to insure its presence in the school-room.

(2) Justice. This is recognized as the chief in the family of secular virtues. It has several forms or species, as, for example, (*a*) honesty, fair dealing with others, respect for their rights of person and property and reputation; (*b*) truth-telling, or honesty in speech—honesty itself being truth-acting. Such names as integrity, uprightness, righteousness, express further distinctions that belong to this staunch virtue.

Justice, while like courtesy in the fact that it looks upon the ideal of the individual, is unlike courtesy in the fact that it looks upon the deed of the individual in a very strict and business-like way, and measures its defects by that high standard. According to the principle of justice, each one receives in proportion to his deeds and not in proportion to his possibilities, wishes, or unrealized aspirations. All individuals are ideally equal in the essence of their humanity; but justice will return upon each the equivalent of his deed only. If it be a crime, justice returns it upon the doer as a limitation of his freedom of person or property.

The school is perhaps more effective in teaching the forms of justice than in teaching those of courtesy. Truth-telling especially receives the full emphasis of all the power of school discipline. Every lesson is an exercise in digging out and closely defining the truth, in extending the realm of clearness and certainty further into the region of ignorance and guesswork. How careful the pupil is compelled to be with his statements in the recitation and how painstaking in his previous preparation!

Justice in discovering the exact performance of each pupil and giving him recognition for it may give place to injustice in case of carelessness on the part of the teacher. Such carelessness may suffer the weeds of lying and deceit to grow up, and it may allow the pupil to gather the fruits of honesty and truth, and thus it may offer a premium for fraud. The school may thus furnish an immoral education, notwithstanding its great opportunities to inculcate this noble virtue of honesty.

The private individual must not be permitted to return the evil deed upon the doer, for that would be revenge, and hence a new crime. All personality and self-interest must be sifted out before justice can be done to the criminal. Hence we have another virtue belonging to this class which is itself an outgrowth of justice—that of respect for law.

(3) Respect for law, as the only means of protecting the innocent and punishing the guilty, is the complement of justice. It looks upon the ideal as realized not in an individual man, but in an institution represented in the person of an executive officer who is supported with legislative and judicial powers.

The school, when governed by an arbitrary and tyrannical teacher, is a demoralizing influence in a community. The law-abiding virtue is weakened, and a whole troop of lesser virtues take their flight and give admittance to passions and appetites. But the wise and just teacher will teach respect for law very thoroughly, on the other hand. A great change has been wrought in the methods of discipline in later years. It is clear that with frequent and severe corporal punishment it is next to impossible to retain genuine respect for law. Only the very rare teacher can succeed in this. Punishment through the sense of honor has therefore superseded for the most part in our best schools the use of the rod. It is now easy to find the school admirably disciplined and its pupils enthusiastic and law-abiding—governed entirely without the use of corporal punishment.

The school possesses very great advantages over the family in this matter of teaching respect for law. The parent is too near the child, too personal to teach him this lesson.

At this point we approach the province of religious duties. Higher than the properly moral duties, or at least higher than the secular or "cardinal" virtues, are certain ones which are called "celestial" virtues by the theologians. These are faith, hope, and charity, and their special modifications.

The question may arise whether any instruction in these duties can be given which is not at the same time sectarian. An affirmative answer will have to show only that the essential scope of these virtues has a secular meaning and that the secular meaning is more fundamental than in the case of the so-called cardinal virtues.

(1) Faith in a theologic sense means the true knowledge of the first principle of the universe. Everybody presupposes some theory or view of the world, its origin and destiny, in all his practical and theoretical dealing with it. Christendom assumes a personal Creator of divine human nature, who admits man to grace in such a way that he is not destroyed by the results of his essential imperfection, but is redeemed in some special way. The Buddhist and Brahmin think that finitude and imperfection are utterly incompatible with the Divine Being, and hence that the things of the world can not be supposed to have real existence. They exist only in our fancy. Here is no grace, no redemption. Nature is not a real existence to those who hold such a theory, and hence for them there can be no natural science.

In Christian countries the prevailing institutions and confessions of faith recognize this belief in a divine-human God—a God of grace—and their people more or less cultivate science. Some persons theoretically deny this belief, but cling to science, which is itself based on the deep-lying assumption that the world is a manifestation of reason. Such skeptics have not yet measured the consequences of their theories and for our purposes may be said to belong to the faith inasmuch as the reality of a finite world presupposes a personal God whose essential attribute is grace. The agnostic too is strenuous in acknowledging the practical importance of the code of moral duties.

The prevailing view of the world in Christian countries is very properly called faith, inasmuch as it is not a view pieced together from the experience of the senses nor a product of individual reflection unaided by the deep intuitions of the spiritual seers of the race.

Faith is a secular virtue as well as a theological virtue, and whoever teaches another view of the world—that is to say, he who teaches that man is not immortal and that nature does not reveal the divine reason, teaches a doctrine subversive of faith in this peculiar sense and also subversive of man's life in all that makes it worth living.

(2) Hope, the second theological virtue, is the practical side of faith. Faith is not properly the belief in some theory of the world, but in that particular theory of the world which Christianity teaches. So hope is not a mere anticipation of some future event, but the firm expectation that the destiny of the world is in accordance with the scheme of faith, no matter how much present appearances may be against it. Thus the individual acts upon this conviction. It is the basis of the highest practical doing in this world. A teacher may show faith and hope in the views of the world which he expresses and in his dealings with his school—in his teaching of history, in his comments on the reading lessons, in his treatment of the aspirations of his pupils. Although none of these things

may be consciously traced to their source by the pupils, yet their instinct will not fail to recognize genuine faith and hope or their lack in the character. Nothing is so difficult to conceal as one's conviction in regard to the origin and destiny of the world and of man.

(3) Finally, Charity is the highest of these virtues, in the sense that it is the concrete embodiment and application of that view of the world which Faith and Hope establish.

The world is made and governed by divine grace, and that grace will triumph in the world. Hence, says the individual, let me be filled with this principle and hold within myself this divine feeling of grace towards all fellow-creatures. Charity is, therefore, not alms-giving, but a devotion to others. "Sell all that thou hast" * * * "and follow me." Faith perceives the principle; Hope believes in it, where it is not yet visible; Charity sets it up in the soul and lives it. There might be conceived a Faith or insight into this principle of divine grace and a Hope that should trust it where not seen, and yet the possessor of this Faith and Hope lack Charity. In that case the individual would acknowledge the principle as dominant, but would not admit it into himself. With Charity all other virtues are implied, even justice.

While courtesy acts towards men as if they were ideally perfect and had no defects, while justice holds each man responsible for the perfect accordance of his deed with his ideally perfect nature, and makes no allowance for immaturity, Charity or loving-kindness sees both the ideal perfection and the real imperfection, and does not condemn, but offers its help, and is willing and glad to sacrifice itself to assist the imperfect in their struggle towards perfection.

The highest virtue, that of loving-kindness or charity, has of all the virtues, the largest family of synonymes: Humility, considerateness, heroism, gratitude, friendliness, and various shades of love in the family (parental, filial, fraternal, and conjugal), sympathy, pity, benevolence, kindness, toleration, patriotism, generosity, public spirit, philanthropy, beneficence, concord, harmony, peaceableness, tenderness, forgiveness, mercy, grace, long-suffering, and many others.

The typical form of this virtue as it may be cultivated in school is known under the name of kindness. A spirit of true kindness made to pervade a school is the highest fountain of virtue. That such a spirit can exist in a school as an emanation from a teacher we know from many a saintly example that has walked in the path of the Great Teacher.

From the definition of this principle it is easy to deduce a verdict against all those systems of rivalry and emulation in school which stimulate ambition beyond the limits of generous competition to the point of selfishness. Selfishness is the root of mortal sin, as theologians tell us, and the lowest type of it is cold unfeeling pride, while envy is the type next to it.

Returning to our first question, we repeat: In a state which has no established church and in a system of public schools that is not permitted to be under the control of sects or denomination, what shall be the fate of dogmatic instruction in morals, especially instruction in that part of morals which rests upon the celestial virtues? Of course the problem is still a simple one in parochial schools and denominational schools. But it is not proper for us to ignore the dangers incurred even in strictly parochial schools. The more strict the denominational control the less likely is there to pervade the school that spirit of tolerance and charity towards others which is the acknowledged deepest taproot of the virtues. Were the community homogeneous in its confession of faith, religious instruction could still properly remain in school. The movement of American society is not, however, in that direction, and it is quite likely that the church must see formal religious instruction, even to the ceremony of reading the Bible, leave the common schools altogether. But a formal reading of the Bible "without note or comment," or a formal prayer on opening school, is surely not religious or moral instruction in any such efficient sense as to warrant a Christian man or woman in sitting down in content and claiming a religious hold on the popular education. Such a delusive content is indeed too prevalent.

It is not the undoing of the separation of church and state even in the common schools, nor the struggle to maintain a frigid and bloodless "non-sectarian," so-called, religion in our schools that is to succeed or to do any good. It is for the churches to rouse themselves in the presence of this danger and proselyte by new means and appliances as well adapted to the present day as the Sunday-school movement was seventy years ago.

It is for the teachers not to claim the right to introduce formal religious ceremonies, but to make all their teaching glow with a genuine faith, hope, and charity, so that pupils will catch from them their view of the world as the only one that satisfies the heart, the intellect, and the will. Let us note the fact that in the mechanical virtues so important to making good citizens, the training in the schools is already admirable. Human freedom is realized not by the unaided effort of the individual, but by his concerted or combined efforts in organized institutions like the state and civil society. Those mechanical virtues make possible the help of the individual in this combination, and fit him for the modern world now bent on the conquest of nature.

The social virtues, justice, politeness, and obedience to law may be equally well provided for although in fact they are not successfully taught in every school.

The celestial virtues can be taught by teachers inspired by those virtues and by none others. The empty profession of such virtues without the devotion of the life to them is likely in the school, even more than elsewhere, to produce the well-known practical result of atheism.

In closing let us call up the main conclusions and repeat them in their briefest expression.

1. Moral education is a training in habits and not an inculcation of mere theoretical views.

2. Mechanical disciplines are indispensable as an elementary basis of moral character.

3. Lax discipline in a school saps the moral character of the pupil. It allows him to work merely as he pleases, and he never can re-enforce his feeble will by regularity, punctuality, and systematic industry. He grows up in habits of whispering and other species of intermeddling with his fellow-pupils, neither doing what is reasonable himself nor allowing others to do it. Never having subdued himself, he will never subdue the world of chaos or any part of it as his life-work, but will have to be subdued by external constraint on the part of his fellow-men.

4. Too strict discipline, on the other hand, undermines moral character by emphasizing too much the mechanical duties and especially the phase of obedience to authority, and it leaves the pupil in a state of perennial minority. He does not assimilate the law of duty and make it his own.

The law is not written on his heart, but is written on the lips only. He fears it, but does not love it. The tyrant teacher produces hypocrisy and deceit in his pupils. All manner of fraud germinates in attempts to cover up shortcomings from the eye of the teacher. Even where there is simple implicit obedience in the place of fraud and the like, there is no independence and strength of character developed.

5. The best help that one can give his fellows is that which enables them to help themselves. The best school is that which makes the pupils able to teach themselves. The best instruction in morality makes the pupil a law unto himself.

Hence, strictness which is indispensable must be tempered by such devices as cause the pupil to love to obey the law for the law's sake.

SPECIAL READING

Education for Leadership in a Democracy /
MICHAEL DEMIASHKEVICH

Who Shapes History, the Masses or Individual Leaders?

Approximately a hundred years ago the intellectuals in almost every country of Western civilization were debating the problem as to which is

"Education for Leadership in a Democracy" is reprinted from Michael Demiashkevich, "Education for Leadership in a Democracy," *An Introduction to the Philosophy of Education*, copyright 1935, permission granted by the American Book Company.

the more influential in shaping history, the individual or the masses. Tolstoy, in *War and Peace*, echoed the controversy.

In the majority of European countries, it fell to the task of bureaucracies to "canalize"—as the expression went—the chaos following in the wake of the Napoleonic Wars. Happily, in every chaos there are germs of a cosmos; but it takes the penetrating and properly trained eyes of really gifted leaders to perceive them. The autocratic hereditary regimes, served by practically hereditary bureaucracies, then prevalent in the majority of Western countries, did not produce the soil in which really constructive leadership could grow, and, as the saying is, it is not the cowl that makes the monk. As a result, the chaos was painfully long. Political philosophers of the time were divided in distributing the blame. Some thought that the popular masses were responsible in the last analysis. Such philosophers believed, as Walter Lippmann seems to believe, that history is made by movements of the popular masses; that "the real law in the modern state is the multitude of little decisions made daily by millions of men." [1] The opposite school of thought maintained that history is made by leaders, by inspired individuals.

It appears that the controversial problem in question has been settled with satisfactory clarity by the history of the last hundred years. This was the century of liberalism during which the masses, or the so-called lower classes, exercised greater political activity and influence than ever before. Yet that century of liberalism seems to have vindicated the theory that it is individual leaders who shape history. The historic lessons on leadership derivable from the World War and its continuing aftermath are particularly illuminating in this respect. England, France, and the United States are the nations in which "circulation of the elite" had been practiced on a larger scale before the war began, and more sincerely during the war, than was the case in such countries as Russia, Germany, Austria-Hungary, or Rumania. Circulation of the elite is the social process which consists in the recruitment and training, on the competitive basis, of future leaders in the various walks of life selected from among the children best endowed or "chosen" intellectually and morally; further, it consists in bringing the right man, the gifted and properly trained man, to the right place by displacing the wrong man from the wrong place. It is scarcely a mere accident that the three first-named countries made in the war a far better showing, on the whole, regarding the supreme national leadership, political, social, and economic, which contributed to the outcome of the war. In this group of belligerent states the circulation of the elite made possible a more effective employment of the potential services of the more capable individuals.

Pre-war Germany had some very capable civil servants, but they were

[1] Walter Lippmann, *Preface to Morals* (New York: Macmillan, 1929), p. 275.

debarred by social barriers from posts of higher authority and remained in subordinate positions, while titled mediocrities possessing "pull" were the masters of Germany. Germany had in the World War many excellent generals; but these were not in the supreme command, at least not during the initial phase of the war—August–September, 1914—which predetermined the final issue. In the closing chapter of the remarkable study of the World War, *Der Welikrieg*, by General Hermann von Kuhl, there are found almost literally repeated such aphorisms as the one attributed to Philip of Macedon: "An army of stags with a lion at their head is better than an army of lions with a stag at their head"; or that found in Aristophanes: "It often happens that less depends upon the valor of an army than upon the skill of the leader." [2] What was true of the higher Imperial German civil and military administration was certainly not less true of the Russian. The new evidence furnished by public and private documents seems to have elevated to the quality of historic truth the opinion professed by many military experts that Germany lost and France won the decisive battle of the Marne of September 6–11, 1914, for the reason that the German armies were commanded at the time by the sickly, nervous, and confused von Moltke, but the French, by the robust and self-possessed Joffre.

Even much more appropriately it might be said that if at the time of the World War Russia had had a more capable ruler than Emperor Nicholas II and Germany a more fit one than Emperor William II, the condition of these two countries and of the world at large would have been in all probability immeasurably better than it is now. Or how differently the February revolution of 1917 in Russia would have turned out if Kerensky had had determination and vision more nearly commensurate with his good intentions, and if the Bolshevist group had been led during the initial phase of its rule by a man of less intrepidity, ruthlessness, and clarity of judgment than Lenin.

But these and similar illustrations of the predominance of the specific gravity of leaders over that of the masses in shaping the historic process may fail to impress some people in a democratic country. The illustrations are taken from the history of autocratically governed countries. Though, in truth, in this case the point relative to the origin of the evidence is beside the point, still it is interesting to recall that the clearly tangible turning-points in the political history of a democratic country such as the United States are connected with the names of individual leaders like George Washington, Abraham Lincoln, Theodore Roosevelt, Woodrow Wilson, Franklin D. Roosevelt. And are not the important stages in the economic history of the United States connected with the names of Vanderbilt, Astor, Rockefeller, Carnegie, Morgan, Ford? Or the

[2] Herman von Kuhl, *Der Weltkrieg 1914–1918* (Berlin: Verlag Tradition, 1929), B. I, S. 45, 46, 47, 61 ff.; B. II, S. 553 ff.

significant phases of the cultural history of the United States with the names of Henry Barnard, Horace Mann, Thomas Alva Edison, Charles W. Eliot?

Great Waste Instead of Great Investment

The devastating result of the false, inflated version of the democratization of education, according to which post-elementary education should be given freely to all in non-selective public schools in non-classified groups, hazardously formed on the basis of the pupils' chronological age, is that it irresistibly degenerates into wasteful lowering of standards of education. The inevitable consequence of this would be the substantial, if not the statutory, abrogation of democracy itself and the establishment of the rule of demagogues and racketeers exploiting the actual, if not advertised, backwardness of the popular masses, fostered through the weakened public schools. Moreover, the masses are then left unprotected by true democratic leadership. Under the regime of an inflated conception of equality of educational opportunity, the elite—that is to say, the gifted and keen children, adolescents, and youths attending public schools—are thrown in with poorly endowed, incurious, and unwilling pupils whom the teachers must try to occupy in some worth-while manner.

Thus the public secondary school in which the capable adolescents should, normally, receive an enriching and stimulating liberal education (in other words, a general cultural education preparing toward no definite vocation but necessary for practicing competent leadership in any vocation), is often forced down to the role of an entertaining establishment for any adolescent of secondary school age. It becomes then impossible to follow in public secondary education the only reasonable policy, which, in the fitting words of Professor F. T. Spaulding, is one of "discriminating selection of those pupils for whom continued schoolwork may mean reasonable profit to the state, rather than an effort to hold all pupils in school indefinitely, regardless of their ability to learn or their willingness to learn." [3] Thus, also, virtual "grade schools and high schools are made out of colleges because a great many young people fail to do their grade and high school work before they go to college." [4] The eager, inquisitive boys and girls ambitious for learning and culture, are then held back, if not entirely submerged, by the crowds professing what a heroine of Sinclair Lewis called the "cheerful antipathy to scholarship." [5]

[3] "A Brief for the Selection of Secondary School Pupils," *The Harvard Teachers Record* (November 1931), p. 106.
[4] J. W. Shepherd, "Our Educational Goose-Step," *The American Scholar* (May 1933), p. 293 ff.
[5] *Ann Vickers, cit.*, pp. 55–56.

Next, the public is disappointed in its colleges. In the words of Professor J. W. Shepherd,[6] "The public sees too little studying, too light an attitude towards life's problems, too much professional incompetence. . . . The final product of the college—its graduates—is being criticized for lack of scholarly knowledge, for lack of cultural attitudes, for lack of leadership, and for lack of ability to do successfully the things demanded by a cold and unsympathetic world." Then, the disappointed public reduces its support to higher educational institutions, and the vicious circle is formed in consequence of which the circulation of the elite is blocked, the commonwealth does not obtain a sufficient supply of gifted and carefully trained potential leaders from among whom it could choose, on the basis of electoral competition and civil service examinations, its actual leaders in the various walks of life. As a result, such a commonwealth, as surely as water flows downward, is weakened in comparison with those commonwealths which have in their educational system an adequate arrangement for preliminary selection and training of their future leaders in public educational institutions.

In order that the elite of a democratic nation may have an appropriate educational opportunity, and the nation an appropriate circulation of the elite, which alone can promise that the right man will be brought to the right place in the service of democracy, it is necessary, then, that equality of educational opportunity should be reduced to its right proportions, and educational opportunity for the elite should be adequately provided.

"Dialectics" of the History of Education for Leadership

The philosopher Hegel teaches that the development of the universe proceeds by the "triad of dialectics" or certain creative contradictions. The triad consists of position (thesis), negation (anti-thesis), and higher unity (synthesis). Thus, for instance, in the moral development of the individual or humanity at large, innocence (position) gives place to doubt (negation) out of which grows conviction or rationally established faith (higher unity). In the physical world, a seed (position) undergoes disintegration through germination (negation) to give life to a plant (higher unity).[7] Some historians, observing how humanity has been in the habit of finding more or less balanced solutions of its problems only after a jump from an extreme into its opposite, have spoken of the Hegelian "dialectical process" in history.

The history of education certainly affords many examples of such a "dialectical process" of contradictions out of which only very slowly and

[6] *Op. cit.*
[7] *Enzyklopädie der philosophischen Wissenschaften im Grundrisse*, Hegels Werke, Bd. VI–VII.

painfully emerge reasonably balanced practices relative to the organization, administration, and method of the educative process. Confining ourselves to the history of education for leadership, it is interesting to remember how in this regard also (as in many other educational matters, for instance in those relative to educational method), *praejudicium antiquitatis*, or the bigotry of tradition, would be replaced by a sort of *praejudicium novitatis*, the bigotry of novelty. Out of the resulting conflicts, there begins only now to emerge in some countries a more or less balanced solution of the problem of education for leadership.

At the beginning of all organized educational effort in each Western country, as well as elsewhere, the primary purpose was almost exclusively the training of leaders. At first the leading members of the community rose to their position through their personal ability and effort, or because they were—in the terminology of Jefferson—"natural aristocrats," the best endowed members of the group. They wished, however, that their children, whom they naturally wanted to succeed them, be trained for leadership through theoretical learning—that is to say, through the assimilation of past experience sufficiently crystallized into theory.[8] In doing so, fathers did not simply try to smooth out for their progeny the rough path of life. They understood also that the tasks of their sons as public authorities were necessarily going to be more difficult than their own, because those tasks of the sons would be complicated by the various improvements and developments made under the fathers, since the imperfection of human kind willed that progress should mean the greater complexity of life. The fathers understood also that it was only through a sequential assimilation of the accumulated experience of the group that the sons could become prepared to exercise safely the inherited authority. Hence, the organization or institutionalization of education. At the dawn of the history of education, then, training for leadership was the only formal intellectual education given. Only much later did it begin to dawn upon the authorities of the tribe, clan, or absolutist national state that it was necessary to do something for the masses in order to make of them more intelligent and more efficient followers. They were intended, however, to receive just a modicum of practical training and much indoctrination.

Thus at the beginning of the history of organized education the opportunity of education toward leadership existed primarily, if not exclusively, for the descendants of "natural aristocrats" who, though already hereditary aristocrats, were still willing and capable of undertaking the hard work necessary at all times in good training for leadership.

---

[8] The term "theory" is taken here to mean a set of guiding principles of action and conduct in specific situations demanding a well-analyzed, clearly understood specific experience; for instance, theory of bridge construction, fortress building, warfare, navigation, government, etc.

But it is rightly said that history is the cemetery of aristocracies. They rapidly enough degenerate into mere "vested interests" which would not relinquish, however, of their own accord the dominant positions inherited from their truly aristocratic forefathers—that is, forefathers who were the members of the group best endowed, intellectually and morally —unless and until such vested interests are forced out by the new "natural aristocracy" rising from the so-called lower strata and supported by the masses. Before this happens, however, education for leadership is monopolized by vested interests. The educative process, serving then the deteriorated progeny of the pristine "natural aristocracy" of intellect and will power, is deliberately facilitated by the allotment of a large place to social adornments, sports, and other occupations not demanding much intellectual ability and effort.

Sooner or later the dissatisfied real elite that happened to be born into the plebeian strata of society, usually assisted indirectly by the blunders, ineptitude, ostentatious satiety, and inefficiency of the self-perpetuating vested interests, succeeds in revolutionizing the chronically dissatisfied lower masses and marching them, literally or figuratively, into the revolt intended to destroy the weakened, degenerated ruling class.

In consequence, another extreme sets in with relation to the accessibility of higher levels of education preparing toward the Periclean leadership, unless the aristocratic tradition is sufficiently shared and endorsed by the masses—as it has been in England, for example—and thus protects the new democracy against harmful equalitarian illusions. Unless a joint check, combining common sense and a reasonable aristocratic tradition, is kept, an inflated doctrine of equality of educational opportunity is produced. Then for a long time this doctrine virtually obstructs the development of the elite through the medium of the public school, until a national crisis demonstrates to the well-intentioned but unimaginative citizenry the wasteful absurdity of the situation. Meanwhile the public school, despite the generous increase of funds given to it by the community, would fail to turn out a reasonably sufficient number of enlightened and patriotic potential leaders, whose presence and competitive public activity would make it impossible for racketeers and demagogues virtually to enslave whole communities and to undermine the very foundations of democracy to the point of creating in many minds the desire for a sort of Fascist, authoritarian, and supposedly paternalistic, unpartisan government.

Such, briefly, seems to have been the thesis (or position) and the anti-thesis (or negation) of the dialectics of the history of education for leadership. But, though this is a historic fact, it is important to insist that there is no fatality about this fact in the sense that it must produce itself everywhere. It did not produce itself in some communities; and where it did, it did so with greatly varying degrees of wastefulness and harm.

Whatever may be the fatality of the development of matter in accordance with the Hegelian dialectics, human society (that is, human minds in their interrelationship) can be free from that fatality, if it is enlightened enough and tries hard enough. The principal difference between matter and mind is that matter is uncritical of itself and its actions. The realm of matter is where facts, such as they are, have the last word; while in society, *i.e.*, in the realm of the interrelationship of human minds, it is a mind that may have the last word over facts when it is clear enough, creative enough, and determined enough to produce new and better facts. Thus the human mind has successfully replaced, in many societies, the facts of cruelty, fanaticism, and injustice with a reasonable measure of tolerance, co-operation, and justice.

Democratic Selection and "Aristocratic" Training of the Elite

To be able to assist toward placing the problem of democratic leadership on the sound basis of circulation of the elite, the school in a democracy must first free itself from the inflated notion of equality of educational opportunity, for this notion results in depriving the nation's "natural aristocracy" of the opportunity adequately to prepare themselves in public educational institutions for proper service to the nation.

It is suggested, therefore, that in order to eliminate the dilemma of the dialectics of the history of education concerning education for leadership, "higher unity" should be substituted for the distortions of education for leadership via the dialectics of the thesis and anti-thesis. Such distortions come either from above and are made by vested interests or they come from below and then they are made by intentionally or unintentionally false friends of democracy. To achieve the higher unity in question, there must be offered a special educational opportunity to "natural aristocrats" from wheresoever they may come. In other words, the elite, or potential future leaders, should be democratically recruited, but should be trained "aristocratically," that is, in the manner which "natural aristocrats" naturally desire—through systematic and exacting intellectual work properly interspersed with physical, aesthetic, and religious activities.

Under such conditions, the future leaders who have received their valuable training, both general and specialized, free in public educational institutions will contract, in a sufficient number of instances, a debt of gratitude toward the nation. Then there will be only a very small place for the quite intelligible suspicion and fear that the popular masses used to have of superior persons as leaders, aloof and contemptuous. The majority of leaders will then be directly and literally flesh from the flesh and bone from the bone of the people. Why is it not a reasonable belief that such leaders, many of whom would have borne the real brunt of life, would understand, at least merely egotistically, that it is not possible to be happy save in a happy world? Why not believe that among such "natural aristocrats," elevated to leadership through the training given them under special provision made by the nation, there would be enough great souls, of whom the Indian philosopher Kalidasa has well said that they are like the skies; they accumulate only in order to spread and distribute? They will be close enough to the people and will understand the people and be understood because they are, in the words of a thinker, "the condensed people." [9]

American Democratic Aristocracy

A unique experience of leadership exercised by a democratically selected aristocracy of the mind and character is furnished by eighteenth-century America. Was not, indeed, the eighteenth-century leadership in this country distinguished by a blending—unprecedented in modern times—of superior intellect and character, disinterested love of letters and science, and democratic sentiment? The leading members of the Continental Congress were precisely men who embodied in themselves this happy blending. Was not such a great democrat as Benjamin Franklin, for instance, not only a member of the committee to draw up the Declaration of Independence and later the first ambassador of the American republic to France, but also the founder of the American Philosophical Society? Small wonder that Benjamin Franklin, skillful not only in practical affairs, both public and private, but at the same time very sensitive to literary and artistic elegancies, was heartily welcome to associate with the intellectual aristocracy of France. Alexander Hamilton advised the people of New York that "the aim of every political constitution is, or ought to be, first to obtain for rulers men who possess the most wisdom to discern, the most virtue to pursue the common good of society," [10] in other words, aristocrats of mind and character.

Jefferson, who, it will be remembered, was the founder of the University of Virginia, distinguished between a natural aristocracy based upon virtue and talent and an artificial aristocracy based upon wealth and birth. He believed that "natural aristocracy" was "the most precious gift of nature," and eminently valuable for the instruction and government of society. He maintained, "That form of government is the best which provides the most effectively for a pure selection of these natural *aristoi* into the offices of government." [11]

The American Commission headed by John Quincy Adams and including Commissioners Bayard, Gallatin, Clay, and Russell, who negotiated

[9] Constantin Brunner, *Die Lehre von dem Geistigen und dem Volk*, cit., S. 57.
[10] *The Federalist*, p. 377.
[11] C. Edward Merriam, *op. cit.*, p. 156.

with the English the treaty of peace in 1814, undoubtedly was also composed of such "natural aristocrats" of excellent culture. To them the Marquis of Wellesley paid a tribute by declaring in the House of Lords that the Americans "had shown a most astonishing superiority over the British during the whole of the negotiations." And James Truslow Adams justly remarks in a comment upon this statement made before the Lords, "It must be recalled that the Americans had been dealing not with the British negotiators but through them with the British Government itself." [12]

Truly, their own intellectual and moral power in achievement, even more than their theory of government and of leadership in a democracy, is an undying monument and an impressive lesson in the unadulterated democratic philosophy of education bequeathed to the American people by their great leaders of the eighteenth and the early nineteenth centuries. Unfortunately, this philosophy of education was subsequently distorted by the inflation of the idea of equality.

Selective Advanced Courses in the High School as an Opportunity for the Elite

The establishment of advanced courses in the high school for the selected, brighter, more ambitious, and more scholastically-minded adolescents should probably be the first step in the direction of selective public education for the elite under the condition of local support and control of public education. With the good will and tact of really competent school superintendents and principals who are converted to the idea, much can be accomplished even without special funds, and without setting up a war between the parents of the more intelligent and those of the less capable students. Why, for example, in large, even non-selective high schools, should not a certain fair percentage of funds and personnel be assigned to the service of the select students? Adolescents found in high schools are often lacking in interest, or in ambition, or in intelligence, or in all of these together, and therefore are not qualified to pursue more difficult systematic studies. To be sure, it is in the end a better policy to occupy such adolescents in public high schools and continuation schools as worthily as possible, rather than leave them at the mercy of the street, only later to spend in the increased budgets of the police force prisons, criminal courts, and the like, whatever savings might be effected by refusing admission to or turning from post-elementary education the incapable or non-studious pupils. But it seems to be also imperative that a certain just percentage of funds and personnel should be set aside for the special care of the elite. Teachers more

[12] James Truslow Adams, *The Adams Family* (Boston: Little, Brown, 1930), p. 156.

suitable for handling the less gifted students should fill about seventy-five per cent of the faculty appointments of non-selective secondary schools and should conduct with the mass of students some suitable work of more elementary nature in the humanities, and of utilitarian, practical nature in mathematics, natural science, and crafts. The other twenty-five per cent of the faculty should be selected and developed in service to appeal to the brighter and keener pupils by the broadness and richness of their general culture as well as by expertness in some definite field or fields of knowledge.

THE AUTHORS

Johann Karl Friedrich Rosenkranz (1805–1879). Famous nineteenth-century Hegelian philosopher who wrote the one systematic treatise on Hegelian philosophy of education, utilizing Hegel's system and categories to explain the nature and form of education as well as its specialized requirements. Born in Magdeburg; graduated from the University of Halle (1824); resident at the University of Berlin, distinguishing himself as a disciple, first of Schleiermacher, and afterward of Hegel (1824–1831); professor of philosophy, University of Halle (1831–1833); professor of philosophy at Königsberg for forty-five years (1833–1879), succeeding Immanuel Kant and Johann Friedrich Herbart in this distinguished chair of philosophy. Wrote extensive works on philosophy and literature. Belonged to the so-called "center" group of Hegelians, midway between Erdmann and Gabler on the one hand, and the extreme left of Straus, Feuerbach, and Bruno Bauer. Among his most prominent works are: *Psychology* (1837); *Critical Explanations of Hegel's System* (1840); edited Kant's *Samtliche Werke* (1838–1842); *History of Kant's Philosophy* (1840); *Life of Hegel* (1844); *Pedagogy as a System* (1848); *Science of Logical Ideas* (1850); *Hegel as the National Philosopher of Germany* (1870); *New Studies* (1875).

Ruric Nevel Roark (1859–1909). Prominent later nineteenth-century educator, dean of a school of education, and college president who wrote one of the most widely used textbooks in education on faculty psychology for teachers with emphasis on the science of the mind and the needed exercise and training of the different mental faculties. Born Greenville, Kentucky, graduate of National University at Lebanon, Ohio (1881); instructor in pedagogy, Lebanon (1881–1885); president, Glasgow Normal School (1885–1889); dean, department of pedagogy, University of Kentucky (1889–1905); honorary fellow in psychology, Clark University (1905–1906); president, Eastern Kentucky State Normal School at Richmond (1906–1909). Major publications are: *Psychology in Education* (1895); *Method in Education* (1899); *General Outline of Pedagogy* (1900); *Economy in Education* (1905).

William Torry Harris (1835–1909). Leading figure in American post Civil War education as superintendent of schools St. Louis, Missouri and as United

States Commissioner of Education, a Hegelian intellectual who founded the St. Louis Philosophical Society and America's first philosophy periodical, *The Journal of Speculative Philosophy*. Born in Connecticut, graduated from Yale (1858); M.A. from Yale "honoris causa" (1869); teacher in the St. Louis public schools, (1857–1867); superintendent of the St. Louis public schools (1868–1880); University Professor of the Philosophy of Education, Washington University, periodic lecturer (1876–1892); Concord Summer School of Philosophy, lecturer throughout New England (1880–1889); United States Commissioner of Education (1889–1906); honorary doctor degrees from the University of Missouri (1890), Brown University (1893), University of Pennsylvania (1894), Yale University (1895), Princeton University (1896); Doctor of Philosophy from the University of Jena (1899). Editor, *Appleton's School Reader* and Appleton's International Education Series; founder, *The Journal of Speculative Philosophy* (1867); translator of second volume of *Hegel's Logic*, titled *Hegel's Doctrine of Reflection* (1881). Major publications: *Introduction to the Study of Philosophy* (1881); *The Spiritual Sense of Dante's Divina Commedia* (1889); *Hegel's Logic or the Genesis of the Categories of the Mind* (1890); *Psychologic Foundations of Education* (1898); *Monograph on Elementary Education in the United States* (1900).

Michael John Demiashkevich (1891–1938). Russian intellectual of peasant birth, escaped from Bolshevik Russia to the United States, staunch supporter of the European Idealistic tradition of education, declared by William Bagley to be the first to use the term "essentialism" to designate an approach to education that is in opposition to progressivism. Born in Orsha, Russia. Graduated from the Imperial Historico-Philological Institute and Imperial Archaeological Institute of Petrograd (1914); Ph.D. in education, Columbia University (1926). Teacher of Russian language and Latin literature, Alexander I Gymnasium, the Deutsche Hauptschule at St. Petri, the Navy College of Petrograd (1914–1923); assistant in the International Institute, Teachers College, Columbia University (1926–1927); visiting scholar at the universities of Grenoble, Paris, Munich, Berlin, and London (1927–1929); professor of education, George Peabody College (1929–1938); summer instructor at Harvard (1933, 1935); summer instructor at University of California at Berkeley (1938). Awarded Laureate, Institut Littéraire et artistique de France. Major publications: *The Activity School* (1926); *Shackled Diplomacy: The Permanent Factors of Foreign Policies of Nations* (1934); *An Introduction to The Philosophy of Education* (1935); *The National Mind: English, French, German* (1938).

Process-Structure Philosophy

Process and structure are, quite logically, the key notions of the thought pattern of Process-Structure Philosophy. They are derived from the discoveries and conceptual constructions of the new physics. First of all, the concept of process is indicated by the evidences from quantum mechanics. The physical world is made up of forces of energy. According to quantum mechanics, it is incorrect to conceive of the world as consisting of simple objects in an absolute and empty space. Objects are not static, self-contained, or simply located, but forms of energy in mass that interact with the environment. Space, on the other hand, is not empty, but consists of fields of electromagnetic forces that pervade the universe. The energy of so-called space and the energy of mass are at root the same. The concept of process is also derived from relativity theory, which adds the dimensions of position and succession, referring to a four-dimensional space, which is best understood as event positions in process. Events are fields of contiguous experience, fields involving interactions of position-environment locations, that is, space-time. The discovery that simultaneity is not absolute but rather circumstantial relative to motions and regions is the confirming evidence of the relativity of events. Thus both quantum mechanics and relativity theory contribute to the generic notion of the primacy of process and energy as the basic fact of nature.

If process and energy are basic to nature, what forms do they take in human experience? Process for human experience consists of personal events in temporal contiguousness, which give subjective and bodily identity by way of the concrescence of heritage to the creativity of the moment. Energy, on the other hand, is the feeling tone of emotion and bodily activities. The human is primarily a feeling being. He feels the energy of the environment through sensation; he feels the energy of himself through emotion. Only a small percentage of energy passes over into cognitions. Yet, these cognitions are the component that civilizes man. Cognitions are the abstractions from interest and focus that function for specialized accomplishments. They are not, however, the raw base of experience. The basis of human experience is feeling, an energy that is at the root of creativity and the power of purpose.

The problem of organizing the data of the new physics leads to the

174

generic notion of structure. Contemporary interest in structure stems from the problems of epistemology that arose when it was realized that sense perception could not envision the world in its elementary forms of energy. The human sees identities and objects, not processes of energy. This means that the human being cognitively structures the data he receives into a system that is relative to his senses and mode of conceptual organization. The determination of identity is not so much a fact of the environment since the environment provides only discrete data. Rather, identity occurs through the organizing capacity of the mind to structure that data. As cognitive psychologist Jerome Bruner remarks:

> The revolution of modern physics is as much as anything a revolution against naturalist realism in the name of a new nominalism. Do such categories as tomatoes, lions, snobs, atoms, and mammalie exist? In so far as they have been invented and found applicable to instances of nature they do. They exist as inventions and not discoveries.[1]

Cognitive psychology becomes the science of identifying structures relevant to environment stimuli, human equipment, and child development. Jean Piaget, for example, identifies not only the place of organized concepts in the development of the child, but also the steps in the organizational process. His most surprising discovery is that objects are not a given structure of infant experience, but something that is acquired and organized as the child learns to separate external events from his own events of egocentrism.

Structure involves the construction of categories from the world of events. In its most advanced stage, structure pertains to the organization of systems of thoughts, theories that guide human endeavors. Man is a generalizing creature. He requires theories in order that he may know how to approach and identify material from research and scholarly endeavor. Raw data without the cognitive system of organization give him no direction in proceeding, no point of reference for integrating the material. Man requires a system of theoretical structure in order to make use of the stimuli he receives from the environment.

Civilizations have developed intellectually as a result of the theories that organize culture and promote the sciences. No great society has existed without them. Such theories provide guidance in all intellectual matters. They are proposed speculatively from the insights provided by new discoveries or derived from general experience, then pursued deductively in order to confirm them and put them to practical use. They explain what is known and direct anticipation. But theories of this type are merely cognitive structures, not actual systems of nature. Thus they cannot exist indefinitely. New theories must replace old ones not because

[1] Jerome S. Bruner, Jacqueline J. Goodnow, and George A. Austin, *A Study of Thinking* (New York: Wiley, 1956), p. 7.

the old theories are proved wrong, but because they no longer explain adequately a growing body of data.

The place of the theoretical outlook in the total man is stated by Albert Einstein:

> Man tries to make for himself in the fashion that suits him best a simplified and intelligible picture of the world; he then tries to some extent to substitute this cosmos of his for the world of experience, and thus to overcome it. This is what the painter, the poet, the speculative philosopher and the natural scientist do, each in his own fashion. He makes this cosmos and its construction the pivot of his emotional life, in order to find in this way the peace and security which he cannot find in the narrow whirlpool of personal experience.[2]

Educational practices that derive from the Process-Structure Philosophy thought pattern reflect its basic themes. Proponents of Process-Structure Philosophy emphasize creativity and structure. However, by creativity they do not mean the operationally defined "divergent thinking" that can be identified by tests and that can be enhanced through education. On the contrary, they believe that creativity is the principle related to human life itself, something that is basic to all experience but never completely understood or controlled. Somehow it rests in feeling, emotion, and insight, and the term "creativity" is merely a designation for something that exists in all individuals in varying degrees. One does not educate directly for creativity. Rather, one educates for a type of definiteness; that is, one provides intellectual conditions that allow for personal identity of direction and thought. To stimulate creativity, the educator can only furnish suggestive cognitive materials, an environment condusive to the exercise of imagination, and opportunities for discovery.

Structure, the second theme of the Process-Structure thought pattern, is the foundation of creativity. There can be no creativity without some kind of structure. Suggestiveness, imagination, and discovery will only evolve out of some form of definiteness. Hence, Alfred North Whitehead remarks that there can be no creative impulse without the sense of importance and definite selections of matter of fact, while Jerome Bruner indicates that a well-prepared mind is necessary for discovery. Don't teach too many subjects, but teach thoroughly those you do teach is Whitehead's maxim for educational definiteness.

Definiteness in cognition is structure, the organization of materials around prominent ideas and relationships. Because structure, unlike creativity, can be taught, teaching must emphasize this component. The teaching of structure centers upon two basic types of subject matter, systems of notation and general ideas. Systems of notation are man's

---

[2] Albert Einstein, "Principles of Research," in *Essays in Science,* Alan Harris (tr.). (New York: Philosophical Library, 1934), pp. 2, 3.

written languages. The first written language is based on words, which are symbolic representations of actions, things, and attributes. This system of notation provides a means for coding and recoding information in a representational system. The goal of education is not merely to permit the student to acquire new and useful words, but to teach him to utilize and understand the representational system, its structure, its grammar, its forms. The second written language is that of mathematics, which symbolically represents relationships and patterns rather than events and objects. Learning the structure of mathematics involves understanding and using its basic concepts: sets, equality, more than and less than, numeration, place value, commutative property, associative property, distributive property, and so on.

The second basic type of subject matter involved in teaching structure is that of general ideas. General ideas are the great organizing notions of civilization—its sciences and humanistic fields. General ideas originate from human feeling of importance and human points of view about the nature of man, society, and destiny. Two dimensions of general ideas must be found in the curriculum. First, the curriculum must contain past general ideas. History is the key to all knowledge, scientific or humanistic, and past general ideas are the basis for understanding history. Students must study the history of science, music, art, and literature in order to discover the general ideas of different historical periods. Present general ideas must also form a significant part of the curriculum. General ideas of modern cultures in various parts of the world are important because they aid the student in understanding the present, which is necessary for world community and cooperation. Students must also gain some insight into the general ideas of their own culture. Such ideas, however, can be understood only by looking philosophically and deeply at that culture. This in-depth study requires a careful examination of the presuppositions of modern technology and science, as well as an attempt to discern the myths of modern culture through literature. Achievement in recognizing general ideas leads to understanding, and this in turn provides wisdom for functioning intelligently in the modern world. The motivating feeling behind such curriculum requirements is that learning should involve excitement and adventure with ideas.

Certain pedagogical notions arise from the Process-Structure thought pattern. The most important of these is the "eureka" notion, which indicates the error of the traditional assumption that education must begin with the simple and proceed through sequential steps to the complex. Because those who adhere to the Process-Structure thought pattern stress the primacy of process and structure in education, they believe that acquisition of the complexities of generalization must often come first. Applied to educational practice, this notion means that the teacher must strive for the student's insightful recognition of structure—

an all-at-once vision of a basic idea or principle—with the acquisition of details and relationships occurring most likely after this has taken place. Preparation, of course, is necessary in order to achieve such insight, but it is a preparation for the anticipation of a key notion rather than a step by step analysis of simple facts. The spiral curriculum suggested by Bruner allows and uses this type of educative experience.

Another pedagogical notion deriving from the Process-Structure thought pattern is the respect for both general and special education. General education is necessary because it provides broad cultural understanding and the place of individual interpretation in it. Special education, on the other hand, involves the study of general principles and their application within a particular specialized field. It aims at coordinating both the special and general elements of education so that the end product is a specialist who excels in one phase of life, but is able to relate his specialty to the general ideas of his time.

PEDAGOGICAL ORIENTATION

The Aims of Education   /   ALFRED NORTH WHITEHEAD

Culture is activity of thought, and receptiveness to beauty and humane feeling. Scraps of information have nothing to do with it. A merely well-informed man is the most useless bore on God's earth. What we should aim at producing is men who possess both culture and expert knowledge in some special direction. Their expert knowledge will give them the ground to start from, and their culture will lead them as deep as philosophy and as high as art. We have to remember that the valuable intellectual development is self-development, and that it mostly takes place between the ages of sixteen and thirty. As to training, the most important part is given by mothers before the age of twelve. A saying due to Archbishop Temple illustrates my meaning. Surprise was expressed at the success in after-life of a man, who as a boy at Rugby had been somewhat undistinguished. He answered, "It is not what they are at eighteen, it is what they become afterwards that matters."

In training a child to activity of thought, above all things we must beware of what I will call "inert ideas"—that is to say, ideas that are merely received into the mind without being utilised, or tested, or thrown into fresh combinations.

In the history of education, the most striking phenomenon is that schools of learning, which at one epoch are alive with a ferment of genius, in a succeeding generation exhibit merely pedantry and routine. The reason is, that they are overladen with inert ideas. Education with inert ideas is not only useless: it is, above all things, harmful—*Corruptio optimi, pessima*. Except at rare intervals of intellectual ferment, education in the past has been radically infected with inert ideas. That is the reason why uneducated clever women, who have seen much of the world, are in middle life so much the most cultured part of the community. They have been saved from this horrible burden of inert ideas. Every intellectual revolution which has ever stirred humanity into greatness has been a passionate protest against inert ideas. Then, alas, with pathetic ignorance of human psychology, it has proceeded by some educational scheme to bind humanity afresh with inert ideas of its own fashioning.

Let us now ask how in our system of education we are to guard against this mental dryrot. We enunciate two educational commandments, "Do not teach too many subjects," and again, "What you teach, teach thoroughly."

The result of teaching small parts of a large number of subjects is the passive reception of disconnected ideas, not illumined with any spark of vitality. Let the main ideas which are introduced into a child's education be few and important, and let them be thrown into every combination possible. The child should make them his own, and should understand their application here and now in the circumstances of his actual life. From the very beginning of his education, the child should experience the joy of discovery. The discovery which he has to make, is that general ideas give an understanding of that stream of events which pours through his life, which is his life. By understanding I mean more than a mere logical analysis, though that is included. I mean "understanding" in the sense in which it is used in the French proverb, "To understand all, is to forgive all." Pedants sneer at an education which is useful. But if education is not useful, what is it? Is it a talent, to be hidden away in a napkin? Of course, education should be useful, whatever your aim in life. It was useful to Saint Augustine and it was useful to Napoleon. It is useful, because understanding is useful.

I pass lightly over that understanding which should be given by the literary side of education. Nor do I wish to be supposed to pronounce on the relative merits of a classical or a modern curriculum. I would only remark that the understanding which we want is an understanding of an insistent present. The only use of a knowledge of the past is to equip us for the present. No more deadly harm can be done to young minds than by depreciation of the present. The present contains all that there is. It is holy ground; for it is the past, and it is the future. At the same time it must be observed that an age is no less past if it existed two hundred years ago than if it existed two thousand years ago. Do not be deceived by the pedantry of dates. The ages of Shakespeare and of Molière are no less past than are the ages of Sophocles and of Virgil. The communion of saints is a great and inspiring assemblage, but it has only one possible hall of meeting, and that is, the present; and the mere lapse of time through which any particular group of saints must travel to reach that meeting-place, makes very little difference.

Passing now to the scientific and logical side of education, we remember that here also ideas which are not utilised are positively harmful. By utilising an idea, I mean relating it to that stream, compounded of sense perceptions, feelings, hopes, desires, and of mental activities adjusting thought to thought, which forms our life. I can imagine a set of beings which might fortify their souls by passively reviewing disconnected ideas. Humanity is not built that way—except perhaps some editors of newspapers.

In scientific training, the first thing to do with an idea is to prove it. But allow me for one moment to extend the meaning of "prove"; I mean —to prove its worth. Now an idea is not worth much unless the propositions in which it is embodied are true. Accordingly an essential part of the proof of an idea is the proof, either by experiment or by logic, of the truth of the propositions. But it is not essential that this proof of the truth should constitute the first introduction to the idea. After all, its assertion by the authority of respectable teachers is sufficient evidence to begin with. In our first contact with a set of propositions, we commence by appreciating their importance. That is what we all do in after-life. We do not attempt, in the strict sense, to prove or to disprove anything, unless its importance makes it worthy of that honour. These two processes of proof, in the narrow sense, and of appreciation, do not require a rigid separation in time. Both can be proceeded with nearly concurrently. But in so far as either process must have the priority, it should be that of appreciation by use.

Furthermore, we should not endeavour to use propositions in isolation. Emphatically I do not mean, a neat little set of experiments to illustrate Proposition I and then the proof of Proposition I, a neat little set of experiments to illustrate Proposition II and then the proof of Proposition II, and so on to the end of the book. Nothing could be more boring. Interrelated truths are utilised *en bloc,* and the various propositions are employed in any order, and with any reiteration. Choose some important applications of your theoretical subject; and study them concurrently with the systematic theoretical exposition. Keep the theoretical exposition short and simple, but let it be strict and rigid so far as it goes. It should not be too long for it to be easily known with thoroughness and accuracy. The consequences of a plethora of half-digested theoretical knowledge are deplorable. Also the theory should not be muddled up with the practice. The child should have no doubt when it is proving and when it is utilising. My point is that what is proved should be utilised, and that what is utilised should—so far as is practicable—be proved. I am far from asserting that proof and utilisation are the same thing.

At this point of my discourse, I can most directly carry forward my argument in the outward form of a digression. We are only just realising that the art and science of education require a genius and a study of their own; and that this genius and this science are more than a bare knowledge of some branch of science or of literature. This truth was partially perceived in the past generation; and headmasters, somewhat crudely, were apt to supersede learning in their colleagues by requiring left-hand bowling and a taste for football. But culture is more than cricket, and more than football, and more than extent of knowledge.

Education is the acquisition of the art of the utilisation of knowledge. This is an art very difficult to impart. Whenever a text-book is written of real educational worth, you may be quite certain that some reviewer will say that it will be difficult to teach from it. Of course it will be difficult to teach from it. If it were easy, the book ought to be burned; for it cannot be educational. In education, as elsewhere, the broad primrose path leads to a nasty place. This evil path is represented by a book or a set of lectures which will practically enable the student to learn by heart all the questions likely to be asked at the next external examination. And I may say in passing that no educational system is possible unless every question directly asked of a pupil at any examination is either framed or modified by the actual teacher of that pupil in that subject. The external assessor may report on the curriculum or on the performance of the pupils, but never should be allowed to ask the pupil a question which has not been strictly supervised by the actual teacher, or at least inspired by a long conference with him. There are a few exceptions to this rule, but they are exceptions, and could easily be allowed for under the general rule.

We now return to my previous point, that theoretical ideas should always find important applications within the pupil's curriculum. This is not an easy doctrine to apply, but a very hard one. It contains within itself the problem of keeping knowledge alive, of preventing it from becoming inert, which is the central problem of all education.

The best procedure will depend on several factors, none of which can be neglected, namely, the genius not denounce it because we are cranks, and like denouncing established things. We are not so childish. Also, of course, such examinations have their use in testing slackness. Our reason of dislike is very definite and very practical. It kills the best part of culture. When you analyse in the light of experience the central task of education, you find that its successful accomplishment depends on a delicate adjustment of many variable factors. The reason is that we are dealing with human minds, and not with dead matter. The evocation of curiosity, of judgment, of the power of mastering a complicated tangle of circumstances, the use of theory in giving foresight in special cases—all these powers are not to be imparted by a set rule embodied in one schedule of examination subjects.

I appeal to you, as practical teachers. With good discipline, it is always possible to pump into the minds of a class a certain quantity of inert knowledge. You take a text-book and make them learn it. So far, so good. The child then knows how to solve a quadratic equation. But what is the point of teaching a child to solve a quadratic equation? There is a traditional answer to this question. It runs thus: The mind is an instrument, you of the teacher, the intellectual type of the pupils, their prospects in life, the opportunities offered by the immediate surroundings of the school, and allied factors of this sort. It is for this reason that the uniform external examination is so deadly. We do first sharpen it, and then use it; the acquisition of the power of solving a quadratic equation is part of the process of sharpening the mind. Now there is just enough truth in this answer to have made it live through the ages. But for all its half-truth, it embodies a radical error which bids fair to stifle the genius of the modern world. I do not know who was first responsible for this analogy of the mind to a dead instrument. For aught I know, it may have been one of the seven wise men of Greece, or a committee of the whole lot of them. Whoever was the originator, there can be no doubt of the authority which it has acquired by the continuous approval bestowed upon it by eminent persons. But whatever its weight of authority, whatever the high approval which it can quote, I have no hesitation in denouncing it as one of the most fatal, erroneous, and dangerous conceptions ever introduced into the theory of education. The mind is never passive; it is a perpetual activity, delicate, receptive, responsive to stimulus. You cannot postpone its life until you have sharpened it. Whatever interest attaches to your subject-matter must be evoked here and now; whatever powers you are strengthening in the pupil, must be exercised here and now; whatever possibilities of mental life your teaching should impart, must be exhibited here and now. That is the golden rule of education, and a very difficult rule to follow.

The difficulty is just this: the apprehension of general ideas, intellectual habits of mind, and pleasurable interest in mental achievement can be evoked by no form of words, however accurately adjusted. All practical teachers know that education is a patient process of the mastery of details, minute by minute, hour by hour, day by day. There is no royal road to learning through an airy path of brilliant generalisations. There is a proverb about the difficulty of seeing the wood because of the trees. That difficulty is exactly the point which I am enforcing. The problem of education is to make the pupil see the wood by means of the trees.

The solution which I am urging, is to eradicate the fatal disconnection of subjects which kills the vitality of our modern curriculum. There is only one subject-matter for education, and that is Life in all its manifestations. Instead of this single unity, we offer children—Algebra, from which nothing follows; Geometry, from which nothing follows; Science, from which nothing follows; History, from which nothing follows; a Couple of Languages, never mastered; and lastly, most dreary of all, Literature, represented by plays of Shakespeare, with philological notes and short analyses of plot and character to be in substance committed to memory. Can such a list be said to represent Life, as it is known in the midst of the living of it? The best that can be said of it is, that it is a rapid table of contents which a deity might run over in his mind while he was thinking of creating a world, and had not yet determined how to put it together.

Let us now return to quadratic equations. We still have on hand the unanswered question. Why should children be taught their solution? Unless quadratic equations fit into a connected curriculum, of course there is no reason to teach anything about them. Furthermore, extensive as should be the place of mathematics in a complete culture, I am a little doubtful whether for many types of boys algebraic solutions of quadratic equations do not lie on the specialist side of mathematics. I may here remind you that as yet I have not said anything of the psychology or the content of the specialism, which is so necessary a part of an ideal education. But all that is an evasion of our real question, and I merely state it in order to avoid being misunderstood in my answer.

Quadratic equations are part of algebra, and algebra is the intellectual instrument which has been created for rendering clear the quantitative aspects of the world. There is no getting out of it. Through and through the world is infected with quantity. To talk sense, is to talk in quantities. It is no use saying that the nation is large,—How large? It is no use saying that radium is scarce,—How scarce? You cannot evade quantity. You may fly to poetry and to music, and quantity and number will face you in your rhythms and your octaves. Elegant intellects which despise the theory of quantity, are but half developed. They are more to be pitied than blamed. The scraps of gibberish, which in their school-days were taught to them in the name of algebra, deserve some contempt.

This question of the degeneration of algebra into gibberish, both in word and in fact, affords a pathetic instance of the uselessness of reforming educational schedules without a clear conception of the attributes which you wish to evoke in the living minds of the children. A few years ago there was an outcry that school algebra was in need of reform, but there was a general agreement that graphs would put everything right. So all sorts of things were extruded, and graphs were introduced. So far as I can see, with no sort of idea behind them, but just graphs.

Now every examination paper has one or two questions on graphs. Personally, I am an enthusiastic adherent of graphs. But I wonder whether as yet we have gained very much. You cannot put life into any schedule of general education unless you succeed in exhibiting its relation to some essential characteristic of all intelligent or emotional perception. It is a hard saying, but it is true; and I do not see how to make it any easier. In making these little formal alterations you are beaten by the very nature of things. You are pitted against too skilful an adversary, who will see to it that the pea is always under the other thimble.

Reformation must begin at the other end. First, you must make up your mind as to those quantitative aspects of the world which are simple enough to be introduced into general education; then a schedule of algebra should be framed which will about find its exemplification in these applications. We need not fear for our pet graphs, they will be there in plenty when we once begin to treat algebra as a serious means of studying the world. Some of the simplest applications will be found in the quantities which occur in the simplest study of society. The curves of history are more vivid and more informing than the dry catalogues of names and dates which comprise the greater part of that arid school study. What purpose is effected by a catalogue of undistinguished kings and queens? Tom, Dick, or Harry, they are all dead. General resurrections are failures, and are better postponed. The quantitative flux of the forces of modern society is capable of very simple exhibition. Meanwhile, the idea of the variable, of the function, of rate of change, of equations and their solution, of elimination, are being studied as an abstract science for their own sake. Not, of course, in the pompous phrases with which I am alluding to them here, but with that iteration of simple special cases proper to teaching.

If this course be followed, the route from Chaucer to the Black Death, from the Black Death to modern Labour troubles, will connect the tales of the mediæval pilgrims with the abstract science of algebra, both yielding diverse aspects of that single theme, Life. I know what most of you are thinking at this point. It is that the exact course which I have sketched out is not the particular one which you would have chosen, or even see how to work. I quite agree. I am not claiming that I could do it myself. But your objection is the precise reason why a common external examination system is fatal to education. The process of exhibiting the applications of knowledge must, for its success, essentially depend on the character of the pupils and the genius of the teacher. Of course I have left out the easiest applications with which most of us are more at home. I mean the quantitative sides of sciences, such as mechanics and physics.

Again, in the same connection we plot the statistics of social phenomena against the time. We then eliminate the time between suitable pairs. We can speculate how far we have exhibited a real causal connection, or how far a mere temporal coincidence. We notice that we might have plotted against the time one set of statistics for one country and another set for another country, and thus, with suitable choice of subjects, have obtained graphs which certainly exhibited mere coincidence. Also other graphs exhibit obvious causal connections. We wonder how to discriminate. And so are drawn on as far as we will.

But in considering this description, I must beg you to remember what I have been insisting on above. In the first place, one train of thought will not suit all groups of children. For example, I should expect that artisan children will want something more concrete and, in a sense, swifter than I have set down here. Perhaps I am wrong, but that is what I should guess. In the second place, I am not contemplating one beautiful lecture stimulating, once and for all, an admiring class. That is not the way in which education proceeds. No; all the time the pupils are hard at work solving examples, drawing graphs, and making experiments, until they have a thorough hold on the whole subject. I am describing the interspersed explanations, the directions which should be given to their thoughts. The pupils have got to be made to feel that they are studying something, and are not merely executing intellectual minuets.

Finally, if you are teaching pupils for some general examination, the problem of sound teaching is greatly complicated. Have you ever noticed the zig-zag moulding round a Norman arch? The ancient work is beautiful, the modern work is hideous. The reason is, that the modern work is done to exact measure, the ancient work is varied according to the idiosyncrasy of the workman. Here it is crowded, and there it is expanded. Now the essence of getting pupils through examinations is to give equal weight to all parts of the schedule. But mankind is naturally specialist. One man sees a whole subject, where another can find only a few detached examples. I know that it seems contradictory to allow for specialism in a curriculum especially designed for a broad culture. Without contradictions the world would be simpler, and perhaps duller. But I am certain that in education wherever you exclude specialism you destroy life.

We now come to the other great branch of a general mathematical education, namely Geometry. The same principles apply. The theoretical part should be clear-cut, rigid, short, and important. Every proposition not absolutely necessary to exhibit the main connection of ideas should be cut out, but the great fundamental ideas should be all there. No omission of concepts, such as those of Similarity and Proportion. We must remember that, owing to the aid rendered by the visual presence of a figure, Geometry is a field of unequalled excellence for the exercise of the deductive faculties of reasoning. Then, of course, there follows Geometrical Drawing, with its training for the hand and eye.

But, like Algebra, Geometry and Geometrical Drawing must be extended beyond the mere circle of geometrical ideas. In an industrial neighbourhood, machinery and workshop practice form the appropriate extension. For example, in the London Polytechnics this has been achieved with conspicuous success. For many secondary schools I suggest that surveying and maps are the natural applications. In particular, plane-table surveying should lead pupils to a vivid apprehension of the immediate application of geometric truths. Simple drawing apparatus, a surveyor's chain, and a surveyor's compass, should enable the pupils to rise from the survey and mensuration of a field to the construction of the map of a small district. The best education is to be found in gaining the utmost information from the simplest apparatus. The provision of elaborate instruments is greatly to be deprecated. To have constructed the map of a small district, to have considered its roads, its contours, its geology, its climate, its relation to other districts, the effects on the status of its inhabitants, will teach more history and geography than any knowledge of Perkin Warbeck or of Behren's Straits. I mean not a nebulous lecture on the subject, but a serious investigation in which the real facts are definitely ascertained by the aid of accurate theoretical knowledge. A typical mathematical problem should be: Survey such and such a field, draw a plan of it to such and such a scale, and find the area. It would be quite a good procedure to impart the necessary geometrical propositions without their proofs. Then, concurrently in the same term, the proofs of the propositions would be learnt while the survey was being made.

Fortunately, the specialist side of education presents an easier problem than does the provision of a general culture. For this there are many reasons. One is that many of the principles of procedure to be observed are the same in both cases, and it is unnecessary to recapitulate. Another reason is that specialist training takes place—or should take place—at a more advanced stage of the pupil's course, and thus there is easier material to work upon. But undoubtedly the chief reason is that the specialist study is normally a study of peculiar interest to the student. He is studying it because, for some reason, he wants to know it. This makes all the difference. The general culture is designed to foster an activity of mind; the specialist course utilises this activity. But it does not do to lay too much stress on these neat antitheses. As we have already seen, in the general course foci of special interest will arise; and similarly in the special study, the external connections of the subject drag thought outwards.

Again, there is not one course of study which merely gives general culture, and another which gives special knowledge. The subjects pursued for the sake of a general education are special subjects specially studied; and, on the other hand, one of the ways of encouraging general mental activity is to foster a special devotion. You may not divide the seamless coat of learning. What education has to impart is an intimate sense for the power of ideas, for the beauty of ideas, and for the structure of ideas, together with a particular body of knowledge which has peculiar reference to the life of the being possessing it.

The appreciation of the structure of ideas is that side of a cultured mind which can only grow under the influence of a special study. I mean that eye for the whole chess-board, for the bearing of one set of ideas on another. Nothing but a special study can give any appreciation for the exact formulation of general ideas, for their relations when formulated, for their service in the comprehension of life. A mind so disciplined should be both more abstract and more concrete. It has been trained in the comprehension of abstract thought and in the analysis of facts.

Finally, there should grow the most austere of all mental qualities; I mean the sense for style. It is an æsthetic sense, based on admiration for the direct attainment of a foreseen end, simply and without waste. Style in art, style in literature, style in science, style in logic, style in practical execution have fundamentally the same æsthetic qualities, namely, attainment and restraint. The love of a subject in itself and for itself, where it is not the sleepy pleasure of pacing a mental quarter-deck, is the love of style as manifested in that study.

Here we are brought back to the position from which we started, the utility of education. Style, in its finest sense, is the last acquirement of the educated mind; it is also the most useful. It pervades the whole being. The administrator with a sense for style hates waste; the engineer with a sense for style economises his material; the artisan with a sense for style prefers good work. Style is the ultimate morality of mind.

But above style, and above knowledge, there is something, a vague shape like fate above the Greek gods. That something is Power. Style is the fashioning of power, the restraining of power. But, after all, the power of attainment of the desired end is fundamental. The first thing is to get there. Do not bother about your style, but solve your problem, justify the ways of God to man, administer your province, or do whatever else is set before you.

Where, then, does style help? In this, with style the end is attained without side issues, without raising undesirable inflammations. With style you attain your end and nothing but your end. With style the effect of your activity is calculable, and foresight is the last gift of gods to men. With style your power is increased, for your mind is not distracted with irrelevancies, and you are more likely to attain your object. Now style is the exclusive privilege of the expert. Whoever heard of the style of an amateur painter, of the style of an amateur poet? Style is always the product of specialist study, the peculiar contribution of specialism to culture.

English education in its present phase suffers from a lack of definite aim, and from an external machinery which kills its vitality. Hitherto in this address I have been considering the aims which should govern education. In this respect England halts between two opinions. It has not decided whether to produce amateurs or experts. The profound change in the world which the nineteenth century has produced is that the growth of knowledge has given foresight. The amateur is essentially a man with appreciation and with immense versatility in mastering a given routine. But he lacks the foresight which comes from special knowledge. The object of this address is to suggest how to produce the expert without loss of the essential virtues of the amateur. The machinery of our secondary education is rigid where it should be yielding, and lax where it should be rigid. Every school is bound on pain of extinction to train its boys for a small set of definite examinations. No headmaster has a free hand to develop his general education or his specialist studies in accordance with the opportunities of his school, which are created by its staff, its environment, its class of boys, and its endowments. I suggest that no system of external tests which aims primarily at examining individual scholars can result in anything but educational waste.

Primarily it is the schools and not the scholars which should be inspected. Each school should grant its own leaving certificates, based on its own curriculum. The standards of these schools should be sampled and corrected. But the first requisite for educational reform is the school as a unit, with its approved curriculum based on its own needs, and evolved by its own staff. If we fail to secure that, we simply fall from one formalism into another, from one dung-hill of inert ideas into another.

In stating that the school is the true educational unit in any national system for the safeguarding of efficiency, I have conceived the alternative system as being the external examination of the individual scholar. But every Scylla is faced by its Charybdis—or, in more homely language, there is a ditch on both sides of the road. It will be equally fatal to education if we fall into the hands of a supervising department which is under the impression that it can divide all schools into two or three rigid categories, each type being forced to adopt a rigid curriculum. When I say that the school is the educational unit, I mean exactly what I say, no larger unit, no smaller unit. Each school must have the claim to be considered in relation to its special circumstances. The classifying of schools for some purposes is necessary. But no absolutely rigid curriculum, not modified by its own staff, should be permissible. Exactly the same principles apply, with the proper modifications, to universities and to technical colleges.

When one considers in its length and in its breadth the importance of this question of the education of a nation's young, the broken lives, the defeated hopes, the national failures, which result from the frivolous inertia with which it is treated, it is difficult to restrain within oneself a savage rage. In the conditions of modern life the rule is absolute, the race which does not value trained intelligence is doomed. Not all your heroism, not all your social charm, not all your wit, not all your victories on land or at sea, can move back the finger of fate. To-day we maintain ourselves. To-morrow science will have moved forward yet one more step, and there will be no appeal from the judgment which will then be pronounced on the uneducated.

We can be content with no less than the old summary of educational ideal which has been current at any time from the dawn of our civilisation. The essence of education is that it be religious.

Pray, what is religious education?

A religious education is an education which inculcates duty and reverence. Duty arises from our potential control over the course of events. Where attainable knowledge could have changed the issue, ignorance has the guilt of vice. And the foundation of reverence is this perception, that the present holds within itself the complete sum of existence, backwards and forwards, that whole amplitude of time, which is eternity.

PSYCHOLOGICAL DIMENSION

The Perfectibility of Intellect / JEROME S. BRUNER

I shall concern myself in what follows with the vexed problem of the perfectibility of man's intellect. Let me consider the matter in the light of four constraints on the exercise of intellect. The first is the nature of knowing itself, as we observe it in intact human beings attempting to gain knowledge. The second derives from the evolution of intellect in primates, including man. The third constraint is imposed by the growth of intellect from childhood to such perfection as man may reach. The fourth has to do with the nature of knowledge as it becomes codified and organized in the society of learned men. It is too broad a task I have set for myself, but unavoidably so, for the question before us suffers distortion if its perspective is reduced. Better to risk the dangers of a rough sketch.

Let me confess that I, indeed any student of human intellect, can hardly pretend that what I say of the reach and range of human intellect is innocent of social, political, and moral consequences. For however one poses the problem whatever one finds must inevitably affect or at least question our conception of what is humanly possible in the cultivation of mind. The issue of the perfectibility of intellect stirs passionate debate. Beware those who urge that the debate is without purpose, that the results of scientific inquiry carry self-evident implications with them. For it is a debate that requires continual renewal lest our educational enterprise fail to fulfill its function either as an agency for empowering human minds or as a reflector of the values of the culture. What the student of human intellect can do is to refresh the debate with estimates of what is possible and estimates of what is the cost of the possible.

Consider first the nature of human intellect as we understand it after a half century of investigation—investigation often more orderly than startling, but yet of a nature that yields a steady knowledge. In most recent years, the quest has yielded more surprising turns as we have undertaken the job of forging compatible links between man's intellect and the computers that are its servants.

Perhaps the most pervasive feature of human intellect is its limited capacity at any moment for dealing with information. There is a rule that states that we have about seven slots, plus or minus two, through which the external world can find translation into experience. We easily become overwhelmed by complexity or clutter. Cognitive mastery in a world that generates stimuli far faster than we can sort them depends upon strategies for reducing the complexity and the clutter. But reduction must be selective, attuned to the things that "matter." Some of the modes of reduction require, seemingly, no learning—as with our adaptation mechanisms. What does not change ceases to register: steady states in their very nature cease to stimulate. Stabilize the image on the retina by getting rid of fine tremor, and the visual world fades away. There is another type of selectivity that reflects man's deepest intellectual trait and is heavily dependent on learning. Man constructs models of his world, not only templates that represent what he encounters and in what context, but also ones that permit him to be beyond them. He learns the world in a way that enables him to make predictions of what comes next by matching a few milliseconds of what is now experienced to a stored model and reading the rest from the model. We see a contour and a snatch of movement. "Ah yes, that's the night watchman checking the windows . . ." Or a patient sits before a physician complaining that vision in one eye is unaccountably dim. Both doctor and patient are involved in kindred activities. If the doctor diagnoses a scotoma, a deadened area on the retina, he does so by a process analogous to the process that leads the patient not to see a "hole" in his visual field, but a dimming, for the victim of a scotoma completes the hole by extrapolating what the rest of the eye is taking in. It is in the nature of the selectivity governed by these models that we come increasingly to register easily on those things in the world that we expect; indeed we assume that the expected is there on the basis of a minimum of information. There is compelling evidence that so long as the environment conforms to the expected patterns within reasonable limits, alerting mechanisms in the brain are quietened. But once expectancy is violated, once the world ceases strikingly to correspond to our models of it (and it must be rather striking, for we ride roughshod over minor deviations), then all the alarms go off and we are at full alertness, thanks to our neural reticular system. So man can not only deal with information before him, but go far beyond the information given—with all that this implies both for swiftness of intellect and for fallibility. Almost by definition, the exercise of intellect, involving as it must the use of short cuts and of leaps from partial evidence, always courts the possibility of error. It is the good fortune of our species that not only are we also highly adept at correction (given sufficient freedom from time pressure), but have learned to institutionalize ways of keeping error within tolerable limits.

The models or stored theories of the world that are so useful in inference are strikingly generic and reflect man's ubiquitous tendency to categorize. William James remarked that the life of mind began when the child is first able to proclaim, "Aha, thingumbob again." We organize experience to represent not only the particulars that have been experienced, but the classes of events of which the particulars are exemplars. We go not only from part to whole, but irresistibly from the particular to the general. At least one distinguished linguist has argued in recent times that this generic tendency of human intellect must be innately human, for without it one could not master the complex web of categorial or substitution rules that constitutes the syntax of language—any language. Both in achieving the economy with which human thought represents the world and in effecting swift correction for error, the categorizing tendency of intelligence is central—for it yields a structure of thought that becomes hierarchically organized with growth, forming branching structures in which it is relatively easy to search for alternatives. The blunders occur, of course, where things that must be together for action or for understanding happen to be organized in different hierarchies. It is a form of error that is as familiar in science as in everyday life.

I do not mean to imply, of course, that man structures his knowledge of the world only by the categorial rules of inclusion, exclusion, and overlap, for clearly he traffics in far greater complexity, too. Witness the almost irresistible urge to see cause and effect. Rather, the categorial nature of thought underlines its rule-bound nature. The eighteenth-century assumption that knowledge grows by a gradual accretion of associations built up by contact with events that are contiguous in time, space, or quality does not fit the facts of mental life. There are spheres where such associative laws operate within limits, as for example with material that is strange and meaningless (the psychologist's nonsense syllables, for example), but for the most part organization is a far more active process of imposing order as by forming a hypothesis and then checking it to be sure.

In the main, we do the greater part of our work by manipulating our representations or models of reality rather than by acting directly on the world itself. Thought is then vicarious action, in which the high cost of error is strikingly reduced. It is characteristic of human beings and no other species that we can carry out this vicarious action with the aid of a large number of intellectual prosthetic devices that are, so to speak, tools provided by the culture. Natural language is the prime example, but there are pictorial and diagrammatic conventions as well, theories, myths, modes of reckoning and ordering. We are even able to employ devices to fulfill functions not given man through evolution, devices that bring phenomena into the human range of registering and computing: phenomena too slow to follow or too fast, too small or too large, too numerous or too few. Today, indeed we develop devices to determine whether the events we watch conform to or deviate from expectancy in comprehensible ways. My colleague George Miller put it well, speaking about computers in his Granada Lecture in 1965: "Mechanical intelligence will not ultimately replace human intelligence, but rather, by complementing our human intelligence, will supplement and amplify it. We will learn to supply by mechanical organs those functions that natural evolution has failed to provide." [1]

The range of man's intellect, given its power to be increased from the outside in, can never be estimated without considering the means a culture provides for empowering mind. Man's intellect then is not simply his own, but is communal in the sense that its unlocking or empowering depends upon the success of the culture in developing means to that end. There is a sense in which, as Professor Lévi-Strauss has taught us, human intellect does not vary in power as a function of the means and technology available to it. For the use of amplifiers of mind requires, admittedly, a commonly shared human capacity, and each society fashions and perfects this capacity to its needs. But there is, I believe, a respect in which a lack of means for understanding one matter places out of reach other matters that are crucial to man's condition whatever his culture.

Let me add one final point before turning to the evolution of primate intelligence. Human beings have three different systems, partially translatable one into the other, for representing reality. One is through action. We know some things by knowing how to do them: to ride bicycles, tie knots, swim, and so on. A second way of knowing is through imagery and

---

[1] George A. Miller, "Computers, Communication, and Cognition," *Advancement of Science,* 21 (January 1965), 417–430.

those products of mind that, in effect, stop the action and summarize it in a representing ikon. While Napoleon could say that a general who thinks in images is not fit to command, it is still true that a thousand words scarcely exhaust the richness of a single image. Finally, there is representation by symbol, of which the typecase is language with its rules for forming sentences not only about what exists in experience but, by its powerful combinatorial techniques, for forming equally good ones about what might or might not exist. Each of these modes has its own skills, its own prosthetic aids, its own virtues and defects, and we shall encounter them again before we are done.

The evolution of primate intelligence is only now beginning to be understood. The evidence today is that the full evolution of human intelligence required for its movement the presence of bipedalism and tool use in early hominids. It is subsequent to these developments that we find a sharp increase in man's cranial capacity and in the size of his cerebral cortex. But the logic of the situation and indirect evidence argues that the development of tool using itself required some prior capacity, however minimal. I have recently observed a film shot in a natural park in East Africa in which a chimpanzee is using a straw, properly wetted in spittle, to insert into a termite hill to extract these insects. A baboon is watching. When his turn comes he tears the termite hill apart. Tool using of the kind found in early hominids is quite plainly a program in which tools are substituted for manual operations in much the same way that the carpenter can substitute a chisel for his forgotten plane, or a knife or even a saw blade. The evidence indicates that the change in tools used in East Africa after the first stabilization of a chopping tool was not very rapid. What was probably more important was the range of programs or activities into which this tool was substituted.

But having said that much, it is well to note that it was not a large-brained hominid that developed the technical-social way of life of the human, but rather the tool-using, cooperative pattern that gradually changed man's morphology by favoring the tool user over the heavy-jawed, smaller brained creature who depended upon his morphology alone. I have commented in passing upon the emergence of tools made to pattern, in contrast to spontaneous tools. It is at this point in human evolution, place it at some multiple of 10^5 years ago, that man comes to depend upon a culture and its technical pool in order to be able to fill his ecological niche. The biologist Peter Medawar comments in a recent Huxley Lecture that it is at about this point that human evolution becomes sufficiently elaborated to merit being called Lamarckian and reversible, rather than Darwinian and irreversible. For what is now being transmitted, over and beyond the human gene pool, is a set of acquired characteristics passed on in the cultural pool of a people. The reversibility, of course, is attested to by many splendid ruins, ruins manned by descendants with genes indistinguishable from their ancestors.

It is folly to speculate about the birth date of language. It seems likely, however, that the capacity that made possible the development of human language, the abstractive, rule-producing gift, must also have had something to do with the programmatic nature of tool using with its rules of substitution. It is not plain how we shall ever be able to reconstruct the matter.

One further feature of the evolution of intelligence relates to impulse control. We have had, in the past decade, several impressive overviews of the evolution of mammalian sexuality, from the familiar laboratory rat, through the ubiquitous macaque monkey, through the great apes, to man. The picture that emerges in the transition from lower mammals through primates is one of decreasing control by the hormonal system and an increasing part played by early experience through intervention of the cerebral cortex. Even before the emergence of higher apes, hominids, and early man, there was a striking increase in control of sexual activity by the central nervous system. With man and his ability to symbolize, the role of the central nervous system is further increased. For what is most striking in the change in sexuality from higher primates to humans is the emergence of what anthropologists speak of as classificatory kinship. In place of the sexual dominance and restricting territoriality of the higher apes, the human species seems early to have developed a pattern involving reciprocal exchange of women outward to neighboring groups, an exchange used in the formation of mutual alliances. The role of this more stable and reciprocal kinship pattern in the upbringing of young must now concern us.

Human beings have a more prolonged and dependent childhood than other primates. Present opinion concerning the origin of this condition is somewhat as follows. As hominids became increasingly bipedal, with the free hands necessary for tool using, there was not only an increase in the size of the brain, but also a requirement of a stronger pelvic girdle to withstand the impacting strain of upright walking. The increased strength of the pelvic girdle came through a gradual closing down of the birth canal, and an obstetrical paradox was produced: a larger brain, but a smaller birth canal for the neonate to pass through. The resolution seems to have been achieved through the cerebral immaturity of the human infant, not only permitting the newborn to pass through the reduced canal, but assuring a prolonged childhood during which the ways and skills of the culture could be transmitted. There are reasonable arguments to be advanced in favor of the view that the direction of evolution in the nervous system of primates from the lowly tree shrews through lemurs and tarsiers and monkeys on to the higher apes and man has been in the direction not only of more cerebral cortex and more tissue for the distance receptors, but also toward the evolutionary selection of immature forms. This tendency to neoteny, as it is called, is particularly notable in man, to the extent that the human brain more closely resembles the fetal brain of the gorilla in some respects than the adult brain of that great ape. And so, to take one index, the human brain is about a quarter of adult size at birth; in rhesus monkeys and gibbons, the job is about finished after six months. And so it is argued that human infancy with its more malleable dependency can be viewed as a prolongation of the fetal period of the earlier primates.

It is not simply the length and dependency of childhood that increases in man, but also the mode of raising young to the requirements of communal life. Let me describe very briefly some salient differences in the free learning patterns of immature baboons and the children of a hunting-gathering group in a roughly comparable ecology (the !Kung Bushmen). Baboons have a highly developed social life in their troops, with well-organized and stable dominance patterns. They live within a territory, protecting themselves from predators by joint action of the strongly built, adult males. It is striking that the behavior of baboon juveniles is shaped principally by play with their peer group, play that provides opportunity for the spontaneous expression and practice of the component acts that, in maturity, will be orchestrated into the behavior either of the dominant male or of the infant-protective female. All this seems to be accomplished with little participation by any mature animals in the play of the juveniles. We know from a variety of experiments how devastating a disruption in development can be produced in subhuman primates raised in a laboratory by interfering with their opportunity for peer-group play and social interaction.

Among hunting–gathering humans, on the other hand, there is *constant* interaction between adult and child, or adult and adolescent, or adolescent and child. !Kung adults and children play and dance together, sit together, participate in minor hunting together, join in song and story telling together. At very frequent intervals, moreover, children are party to rituals presided over by adults—minor, as in the first haircutting, or major, as when a boy kills his first kudu buck and goes through the proud but painful process of scarification. Children, besides, are constantly playing imitatively with the rituals, implements, tools, and weapons of the adult world. Young juvenile baboons, on the other hand, virtually never play with things or imitate directly large and significant sequences of adult behavior.

Note, however, that among the !Kung one virtually never sees an instance of "teaching" taking place outside the situation where the behavior to be learned is relevant. Nobody "teaches" in our prepared sense of the word. There is nothing like school, nothing like lessons.

Indeed, among the !Kung there is very little "telling." Most of what we would call instruction is through showing. In the end, everybody in the culture knows nearly all there is to know about how to get on with life as a man or as a woman.

The change in the instruction of children in more complex societies is twofold. First of all, there is knowledge and skill in the culture far in excess of what any one individual knows. And so increasingly there develops an economical technique of instructing the young based heavily on *telling* out of context rather than *showing* in context. The result of "teaching the culture" can, at its worst, lead to the ritual, rote nonsense that has led generations of critics to despair. But school imposes indirect demands that may be one of the most important departures from indigenous practice. It takes learning, as we have noted, out of the context of immediate action just by dint of putting it into a school. This very extirpation makes learning become an act in itself, freed from the immediate ends of action, preparing the learner for that form of reckoning that is remote from payoff and conducive to reflectiveness. In school, moreover, one must "follow the lesson," which means one must learn to follow either the abstraction of written speech—abstract in the sense that it is divorced from the concrete situation to which the speech might originally have been related—or the abstraction of language delivered orally but out of the context of an on-going action. Both of these are highly abstract uses of language.

It is no wonder, then, that many recent studies report large differences between "primitive" children who are in schools and their brothers who are not: differences in perception, abstraction, time perspective, and so on.

Let me now describe very briefly some of the major aspects of intellectual growth as we observe it in the growing child. The first and most general thing that can be said is that it does not flow smoothly, but rather in spurts of rapid growth followed by consolidation. The spurts in growth seem to be organized around the emergence of certain capacities, including intellectual capacities. These latter have about them the character of prerequisites: one thing must be mastered before the child can go on to the next. Many of them are directed to two ends: the maintenance of invariance and the transcending of momentaneousness in registration and response. Let me say a word about each.

By invariance, we mean the recognition of kinship and continuity in things that are transformed either in location or appearance or in the response they evoke. The child must first learn to distinguish that objects have a persistent identity beyond the identity endowed upon them by the action one takes toward them. He then learns that an object persists beyond one's visual or tactile contact with it so that out of sight is not out of mind and a new appearance is not a new thing. He must then travel the long road of decentration, as Piaget (who has taught us so much about mental development) calls it: being able to represent things not only from the egocentric axis, but from other vantage points, personally as well as geometrically. In time, the child moves (at least in our culture) from a representation of the world through action to a representation based very heavily upon the appearance of things. Water poured from a standard beaker into one that is longer and thinner is now said by the four-year-old to be more water because it is "taller than before." In time, the child recognizes that there is constancy across change in appearance. What he is doing in the process of mastering invariance is, of course, constructing increasingly stable models of the world, increasingly comprehensive ones capable of reducing the surface complexity of the world to the limits of his capacity for dealing with information. In good season, and always with help from the culture, the child develops models or modes of representation that are far more symbolic or linguistic in nature. The growth of invariance, then, takes place with the development of the enactive, ikonic, and symbolic representations we examined earlier. Students of the developmental process agree in broad outline about this progress, though the details and the terminology differ as one travels west from Moscow to Geneva to Paris to Cambridge to Denver to Berkeley.

With respect to transcending momentaneousness, let me illustrate by citing a child, age five, who said of the larger of two half-filled beakers that it was fuller than the other, a moment later that it was also emptier, and then a moment later in answer to a question that it could not be both fuller and emptier. He worked with a consistent logic and saw no contradiction. The logic was self-sufficient for each episode and the three in question were not put together to make possible the recognition of contradiction. The bigger glass was fuller because it appeared to have more water; the bigger was also emptier because it appeared to have more empty space; a vessel could not be both emptier and fuller because, to cite the product of the child's *Sprachgefühl*, "that's silly." Again, development provides models that permit the child to sense coherence over larger and larger segments of experience, time- and space-binding representations that permit wider ranges of connection.

Save in the artificial setting of the school, dominated as it is by telling and a lack of guiding feedback, there is an extraordinary property of self-reward about the act of learning during growth. The satisfaction of curiosity seems to be self-rewarding among all primates. So, too, the development of competence. More uniquely human, finally, is that mysterious process whereby human beings pattern themselves on another and gain satisfaction by maintaining the supposed standard of their model. The three self-rewarding processes provide a motor for growth that is stalled only by repeated failure or by an inability to determine how one is progressing at a task. This does not mean, of course, that what a child learns is what is most empowering of his capacities but, rather, what happens to be available. It is here that the innovation of school and teacher can be critically important.

Consider now the nature of codified knowledge as it might affect our views about the perfectibility of intellect. The past half century has surely been one of the richest as well as the most baffling in the history of our effort to understand the nature of knowledge. Advances in the foundation of mathematics and logic, in the philosophy of science, in the theory of information processing, in linguistics, and in psychology—all of these have led to new formulations and new conjectures.

Perhaps the greatest change, stemming principally from the revolutions in physics, is in our conception of what a theory is. For Newton, inquiry was a voyage on the sea of ignorance to find the islands of truth. We know now that theory is more than a general description of what happens or a statement of probabilities of what might or might not happen—even when it claims to be nothing more than that, as in some of the newer behavioral sciences. It entails, explicitly or implicitly, a model of what it is that one is theorizing about, a set of propositions that, taken in ensemble, yield occasional predictions about things. Armed with a theory, one is guided toward what one will treat as data, is predisposed to treat some data as more relevant than others. A theory is also a way of stating tersely what one already knows without the burden of detail. In this sense it is a canny and economical way of keeping in mind a vast amount while thinking about a very little.

Discussing the organization of thought, Whitehead remarks in *The Aims of Education*, "Mankind found itself in possession of certain concepts respecting nature—for example, the concept of fairly permanent material bodies—and proceeded to determine laws which related the corresponding percepts in nature. But the formulation of laws changed the concepts, sometimes gently by an added precision, sometimes violently. At first this process was not much noticed or at least was felt to be a process curbed within narrow bounds, not touching fundamental ideas. At the stage where we now are, the formulation of the concepts can be seen to be as important as the formulation of the empirical laws connecting the events in the universe as thus conceived by us."[2] What is perhaps most important about this way of viewing theory is the attitude it creates toward the use of mind. We now see the construction of theory as a way of using the mind, the imagination, of standing off from the activities of observation and inference and creating a shape of nature.

It can also be said of knowledge that, though it is constrained by the

[2] Alfred North Whitehead, *The Aims of Education and Other Essays* (New York: Macmillan, 1929).

very mode of its expression, it can be expressed in various modes. There is a continuity between knowing how to operate a seesaw, being able to describe a balance beam and cause it to balance with weights placed differentially on either side, knowing that three ounces six inches from the center of the balance will be equal to six ounces at three inches or two ounces at nine inches or eighteen ounces at one inch, and finally, knowing Newton's conception of moments. This partial isomorphism between more and less abstract ways of knowing something, though it gives the appearance of great obviousness, has implications that are all too easily overlooked.

Let me comment on a point that has preoccupied Dr. Oppenheimer: the connexity of knowledge. There is an implosion of knowledge just as there is an explosion. As observations have become more numerous, the ways in which they may be integrated and connected by powerful theories have also increased. Where the danger lies, of course, is in the possibility that fewer men will come to know the larger and more comprehensive domains to which such theories can be related. But there is reason to question such an eventuality. For it may be that the technologies now being devised for storing, relating, and retrieving information may change the very texture of the intellectual community. Crude though its present conception may be, the idea of a society of scholars connected to a data base through computational devices and programs that can quickly retrieve related information, suggests that we may have automatic servants and assistants vital to the pursuit of connection. We can begin to envisage ways of making knowledge less inert and discrete than it is now, when placed on the shelves of libraries or within the pages of our journals. What is required is a means of constantly rearranging and reordering knowledge in a fashion to reflect the theoretical advances and hypotheses current in the intellectual community that uses the knowledge.

The disciplines of learning represent not only codified knowledge but ways of thought, habits of mind, implicit assumptions, short cuts, and styles of humor that never achieve explicit statement. Concentrations of these ways of thought probably account for the phenomenal productivity in ideas and men of, say, the Cavendish Laboratory under Rutherford or Copenhagen under Bohr. For these ways of thought keep knowledge lively, keep the knower sensitive to opportunity and anomaly. I draw attention to this matter, for studies in the history of knowledge suggest that deadening and banalization are also characteristics of knowledge once it becomes codified.

I apologize for this headlong dash through the domain of cognition and, indeed, beg your forbearance for the major omissions, particularly one. I have concentrated on right-handed knowledge and given short shrift to the left hand—to the disciplines of art, of poetry, of history, of drama, and of metaphysics. Several implications follow from the account that I have given that bear not only upon the perfectibility of man's intellect, but also upon the process of its perfecting. Let me in conclusion, then, comment upon a few of these.

In speaking of the nature of intellectual functioning, its evolution, its growth, and its codified products, I have placed heavy emphasis upon the role of models or theories that human beings build to render the varieties of experience into some manageable and economical form. Man creates theories before he creates tools. His capacity and skill for catching the invariances of the world around him probably underlie not only his success as a tool user and tool maker, but also his use of that powerful instrument for expression and thought, human language. His myths, his art, his ritual, his sciences are all expressions of this deep-lying tendency to explicate and condense, to seek steady meaning in capricious experience.

Many scholars in this country and abroad have been involved this past decade in what has come popularly to be called the "curriculum revolution," the effort to start children younger and more effectively on the way to grasping the more powerful ideas embodied in the learned disciplines. And indeed it is a revolution in at least one obvious respect: the union of men at the frontiers of knowledge with those charged with instructing the young, the two working jointly on the conversion of learning into a form comprehensible and nutritious to the young. The effort is also recentering the work of psychologists and others concerned with the development of children, though we are only beginning to understand the means whereby intellectual development can be assisted. It is in this activity that I see a fresh approach to the perfectibility of intellect. Let me explain.

Once granted that a principal task of intellect is in the construction of explanatory models for the ordering of experience, the immediate problem then becomes one of converting the most powerful ways of knowing into a form that is within the grasp of a young learner. Let curriculum consist of a series of prerequisites in knowledge and in skill, to be mastered with an in-built reward in increased competence as the learner goes from one step to the next. Such a view assumes that for any knowledge or empowering skill that exists in the culture there is a corresponding form that is within the grasp of a young learner at the stage of development where one finds him—that any subject can be taught to anybody at any age in some form that is both interesting and honest. Once mastered in that appropriate form, the learner can go on to more powerful, more precise forms of knowing and of using knowledge. It is already reasonably clear that this can be done in mathematics and science—though we are very, very far from doing it well. But it is also the case that reading simpler poetry brings more complex poetry into reach, or that reading a poem once makes a second reading more rewarding.

The conception of a curriculum as an effort to go more deeply and more powerfully and more precisely into a body of knowledge before one risks traveling more widely carries with it a self-limiting but benign constraint. One must choose the subjects one teaches from domains of knowledge robust and deep enough to permit such revisits. But it is not so much the subject matter that is at issue. The more "elementary" a course and the younger its pupils, the more serious must be its pedagogical aim of forming the intellectual powers of those whom it serves. It is as important to justify a good mathematics course by the intellectual discipline it provides or the honesty it promotes as by the mathematics it transmits. It cannot do one without the other.

Invention is required if one is to proceed in this way. How convert knowledge into the form that is within the grasp of a learner, so that he may be tempted on? Recall the three modes of knowing characteristic of human cognitive operations—by action, by image, and by symbol. One approach to the task that has proved moderately successful is to begin a sequence of learning with an enactive representation—learning inertial physics by operating levers, learning music by composing and playing in a highly simplified musical notation, and so on. One goes beyond that to intuitive, image-laden forms, as with intuitive geometry or the kind of visual aids by which formal logic can be rendered in Venn diagrams, and finally to the increasingly abstract symbolic modes of a field of learning.

A more difficult task is to instill early in the learner what in effect is a balance between impatience with the trivial as proof against clutter and an open spirit toward what might be but is not obviously relevant. Here again, the experience of those who have worked on constructing curriculum suggests that one plunge right in. Short of that, it is difficult to accomplish anything. One starts concretely trying to give some feeling for the way of thought that is a discipline and one often succeeds. Again, it is as with musical instruction where one gives the learner the simplest possible Mozart rather than a scale so that as early as possible he may sense what music is.

Above all, what emerges from the past decade of experimenting with instruction is the importance of increasing the child's power of thought by inventing for him modes of access to the empowering techniques of the culture. The nature of a school as an instrument for doing this is very unclear. The perfecting of intellect begins earlier than we thought and goes communally from the outside in as well as growing from within. Perhaps the task of converting knowledge into a form fit for this function is, after all, the final step in our codification of knowledge. Perhaps the task is to go beyond the learned scholarship, scientific research, and the exercise of disciplined sensibility in the arts to the transmission of what we have discovered. Surely no culture will reach its full potential unless it invents ever better means for doing so.

SOCIAL CONCEPTS DIMENSION

Education for Intercultural Understanding /

F. S. C. NORTHROP

Education must fit men to understand and solve the inescapable problems of our time. Any consideration of the character of education, therefore, must begin with an analysis of these problems.

Even at the cost of becoming repetitious, it must none the less be reiterated that the most pressing problem centers in the atomic bomb. The presence of this bomb in our midst raises the question whether we will have any time to face the other pressing problems of our world. The next war will truly be a war to end all future wars, since it will be a war which ends all possible warriors.

Nevertheless, the atomic bomb itself is not the real danger. For the atomic bomb will not hurt civilization unless men direct it to such ends. This means that the problem centers not in scientific technology but in moral philosophy and the social sciences. It is the latter subjects which create social conceptions—economic, political, religious and philosophical—necessary to generate the social controls requisite for directing the use of scientific technology to constructive ends.

To note this, however, is to become aware that the problem confronting our world is even more serious than the presence of the atomic bomb might indicate. For when we turn to the economic, political, and religious doctrines defining the type of social organization which the different nations, peoples and cultures in the world deem good, we find not agreement but deep-rooted conflict. The Latin-American conception of the good society differs from the Anglo-American one; the American conception of appropriate economic and political organization differs from that of the Labor Government in Great Britain. The ideology of the democracies west of the Rhine differs from the communist ideal of economic democracy of Soviet Russia, and the traditional culture of the West has been at loggerheads with the traditional culture of the East.

"Education for Intercultural Understanding" is reprinted from F. S. C. Northrop, "Education for Intercultural Understanding," The Journal of Higher Education, Vol XVIII, No. 4 April 1947. Reprinted by permission from F. S. C. Northrop, the Princeton Bicentennial Committee, and The Journal of Higher Education. This chapter was first read in the Symposium on The University and its World Responsibilities on February 19, 1947, in connection with the Bicentennial Program of Princeton University.

Everywhere in the realm of ideals to which we must turn if we are to control the atomic bomb, we find basic disagreement and conflict rather than agreement and mutual trust.

Furthermore, these differences in the social ideals to be used in setting up the social controls necessary to direct atomic energy to constructive ends are Oriental as well as Occidental in their character and focus. It is no longer the case that war is likely to break out in a serious form only in Europe. The ideologies of the nationalistic nations of the West have now spread to Asia. Thus nationalistic wars of the Western type are as likely to start in Korea or Java or Northwest China or India as in the Balkans or in the Rhineland. Conversely, Oriental peoples and values are pressing upon the West for recognition in their own right. The Japanese, Chinese, Indians and Javanese are insistent upon bringing their political, economic, and traditional cultural weight to bear upon the West as well as to receive values from the West. This means that as time goes by, traditional Oriental ideological issues are more and more going to become Western issues also.

From these considerations certain conclusions follow immediately. An education which would fit men to meet the problems of the contemporary world must acquaint men not merely with Western civilization but with all the major civilizations of our world. Even within its treatment of Western civilization, it must do more than convey the economic, political, and religious doctrines of our particular culture and period in the Western world. This means, to be more specific, that a department of economics in any university cannot restrict itself to the economic science of Jevons and the Austrian School, rooted in pre-Kantian British empirical philosophy. It must also convey the theory of economics of Historismus, rooted in the historical philosophy of Hegel, and the labor theory of the economic science of Marx, rooted in Marxian dialectical materialism. Similarly, a department of religion must do more than merely convey one conception of religion, the theistic Western one, and within theism merely one type of theistic religion, namely Christianity, and within Christianity merely one form of that, namely, modern Protestantism or medieval Roman Catholicism.

What must be said with all the emphasis at one's disposal is that our very existence as human beings depends upon whether during the next ten or fifteen years we can learn to understand each other and resolve the ideological conflicts which divide us internationally. For this undertaking we must first thoroughly understand the differing cultures and their respective differing and often conflicting economic, political, and religious normative ideological theories. It is these theories which define what a specific culture regards as good and which prescribe the type of social organization to which it will agree in a conference of the United Nations. Consequently, if these conferences are ever to succeed, men in different parts of the world must receive an education which enables them to understand the other person's culture and ideology as well as their own, an education which gives a clear conception of the basic problem to which the conflicting ideologies are differing answers. Only if these basic problems, as thus clearly defined, are faced and then resolved, can a really constructive program for peace, grounded in understanding and knowledge rather than bickering and threats and verbal futile compromises, be achieved.

If this be accepted, a second question arises immediately. What character must the curriculum in our educational institutions take on? Obviously, everything which the sciences of anthropology and sociology tell us concerning the world's different cultures must be taught. This is obvious and axiomatic. Something more, however, is required. A culture is not merely the facts which an anthropologist observes by a careful use of the objective methods of science. It is also the concepts and theories by which these facts are understood by the people indigenous to this culture.

It is with respect to the concepts and theories in terms of which the people of a given culture themselves understand their own empirically present cultural practices and institutions that contemporary anthropology and sociology are weak. This, moreover, is a serious weakness so far as the present situation in our world is concerned. For the failure of peoples from different nations and cultures to agree on social controls to avoid the present dangers, centers not in the fact that their empirical practices and institutions are different, but centers instead, in considerable part, in a difference in the normative theories from the standpoint of which they judge their own and all other empirical social institutions. Thus the normative theories indigenous to the respective cultures are at the heart of the difficulty, and an anthropological and sociological science which neglects these normative theories misses the fundamental problem of the contemporary world.

This fact is so important that it may be worth our while to indicate precisely why this weakness in the anthropological and sociological sciences has occurred. The reason is that these sciences have arisen in the modern culture of the modern Western world. They have brought to the formation of their own methodology and their own conceptual apparatus the philosophical assumptions of this modern culture. No one for a minute can suppose that Spencerian sociology is independent of the philosophy of Spencer; nor can anyone suppose that the Comtian sociology has an independence of the Comtian philosophy. The same is true of all the major anthropological and sociological sciences of our modern Western world. Each has developed a set of technical concepts in terms of which the institutions of different cultures are classified and investigated. Thus all the facts of these other cultures are translated into the conceptual framework of a modern Western sociological science and its modern Western culture. Hence, what one obtains often is not the ideology of the native culture that is being investigated but the empirical facts of this culture brought under the ideology of modern Western sociologists and their particular cultural and philosophical assumptions.

There is but one cure for this state of affairs. The methods of the modern logic of systems must be introduced into anthropology and sociology. This method works with a technique which leaves one's postulates indeterminate, through the methodological procedure which one uses, permitting one to approach a given culture and to allow the institutions of that culture and the conceptual interpretation and evaluation put upon those institutions by the people in the culture in question to determine the conceptual framework in terms of which that culture is understood. This permits us to have an anthropology and a sociology in which the different cultures of the world will be understood in terms of the conceptual framework and apparatus of the ideological theories of the people who created those cultures.

It is precisely such a designation of the respective normative theories of the major nations and cultures in the world today which was attempted, in a rough sort of way and in a preliminary fashion, in *The Meeting of East and West*. Despite all the errors of detail inevitable in so extensive a study carried through by one person, which experts in the special fields discussed will undoubtedly correct, this study none the less demonstrates that it is possible at the present time in our universities to inaugurate a course which will acquaint men with the intercultural problem of the world as a whole and bring them to other cultures and the presuppositions of these other cultures in a mood of sympathetic understanding. This alone will go a long way toward removing the dangers of the contemporary world. For if people thus educated should go into the government or into the meetings of the United Nations, they would, at least, give the representatives of other countries the feeling that, even when differences of opinion on ideological matters arise, the ideological assumptions of cultures other than one's own were sympathetically understood. In such an atmosphere of mutual respect and sympathetic understanding, the practical problem of setting up international agreements sufficient to control the technological discoveries of science could be solved.

If education is to be effective, however, an entirely new type of training of both scholars and students is necessary. Both scholars and students must be trained to think deductively, as well as inductively. Only if men learn how to think deductively, can they acquire the tolerant attitude and the openmindedness necessary to comprehend the empirical cultural practices and institutions of a given people from the standpoint of the ideological assumptions of that people themselves. For each culture is a set of empirical social institutions and practices interpreted by a certain set of philosophical premises. To understand a given culture is to know its premises and to put oneself, at least tentatively, both imaginatively and sympathetically into the standpoint of its premises. Training in the usual textual empirical inductive methods of the traditional research of the historians and in the inductive methods of empirical science is quite inadequate for this. In fact, it is not too much of an exaggeration to say that the weakness of much of contemporary education concerning the needs of our world, centers in the curse of the inadequacy of the traditional historical method in scholarship.

This method, because of its excessively inductive character, paying attention to texts and source materials and the words in texts, is continuously misleading the scholar and those who read his conclusions. The inductive character of the traditional historical method brings the historian and the social scientist to the subject matter of history and of a given culture without the technical, theoretical concepts and assumptions of the people in question which are necessary to understand it. Thus, if the traditional scholar really uses his inductive method according to the sound prescriptions of this method, he comes out with nothing more than a lot of neutral, colorless facts. All the ideas and technically grasped theories necessary to comprehend these facts are lost. This is the reason why most of the current anthropological and sociological sciences and practically all of the results of the historical scholarship dealing with the different cultures of the world throw so little light on the perplexing problems of our time, which are so inescapably ideological in their character.

Actually, however, the errors of the present scholarship of our universities in the social sciences and the humanities are even worse than this. It is impossible even to record and classify the facts of history or of the diverse practices and institutions of different peoples without bringing these facts under concepts and theories. The only way to get pure facts, independent of all concepts and theory, is merely to look at them and forthwith to remain perpetually dumb, never uttering a word or describing what one sees, after the manner of a calf looking at the moon. For the moment one reports what one observes, at a meeting of historians or in a book written for sociologists, at that moment one has not pure facts but facts brought under concepts, and hence theory. Thus the social scientist's or the historian's aim at pure fact is a snare and a delusion. What one gets are not facts, but facts brought under some often uncritically examined, unconscious, theoretical assumptions of the sociologist or historian in question. As a rule, these theories are very speculative, since neither the social scientist nor the historian has the training or the method necessary to understand the technical, economic, political, theological and philosophical theories which are being exemplified in the facts. Even if his theories are more critically examined, they are, none the less, his theories. Rarely are they the theories used by a people to conceive and evaluate the empirical facts exhibited in their social practices and cultural institutions.

Nor is this all. The followers of the inductive and the historical method, because of the excessively verbal character of the texts which they take as sufficient sources, are continually confusing an identity of words used in different philosophies and different cultures with an identity of meaning. The fact, for example, that Locke speaks of a law of nature, even referring to Hooker when he does so, offers little proof of the thesis that Locke means by a law of nature what Hooker means or that Locke derived his meaning from Hooker. There will be no cure for these errors until people are trained to think deductively in the social sciences and history, as they are trained to do in the natural sciences and in philosophy when these are properly understood. Whenever one finds Locke talking about reason or about mind or using any other word used by any previous scholar, one must immediately ask oneself the question, "What, upon the premises of Locke's philosophy, must this word mean?" Only if one learns to think deductively in terms of the premises of a given philosopher's philosophy, can one learn to know what he means by the words he uses.

To learn to think deductively, as well as inductively, will not merely give us a complete and thorough scholarship. It is also necessary in order sharply to state the issues and conflicts of our world and thereby to understand precisely the basic nature of the problems with which we are concerned. To make this explicit, let us examine the classical normative theory of the culture of the United States and that of contemporary communist Russia.

The theory of the United States is made roughly explicit when one designates the postulates of its economic science, its political theory, its predominantly Protestant Christianity, and so on. Its economic science was formulated by Jevons, and later modified slightly by the Austrian School. Its traditional political philosophy goes back to John Locke. Its Protestantism, in so far as its doctrine departs from the doctrine of Thomistic medievalism, is a conception of the Christian religion rooted in the assumptions of modern philosophy. When one examines, technically and specifically, each of these doctrines which are deductively formulated theories, one finds that the basic postulates of the traditional cultures of the United States are not three independent sets of postulates but that instead they are interconnected in a single set of basic ideas and postulates. This common set of postulates joining the economic, political, and religious doctrines into one doctrine of a single culture is one's philosophy. This philosophy is, roughly, pre-Kantian British empiricism.

The technical economic theory, political theory, and religious, or antireligious, doctrines of contemporary communist Russia are similarly rooted in an underlying philosophy, that of Karl Marx. Marxian philosophy, as is well known, is Hegelian in its dialectical theory of history and Feuerbachian in its materialistic conception of the content of history.

To understand the ideologies of the United States and contemporary Russia thus deductively is to be in a position to formulate sharply the ideological problem at the basis of the perpetual impasses which arise between Russian delegates and the delegates of the United States in the United Nations. The economic, political and underlying philosophical premises defining the idea of the good society in the traditional cultures of the United States and of contemporary communistic Russia are self-contradictory. The hedonistic or psychological postulates of the economic science of Jevons and the Austrian School contradict the labor theory of economic value of Karl Marx. The political axioms of the present constitution of the U.S.S.R. contradict the axioms of the Declaration of Independence and the Constitution of the U.S.A. Similarly, the underlying postulates of pre-Kantian British empirical philosophy are incompatible with the post-Kantian philosophical assumptions of Hegel and Marx.

This means that the conflicts between delegates of the U.S.S.R. and the U.S.A. in the United Nations are truly serious conflicts, much more serious than most people have supposed, and that they cannot be resolved either by practical compromises alone or by a mutual understanding of each other's position and premises alone. In fact, the more the contemporary Russians and Americans come to understand each other's premises, the more the intensity of the conflict will exhibit itself. For when the basic assumptions of two different faiths contradict each other, reconciliation by practical expedients is unlikely, and reconciliation by mutual understanding is unequivocally impossible. Contradictories cannot be reconciled.

There is, however, a way of resolving such a difficulty. Only, however, by learning to think deductively and thus becoming capable of formulating such an international conflict in precise theoretical terms, can the way out be found. A clue appears, by way of contrast, if one examines certain other differences in philosophical premises when one applies the deductive method of inquiry to the diverse major cultures of the world. Then a situation other than that illustrated by the United States and Russia often arises. For example, in *The Meeting of East and West*, it has been shown that the basic philosophical premises and attendant economic, political and religious doctrines underlying Oriental civilization are different from those at the basis of Western civilization, and yet these differing assumptions do not contradict one another. Thus the problem of reconciling the East and the West presents no serious logical or theoretical difficulty. It entails merely enlarging the ideology of the one to include that of the other. This, to be sure, is by no means an easy task, since it involves far-reaching changes, especially with respect to the all-sufficiency and perfection of the traditional claims of one's own religion and one's own political and economic doctrines.

But where the basic assumptions do not merely differ but contradict each other, as in the case of the social ideals of the Soviet Russians and the Americans, the changes must be even greater and are far more difficult to achieve, not merely practically but also theoretically. For a contradiction cannot be resolved by enlarging the ideological concept of one people to include that of the other. One set of assumptions does not permit the inclusion of its contradictory.

Such a desperately serious ideological conflict can be resolved, nevertheless. Similar problems occur continually in the deductively formulated, experimentally verified theories of the natural sciences, and the technique for resolving them is well known. One must pass from the assumptions of both of the contradictory theories to a new set of philosophical premises which takes care of the facts supporting the two contradictory theories, without contradiction. This means that there can be no real intellectually constructive solution of the conflicts between democracies rooted in pre-Kantian philosophy and communistic Russia rooted in post-Kantian and post-Hegelian Marxism without passing on to a new set of assumptions which can take care of the merits of the communistic and the traditional democratic theories without contradiction.

Hence, the capacity to think about empirical data deductively, as well as inductively, must be made the primary concern of contemporary education. Before this capacity is obtained by both scholar and student, little can be accomplished. More of the present excessively inductive and textually verbal pseudo-scholarship has the effect of merely throwing dust into the eyes of both the scholars and the readers. The more information which they gather by these means, the less use they can make of it, the more overwhelmed intellectually they are by it, and the less capable they are of understanding it.

Nevertheless, the capacity to think theoretically and deductively is by itself of no use, unless one understands the technical content which goes into the deductively formulated theories of the different cultures of the world. For this understanding, one must be a master in the subjects to which these deductively formulated theories refer. To this end a mere mastery of languages and of dictionaries is quite insufficient. It is as absurd to suppose that a Ph.D. degree in philology or linguistics fits one to understand the philosophy of China as it would be to suppose that a Ph.D. in German fits one to understand the German texts of Einstein's theory of relativity. The basic cultural and ideological differences of our world go down to basic philosophical difficulties, and only scholars trained in the problems of philosophy and in the alternative answers to these problems, each one of which is reasoned out deductively, can hope to be competent to convey the standpoints of the cultures of either the East or the West.

But even more than an understanding of philosophy with the training in deductive thinking with respect to the theories of philosophy is required. One must also know technically the specific economic doctrines, such as the Austrian psychological theory of economic value or the Marxian labor theory of economic value, which go with these respective philosophies. The same is true for technical political and theological doctrines.

It will be said immediately that this is impossible for any one scholar or any one mind. There is no answer to this objection if the methodology of scholarship is purely inductive and verbal and textual. To acquiesce in the latter conclusion is to doom our civilization and mankind to extinction under a rain of atomic bombs within the lifetime of the younger generation.

There is no need to acquiesce in this counsel of doom from contemporary scholars. There is nothing whatever to prevent the introduction of a thoroughly adequate course in the methods of thinking, both inductively and deductively, in the freshman year in any college or university. Part of such a course could be very profitably pushed back into the high schools and preparatory schools. During the last semester in Yale College, such a course, within the limits of one-half year, was taught to a class of six hundred, more than 50 per cent of whom were Freshmen. Providing the capacity to think deductively is mastered, there is no reason, so far as the restrictions of time are concerned, why any good student having subsequent year-courses in deductively presented philosophy, economics, politics and religion illustrated with concrete inductive materials, could not be taken to the basic concepts and postulates of the major philosophical, economic, political and religious doctrines of the major cultures of the world with a thoroughness which would permit him sympathetically to understand all of these doctrines and later to master them technically.

This is not achieved at the present time because of the exclusively inductive character of the historical method in the humanities and the traditional methods of the social sciences. The students are so overwhelmed with empirical information which is not theoretically digested, even by the professors who present it to them, that they never find the key concepts and postulates defining the theoretical standpoints and evaluations of the different peoples and ideologies. An early training in the capacity to think deductively will enable both scholars and students to understand the facts they come upon and to distinguish basic notions in any field from secondary, derived notions. Actually, this enlarged kind of training, permitting any person to know technically philosophy, economics, politics and theology, not only for his own culture but also for the major cultures, could be achieved in a shorter time educationally than the present confusing methods and educational procedures require. The result would be that both scholars and students would be able to handle philosophical, economic, political and theological ideas in history and in the diverse cultures of the world more like expert philosophers, economists, political scientists and theologians, with the technical knowledge needed to understand them.

All this, even, is not enough. One people's ideology will, so far as the prescriptions up to this point indicate, be as valid as that of any other people's, even including the Germans', held spellbound by Hitler. Nor will these ideologies be fully appreciated as the people of any one of these ideologies actually feels it and loves it, if one merely grasps it technically.

Properly to understand any culture means not merely to know the basic philosophical premises defining its standpoint but also to be convinced that these philosophical premises are, for the people in question, a reasonable scientific generalization from the empirical data of their limited experience. Never is any culture understood, even when its indigenous ideology is grasped, unless the facts which led to its particular ideology are also ascertained. This means that the philosophy of any specific culture is grounded in its science, even when the people in question may be what we, in the West, have falsely called "primitive," without science in our more sophisticated form. Any people notes the facts of experience and generalizes from these facts to a philosophy. Consequently, no philosophy of culture is completely understood unless the empirical facts behind the generalization are also ascertained.

This means that the present separation of the social sciences and humanities from the natural sciences must be unequivocally repudiated. No humanistic doctrine in any culture is understood unless the underlying philosophy of that culture is understood. No underlying philosophy is sympathetically and emotionally apprehended unless the empirical evidence and the process of generalization, essentially scientific in character, taking the people in question from the empirical facts noted by them to their basic philosophy, are also grasped. In short, as Socrates and Plato noted long ago, one's philosophy of the good in the social sciences and humanities is one's philosophical generalization of the empirically true in the natural sciences.

An education which connects the technical philosophical systems of the differing cultures and ideologies and their attendantly different economic, political, religious and aesthetic ideas of the good with their scientific empirical background will not merely reconcile the humanities and the sciences, so that as the natural sciences produce new technological instruments, the humanistic social ideas necessary for the good control of these instruments will be present; but it will also provide an empirical, scientifically verifiable criterion indicating which set of philosophical premises has the generality and the deductive fertility sufficient to take care of all the facts noted by all the peoples of the differing cultures of the world. Thereby, ideological and cultural relativism, with its attendant demoralization with respect to international norms valid for all nations, can be transcended and escaped.

If the grounding of one's philosophy of culture in an empirically verified philosophy of natural science is not to be misunderstood, it must be emphasized that natural science must be taken in the broadest sense. This broad sense must include the empirical generalizations of so-called primitive peoples. It must also include the more purely empirical, qualitative, natural history type of natural science as well as the more theoretical, quantitative, mathematical type. Also, it must specify how these two types of scientific knowledge are related.

To this end, purely empirical data in natural science must be clearly distinguished from inferred hypothetically and theoretically designated factors. Through all cultures, the purely empirical data of nature are the same, for the most part. It is largely what is scientifically inferred from some of these empirical data which makes the ideology of one culture different from that of another. A clear understanding of this situation should go far to sustain an attitude of tolerance toward philosophies of culture other than one's own.

What happens is that people are continually identifying inferred factors in their scientific and cultural philosophy with purely empirically given data. The therapeutic for this prevalent disease is an inquiry, such as Bishop Berkeley pursued in his *Principles* and his *Dialogues between Hylas and Philonous,* concerning the nature of purely empirically given fact. Such an inquiry shows conclusively that pure fact is merely the immediately apprehended continuum of experience, differentiated by the sensuous qualities delivered by the senses. The latter qualities are not common-sense external objects, unobservable scientific objects, or theistic religious objects; they are, instead, aesthetic objects in the sense of the impressions of early French impressionistic art.

This means that if natural science is to include and convey most effectively the qualitative, purely empirical part of its knowledge, it and our university teachers must use impressionistic art. For impressionistic art, like much of the landscape painting of the Chinese, is the instrument *par excellence* for conveying the purely empirical data from which the theoretical generalizations of science and its attendant philosophy of culture are made.

In other words, an effective education for intercultural understanding must include, in addition to the five subjects previously noted, at least one course in the different types of the world's art. These types must encompass the Chinese intuitive and the modern Western impressionistic forms, both of which are supreme for conveying the purely empirical component of one's philosophy of science and culture. They must also embrace the more symbolic classical types of Western art, which are superb for the conveying of the theoretically inferred component of one's philosophy of science and culture. These diverse types of art can both exhibit literal scientific and philosophical truth known purely empirically and add persuasion to the analogical presentation of scientifically philosophical truth expressed literally only by more theoretical and mathematical means.

Such an education should be able to capture the hearts as well as the minds of men the world over, thereby adding affection to intellect and action in world understanding.

SPECIAL READING

The Developing Imagination / NORTHROP FRYE

I am not . . . an expert in the field with which my lecture is concerned. My own preparatory education I regarded, rightly or wrongly, as one of the milder forms of penal servitude, and it was fortunate for me that in my easygoing days I could enter school at grade four and the University of Toronto from grade eleven. So I probably owe my present interest in education to the fact that I had so little of it. However, I have acquired the seniority which is the natural reward of survival, and I now find myself sitting on committees concerned with every stage of the education continuum from kindergarten to graduate school.[1] I still do not know very much about what is taught in Ontario high schools, especially in the upper grades which I never reached, but I do know something of what is said at Ontario high school commencements, as I have said a fair amount of it myself. I propose therefore to take the commencement perspective rather than the classroom perspective, and to confine myself to the only area of learning in which I can claim any scholarly competence, which is that of English language and literature.

I teach literature at the upper university levels, and in recent years

[1] This paper is closely related to my introduction to the reports of the study committees appointed by the Joint Committee of the Board of Education of Toronto and the University of Toronto (*Design for Learning*, University of Toronto Press, 1962).

have given most of my attention to the theory of criticism. In the old humanist days, when literary training was confined to the classical languages, contact with one's own literature was left largely to what was called "taste," a by-product rather than a definite subject of education. When modern literatures became a subject of academic study, toward the latter half of the nineteenth century, the philological scholarship developed in the classics was naturally first applied to them. Since then, scholarship in modern literature has become a flourishing enough discipline, but we have not yet evolved a literary criticism which is solidly based on this scholarship, which clarifies its central principles, brings its assumptions into the open, and provides a view of the whole subject giving proportion and context to its more restricted achievements.

We have not even evolved a theory of criticism which can distinguish the genuine from the useless in scholarship itself. This distinction is left to the common sense of the scholar, which is usually but by no means invariably the best place to leave it. We still encounter students who have been awarded Ph.D.'s for theses on made-up subjects that are of no use to anyone, least of all the student. We can say that the supervisor of such a thesis has been a fathead, but in the absence of critical theory we cannot speak of academic malpractice. There is a bewildering amount of scholarship and commentary and piecemeal criticism today—far too much for anyone to keep up with more than odd bits of it—but very little understanding of the central principles of the study of literature. Our critical theory, as reflected in our teaching at all levels, is still largely the old "taste," or "appreciation," reinforced by a variety of "backgrounds," biographical, historical, and linguistic, none of which seem to contribute directly or systematically to the problem described in Wordsworth's *Prelude* as the impairing and restoring of taste.

Although most literary scholarship, good or bad, is intelligible only to fairly advanced university students, it is natural that its unpruned vine, a wild tangle of foliage with few identifying flowers or fruits, should be creeping around the schools as well, in the form of explicatory and other teaching methods. But the issues involved are more important than that. In the first place, the only guarantee that a subject is theoretically coherent is its ability to have its elementary principles taught to children. In the second place, literature cannot be directly taught or learned: what is taught and learned is the criticism of literature, and whatever is hard to understand about the place of literature in education owes its difficulty to the confusion of critical theory. I sympathize entirely with the plea for a more synoptic view of the different subjects taught to children, but how can literature (that is, criticism) enter into such a synoptic view until it has acquired a synoptic view of itself? We are asked to define a pachyderm when we are still collecting blind men's impressions of an elephant.

The subject generally referred to, in English-speaking countries, as "English" means two things. It is the name of a literature which is part of one of the major arts, and it is the mother tongue, the normal means of understanding anything that is not mathematical. Mr. MacKinnon has dealt mainly with the latter aspect; my own chief interest is in the former. I am aware of the dangers of trying to split the mind up into separate faculties, but the different directions that the mind faces, so to speak, surely do need to be distinguished. The faculty addressed by English as a literature is the imagination. At least, that is what the great Romantic critics call it, and I am not aware that the conception has been altered except for the worse. The faculty addressed by English as the mother tongue is one that is often associated, sometimes correctly, with the reason. I should prefer to call it something more like "sense." It is the power of apprehending what is presented to us by experience, the recognition of things as they are. It is the reality principle that we appeal to as the standard of the "normal" in behavior, and it is the basis of the scientific attitude to nature or the external world. The arts, including literature, are not so much concerned with the world as it is: their concern is with the world that man is trying to build out of nature, and the imagination they appeal to is a constructive power, which is neither reason nor emotion, though including elements of both.

It seems to me that there are a primary and a secondary phase of learning which correspond roughly, though by no means exactly, with the chronological stages of our elementary and secondary schools. There is also a tertiary phase, which has a much less direct parallel with post-secondary education, especially in the university. In each phase there is a conservative and a radical aspect of learning, a power of consolidating and a power of exploration and advance. In the primary phase the consolidating or conservative power is memory, and the exploring or radical power is what we have just called "sense." The memory preserves the facts transmitted in text or notebook; but facts, when really understood, are illustrations of principles, and the principles are what the "sense" attempts to grasp. The dull teacher, and the dull student, depend as much on memory and use as little "sense" as possible; and even the good student will rely on his memory to help him through the subjects in which he is less interested. What the memory holds we call content; what sense holds is structure. The good teacher is distinguished from his mediocre colleagues mainly by the efforts he makes to transform content into structure, to help his students to see significant patterns in facts, and to encourage the child to ask "Why?" with more purpose and direction than he ordinarily employs with that word.

Mathematics and the physical sciences are the most theoretically coherent of all the subjects of education, and we can see the supremacy of structure to content most clearly in them. They also best illustrate the fact that the natural shape of elementary teaching is deductive. Elementary science consists of principles so well established that no experiment could do more than simply illustrate them, and almost anything the child encounters in ordinary experience, such as the fact that he gets warmer when he runs, may be used as an illustration of a scientific principle. The teaching of elementary science can be considerably simplified once its deductive shape is realized, and it can also be brought down to the capacities of the youngest learners. (Of course saying that elementary science is presented deductively is not saying that experiment and direct observation are unimportant, at any stage. I knew of one school principal who held that children should not attempt experiments, on the ground that they work out better when adults did them; hence his students were compelled to stand helplessly by while their rivals in the next precinct were rigging up various gadgets including a burglar alarm, which, after several teachers had walked into it, finally caught a burglar.)

In history, and in at least political geography, the deductive pattern is more difficult to bring out. In Spenser's allegory of the House of Alma, in *The Faerie Queene,* history is entrusted to an old man in the back of the brain called "good memory" (Eumnestes), and it is hardly possible to avoid committing to memory a large number of dates and facts and names before much of a significant pattern can be glimpsed behind them. History, as Burke pointed out long ago, is, along with politics, naturally empirical and inductive in shape, and the difficulty in fitting it into elementary education is greater in consequence. The process may be easier when society is committed to an a priori and deductive view of history, as the Soviet Union is. Complaints that citizens of the democracies, in comparison with Communists, do not know what they really believe in, reflect what may be ultimately a problem of elementary education.

The teaching of literature in school will clearly depend for its tactics on whether literature (or criticism, as above) is naturally deductive in shape, like the physical sciences and mathematics, or naturally inductive, like history. The work I have done on critical theory has convinced me that literature is, like mathematics, mainly structure rather than content, and that the teaching of it, or criticism, can follow a deductive pattern. If I am right, the role of literature in the educational process should become much clearer, and its teaching greatly simplified.

In childhood the imagination is a third force, playing a role subordinate to memory and sense in the schoolroom, if not in the child's mind. In the child's mind it is extremely active, but it is not yet a constructive power: it is still on the level of what Coleridge and other critics distinguish as fancy, a stylizing and modifying of the actual conditions of the child's life, a kind of primitive realism. We can see this fanciful quality in children's pictures and poems, though our critical concepts are usually too vague to separate it from anything else in the "creative" area. The word "creative" is one of the most elastic and elusive metaphors in the language, as befits its theological origin. In any case it is memory and sense that take the lead in learning the techniques of reading and writing.

Those who never get beyond the primary phase of learning illustrate the child's situation in a petrified adult form. They often assume that good memory is equivalent to high intelligence, and (at least recently) that high intelligence is dramatized in the kind of television program in which the possessor of a great deal of noncontroversial information is rewarded with encyclopedias. They also regard literature and the arts as not strictly educational, but as either "frills" on education or as fanciful, concerned with the relaxing or amusing of the mind. In their conception of society, the creative man follows the practical one at a respectful distance. They also tend to make associative judgments, attaching the content of picture or poem to their experience instead of grasping the formal unity of the work. The suggestion that the arts are radically constructive, that they cannot always be directly related to the recognition of reality, but create their own kind of reality, is one that they normally resist or resent.

I referred above to the humanist tradition in education, a form of education based primarily on literature. The strength of humanism lay in its exploitation of a central fact about literature: that the arts do not, like the sciences, evolve and improve, but revolve around classics or models. Like most such principles, this one could be and often was frozen into a sacrosanct dogma, and those who held it in this form give us a sharp sense of its limitations. The Elizabethan Roger Ascham wrote *The Scholemaster* to explain how Latin could be taught by using Cicero as a model. Toward the end of his book he considers, reluctantly, the question whether Cicero really is an example of what he calls "the vnspotted proprietie of the Latin tong . . . at the hiest pitch of all perfitenesse." He is not slow to give his answer:

> For he, that can neither like *Aristotle* in Logicke and Philosophie, nor *Tullie* in Rhetoricke and Eloquence, will from these steppes, likelie enough presume, by like pride, to mount hier, to the misliking of greater matters: that is either in Religion, to haue a dissentious head, or in the common wealth, to haue a factious hart: as I knew one a student in Cambrige, who, for a singularitie, began first to dissent, in the scholes, from *Aristotle*, and sone after became a peruerse *Arian*, against Christ and all true Religion.

Nevertheless, the humanist theory of models worked fairly well in literary education, because it is broadly true for literature, and in addition it had the great advantage of being deductive in shape, giving the student a few central texts and extracting from them a set of principles he could apply in all his reading, and more particularly in all his writing. But, of course, the humanist theory was inadequate for the inductive sciences, where classical authority has no functional place.

Humanistic education was directed toward the past: the essential standards and values already existed in certain classics, and they could be applied to present use. Its curriculum, as the quotation from Ascham indicates, could be taught with the greatest confidence in both the subject matter and the ethical validity of its classics. There they were, dignified and eminently visible. Education slowly began to change its center of gravity from literature to science about a century ago, and this meant a change to an education directed not toward the past but toward a present and an unknown future, where anything we now know may be rendered obsolete by coming discoveries. Hence the social and moral values established by education have tended to become interim values. Many educators have naturally attempted to transfer the public confidence in education from the past to the present and future, from establishment to process, to new programs of what has been alternately called education for today and education for tomorrow. But an uncertainty about the content and the purpose of education, a sense of lost values, and an uneasiness about the loss are plain for anyone to see. I am not proposing any "return" to humanism as a cure for this; still, the question naturally suggests itself: is there anything permanent in humanism, and appropriate at least to the literary part of education today, that can be re-established with its present context?

We notice that literature is, by its very nature, intensely allusive: its classics or models, once recognized as such, echo and re-echo through all subsequent ages. Whitman urged us to make less of the wrath of Achilles and develop new themes for a new world, where the Muse would be invoked to sing of the righteous wrath of an American democrat. But allusions to Homer in writers even more recent than Whitman carry the same weight of authority that they carried in Milton's day, and Whitman's view clearly does not fit the facts of literary experience. It looks as though that experience were not a random one, but radiated from a center where the great classics, including Homer, are to be found. Literature revolves around certain classics or models because it is really revolving around certain structural principles which those classics embody. The problem of imitation or mimesis in literature has two aspects. The traditional imitation of nature (or action, or life, or experience) refers primarily to content, but as far as his form is concerned, what the poet imitates are the conventions and genres of literature as he finds them. This latter aspect of literature is so neglected in our teaching of it that we tend to make naïve judgments on literature which assume that literary works form a kind of continuous allegorical commentary on the society contemporary with them. Thus if a dramatist writes a play without succeeding in giving it any dramatic shape, he can always say that its shapelessness reflects the chaos of our time. It does nothing of the kind, of course: what it reflects is probably the practice of a better dramatist who gives a skillful illusion of shapelessness, and that practice in its turn reflects, not the chaos of our time, but a stage in the development of certain twentieth-century dramatic conventions.

The humanist theory, in its earliest stages, based the study of literature on precept and example. It was the *sententiae,* the profound axioms of the human situation, that were especially prized in the great writers, and the stories they told were *exempla,* or illustrations of the same kind of thing. This approach puts literature at the service of certain social and moral ideals assumed to be permanently valid. No doubt it is an important function of literature, especially in childhood, to reinforce with its peculiar resonance the kind of attitudes we want our children to accept. I have been fascinated by Mr. MacKinnon's account of the effectiveness of television commercials as teaching techniques, which are also based on *sententiae,* in the form of advertising slogans, and pretend to have the same kind of moral urgency. Apparently Marxism, in its latter or post-Lenin phase, holds much the same conception of the social role of literature. Granting that there are better forms of such an approach, they would still be primarily rhetorical, training the student in English as the mother tongue, and only incidentally in English as part of a major art. We need along with this a genuinely literary conception of English, based on structure rather than content, on insight rather than memory, one which will give literature its own proper independence instead of making it an adjunct of accepted modes of life and manners.

One essential aspect of literary training, and one that it is possible to acquire, or begin acquiring, in childhood, is the art of listening to stories. This sounds like a passive ability, but it is not passive at all: it is what the army would call a basic training for the imagination. It is the opposite of the sententious approach, because the mind is directed toward total structure, not to piecemeal content. Concentrating on a story separates the work of the reason, which proceeds by argument and thesis, by aggression and dialectical conflict, from the proper work of the imagination, where there are no assertions and no refutations. The storyteller asserts nothing: he lays down postulates. The postulates may be, for example, that a little girl goes to sleep outdoors one afternoon, sees a rabbit run past her, sees him take a watch out of his pocket and mutter something about being late for an appointment, and follows him as he disappears down a rabbit-hole. Very well: these are the storyteller's postulates; we listen to the story to see what he does with them. We learn to suspend judgment until more data are in—a useful habit of mind in itself. We learn not to argue or raise objections before our perspective is in focus, and when all objections are still only prejudices. (The appropriate Socratic dialogue would run somewhat as follows: "But that's silly; rabbits don't talk or look at watches." "Well, they do in this story: now shut up.") If in later years we are confronted with nonobjective painting, twelve-tone music, or the theater of the absurd, our early training should help us to try to grasp first of all the totality of what is presented. Failing such training, we are apt to try to assimilate the work of art to the discursive and argumentative structures of words that we are more familiar with, and ask such questions as: What is he trying to get across? Why can't somebody explain to me? and the like.

The next question is what stories it is particularly appropriate for a child to listen to, and here we come back again to the fact that literature is allusive, and seems to radiate from a center. Literature develops out of, or is preceded by, a body of myths, legends, folk tales, which are transmitted by our earlier classics. In our tradition the most important groups of these myths are the biblical and the classical, and it is essential to acquire some knowledge of both as early in life as possible. One reason for doing so is sheer convenience: these stories are so endlessly alluded to and commented on that one has no landmarks in literature without them. To grow up in ignorance of what is in the Bible or Homer is as crippling to the imagination as being deprived of the multiplication table. But convenience in understanding allusions is not the really important reason for knowing the sources of them.

The really important reason, as far as literature is concerned, is that there are only a certain number of ways (structural principles) in which stories can be told, and familiarity with two major mythologies, the Greek and the biblical, puts us in command of all of them. In other words, there really is a deductive principle in literature which can be exploited for educational purposes. All stories in literature are developments of fundamental fictional shapes which can be studied most clearly in myths and folk tales. The reason why writers are so persistently fascinated by myth and folk tale is not antiquarianism, but the fact that, like still life in painting, they illustrate the formal characteristics of their art most clearly. Some students of mine now in secondary schools tell me that they have had a good deal of success in teaching the writing of fiction by using the principle that I call "displacement," giving their students a myth or a Grimm fairy tale and asking them to translate each detail of it into a plausible or realistic incident, while preserving the structure intact.

From familiarity with the traditional stories of our culture we may gradually acquire a sense of the categories of stories, which I should classify as four in number: the romantic, the comic, the tragic, and the ironic. Of these, comedy and romance are primary; tragedy and irony more difficult, because more ambivalent in tone. Once again, those who never get past the primary phase of learning seldom read anything with genuine pleasure that is not a comedy or a romance. The next step is to get a sense of structure as exhibited in the conventions and genres of literature. We notice that when we read deliberately for relaxation, we turn to highly conventionalized stories where the general structure is known in advance, such as the detective story, the Western, or the even more predictable dramas of television.

The distinction between the structure and the texture of fiction, which criticism has only begun to recognize, is of major importance in determining the sequence of reading. The really difficult writers who have to be reserved for the university, such as Proust or Conrad or the later Henry James, are as a rule more difficult in texture, but keep to much the same principles of structure as the writers we are more inclined to take to bed with us. Complex writers attract a great deal of rather myopic commentary, based entirely on texture, which with a better training in structure might be less necessary for students to read, or, if they become advanced students, to write. Works of universal appeal and of great and immediate communicative power are usually simple in texture as well as structure. Hence they, or something in them, are primary in the educational sequence.

The traditional humanists identified such works with the classics of Greek and Latin literatures: this identification is still going strong in Matthew Arnold's essay "The Choice of Subjects in Poetry." We need a broader principle of the same type, such as the real principle that underlies Tolstoy's *What is Art?*

In its present form Tolstoy's theory is a tissue of exclusive value judgments based on nonliterary values—in other words it is critically neurotic. But it would make a good deal of sense if transformed into an educational theory, used to establish the central texts that could be used with profit by children and others of limited imaginative experience. We have all met or heard of people of little formal schooling, who know the Bible and a few English classics and give the impression of essentially educated people. I suggest that the impression is based, not on sentimental illusion, but on the facts of literary education. And it is still possible to say that one who does not know the central classics of his own language and cultural tradition gives the impression of an ignoramus, regardless of what else he knows.

In the secondary phase of education, the radical and conservative aspects of learning become more conceptual. They are now closer to the radicalism and conservatism distinguished by John Stuart Mill in the political thought of his day, and in fact they are most easily seen at work in the social and political area. In the secondary phase the radical side of the mind wants to know what good or what use an idea or institution is, whether we could get along without it, what it has to say for itself even if generally accepted. The conservative side wants to know why the idea or institution exists, why it has been accepted if wrong, what significance is in the fact that it has existed. Thus the secondary phase revolves around the problem of symbolism, of the relation of appearance to reality, and its aim is not simply the formation of an intelligence, as in the primary phase, but the formation of a critical intelligence, the intelligence of a responsible citizen in a complex modern democracy.

In this phase the growing imaginative power forms a natural alliance with the conservative side of learning. The radical side is utilitarian, aggressive, argumentative, appealing to what it regards as reason or common sense, and it is frequently anti-imaginative. It is impressed by the actuality of the present, as the conservative side is by the inadequacy of the present to what one's deeper desires demand. The imagination is no longer fanciful, and it is not yet a fully constructive power, but moves most freely among the monuments of its own magnificence. It is bound intellectually to tradition, and emotionally to nostalgia. The problem in our society recently tagged with the phrase "two cultures" refers to a natural division in the mental attitudes of most of our educated citizens. It is considerably oversimplifying the problem to identify the two attitudes with the sciences and the humanities respectively.

In stressing the importance of myth and of biblical and classical stories in primary literary education, I am agreeing to some extent with the outline of an "articulated English program" recently proposed by a committee of the Modern Language Association. Mr. MacKinnon refers to this in passing, but without much enthusiasm, and it is clear that it does not, for him, solve the problem of relating literary to other aspects of education. My own feeling is, once again, that whatever separates literature from the rest of education reflects the confusion of critical theory. As long as a story is just a story, the real separation involved is the separation of fiction from fact—in itself, of course, a healthy and necessary separation. But some stories are more obviously just stories than others. The radical side of our critical intelligence may assert that the story of the Garden of Eden in Genesis is on precisely the same plane of reality as the Garden of the Hesperides in Homer. But the conservative side, aided by the imagination, realizes that the myth of creation and fall in Genesis has been and still is an informing principle of our religious, social, and even philosophical thought, whether we are conscious of its role in those areas or not.

The extent to which our thinking is molded by informing principles articulated in poetic myths is still largely an unexplored subject in literary criticism. It is most highly developed, I think, in the criticism of American literature, but the books that set it forth are difficult books, addressed to advanced scholars, and have not made much headway into the educational system. Still, most serious students of American literature are aware that *Huckleberry Finn, Moby Dick, The Scarlet Letter, Wal-*

den, the tales of Poe, and others can be studied not only as works of literature but as focal points of a cultural imagination, and that as such they make American history, politics, religion, and social life more intelligible. Literary works which express these informing social myths most clearly are the works which have prior claim on the educator's attention, whenever they can be read or adapted for reading. They are not invariably the books of greatest literary value, though they always have some value: they would include, for instance, *Uncle Tom's Cabin.*

It is of course true that a great deal of trash which passes as literature, or at least as entertaining reading, also articulates social myths with great clarity. I read many of the novels of Horatio Alger at an early age, and as I have a good verbal memory, a journey round my skull would unearth a great many pages of some of the most pedestrian prose on record. I wish very much that a surgical operation could remove it and substitute something better, but still Alger probably did me no permanent damage, as I was never inspired to adopt the virtues of his heroes, and this leads me to hope that the children of today may emerge similarly unscathed from their similar experiences. I feel that a well-planned literary education would give us a standard by which to measure such writing. By a standard I do not mean only a standard of quality or value, which any literary education worth anything at all would give: I mean also a standard of comprehension, an understanding of it not merely as bad writing but as shoddy mythology. The benefits of having such a standard of comprehension extend far beyond literature. I should think, for example, that the doctrines of Mr. Buckley or Senator Goldwater would have little appeal to a society in which the high school graduates knew something about the working of pastoral myth in the political imagination.

I am well aware that what I suggest bears a close resemblance to one of the worst and most futile ways of teaching literature. This is the practice of reducing every work of imagination to a sociological document, studying Henry James or Faulkner merely as illustrating some dismal clichés about cultural decline in New England or the Old South. The emphasis I should prefer is the exact reverse of this. Historians and social scientists give most of their conscious attention to inductive procedures, the collecting of facts and evidence. They give much less attention to the conceptions that give shape and organization to the books they write, conceptions which are therefore largely unconscious, but are revealed in such things as the choice of metaphors and analogies. These conceptions are really myths, using the word "myth" in its proper sense of an informing verbal structure, and literature enables us to understand what these myths are. As I have maintained elsewhere, literature has an informing relation to the verbal disciplines somewhat analogous to the relation of mathematics to the physical sciences.

The same principles would apply to the study of English as a foreign or second language. Looking at English or American culture from the outside gives one a different perspective on it, certainly. French poets found not only an American but a universal cultural significance in Poe that we have been slow to discover for ourselves, and Lenin's view of Jack London has given him an importance in Russia that he has never had in his own country. But while the perspectives are different, they are not irreconcilably different. We are committed to our own society, but education ought to give us more detachment, to impress us with the importance of satire and denunciation and protest in a healthy culture. A study of the same culture that begins in detachment or even hostility would naturally tend, in itself, to greater sympathy or even a sense of participation. We all know, vaguely, that *Robinson Crusoe* is one of our educational "classics," but a citizen of Asia or Africa might spot more quickly than we the cultural myth that helps to make it a classic. Crusoe lands on his island and instantly opens a journal and a ledger, though all he has to put in the latter are the pros and cons of his situation. He domesticates some animals and ensures himself some privacy—he has no need for privacy, but an Englishman's home is his castle. He catches his man Friday and proceeds to convert him, without the slightest sense of incongruity, to his own brand of modified Presbyterianism. He is the British Empire in action, imposing its own pattern wherever it is, and never dreaming of "going native." The African or Asian is familiar with the social results of Western expansion: if he reads *Robinson Crusoe* he is seeing the same process from the inside, as a conceivable way of life. He may not like its effects any better, but he can see its causes as human and not demonic, and I doubt if education can do much more than that for the brotherhood of man.

These two cultural impulses, a growing detachment from what we possess and a growing sympathy with what is alien, are equally essential in a world like ours. It is reassuring to find a naïve enthusiasm for yoga or Zen Buddhism in the United States: it would be disturbing to find it in India or Japan. The members of the Athenian assemblies who authorized the expedition to Syracuse and the massacre of Mytilene did not know that their culture would come to symbolize sweetness and light, the triumph of reason and beauty over the arid fanaticism of the moral will. But such is the healing power of what is called aesthetic distance. I think that if Hellenism can come to symbolize a love of beauty, and Hebraism a moral energy, the cultural heritage of the English-speaking nations can also come to symbolize a sense of individual freedom which is one of the permanent achievements of human history, and will remain so however dark and troubled our future may become. But it is not for us to dwell on this: our sustained admiration must be rather for other cultures, with hope that we may give some cause, at least to posterity, for admiration of our own.

There are many other aspects of literary education than those of myth and fiction which I have no space to develop. We are greatly confused at present by the notion that prose is the language of ordinary speech, and that poetry is an unnatural and perversely ingenious method of distorting prose statements. We can get a better progression if we realize that the language of ordinary speech is no more prose than it is poetry. The language of ordinary speech is an unshaped associative babble, a series of asyntatic short phrases, and it is psychologically a monologue, designed for expression and not primarily for communication. As it develops toward communication, it can be conventionalized in either of two ways. The direct and simple way is to put a pattern of recurrence on it and turn it into verse. The more difficult and sophisticated way is to put a logical pattern on it and turn it into prose. Developed techniques of verse usually precede developed techniques of prose in the history of literature, because verse is the more primitive of the two. If we listen to small children, we soon realize that their chanting speech has at least as much verse in it as prose. If we mark the essays of college freshmen, we soon realize that we are usually not reading prose, but a series of phrases for which the only appropriate form of punctuation is the dash. The conviction that written language is normally prose, that its unit is the sentence, and that a period goes at the end of it is one that twelve years of concentrated teaching often fails to evoke. The simplest form of literary expression, and the one most readily accessible to children, is, I should think, accentual verse, of the kind that we find in nursery rhymes, and which illustrates the affinity of poetry with dance and song and bodily energy. A lucid prose style accompanies the sense of the complete reality of other people, and its development is a long-range one.

It is partly because of the rhythm of speech in childhood, and partly because of the central role of memory in elementary learning, that sequential and rhythmical catalogues, from the multiplication table to the monarchs of England, are easier for children than for most adults. In this respect children resemble the poets of primitive societies, who are culturally in a parallel situation, unlocking their word hoards to chant their memorized songs of ancestral legends, place names, neighboring tribes and alliterating kings.

In simpler societies this power of memory is the basis of a poetic power of an extraordinarily spontaneous and plastic kind. We find it in ballads and folktales, where motifs and refrains are constantly interchanging and developing new variants. We find it in the formulaic oral epic, with its basis of stock themes and metrical units, described in Professor Lord's fascinating book, *The Singer of Tales* (Cambridge,

Mass., 1960). We can find it in other arts, as in some schools of Oriental painting, which develop out of what are essentially memorized subjects. Many of the strongest cultural movements of our time seem to be headed in a somewhat similar direction: in action painting, in the genuine forms of jazz music, in certain poetic developments often and not too accurately associated with the term "beat." Professor Lord has shown for the formulaic epic that spontaneity shrivels instantly at the touch of education, or at any rate of book learning, and some of the contemporary phenomena just listed seem to have a strongly anti-intellectual slant to them. Yet the analogies between the primitive and the childlike may need further exploration in an age where there are so many media of education that circumvent the normal book learning processes and cut straight through to a direct and primitive response of eye and ear. I know little of such matters, but there seems to me to be a gap between education and one important aspect of contemporary culture, and of imaginative power in general, that educational theory and practice have not to my knowledge yet bridged.

I spoke at the beginning of a tertiary phase of education. This phase, which is considerably more of an ideal than a fact, is symbolized, and perhaps occasionally achieved, by the liberal-arts program in the university, and by the four-year withdrawal from ordinary society which is devoted to it. Here the consolidating and exploring aspects of the mind take on still another relationship. The conservative aspect is now the awareness of the society that the student is living in, the knowledge of its institutions, conventions, and attitudes which enables him to take his rightful place in it. This is the end of all that aspect of education covered by such terms as "preparation for life" or "adjustment" to it. Over against this, in the ideally educated mind, is the awareness that the middle-class mid-twentieth century North American society we are living in is not the real form of human society, but the transient appearance of that society. The real human society is the total body of human achievement in the arts and sciences. The arts are perhaps more concerned with what humanity has done, the sciences perhaps more concerned with what it is about to do, but the two together form the permanent model of civilization which our present society approximates. This model is our cultural environment, as distinct from our social environment. The educated man is the man who tries to live in his social environment according to the standards of his cultural environment. This gives him some detachment about his own society, some understanding of the forces that make it change so rapidly, and some ability to distinguish its temporary expedients from its permanent values. It is unnecessary to labor the point that an age as revolutionary as ours, in which we have to adjust quickly and constantly to radical changes or disappear from history, needs such elements in its education.

In this final phase the imagination moves over to the exploring or radical side of the mind, and comes into its own. It is now a fully developed constructive power: It is informed by what Whitehead calls the habitual vision of greatness, and its activity in the world around it is to realize whatever it can of that vision. It operates in society in much the same way, working from conception to realization, that the artist works on his art, which is what Blake meant by saying that the poetic genius of man is the real man. The immediate purpose of teaching literature to children and adolescents is not to persuade them to appreciate or admire works of literature more, but to understand them with a critical intelligence blended of sympathy and detachment. Detachment without sympathy is Philistinism; sympathy without detachment is accurately called uncritical. But the ultimate purpose of teaching literature is not understanding, but the transferring of the imaginative habit of mind, the instinct to create a new form instead of idolizing an old one, from the laboratory of literature to the life of mankind. Society depends heavily for its well-being on the handful of people who are imaginative in this sense. If the number became a majority, we should be living in a very different world, for it would be the world that we should then have the vision and the power to construct.

THE AUTHORS

Alfred North Whitehead (1861–1947). World famous mathematician and philosopher, developed a metaphysics of process from the new physics; educator and consultant in British education. Born in Ramsgate, England; graduated from Trinity College, Cambridge University (1884); M.A., Trinity College (1887); D.Sc., Trinity College (1905); lecturer and later senior lecturer on mathematics, Trinity College (1885–1910); lecturer on applied mathematics and mechanics, University College, University of London (1910–1914); professor of applied mathematics at the Imperial College of Science and Technology, Kensington (1914–1924); dean of the faculty of science, Imperial College (1921–1924); professor of philosophy, Harvard University (1924–1936); professor emeritus, Harvard University (1936–1947). Awarded the James Scott Prize of the Royal Society, Edinburgh (1922); the Sylvester Medal of the Royal Society, London (1925); the Butler Medal, Columbia University (1930); the Order of Merit from the British Crown (1945). Major publications: *A Treatise on Universal Algebra* (1898); *Principia Mathematica*, in collaboration with Bertrand Russell (1910–1913); *The Organization of Thought* (1916); *The Principles of Natural Knowledge* (1919); *The Concept of Nature* (1920); *The Principle of Relativity* (1922); *Science and the Modern World* (1926); *Religion in the Making* (1926); *The Aims of Education* (1928); *The Function of Reason*

(1929); *Process and Reality* (1929); *Adventures of Ideas* (1933); *Modes of Thought* (1938).

Jerome Seymour Bruner (1915–   ). Cognitive psychologist of perception, thinking, and child growth; founder of the Center for Cognitive Studies at Harvard; introduced the work of Sem Vygotsky to American psychologists and became the liaison between Americans and Jean Piaget of Geneva. Born in New York City; graduated from Duke University (1937); M.A. and Ph.D., Harvard University (1941); associate director, Office of Public Opinion Research (1943–1944); overseas branch, United States Office of War Information (1944–1945); lecturer in psychology, Harvard University (1945–1948); associate professor, Harvard (1948–1952); professor of psychology, Harvard (1952–   ). Member of the White House Committee on Education (1962–1964); honorary Officier de l'Instruction Publique, France; honorary foreign fellow, Federation Suisse de Psychologie; Distinguished Scientific Award, American Psychological Association (1962); consultant, Educational Services Incorporated. Major publications: *A Study of Thinking* (1956); *The Process of Education* (1960); *On Knowing: Essays of The Left Hand* (1962); *Toward a Theory of Instruction* (1966); *Studies in Cognitive Growth* (1966).

Filmer Stuart Cuckow Northrop (1893–   ). Philosopher of the theories and methods of the new physics and natural sciences; redirected his attention to legal, ethical, and cultural experience as Sterling Professor of Philosophy and Law in the Graduate School of Yale University. Born in Janesville, Wisconsin; graduated from Beloit College (1915); M.A., Yale University (1919); M.A., Harvard University (1922); Ph.D., Harvard University (1924); postgraduate study at the University of Freiburg, Germany; Trinity College, Cambridge University; Imperial College of Science and Technology, London University; at Yale University was instructor in philosophy (1923–1926); assistant professor (1926–1929), associate professor (1929–1932), professor of philosophy (1932–1947), and professor emeritus (1947–   ). Founding fellow of the East-West Philosophers' Conference; member of the advisory board, International World Federalist; Order of Aztec Eagle, Government of Mexico. Major publications; *Science and First Principles* (1931); *The Meeting of East and West* (1946); *The Logic of the Sciences and Humanities* (1947); *The Taming of the Nations* (1952); *European Union and United States Foreign Policy* (1954); *The Complexity of Legal and Ethical Experience* (1959); *Philosophical Anthropology and Practical Politics* (1960); co-editor with Mason Gross, *Alfred North Whitehead: An Anthology* (1953).

Northrop Frye (1912–   ). Developed a comprehensive theoretical system of literary criticism⁻ on the model of constructionism in the new physics; concerned with literature as the history of schematic forms in myth-making created by man's imagination; literary education must not be the mere teaching of literature but the intellectual criticisms and forms of it. Born in Sherbrooke, Quebec; graduated from Emmanuel College, University of Toronto (1933); ordained in the United Church ministry (1936); M.A., Merton College, Oxford University (1940); instructor in English, Victoria College,

University of Toronto (1940–1959); principal, Victoria College (1959–1966); professor of English, University of Toronto (1966). Awarded the Lorne Pierce Medal in Canadian literature (1958). Major publications: *Fearful Symmetry: A Study of William Blake* (1947); *Anatomy of Criticism: Four Essays* (1957); *The Well-Tempered Critic* (1963); *The Educated Imagination* (1963); *Fables of Identity: Studies in Poetic Mythology* (1963); *A Natural Perspective: The Development of Shakespearean Comedy and Romance* (1965); *The Modern Century* (1967); Editor, *Design for Learning*, Toronto Board of Education and the University of Toronto (1962).

Logical-Science
Philosophy

GENERIC NOTIONS AND BASIC THEMES

The key theme in the Logical-Science thought pattern is that of verification and proof. Careless thinking can lead to ambiguity and false notions. The mind requires a special kind of order before it can arrive at conclusions and determine facts. This order is provided by two kinds of constraints, scientific and mathematical. The first is empirical evidence, which stems from the data of the specialized sciences. The sciences are separate specialized fields, each with an established body of knowledge and individual methods of research. The essential contribution of the sciences is confirmations deriving from observation and inductive logic. The second group of constraints are those imposed by the logical proof of formal analyses and mathematical logic. In this case, the logician, using the propositional function in mathematics, follows a pattern of logical discourse involving the arrangements of theorems from postulates.

The underlying assumption of this thought pattern is that an intellectual culture should be provided in which the specialized sciences can function freely and be honored for the knowledge they acquire. Although the theme of science is not new, the Logical-Science philosophers have reinterpreted it to emphasize the specialized work of independent fields. The primary momentum toward this new interpretation was provided by the recognition that the problems of the new physics can be solved by specialized fields, each performing research in its own area. By logically separating issues, by allowing the different specialities to research their own problems, Logical-Science intellectuals have managed to settle questions of particular interest in the quest for certainty. However, they do recognize that the model of one field can be used as a model for another.

Logical-Science philosophers believe that the great obstruction to the scientific enterprise in contributing to human life is philosophizing; that is, uninformed people expounding superficial generalities about the nature of reality and values. A person who philosophizes makes all kinds of extravagant statements about situations without any conceivable evidence or means of confirmation. In this view such a person overgeneralizes; he applies a particular idea to areas in which it does not belong.

As a result, he creates a complete misconception of the situation, producing confusion and ambiguity. This mutilation of truth can only be ended if people, scientists, laymen, and philosophers, can be made to stop philosophizing. Logical-Science philosophers feel that if people can be trained to follow the correct rules of language usage, most problems can be solved or left to those with the means to solve them. Once these rules are instilled, no one will be able to generalize beyond the facts and the evidences at hand.

The Logical-Science thought pattern places great emphasis on the role of language in modern life. For these thinkers, language is a social convention, a public system of communication, which develops from the process of human socialization. Language provides society with its main source of meaning, the meaning related to what man experiences with his senses, that is, objects and states of affairs. Participants in human communication are obliged to follow the rules of common usage.

The significance of language lies in its units of meaning, words and sentences. Although phonemes are the smallest units of a language, they do not convey meaning, and therefore are not primary factors in correct language usage. Words, which stand for things and objects, are the smallest meaningful units, arbitrary symbols that eventually become conventional symbols. Sentences, on the other hand, are labels assigned to situations or states of affairs. To have meaning, they must assert something. When they assert something, they are propositions. All complex sentences can be reduced to simple sentences, separate units of meaning that entail nothing but a subject and predicate. The function of philosophy is to analyze the various language units, to examine the meaning of words to see if there are things in nature that correspond to them, to check simple sentences to see if the propositions are true (either logically or empirically) or false.

Some sentences, however, when analyzed, turn out to be neither true statements nor false statements. A single word in a sentence may be meaningless, thus depriving the entire sentence of meaning. Or, the sentence may not be a proposition because it does not assert anything of a true or false nature. For example, some sentences are emotive statements, which simply indicate the feelings of the speaker. They do imply the facts of the speaker's feelings, but they are not considered cognitive statements in the universal sense because they do not convey knowledge about the depersonalized state of the world. Problems arise when emotive statements appear to have the form of propositions and people believe them to be cognitive. Such confusion most commonly occurs in the case of metaphysical speculations or assertions of values.

Logical-Science philosophers believe metaphysical speculations are unworthy of attention since they can be proved neither true nor false. Questions of value, on the other hand, have aspects of cognitive content.

The expressive, descriptive, and imperative functions of value statements convey some kind of meaning. The analytical work of philosophy is necessary to clarify this meaning. Scientific work pertaining to statements of value is also needed. Since value statements express personal preferences, and these preferences result from socialization, the sciences, especially sociology and social psychology, can study and gather empirical evidence about them.

Education, according to Logical-Science philosophers, concerns questions relating to value judgments. Hence, analysis of educational value judgments and empirical evidences on socialization is needed. Two major kinds of decisions pertaining to value judgments must initially be made in education. They are decisions of "goods as ends," which relate to the basic goals of education, and decisions of "goods as means," which relate to methods of education. Decisions concerning "goods as ends" are made on the basis of the consensus of the attitudes of society. The human socialization process invariably produces common preferences for very general educational aims and endeavors. Science can take these general expectations and produce a taxonomy of educational objectives. In contrast, decisions concerning "goods as means" are not settled by consensus, but by experts in appropriate fields of educational research. It is the experts in curriculum, methods, learning theory, and so on, who indicate the correct procedures in education.

Although the analysis of value judgments is the only area of philosophy that can be related directly to education, nevertheless Logical-Science philosophers suggest that education should strive for the attainment of cognitive skills rather than values. Herbert Feigl, among others, indicates that the objective of the school should be a broad (but not superficial) knowledge on the part of the student, achieved by the clustering of the specialized studies around a nucleus of basic subjects with emphasis on problems of language.[1] Most Logical-Science philosophers concur with this emphasis. Some even attempt to prove that this is the correct goal by definition by using an analogy. They say: Geometry is the application of axioms. When you question the axioms, this is not geometry but something else. Education has similar definitional restrictions. When one talks about individual differences, social needs, or political reforms, this is not education but something belonging to psychology, sociology, and political science. Education by definition is not the attaining of long-range political or social ends but of short-range achievements; learning to read, write, and perform adequately in arithmetic.

Three themes concerning educational practice are prominent in the

[1] Herbert Feigl, "Aims of Education for Our Age of Science: Reflections of a Logical Empiricist," *Modern Philosophies of Education* (National Society for the Study of Education, 1955).

Logical-Science thought pattern. The first is the great emphasis on skills in education. Since little attention is given to generalities, education must stress the smaller units of meaning, those that can be tested in manners of performance. The emphasis must be on procedural activities that require a high degree of ability and training; that is, skillful behavior, mathematical or scientific. A student goes to school to acquire reading skills, language skills, and arithmetic skills. In advanced work, he is to attain the skills used by experts in particular specialized fields. The notion of ability and skill go hand in hand with the aim of specialized and expert knowledge.

The second educational theme that affects practice is the notion of "the end of ideology," popularized in works of political science and economics. Issues of ideology are viewed as meaningless in today's world, serving only to confuse the primary questions related to facts and evidences. An individual may emotionally embrace an ideology, but it has no significance to clear cognitive reasoning. Logical-Science philosophers insist that students must be taught to oppose all ideologies on the grounds that they are nonsensical generalities. Training for precise thinking and clarity must replace any ideological considerations.

The third theme is education for specialization. Expert knowledge and "know how" are essential aspects of the Logical-Science thought pattern. Thus, educational practices must center on training for specialization. The best program is one in which students with specialized abilities are taught by specialists, and in which attention is given to proper empirical and mathematical language usage. Team teaching has been used effectively to this end.

PEDAGOGICAL ORIENTATION — PHILOSOPHY OF SCIENCE

Philosophy in Educational Research   /   ERNEST NAGEL

The word "philosophy" is notoriously ambiguous. Indeed, even the more definite label "philosophy of science" in its current usage does not designate a precisely delimited area of study, but on the contrary covers a variety of concerns between which there is often only a tenuous connection. Nevertheless, the task widely assumed to be distinctive of philosophy since its beginnings in Western thought has been to assess and systematically relate from some integrating perspective the diversity of human knowledge and experience. Although as will soon be evident I have serious reservations about the way this unifying function has frequently been performed by philosophers, the general spirit of this view of the office of philosophy inspires the present paper. On the other hand, my familiarity with the substantive materials of educational research is at best peripheral; and I offer these reflections of the philosophy of educational research with the acute sense that I have ventured on territory upon which it would be far wiser for me not to tread. But in any event, I must first take some space to indicate a bit more fully how I envisage the task of philosophy in general and of the philosophy of science in particular, as an essential preliminary to a brief outline of what seems to me a possible role of philosophy in the study of educational problems.

I.

According to an ancient and still influential tradition, philosophy is the fundamental, because most general, science of existence. Its major objective is to discover the basic kinds and structures of reality, and to establish by way of an infallible insight into the nature of things the necessary principles that constitute the intellectual foundations of all knowledge of specialized subject matters. This conception of the aim and method of philosophy has been increasingly on the defensive since the rise of modern science, and especially since developments within pure mathematics and physics have undermined the authority of appeals to allegedly self-evident truth for validating claims to knowledge. Nevertheless, this conception of philosophy has been enjoying a flourishing renaissance in recent years, a revival not without a following among students of education. Moreover, even before this revival, many thinkers who have neglected these ancient pretensions of philosophy concerning matters belonging to the province of the positive sciences, have continued to advance analogous claims for the competence of philosophy to establish the ultimate moral norms and objectives of both individual and social behavior.

The prospects for this conception of philosophy seem to me hopeless, though because of lack of time I must be dogmatic in stating my dissent. I do not believe, in the first place, that truth-claims about the occurrence of events and processes, or about relations of dependence between events, can be established by a logic of procedure other than the one used in a relatively crude fashion in ordinary affairs and employed in a more or less refined manner in the various positive sciences. Insofar as philosophers profess to base their cognitive claims about the nature of things on the methods of empirical science, they are themselves empirical scientists; and their claims must be judged by the same logical standards that are operative in specialized areas of inquiry—standards which, by and large, are not even approximately satisfied by such claims made by exponents of *philosophia perennis*. The supposition that philosophy can supply the foundational principles upon which genuine knowledge of any sector of the world must rest therefore seems to me thoroughly mistaken, and to be belied by the actual history of thought. Nor do I believe, in the second place, that the cognitive issues generated in assessing moral choices or the worth of proposed human ideals can be resolved by invoking a different logical method from the one employed in the positive sciences. In my view, therefore, philosophy does not possess a distinctive procedure for certifying propositions about human values, and philosophers *qua* philosophers are not in a privileged position to make warranted pronouncements about human nature and the proper goals of human effort.

But if the notion of philosophy as the master architectonic science is a blunder, as I think it is, is there a viable alternative to it? I believe there is. For although there does not seem to me to be any *subject matter* that is distinctively and inherently philosophical, there is a large if vaguely demarcated class of *questions,* many of which arise in connection with every specialized subject matter, that are generally regarded as being characteristically philosophical. They are so regarded not simply because they happen to be discussed for the most part by those who are philosophers by profession, since in point of fact such questions are frequently pursued by thinkers in almost every domain of professional activity. The questions are held to be philosophical because they deal with *foundational* problems and more specifically with *foundational problems of knowledge*—with the analysis of ideas central to some particular area of thought as well as with the general conditions under which discourse is meaningful; with the grounds of beliefs dominating some department of inquiry as well as with the logic implicit in evaluating the worth of evidence; or with the relations of one branch of knowledge to some other branch as well as with the general principles presupposed in integrating the conclusions of specialized inquiries into a unifying perspective upon the diverse materials of human experience. For example, one is tackling a philosophical question in this sense when one attempts to clarify such notions as that of cause or energy in physics, growth. or adaptation in biology, instinct or purpose in psychology, democracy or property in political science, and responsibility or self-development in moral theory. Again, one is raising a philosophical question when one asks whether the law of effect in psychology has the status of an empirical generalization or that of a definitional truth, what is the rationale for punishing those guilty of criminal offenses, and in what respects the logic employed in supporting the contention that litigants at law should receive treatment irrespective of their race is similar to or differs from the logic used to warrant the claim that blue-eyed human parents have blue-eyed children. Once more, it is a philosophical problem to determine in what way admitted facts of psychology are contingent upon the findings of physics and biology, or to assess the bearing of current knowledge in the natural and social sciences upon some proposed ideal for human conduct.

It will be evident that on this conception of the role of philosophy, its task is not to add to our knowledge of the *primary subject matters* explored by the various branches of substantive inquiry, neither in the form of propositions about individual happenings nor in the form of general statements about the regularities with which things happen. On this conception the task of philosophy is to be a *critique* of cognitive claims, with the intent, in part, to purge our ideas and beliefs of unclarities and dubious assumptions, in part to make us self-conscious about the nature and grounds of our intellectual commitments, and in part to enlarge the angle of our vision by suggesting alternative ways to unreflectively habitual ones for organizing and bringing into mutual relations various detailed portions of our knowledge. It will also be evident, however, that on this conception of philosophy, competent philosophical inquiry requires both considerable familiarity with the substantive content and the procedures of specific inquiries, as well as some mastery of techniques of logical analysis. That is why, although in my opinion much of the best work in the philosophy of science has been done by philosophically minded scientists, most practicing scientists neither give serious consideration to philosophical questions nor are they able to discuss such questions in a mature manner. That is also why philosophers who have developed some sensitivity to logical issues and some skills in resolving them as part of their professional training are often particularly well-equipped to deal with at least certain types of problems in the philosophy of science.

In my view, therefore, philosophy can serve as an integrating discipline, even if not quite in the traditional sense, by articulating, assessing, and thereby perhaps helping to reorganize the logical organization of our knowledge, and the logical principles employed in establishing cognitive claims. At any rate, this is the central concern of the philosophy of science, despite the fact that philosophical discussions of science often appear to deal with a miscellany of unrelated themes. There are many ways of classifying these themes, especially when the word "science" is used broadly, as I propose to use it here, not only for the various conventional divisions of inquiry into natural and social phenomena, but for any areas of reflective thought, including the domain of moral deliberation, in which cognitive claims stated in propositional form can be significantly made. However, without pretending to offer an exhaustive listing of major problems that are considered in the philosophy of science—indeed, I am deliberately excluding from this account questions in the sociology of knowledge which deal with certain factual matters concerning the mutual relations of science and society, and which are sometimes subsumed under the philosophy of science—I have found the following three-fold classification useful for indicating the office of philosophy as a critique of discursive thought.

1. Problems relating to the evaluation of evidence. Under this heading belong, among other things, analyses of the requirements for significant observation and experiment, of the various canons for estimating the probative force of evidential statements, of the nature and rationale of probable inference, and of principles for judging the competence of decisions between alternative policies.
2. Problems relating to the explication of concepts. This rubric covers such matters as the examination of varieties of definitional procedures, of the criteria for the empirical significance of statements, of the logic of classification and measurement, and of the logical requirements for generalizing the applicability of ideas.
3. Problems relating to the construction of systematic bodies of knowledge. Under this label are included discussions of the types and functions of general statements, of patterns of explanation and prediction, of the role of analogies and models in the expansion of knowledge, and of the logical conditions for assimilating different branches of inquiry into a common intellectual framework.

These groups of problems are in general not independent of one another, even though it is often the case that some thinkers are more attracted to one group, or are better equipped to deal with some of the specific questions subsumed under it, than to another group. Moreover, each of these convenient divisions also contains not only discussions of the general problems I have mentioned, but also discussions of special forms of these problems in the context of some concrete branch of inquiry. But I hope I have said enough to suggest that the philosophy of science, or philosophy as a critique of reflective thought, can play a significant role in every domain in which a quest for responsibly grounded knowledge is actively pursued.

II.

I must now indicate in what way philosophy so construed may be pertinent to the enterprise of educational research. If I can judge from the small fraction of its literature with which I am familiar, educational research is addressed to two roughly distinguishable sets of problems. The first group of questions are empirical or factual in the narrow sense of these words. They deal with such matters as the testing of traditional or proposed techniques of instruction and learning, the development of reliable measures for various types of ability and achievement, the effectiveness of some designated course of study and training for achieving a stated aim, or the optimal structure of various administrative units in the organization of educational institutions. The second set of problems is often regarded as the distinctively philosophical of foundational sector of educational research. These problems are in the main concerned with formulating, analyzing, and to some extent justifying less inclusive educational objectives and policies, in part in the light of various biological, psychological, and sociological assumptions about human capacities, in part under the influence of more or less explicitly avowed moral and social ideals. Although these problems raise some issues that can be resolved only by reference to ostensible matters of fact, so that those issues can in principle be settled in an admittedly objective manner, these problems also involve questions concerning the comparative worth of alternate and frequently incompatible human aspirations and moral standards. In consequence, this area of educational research is faced by most of the difficulties that confront those who attempt to supply a rational basis for moral choice and value judgments.

1. Insofar as educational research is a branch of positive science, a philosophical critique can contribute to its development in a fashion quite analogous to the way such a critique functions in other positive inquiries. I do not feel qualified to cite chapter and verse in this connection. But at the risk of appearing presumptuous, I do want to mention some pertinent though elementary considerations in the logic of science, greater familiarity with which on the part of those engaged in positive educational research is eminently desirable.

a. In the first place, the simplicistic Baconian conception of science still seems to dominate much empirical research in this area, so that the assiduous collection of data, uninformed by a clearly formulated and consciously entertained controlling hypothesis, is often taken to be the paradigm of sound inquiry. This state of affairs is not improved by the circumstance that unacknowledged assumptions may enter critically into the interpretations which the investigator places upon his data. Although no one can be explicitly aware of all the tacit assumptions one is making in the conduct of any inquiry, it is well to realize that one is always operating within some framework of presuppositions, and to be habitually on the lookout for those that are highly questionable. This point seems to me especially important in a domain, such as the study of human behavior, in which theoretical notions are frequently taken for granted that are still not firmly established. The rather prominent fluctuations of fads and fashions in educational practice, though presumably each is based on the findings of allegedly "scientific" research, provide some evidence that many of those findings are not the conclusions of a critically conducted inquiry.

b. It is also my impression, in the second place, that although research techniques are often employed in this domain with undoubted mechanical expertness, those who use them do not always possess a mature understanding of their intellectual tools. For example, they are in general not sensitive to the limitations of various types of quantitative scales currently in use, and are sometimes not aware of even such fundamental points as that the relative magnitudes of numerical differences on an ordinal scale are without significance. Similarly, they apply many statistical formulas in drawing inferences from data, without much thought to the fact that while those formulas may be valid within the framework of theoretical assumptions in which the formulas are derived, these assumptions may not always be realized with a sufficient degree of approximation to warrant the inferences. Moreover, there is often only a dim conception of the nature of controlled experiment, so that general propositions are asserted on the basis of ostensibly confirmatory data that do not provide competent support for those conclusions. In any event, there is a frequent neglect of the fundamental canon of experimental reasoning that the mere agreement of factual data with a given hypothesis does not constitute cogent evidence for the latter, if those data are also compatible with equally plausible competing hypotheses.

2. But I must turn to the second group of problems in educational research.

a. I introduce my first point with the obvious reminder that since proposed educational objectives and practices may in part be based on allegedly warranted conclusions of some other branch of inquiry, some consideration deserves to be given to the question whether those conclusions are indeed solidly grounded. Now the physical sciences, and to a lesser extent the biological ones, have been operating during a fairly long period with standards of workmanship that have yielded intellectual products which have proved to be generally reliable; and there is therefore a reasonable presumption that the conclusions accepted from these sciences are firmly grounded. However, this cannot be said about psychology, a major source of many of the assumptions upon which educational objectives and practices are supported. For although there are currently differing "schools" of psychology, there are today no comparable "schools" of physics. Accordingly, so long as there are such schools, so long as competently trained students disagree in their interpretations of psychological data because of their adherence to differing psychological theories, educational objectives and practices based (even if only partially) on such disputed matters may often be only the expressions of partisan commitments in a warfare of psychological schools. Moreover, there are reasons for suspecting that some of these current schools, such as variant forms of psychoanalysis or of behaviorism, are in turn elaborations of antecedently adopted general assumptions (or "philosophies") about the "real" nature of man—assumptions which may be too vague to be capable of either proof or disproof by experiment, but which may nonetheless significantly color the selection and formulation of observed data. There is a manifest circularity in advocating a conception of human nature on the ground that the conception is in conformity with the facts of psychology, if those facts are themselves the products of an interpretation of empirical data that is controlled by such antecedent assumptions about the nature of man. It is evident that a philosophy of educational objectives erected on the foundations of such a conception of human nature has an empirical backing that may be largely specious, and may in fact only serve as window dressing for a conception that is wholly an a priori construction.

The point I am therefore concerned to make is that a philosophical critique of the ostensibly empirical assumptions upon which conceptions of human nature underlying proposed educational objectives are based can render a vital service to educational research. An indispensable prerequisite for such a critique in the present connection is competent familiarity with the special discipline (which is not necessarily psychology) into whose province the assumptions under discussion fall. But a no less essential requirement is logical maturity, combined with a sensitivity to shifts in meaning that words may undergo as they are moved from one context of usage to another. I have already said something about logical maturity, and will therefore illustrate only the second part of this latter requirement. Consider, for example, the transformations in the meaning of the word "development" when it is transplanted from biological to psychological to moral contexts, as in the following sequence: "development of an embryo," "development of an idea," "development of human individuality." In the first of these phrases, the word is used in an exclusively descriptive or nonevaluative sense, and refers to some series of definite stages in the "natural" formation of increasingly more complex organic structures. In the second phrase, the word is again used in an essentially nonevaluative fashion, to designate some sequential elaboration of a notion, whether in the direction of its explicit formulation, the derivation of some of its logical consequences, or its extended application to various types of problems. In the third phrase, the word is employed in an unmistakable approbative or evaluative sense, though without any clear indication of the direction of the changes that ostensibly merit commendation. However, despite these alterations in meaning, there is a considerable carry-over to other contexts of the sense of the word as used in the biological domain. There is thus a temptation, to which some thinkers have indeed succumbed, to assume, for example, that the development of human individuality is a biological rather than a distinctive moral notion, and to believe that the word "development" when employed in discussions of educational ideals is as nonevaluative as when it is employed in biology. More generally, the occurrence of an expression in a variety of contexts with somewhat altered though apparently "continuous" meanings is often a sign that some analogy whose terms are borrowed from one domain is being exploited in some other area. But while analogies may have great heuristic value, their use may also conceal crucial differences between the allegedly analogous traits of different subject matters, and may therefore be misleading. To call attention to analogies that may control the discussion of educational objectives, to make explicit the tacit assumptions employed in this domain, to examine their credentials, is one important task that a philosophical critique can undertake.

b. A second though related task that such a critique can perform is to reveal elements of a sterile utopianism and of an ineffective sentimentalism that may present in actual or proposed educational ideals, by examining, on the one hand, current assumptions about the relations of means to ends, and on the other hand the coherence of envisaged ideals of educational practice with the acknowledged facts about the human materials of education. Educational objectives are often defended by reference to biological and psychological information concerning human capacities, without serious consideration of the nature of the social institutions in which those capacities will presumably manifest themselves. In consequence, specific educational ends may be proposed, as if those ends could be realized irrespective of what social mechanisms other than the schools are in operation or what objectives other than educational ones are being pursued in the society under discussion. Thus, even a relatively definite educational ideal such as universal literacy will in practice have a different specific content, according to the composition of the community in which that ideal is adopted and according to the uses to which literacy is put because of the institutional arrangements of the community. Moreover, the assumption is commonly made that objectives can be chosen in a principled manner, independently of the means through which those objectives may be realized. However, this assumption rests on a serious error of oversight, of neglecting the elementary point that the consequences produced by two different means are never precisely the same, and that the *total* ends achieved through the use of distinct means are not identical. For example, there undoubtedly are different ways of teaching children how to read, and one of these ways may be regarded as the preferable one because its adoption leads to a more rapid acquisition of reading skills than do the alternative ways. However, even if maximum speed of acquiring such skills is a desideratum, the method of teaching that achieves this result is not necessarily the most desirable one. For the use of that method may have other consequences as well (e.g., it may generate a tendency to misspell, or a questionably sound habit of reading all texts at the same rate). Such possible "side-effects" must not be ignored, for they are obviously included in the total end achieved through the use of that method. We are therefore foolishly utopian if we think that ends can be properly adjudicated without consideration of means for attaining them.

But inversely, educational objectives need to be examined for their compatibility with what is presumably known about the capacities and the aspirations of those for whom the objectives are being proposed. I must content myself with but one example of what I have in mind. Some contemporary thinkers maintain that in a society whole-heartedly dedicated to democratic ideals, all schools inclusive of college should seek to generate a sense of common heritage by requiring all students to follow a *uniform* course of study in the sciences and the humanities. According to these thinkers, schools betray the democratic ideal when they are organized to provide one type of instruction for those likely to enter one of the so-called professions, and a different course of instruction for those headed for more "practically" oriented careers; and an identical "liberal" education is therefore recommended as a right and a duty for all citizens of a democratic society. For the purposes of the present discussion, I will take for granted the desirability of a widespread familarity with the heritage of thought and artistic expression that is our portion as members of a liberal civilization; and I agree that it would be undemocratic to deny equal educational *opportunities* to those possessing the *requisite and comparable aptitudes* for preparing themselves for desired careers. But I also think it is muddled of well-intentioned sentimentalism to argue that a genuinely democratic ideal demands a system of public education which gives the *same* training to everyone, irrespective of individual differences in capacity and aspiration, and that this ideal is compromised when provision is made in courses of study even in elementary and secondary schools for those to whom a stress on various "practical" subjects is more congruous with their abilities and ambitions than is an exclusive emphasis on the purely theoretical content of the sciences and humanities. A uniform requirement with respect to the content of instruction leads to a debasing of that content if, as no one seriously disputes, there are important differences in the individual capacities of students. Moreover, if a democratic society is directed toward the moral ideal that all men be given equal opportunities for realizing their distinctive talents, uniformity in respect to the content of education for everyone contributes to the defeat of that ideal, since it can impede students from preparing themselves for careers congruent with their individual gifts.

c. Thus far I have been stressing the purgative role of philosophic criticism. However, as has been often and justly noted, we cannot live on disinfectants alone; and although I do not believe that philosophers have special prerogatives in matters concerned with values, neither are philosophers necessarily disqualified for discussing them. My concluding remarks are therefore intended to suggest briefly a positive contribution that philosophy can make to the articulation of what in my judgment is an important educational objective.

I must prepare the ground for my suggestion by mentioning the familiar fact that in almost every field of inquiry specialization is increasing at an accelerated rate, and that in consequence there is some basis for the frequently expressed alarm that the incapacity for communicating with one another which was finally exhibited by the ancient builders of the tower of Babel is a fate that also threatens ourselves. Moreover, partly as a consequence of this increasing specialization and of the attendant difficulties that a nonspecialist experiences in trying to understand current scientific theories, and partly because responsibility for many of our current ills is frequently laid at the door of modern science, there is a widespread conviction that the sciences are not humanistic disciplines. Despite the many admittedly beneficial contributions that technologies based on scientific theories have been making to the enhancement of human life, the traditional hostility between the sciences and the humanities has become intensified.

It would take many volumes to fill in with some degree of adequacy this thumbnail sketch, and to examine the complex issues that are generated by the situation it describes. The only one of these problems I have time to mention is that of finding some integrating perspective from which to view the various compartmentalized scientific inquiries, and thereby of achieving a just appreciation of the significance of the scientific enterprise in the economy of human concerns. It is to this problem that I want to address myself briefly. It seems to me that there are just two major ways in which a unified view of science and of the knowledge it achieves can be obtained. The first is to find comprehensive substantive principles, with the help of which the innumerable items of information amassed in specialized inquiries can be exhibited as details in an intelligible pattern of relations. For example, Newton effected such a unification of the then current knowledge of mechanical phenomena through the introduction of his axioms of motion and theory of gravitation. In my opinion, however, a comparable unification for the entire range of our present knowledge is not likely to occur in the foreseeable future. But in any event, a unification of this sort is something that must await further scientific advances; and as I have already indicated, philosophy can contribute little if anything to achieve that objective.

The second way for integrating knowledge is to exhibit the findings of the sciences as well as the warranted cognitive claims made in other contexts of human concern as the products of a common intellectual method. If there is a logic of inquiry that is canonical for investigations into all subject matters (as I believe there is, though I can assert this here only dogmatically), and since in point of fact philosophers are often particularly concerned with articulating its features and examining its credentials, philosophy can render an important service in such a task of integration. But I hasten to add that it is a task which philosophers cannot undertake unaided.

My suggestion pertinent to the present context therefore is that philosophers can play a constructive role in the detailed formulation of a central educational objective. That objective, when stated in general terms, is to replace intellectual habits which tend to make men accept and retain unexamined beliefs by intellectual habits that place a premium on responsibly based thought. However, if this general objective is to be realized, the character of cogent reasoning must be set forth clearly, not simply in the abstract but in the context of teaching the concrete materials of various specialized domains of inquiry. In short, I believe that a supreme educational objective can be realized only if both the sciences and the humanities are presented to students not simply as miscellaneous bodies of useful and enlightened information, but as the fruits of a characteristically human method of intelligence. For organizing such presentations, there is needed expert familiarity with the accredited outcome of educational research, and expert familiarity with the relevant distinctions and principles of logic. By participating in such a cooperative reorganization of the content of instruction, philosophy can make what I think is an invaluable contribution to educational practice and theory. In this way, philosophical criticism can be of constructive aid in exhibiting the unity of the logical foundations of our knowledge, and in showing that the various sciences, like the disciplines traditionally designated as the humanities, are the interrelated products of a single, intellectually liberating and humanistic enterprise.

PEDAGOGICAL ORIENTATION— LINGUISTIC CRITICAL PHILOSOPHY

What is an Educational Theory?
DANIEL J. O'CONNOR

In the strictest sense of the word, a theory is an established hypothesis or, more usually, a logically connected set of such hypotheses whose main function is to explain their subject matter. The object of this discussion is to find out what can be said about theories in education. For

"What is an Educational Theory?" is reprinted from D. J. O'Connor, "What is an Educational Theory?" in An Introduction to the Philosophy of Education, London: Routledge and Kegan Paul, Ltd., 1957. Permission granted by Routledge and Kegan Paul, Ltd., and Philosophical Library.

the word 'theory' is apt to be used there very freely but more loosely than in most other contexts. It will therefore be worthwhile finding out, if we can, both the different senses in which the term occurs there and also the extent to which it is used in its primary sense of an explanatory conceptual framework based on experience and when it is used only in some derivative and weakened sense. Because of the success of scientific modes of explanation, the word 'theory' has come to be a prestige word. Like most such words, it is used more often for its prestige value than for its strict descriptive sense. An examination of this kind will tell us when we are to take the word 'theory' seriously in an educational context and when we need not do so.

Most people would agree that education is not itself a science. It is rather a set of practical activities connected by a common aim. But such activities often have their theoretical justification in some scientific theory. Indeed, the more reliable and efficient a system of education becomes, the more firmly will its techniques and aims be grounded in scientific findings. In this respect, the practice of education may be compared with the practice of medicine or of engineering. Medicine again is not itself a science. It aims not at the increase of knowledge but at a practical result, the prevention and cure of disease. However, in order that doctors can carry out this task effectively, they have to make use of the relevant scientific discoveries in their practical techniques; and they have themselves to know a certain amount of the sciences that bear upon their work. In particular, they must know a good deal of anatomy and physiology, the sciences of the structure of the body and of its working. Again, if we look not at the physicians and surgeons themselves but at the medical research workers who develop the tools of the doctors' trade, we find that many of them are pure scientists and perhaps not even medically qualified. The growing points of medical knowledge lie largely in pure science, in physics, chemistry and physiology rather than in the day to day activities of the consulting room and the operating theatre.

The same is true of the relation between the practical techniques of the engineer and the theoretical discoveries of the scientist and the mathematician. If no more mathematics and physics was known today than was known three hundred years ago, we should be without practically all the mechanical advances that have marked off the nineteenth and twentieth centuries from the rest of history. There were of course doctors, surgeons and engineers in the ancient and medieval worlds. They had to work without the scientific equipment of their present-day counterparts and, as a result, the scope of their work and its efficacy was immeasurably less than that of modern doctors and engineers. Their skill and knowledge was based on what they and their predecessors could find out by trial and error in the course of their practice. This traditional skill and knowledge was rarely based on any sort of experimentally verified findings and in the case of medicine contained as a result a good deal of superstition and nonsense. (Doctors and educators, unlike engineers, are not restrained by the nature of their failures from allowing their practice to outstrip its theoretical basis.)

How far can we use this analogy between education and other practical arts with a scientific basis? It might be tempting to suppose that since the sciences on which education rests are not in the advanced state of chemistry, physics and mathematics, great advances in educational theory and practice may be expected when the sciences of psychology and sociology attain maturity. Perhaps twentieth-century education is in the primitive condition of the engineering and medicine of the seventeenth and eighteenth centuries. We have made some advances in the relevant social sciences but so far, the advances have been modest ones and even so, they have not been properly applied in the service of education. More perfect knowledge and more systematic application of theory to practice may perhaps be expected to bring about an educational revolution. Some people would no doubt be willing to support this point of view but I think that there are good reasons for supposing that it is far too optimistic about the future and, moreover, far too pessimistic about the present.

What then is wrong with the proposed analogy? In one sense, the comparison is a fair one. Education like medicine and engineering, is a set of practical activities and we understand better how to carry them out if we understand the natural laws that apply to the material with which we have to work. Indeed, if we were quite ignorant of these laws, the limits of our successful practice would be very narrow. But some of the regularities of nature are much more easily known than others. Men lived successfully for many thousands of years and developed great civilizations without more than a very superficial acquaintance with the laws of mechanics and without knowing anything at all of electro-magnetism, chemistry or physiology. The laws of these sciences are not to be grasped by casual observers. Mere observation, however careful and persistent, is not enough. It needs patient and orderly *experiment* in order to make any headway at all in these fields. That is to say, observations must be made under conditions controlled and systematically varied by the observer and directed by his hypotheses. Such sciences also require techniques of accurate measurement and devices for extending the normal reach of observation, microscopes, galvanometers, spectrographs and the like. Thus they can develop only gradually and in a civilization that puts a high value on this sort of knowledge.

But it is, to some extent, quite different in the sciences of man. One of the reasons why psychology, economics, sociology and the rest of the studies that we call social sciences developed so late is, paradoxically, just that we can learn a good deal about them by casual observation, provided that it is intelligent and critical. The rough regularities of behaviour and experience that we can all notice in ourselves, our friends and our animals are sufficient to give us all a modest stock of psychological knowledge. We know roughly how we learn, how we are motivated, how our emotions work and so on. Such knowledge is very limited, inaccurate and unorganized but it is sufficient to enable us to live our lives more or less successfully in contact with other people. So too with the other social sciences. As long as social and economic organization remains at a fairly elementary level, we can understand the operation of social and economic laws well enough to keep our institutions in control. When there is an economic crisis in a South Pacific island it is likely to be due to something obvious and inevitable like a crop failure rather than to some unexpected outcome of government policy or the defects of the monetary system.

There is thus an important difference between the laws of nature and the laws of human nature. The regularities of human and animal behaviour are clear in rough outline to an intelligent observer. But the regularities of nature lie, for the most part, beneath the surface of things and have to be painfully elucidated by the standard methods of science. This is one of the reasons why education has been a successful enterprise for many thousands of years while medicine and engineering have only recently attained maturity. A good teacher knows enough of the workings of human nature from common experience to enable him to teach effectively.

Considerations of this sort are sometimes used to discredit the social sciences and in particular, the science of psychology. But I certainly do not wish to suggest that the sciences of man are unimportant or trivial. Indeed it is just because they seem so obvious at their superficial levels that it is easy to be dangerously complacent or dogmatic about our supposed knowledge of ourselves. The accounts of human nature in educational theory from Plato to Froebel are a good example of the dangers of relying on pre-scientific psychology for our beliefs about man. Although intelligent reflection on a wide experience may give us the capacity for successful day-to-day dealings with our fellows, it will certainly not suffice for all the social occasions of a complex modern society. In just the same way, a shrewd business sense that might make a man wealthy in ancient Athens or the Solomon Islands would not be a substitute for the specialist knowledge needed by an economic adviser to the Treasury.

There is a sense in which the development of the sciences of man, like that of the natural sciences, has been determined by social conditions. The rise of modern psychology, economics and sociology has been helped by the fact that social organization has grown so complicated in the last hundred years that our rule of thumb, commonsense knowledge of man has proved quite inadequate. A very intricate economic organization will easily get out of control unless the forces at work in it are understood. Thus modern economic theory has been in part a response to the demands of an increasingly complex economy. So also modern psychological theory has arisen, partly at least, to meet the requirements of administrators for whom the problems offered by industry, mental health and education were rapidly outgrowing the crude psychological opinions common to intelligent men.

It is easy to see how this has happened in the case of education. There is no reason to suppose that the average effectiveness of the teaching given in ancient or medieval times was very much less than that of our present-day schools. No doubt, the teachers of those days used methods that would nowadays be recognized as time-wasting and inefficient but by and large they achieved their aims, such as they were. And when we look at the Greek or medieval achievements in art, literature and philosophy, it certainly does not become us, as twentieth-century critics, to despise the educational systems that furthered them. Yet it is obvious that those educational methods would not give the results that we look for today. Ancient and medieval teachers could afford to rely on traditional commonsense methods of teaching because the material on which they had to work was a small body of students selected by rank or talent. Modern education, on the other hand, is given indiscriminately to the whole of the child population. Moreover, while the teacher in former times had only to impart a limited body of knowledge and skill, modern teachers have somehow between them to ensure that the whole of contemporary knowledge is transmitted at least to sufficient numbers of students to guarantee that it will be preserved and furthered. They have also to see that practically everyone, however ill-suited by capacity or interest, can read and write sufficiently to fill up forms and understand official instructions. (Illiteracy is not, as is often pretended, a cultural problem; but it can be a serious social problem in a complex modern society.)

Thus two of the basic aims of education nowadays require that educational methods shall be as efficient as possible. For this purpose, it is necessary that what we know of the sciences of man shall be applied to ensure this increased efficiency. Thus the analogy between education and applied skills like medicine or engineering is imperfect. Even to be efficient on a small scale, medicine and engineering must be based on natural science. But education demands this only when it has so increased in scale and complexity that the laws of human nature that are patent to intelligent observers prove an inadequate theoretical basis and need to be supplemented or replaced by the sciences of man.

Before we consider the extent to which these sciences are applied in educational theory and practice, it will be useful to look at the ways in which the social sciences are supposed to differ from the natural sciences. For we have based the discussion of theories and explanation in the previous chapter on the ways in which these concepts occur in the natural sciences. We did so because sciences like physics, chemistry and astronomy are the standard cases of well-developed sciences so that the clearest and best established uses of terms like 'theory' and 'explanation' will be found there. Now we want to know how far the uses of these terms in education conform to these standard uses and how far they are weakened and derivative.

In the first place, it is well to remember that the history of the social sciences is a short one. Psychology as an experimental science has a history of less than a hundred years. Previously it had been a branch of speculative philosophy. We cannot foresee at this date how far it may progress in the future. Possibly our present-day psychology, like chemistry in the early nineteenth century, is on the threshold of a spectacular period of progress. But it may be that the subject matter of psychology and its methods can never give us this sort of systematic development. Only the future history of the science can tell us that. What we can do is to look at the sort of differences that obviously exist at present between psychology and the other sciences of man on the one hand and the sciences of nature on the other.

We must not start however by making too sharp a division between the sciences of man and the sciences of nature. Man is a part of nature. His body is as much subject as are the other parts of nature to the laws of physics, chemistry and biology. And if we look at the relations between the sciences, we do not find that there is any sharp discontinuity between the sciences peculiar to man and those common to man and the rest of nature. The laws of physics set the framework within which the laws of chemistry may be found. Chemistry sets a similar framework for biology and biology for psychology. In the same way the laws of psychology are the limits within which the specialized sciences of man, economics, sociology and the rest can be understood. Thus the sciences can be regarded as having the same sort of relation to each other as the members of a set of Chinese boxes, the more general and abstract studies setting the limits for the more specialized. In this way there is a clear continuity between the sciences of man and the sciences of nature, just as there is a clear continuity between man himself and the rest of the universe. But having recognized this continuity, it is helpful in trying to understand the nature of theories about man, to trace whatever differences there may be between the social and the natural sciences.

The most obvious of these differences is the one I have referred to already: the main laws of the sciences of man are more obvious or at least less surprising than those of the sciences of nature. Indeed, the social sciences might be satirically defined as those sciences which tell us nothing that we do not know already. This description, in spite of being a rhetorical exaggeration, is not entirely misleading. Being men, we have every opportunity for observing the main trends of human experience and behaviour. And living in societies, we have a privileged viewpoint on the workings of societies. This inside knowledge of the subject matter of the social sciences has both advantages and drawbacks. Although it gives us some sort of rough and ready knowledge of the uniformities of human behaviour, it inhibits us from looking at them with the objective eye that the scientist needs. Moreover it is liable to make us complacent about the value and range of our common understanding of man. The layman is more suspicious of the psychologist than he is of other scientists just because he is unwilling to believe that the knowledge of man can be an intellectual speciality.

The extent to which psychology, to take only one example, conforms to this satirical description of a social science [1] may be tested by reading any standard elementary text-book on the subject. Those psychological discoveries that come as a surprise to us will be found, in general, to come from two different sources. Either they originate from the laboratory of the physiologist and so are not, properly speaking, part of psychology at all, or they come from the speculations of the psychiatrists. And these, however surprising they may be, are supported by such flimsy evidence that they can hardly rank as scientific discoveries.[2] Yet in spite of this, psychology is not a negligible collection of truisms in a scientific guise. It is an important and rapidly developing science with rewarding applications in many different fields. What is the explanation of this apparent contradiction?

In so far as psychology merely confirms common human opinion on man's nature, it serves three important scientific ends. In the first place, it makes this common knowledge *precise*. Secondly, it gives us an orderly account of the *evidence* for it. Our common knowledge of human nature is both vague and unsupported by adequate evidence and so cannot really rank as *knowledge* at all. It should rather be called belief or opinion. And opinons of this ill-defined and ill-supported kind cannot be reliably applied. Thirdly, the experimental psychologist can often show how the different ways in which we behave can be related together. He can thus *systematize* common opinion on these matters which in its ordinary forms tends to be piecemeal and unorganized. Thus psychology

---

[1] The obvious exception to this rule seems to be social anthropology. Here we learn a great deal that is surprising and strange about the customs of men in societies very different from our own. But these surprising facts are the *material* of the anthropologist not his *conclusions*. They do however illustrate the tendency of human behaviour to take on different forms in different circumstances. This point is referred to below.

[2] For a useful critical discussion of the evidence for psychotherapy, see H. J. Eysenck, *Uses and Abuses of Psychology*, Chapter 10, and D. O. Hebb, *Organization of Behavior*, Chapter 10.

introduces into our everyday knowledge of human nature the characteristically scientific notes of precision, evidence and system and so justifies
its claim to be the science of experience and behaviour. I have chosen to
speak of psychology here as it is the science most clearly germane to
education. But the same sort of advance from commonsense opinion to
scientific knowledge occurs in the other social sciences.

There is a second obvious way in which the laws of the sciences of
man differ from those of the sciences of nature. We regard the laws of
nature as permanent and immutable features of the world, the same
today as they were in the Old Stone Age. We have indeed no conclusive
proof that they never will alter in the future or that they never have done
so in the past. But we have good evidence for supposing that such
variations, if they occur at all, are so slight or so infrequent as not to
demand that we take account of them. But this is not quite the position
with the sciences of man. The question 'Can we change human nature?'
as it is popularly asked is a vague one. But it can be put in a form that is
in principle capable of being answered by observational evidence,
though the evidence might be very difficult to obtain. For our purposes,
however, the interesting feature of the question is that it is not obviously
absurd. We should never think of asking 'Can we change the laws of
chemistry?'

There are several ways in which the laws of human nature might seem
to be changeable. Because the sciences of man lie, as it were, in a matrix
of non-human sciences, the laws of human nature depend to a largely
unknown degree on the laws of physics, chemistry and biology. These
sciences might therefore be applied to alter human nature as we know it.
For example, applications of genetics to human breeding might conceiv-
ably alter man to the extent that wheat or maize has been altered by
systematic plant-breeding. Or mutations might be induced in men, accidentally or by design, which might bring entirely new hereditary characters to mankind. The possibilities of this sort are numerous but so far,
perhaps fortunately, they have been exploited only in imagination by the
writers of utopian novels or science fiction. (Aldous Huxley's *Brave New
World* is the best known example.) Such genetic changes, if they occurred, would tend to bring about changes in social structure. For
example, systems of representative democracy as we know them are
possible only because the native abilities of mankind are distributed as
they are. A society in which 95 per cent of the population were mentally
defective and 5 per cent of high intellectual gifts would not be a
representative democracy. (It would far more probably be a slave state.)

Just as innate human tendencies have an influence on the structure of
society, so social structure can influence the ways in which our hereditary capacities develop and show themselves in action. An important
justification of large scale educational reforms is precisely the reasonable

hope that altered social conditions will bring out features of human nature which are masked or discouraged by other kinds of educational organization.

Of course, in neither of these two cases could we properly say that the *laws* of human nature had altered. It would be rather that man, like any other part of nature, responds differently to different conditions and by altering the conditions we can provide new occasions in which previously hidden capabilities can be developed.

The extent to which we can do this points to a third difference between the natural and the social sciences. The scope of experiment is greatly limited in the social sciences. There are two main reasons for this. The first is a matter of morals. When we experiment with human material, the varying conditions to which we subject our material are restricted by the welfare of the human beings on whom we are working and by what we recognize to be their rights. In the second place, it is technically very difficult for obvious reasons to vary social conditions on any large scale. Thus the possibility of observation under controlled conditions is naturally restricted in the sciences of man. We are therefore compelled to rely largely on *comparing* what we can observe under conditions familiar to us with what we can observe under rare or unfamiliar conditions. We compare the behaviour of normal adults with that of children, savages or psychotics, or the structure of our own social system with that of societies very different from our own. This will tell us something but it is naturally much less effective than systematic experiment would be, were this possible.

Perhaps the most important of the differences between the natural and the social sciences lies in their respective levels of development. T. H. Huxley, the great Victorian biologist, suggested a very useful analysis of the development of a science into three stages. The first stage is shown at the level of commonsense knowledge of a subject as, for example, the ordinary man's casual knowledge of plants. The second stage is that of natural history exemplified by, say, the amateur botanist who finds the collection and classification of plants an interesting pastime. The third stage of a fully developed science is reached when the whole of the plant world and its environment is understood by the biologist as a complex system of interacting causes and effects. These three phases are not, of course, sharply distinct and the third stage of any science is never completely achieved. Natural history, the second stage, is the descriptive and classificatory phase of a science. It falls roughly into two parts: (*a*) careful and exact observation and recording of facts; (*b*) the intelligent classification of these facts to reduce them to a manageable and comprehensible order. The social sciences are, for the most part, in this second phase of development and in some of them development has not gone far enough for us to know if the third stage will ever be possible. Social science in its present state is little more than the natural history of man.

These are the most important differences between the natural and the social sciences.[3] We can point also to others in techniques of measurement, in the precision with which the technical terms of the science can be defined, in the kinds of explanation used, in the degree to which theories can be systematized; and so on. Some of these differences are due to the nature of the material with which the scientist has to work and some of them are due to the stage of development that the science has reached. Only the future development of the sciences can tell us how fundamental these differences are. But in considering the status of educational theories we have to take the social sciences as they are at present.

I now come to the main question with which this chapter is concerned: How far should educational theories properly be called 'theories'? And what kind of theories are they? I suppose that it will have been obvious from what was said earlier that theories in education do not, in general, conform to the models that we find in a well-developed natural science. We have discussed very briefly some of the reasons for this. Nevertheless, it would be absurd to deny that education has a theoretical basis. What we should be clear about however is what job these educational theories do if they do not have the logical status of standard scientific theories.

If we read a text-book on educational theories or the history of educational ideas, we can find three quite different sorts of statement which have been put forward as a basis for educational practice.[4] These kinds of statement are different in the sense that they belong to distinct logical families and for that reason need to be supported in quite different ways. Often indeed we find that the three kinds are mixed up together in the writings of a single man so that it is not easy to judge the value of what he is saying until we have distinguished the different logical components and evaluated them separately. First, there is often a *metaphysical* part to educational writings. This occurs most obviously in the writings of Plato and the medieval scholastics and, in modern times,

---

[3] It is sometimes claimed by writers on the methodology of the social sciences that the question of 'free will' and the problem of value judgments present peculiar difficulties for the social scientist. These are old fallacies which are unfortunately still believed by some. I mention them here only for this reason. 'Free will' presents a philosophical problem which has no bearing on factual question of how far the *statistical* predictions of the social scientists are reliable. And though value judgments may form part of the social scientist's *material*, they do not, if he is a good scientist, influence his *conclusions*. They may, of course, affect the methods he adopts but no more so than they may affect the methods of the chemist or the biologist.

[4] It is a useful elementary exercise in philosophical criticism to read some standard texts on education with the object of detecting the different kinds of statement which occur there. On the whole, the better the writing, the easier it will be to recognize its different components.

in the educational theories of Christian writers. Statements of this kind are not believed, in the first place, just because they form part of an educational theory. They are accepted rather because they feature in a philosophy or a theology which is already believed on other grounds. But they occur in educational writings naturally enough because they are the sort of statements which seem to have an important bearing on education. Many of Plato's educational proposals, for example, are based on the beliefs that man is essentially a soul or spirit in a temporary association with a material body, that this soul was created before the body and will survive its dissolution and that the real object of education is 'improvement of the soul'. This belief in a radical distinction between soul and body is, of course, a metaphysical one. It has never been demonstrated by any recognized process of argument. Nor can we even be sure what sort of argument could establish it. Christianity took over from Platonism this belief in an immaterial and immortal soul in a temporary relation with a material and corruptible body. And it has added a more precise and circumstantial account than Plato's of the divine origin of souls and their destiny. Moreover, it has supplemented this with an explanation of the relation of man to God in terms of the doctrines of the incarnation, grace and salvation. Whether true or false, all of these doctrines, Platonic and Christian alike, are metaphysical in the sense in which we have understood this word. Nevertheless, they have had an enormous influence on the aims and methods of education. And it is easy to see why this has been so. If we hold that every human being is an immortal soul, created by God for an eternal destiny and placed here on earth in a state of probation, this belief has an important effect on the aims and content of the educational system that we shall be prepared to support.[5] We have seen that the main difficulty about claims of this kind is that there is no well-established way of confirming them. It is therefore impossible to say exactly what is being claimed or even to be sure that such statements have any cognitive meaning at all. Propositions

---

[5] The following point is important but is put here in a footnote because it may be found difficult. It is not possible to deduce statements about the aims of a system of education or its curriculum from any purely *philosophical* statements. This follows from an obvious extension of Hume's principle, namely, that the evidence for any conclusion must contain statements of the same logical sort as the conclusion itself. There is a sense in which a practical policy for education can 'follow from' a psychological theory about human motivation, for example, or the learning process. But it does not follow from it in any logical sense. It is merely that if we know or think that we know something about the motives governing human conduct, it would be foolish not to take advantage of this knowledge in planning the educational system just as it would be foolish not to use our knowledge of hydrostatics in designing a system of plumbing. In a similar way, philosophical statements *which are metaphysical* can have practical consequences for education *just because such statements purport to be factual as well as philosophical.* The difficulty, as we have seen, is that these 'facts' are of a peculiarly inaccessible kind. This point is of considerable importance for the philosophy of education.

of this kind do not always show their character on their faces. But they may usually be recognized because however much they may look like ordinary statements of fact, they are basically unlike them in at least one way: they cannot either be confirmed or refuted by evidence which can be collected, checked and assessed by established and publicly recognized methods. It is important that, whether or not we suppose that such statements are meaningful or provable, we should at least be able to recognize them. For it is hardly possible to understand them if we do not appreciate their logical status.

The second type of statement embodied in educational theories consists of *judgments of value*. These are inevitable in any system of education, though they are sometimes disguised so that the very proponents of an educational system may be imperfectly aware of the values that guide their practice. Part of the use of philosophical criticism of an educational theory is to dissect out and make plain its guiding values. Most of the catchwords and slogans of the educational reformer are fossilized value judgments: 'education according to nature', 'education for democracy', 'equality of opportunity', 'education for citizenship' and the rest. It is of the greatest importance that directives of this sort should not remain mere slogans. They should be explicitly formulated, related to practice and *recognized for what they are*. An undiagnosed value judgment is a source of intellectual muddle. Once we recognize it, we realize that it is not 'self evidently true' and beyond all criticism. For however important and inevitable our valuations are, we have seen that their justification is a very perplexing philosophical problem. If we realize this we shall tend not to be dogmatic or fanatical about them.

The third component of educational theories is *empirical*, being capable of being supported by the evidence of observable fact. Empirical components of educational theories are, in general, of two different kinds. The first of these is relatively common in the writings of those theorists who lived before psychology became established as an experimental science. They consist of recommendations for educational practice. These recommendations may of course be made on theoretical grounds but they have been adopted rather because of their efficiency in giving results. The influence of educational reformers like Pestalozzi, Froebel and Montessori is due more to their precepts and their practical achievements than to their theoretical teachings. A new practical approach to teaching is more influential than a new theory about teaching. Ideally of course a new technique should be capable of being justified by theoretical considerations as it usually is in engineering or medicine, just as a new theory, if it is genuinely a theory, should result in practical advantages when it is applied in the classroom. But we do not find that the connexion between most educational theories and their practice is as close as this. It is rather similar in this respect to the present state of psychotherapy where there are a number of different therapeutic techniques in use, each with its theoretical background. It is found that although the theories are incompatible with one another, the techniques as used by skilled practitioners all seem to produce sufficient results to justify their continued use. And this would be impossible if the techniques were in fact tied as closely to their supposed theoretical foundation as is the case with physical or chemical theory and its applications. We must rather suppose that the theories of the psychiatrists are rationalizations of their practice rather than genuine reasons for them.

The same seems to be true of much of the so-called theory underlying established educational practice. The fact that a well conducted school using the Dalton plan or Montessori or Froebel methods produces good results is, of itself, no justification whatever of the supposed theoretical background of these practices. If indeed a representative group of schools using, say, project methods of teaching consistently got better results than a comparable group of schools using other methods, that would be some evidence in favour of Dewey's educational theories which the project method was designed to apply. But no very convincing evidence of this sort seems to be available at present.[6] The cumulative effect of new proposals for teaching techniques is of course considerable over long periods of time. The teaching practice and curriculum of a present-day primary school is very different from those of a similar school of seventy years ago. And these differences are due to the ingenuity and hard work of many educational reformers. But the adoption of these different improvements in the art of teaching does not commit anyone to adopting the often elaborate 'theoretical' justifications of the new methods. The introduction of a new teaching method has often been more like the empirical insight of a herbalist in the early stages of medicine. Practice comes first; but its theoretical justification has to wait for the scientific development that can explain its success. Thus educational theories which preceded the rise of a scientific psychology (when they were not metaphysical speculations or ethical judgments) were more or less acute guesses at explaining successful practice. Some of them were acute and systematic but mistaken like the psychology of Herbart.[7] Some were unsubstantiated conjectures, like Montessori's views on the training of the senses. Some, like Pestalozzi's doctrine of *Anschauung*, were unintelligible adaptations of metaphysical concepts. Many of such theorists indeed seem to have taken to heart the rule of method by which Rousseau attempted to explain the nature of man: 'Let us then begin by laying facts aside, as they do not affect the question.' It

[6] For recent work of this kind, see the references cited by W. D. Wall in his lecture *Teaching Methods: Psychological Studies of the Curriculum and of Classroom Teaching* in University of London Institute of Education Studies in Education No. 7.

[7] For a good example of philosophical criticism of a standard 'educational theory', see C. D. Hardie's analysis of Herbart in *Truth and Fallacy in Educational Theory*.

is not therefore surprising that the results were unsatisfactory. Usually however these abortive theories were just glosses on fruitful innovations in educational practice. It was the practice that mattered.

But the development of a scientific psychology has put us in the position where we no longer have to rely on practice to suggest theory. It may, of course, still do so but it is *experiment* rather than practice which now suggests theory. The relationship between theory and practice has become a reciprocal one. Theory directs practice and practice corrects theory. Present-day knowledge of perception, learning, motivation, the nature of 'intelligence' and its distribution and development, the causes of educational backwardness, and many other matters of this kind enable us to amend educational practice in the expectation of improved results. We have, in other words, a body of established hypotheses that have been confirmed to a reliable degree. They enable us to predict the outcome of their application and to explain the processes that we are trying to control. They are, to that extent, genuine theories in the standard scientific sense of the word. Even so, they do not approach the theories of the physical sciences in their explanatory power. For example, learning theory is one of the best developed fields of psychology. The processes of human and animal learning have been very thoroughly studied by experimental methods for over fifty years. The great mass of accumulated results of this work has greatly improved our understanding of how we learn but it has not yet been condensed into a single overall theory. There are several theories of learning all of which seem to be compatible with most of the known facts without being necessitated by them. No one of them fits the facts so perfectly as to exclude all its rivals. What are still needed are crucial experiments which will enable the psychologists to decide between one theory and another.[8] Thus even the best examples of theories in the sciences of man are less closely tied to their supporting facts than theories in the sciences of nature.

We can summarize this discussion by saying that the word 'theory' as it is used in educational contexts is generally a courtesy title. It is justified only where we are applying well-established experimental findings in psychology or sociology to the practice of education. And even here we should be aware that the conjectural gap between our theories and the facts on which they rest is sufficiently wide to make our logical con-sciences uneasy. We can hope that the future development of the social sciences will narrow this gap and this hope gives an incentive for developing these sciences.

---

[8] For an excellent account of the relation of contemporary learning theory to education, see R. W. Russell, *How Children Learn*, in University of London Institute of Education Studies in Education No. 7.

The Chemistry of Learning / DAVID KRECH

American educators now talk a great deal about the innovative hardware of education, about computer-assisted instruction, 8 mm cartridge-loading projectors, microtransparencies, and other devices. In the not too distant future they may well be talking about enzyme-assisted instruction, protein memory consolidators, antibiotic memory repellers, and the chemistry of the brain. Although the psychologists' learning theories derived from the study of maze-running rats or target-pecking pigeons have failed to provide insights into the education of children, it is unlikely that what is now being discovered by the psychologist, chemist, and neurophysiologist about rat-brain chemistry can deviate widely from what we will eventually discover about the chemistry of the human brain.

Most adults who are not senile can repeat a series of seven numbers—8, 4, 8, 8, 3, 9, 9—immediately after the series is read. If, however, they are asked to repeat these numbers thirty minutes later, most will fail. In the first instance, we are dealing with the immediate memory span; in the second, with long-term memory. These basic behavioral observations lie behind what is called the two-stage memory storage process theory.

According to a common variant of these notions, immediately after every learning trial—indeed, after every experience—a short-lived electrochemical process is established in the brain. This process, so goes the assumption, is the physiological mechanism which carries the short-term memory. Within a few seconds or minutes, however, this process decays and disappears; but before doing so, if all systems are go, the short-term electrochemical process triggers a second series of events in the brain. This second process is chemical in nature and involves, primarily, the production of new proteins and the induction of higher enzymatic activity levels in the brain cells. This process is more enduring and serves as the physiological substrate of our long-term memory.

It would follow that one approach to testing our theory would be to provide a subject with some experience or other, then interrupt the short-term electrochemical process immediately—before it has had an opportunity to establish the long-term process. If this were done, our subject should never develop a long-term memory for that experience.

"The Chemistry of Learning" is reprinted from David Krech, "The Chemistry of Learning" adapted from a speech to Three National Seminars on Innovation, sponsored by the U. S. Office of Education and the Charles F. Kettering Foundation, in Honolulu, July 1967, printed in the Saturday Review, January 20, 1968. Copyright 1967 Saturday Review, Inc.

At the Albert Einstein Medical School in New York, Dr. Murray Jarvik has devised a "step-down" procedure based on the fact that when a rat is placed on a small platform a few inches above the floor, the rat will step down onto the floor within a few seconds. The rat will do this consistently, day after day. Suppose that on one day the floor is electrified, and stepping onto it produces a painful shock. When the rat is afterward put back on the platform—even twenty-four hours later—it will not budge from the platform but will remain there until the experimenter gets tired and calls the experiment quits. The rat has thus demonstrated that he has a long-term memory for that painful experience.

If we now take another rat, but this time *interfere* with his short-term memory process *immediately after* he has stepped onto the electrified floor, the rat should show no evidence of having experienced a shock when tested the next day, since we have not given his short-term electrochemical memory process an opportunity to initiate the long-term protein-enzymatic process. To interrupt the short-term process, Jarvik passes a mild electric current across the brain of the animal. The current is not strong enough to cause irreparable harm to the brain cells, but it does result in a very high level of activation of the neurons in the brain, thus disrupting the short-term electrochemical memory process. If this treatment follows closely enough after the animal's first experience with the foot shock, and we test the rat a day later, the rat acts as if there were no memory for yesterday's event; the rat jauntily and promptly steps down from the platform with no apparent expectation of shock.

When a long time-interval is interposed between the first foot shock and the electric-current (through the brain) treatment, the rat *does* remember the foot shock, and it remains on the platform when tested the next day. This, again, is what we should have expected from our theory. The short-term electrochemical process has now had time to set up the long-term chemical memory process before it was disrupted.

Some well known effects of accidental human head injury seem to parallel these findings. Injuries which produce a temporary loss of consciousness (but no permanent damage to brain tissue) can cause the patient to experience a "gap" in his memory for the events just preceding the accident. This retrograde amnesia can be understood on the assumption that the events immediately prior to the accident were still being carried by the short-term memory processes at the time of the injury, and their disruption by the injury was sufficient to prevent the induction of the long-term processes. The patient asks "Where am I?" not only because he does not recognize the hospital, but also because he cannot remember how he became injured.

Work conducted by Dr. Bernard Agranoff at the University of Michigan Medical School supports the hypothesis that the synthesis of new brain proteins is crucial for the establishment of the long-term memory process. He argues that if we could prevent the formation of new proteins in the brain, then—although the short-term electrochemical memory process is not interfered with—the long-term memory process could never become established.

Much of Agranoff's work has been done with goldfish. The fish is placed in one end of a small rectangular tank, which is divided into two halves by a barrier which extends from the bottom to just below the surface of the water. When a light is turned on, the fish must swim across the barrier into the other side of the tank within twenty seconds—otherwise he receives an electric shock. This training is continued for several trials until the animal learns to swim quickly to the other side when the light is turned on. Most goldfish learn this shock-avoidance task quite easily and remember it for many days. Immediately before—and in some experiments, immediately after—training, Agranoff injects the antibiotic puromycin into the goldfish's brain. (Puromycin is a protein inhibitor and prevents the formation of new proteins in the brain's neurons.) After injection, Agranoff finds that the goldfish are not impaired in their acquisition of the shock-avoidance task, but, when tested a day or so later, they show almost no retention for the task.

These results mean that the short-term memory process (which helps the animal remember from one trial to the next and thus permits him to learn in the first place) is not dependent upon the formation of new proteins, but that the long-term process (which helps the animal remember from one day to the next and thus permits him to retain what he had learned) is dependent upon the production of new proteins. Again, as in the instance of Jarvik's rats, if the puromycin injection comes more than an hour after learning, it has no effect on later memory—the long-term memory process presumably has already been established and the inhibition of protein synthesis can now no longer affect memory. In this antibiotic, therefore, we have our first chemical memory erasure—or, more accurately, a chemical long-term memory preventative. (Almost identical findings have been reported by other workers in other laboratories working with such animals as mice and rats, which are far removed from the goldfish.)

Thus far I have been talking about disrupting or preventing the formation of memory. Now we will accentuate the positive. Dr. James L. McGaugh of the University of California at Riverside has argued that injections of central nervous system stimulants such as strychnine, picrotoxin, or metrazol should enhance, fortify, or extend the activity of the short-term electrochemical memory processes and thus increase the probability that they will be successful in initiating long-term memory processes. From this it follows that the injection of CNS stimulants immediately before or after training should improve learning performance. That is precisely what McGaugh found—together with several additional results which have important implications for our concerns today.

In one of McGaugh's most revealing experiments, eight groups of mice from two different hereditary backgrounds were given the problem of learning a simple maze. Immediately after completing their learning trials, four groups from each strain were injected with a different dosage of metrazol—from none to five, 10, and 20 milligrams per kilogram of body weight. First, it was apparent that there are hereditary differences in learning ability—a relatively bright strain and a relatively dull one. Secondly, by properly dosing the animals with metrazol, the learning performance increased appreciably. Under the optimal dosage, the metrazol animals showed about a 40 per cent improvement in learning ability over their untreated brothers. The improvement under metrazol was so great, in fact, that the dull animals, when treated with 10 milligrams, did slightly better than their untreated but hereditarily superior colleagues.

In metrazol we not only have a chemical facilitator of learning, but one which acts as the "Great Equalizer" among hereditarily different groups. As the dosage was increased for the dull mice from none to five to 10 milligrams their performance improved. Beyond the 10-milligram point for the dull mice, however, and beyond the five-milligram point for the bright mice, increased strength of the metrazol solution resulted in a deterioration in learning. We can draw two morals from this last finding. First, the optimal dosage of chemical learning facilitators will vary greatly with the individual taking the drug (There is, in other words, an interaction between heredity and drugs); second, there is a limit to the intellectual power of even a hopped-up Southern Californian Super Mouse!

We already have available a fairly extensive class of drugs which can facilitate learning and memory in animals. A closer examination of McGaugh's results and the work of others, however, also suggests that these drugs do not work in a monolithic manner on something called "learning" or "memory." In some instances, the drugs seem to act on "attentiveness"; in some, on the ability to vary one's attacks on a problem; in some, on persistence; in some, on immediate memory; in some, on long-term memory. Different drugs work differentially for different strains, different individuals, different intellectual tasks, and different learning components.

Do all of these results mean that we will soon be able to substitute a pharmacopoeia of drugs for our various school-enrichment and innovative educational programs, and that most educators will soon be technologically unemployed—or will have to retool and turn in their schoolmaster's gown for a pharmacist's jacket? The answer is no—as our Berkeley experiments on the influence of education and training on brain anatomy and chemistry suggest. This research is the work of four—Dr. E. L. Bennett, biochemist; Dr. Marian Diamond, anatomist; Dr. M. R. Rosenzweig, psychologist; and myself—together, of course, with the help of graduate students, technicians, and, above all, government money.

Our work, started some fifteen years ago, was guided by the same general theory which has guided more recent work, but our research strategy and tactics were quite different. Instead of interfering physiologically or chemically with the animal to determine the effects of such intervention upon memory storage (as did Jarvik, Agranoff, and McGaugh), we had taken the obverse question and, working with only normal animals, sought to determine the *effects* of memory storage on the chemistry and anatomy of the brain.

Our argument was this: If the establishment of long-term memory processes involves increased activity of brain enzymes, then animals which have been required to do a great deal of learning and remembering should end up with brains enzymatically different from those of animals which have not been so challenged by environment. This should be especially true for the enzymes involved in trans-synaptic neural activity. Further, since such neural activity would make demands on brain-cell action and metabolism, one might also expect to find various morphological differences between the brains of rats brought up in psychologically stimulating and psychologically pallid environments.

I describe briefly one of our standard experiments. At weaning age, one rat from each of a dozen pairs of male twins is chosen by lot to be placed in an educationally active and innovative environment, while its twin brother is placed in as unstimulating an environment as we can contrive. All twelve educationally enriched rats live together in one large, wire-mesh cage in a well lighted, noisy, and busy laboratory. The cage is equipped with ladders, running wheels, and other "creative" rat toys. For thirty minutes each day, the rats are taken out of their cages and allowed to explore new territory. As the rats grow older they are given various learning tasks to master, for which they are rewarded with bits of sugar. This stimulating educational and training program is continued for eighty days.

While these animals are enjoying their rich intellectual environment, each impoverished animal lives out his life in solitary confinement, in a small cage situated in a dimly lit and quiet room. He is rarely handled by his keeper and never invited to explore new environments, to solve problems, or join in games with other rats. Both groups of rats, however, have unlimited access to the same standard food throughout the experiment. At the age of 105 days, the rats are sacrificed, their brains dissected out and analyzed morphologically and chemically.

This standard experiment, repeated dozens of times, indicates that as the fortunate rat lives out his life in the educationally enriched condition, the bulk of his cortex expands and grows deeper and heavier than that of his culturally deprived brother. Part of this increase in cortical mass is accounted for by an increase in the number of glia cells (specialized brain cells which play vital functions in the nutrition of the neurons and, perhaps, also in laying down permanent memory traces); part of it by an increase in the size of the neuronal cell bodies and their nuclei; and part by an increase in the diameters of the blood vessels supplying the cortex. Our postulated chemical changes also occur. The enriched brain shows more acetylocholinesterase (the enzyme involved in the trans-synaptic conduction of neural impulses) and cholinesterase (the enzyme found primarily in the glia cells).

Finally, in another series of experiments we have demonstrated that these structural and chemical changes are the signs of a "good" brain. That is, we have shown that either through early rat-type Head Start programs or through selective breeding programs, we can increase the weight and density of the rat's cortex and its acetylocholinesterase and cholinesterase activity levels. And when we do—by either method—we have created superior problem-solving animals.

What does all of this mean? It means that the effects of the psychological and educational environment are not restricted to something called the "mental" realm. Permitting the young rat to grow up in an educationally and experientially inadequate and unstimulating environment creates an animal with a relatively deteriorated brain—a brain with a thin and light cortex, lowered blood supply, diminished enzymatic activities, smaller neuronal cell bodies, and fewer glia cells. A lack of adequate educational fare for the young animal—no matter how large the food supply or how good the family—and a lack of adequate psychological enrichment results in palpable, measurable, deteriorative changes in the brain's chemistry and anatomy.

Returning to McGaugh's results, we find that whether, and to what extent, this or that drug will improve the animal's learning ability will depend, of course, on what the drug does to the rat's brain chemistry. And what it does to the rat's brain chemistry will depend upon the status of the chemistry in the brain to begin with. And what the status of the brain's chemistry is to begin with reflects the rat's early psychological and educational environment. Whether, and to what extent, this or that drug will improve the animal's attention, or memory, or learning ability, therefore, will depend upon the animal's past experiences. I am not talking about interaction between "mental" factors on the one hand and "chemical" compounds on the other. I am talking, rather, about interactions between chemical factors introduced into the brain by the biochemist's injection or pills, and chemical factors induced in the brain by the educator's stimulating or impoverishing environment. The biochemist's work can be only half effective without the educator's help.

What kind of educational environment can best develop the brain chemically and morphologically? What kind of stimulation makes for an enriched environment? What educational experiences can potentiate the effects of the biochemist's drugs? We don't know. The biochemist doesn't know. It is at this point that I see a whole new area of collaboration in basic research between the educator, the psychologist, and the neurobiochemist—essentially, a research program which combines the Agranoff and McGaugh techniques with our Berkeley approach. Given the start that has already been made in the animal laboratory, an intensive program of research—with animals and with children—which seeks to spell out the interrelations between chemical and educational influences on brain and memory can pay off handsomely. This need not wait for the future. We know enough now to get started.

Both the biochemist and the teacher of the future will combine their skills and insights for the educational and intellectual development of the child. Tommy needs a bit more of an immediate memory stimulator; Jack could do with a chemical attention-span stretcher; Rachel needs an anticholinesterase to slow down her mental processes; Joan, some puromycin—she remembers too many details, and gets lost.

To be sure, all our data thus far come from the brains of goldfish and rodents. But is anyone so certain that the chemistry of the brain of a rat (which, after all, is a fairly complex mammal) is so different from that of the brain of a human being that he dare neglect this challenge—or even gamble—when the stakes are so high?

SOCIAL CONCEPTS DIMENSION

Some Contributions of Sociology to the Field of Education / NEAL GROSS

The purpose of this paper is to delineate *for the educational practitioner* some specific contributions of sociological analysis to the field of education. We propose to focus on a limited set of substantive sociological contributions that teachers, supervisory personnel, school principals, or school superintendents may find of value in dealing with their work environment in a more realistic and effective manner.

Of the many approaches possible in describing some "practical contributions" of sociology to the field of education, the following procedure has been adopted. Specific contributions will be discussed under three headings that constitute sociological perspectives in the examination of school systems as functioning social systems. The first is that educational

"Some Contributions of Sociology to the Field of Education" is reprinted from Neal Gross, "Some Contributions of Sociology to the Field of Education," *Harvard Educational Review*, 29, Fall 1959, 275–287. Copyright © 1959 by President and Fellows of Harvard College.

relationships occur in the context of a formal organizational setting. Students, teachers, supervisors, principals, and school superintendents interact as incumbents of positions in a social system which has an organizational goal, the education of children. To accomplish this task the work that goes on in a school must be assigned, coordinated, and integrated. Educational practice involves a number of people in a complicated division of labor; this necessitates networks of role relationships within an organizational environment. The second perspective derives from the fact that the basic work of the school, the educational transaction, takes place primarily in a relatively small social system, the classroom. The third perspective emerges from an observation that the sociologist would make about the school as a social system: Like all organizations, it is influenced by forces external to it. The impact of these external factors on the functioning of the school therefore comes under his scrutiny as a focal point of inquiry. It is from these three limited perspectives [1]—the school system as a formal organization, the classroom as a social system, and the external environment of the schools—that we propose to delineate some contributions of sociology to practitioners in the field of education.

The School System as a Formal Organization

A school system from a sociological point of view shares many common characteristics with other kinds of large-scale organizations. Two of these are of special relevance for our purpose. The first is that a school system, like business firms and hospitals, has an organizational objective. It is a goal-directed social system. Second, it contains a network of interrelated positions (for example, teachers, supervisors, and administrators) that are directly linked to the accomplishment of the organizational goal.

According to the "organizational model" for public schools, the business of the school is to impart knowledge and skills to students and therefore teachers are employed for this purpose. The function of supervisors is to help teachers to do a more effective job, and the formal duties of school administrators are to coordinate and integrate the diverse activities of the school. The incumbents of these positions have certain rights and obligations in their relationships with incumbents of other positions with whom they interact. Implicit in discussions of these aspects of the organizational structure of the school are two assumptions that deserve empirical examination. The first is that there is basic agree-

---

[1] For other perspectives and an examination of needed research in the sociology of education see Orville G. Brim, Jr., *Sociology and the Field of Education* (New York: Russell Sage Foundation, 1958), and Neal Gross, "The Sociology of Education," in Robert K. Merton, Leonard Broom, and Leonard S. Cottrell, Jr. (eds.), *Sociology Today* (New York: Basic Books, 1959).

ment on the organizational objective of the schools. The second is that there is agreement on the rights and obligations associated with the various positions in education. Sociological analysis suggests that both assumptions may in fact be tenuous in many school systems, and that lack of agreement on educational objectives and role definition may constitute major dysfunctional elements in the functioning of the school and may affect the gratification educators derive from their jobs.

The formal organizational goal of public school systems is vague and is characterized by ambiguity. This observation emerges from a comparison of school systems with other types of organizations, for example, a business firm. The formal organizational goal of a business firm is unambiguous: to produce products or services for a profit. Labor unions may fight with management over the distribution of profits but typically there is no quarrel over the organizational goal itself. The situation is quite different, however, when an effort is made to specify the organizational objective of a school system. "To educate children" is a largely meaningless statement unless the purposes of the education are specified. And here lies the difficulty.

The specification of educational purposes invokes value issues such as the respective responsibilities of the home and the school or the meaning of a "good education." Whether the schools should give greater primacy to the intellectual, social, or emotional development of the child; whether or not they have the responsibility to impart moral values; whether the schools have different obligations to the "typical" and "atypical" child; whether they should encourage or discourage the questioning of the status quo; whether driver education, physical education, and courses in home economics and family living are legitimate or illegitimate functions of the school—each of these is a value question on which there may be contradictory points of view within and outside of school systems. An unpublished Harvard study involving personnel at different levels in eight New England school systems revealed dramatic differences in the beliefs teachers hold about educational goals and revealed that principals and teachers frequently do not share common views about educational objectives. Striking disagreements between superintendents and school boards have also been uncovered in regard to certain educational objectives.[2] Research evidence [3] further indicates that one of the major sources of pressures to which school administrators are exposed consists in conflicting viewpoints in their communities about school objectives and programs. Educational practitioners need to recognize that a fundamental source of controversy within the schools may be related to basic and unrecognized value conflicts over its organizational objectives. These differences in beliefs are infrequently brought to the surface for frank

[2] Neal Gross, *Who Runs Our Schools?* (New York: Wiley, 1958), pp. 113–125.
[3] *Ibid.*, pp. 45–60.

and open discussion. They may constitute basic blocks to effective group action and harmonious social relationships.

The second "organizational assumption," that there is agreement on the role definition for educational positions, also appears to be suspect. Although textbooks in education glibly speak about the role of the teacher and of the school administrator as if everybody agreed on what they are, and many educational practitioners make this assumption, the organizational fact in many school systems may be that those people who work together frequently do not share similar views about the rights and obligations associated with their positions.

Should teachers be expected to attend PTA meetings regularly? Does the teacher's job include the counseling function? What are the teacher's obligations to the especially bright or especially dull child? Or the problem child? What are the teacher's obligations in handling discipline problems? Should teachers be expected to participate in in-service training programs? Does the teacher have the right to expect that the administrator will always support him when parents complain about his behavior? On these and many other phases of a teacher's job there may be considerable disagreement between principals and teachers as well as among teachers.

The findings of a study concerned with the role definition of approximately 50 per cent of the superintendents and school board members in Massachusetts revealed a basic lack of agreement over the division of labor between them.[4] On the issue of hiring new teachers, seven out of ten superintendents interviewed reported that the arrangement they desired was this: when a new teacher was to be hired, the school board should act *solely* on the nominations of the superintendent. But only one out of five of the school board members agreed with them. How about the selection of textbooks? Nearly nine out of ten superintendents felt that the school board should always accept the recommendation of the superintendent in choosing a textbook. But less than one-half of the school board members agreed. What about teacher grievances? Nearly 90 per cent of the superintendents believed that teachers should always bring their grievances to the superintendent before they went to the school board. Only 56 per cent of the school board members agreed. What should the procedure be when a community group wishes to use school property? Nine out of ten school superintendents thought that this decision should be the superintendent's responsibility. Nearly one-half of the school board members, however, felt that these decisions should be made by the school board. What about recommendations for salary increases for school system employees? Over two-thirds of the superin-

---

[4] Neal Gross, Ward S. Mason, and Alexander W. McEachern, *Explorations in Role Analysis: Studies of the School Superintendency Role* (New York: Wiley, 1958), p. 124.

tendents felt that the superintendent should make all such recommendations. Only one-third of the school board members agreed with them.
These findings imply that in many school systems disagreements over the
rights and obligations associated with educational positions may constitute basic sources of stress in the school system. They also suggest that
intra-role conflicts appear to be "built into" many educational positions.

By an intra-role conflict we mean conflicting expectations to which an
individual is exposed as a consequence of his occupancy of a *single*
position. Teachers are frequently exposed to conflicting expectations
from their principal and supervisors, from guidance personnel and their
principal, from parents and administrators, and even from students in
their classrooms. School principals are exposed to conflicting expectations from their superintendent and their staff over such matters as the
supervision of classroom instruction and the handling of discipline problems. School administrators are confronted with conflicting expectations
among their school staff. For example, some teachers expect their principal to make all important decisions affecting their welfare, but other
teachers expect to participate in such decisions.[5] In addition, parents and
teachers frequently hold contradictory expectations for the principal's
behavior in regard to student promotion and discipline practices. It is the
school superintendent, however, who probably is exposed most frequently to intra-role conflict. A major source of these conflicting expectations arises from the differential views held by his school board and his
staff for his behavior. Whose views should he support when the school
board and the staff hold conflicting expectations for his behavior on such
issues as the size of the school budget or promotion policies? Superintendents, like school principals, must also frequently deal with differential expectations among the teaching staff. And their most difficult problems may emerge from conflicting expectations held by their school
board members for their performance.

To sum up: Viewing school systems as organizations from a sociological perspective suggests major organizational barriers to their effective
functioning. We have emphasized two of these blocks: lack of agreement
on organizational goals and lack of consensus on the role definitions
associated with educational positions.

The Classroom as a Social System

Parsons, in a recent paper, presents a provocative theoretical analysis
of the school class as a social system from the viewpoint of its functions

[5] Melvin Seeman, "Role Conflict and Ambivalence in Leadership," *American
Sociological Review*, 18 (August 1953), 373–380; also see Charles E. Bidwell, "The
Administrative Role and Satisfaction in Teaching," *Journal of Educational Sociology*,
29 (September 1955), pp. 41–47.

for American society.[6] Coleman's analysis of the structure of competition in the high school and its influence on academic achievement clearly has implications for isolating forces that influence the "academic output" of the classroom.[7] These analyses, plus those of sociologists like Gordon [8] and Brookover,[9] suggest the importance of a sociological perspective in examining the structure and functioning of the classroom as a social system.

At this stage of sociological and sociopsychological inquiry on the classroom as a social system, the major empirical contributions of the sociologist have undoubtedly been to draw attention to the sociometric structure of the classroom and to isolate basic sources of strain and tension to which teachers are exposed in the classroom. Sociometric studies reveal that classrooms typically contain "stars" and "isolates," and they have uncovered factors that affect student interpersonal relations in the school class.[10] Of especial importance to educators is the finding that teachers appear to misperceive frequently the interpersonal relationships among students in their classrooms.[11] They do not show high sensitivity to the way children actually react to each other and they frequently allow their own biases toward students to hinder a correct assessment of the "sociometric facts of life."

A second sociological contribution to the understanding of classroom behavior stems from the isolation of some potential sources of strain for the classroom teacher. One source of stress is the collision between the authority structure of the school and the professional status of the teaching staff. A school system must provide for the coordination and integration of the work of its members. Someone has to assign responsibilities, see that tasks are accomplished, and have the power to sanction teachers and students for deviant behavior. The elementary school prin-

[6] Talcott Parsons, "The School Class as a Social System: Some of Its Functions in American Society," *Harvard Educational Review,* 29 (Fall 1959), 297–318.

[7] James S. Coleman, "Academic Achievement and the Structure of Competition," *Harvard Educational Review,* 29 (Fall 1959), 330–351.

[8] C. Wayne Gordon, *The Social System of the High School: A Study in the Sociology of Adolescence* (New York: Free Press, 1957).

[9] Wilbur B. Brookover, "The Social Roles of Teachers and Pupil Achievement," *American Sociological Review,* 8 (August 1943), 389–393.

[10] See Lloyd A. Cook, "An Experimental Sociographic Study of a Stratified 10th Grade Class," *American Sociological Review,* 10 (April 1945), 250–261; Otto H. Dahlke and Thomas O. Monahan, "Problems in the Application of Sociometry to Schools," *School Review,* 57 (April 1949), 223–234; Robert J. Havighurst and Bernice L. Neugarten, *Society and Education* (Boston: Allyn and Bacon, 1957); and August B. Hollingshead, *Elmtown's Youth* (New York: Wiley, 1949).

[11] Merl E. Bonney, "Sociometric Study of Agreement between Teacher Judgments and Student Choices: In Regard to the Number of Friends Possessed by High School Students," *Sociometry,* 10 (May 1947), 133–146; and Norman E. Gronlund, "The Accuracy of Teachers' Judgments concerning the Sociometric Status of Sixth-Grade Pupils," *Sociometry,* 13 (August 1950), part 1, 197–225; part 2, 329–357.

cipal, for example, as the formal leader of his school has to make room assignments and final decisions about the disposition of discipline problems. He must also see that the educational experiences of the child in the first grade are integrated with those he receives in the second and third grades. This requires some type of control over the work content and work output of teachers at each of these levels. Their classroom behavior is part of his concern. The authority structure, however, conflicts with another characteristic of school organization—the school is staffed with professional personnel. A professional worker is supposed to have autonomy over his own activities. This implies that the teacher should have considerable freedom in the manner in which he conducts his classes and in the skills and knowledge which he imparts to his students. It is this built-in source of strain that in part accounts for the "social distance" that frequently exists between school principals and their teachers and for the charge—by teachers—that administrators upset "their" classes. The clash between the authority structure and the professional status of teachers is also undoubtedly reflected in the latent and overt opposition of teachers to the introduction of new educational practices.

A second source of strain derives from the differential norms held by teachers and students for the student's behavior. Gordon's analysis [12] of a high school suggests the differential frames of reference that may be operating in many classrooms. His analysis indicates that teachers expected students to perform in a manner that approximated their knowledge and ability potential. But students' expectations were in part based on the informal social structure and values of the students. He indicates that student stereotypes had an important influence on the "roles" students assigned each other and played themselves, and that these stereotypes therefore affected their role performance. When student-defined and teacher-defined roles and values were incompatible, the net result was strain for the teacher in his transactions with students.

Another contribution of a sociological perspective on classroom behavior is demonstrated by the current work of Lippitt and his associates at the University of Michigan on the "socially unaccepted" child in the classroom. In addition to showing the need for a typology of such children, their studies suggest the powerful group forces operating on the unaccepted child. The major barriers to changing his behavior may be in the classroom, rather than or in addition to forces within the child. This finding has important implications for teachers and also for school guidance practices which are usually based on the assumption that individual counseling is the only way to change a student's behavior. The

[12] Gordon, *op. cit.*

observation that the attributes and stereotypes of classmates as well as the teacher are barriers to behavior changes is one demanding rigorous exploration.

In addition, sociological analysis strongly suggests that the attitudes and behavior of the individual are strongly linked to those groups to which he belongs or aspires. These reference groups constitute "anchoring points" which have to be considered in inducing changed behavior. For the classroom teacher, the important consequence of this observation is that to deal effectively with a child may require isolating group forces that are constraining his behavior and inducing changes in clique norms and values.

The External Environment of the School

A school system does not exist in a vacuum. Its existence and functioning depend in part on its outside world, its external environment. This sociological point of view has many implications for the analysis of school systems.

One implication is that changes in the larger social system of the community materially affect the composition of the student body in a school system, and therefore may require modifications in the curriculum. The heavy migration of the rural population in the South to metropolitan centers implies that many large city school systems need to undertake a critical review of the ability of their school program to meet the needs of the school's changed clientele. The empty school buildings in the center of many cities and the needed new school buildings in suburban areas, associated with the recent "flight to the suburbs," suggest the need for a metropolitan approach to school planning, a concept infrequently considered in educational circles. In short, the educational implications of demographic studies require considerably greater attention by educators.

A second aspect of the external environment of public school systems to which sociologists have given considerable attention is the social class structure of communities. Studies in this area [13] reveal that most aspects of school functioning are influenced by social class phenomena. Research on social class strongly supports the notion that teacher grading practices and the criteria which teachers apply to children are related to the social class placement of the child and the teacher. The mobility aspirations of

---

[13] For a summary of these studies see Wilbur B. Brookover, *A Sociology of Education* (New York: American Book, 1955); and Havighurst and Neugarten, *op. cit.* For a critical appraisal of some of this literature see Neal Gross, "Social Class Structure and American Education," *Harvard Educational Review*, 23 (Fall 1953), 298–329.

children, the drop-out rate, participation in extra-curricular activities, dating behavior, and friendship patterns are in part accounted for by the socio-economic characteristics of the child's family.

A third "external environment" factor that has important implications for the public schools is the power structure or structures of the community.[14] School systems absorb a large portion of the local tax dollar and the influence of informal and formal power agents in the community on educational budgetary decisions is without doubt a basic influence on the quality of the staff and the program of a school system. It is not surprising that national meetings of educational administrators usually have sessions devoted to "techniques for studying community power structure" and that sociologists are invited to participate in them.

A fourth contribution of sociology to the understanding of the external environment of the schools is the analysis of the basic link between the community and the schools—the school board. Charters has questioned the assumption, frequently found in the educational literature, that the disproportionate incidence of school board members from upper socio-economic strata results in "a conservative bias" in public education.[15] Sociological research has demonstrated the impact of the behavior of school board members and of their motivation for seeking election to this position on the superintendent's job satisfaction and his job performance. The effect of such factors as religion, occupation, and income on the school board member's behavior as well as the pressures to which school administrators are exposed by their school boards have also been examined. These findings lead to the general conclusion that a crucial, but frequently neglected, variable influencing the operation of the school is the behavior of the small group of laymen who are its official policy-makers.[16] This conclusion has had many important ramifications, one of which is the National School Board Association's current effort to improve the "quality" of school board members.

A fifth sociological contribution emerges from the analysis of inter-role conflicts to which educational personnel are exposed as a consequence of their occupancy of positions in schools and in other social systems.

---

[14] See, for example, Robert E. Agger, "Power Attributions in the Local Community," *Social Forces*, 34 (May 1956), 322–331; Floyd Hunter, *Community Power Structure: A Study of Decision Makers* (Chapel Hill: University of North Carolina Press, 1953); Peter Rossi, "Community Decision Making," *Administrative Science Quarterly*, 1 (March 1957), 415–441; and Robert O. Schulze, "The Role of Economic Dominants in Community Power Structure," *American Sociological Review*, 23 (February 1958), 3–9.

[15] W. W. Charters, Jr., "Social Class Analysis and the Control of Public Education," *Harvard Educational Review*, 23 (Fall 1953), 268–283.

[16] For a report of the specific findings leading to this conclusion, see Gross, *Who Runs Our Schools?*, *op. cit.*

Getzels and Guba [17] found that many of the expectations linked to the teacher's position conflict with other positions he occupies, and that some of these conflicts are a function of local school and community conditions.

The school superintendent's position is especially exposed to inter-role conflict. His job and the way he carries it out influence in some way virtually all members of the community. In dealing with him, members of his church, his personal friends, members of other organizations to which he may belong, and, of course, his wife and family, are inclined to identify him not only as a fellow church member, for example, but as a fellow church member who is at the same time the superintendent of schools.

Some unpublished findings of the School Executive Studies [18] shed light on the kinds of inter-role conflicts to which school superintendents are exposed. Twenty per cent of the superintendents reported that they faced incompatible expectations deriving from their simultaneous occupancy of positions in the *educational and religious systems*. The formal leaders and certain members of their church expected them to act in one way regarding certain issues, while other individuals and groups expected contrary behavior. One Catholic superintendent said that he faced situations like this all the time:

> Sometimes, the situation gets pretty touchy. I want to keep good relations with the Church. Don't forget—most of my school committee members and the local politicians belong to my church. Take this for example: one of the Catholic groups wanted to let the kids out early from school. They were having some special meetings, and they wanted the kids to be there. I knew that wouldn't be right. It wasn't fair to the other kids. So what did I do? I refused to give an official o.k. to the request, but at the time I simply winked at it [letting them out early]. I would have offended them if I'd stopped the kids from going, and I just couldn't afford to do that. It really left me bothered. Should I have stopped it? Legally, I could and I would have been right. But I know I would have had hell to pay.

Another superintendent, a Protestant, told the interviewer:

> [My] minister wants all kinds of special favors because I am a member of his church. He expected me to turn over our gym to the church basketball team. He wanted me to support his idea of giving out a Bible to each public school child. He told me that he thought I ought to see that more of

---

[17] J. W. Getzels and E. G. Guba, "The Structure of Roles and Role Conflict in the Teaching Situation," *Journal of Educational Sociology*, 29 (September 1955), pp. 30–40.

[18] For other findings of the School Executive Studies, see Gross, Mason, and McEachern, *op. cit.*; and Gross, *Who Runs Our Schools?, op. cit.*

'our people' get jobs in the school. None of these are fair requests. I'm supposed to represent all the people, and I want to use the criterion of 'what's best for the schools,' not 'what's best for my church.' I might give him the gym, but it would be worth my job to give in on the Bibles in this community. I try not to play favorites, but sometimes it's hard to know what is the right thing to do.

Of perhaps as great personal and emotional significance to superintendents are the role conflicts arising from the expectations of their *personal friends* which are incompatible with those held by other individuals and groups in the community. Thirty-five percent of the superintendents reported conflicts of this kind.

Although some superintendents said that their "personal friends" expected special consideration in the areas of personnel decisions and the allocation of school contracts, more often the superintendents said that their friends expected special consideration for their children. These included requests that teachers be reprimanded for treating their children unfairly, that their children be transferred to a school in another district, that transportation be provided for children who are not entitled to it, that their children be promoted against the best judgment of the teacher and principal involved, and so on. Each of these "special consideration" expectations is incompatible with procedures and principles which the superintendent is expected to follow and which are set by the school board, by the teachers, and by PTA groups. Undoubtedly there are many requests of this kind which superintendents automatically ignore or refuse and which they did not mention in the interview; it is when these requests come from personal friends and when these friends expect the superintendent to make particular concessions, that the superintendents describe them as "role conflict" situations.

One superintendent said:

[One of the] nastiest aspects of my job is bus transportation. Good friends of mine have the nerve to telephone me, the superintendent of schools, and ask that a bus pick up their children, when they know, and I know, and the bus driver knows, that they live within the one-mile limit. I tell them I don't drive the bus. I'm just superintendent of schools. Talk to the bus driver. They think I'm saying okay, and I guess I am if you come right down to it. Someday I guess I'll get into trouble when someone who doesn't have the gall to come to me goes to the committee and says 'so and so, the superintendent's friend, has his kids picked up. Why can't I have mine?' It's all in the game and sometimes the game is rough.

A third role conflict situation frequently mentioned involved the *superintendency and the father positions.* Forty-eight per cent of the superintendents described conflicts of this type.

The superintendents reported a wide variety of situations in which their children expected one thing and others expected something quite different. One superintendent who was greatly troubled by problems in this area described his situation in this way:

> You know one of the worst things about this job that you never think of before you get into it is its effect on your children. You don't have time for your children. You have to be out every night and it just isn't fair to them. They don't like it; they resent it. And then the kids have a cross to bear. Either they get especially soft or especially rough treatment by the teachers. And the teachers are just waiting for you to throw your weight around.
>
> For example, my boy has told me certain things about one of his teachers —the way she behaves in the classroom. He's an honest youngster so I have no reason to doubt him, and if I were not the superintendent you can be darn sure I'd raise a lot of cain. But as the superintendent I'm not supposed to invade a teacher's classroom. So I try to support the teacher even though I know she is in the wrong. I feel pretty mean about this, but what else can I do? I hope my boy will understand the situation better later on.

Eighteen percent of the superintendents mentioned inter-role conflicts stemming from incompatible expectations held for their behavior as a *member of a local community association and as the superintendent.* For example, in many communities certain local organizations to which the superintendent belonged expected him to allow them to use the time of students and staff to achieve their own organizational objectives, whereas the professional school staff expected him to protect the schools from this type of "invasion." School superintendents are exposed to requests for school children to be active in fund raising activities, for the school band to play in parades, and for the schools to participate in youth activities. Local community groups expect the superintendent to facilitate their use of these school resources. On the other hand, many superintendents know that one of the major complaints of their faculty is that this type of activity frequently disrupts classroom activities and planned school programs. This constitutes a difficult area of decision making, especially when the organization in question has a powerful voice in community affairs.

These findings support the proposition that inter-role conflicts stemming from occupancy of positions in the school system and in the environment external to it constitute a basic source of potential stress for the educator.

There are dangers to be avoided as well as benefits to be derived from the closer alignment between the fields of sociology and education. One of these dangers is to overgeneralize sociological research findings that apply to a single case or a small population to American education or American society when there is no logical basis for such induction. Sociologists as well as educators have erred in this respect. A second pitfall is the uncritical acceptance of unverified pronouncements of sociologists as verified propositions. There are many statements to be found in textbooks of educational sociology that are speculative in nature and which are not based on rigorous research evidence. Hunches and speculations need to be distinguished from verified propositions. A third danger is the acceptance of sociological research findings without critical examination of their assumptions, the adequacy of their research methods, and their conclusions. The literature on the influence of social class structure in American education is permeated with each of these, as well as other, pitfalls in the sociology-education mating process. The educational practitioner needs to be aware of these difficulties in his utilization of sociological analyses of educational problems.

These precautionary observations lead to the consideration of the major contribution of the sociologist to educational practitioners. The teacher or school administrator must constantly bear in mind that he is working in a complex environment in which many variables are at play. The forces are multidimensional and his environment, although it shares common features with the situation confronting other educational practitioners, has many unique features. The sociologist, however, usually defines his problem so that he is working with one or a few independent variables (for example, social class or leadership structure) and one dependent variable (for example, academic achievement or sociometric choice), and he attempts to control other variables that may be influencing the relationships he is investigating. Of necessity he must simplify his problem so he can deal with it. He usually assumes multiple causation but his methodological tools allow him to deal with only a very limited number of the forces that may account for the phenomena he is trying to explain. He never deals with *all* the variables that the practitioner probably needs to take into account in his decision making. Further, the research findings of the sociologist may not be applicable to the particular set of conditions confronting the practitioner. Research findings based on a sample of suburban school systems may not hold for city school systems. These considerations lead to the following point of view about the sociologist's major contribution to the educational practitioner. What the sociologist has to offer is basically a series of sensitizing and analytic concepts and ideas based on theoretical and empirical analysis that will allow the practitioner to examine in a more realistic and more incisive way the multiple forces operating in his social environment. The sociologist cannot make the educational practitioner's decisions for him, nor can the sociologist's research findings based on one population be applied to any educational population indiscriminately. The practitioner's task is to assess the various forces that have a bearing on the achievement of his objectives, assign them relative weights, and make a decision based on these calculations. The basic sociological contribution is to add to the educator's kit of intellectual tools a set of sociological insights and concepts that will allow him to take account in his decision-making organizational, cultural, and interpersonal factors at work in his environment.

SPECIAL READING

Can There Be a Normative Philosophy of Education?   /

PATRICK SUPPES

1. *Negative Answers.* The complex question of whether there can be a normative philosophy of education does not have a simple affirmative or negative answer. We must expand upon the meaning of the question, draw distinctions, and delineate a position in any attempt to provide an answer. A good place to begin is to indicate major senses in which there can be no normative philosophy of education.

One such sense is that of claiming that the philosopher has special access to knowledge distinct from that of the scientist or the ordinary man, which will enable him to establish the fundamental principles of philosophy of education by special methods of knowing. Such a position goes back to the cabalism of ancient priesthoods. The priest is supreme and sacred because he has secret and special access to fundamental knowledge. Much of the great historical tradition of metaphysics seems to be a direct heir to this priestly tradition. In many parts of the world, there are still those who would maintain that the philosopher's proper role is to establish a system of metaphysics by special methods of argument and perception, including in such a system the fundamental principles of a philosophy of education. However, most philosophers in the Anglo-Saxon tradition would not take seriously such claims. This would apply to rationalistic claims of having direct intuitive access to principles of knowledge, as well as similar claims of direct intuitive knowledge of moral principles.

A more sophisticated argument, and one more difficult to deal with, is that there is one special preserve of knowledge from which at least parts of a philosophy of education would come; this is the claim that *a priori* synthetic propositions can be established. Although Kantianism is undergoing a vigorous revival, it is difficult to take it seriously in analyzing

"Can There Be a Normative Philosophy of Education?" is reprinted from Patrick Suppes, "Can There Be a Normative Philosophy of Education?" *Proceedings of the Twenty-Fourth Annual Meeting of the Philosophy of Education Society*—Santa Monica, April 7–10, 1968. Permission granted by the Philosophy of Education Society.

special areas of philosophy like the philosophy of education. Because I know of no philosopher of education who is concerned systematically to defend *a priori* synthetic propositions, I dismiss without further consideration the development of a normative philosophy of education with *a priori* synthetic underpinnings.

A third more powerful and more important line of negative argument is the claim that no injunctions as to what ought to be done in education either in teaching moral principles or in guiding child development for society's needs can be derived from purely factual considerations. The negative answer in this case is that from purely factual considerations or purely empirical evidence, it is not possible to infer a normative philosophy. The claim is that if we limit the grounds of philosophical principles to purely empirical matters, we can make no inference to normative principles. To do so is to commit the naturalistic fallacy. We shall have more to say about the naturalistic fallacy later, but let me say in passing that these claims concerning the derivation of *ought* statements from purely factual statements, which originate with G. E. Moore and which have been frequently analyzed by philosophers in this century, are seldom given a serious logical and semantic treatment in the context of an analysis of moral principles or the epistemological foundation of such principles. (Systematic logical analysis of these matters of inference under the heading of deontic logic is another matter.) Although the logical aspects of the matter have not been treated with any great depth or elegance by philosophers of education such as D. J. O'Connor or Alan Montefiore, there is considerable intuitive appeal to the claim that educators cannot derive normative principles from factual considerations without committing the naturalistic fallacy.[1]

Each of these negative answers I am willing to accept. To the extent that demands for a normative philosophy of education violate them, I am skeptical of being able to satisfy them. I say this, however, with one reservation. I am skeptical that a really firm distinction between normative and non-normative statements can be drawn, just as I am skeptical of drawing a like distinction between analytic and synthetic statements. The arguments that surround the naturalistic fallacy have received much attention. It seems to me it will be more productive in the near future at least to assign moral principles the rather indefinite epistemological status already possessed by general mathematical principles and many of the more general principles of physics. The axioms of a standard version of set theory, for instance, can serve an important and fundamental role of organization and clarification of the structure of mathematics even when there is no clean agreement about the epistemological status of the

[1] D. J. O'Connor, *An Introduction to the Philosophy of Education* (London: Routledge and Kegan, Paul, 1957). Alan Montefiore, "Moral Philosophy and the Teaching of Morality," *Harvard Educational Review*, 35 (Fall 1965), 435–449.

axioms themselves. Similar systematic investigations of normative principles, as in the philosophy of education, should prove fruitful, even if there is continued controversy about the status of the principles themselves. This way of looking at the subject is expanded upon below.

2. *Affirmative Answers.* From another standpoint, to accept only negative answers to the question that is the title of this paper seems absurd. In some sense, even if it is not always a precise and clear sense, there must be a normative philosophy of education, just because practical decisions must be made daily about how education is to be organized, what curriculum is to be taught, and what the aims of the curriculum should be. We may wish to charge that the philosophy that dominates practice is inchoate or even inconsistent, but the charge that it is bad philosophy is distinct from the charge that there can be no philosophy of education.

Without trying to encompass all practical levels of decision-making in schools which involve some use of philosophical principles, it seems to me that there are at least three levels at which normative principles must be applied in education. The first and most general level is that of setting general aims of education. A useful catalogue of general aims has been provided by O'Connor.[2] Here is the list.

1 to provide men and women with a minimum of the skills necessary for them (a) to take their place in society and (b) to seek further knowledge;
2 to provide them with a vocational training that will enable them to be self-supporting;
3 to awaken an interest in and a taste for knowledge;
4 to make them critical;
5 to put them in touch with and train them to appreciate the cultural and moral achievements of mankind.

Probably like most of you, I am not entirely happy with this list. I give it here only as an example of the kind of thing one can mean by general aims. It is not my purpose in this paper critically to set forth a more systematic set of general aims.

However, once a set of general aims is accepted, and hopefully on a rather explicit basis, the next requirement is to allocate the economic resources of the school system or other school unit to the various aims of education. The normative principles of allocation take us far beyond general aims of education to much more complex and difficult questions of relative distribution and emphasis. As yet, there has been little explicit discussion in education of these normative principles of relative allocation, but as I shall attempt to show later, the contemporary literature of

[2] *Ibid.,* pp. 8–9.

normative economics and decision theory can teach us much about how such principles can be formulated and what the difficulties of complete formulation are. My only point at the moment is to emphasize that normative principles are always at work, implicitly or explicitly, in decisions about allocations of scarce resources. Pious talk about general aims of education do not amount to much if the serious problems of relative allocation are not dealt with systematically.

The third and most particular application of normative principles that I would mention is the set of decisions about what particular curriculum to teach and what sequence of topics to follow within a subject, given a particular allocation of resources to that subject. Given a fixed amount of money to be spent, for example, on a mathematics curriculum, it is still a matter for decision and therefore for the application of systematic normative principles to decide what kind of mathematics our students should be taught. Even more serious and more controversial are similar questions about the kind of history or civics or social studies that should be offered to our students. Currently, difficult questions about the appropriate and proper emphasis that should be given to Negro history are at the forefront of many discussions. In many cases substantive decisions about curriculum can take place relatively independent of economic considerations and therefore their guiding principles need to be separated and given a distinct place among the systematic normative principles of education.

In my own view, too much of the philosophy of education has centered on problems of moral philosophy and the teaching of morality in the schools. This is a point I want to expand on.

3. *Non-moral Normative Principles.* Because the discussion of moral principles and the teaching of morality have dominated so much of the philosophy of education, it seems wise to give a very explicit emphasis to the importance, particularly the practical importance, of non-moral normative principles. It is essential not to be misunderstood on this point. In many cases of non-moral normative principles some minor aspect of moral judgment may enter, but the thrust of such principles is in general to be neutral with respect to moral questions and to be concerned with other normative questions. To ask what mathematics ought to be taught to students in the sixth grade is not really to ask a moral question, even though the sentence is an *ought* statement. The principles by which we attempt to settle the question are not generally part of what would be called moral principles. I realize, however, that some may wish to claim that at the highest level in these analyses, problems of morality will still enter. I don't wish to make a direct argument about this; there is probably a sense in which such a claim is correct. On the other hand, there are a number of normative principles which enter into the philosophy of education and the systematic decisions that are taken by all

educational units and systems, and which are not primarily or essentially moral in character.

Here are two very simple but concrete examples from my own experience. Because of the great importance now attached to reading, in some elementary schools it is customary to schedule most of the reading work in the morning when the children are assumed to be most susceptible to learning and most likely to pay attention to the teacher and the lessons. Social studies, science, and mathematics, which mainly means arithmetic, are taught later in the day, often primarily in the afternoon. The kind of inference and argument that goes into this decision looks something like the following:

1) The most important part of the curriculum should be taught when the students are likely to make the best progress in learning.
2) Reading is the most important part of the elementary-school curriculum.
3) Students are likely to make the most progress in learning during the first hours of school, i.e., in the morning.
4) Therefore, reading should be taught in the morning.

The one premise of this argument that is a normative principle is evident. One might, however, also claim that the premise asserting that reading is the most important part of the curriculum expresses in the indicative mood a normative principle, or at least depends on such a principle. Whatever the view of this matter, it does seem fairly defensible that in the ordinary sense of moral principles neither premise (1) nor (2) would be regarded as a moral principle, and yet at least one of them is a normative principle, and possibly both are.

I don't want to give the impression that arguments involving normative principles can always assume the simple form of the one just given. It would be useful to consider a slightly more complicated example to illustrate two points: first, that the argument is not necessarily deductive in character but can be probabilistic in terms of inference; and secondly, that specific evaluation of alternative courses of action is required and is a particular point at which normative considerations enter.

In this example, consider the administrator who is concerned to introduce a new reading program in his school system. He thinks well of reading programs A and A' but he personally favors A over A'. On the other hand, he knows that there are complexities in getting either program adopted. Two layers of reviewing committees are required and because of the many competing ideas in front of the committees, it is essential for him to pick either A or A' from the beginning and to stick with it through the committee decisions if he is to have any chance of getting either A or A' adopted. He estimates the possibility that A would pass Committee 1 as at least p, which we shall write as $P(A_1) \geq p$. Also given that program

A passes Committee 1 he believes that it has at least probability q of passing Committee 2, which we shall write as

$$P(A_2 \mid A_1) \geqq q.$$

Also because of administrative procedures the chance of passing Committee 2 if Committee 1 is not passed is essentially 0. On the supposition that the hurdle of Committee 2 is the last hurdle before adoption of program A, we can then use the following probabilistic argument to estimate the chances $P(A)$ of adopting program A:

$$
\begin{array}{ll}
(1) & P(A_1) \geqq p \\
(2) & P(A_2 \mid A_1) \geqq q \\
(3) & P(A \mid A_2) = 1 \\
\hline
\therefore (4) & P(A) \geqq pq.
\end{array}
$$

A corresponding argument holds for the probability of adopting program A'.

$$
\begin{array}{ll}
(1) & P(A_1) \geqq p' \\
(2) & P(A_2' \mid A_1') \geqq q' \\
(3) & P(A' \mid A_2') = 1 \\
\hline
\therefore (4) & P(A') \geqq p'q'.
\end{array}
$$

We can now see why explicit quantitative principles of evaluation are needed in order for the administrator to decide which program he should support before the two committees. Let us write $v(A)$ for the value of A and $v(A')$ for a'. The administrator may now express his preference for A over A' in terms of the greater educational value of A' by the inequality, $v(A) > v(A')$. Suppose however, that in terms of the probability of committee actions he believes as follows:

$$p' > p,$$
$$q' > q,$$

and so

$$p'q' > pq.$$

He is then faced with a delicate problem of evaluation because the expected value of program A is at least $pqv(A)$ and the expected value of program A' is at least $p'q'v(A')$, and from the inequalities we have stated he cannot infer which program has the greater expected educational value. Quantitative principles of evaluation are needed for this purpose. The necessary normative principles of evaluation would not ordinarily be thought of as moral principles but at the same time they would be regarded as indubitably normative. I shall have something more to say below about quantitative principles of evaluation.

The point of these two examples is just to illustrate that in the context of decisions that must be made, a variety of normative principles, some major and significant, some minor and almost trivial, must enter into educational practices. Making explicit these normative principles is in my own judgment one of the major tasks of the philosophy of education, a task that has been unduly neglected to the almost exclusive consideration of general aims of education, problems of moral philosophy, and the teaching of morality.

4. *The Model of Normative Economics.* Analytical philosophers such as O'Connor and Montefiore have performed a considerable service in removing some of the rubbish that lies in the way of a constructive philosophy of education, to paraphrase a famous remark of Locke's; but as they both admit, it is certainly true that the contributions of contemporary analytic philosophy to the philosophy of education have been mainly negative in character. They have been of great help in analyzing fallacious arguments and in showing why in a relatively precise way vague ideas are indeed vague. But their positive contribution is almost negligible to a constructive philosophy of use to educators forced to make practical decisions at all the various levels I have mentioned. The situation, however, is not unusual. Exactly the same is true of the general domain of moral philosophy. In my own view, the reasons why this is true are intrinsic in the methods and approach of analytic philosophy; and if we seek to erect a constructive normative philosophy of education, we must look elsewhere for methods and models. Surely one of the best places to look is in the literature of modern normative economics, which has been very much concerned to make explicit and precise the principles of individual choice and social decision-making. From the point of view of this paper, it is important to be clear about the differences between these investigations in economics and the work in moral philosophy of the past two decades. The theoretical economists concerned with the normative principles that should form the foundation of economics and political theory have been little concerned with the epistemological foundation of the principles considered. Rather, they have given detailed scrutiny to their consequences and to the formal interplay between various sets of principles. As an example, consider the standard axiom that the method of making social decisions should not be dictatorial, i.e., according to the preferences simply of one member of the society. I cannot recall reading a single systematic epistemological discussion of the status of this principle. Economists have assumed that at least most intelligent readers would accept the principle. Consequently, they have been concerned to use it in a subtle way in its relation to other principles rather than to flay at the obvious and argue for its acceptance. As a second example, consider the principle of Pareto optimality. Roughly speaking, this principle asserts that one social decision should

be preferred to another if the first decision would lead to a social state in which everyone is at least as well off as in the second state and some persons are better off. In economic and political terms it is difficult to think of anyone's objecting to the soundness of this principle, although it is a relevant philosophical question to ask why we accept it or what more general principles might lead to its acceptance. My point, of course, is not to argue against the investigation of the epistemological foundations of universally accepted principles, but rather to argue that in the philosophy of education, as in moral philosophy, a balance now needs to be struck in the other direction. We need an intensive investigation of a wide range of principles in terms of their consequences and their logical inter-relationships, not of their foundations.

In citing these two examples it might appear that I am suggesting that it will be a simple matter of universal agreement to write down the normative principles of decision-making required in education. I do not wish to suggest anything of the kind and I emphasize that this is not at all the case in economics and political theory. Because we can get everyone to agree on Pareto optimality, it does not follow that a sufficient set of principles to apply on any broad basis can be agreed upon. We are faced with the problem clearly apparent in the principle of Pareto optimality: the principle is seldom applicable. In other words, the principles that can be readily agreed upon are not sufficiently discriminating to permit a unique alternative or even a small set of alternatives to be selected for adoption. It might be thought that this was always the situation and there was never any problem of having too many principles to apply. However, as the paradoxical consequences of various principles in economics and decision theory have clearly shown, our naive intuitions about rationality or justice are often inconsistent when we attempt to make them explicit. In other words, the set of principles we are prepared to adopt on a naive and unreflective basis is too large a set in the sense that no course of action or alternative before us is able to satisfy all the principles simultaneously. The existence of such paradoxical sets of principles is relatively new in philosophy in the context of decisions or the analysis of political theory, but it is an old story in the foundations of mathematics, where apparently obvious principles that all would accept, such as the axiom that permits us to form the collection of objects having a given property, can lead to a contradiction.

It is important to be clear about the kind of conflict of principles that is at issue here. It is an everyday matter in education for conflict of principles to arise among various groups interested in the curriculum concerning what should be taught to students. Strongly held views on sex education, on the teaching of religion, or on the open discussion of politics can be found in many quarters. Such conflict is another sort of problem for the philosophy of education, not one that I shall consider in detail here. I shall simply remark in passing that adequate analysis of the conflict is missing from the philosophy of education just as it is from many contemporary theories of politics, which disdain any explicit concept of power. In the present context, however, the conflict of principles I have in mind is the conflict of principles within a given individual or social group. Revealing the implicit principles held by the individual or group leads to the result that the full set of principles is inconsistent. An examination of such inconsistencies can be, I believe, one of the more fruitful avenues of progress in the philosophy of education. Consistency of principles is a necessary condition that almost all men accept. It can be imposed and exploited without further analysis of the epistemological status of the principles. The close articulation of principles in the philosophy of education can have the kind of beneficial effects found in other philosophical endeavors, ranging from the foundations of mathematics to contemporary formulations of decision theory and normative economics.

In this sense, my appeal is for an old-fashioned philosophy of education, a constructive endeavor to supplement current negative efforts at clarification.

I realize that it may be well and good to call for such articulation of principles in the philosophy of education, but to leave the matter there is to leave the discussion very close to the arid plane of most general discussions in the philosophy of education. If we examine the particular principles much debated and argued about in normative economics, it is easy to see that these principles have a close relation to moral philosophy, and yet they have their own distinctive character and formulation. For example, consider the principle that the method of social decision shall not be dictatorial, that the choice between two alternatives shall be independent of the preferences for other alternatives, or that whenever possible, a Pareto-optimal action should be adopted. These are principles that make sense in the context of moral philosophy and yet have a distinctive political or economic feel about them. We should expect the same of normative principles of education. This point I now want to explore in greater depth.

5. *Antinomies of Education.* The antinomies of mathematics, ranging from Russell's paradox to the antinomy of the liar, have been a source of ever deeper investigations into the foundations of mathematics during this century. The philosophy of mathematics is indeed the one subject in which a very great and notable progress in philosophy is apparent over the course of the past hundred years. In the last decade or two, antinomies that arise in normative economics or in rational decision-making have again been the source of many important and exact investigations. The existence of antinomies in education has not had a corresponding effect but has been the source mainly of acrimonious debate and polemic.

Here are four closely related antinomies of education that need far deeper analysis than they have yet received. For uniformity of terminology, I shall call each of them by the term that relates to the child-centered side of the antinomy rather than to the content- or the curriculum-oriented side. This corresponds in moral philosophy and epistemology to talk about the antinomy of freedom rather than the antinomy of necessity.

Antinomy of Adjustment. On the one hand, the principle is asserted that the school, particularly the elementary school, should be organized to provide the maximum amount of personal and social adjustment for the individual child. On the other hand, the principle is asserted that the school should be organized to provide the maximum amount of *achievement* on the part of the individual child. When these two principles are joined with some fairly widely accepted factual statements, an antinomy or contradiction is easily derived.

Antinomy of Method. The principle is asserted that in teaching we should maximize learning and problem-solving techniques independent of content, and selection of curriculum material should maximize student involvement and motivation. On the other hand, the principle is asserted that we should maximize the *content* of the curriculum in order to prepare students for specific jobs with specific skills or to provide them with a particular historical and cultural background. Dewey's *How We Think* is a typical defense of method, and the Hutchins' program of great books a defense of content.

Antinomy of the Child. The principle is asserted that the school, particularly the elementary school, should be centered entirely on the child and not on the curriculum. On the other hand, the principle is asserted that the schools should at all times emphasize the *curriculum,* because teaching the curriculum is the proper function of the schools, while the personal development of children is the responsibility of other segments of society.

Antinomy of Freedom. The principle is asserted that the schools should endeavor in all ways to develop freedom of speech, thought, and choice. On the other hand, the principle is asserted that the schools should endeavor in all ways to develop a sense of *discipline* and criticism that satisfies the highest possible intellectual standards.

The existence of these four antinomies and others in the fundamental concepts of education does not mean that the daily business of education cannot go forward. It can and it will, but their existence does mean that a first order of business for the philosophy of education is to formulate the foundations in a way that avoids any antinomies. In the case of mathematics, for example, the explicit efforts to avoid the antinomies of set theory have led to profound investigations into the nature of mathematics. What we still lack in education, in comparison to mathematics, is a set of concepts that are formulated with sufficient precision. However, the task is by no means hopeless. The recent clarifications of very similar problems in normative economics should give heart to all of us in education.

There is another aspect of the antinomies that is important. The acceptance of either side of one of the antinomies represents an extreme position. Most of us feel that the proper position is somewhere between the two extremes. Acceptance of a mean position leads to a rejection of simplistic ideologies of education. What is not sufficiently recognized by those who would tread the middle of the road is that we have not yet solved the more complex and subtle intellectual problems of formulating and establishing an intellectual foundation for that middle ground. There are a number of ways of illustrating this point. I choose a mathematical aspect of the problem. A compromise position between the extremes of any one of the antinomies will not be fully articulated until the explicit problem of optimization or minimization is solved. This is the problem of formulating the relevant concepts in measurable terms. How much freedom and how much disciplined inquiry? How much adjustment and how much achievement? It is only twaddle to talk about educationally viable solutions of any permanent value until more systematic and deeper analyses of the relevant fundamental concepts can be given.

I would like to try to illustrate the difficulties we quickly encounter by giving a deliberately oversimplified formal version of the antinomy of freedom. We shall assume only that agreement may be reached in judging whether one of two curriculum schemes permits more freedom of speech, thought, and choice on the part of the student. Thus I write xFy to mean that curriculum x is more free than curriculum scheme y. A more refined system of measurement is not assumed. Correspondingly I write xDy when scheme x is judged to contain or promote more disciplined and critical inquiry than scheme y. I write xCy when the number of significant choices given the student is judged to be greater under scheme x than under scheme y, and I write xLy when it is judged that more is learned under scheme x than under scheme y in terms of direct behavioral measures of learning.

The following postulates about the relations C, D, F, and L are then made, for a generous but finite set X of curriculum schemes.

Postulate 1.   *The relations* C, D, F, *and* L *are transitive on* X.
Postulate 2.   *The relations* C, D, F, *and* L *are asymmetric on* X.
Postulate 3.   *The relations* C, D, F, *and* L *are connected on* X.

(This means, for example, that for x and y in X if $x \neq y$ then xCy or yCx.)

Postulate 4.   *If* xCy *then* xFy *for any* x *and* y *in* X. (This postulate says that greater choice implies greater freedom.)

Postulate 5. If xDy *then* xLy *for any* x *and* y *in* X. (This postulate says that greater discipline implies greater learning.)

Postulate 6. Max C $\neq$ Max L, *where* Max C *is the scheme* x *such that for all* y $\neq$ x, xCy, *and* Max L *is defined similarly.* (This postulate says that the scheme with the greatest freedom of choice is not identical with the scheme with the greatest potential for learning.)

The Principle of Freedom says that we must choose as our curriculum scheme Max F. The Principle of Discipline and Criticism says that we must choose as our curriculum scheme Max D. It follows from our six postulates that Max F $\neq$ Max D, and an antinomy of decision results, for our two principles of decision are in direct conflict. The system of postulates I have laid down is admittedly highly schematized and much too simple, but it does illustrate one fundamental point. It is relatively easy to lay down principles which are perhaps too simple but still reasonable and which lead directly to an antinomy. It is far harder to take the next step and indicate the explicit principles that should be used to select a curriculum scheme between the two extremes.

As I have already said, I do not mean to suggest that the everyday business of education can wait on an adequate analysis, but the first step forward in any domain of philosophy or science is to recognize in clear and certain terms what fundamental problems exist that are as yet unsolved. Clearly stated normative principles to deal with the antinomies of education are for me the most urgent need of contemporary philosophy of education.

THE AUTHORS

Ernest Nagel (1901–   ). One of America's most famous philosophers of science in the Positivist and Logical Empiricist tradition, master of the philosophical technique of symbolic logic, philosopher of the methodology of science. Born Novemesto, Czechoslovakia; came to the United States in 1911. Graduated from the City College of New York (1923); M.A., Columbia University (1925); Ph.D. in philosophy, Columbia University (1931). Teacher in the public schools of New York City (1923–1929); instructor in philosophy, City College of New York (1930–1931); instructor, Columbia University (1931–1937); assistant professor, Columbia (1937–1939); associate professor, Columbia (1939–1946); professor of philosophy, Columbia (1946–1955); John Dewey Professor of Philosophy (1955–1966). Awarded the Butler Silver medal, Columbia University (1954); American Council Learned Society Prize for Distinguished Scholarship (1959). Editor, *The Journal of Philosophy* (1939–1956); editor, *Journal of Symbolic Logic* (1940–1946); editor, *Philosophy of Science* (1956–1959). Major publications: *Principles of the Theory* *of Probability* (1939); *On the Logic of Measurement* (private printing); *Sovereign Reason* (1954); *Logic Without Metaphysics* (1957); *Structure of Science: Problems in the Logic of Scientific Explanation* (1961); co-authored with J. R. Newman, *Godel's Proof* (1958); co-authored with R. B. Brandt, *Meaning and Knowledge* (1965).

Daniel John O'Connor (1914–   ). British philosopher of critical language analysis, amending strict Logical Positivism, published the most influential text in linguistic critical philosophy and philosophy of education. Born in Seattle, Washington. Graduated from Birkbeck College, University of London (1933); served with various branches of the Civil Service for the British Commonwealth (1933–1946); Commonwealth Fund Fellow in philosophy, University of Chicago (1946–1947); professor of philosophy, University of Natal, South Africa (1949–1951); professor, University of Witwatersrand, Johannesburg (1951–1952); lecturer in philosophy, University College of North Staffordshire (1952–1954); professor of philosophy, University of Liverpool (1954–1957); professor of philosophy, University of Exeter (1957–   ); visiting professor, University of Pennsylvania (1961–1962). Major publications: *John Locke* (1952); co-authored with A. H. Basson, *Introduction to Symbolic Logic* (1953); *An Introduction to the Philosophy of Education* (1957); edited, *A Critical History of Western Philosophy* (1964).

David Krech (1909–   ). Distinguished psychologist of the physiological foundations of human and animal behavior, learning, and perception; noted researcher in the chemistry of the brain. Born in Grodno, Poland; came to the United States in 1913. Graduated from New York University (1930); M.A., University of California (1931); Ph.D. in psychology, University of California (1933). National Research Council fellow in the biological sciences, University of Chicago (1933–1934); assistant professor, University of Chicago (1934–1937); resident associate, Swarthmore College (1937–1938); instructor, Colorado University (1938–1939); social science analyst, U. S. Department of Agriculture (1941–1942); assistant professor of psychology, Swarthmore College (1945–1946); assistant and associate professor, University of California at Berkeley (1946–1951); professor of psychology, University of California (1951–   ). Fulbright professor (1949–1950, 1963–1964); at University of Oslo, Norway (1949–1950); visiting professor at Harvard (1950–1951); University of Nijmegan, Holland (1962–1963). Major publications: co-authored with R. S. Crutchfield, *Theory and Problems of Social Psychology* (1948) and *Elements of Psychology* (1958); co-authored with R. S. Crutchfield and E. L. Ballachey, *The Individual in Society* (1963).

Neal Gross (1920–   ). The most prominent specialist in the sociological analysis of education, applies the tools of analysis and science methodology to clarify the function of the educational organization, the roles of professional educators, and the organization of the school. Born in San Antonio, Texas. Graduated from Marquette University (1941); M.A., Iowa State College (1942); Ph.D. in sociology, Iowa State College (1946); honorary M.A., Harvard (1956). Assistant professor of sociology, Iowa State College

(1946–1948); associate professor, University of Minnesota (1948–1951); lecturer in education and sociology, associate professor, Harvard Graduate School of Education (1951–1958); professor of education and sociology, Harvard Graduate School of Education (1958–1968); professor of education and sociology, dean of the Graduate School of Education, University of Pennsylvania (1968–   ). Consultant, Ford Foundation (1961–1962); fellow, Center for Advanced Study in Behavioral Sciences (1957–1958); Ford Foundation Special Award (1963–1964). Major publications: *Who Runs Our Schools?* (1958) co-authored with W. S. Mason and A. W. McEachern, *Explorations in Role Analysis* (1958) co-authored with R. E. Herriott, *Staff Leadership in Public Schools* (1965).

Patrick Suppes (1922–   ). Logician, mathematician, and philosopher of science, has endeavored to apply the models of mathematics to certain specialized problems in the social sciences and topics in the humanities. Born in Tulsa, Oklahoma. Graduated from the University of Chicago (1943); Ph.D. (Wendell T. Bush fellow), Columbia University (1950); instructor, Stanford University (1950–1952); assistant professor, Stanford (1952–1955); associate professor, Stanford (1955–1959); professor of philosophy and statistics, Stanford (1960–   ); associate dean, School of Humanities and Social Sciences, Stanford (1958–1961). Major publications: *Introduction to Logic* (1957); *Axiomatic Set Theory* (1960); co-authored with S. Hill, *First Course in Mathematical Logic* (1964); co-authored with D. Davidson, *Decision Making: An Experimental Approach* (1957); co-authored with R. C. Atkinson, *Markov Learning Models for Multiperson Interactions* (1960). Co-authored with others, elementary schools books in mathematics, *Geometry for Primary Grades* (1959), *Sets and Numbers* (1961). Editor, with L. Henkin and A. Tarski, *The Axiomatic Method* (1959); editor, with K. J. Arrow and S. Karlin, *Mathematical Methods in Social Sciences* (1960); editor, with E. Nagel and A. Tarski, *Methodology and Philosophy of Science* (1962); editor, with J. Criswell *et al.*, *Mathematical Methods in Small Group Processes* (1965).

Ordinary Language
Philosophy

GENERIC NOTIONS AND BASIC THEMES

U nderlying the Ordinary Language thought pattern are the influences of Logical-Science Philosophy and of philosophy's search for its own identity. From Logical-Science Philosophy comes the continued interest in language analysis, the call for some standard for identifying the true and false, and the ideal of specialization. However, the Ordinary Language philosophers have rejected the Logical-Science thought pattern's heavy reliance on science and mathematics for evidence and proof of philosophical statements. Most of the important scholars dealing with philosophy had been scientists in the Logical-Science tradition, who insisted that the ultimate source of truth rested in the scientific and mathematical disciplines. Ordinary Language philosophers, who wished philosophy to become an autonomous discipline, independent of other fields of knowledge, have developed a program for identifying truth that uses only philosophical materials. Although it is true that many philosophers turned to Ordinary Language Philosophy as a means for solving some unsettled questions in philosophy, its primary appeal has been its promise of specialization, its desire to put philosophy on an equal intellectual footing with the sciences and mathematics.

The thought pattern of Ordinary Language Philosophy has two generic notions: the acceptance of absolute truth, and the assumption of the priority of reason. The absolute truth that Ordinary Language philosophers refer to is not a system of eternal dogmas or lasting statements about reality, but the facts of nature as they are. Truth is merely that which is, a condition of nature, absolute and nonrelative. Verification, the activity that scientists perform, does not change truth. Truth is prior to test and verification and is something that philosophers can determine. Ordinary Language philosophers ask us to recognize that truth has a unique existence, that it is not a mental or psychological affair, that it is not a result of human operations. Truth is truth by philosophical logic. It is simply incorrect to say that truth is that which is untrue.

The second generic notion is the priority of reason, the relationship persons have to the absoluteness of truth. Since verification and confirmation are virtually secondary and limited processes in the context of truth, reason must be primary in human knowing. Ordinary Language philosophers do not believe that mathematics and formal logic should be primary, but rather the reason of knowing the truth and being able to justify and argue for it rationally.

"Doing philosophy," the expression Ordinary Language philosophers use to describe their work, involves a unique method deriving from the two generic notions. The method is not a well-defined procedure following externalized steps. It is a method of language analysis for the purpose of recognizing truth. The method follows from the presupposition that natural language produces confusion and misleading suggestions. Although truth is absolute and present, it can be clouded and blurred by common mistakes in the use of language. The philosopher must analyze ordinary language usage to clear up misleading or mistaken categories. The problem lies with "words" and "sentence-factors," not with the formal syntax of sentences. That is, philosophical problems must be solved by analyzing the logical behavior of words and by trying alternate sentence-factors in different expressions in order to identify the correct use of the terms.

This method produces an unusual result in the form of the contention that a conclusion is not an exposé of truth but a revelation of it. The goal is not a verbal formulation, but truth revealed and laid bare by analysis. A characteristic of this movement is its answerlessness. Analysis simply does not give propositional accounts of truth. Truth is already present, it does not need a verbalization. In the words of A. J. Ayer, "the important work consists not in the formulation of an answer, which often turns out to be almost platitudiness, but in making the way clear for its acceptance." [1]

A second dimension to the philosophical method as perceived by the Ordinary Language philosophers, relates to the topics of philosophy. Since philosophy is a distinctive discipline, it requires phenomena that are its own specialized concern. Philosophers have always dealt with the areas of epistemology, moral philosophy, and metaphysics, and these can be interpreted as the exclusive domains of the specialty of philosophy. Doing philosophy therefore, can be construed as language analysis of a problem in one of these areas.

According to the Ordinary Language philosophers, information on philosophical problems cannot be found in the sciences, in psychology or the sociology of knowledge. The sources must lie in philosophy itself, in the voluminous data provided by the writings of the great philosophers —Plato, Aristotle, Aquinas, Kant—and of contemporary philosophers who are doing philosophy. Since the truth is absolute and already present, there is no new knowledge to discover. Instead, the task of philosophers is to analyze what is already known. In the words of

[1] A. J. Ayer, *The Problem of Knowledge* (Baltimore: Penguin, 1956), p. 133.

Ludwig Wittgenstein, "The problems are solved not by giving new information, but by arranging what we have always known." [2] All the evidence that bears upon a philosophical problem is already available. It merely needs a Socrates to bring it forth. On the basis of philosophy's unique methodology, data, and topics philosophers have built a convincing case for the specialization of philosophy.

The requirements of "a discipline" have been carefully defined by Ordinary Language philosophers. One field that does not meet these requirements is education. Education is not autonomous or self-perpetuating as is, for example, philosophy. It has no specialized subject matter or vocabulary, and it does not deal with only one group of phenomena. Education draws on many disciplines, as well as on experiences outside those disciplines. It has no concise method for acquiring data, and no set laws and principles to order the data, once collected. Education thus in no sense can be considered a discipline.

Philosophy is one of the fields that can make an important contribution to education, just as psychology, sociology, history, and other disciplines can also contribute. Philosophy aids education, not by constructing a world view or philosophy of education, however, but by doing philosophy on educational problems in the philosophical areas of epistemology and moral philosophy. Philosophical analysis in moral philosophy can clarify issues in moral education, whereas analysis in epistemology can expose the meanings of teaching, knowing, and other related concepts. It is a misnomer, then, to speak of "philosophy of education." Instead, one should always refer to "philosophy *and* education."

Unlike the Logical-Science philosophers, Ordinary Language philosophers do not conceive of moral philosophy, one of the two areas in which they believe philosophical study can help education, as the clarification of such emotive words as "right" and "ought." Rather, they believe moral philosophy involves language analysis aimed at grasping the nature of morality itself. The philosophical method of analysis is used to reveal the absolutes or universals of morality. The important words and phrases in the search for this relevation are: "obligation," "blameworthiness," "free choice," "responsibility," "moral rules and principles," and "doing one's duty." Ordinary Language philosophers seek to use analysis to clarify the universal codes, rules, and principles of morality that are as much a part of nature as truth itself. Education can profit from such philosophical endeavor because such work supplies education with the recognition of the reasonableness of morality, and the clarification of the requirements for specific moral training of youth.

The second area in which philosophy makes a contribution to education is epistemology. Epistemological analysis clarifies the educational

[2] Ludwig Wittgenstein, *Philosophical Investigations*, G. E. M. Anscombe, (tr.) (Oxford: Blackwell, 1953), p. 47.

conditions surrounding the knowing of absolute truth and related academic achievements. The philosophical procedure involved is the linguistic examination of words and sentence-factors that reflect educational contexts. Analysis of the words "teaching," "telling," "knowing," "believing," "knowing how," and "understanding" helps to identify the procedures that are at work in education by clarifying particular meanings and the limitations surrounding certain processes. Educators uncertain of the connotation of the word "teaching," for example, can better comprehend its true meaning by following Israel Scheffler's analysis that interprets "teaching" as a manner of doing something. This suggests that the word has both an intentional use (directed toward a goal and requiring effort) and a success use (expectation of a successful outcome).[3]

The Ordinary Language Philosophy thought pattern implies certain educational practices. Analysis has focused specifically on three main areas: knowing that, conduct or performance, and knowing how to do something. Through analysis, each of these areas has been shown to be distinct, and each requires different procedures of teaching and learning. The first, "knowing that," in the strictest sense of the term, involves the truth condition of knowledge. This kind of "knowing" cannot be taught by lecturing or telling. It is an outgrowth of reasoning. The most a teacher can do is promote knowing. Ordinary Language philosophers strongly oppose lecturing as an educational practice. The second concern is the teaching of conduct, which involves two activities, rational discourse with reference to reasons in morality and activities where students can learn the dispositions to act rightly. Finally, the analysis of "knowing how to" reveals the importance of teaching skills. Telling may aid in the acquisition of skill, but repetition, practice, and even demonstration are also needed.

According to Ordinary Language philosophers, educational practice will vary according to the clarification of different sets of educational phenomena. However, one practice central to all educational tasks, is the use of reason in discourse and action. A teacher must utilize reason in teaching, must provide incidents requiring the critical quest for reasons, must get students involved in making claims and supporting such claims by rational procedures. Reason lies at the heart of the educational process whether attention is directed to intellectual or moral achievements.

[3] Israel Scheffler, *The Language of Education* (Springfield Ill.: Thomas, 1960), pp. 60–75.

Conditions of Knowledge / ISRAEL SCHEFFLER

The development and transmission of knowledge are fundamental tasks of education, while analysis of its nature and warrant falls to that branch of philosophy known as epistemology, or theory of knowledge. An adequate educational philosophy must not only address itself to epistemological problems in their general form but must also strive to view these problems from the perspective of educational tasks and purposes. . . .

Cognitive and Educational Terms Related

How are the cognitive terms *knowing* and *believing* related to the educational terms *learning* and *teaching?* The question is not as simple as it may seem, and our consideration of it in this section will introduce several points of relevance throughout our discussions.

We might, as a result of attending to certain simple cases, suppose *learning that* to imply *knowing that.* If a student, for example, has *learned that* Boston is the capital of Massachusetts, we should normally say he has come to *know that* Boston is the capital of Massachusetts. Yet we cannot generalize from such cases that whenever a person X has learned that Q, he has come to know that Q.

Consider a student in some distant age or culture in which disease has been attributed to the action of evil spirits. Such a student may well have learned from his tutors that disease is caused by evil spirits, but we should not be willing to describe him as having come to know that disease is caused by evil spirits. *He* may, to be sure, have been perfectly willing to say "I *know* that evil spirits cause disease," but nonetheless *we* will not wish to describe him as having come to know that evil spirits cause disease, for we should then ourselves be admitting that evil spirits *do* cause disease. For us to say that some person knows that such and such is the case is, in general, for us to commit ourselves to the embedded substantive assertion that such and such *is* the case. Where such a commitment is repugnant to us, we will accordingly avoid attributing knowledge, though we may still attribute belief. In the present case, we will deny that the student in question has come to know that evil spirits cause disease, but we may safely describe him as having come to believe that evil spirits cause disease, for our belief attribution does *not* commit us to the substantive assertion in question. In our earlier example, by contrast, since we were perfectly willing to agree that Boston is the capital of Massachusetts, the stronger attribution of knowledge to the student did not commit us to an embedded substantive claim we found repugnant.

We are thus led to contrast *learning that* and *knowing that* in the following way: To say that someone has come to know that Q, commits us generally to the substantive assertion represented by "Q." For example, if we say of a pupil that he has come to know that Cornwallis surrendered at Yorktown, we are ourselves committed to the substantive assertion, "Cornwallis surrendered at Yorktown." To say that someone has learned that Q, does not so commit us; we are, in general, limited only to the claim that he has come to believe that Q.[1]

There are, to be sure, certain uses of *learning that* which do, in fact, commit us substantively in the manner we have been discussing. Consider the following statement, for example: "Reporters, after extensive investigation, learned that secret negotiations had been in progress for three weeks before the agreement was announced publicly." The force of "learned that" in this statement approximates that of "found out that" or "discovered that," which do commit us substantively. We may label such a use of "learn that," a *discovery use*, and contrast it with the *tutorial use*, in which the expression refers (without committing us substantively) to what people come to believe in consequence of schooling. The existence of the tutorial use suffices to show that a *learn that* attribution does not, in general, commit us to the embedded substantive assertion. And as we saw earlier, this is sufficient to *block* the generalization that what X has learned he has come to know, permitting only the weaker generalization that what X has learned he has come to believe.

The weaker generalization, in other words, unlike the stronger one, frees us from commitment to repugnant substantive claims in all those cases where we attribute *learning that* tutorially but reject the content learned. The student mentioned earlier may well be admitted to have learned, and to have believed, that evil spirits cause disease, but he cannot well be admitted to have come to know this. Suppose, now, that we consider all and only those cases where (i) X has learned that Q, and where (ii) we concur with the substantive assertion represented by "Q." Should we be willing in all these cases, at least, to say that X has indeed come to know (and not merely to believe) that Q?

---

[1] The letter Q occurs here, and in discussions to follow, sometimes framed by quotation marks, sometimes not. The letter *without* quotation marks stands in place of a sentence, fully displayed at the location of the occurrence in question. The letter *with* quotation marks, on the other hand, stands in place of a name of the sentence in question—typically, in place of the sentence-name which consists of the sentence itself framed by quotes.

This question raises a point of general importance regarding the attribution of knowledge: Some writers on the subject have recognized a weak and a strong sense of *know that*.[2] The answer to our question will depend on which sense we have in mind. In the weak sense, *knowing that* depends solely on having true belief; in the strong sense, it requires something further—for example, the ability to back up the belief in a relevant manner, to bring evidence in its support, or to show that one is in a position to know what it affirms. If we take the weak sense of *know that*, we shall then answer our question in the affirmative. If X has learned that Q and has therefore come to believe that Q, and if, further, we are willing to concur with the claim made by "Q" (i.e., to affirm it as true), we must acknowledge that X has come to believe truly, hence to know (in the weak sense) that Q.

If we take the strong sense of *know that*, however, we must answer our question in the negative. For a person may believe correctly or truly that Q, and yet lack the ability to provide adequate backing for his belief or to show that he is in a position to know that Q. Though he has learned that Q and has come to believe truly that Q, he will then not *really* know, or know in the strong sense, that Q. He has, for example, learned in school that $E = mc^2$, but cannot, unless he can supply suitable supporting reasons, be said to know (in the strong sense) that $E = mc^2$.

We may summarize our discussion to this point as follows: If X has learned that Q, he has come to believe that Q. If we deny "Q," we will directly rule out that X has also come to know that Q, no matter how well X is able to support "Q." On the other hand, if we grant that "Q" is true, it is not directly ruled out that we shall say X has come to know that Q. We shall, indeed, say this immediately if we employ the weak sense of *know*, but only upon the satisfaction of further conditions if we employ the strong sense of *know*.

Often, perhaps typically, however, we do not make a direct test to determine whether these further conditions have indeed been satisfied; we operate rather on general presumptions that seem to us plausible. The presumption that the relevant conditions have been satisfied varies, for example, with the difficulty, technicality, or complexity of the subject. Thus, it seemed quite natural to us earlier to say that a student who has learned that Boston is the capital of Massachusetts has indeed come to know this. Nor does this seem to be simply a result of using the weak sense of *know*. The question "He has learned it, but does he really know it?" springs less easily to our lips in this case than in the case of "$E = mc^2$." For what sort of complex technical backing could possibly be needed here? Granted that the strong sense of *know* is operative, we are more likely to presume, on general grounds, that a student who has

[2] For example, Jaakko Hintikka, *Knowledge and Belief* (Ithaca, N.Y.: Cornell University Press, 1962), pp. 18–19.

learned a "simple" fact can support it appropriately than we are likely to make the same presumption for a relatively "complex" or technical affirmation.

Another source of variation seems to be the method by which the belief has been acquired. To have merely been made aware or informed by somebody that Q leaves open the practical possibility that one does not really know (in the strong sense) that Q, even where "Q" is true. To have found out for oneself that Q, lends greater credence to the presumption that one really has come to know that Q, for it suggests, though it does not strictly imply, that one has been in a good position to realize that Q, either relatively directly or on the basis of clues or reasons pointing to "Q."

This suggests why the discovery use of *learning that* seems to imply *knowing that* in the strong sense. Consider again our reporters, who learned (found out) after extensive investigation that the negotiations had been in progress for three weeks before the publicly announced agreement. The question "Granted they found out, but did they really know?" does not strike us as immediately relevant or natural. Those educators who stress so-called discovery and problem-solving methods in schooling may, in fact, be operating upon the general presumption that such methods lead to strong knowing as an outcome. And emphasis on *teaching*, with its distinctive connotations of rational explanation and critical dialogue, may have the same point: to develop a sort of learning in which the student will be capable of backing his beliefs by appropriate and sufficient means. To have learned that Q as a consequence of genuine teaching, given that "Q" is true, does seem to lend some weight to the presumption that one has come to know.

The notion of "teaching," unlike "learning," has, typically, *intentional* as well as *success* uses.[3] That is to say, teaching normally involves trying, whereas learning does not. To say of a child that he is learning to walk, that he is learning several new words every day, that he is learning how to conduct himself socially, that he is learning to express himself well in speech, does not in itself normally convey that he is *trying* to accomplish these things. It does not even convey that he is engaged or occupied in them, in the sense of thinking of what is going on, focusing his attention, and acting with care. Learning, it might thus be said, is not an *activity* but rather more nearly a *process*. We may surely distinguish the different stages of a process, and we may separate those situations in which the process has run its course to completion from those in which it has not. But such analyses do not presuppose either deliberateness or intention, although the latter *may*, in particular circumstances, be involved. We

[3] On this point, see Israel Scheffler, *The Language of Education* (Springfield, Ill.: Charles C. Thomas, 1960), pp. 42, 60–61.

can try to learn this or that, but we often learn without trying at all; there is, moreover, no general presumption that any given case of learning is intentional.

Teaching appears quite different, by comparison. To say of someone that he is teaching conveys normally that he is engaged in an activity, rather than caught up in a process. It is to imply contextually that what he is doing is directed toward a goal and involves intention and care. He is, in short, trying, and what he is trying to bring about represents *success* in the activity, rather than simply the end-state of a process. We can, to be sure, speak of so-called "unintentional teaching," in which a person actually brings about a certain sort of learning, although without trying or even awareness on his part. But such reference will require that the word *teaching* be suitably qualified (e.g., by the word *unintentional*), or that supplementary explanation of the case be offered. Without such further information, a bare ascription of *teaching* contextually implies intention, whereas a success use of the verb (e.g., "Jones has taught his son how to swim") signifies intention brought to successful fruition.

What does teaching have as its goal? What does a person engaged in teaching intend or try to bring about? Obviously, an appropriate bit of learning. In the particular case of *teaching that* with which we have so far been concerned, a person X teaching Y that Q, is trying to bring about Y's learning that Q. As we have seen, this involves Y's coming to accept "Q" or to believe that Q. If X has been successful in teaching Y that Q, Y has indeed learned that Q, has come to believe that Q.

The converse, of course, does not hold: One may learn that Q without having been taught it by anyone. Furthermore, we must not suppose that teaching can be *reduced to* trying to achieve someone's coming to believe something. One may try to propagate a belief in numerous ways other than teaching—for example, through deception, insinuation, advertising, hypnosis, propaganda, indoctrination, threats, bribery, and force. Nor must we be quick to identify teaching with schooling generally, for formal agencies of schooling have employed and often do employ methods other than teaching—for example, indoctrination, suggestion, threats, and force. Thus, if we think of *learning that* as referring to the acquisition of belief just in the context of schooling, we still cannot take teaching as simply directed toward learning as its goal, although teaching does have learning as its goal.

What distinguishes teaching, as we remarked earlier, is its special connection with rational explanation and critical dialogue: with the enterprise of giving honest reasons and welcoming radical questions. The person engaged in teaching does not merely want to bring about belief, but to bring it about through the exercise of free rational judgment by the student. This is what distinguishes teaching from propaganda or debating, for example. In teaching, the teacher is revealing his reasons for the beliefs he wants to transmit and is thus, in effect, submitting his own judgment to the critical scrutiny and evaluation of the student; he is fully engaged in the dialogue by which he hopes to teach, and is thus risking his own beliefs, in lesser or greater degree, as he teaches.

Teaching, it might be said, involves trying to bring about learning under severe restrictions of *manner*—that is to say, within the limitations imposed by the framework of rational discussion. Since teaching that Q presupposes that the teacher takes "Q" to be true (or at least within the legitimate range of truth approximation allowable for purposes of peda-gogical simplification and facilitation) and since the activity of teaching appeals to the free rational judgment of the student, we might say that the teacher is trying to bring about knowledge, in the strong sense earlier discussed. For the presumption is that a person who is encouraged to form his beliefs through free rational methods is likely to be in a position to provide proper backing for them. The teacher does not strive merely to get the student to learn that Q, but also to get him to learn it in such a way as to know it—i.e., to be able to support it properly.

We must, however, admit that there will generally be differences of opinion as to the success or failure of the whole teaching operation. Cross-cultural cases provide the clearest illustrations. Consider the teacher of a distant age who strove to teach that evil spirits cause disease. He was (we have said) *trying* to get his students really to know this. Now we may admit that he was successful in getting them to believe that evil spirits cause disease and even in supporting this belief in a way that may have been reasonable in their cultural environment. We cannot, however, admit his *success* in getting his students to *know* that evil spirits cause disease, for *we* hold this doctrine to be false.

Is there not a difficulty here from the point of view of appraisal of teaching? We want to distinguish successful from unsuccessful teaching in this ancient era, but our present analysis forces us to judge all of it (at least with respect to such false doctrines as we have been considering) to have been uniformly unsuccessful. To meet this problem, we may pro-pose a secondary or "subjective" notion of success to supplement the primary or "objective" notion we have been using. According to this secondary or subjective notion of success, we assume that the truth of the doctrine taught is to be judged from the teacher's point of view; we also judge the question of proper backing in a way that makes allowances for the prevalent standards and available data in the culture in question. Then we judge success in the normal manner. We can now make the wanted cross-cultural distinctions between successful and unsuccessful teaching even where, from an objective point of view and judged from our standpoint, it has been unsuccessful.

Any teaching is geared to what the teacher takes to be true, and his aim is not merely that his student learn what he takes to be true but that he be able to support it by criteria of proper backing taken to be authoritative. Insofar as the teacher is *teaching*, he is, in any event, risking his own particular truth judgments, for he is exposing them to the general critique of these criteria and to the free critical judgment of the student's mind.

One point of general importance should be especially noted. *Knowing that* attributions reflect the truth judgments and critical standards of the speaker; they commit him substantively to the beliefs he is assigning to others, and they hinge on the particular criteria of backing for beliefs, which he adopts. Thus, unlike attributions of *belief, learning that,* and *teaching that,* they reveal his own epistemological orientation to the items of belief in question; in this sense, they do more than merely describe the person to whom knowledge is being attributed.

We have, in sum, connected the educational ideas of learning and teaching with the cognitive ideas of knowledge and belief, as follows: Learning that Q involves coming to believe that Q. Under certain further conditions (truth of "Q" and, for the strong sense of *knowing*, proper backing of "Q"), it also involves coming to know that Q. Teaching that Q involves trying to bring about learning that (and belief that) Q, under characteristic restrictions of manner, and, furthermore, knowing that Q, as judged by the teacher from his own standpoint.

Now, there are certain classes of counterexamples that might be offered in opposition to these generalizations. A student might say, in reporting what he had learned on a certain day, "I learned that the gods dwelt on Olympus," or, if a student of philosophy, "I learned that the world of sense is an illusion." These reports might indeed be true, without the student's actually coming to *believe* that the gods dwelt on Olympus or that the world of sense is an illusion. Such reports are, however, plausibly interpreted as elliptical. What is really intended is, "I learned that it was believed (by the Greeks) that the gods dwelt on Olympus," or, "I learned that it was said (by such and such a philosopher) that the world of sense is an illusion."

Another sort of counterexample is provided by the case of X, who is teaching Y that metals expand when heated but who does not really care whether Y believes this or not. He is not trying to get Y to believe or to qualify (from his point of view) as knowing that metals expand when heated. He is only preparing Y to do what is necessary to pass the end-term examination. He may not even care about that; he may only be trying to get through the day. First, as to the latter case, it is quite possible for a *teacher* not to be engaged in *teaching* at a given time. To be called a teacher is, typically, to be described as having a certain institutional role in the process of schooling, rather than as engaging in teaching activity; we must avoid the assumption that whatever a teacher does on the job is properly describable as teaching. Secondly (as to the former case), we might well differentiate teaching Y that metals expand when heated from teaching Y how to handle examination questions relating to this subject in order to facilitate passing. It is, in fact, possible to do one of these without doing the other; from the time of the Sophists (at least), it has been recognized that teaching might be geared not toward knowledge of propositions taken as true but rather toward the acquisition of skills in handling the outward manifestations of such knowledge. There are analogous cases, moreover, where the latter aim is quite respectable—for example, where teaching is geared toward the development of skills in handling and applying theories rather than toward acceptance of these theories as true.[4]

Ranges of Cognitive and Educational Terms

Our discussion of the previous section dealt with certain general connections between the educational terms *learning* and *teaching* and the cognitive terms *knowing* and *believing.* Our discussion was restricted, however, to comparable uses of these terms—i.e., *learning that, teaching that, knowing that,* and *believing that.* We must now turn to the question of their several ranges of use, which differ in important ways. We shall then have a clearer idea of the landscape within which our previous considerations may be located. Further, we shall find reason to avoid identifying the range of *education* with the range of *knowledge.* Following our exploration of the larger territory, we shall turn to detailed analyses of the region where educational and cognitive ranges overlap.

We may begin by suggesting that *know* is a term of wider range than *believe.* We can speak not only of *knowing that* but also of *knowing how to;* we can speak only of *believing that.* We may say not only "X knows that Napoleon was defeated at Waterloo" but also "X believes that Napoleon was defeated at Waterloo." However, though we may say "X knows how to ride a bicycle," we *cannot* say "X believes how to ride a bicycle." This fact may be conveniently formulated by labeling the *that* use *propositional* and the *how to* use *procedural,* and saying that whereas there is a propositional use of both *know* and *believe,* there is a procedural use only of *know.*

It must immediately be acknowledged, to be sure, that we have the construction *believing in* but not *knowing in.* X may be said to believe in God, in God's benevolence, in the future of the U.N., in democracy, or in John Jones. However, it seems possible to suggest plausible interpreta-

---

[4] The criticisms of Marcus Brown, "Knowing and learning," *Harvard Educational Review,* XXXI (Winter 1961), 10–11, and note 19, thus seem to me to be taken care of.

tions of *believing in* as propositional, in context: To believe in God is, in many typical contexts, for example, to believe that there is a God; to believe in God's benevolence is to believe that God is benevolent; to believe in the future of the U.N. is to believe that the U.N. has a future; to believe in democracy is to believe that democracy is good or that it has a future; to believe in Jones is to believe that Jones will satisfy the trust placed in him or the hopes for his good performance or achievement. There is, it would appear, no single formula of reduction for *believing in* statements; yet, with the help of contextual clues, it does seem plausible to suppose that reduction can be carried through along the lines just suggested, singly or in combination.

Assuming such reduction, belief will be construable as solely propositional, while knowing will clearly be not only propositional but also procedural. Nor is an extra procedural use the only prima facie indication of a wider range for *know* as contrasted with *believe*. We can speak, first of all, of knowing why there are tides but not of believing why there are tides, of knowing who committed the murder, or how or when it was committed, but not of believing who did it nor of believing how or when it was done. We can, to take a second set of examples, speak of knowing chess, music, or Scrabble but not of believing chess, music, or Scrabble. The first set of cases involves implicit reference to *questions* of one or another sort ("Why are there tides?" "Who committed the murder?" etc.); we will tag these as *question* uses. The second set we will label as *subject* uses, since they refer to the "subjects" chess, music, etc.

It is true that for some subjects we can also apply *belief* notions. For example, we can speak not only of knowing the theory of evolution but of believing the theory of evolution. Nonetheless, we cannot apply *belief* notions analogously throughout the whole category of knowable subjects —e.g., to chess or music.

Moreover, even in cases of subjects where *belief* does apply, it is propositional where the corresponding knowing is *not;* it is, furthermore, not implied by (nor included in) the corresponding *knowing,* as is the case with propositional uses. That is to say, *knowing that* metals expand when heated implies *believing that* metals expand when heated, but knowing the theory of evolution does not imply believing the theory of evolution. To say that someone believes the theory of evolution is to say he accepts it or takes it as true. To say he knows it is, normally, to say not *more* than this but something *different:* it is to say rather that he is acquainted with this theory or that he can recognize, handle, and perhaps state it. To *believe* a theory is, in short, to believe *that* it is correct or true; to *know* a theory is *not* to know *that* it is correct or true. The relevant sense of *know* is different from that of the *propositional* use we have discussed.

Now it may, in fact, be suggested that subject and question uses of *know* are reducible to procedural ones: To *know a theory* is to *know how to* formulate and possibly work with it; to *know why* there are tides is to *know how to* answer correctly the question why there are tides. Alternatively one might propose to reduce question uses, at least, to propositional ones, taking "X knows who the murderer is" as "There is a true answer to the question 'Who is the murderer?' and X knows that this answer is true." These suggestions may be thought plausible or they may not, but we need not decide whether they are adequate, at least for our present purposes. It is sufficient if we recognize that belief may be interpreted as, in any event, propositional. On the other hand, knowing is not always propositional; it is not always, nor always reducible to, *knowing that*. Even if the above mentioned reductions were to be carried out, we should still be left with a procedural as well as a propositional use of *know*. Nor could it be plausibly proposed to reduce the procedural use itself to the propositional: To what *knowing that* expression would "knowing how to type" correspond?

The range of *knowing* may thus be said to be larger than that of *believing*. If we now turn to the terms *learning* and *teaching*, we find that they are applicable in all the cases so far discussed; they are not limited to simply propositional uses. The student may learn or be taught that Napoleon was defeated at Waterloo. He may learn or be taught how to ride a bicycle or how to type. He may learn or be taught why there are tides. He may learn or be taught chess or the theory of evolution. Since, however, the notion of belief is not applicable in any but the first and the last of these cases (i.e., believing that Napoleon was defeated at Waterloo, believing the theory of evolution), it cannot be generally tied to learning and teaching as it was in the specifically propositional cases earlier discussed. Taking learning first, we cannot say, for example, that if X has learned how to type, he has come to believe how to type, as we *can* say that if he has learned that Napoleon was defeated at Waterloo, he has come to believe it. We cannot say that if X has learned why there are tides, he has come to believe why there are tides. Nor can we say he has come to believe chess if he has learned chess. Rather, we need to say that if he has learned how to type, he has come to know how to type; if he has learned why there are tides, he has come to know why there are tides; if he has learned chess, he has come to know chess. Moreover, even though it *is* possible to speak of believing the theory of evolution, as it is not possible to speak of believing chess, it is false to say that if X has learned the theory, he has come to believe it; we should rather say he has come to know the theory—which, as we have seen, is a different thing from coming to accept the theory as true.

Analogously, we cannot introduce belief into our general account of teaching as we did earlier. For example, we cannot say that, in teaching Y how to type, the teacher is trying to bring about Y's believing how to type. Rather, we need to say he is trying to get *Y* to know how to type. Similarly, he wants the student to know the theory of evolution, or chess, or why there are tides.

The main result to be noted is that, while the range of *knowing* is larger than that of *belief, learning* and *teaching* are at least as large in range as *knowing*. Education outstrips belief in its range, we might say, concerned as it also is with the development of skills, procedural techniques, subject familiarity—in short, with everything that might be characterized in terms of knowing. Nonetheless, we must not suppose that the range of education coincides with that of knowing. In fact, it goes beyond it; the concepts of learning and teaching are applicable in cases where *knowing* is not.

This point may be introduced by the consideration that *learning to* and *teaching to* have no counterparts such as *believing to* or *knowing to*. The child, for example, may *learn to* be punctual or be *taught to* be punctual, but he cannot then be said to *believe* or *know to* be punctual. His learning here is best thought of not in terms of knowledge but rather in terms of active propensities, tendencies, or habits of conduct. He has not necessarily nor simply come to believe something new, nor has he simply or necessarily achieved a new procedural facility or a new subject familiarity. He has, rather, acquired a new trait or pattern of action. His conduct now, though not before, is characterizable as generally displaying punctuality.

The *learning to* and *teaching to* expressions are, furthermore, not limited to the case of active propensities; they extend also to other cases, which are difficult to classify but which might perhaps be here labeled *attainments:* The child might, for instance, learn to *appreciate* music or to *understand* the relation between multiplication and addition, but he could not be said to *believe* or to *know to* appreciate or understand. So in respect of attainments as well as propensities our educational terms outstrip *knowing* in range.

But perhaps to understand something is reducible to knowing it, so learning to understand X is learning to know X. While, however, there may indeed be contexts in which knowing X conveys the connotation of understanding X, it does not seem plausible to make the proposed *general* reduction. A person may say without contradiction, "I know the doctrines of the existentialists, but I don't understand them." Or we may say of a child, "He knows Newton's laws (or Shakespeare's plays) but doesn't yet understand them." The limits of such knowing are perhaps elastic, involving at times familiarity, recognition, acquaintance, and ability to formulate, paraphrase, and use but not in every case including understanding. What constitutes understanding if it is not simply familiarity or skill of a certain sort is a separate question. Some have suggested that understanding involves something analogous to perception: seeing the point. Or it might be construed to include having explained or paraphrased the doctrine in question in special terms, initially intelligible to the person. Or, again, it might be thought to require a certain degree of experience or maturity (as in understanding Shakespeare's plays). However we interpret it, it seems *not* to reduce to the subject use of *know*.

It might now be suggested that, although there are no *believing to* or *knowing to* locutions, a certain kind of *believing that* or *knowing that* accompanies *learning to*. The idea, in effect, may be to reduce the latter to *learning that:* The child who has learned *to* be punctual has come to believe or know *that he ought to* be punctual; the child who has learned to appreciate music has come to believe or know that he ought to appreciate music; having learned to understand multiplication, he has come to know that he ought to understand multiplication.

This suggestion does not, however, seem to be tenable. Certainly, the converses fail even though in some contexts we interpret, for example, the child's knowing that he ought to be punctual as implying that he is punctual. But even the inferences from *learning to* statements to the proposed *believing that* or *knowing that* statements break down. A boy may learn to bite his nails or to smoke without coming to believe or to know that he ought to bite his nails or to smoke. A person may come to appreciate a painting or to understand the concepts of atomic theory without holding that he ought to; indeed, the question may be raised whether it can meaningfully be said that one ought to appreciate or understand, as distinct from trying to appreciate or understand. Nor, in coming to appreciate a painting, does a person always come to believe that it is a *good* painting; and surely the converse here fails also. (Appreciation may, to be sure, involve liking, but liking is itself not reducible to a belief in the goodness of the object.)

Finally, it might be suggested that *learning to* is really *procedural*, a matter of acquiring more or less complex skills or techniques, describable in terms of *knowing how*. There are some examples in which this suggestion seems to find a plausible interpretation: To say that someone has learned to swim or to drive a car is indeed to say that he has come to know how to swim or to drive—he has acquired swimming or driving skills. These are, however, cases in which the *learning to* expression could well be supplanted by *learning how to:* To have learned to swim or to drive is to have learned how to swim or to drive. Not every case of *learning to* can, however, be thus rewritten in terms of *learning how to,* nor can it be interpreted as a matter of acquiring some relevant bit of know-how. To learn to be a good neighbor or citizen is not the same as learning how to be a good neighbor or citizen. To learn to pay one's debts is not the same as learning how to pay one's debts; it is not, for example, simply the sort of thing that is involved in learning the proper use of a checkbook.[5] Learning various techniques for ensuring one's punctuality is not yet learning to be punctual. To acquire a skill is one thing, to acquire a habit or propensity quite another.

The case seems even stronger with respect to what we have called *attainments*. For, whereas active propensities often have strictly associated techniques (e.g., a person who enjoys swimming and swims regularly knows how to swim), attainments do not have strictly associated techniques. A person who appreciates music is not properly said to know how to appreciate music; one who understands quantum theory is not well described as knowing how to understand quantum theory. (It would certainly seem strange if someone said that he knew very well *how* to appreciate music but didn't choose to, or that he knew *how* to understand quantum theory but hadn't in fact understood it lately.) Certainly there are techniques *embedded* in attainments: One who understands quantum theory knows how to read, and one who appreciates music knows how to listen. But these bits of know-how are not strictly associated; they are not equivalent to knowing how to *understand*, and knowing how to *appreciate*, respectively. Understanding and appreciation cannot, it would seem, readily be said to be exercises of technique or know-how, as swimming might be said to be an exercise of swimming know-how. For there seems to be no such thing as an *understanding know-how* or an *appreciating know-how*. Much less can learning to understand or to appreciate be suggested to reduce to mere acquisition of such know-how.

Skills, or procedures and elements of know-how, carry with them a cluster of associated notions that do not all apply *either* in the case of propensities *or* in the case of attainments. First of all, a skill or element of know-how, once acquired, may or may not be exercised, given the relevant opportunities; a person may be said to have a skill or the relevant know-how even though he never (or very rarely) exercises it after having acquired it, although he has ample opportunity to do so. There are many people who have learned and who know how to swim but who do not any longer swim at all, or only very rarely, though they have the chance. We may conjecture that their technique is rusty, but we do not feel compelled to deny that they *can* swim. By contrast, a person who has the habit or trait of punctuality is a person who *is* generally punctual on relevant occasions. If a person who had been punctual began to show up late for all, or nearly all, of his appointments and continued thus consistently for an appreciable length of time, we should wish to say he had lost the habit of punctuality. A person could not claim still to be punctual on the grounds that he had once been, though for a long time he had never, or hardly ever, arrived anywhere on time. In

[5] See Scheffler, *The Language of Education*, p. 98.

short, it is quite possible to say that X knows how to swim but never does; it would, however, strike us as self-contradictory to say that X has the habit of punctuality but never shows up on time. For attainments, the very notion of repeated performance is suspect: We may speak of one who knows how to swim as swimming every Tuesday, of a punctual student as showing up on time to class twenty times in a row. But what would it mean to say of a person who understands the quantum theory that he had understood it every Tuesday last month, or of a person who appreciates modern art that he had appreciated it twenty times in a row?

Secondly, in the case of skill or know-how a person may clearly decide not to exercise it. There is nothing puzzling in saying that a man knows how to play tennis but chooses not to. An analogous description is indeed possible also for habits, for a man may deliberately control his own propensities on particular occasions; a smoker may decide not to smoke now, for example. There seems, however, to be no such analogue for attainments: A person with an understanding of quantum theory cannot choose not to understand it; one who appreciates poetry cannot decide not to appreciate poetry on Mondays. Even for habits, moreover, the analogy is limited; where control goes far enough, it turns into elimination of the habit in question.

Thirdly, the notion of practice seems clearly relevant to skills and know-how; they are, indeed, typically built up through repeated trials or performances. Analogously, we may speak of habits, too, as being formed through repeated trials; through smoking again and again one may, for example, develop a genuine smoking habit. A parallel description seems, however, out of the question in the case of attainments. One cannot develop an understanding of the quantum theory by understanding it over and over again, nor can one strengthen or deepen one's understanding by repeated performances of understanding; the very notion of repeated performances is here suspect, as argued above. It makes sense to tell a student to practice playing a certain piece of music; it makes no sense to tell him to practice appreciating what he plays.

Finally, the notions of proficiency or mastery seem peculiarly applicable to skills. One may attain proficiency in driving or become a master in chess, but one cannot well be described as proficient in punctuality or honesty nor as having become a master of the habit of taking a walk before breakfast. Neither can one be said to be proficient in understanding a theory nor to have mastered the appreciation of Bach. A person may have more or less understanding of a topic, he may appreciate a poem less or more, but he cannot be called a good understander or appreciator as he might be called a good driver, typist, or chess-player. Similarly, a person's habit of smoking or of fingernail-biting may be weak or strong, deeply or less deeply ingrained, easy or difficult to break, but he cannot well be described as a good smoker or fingernail-biter.

The upshot is that neither propensities nor attainments can well be assimilated to the category of skills or know-how, nor can *learning to* and *teaching to* be construed as really procedural. It follows that the range of educational concepts is not only larger than that of belief, as we saw earlier; it is also larger than that of knowing. Education outstrips cognitive notions altogether in its range, embracing, as we have seen, also the formation of propensities and traits, and the development of understanding and appreciation.

Illustrative Definition of Propositional Knowledge

Having seen the wide range of educational notions, we now turn to a consideration of that part of the range which overlaps the range of *knowing*. The case of knowing that has figured most prominently in classical discussions in epistemology is the propositional case, and to this we address ourselves first. We shall find it convenient to introduce here a sample definition of *knowing that* as an anchor for our future discussions of the propositional case. This definition sets three conditions for *knowing that*, and we shall refer to these as the *belief* condition, the *evidence* condition, and the *truth* condition.[6]

X knows that Q
if and only if
(i) X believes that Q,
(ii) X has adequate evidence that Q,
and (iii) Q.

This definition takes all three stated conditions as jointly defining *knowing that* and thus corresponds to the "strong sense" of *know* discussed early in the first section of the present chapter. The "weak sense" is easily gotten by simply omitting condition (ii). . . .

The Absoluteness of Truth

. . . It is important to distinguish the absoluteness of truth from the fixity of natural processes, for the two ideas are quite independent. Truth is an attribute of statements, beliefs, propositions, or ideas, not an attribute of things, processes, or events generally. To say that truth is absolute is to say that *whatever* true statements or ideas affirm is unqualifiedly in fact the case; no further requirement is made that true statements must affirm only *constancies* or *fixities*. The facts of change,

[6] Variants of this definition may be found in Roderick M. Chisholm, *Perceiving: A Philosophical Study* (Ithaca, N.Y.: Cornell University Press, 1957), p. 16, and in D. J. O'Connor, *An Introduction to the Philosophy of Education* (New York: Philosophical Library, 1957), p. 73.

whatever they may be, render their true descriptions true absolutely. Fluid historical processes or transient historical events do not require fluidity or transiency in the truth of their true descriptions: We have already seen the absurdity of supposing it to be initially true and thereafter false that Galileo at some point in time dropped iron balls from the tower of Pisa. Conversely, the absolute truth of the statement that the First World War began in 1914 does not imply that the First World War's beginning is somehow timeless and fixed, that the War is, somehow, always in a state of incipiency. Spatial as well as temporal qualifications of all sorts apply to things describable by true statements, but this does not imply that the truth itself must be similarly qualified. If it rained in Mexico City on April 7, 1934, the sentence "It rained in Mexico City on April 7, 1934" is not just true in Mexico City; it is simply true. Analogously, it is not just true on April 7, 1934; it is simply true. Insofar, then, as a relativistic doctrine of truth is motivated by the desire to stress the "fluidity" of history and the pervasiveness of natural change, the same purpose can perfectly well (and with enormously less logical strain) be accomplished by an absolute doctrine of truth.

It may, however, in spite of all we have said, be objected that there is a particular class of statements whose *truth* clearly does change with time, place, or person. Consider the following three sentences, for example:

(i) Today is Sunday.
(ii) This city has three daily newspapers.
(iii) I am a Republican.

Clearly neither (i), nor (ii), nor (iii) is invariably true. (i) is true only on Sundays. (ii) is true only in such cities as have three daily newspapers. (iii) is true only when said by a Republican.

It may, in reply, be said that these sentences are all, in a basic sense, incomplete or indeterminate. They do not, in themselves, succeed in making definite assertions, for the grammatical subjects of their respective attributions, i.e., *Today, This city,* and *I,* have no fixed references. How can any of these sentences be evaluated for truth, when it is not clear to what thing its attribution is being made? Suppose one said "X is a Republican." Would it be anything more than the *schema* of an assertion? Surely such a schema has no fixed truth or falsity (no fixed truth-value, to put it briefly) but may be transformed into an indefinite number of statements with fixed truth-values when the variable "X" is replaced by a name or description, or when the whole is prefixed by "For all X," or "There is an X, such that." The absolute theory of truth is not a denial that *schemas* are thus variable with respect to truth, but schemas should not be confused with genuine assertions or statements.

It is of course true that (i), (ii), and (iii) are, in one sense, more determinate than schemas with variables such as "X," "Y," etc. The word *today*, for example, though it varies in reference, as does "*X*," nonetheless *acquires* a definite reference *in the context of its utterance*, unlike "*X*." That is to say, when a particular speaker assertively utters the words "Today is Sunday," *today* refers to the day on which this particular utterance itself falls. Analogously, *this city* refers, on the occasion of utterance, to the city in which the utterance takes place, and *I* refers, when uttered, to the speaker who utters it. Nevertheless, the forms (i), (ii), and (iii), considered apart from utterance, do not succeed in making an assertion any more than does a pure schema. Moreover, as soon as such a form does yield an assertion, through actual *utterance*, not only do its purported references become determinate, but its truth-value is fixed. The utterance, *on a given occasion*, of "Today is Sunday" is thus true or false absolutely, even though the same form of words makes a different assertion when uttered on another day.

The variable indicator words,[7] *today, this, I,* and so forth, may of course be supplanted altogether by nonindicator expressions with definite references; in this way, a fixed truth-value is attained which is preserved even when the same form of words is repeated in other circumstances. When "Eisenhower is a Republican" thus replaces Mr. Eisenhower's own utterance "I am a Republican," its truth-value is fixed not only as an utterance but as a repeatable form of words. The general point is clear: Provided we have a genuine statement or assertion, its truth-value is fixed.

A peculiarity of the notion of absolute truth is that it seems to be totally "transparent," i.e., to add nothing to the facts in question. *That's true* is, like *yes*, just a mode of assent to a statement understood in context; it is a way of re-asserting the statement itself without literally repeating it. Further, the sentence "It is true that Columbus discovered America" seems to say nothing more than *Columbus discovered America;* the prefix *It is true that* is just a device to provide emphasis. Finally, even where we make *attributions* or *predications* of truth, as, for example, in "The statement 'Columbus discovered America' is true," or "The first statement on page 374 of Volume 7 of the Britannica is true," we seem to be affirming nothing more than what the respectively *mentioned* statements themselves affirm: In each case, both mentioned statement and truth attribution are true together or false together (though in the Britannica example we may not even know in what form of words the mentioned statement consists). The truth attribution is thus itself correct if and only if the sentence to which truth is attributed expresses what is, in fact, the case. The same facts which make the latter sentence true also make the truth attribution itself true.

---

[7] See Nelson Goodman, *The Structure of Appearance* (Cambridge, Mass.: Harvard University Press, 1951), pp. 287 ff. for a systematic treatment of indicators.

The "transparency" of absolute truth, though perhaps hard to grasp, involves no fundamental logical difficulties. The logician Alfred Tarski has, in fact, formulated a criterion of truth that incorporates this feature and points up the differentiation of truth from relative notions of confirmation.[8] The criterion of Tarski forms the basis of an explicit argument by R. Carnap that even if we give up the ideal of conclusive confirmation, that is, *certainty,* we need not give up the absolute notion of *truth.*[9] A review of Tarski's proposal and of Carnap's argument will close the present chapter.

Tarski calls his criterion the *semantic criterion of truth,* since it treats truth in the sense of an *attribution* to certain sentences and links it to what is described by those sentences, semantics having to do with the relations between language and reality. His inspiration is Aristotle's doctrine: "To say of what is that it is not, or of what is not that it is, is false, while to say of what is that it is, or of what is not that it is not, is true."[10] Tarski takes this idea to have a modern formulation in the statement: "The truth of a sentence consists in its agreement with (or correspondence to) reality."[11]

In connection with the particular sentence "Snow is white," Tarski says the following equivalence, expressing the requisite correspondence, must hold under any adequate definition of truth:

> The sentence "Snow is white" is true if, and
> only if, snow is white.

Generalizing, he maintains that all equivalences of the following form must hold:

> "_____" is true if, and
> only if, _____

(provided both blanks are filled by the same sentence, under a fixed interpretation, and belonging to the language of the formula itself). The left blank, having quotation marks around it, forms a *name* of whatever sentence is inserted in it, while the right blank does not. The sentence inserted on the right thus expresses a factual condition or state of affairs which holds if and only if the sentence itself (named on the left) is true. (For the use of quotation marks on the left, any other naming device may, moreover, be substituted, provided it names the sentence on the right.) The formula as a whole represents Tarski's criterion.

[8] Alfred Tarski, "The Semantic Conception of Truth," *Philosophy and Phenomenological Research* (1944). Reprinted in Herbert Feigl and Wilfrid Sellars, *Readings in Philosophical Analysis* (New York: Appleton-Century-Crofts, 1949), pp. 52–84.

[9] Rudolf Carnap, "Truth and Confirmation," in Feigl and Sellars, *op. cit.,* pp. 119–127.

[10] Aristotle, *Metaphysics,* Book IV, Chapter 7.

[11] Feigl and Sellars, *op. cit.,* p. 54.

This criterion is *not* a definition of truth, for it contains blanks and is thus only a schema, not a statement, while every actual statement formed by filling in its blanks is insufficiently general to serve as a definition. Nonetheless, it represents a condition that must, according to Tarski, be satisfied by any adequate definition of truth. Any such definition, in other words, needs to be such that all sentences formed in accord with the criterion formula follow from the definition. For our purposes, it is not necessary to go into the technicalities of Tarski's own *definition,* as distinct from his criterion. For the criterion, if it is indeed taken as a necessary condition of truth, is itself sufficient to show the independence of truth from confirmation and to indicate the force of the absolute construal of truth, which it represents.

The criterion, in effect, shows the attribution of truth to a sentence to be tantamount to asserting the sentence itself and hence to be "transparent" in the sense earlier discussed. The criterion offers, however, no method for deciding whether to affirm the sentence in the first instance; it does not tell us, for example, whether snow *is* white. It says only that "whenever we assert or reject this sentence, we must be ready to assert or reject the correlated sentence . . . ' "Snow is white" is true.' " [12] Since true sentences are, however, indefinitely varied, is it any wonder that a unitary method for *ascertaining* truth is a difficult, perhaps impossible, objective? In any event, the criterion is itself sufficient to show that there is no more mystery in truth than in the various sentences themselves asserted to be true. As W. V. Quine has remarked, "Attribution of truth in particular to 'Snow is white', for example, is every bit as clear to us as attribution of whiteness to snow." [13] To put it metaphorically, *truth* is an indirect reflection of the facts themselves, and the *absoluteness of truth* is merely a reflection of the intelligibility of factual descriptions which are not relative to the state of a person's knowledge or belief: We understand perfectly well the question "Is snow white?" and do not need to ask "White for whom?"

Rudolf Carnap, building on Tarski's theory, stresses the difference between truth and confirmation, and the immunity of truth to objections against certainty. Carnap's argument may be presented (in slightly altered form) by reference to the following three sentences:

(i) The substance in the vessel at time t is alcohol.
(ii) "The substance in the vessel at time t is alcohol" is true.
(iii) X believes (confirms, accepts) now, that the sentence "The substance in the vessel at time t is alcohol" is true.

[12] *Ibid.,* p. 71.
[13] Willard Van Orman Quine, *From a Logical Point of View* (Cambridge, Mass.: Harvard University Press, 1953), p. 138. See Chapter VII of this book for further discussion of the semantic conception.

Following Tarski, (i) holds if, and only if, (ii) does. But the same can clearly not be said of (i) and (iii). For it is obviously possible that the vessel may contain alcohol at t while X believes (confirms or accepts) now, that the sentence "The substance in the vessel at time t is alcohol" is false. Conversely, it is also possible for X to hold the sentence in question to be true even though the vessel does not contain alcohol at t but rather water. It follows that (ii) also diverges from (iii), for (ii) holds just in those conditions under which (i) does. Thus, the sentence "The substance in the vessel at time t is alcohol" may be true but not believed by X to be true, and vice versa. Truth is therefore one thing, and being believed, accepted, or confirmed as true is quite another.

Many have argued, says Carnap, that the semantic (or absolute) notion of truth should be abandoned, for scientific purposes at least, since it can never be decided *with certainty* for any empirical sentence S, that S is true or false. Granted, says Carnap, that such certainty is out of the question, does it follow that truth is therefore inadmissible? Such an inference would apparently hinge on the principle: "A term (predicate) must be rejected if it is such that we can never decide with absolute certainty for any given instance whether or not the term applies." [14] But clearly, argues Carnap, this principle "would lead to absurd consequences." For if we cannot decide the application of *true* in b) with certainty, then, by the same token, we cannot decide *alcohol* in a) with certainty; conversely, if we could be certain about the term *alcohol* in a), we could equally be certain about *true* in b). If we follow the above principle in rejecting *true*, we shall also need to reject all empirical terms as well.

The principle may then be replaced by the following weaker version: "A term (predicate) is a legitimate scientific term . . . if and only if a sentence applying the term to a given instance can possibly be confirmed to at least some degree." [15] The latter version no longer has the absurd consequences of its predecessor. Clearly, it legitimizes the term *alcohol*, but also, by the same token, the term *true*.

The large consequence of the foregoing considerations is that even if we totally reject certainty as a condition of knowledge, we need not also reject (absolute) truth. To attribute knowledge that Q, is not only to attribute belief that Q but also to affirm that Q—in effect, to affirm also that "Q" is *true*, in the absolute sense of the term. To be sure, we cannot claim *infallibility* for our knowledge attributions; any of these may turn out to be mistaken. But the latter are no worse in this regard than any of our *other* factual attributions. And if we allow ourselves to make other such attributions, though they are admittedly fallible, how can we deny ourselves the right to make knowledge attributions, in particular?

[14] Feigl and Sellars, *op. cit.*, p. 123.
[15] *Ibid.*, p. 123.

Since we cannot, in general, be obliged to do what is impossible for us to do, we cannot be obliged to attain certainty in *any* case of empirical fact. We *can*, however, be expected to fashion our attributions in accordance with the evidence available to us, and to treat them as subject to public criticism and to revision upon the emergence of contrary evidence.

The possibility of such revision, *presently* contemplated, is indeed what makes our current factual attributions incapable of absolute assurance. But this bare *possibility* is no reason at all either for controverting the evidence available *now* or for refraining from judgment altogether. When and if contrary evidence emerges, we shall then have good reason to revise our present judgments, but, meanwhile, the mere fact that contrary evidence may emerge later constitutes no reason for present revision. Knowledge attributions, in sum, are no different from other factual attributions with respect to certainty. Our job is not to judge the truth infallibly but to estimate the truth responsibly.

We turn now from discussions of the truth condition of propositional knowledge to a consideration of the evidence condition.

The Evidence Condition

In the sample definition of propositional knowledge, X was required to have *adequate evidence* that Q, as one condition of his *knowing* that Q. This "evidence condition" was intended to formulate more precisely the idea that knowing in the *strong sense* is more than just true belief, involving also the ability to justify or back up the belief in appropriate manner.

The force of the evidence condition may be illustrated historically by reference to St. Augustine's theory of teaching. Augustine argues against the idea that the teacher transmits *knowledge* through words. Words are signs referring to reality, he says, and knowledge is not a matter simply of having the words. It requires also a personal confrontation with the reality to which the words refer. Without such confrontation, the student may, at best, acquire belief, but not knowledge. The teacher thus cannot be thought literally to be conveying *knowledge* to the student by means of his words. Rather, he *prompts* the student to confront reality for himself, in such a way as to acquire knowledge. "The import of words," says Augustine, "—to state the most that can be said for them—consists in this: they serve merely to suggest that we look for realities" (p. 154).[16] If someone tells me that Q, but I fail to find the realities to which "Q"

---

[16] Saint Augustine, "The Teacher," included in Kingsley Price, *Education and Philosophical Thought* (Boston: Allyn and Bacon, 1962). Page references to Augustine in the text relate to "The Teacher" in *Education and Philosophical Thought* throughout.

refers, I can at best believe—I cannot know—that Q. "I do not know all I believe," says Augustine, "But I am not for that reason unaware how useful it is to believe also many things which I do not know" (p. 155). Knowing, for Augustine, is a stronger notion than belief. It comes "not through words sounding in the ear, but through truth that teaches internally" (p. 154). When teachers have explained, he says, "by means of words, all those subjects which they profess to teach, and even the science of virtue and wisdom, then those who are called pupils consider within themselves whether what has been said is true" (p. 158).

The pupil who *knows,* Augustine seems to say, is not just someone who *has a belief which is true,* even if he has the belief on the highest authority (he uses Biblical examples). He must further have considered within himself whether what has been said is true. He must have engaged in a personal process of *evaluating* the belief in question, by reference to his own source of "interior truth." If we consider just this emphasis in Augustine's doctrine, apart from the further metaphysical and religious interpretation which he gives it, we can see the point of the evidence condition. It serves to distinguish genuine knowing from mere true belief, by reference to appropriate evaluation of the belief by the believer: The surplus strength of knowing consists, in short, in the knower's having adequate evidence for the belief in question. . . .

To summarize, when we judge that someone has adequate evidence, we are judging that he has an evidential argument which he understands. In saying he knows, we are not merely ascribing true belief but asserting that he has proper credentials for such belief, the *force* of which he himself *appreciates.* We are thereby certifying certain general abilities that carry over to other situations and that are most clearly evidenced in innovation.

PEDAGOGICAL ORIENTATION — MORAL PHILOSOPHY

Toward a Philosophy of Moral Education   /

WILLIAM K. FRANKENA

What can philosophy contribute to education? A philosopher, looking at the present state of education, might answer, "A great deal." His colleague in education, looking at the present state of philosophy, might reply, "Not much." If they did, both would have some *raison,* but also

"Toward a Philosophy of Moral Education" is reprinted from William K. Frankena, "Toward a Philosophy of Moral Education," *Harvard Educational Review,* 28, Fall 1958, 300–313. Copyright © 1958 by President and Fellows of Harvard College.

some *tort*. How much each would have of each I shall, however, not seek to determine, for I do not propose here to use the direct method (as it is called in education) of dealing with our question. That is, I shall not say explicitly in general terms what philosophers, in virtue of their special training, can do to help educators. Instead I shall use the indirect method—I shall attempt, as a philosopher, to make a contribution to education or, rather, to the philosophy of education. In other words, I shall try to answer the question, "What can philosophy contribute to education?" ostensively, by giving an example or what science teachers call a demonstration.

I offer my contribution in much the same humble spirit in which Locke sent his *Thoughts Concerning Education* "abroad into the world." "I am so far from being conceited of anything I have here offered," he says,

> that I should not be sorry . . . if someone abler and fitter for such a task would in just treatise of education . . . rectify the mistakes I have made in this. . . . However, the meanness of these papers, and my just distrust of them, shall not keep me, by the shame of doing so little, from contributing my mite, when there is no more required of me, than my throwing it into the public receptacle.

Now, I am primarily a moral philosopher, and, if I have any mite to contribute, it must be in this capacity. One such mite would be to write a disquisition in moral philosophy for educators to use in thinking about the aims and methods of education, much as one might compose a book on mathematics for engineers. D. J. O'Connor has written just such an essay in Chapter three of his recent *Introduction to the Philosophy of Education*. Another would be to work out a whole theory of the ends and means of education myself, so far as this can be done by applying the findings of moral philosophy as I see them. A third would be to apply these findings to a part of the problem of education to which moral philosophy seems particularly relevant, namely, that of moral education. It is the third of these mites that I propose to throw into the public receptacle now.

The topic of moral education has had a great deal of attention from educators during the last few decades, sometimes under the unlovely label of "character education" and sometimes under the confused and confusing caption of "moral and spiritual values." Yet, as some of these educators themselves insist, ". . . the present character education movement is uncertain as to theory, . . . not sure of its direction." [1] "What character education really is and what its objectives are have not yet been fully agreed upon." [2] As J. S. Mill says in his *Autobiography*, ". . .

---

[1] G. H. Betts and G. E. Hill, as quoted by H. C. McKown, *Character Education* (New York: McGraw-Hill, 1935), p. 12.

[2] J. D. Redden and F. A. Ryan, *A Catholic Philosophy of Education* (Milwaukee: Bruce, 1942), p. 262.

the moral influences [in education] which are so much more important than all the others, are also the most complicated, and the most difficult to specify. . . ." [3] At any rate, there has been, to my knowledge, no significant philosophical book on moral education since those of Dewey and Durkheim were written forty or fifty years ago—unless we count Russell's *Education and the Good Life,* which is itself over thirty years old.[4] Moral philosophers cannot cast stones at educators, however, for a reading of their works during this period turns up very few references to moral education. F. C. Sharp and R. B. Perry are almost unique in dealing with it.[5] Yet, if philosophy is or includes the general theory of education, as Dewey and his followers like to say, then moral philosophy is or includes the general theory of moral education. Indeed, this is being recognized by the most recent moral philosophers, some of whom have never read Dewey. Particularly is this true of a school of writers on ethics who belong to the post-war movement in philosophy which has grown up under the influence of G. E. Moore and Ludwig Wittgenstein. One of these writers, R. M. Hare, regards the problem of moral teaching as especially crucial for ethics. He writes, "The question 'How shall I bring up my children?' . . . is one to the logic of which, since ancient times, few philosophers have given much attention." He then proceeds to give it a good deal of attention, arguing that it is in connection with this question "that the most fundamental moral decisions of all arise; and . . . that the most characteristic uses of moral words are to be found." [6] The other English moralists of this school are S. E. Toulmin, S. N. Hampshire, and P. H. Nowell-Smith; other members or near-members are K. Baier in Australia, and H. D. Aiken, P. Edwards, A. I. Melden, and J. Rawls in this country.

It is with the works of these as well as of other contemporary moral philosophers in mind, together with those of classical writers, that I propose to discuss the problem of moral education. Without meaning to disparage them unduly, I shall somewhat neglect the views of Dewey and his followers, partly because, though very much alive, they belong to an earlier day—to the day when philosophers were either idealists, realists, or pragmatists. It is time that later developments in ethics and

[3] J. S. Mill, *Autobiography* (London: Longmans, Green, Reader and Dyer, 1873), p. 38.

[4] J. Dewey, *Moral Principles in Education* (Boston: Houghton Mifflin, 1909), *Democracy and Education* (New York: MacMillan, 1916); E. Durkheim, *L'Education Morale* (Paris: F. Alcan, published in 1925 but written in 1902–1903). I do not mean to disparage J. L. Childs' *Education and Morals* (New York: Appleton-Century-Crofts, 1950), but it is not a book on moral education in the sense here in question.

[5] F. C. Sharp, *Education for Character* (Indianapolis: Bobbs-Merrill, 1917); *Ethics* (New York: Century, 1928), pp. 260–266; R. B. Perry, *Realms of Value* (Cambridge: Harvard University Press, 1928), pp. 428–431.

[6] R. M. Hare, *The Language of Morals* (Oxford: Clarendon, 1952), p. 74.

general philosophy made their influence felt in education. I take it that is the conviction under which this symposium was organized.

In what follows, therefore, I shall cover the ground usually traversed in studies of moral education, trying as a philosopher to clarify the tasks involved in teaching morality to our children, but without saying much about the methods by which they are to be accomplished. My point will be that moral education includes teaching, learning and espousing, not only a particular morality, but the very art or idea of morality itself.

I.

Socrates and his contemporaries conceived of the problem of moral education as that of teaching "virtue," and Socrates at least was troubled about the method and even the possibility of teaching this, on the ground that the most virtuous parents so often have vicious sons (he did not seem to be worried about daughters). Preachers' sons are too often wicked, and psychologists' sons too often maladjusted. In short, parent-generations have not succeeded in ensuring the conformity to their standards of the conduct of their offspring. Suppose we similarly conceive the problem as that of producing in our children the kind of behavior that we call virtuous. Now Socrates, since he held that we always do what we think right, thought the problem was simply that of passing on a knowledge or true opinion about what is virtuous. If we can do this, he thought, we can secure the future. But most subsequent moral philosophy has doubted the "Socratic paradox" (although much recent educational philosophy does seem to imply a similar optimism about human nature). It has not been persuaded that knowledge is enough, even though it may not agree that love is enough either. We may perhaps take for granted, then, that the problem of producing virtue in the next generation is a twofold one: (1) that of handing on a "knowledge of good and evil" or "knowing how" to act, and (2) that of ensuring that our children's conduct will conform to this "knowledge." For convenience I shall call these two tasks respectively Moral Education X and Moral Education Y, referring to them familiarly as MEX and MEY.

We might try to lick this twofold problem by working out a complete set of rules (or even a casuistry) in advance, drilling it into our children, and then drilling in also an unquestioning obedience. Descartes remarks that God could have done this and chose not to, but we might still try it though we can not hope wholly to succeed. Indeed, some such drastic approach is adopted in different ways by primitive and other tradition-bound societies on the one hand and by totalitarian societies on the other. But such an approach involves employing one or more of the following techniques: (a) a drastic restriction on freedom of action, speech, and thought, (b) a full use of effective sanctions, (c) an austere and rigoristic exclusion of temptations and of new varieties of enjoyment or satisfaction, (d) a sharp resistance to the incursion of new knowledge or novel situations, and (e) a liberal admixture of propaganda and the like. Such techniques have been used in Sparta, Japan, Germany, and Russia, and described in *Brave New World* and *1984*. Like the Athenians of Socrates' day, however, we conceive ourselves as having put them behind us. In fact, as a little attention to our mass media shows, our society is one with a maximum of temptation and a minimum of control, wide open to the impact of science, of critical or even irresponsible reflection, and of novelty. We seem to have set ourselves the task of showing that such an open society is both good and viable. No doubt, we have not yet established this conclusively, but we may well take the position that, until such a society is proved to be either not viable or not ideal, as jeopardizing unduly our future here or in a hereafter, we are honorbound to strive for its realization. We might even argue that it is only such a society that is moral in its dealings with the individual, and that it is only in such a society that morality can be the kind of a guide which it is designed to be. In any event, our acceptance of a way of life which permits or promotes freedom, knowledge, and novelty of goods and of situations as actual or ideal sets us our task. However we may prize virtue, we cannot use the techniques mentioned to secure it, except within narrow limits, yet we must succeed in teaching it without such helps, else we shall fail in our entire enterprise.

I say this, not because I know how we can succeed, but to help us get clearer about our problem. With this background, let us see what is involved in MEX and MEY.

II.

MEX cannot consist of a long list of specific instructions to our children for all of the situations into which they may fall. It must consist, rather, in teaching them certain principles or ends by which they may guide their conduct in those situations. For teaching these rules or ends either the direct or the indirect methods may be used. That is, we may formulate the rules or ends quite explicitly and seek to inculcate them into our children, as the Israelites were commanded to do by Moses:

And these words which I command thee this day . . . thou shall teach . . . diligently unto thy children, and shalt talk of them when thou sittest in thine house, and when thou walkest by the way, and when thou liest down, and when thou risest up.[7]

[7] *Deut.* 6:7.

Or we may tell our children or otherwise instruct them, perhaps by example, what to do in this particular case and in that particular case until they begin to discern the rule or the end involved for themselves. Either way, the point is to teach them ends or principles, "that they may do them in the land which I the Lord shall give them," for, like Moses, we shall not be there to lead them.

Yet the point of moral instruction *is* to put the child in the position of being able to decide what he should do in each situation he may come up against; and, for this, it is necessary but not sufficient to teach him the ends or principles involved. We must also supply him with the knowledge required to apply the principle or to realize the end in question, or with the ability to acquire this knowledge for himself. Roughly speaking, as Aristotle and many others have pointed out, the process of determining what one should do takes the form of a "practical syllogism." There is (a) the rule or end, for example, that of keeping one's promises or of not harming anyone. There is (b) the factual knowledge that one has tacitly or openly made a certain promise, or that certain actions will cause harm to certain people. And there is (c) the conclusion that one should or should not do a certain deed. Thus, if our children are to be able to come to right conclusions about what to do, they must have or be able to get the kind of factual knowledge involved in (b). This means that their moral education must include a training in history and science; we must teach them whatever we know that may be relevant to the solution of their moral problems, and train them to go to find out whatever more they need to know. In this sense at least all intellectual education is moral, as Professor Broudy has remarked in his book,[8] and a moral education includes an intellectual one.

In other words, the task of moral education is not simply to inculcate virtuous principles and good intentions. It is not the road to heaven, but the road to hell, that is said to be paved with good intentions, and the substance of this saying is that we can only be sure of being on the right road when we are guided by factual knowledge as well as by moral principle. As Aquinas puts it, ". . . in order that a choice be good, two things are required. First, that the intention be directed to a due end. . . . Second, that man choose rightly those things which are means to the end. . . ."[9] Russell makes the same point when he says that the good life is one inspired by love and guided by knowledge.[10]

I do not mean to suggest, of course, that the sole ground for an intellectual or scientific education is a moral one; after all, as Matthew Arnold said, morality is only three-fourths of life. But there is a moral

[8] H. Broudy, *Building a Philosophy of Education* (Englewood Cliffs, N.J.: Prentice-Hall, 1954), p. 409.

[9] *Summa Theologica*, Pt. I of Pt. II, Ch. XII, Q. 58. Art. 4.

[10] B. Russell, *What I Believe* (New York: Dutton, 1925), Ch. II.

justification and need, along the lines just indicated, for a very considerable factual and intellectual training.

So far, however, we have been supposing that the problem in MEX is simply to pass on a set of moral principles which is adequate for all occasions, provided only that we also pass on the knowledge and the intelligence needed to apply them. Actually the problem is much more complex than this.

(1) Whether we use the direct or the indirect method of moral instruction, we can do so in either of two ways. We can simply "internalize" in our children certain beliefs about how to act, without any indication of any reasons which may lie behind them. That is, we might conceive of moral education in a "Theirs not to reason why" spirit and we might even use such techniques as drill, propaganda, and hidden persuasion. On the other hand, we might take the position that we must teach the reasons as well as the conclusions. Now, there is, no doubt, a period in the life of a child when such appeals to reason are pointless. Says Felix Adler, "The right to reason about these matters cannot be conceded until after the mind has attained a certain maturity. . . . The moral teacher . . . is not to explain [to the child] why we should do the right. . . ." [11] Plato agreed, and thought it the function of a proper education in poetry and music to use this period in schooling the youth to approve what is to be approved and condemn what is to be condemned, "while he is still too young to understand the reason," that "when reason comes, he will greet her as a friend with whom his education has made him long familiar." [12] The question is not whether the introduction of reasons is to begin at birth, but whether it is to begin as soon as it is feasible or is to be put off as long as it can be, perhaps forever.

It should be noted here that to give the child reasons along with his moral instructions does not necessarily entail going on to stimulate in him a full-fledged critical reflection about morality of the sort that G. H. Palmer has in mind when he argues against "ethical instruction" in the schools.[13] This is shown, it seems to me, by the interesting (if sometimes misguided) examples of moral reasoning used on Johnny by his teachers in the NEA booklet on *Moral and Spiritual Values in the Public Schools* (1951), and perhaps even better by the fact that the Navaho almost automatically give reasons along with their prescriptions about what to do, but without any invitation to criticism.[14]

[11] F. Adler, *The Moral Instruction of Children* (New York: Appleton, 1901), pp. 13–15.

[12] *Republic*, 402a.

[13] G. H. Palmer, *Ethical and Moral Instruction in the Schools* (Boston: Houghton Mifflin, 1908), Ch. I.

[14] On the Navaho see J. Ladd, *The Structure of a Moral Code* (Cambridge: Harvard University Press, 1957), Ch. XI. They do not, however, offer reasons to

Now, most recent educational philosophy has insisted on the importance in moral as well as in other education of developing and appealing to the child's reason whenever possible. With this I agree, at least to the extent of believing that a reference to reasons in morality must be made in the schools, even if criticism and moral philosophy are to be put off until college, as Aristotle thought. For, as recent ethical writers have been pointing out, it is the very genius of morality to appeal to reason. To make a moral judgment is to claim that it is justified, that a case can be made for it. As Philip Rice writes in *On the Knowledge of Good and Evil*, "Even though the sentence containing the word 'ought' does not itself state the . . . reasons, it suggests that there are reasons, . . . and that the conclusion is dictated by them. . . ." [15] Thus, if the parent, speaking as a moral being, says, "You ought to do so and so," it is appropriate for the child to ask, "Why?", and the parent must be prepared, as soon as the child can understand, with some kind of answer, and not just with any kind of answer but with one which will indicate to him what reasons are supposed to count in morality. R. S. Peters even goes so far as to say, in criticizing Freud, "But customary and obsessive behavior is not morality, for by 'morality' we mean *at least* the intelligent following of rules the point of which is understood." [16]

This point may be pushed a bit farther. It is characteristic of a moral judgment, not only to imply reasons, but to claim a basis in considerations of fact which are objectively valid.[17] Hence the reasons adduced by a teacher must not be recognizable to the pupil as mere propaganda calculated to win his assent; they must be such as will bear whatever investigation the pupil may make, else his adherence to the moral enterprise and his virtue will alike be jeopardized.

Thus, even if MEX cannot be said to call for the handing down of a full-scale philosophical or theological theory of the ultimate grounds of moral obligation, it must involve communicating as early as possible at least some sense of the rationale of our judgments of right and wrong. Else our youth can hardly be expected to recognize reason as a friend, even when she comes, for his education will not have made him familiar with her. "The old-fashioned school," says W. T. Harris, "regarded obedience to authority the one essential; the new ideal regards insight into the reasonableness of moral commands the chief end." [18] On this

children in their early years. Cf. p. 271. The examples in the NEA booklet seem to me misguided because they confuse reasons which are merely motivating (which belong to MEY) and reasons which are morally justifying (which belong to MEX).

[15] P. B. Rice, *On the Knowledge of Good and Evil* (New York: Random House, 1955), p. 111; Cf. K. Baier, *The Moral Point of View* (Cornell University Press, 1958), pp. 222, 280; P. H. Nowell-Smith, *Ethics* (Baltimore: Penguin, 1954), p. 161.

[16] R. S. Peters, *The Concept of Motivation* (London: Routledge, 1958), p. 87.

[17] See M. Mandelbaum, *The Phenomenology of Moral Experience* (New York: Free Press, 1955), pp. 243–257.

[18] Editor's Preface to Adler, *op. cit.*, p. vi.

point, with or without the grace of Dewey, the new school and the new moral philosopher see eye to eye.

This means that we parent-teachers must ourselves have some sense of the rationale of moral commands, and for this we may well go to the moral philosophers, even if our children are to be held back from doing so. We must be prepared, however, to find that they disagree profoundly among themselves about what this rationale is, and, while we can learn much from them, we shall have to a considerable extent to rely on what Rice calls our own "global sense of directedness" which was made a part of our "second nature" by our own teachers and "by long buffeting from the world," [19] and without which we shall not be able to benefit from the study of moral philosophy anyway.

(2) The need of building this global sense of moral direction into the second nature of the next generation is reinforced by another consideration, namely, the occurrence of conflicts of duties. Unless the morality which we propose to teach our children is unusually circumspect, it will contain principles which may come into conflict in their experience. In fact, most practical moral problems consist, not simply in applying a given principle, but in resolving conflicts between principles, as in the tragic case of Antigone or in Sartre's example of the young man who "was faced with the choice of leaving for England and joining the Free French Forces . . . or remaining with his mother and helping her to carry on." [20] In such situations, one has one's learned stock of principles. One has also, let us suppose, a well-trained intellect and an excellent supply of relevant information. But, using this information and this intelligence, one still finds a conflict between principles P and Q. If one has also been taught another principle, R, which gives P precedence over Q, all is well, but this is not always the case. Then one must make what Hare calls a "decision of principle"—one must somehow formulate a rule for dealing with the situation in question. This means that we must not only teach our principles and the knowledge required to apply them, but must also prepare the younger generation for a certain creativeness or originality in solving moral problems. We must somehow give them the ability to decide what to do when the answer does not follow from principles learned together with relevant factual information.

(3) This same ability is called for in dealing with another exigency with which new generations are often faced—that of revising or abandoning learned principles in the light of new situations and new knowledge or insight. Perhaps the Socratic-Christian doctrine that it is never right to harm even one's enemies can be regarded as such a revision of a previous rule, or the more recent view that punishment is not retributive

---

[19] Cf. Rice, *op. cit.*, pp. 186, 190 f., 194 f.
[20] J. P. Sartre, *Existentialism* (New York: Philosophical Library, 1947), p. 29.

but prospective or therapeutic in function. Other reformulations of long-accepted principles may be forced on us by recent work in depth or in social psychology, or even by developments in biophysics. And, unless we mean to leave this sort of moral reform entirely to fortune and sporadic genius, we must try to prepare our successors to sense when such a revision of principle is called for and along what lines.

From these considerations it follows that with all our giving of principles we must give understanding and initiative. We must, in teaching principles, try to communicate a sense of their rationale, and along with this a sense of the direction in which to look in cases of conflict or in the event of radically new knowledge or situation; and, at the same time, as Hare emphasizes, we must provide "ample opportunity of making the decisions—by which [principles] are modified, improved, adapted to changed circumstances, or even abandoned if they become entirely unsuited to a new environment." [21] To do this will not be easy for us, for our own generation seems not to have been adequately prepared by its parent-teachers for coping with the changes which have occurred and are occurring. Our own moral education has been wanting either on the side of moral direction or on the side of opportunity for moral decision or both—as well as in the matter of relevant intellectual discipline and factual knowledge. Else neither the existentialism nor the medievalism which we have with us could have arisen.

(4) There is a fourth complication in the program I am calling MEX, one which is implicit in the three just discussed, namely, that of rearing autonomous moral agents. This notion of autonomy is a difficult one. It seems clear that morality is a guide to life of a peculiar sort in that it allows the individual to be, indeed insists on his being, self-governed in the sense, not only of determining what he is going to do, but of determining what it is that he should do. This feature of morality has been stressed by Kant, Durkheim, and many recent writers. In some of the recent writers, however, this autonomy of the individual is misconstrued; it is taken to mean that the individual can create his own standards, and that there is no sort of authority which he must respect. This is the well-known view of Sartre, but something like it seems to be implied by Nowell-Smith when he concludes his book by saying,

> The most a moral philosopher can do is to paint a picture of various types of life . . . and ask which type of life you really want to lead. . . . The questions 'what shall I do?' and 'what moral principles should I adopt?' must be answered by each man for himself; that at least is part of the connotation of the word 'moral.' [22]

[21] Hare, *op. cit.*, p. 76.
[22] Nowell-Smith, *op. cit.*, p. 319 f; cf. Hare, *op. cit.*, p. 77 f.

But to say that a developed moral agent must make up his own mind what is right, and not simply accept the dictates of an external authority, is not to say that he can make a course of action right by deciding on it, or that whatever life he chooses or prefers to live can be claimed by him to be *ipso facto* morally right or good; any more than to say that a developed rational man must make up his own mind what is true, and not merely accept the declarations of another, is to say that he can make a statement true by believing it, or that whatever system he chooses or prefers to believe can be claimed by him to be *ipso facto* intellectually justified. Being autonomous does not mean being responsible to no transpersonal standard in morality any more than in science. In both cases one is involved in an interpersonal enterprise of human guidance (in morality of action, in science of belief) in which one is self-governing but in which one makes judgments ("This is right," "That is true") which one is claiming to be warranted by a review of the facts from the impersonal standpoint represented by that enterprise and shared by all who take part in it—a claim which is not merely an assertion of what one chooses or prefers, and may turn out to be mistaken.

In morality, then, as in science, we must impart to those who come after us a certain difficult but qualified independence or self-reliance of judgment. This and the other three complications in the problem of MEX, however, add up to much the same thing—that there is a Moral Direction or Way which transcends the individual, and within which he stands or claims to stand on his own feet when he makes moral judgments which are not second-hand. I do not conceive of this quite after the manner of C. S. Lewis in *The Abolition of Man,* but with certain judicious modifications much of what he writes about the Tao, as he calls it, seems to me correct, as when he argues that even the moral innovator must speak from within the Tao if what he says is to have any moral force. This Way is for each generation more or less embodied in a set of rules, principles, ideals, or virtues, and this set is what it must proceed to teach to the next generation; but moral education does not consist simply in passing it on intact. Its important task is, rather, in and through the teaching of these ideals or rules, to instill a sense of the Way or Point of View which is involved in morality, and to prepare its pupils to stay self-reliantly within this Way even when the map we have been using turns out to be unclear or inaccurate.

About the nature of this Way recent moral philosophy seems to me in certain respects misleading,[23] but it nevertheless has much to say that is helpful. For example, apart from the existentialists, most writers are agreed that the moral approach to questions about action involves being

[23] See my article, "Obligation and Motivation in Recent Moral Philosophy," in A. I. Melden (ed.), *Essays in Moral Philosophy* (Seattle: University of Washington Press, 1958).

objective, impartial, fact-facing, willing to see one's maxims acted on by everyone even when this is to one's own disadvantage, etc., and in this they seem to be correct. Then teaching the Moral Way, insofar as this falls in the province of MEX, must include imparting an intellectual capacity for this kind of open-mindedness with respect to facts and persons. For the rest, it seems to me that Kant came as near to character-izing the Moral Way as anyone has when he stated "the practical imperative" as follows: "So act as to treat humanity, whether in thine own person or in that of any other, in every case as an end withal, never as means only." [24]

III.

In short, if the method of MEX is the teaching of a particular morality, its goal must be to get across a grasp of the art of morality itself which it is the endeavor of moral philosophy to elucidate. Like Zeus in the myth ascribed to Protagoras by Plato (surely one of the neglected classics on our subject), each generation must send its Hermes (education) to bring the institution of morality to the next, "to the end that there may be regulation of cities and friendly ties to draw them together." [25] With this, our discussion of MEX has completed its course, and we may take a look at MEY. We must be relatively brief about this, and that is regrettable, for MEY, like the month when this was written or any beautiful woman of the same name, is always an interesting subject.

The object of this part of moral education is to keep the youth from replying, "I can but I won't," when Duty whispers low, "Thou must." In W. T. Harris' words, where the job of MEX is "the formation of right ideas," that of MEY is "the formation of right habits," [26] that is, the developing of dispositions which will lead one both to ask what the right is and to act accordingly. First among such dispositions are the moral virtues. These, as Aristotle held, are habit of using the "intellectual virtue" or ability developed in MEX to determine what is right, and of choosing it deliberately because it is right. They are of two kinds. There are somewhat restricted first-order ones such as honesty and veracity; and there are more general second-order ones such as conscientiousness, integrity, and moral alertness. Both kinds are acquired by practice; as Aristotle said, "we become just by doing just acts, temperate by doing temperate acts, brave by doing brave acts." [27] Character education, prop-erly so-called, which must be part of what Professor Ducasse calls

[24] I. Kant, *Fundamental Principles of the Metaphysic of Morals* (London: Long-mans, Green, 1907), Section II.
[25] Protagoras, 322c.
[26] Harris, *op. cit.*, p. v.
[27] *Nicomachean Ethics*, II, i, 4.

education of the will, consists of thus building into the young such dispositions as these.

Another kind of disposition must be mentioned, however. Besides these dispositions to act *from* duty, as Kant puts it, or *because* duty requires, there are others which dispose us to do *such actions as* duty requires, or even to do good deeds which are beyond the strict call of duty, but to do them simply because we want to, for instance, benevolence or gratitude. Aristotle would give honor as the chief of these morality-supporting motives. Kant would object to including attention to any such motives as a part of moral education, because he thought a moral man should always act solely from a sense of duty, but to me, as to Friedrich Schiller and so many others, this seems a hard doctrine, and moreover one which somewhat gratuitously increases the chances that our youth will say "I won't". I should hold, therefore, as Russell does, that the cultivation of such dispositions and the weakening of contrary ones (e.g. fear and hatred), so far as this is possible, is a proper part of moral education. It is what Professor Ducasse calls education of the heart, and perhaps he would not agree that it belongs under *moral* education, since he seems to limit this to education in justice, but I am taking it to include education in goodness too.

In addition to cultivating these "internal sanctions" of morality, as Mill called them, MEY can also make use of such "external sanctions" as punishment or reward (legal, parental, or scholastic) and praise or blame. These are all means of keeping young people on the straight and narrow path, not by changing their motivations, but by using those they already have. To quote Nowell-Smith again, "Pleasure and pain, reward and punishment are the rudders by which human conduct is steered, the means by which moral character is moulded. . . . Moral approval and disapproval play the same role." [28]

This passage makes the point, though it overstates it. The use of the political sanction or power of the state, however, hardly seems a proper part of moral education, for it is of the nature of morality to seek to regulate human behavior without using such power. It may be necessary for the state to back up certain of the demands of morality, but its doing so is not part of the spirit of morality and is necessary only because moral education is not wholly successful. Nowell-Smith, Hare, and others seem to regard punishment of *some* sort as a normal instrument of moral education, but Locke was very chary of its use, as Russell is. It rarely does good and often does harm, he thought; the means to use are praise and blame. "Esteem and disgrace are, of all others, the most powerful incentives to the mind, when once it is brought to relish them." [29] Russell

[28] Nowell-Smith, *op. cit.,* p. 304.
[29] Locke, *op. cit.,* para. 56.

remarks that this relish comes very early, and that "from this moment the educator has a new weapon" which is "extraordinarily powerful," but he adds that "it must be used with great caution." [30] Like most recent educational theorists he prefers to emphasize what Hare, somewhat disparagingly perhaps, calls "other more up-to-date methods." [31]

I shall, however, stick to general theory and not try to evaluate the use of specific kinds of external sanctions. They are all ways of *making* it to an individual's interest to do what is or is regarded as right by some sort of *ad hoc* action, and, while it is clear that morality would like to make its way without them, it is not easy to see how moral education and guidance can get on without anything of the sort. How else, for instance, can it secure the kind of practice which Aristotle says is necessary to produce the habits of justice and temperance, especially when reason cannot yet be used and emulation and generosity do not suffice? We may give up punishment and reward, and limit ourselves to the use of such expressions as "You did right," "But that would be wrong," or "Good boys don't do things like that," but even then we are not simply instructing, we are also appealing to the relishes of esteem and disgrace. This is a sanction which seems almost to be inherent in the use of moral language, and, indeed, Bentham calls it "the moral sanction." That is part of the reason why some contemporary philosophers have been able to make so much of the "emotive meaning" of ethical terms.[32]

Another technique which moralists have often used is not to *make* virtue profitable in this way but rather to *show* that it is profitable or make people *believe* that it is—to prove to the individual, or otherwise lead him to believe, that the world is so constituted as to visit his iniquity, not only on his children and his children's children unto the fourth generation of them that hate morality, but on him. Here enter many gambits which I cannot recite but which are familiar to readers of Plato, Butler, and Hume, as well as of more ordinary moral literature, among them the religious appeal to punishments and rewards in a hereafter. Which of these are sound arguments and which involve what Bergson called myth-making I shall not try to determine. Like Professor Ducasse, I am not convinced that a religious sanction in the form indicated is necessary to morality, and in any case it cannot be appealed to in our public schools. Moreover, I believe that any attempt to prove that being virtuous is always profitable to every individual is and must remain inconclusive, though it may go a long way. But, for so far as it goes, I see no reason why such an attempt should not be included as a

[30] B. Russell, *Education and the Good Life* (New York: Boni and Liveright, 1926), p. 97.

[31] Hare, *op. cit.*, p. 75.

[32] E. g. C. L. Stevenson, *Ethics and Language* (New Haven: Yale University Press, 1944).

part of MEY, at least when it relies on honest argument and not on propaganda—provided that it is not construed as an attempt to give a justification for what is claimed to be right but only as a way of securing the motivation for doing it. Even then, however, it must be made carefully, for the cause of morality will be endangered if the individual is led to think that virtue's promise of profit is its only inducement. That virtue is its own reward is a hoary adage, but it has a present meaning.

Whatever the methods used in MEY, its main concern must not be merely that the individual shall be disposed to act in accordance with certain principles or ideals of right and wrong which have been taught to him in MEX. As the final goal in MEX must be to get across an understanding of the Moral Way and its direction, so the final goal in MEY must be to dispose the individual to follow this Way in spite of contrary temptations, conflicts of duty, or novel situations. Plato thought that we invariably pursue the Idea of the Good, and that our only problem (and hope) in moral education is to understand this Idea or gain true opinion from someone who does. But perhaps there is no such Idea of the *Good* which we can come out of the Cave one day to know in all its glory, and perhaps our problem is rather to understand the Idea of *Morality* as a kind human guidance and to bring about a devotion to it (for such understanding and devotion hardly seem to be natural). It is here that MEX and MEY meet and marry, for of course they are of opposite sexes and bound to fall in love at first sight.

This means that, as MEX must not be occupied simply with teaching a specific set of principles like truth-telling and promise-keeping, but especially with developing a "global sense of moral directedness," and an *ability* to think objectively and impartially, so MEY must not be wholly concerned with developing first-order dispositions like honesty, but more generally with cultivating such second order dispositions as integrity, self-control, and a *readiness* to be governed by impartial and objective thinking and fact-finding.

In saying all this I have been talking as if MEX and MEY are two independent programs of education which meet only at the end. And, indeed, they are distinct and must not be confused. But, of course, they are just two aspects or parts of a single process of moral education, which is going on all the time (just as moral education as a whole is an aspect or part of a yet larger single process of total education), and which has a single ideal of which theirs are components. Really MEX and MEY do not get together only at the end; they are in love and married all the time. Any actual program of moral education must consecrate this marriage at every step, though it must also remember which is husband and which wife.

I have also been talking as if moral education is a log with the older generation at one end and the younger at the other. But, of course, much of it is really a process of self-discipline and self-education.

One thing seems essential if this double program (or "fused curriculum") of moral education is to succeed. This is that we should become aware of others as persons and have a vivid and sympathetic representation in imagination of their interests and of the effects of our actions on their lives.[33] Josiah Royce called this imaginative realization of the feelings of our neighbors "the moral insight," for he believed that one who has it will at once see his duty and feel impelled to act on it. Even his friendly enemy, William James, in "On a Certain Blindness in Human Beings," says much the same thing. "This higher vision of an inner significance in what, until then, we had realized only in the dead external way, often comes over a person suddenly; and, when it does so, it makes an epoch in his history."[34] Earlier we stressed the importance in moral education of factual knowledge and scientific intelligence, but these still proceed in "the dead external way," and something more is needed—a "higher vision" or realizing insight into life which pierces the "great cloudbank of ancestral blindness weighing down upon us." This moral imagination of the lives of others is the one thing needful above all else; perhaps it cannot be taught in any literal sense, but any endeavor of moral education is sadly wanting if it fails to do what can be done to develop it or bring it about. If religion has any direct bearing on moral education, it must be here; James, in fact, calls this "widening of vision" an "increase of religious insight."[35]

IV.

So much for the goals or tasks of moral education as a philosopher sees them. I have not said much about methods. This is mainly a matter for psychologists and educational scientists, though I may add that such philosophers as Russell have much to say here that is helpful. One general remark I must make, namely, that the methods of moral education must be moral. That is, the actions of parents and teachers in dealing with children and pupils must themselves be right by moral standards. Because the end is virtue it does not follow that every means is justified. In fact, the use of immoral means is certain to preclude the realization of the end when the end is morality.

Little also has been said to help solve in any specific way the problem of "the early corruption of youth," as Locke called it, which has been the

[33] Cf. D. D. Raphael, *Moral Judgement* (London: Allen and Unwin, 1955), pp. 105–110.

[34] J. Royce, *The Religious Aspect of Philosophy* (Boston: Houghton Mifflin, 1885), Ch. VI, Sect. V; cf. W. James, *On Some of Life's Ideals* (New York: Holt, 1899), pp. 18–20, 45–50, 93–94.

[35] James, *op. cit.*, p. 64. Cf. pp. 65, 88. The other phrases quoted in this paragraph come from p. 52.

burden of complaint of every parent-generation since Adam or at least since Hesiod. Indeed, I doubt that this is a matter in which philosophers have any special competence; even moral philosophers must leave it largely to parents, churches, schools, and psychologists. Even with all these doing their best within the framework of what has been said here, the motto of moral education must always be that of the Michigan football teams of yesteryear—"Punt, pass, and pray." It is part of the essence of morality, as of democracy and the American system of education, to run the risk of failure. We shall then always have a Socrates who fusses about our inability to succeed in teaching virtue, but perhaps we shall always also have a Protagoras to point out in reply that he who appears to be the worst of those we have tried to bring up would appear to be a master of virtue if we could compare him with men who have had no education or laws or moral restraints, for example, the savages of the poet Pherecrates. "If you were living among such men as this," Protagoras says to Socrates, "you would be only too glad to meet with Eurybates and Phrynondas [two notorious rogues, according to the footnote in my edition] and you would sadly long to revisit the juvenile delinquents of this part of the world." [36] To put the failures of moral education in perspective we need only to try to envisage what an absolute state of nature would be like. Did we not succeed so well as we do, human history would consist in a succession of generations of vipers, if it could last long enough for any children to be born at all.

However, even though philosophy cannot solve the problem of juvenile delinquency, if I may claim anything for the mite which I hereby throw into the public receptacle, it is to have shown that moral educators (which, as Protagoras pointed out, we *all* are) may well consult the works of moral philosophers, especially if moral philosophers will keep in mind the problems of moral education, as they are once more beginning to do.

[36] Plato, *op. cit.*, 327d.

PSYCHOLOGICAL DIMENSION

Some Contributions to the Theory of Innate Ideas /
NOAM CHOMSKY

I think that it will be useful to separate two issues in the discussion of our present topic—one is the issue of historical interpretation, namely,

"Some Contributions to the Theory of Innate Ideas" is reprinted from Noam Chomsky, "Some Contributions to the Theory of Innate Ideas," *Synthese*, Volume 17, March 1967, pp. 2–11. Permission granted by D. Reidel Publishing Company, Dordrecht-Holland.

what in fact was the content of the classical doctrine of innate ideas, let us say, in Descartes and Leibniz; the second is the substantive issue, namely, in the light of the information presently available, what can we say about the prerequisites for the acquisition of knowledge—what can we postulate regarding the psychologically a priori principles that determine the character of learning and the nature of what is acquired?

These are independent issues; each is interesting in its own right, and I will have a few things to say about each. What I would like to suggest is that contemporary research supports a theory of psychological a priori principles that bears a striking resemblance to the classical doctrine of innate ideas. The separateness of these issues must, nevertheless, be kept clearly in mind.

The particular aspect of the substantive issue that I will be concerned with is the problem of acquisition of language. I think that a consideration of the nature of linguistic structure can shed some light on certain classical questions concerning the origin of ideas.

To provide a framework for the discussion, let us consider the problem of designing a model of language-acquisition, an abstract 'language acquisition device' that duplicates certain aspects of the achievement of the human who succeeds in acquiring linguistic competence. We can take this device to be an input-output system

$$\text{data} \rightarrow \quad \text{LA} \quad \rightarrow \text{knowledge}$$

To study the substantive issue, we first attempt to determine the nature of the output in many cases, and then to determine the character of the function relating input to output. Notice that this is an entirely empirical matter; there is no place for any dogmatic or arbitrary assumptions about the intrinsic, innate structure of the device LA. The problem is quite analogous to the problem of studying the innate principles that make it possible for a bird to acquire the knowledge that expresses itself in nest-building or in song-production. On a priori grounds, there is no way to determine the extent to which an instinctual component enters into these acts. To study this question, we would try to determine from the behavior of the mature animal just what is the nature of its competence, and we would then try to construct a second-order hypothesis as to the innate principles that provide this competence on the basis of presented data. We might deepen the investigation by manipulating input conditions, thus extending the information bearing on this input-output relation. Similarly, in the case of language-acquisition, we can carry out the analogous study of language-acquisition under a variety of different input conditions, for example, with data drawn from a variety of languages.

In either case, once we have developed some insight into the nature of the resulting competence, we can turn to the investigation of the innate mental functions that provide for the acquisition of this competence. Notice that the conditions of the problem provide an upper bound and a lower bound on the structure that we may suppose to be innate to the acquisition device. The upper bound is provided by the diversity of resulting competence—in our case, the diversity of languages. We cannot impose so much structure on the device that acquisition of some attested language is ruled out. Thus we cannot suppose that the specific rules of English are innate to the device and these alone, since this would be inconsistent with the observation that Chinese can be learned as readily as English. On the other hand, we must attribute to the device a sufficiently rich structure so that the output can be attained within the observed limits of time, data, and access.

To repeat, there is no reason for any dogmatic assumptions about the nature of LA. The only conditions we must meet in developing such a model of innate mental capacity are those provided by the diversity of language, and by the necessity to provide empirically attested competence within the observed empirical conditions.

When we face the problem of developing such a model in a serious way, it becomes immediately apparent that it is no easy matter to formulate a hypothesis about innate structure that is rich enough to meet the condition of empirical adequacy. The competence of an adult, or even a young child, is such that we must attribute to him a knowledge of language that extends far beyond anything that he has learned. Compared with the number of sentences that a child can produce or interpret with ease, the number of seconds in a lifetime is ridiculously small. Hence the data available as input is only a minute sample of the linguistic material that has been thoroughly mastered, as indicated by actual performance. Furthermore, great diversity of input conditions does not lead to a wide diversity in resulting competence, so far as we can detect. Furthermore, vast differences in intelligence have only a small effect on resulting competence. We observe further that the tremendous intellectual accomplishment of language acquisition is carried out at a period of life when the child is capable of little else, and that this task is entirely beyond the capacities of an otherwise intelligent ape. Such observations as these lead one to suspect, from the start, that we are dealing with a species-specific capacity with a largely innate component. It seems to me that this initial expectation is strongly supported by a deeper study of linguistic competence. There are several aspects of normal linguistic competence that are crucial to this discussion.

I. Creative Aspect of Language Use

By this phrase I refer to the ability to produce and interpret new sentences in independence from "stimulus control"—i.e., external stimuli or independently identifiable internal states. The normal use of language is "creative" in this sense, as was widely noted in traditional rationalist linguistic theory. The sentences used in everyday discourse are not "familiar sentences" or "generalizations of familiar sentences" in terms of any known process of generalization. In fact, even to speak of "familiar sentences" is an absurdity. The idea that sentences or sentence-forms are learned by association or conditioning or "training" as proposed in recent behaviorist speculations, is entirely at variance with obvious fact. More generally, it is important to realize that in no technical sense of these words can language use be regarded as a matter of "habit" or can language be regarded as "a complex of dispositions to respond."

A person's competence can be represented by a *grammar*, which is a system of rules for pairing semantic and phonetic interpretations. Evidently, these rules operate over an infinite range. Once a person has mastered the rules (unconsciously, of course), he is capable, in principle, of using them to assign semantic interpretations to signals quite independently of whether he has been exposed to them or their parts, as long as they consist of elementary units that he knows and are composed by the rules he has internalized. The central problem in designing a language acquisition device is to show how such a system of rules can emerge, given the data to which the child is exposed. In order to gain some insight into this question, one naturally turns to a deeper investigation of the nature of grammars. I think real progress has been made in recent years in our understanding of the nature of grammatical rules and the manner in which they function to assign semantic interpretations to phonetically represented signals, and that it is precisely in this area that one can find results that have some bearing on the nature of a language-acquisition device.

II. Abstractness of Principles of Sentence Interpretation

A grammar consists of syntactic rules that generate certain underlying abstract objects, and rules of semantic and phonological interpretation that assign an intrinsic meaning and an ideal phonetic representation to these abstract objects.

Concretely, consider the sentence 'The doctor examined John.' The phonetic form of this sentence depends on the intrinsic phonological character of its minimal items ("The," "doctor," "examine," "past tense," "John"), the bracketing of the sentence (that is, as [[[the] [doctor]] [[examined] [John]]]), and the categories to which the bracketed elements belong (that is, the categories "Sentence," "Noun-Phrase," "Verb-Phrase," "Verb," "Noun," "Determiner," in this case). We can define the "surface structure" of an utterance as its labeled bracketing, where the brackets are assigned appropriate categorial labels from a fixed, universal set. It is transparent that grammatical relations (e.g., "Subject-of," "Object-of," etc.) can be defined in terms of such a labeled bracketing. With terms defined in this way, we can assert that there is very strong evidence that the phonetic form of a sentence is determined by its labeled bracketing by phonological rules that operate in accordance with certain very abstract but quite universal principles of ordering and organization.

The meaning of the sentence "the doctor examined John" is, evidently, determined from the meanings of its minimal items by certain general rules that make use of the grammatical relations expressed by the labeled bracketing. Let us define the "deep structure" of a sentence to be that labeled bracketing that determines its intrinsic meaning, by application of these rules of semantic interpretation. In the example just given, we would not be far wrong if we took the deep structure to be identical with the surface structure. But it is obvious that these cannot in general be identified. Thus consider the slightly more complex sentences: "John was examined by the doctor"; "someone persuaded the doctor to examine John"; "the doctor was persuaded to examine John"; "John was persuaded to be examined by the doctor." Evidently, the grammatical relations among *doctor, examine,* and *John,* as expressed by the deep structure, must be the same in all of these examples as the relations in "the doctor examined John." But the surface structures will differ greatly.

Furthermore, consider the two sentences:

someone expected the doctor to examine John
someone persuaded the doctor to examine John.

It is clear, in this case, that the similarity of surface structure masks a significant difference in deep structure, as we can see, immediately, by replacing "the doctor to examine John" by "John to be examined by the doctor" in the two cases.

So far, I have only made a negative point, namely, that deep structure is distinct from surface structure. Much more important is the fact that there is very strong evidence for a particular solution to the problem of how deep and surface structures are related, and how deep and surface structures are formed by the syntactic component of the grammar. The details of this theory need not concern us for the present. A crucial feature of it, and one which seems inescapable, is that it involves formal manipulations of structures that are highly abstract, in the sense that their relation to signals is defined by a long sequence of formal rules, and that, consequently, they have nothing remotely like a point by point correspondence to signals. Thus sentences may have very similar underlying structures despite great diversity of physical form, and diverse underlying structures despite similarity of surface form. A theory of language acquisition must explain how this knowledge of abstract underlying forms and the principles that manipulate them comes to be acquired and freely used.

III. Universal Character of Linguistic Structure

So far as evidence is available, it seems that very heavy conditions on the form of grammar are universal. Deep structures seem to be very similar from language to language, and the rules that manipulate and interpret them also seem to be drawn from a very narrow class of conceivable formal operations. There is no a priori necessity for a language to be organized in this highly specific and most peculiar way. There is no sense of "simplicity" in which this design for language can be intelligibly described as "most simple." Nor is there any content to the claim that this design is somehow "logical." Furthermore, it would be quite impossible to argue that this structure is simply an accidental consequence of "common descent." Quite apart from questions of historical accuracy, it is enough to point out that this structure must be rediscovered by each child who learns the language. The problem is, precisely, to determine how the child determines that the structure of his language has the specific characteristics that empirical investigation of language leads us to postulate, given the meagre evidence available to him. Notice, incidentally, that the evidence is not only meagre in scope, but very degenerate in quality. Thus the child learns the principles of sentence formation and sentence interpretation on the basis of a corpus of data that consists, in large measure, of sentences that deviate in form from the idealized structures defined by the grammar that he develops.

Let us now return to the problem of designing a language acquisition device. The available evidence shows that the output of this device is a system of recursive rules that provide the basis for the creative aspect of language use and that manipulate highly abstract structures. Furthermore, the underlying abstract structures and the rules that apply to them have highly restricted properties that seem to be uniform over languages and over different individuals speaking the same language, and that seem to be largely invariant with respect to intelligence and specific experience. An engineer faced with the problem of designing a device meeting the given input-output conditions would naturally conclude that the basic properties of the output are a consequence of the design of the device. Nor is there any plausible alternative to this assumption, so far as I can see. More specifically, we are led by such evidence as I have mentioned to suppose that this device in some manner incorporates: a phonetic theory that defines the class of possible phonetic representations; a semantic theory that defines the class of possible semantic representations; a schema that defines the class of possible grammars; a general method for interpreting grammars that assigns a semantic and phonetic interpretation to each sentence, given a grammar; a method of evaluation that assigns some measure of 'complexity' to grammars.

Given such a specification, the device might proceed to acquire knowledge of a language in the following way: the given schema for grammar specifies the class of possible hypotheses; the method of interpretation permits each hypothesis to be tested against the input data; the evaluation measure selects the highest valued grammar compatible with the data. Once a hypothesis—a particular grammar—is selected, the learner knows the language defined by this grammar; in particular, he is capable of pairing semantic and phonetic interpretations over an indefinite range of sentences to which he has never been exposed. Thus his knowledge extends far beyond his experience and is not a "generalization" from his experience in any significant sense of "generalization" (except, trivially, the sense defined by the intrinsic structure of the language acquisition device).

Proceeding in this way, one can seek a hypothesis concerning language acquisition that falls between the upper and lower bounds, discussed above, that are set by the nature of the problem. Evidently, for language learning to take place the class of possible hypotheses—the schema for grammar—must be heavily restricted.

This account is schematic and idealized. We can give it content by specifying the language acquisition system along the lines just outlined. I think that very plausible and concrete specifications can be given, along these lines, but this is not the place to pursue this matter, which has been elaborately discussed in many publications on transformational generative grammar.

I have so far been discussing only the substantive issue of the prerequisites for acquisition of knowledge of language, the a priori principles that determine how and in what form such knowledge is acquired. Let me now try to place this discussion in its historical context.

First, I mentioned three crucial aspects of linguistic competence: (1) creative aspect of language use; (2) abstract nature of deep structure; (3) apparent universality of the extremely special system of mechanisms formalized now as transformational grammar. It is interesting to observe that these three aspects of language are discussed in the rationalist philosophy of the 17th century and its aftermath, and that the linguistic theories that were developed within the framework of this discussion are, in essence, theories of transformational grammar.

Consequently, it would be historically accurate to describe the views regarding language structure just outlined as a rationalist conception of the nature of language. Furthermore, I employed it, again, in the classical fashion, to support what might fairly be called a rationalist conception of acquisition of knowledge, if we take the essence of this view to be that the general character of knowledge, the categories in which it is expressed or internally represented, and the basic principles that underlie it, are determined by the nature of the mind. In our case, the schematism assigned as an innate property to the language acquisition device determines the form of knowledge (in one of the many traditional senses of "form"). The role of experience is only to cause the innate schematism to be activated, and then to be differentiated and specified in a particular manner.

In sharp contrast to the rationalist view, we have the classical empiricist assumption that what is innate is (1) certain elementary mechanisms of peripheral processing (a receptor system), and (2) certain analytical mechanisms or inductive principles or mechanisms of association. What is assumed is that a preliminary analysis of experience is provided by the peripheral processing mechanisms and that one's concepts and knowledge, beyond this, are acquired by application of the innate inductive principles to this initially analyzed experience. Thus only the procedures and mechanisms for acquisition of knowledge constitute an innate property. In the case of language acquisition, there has been much empiricist speculation about what these mechanisms may be, but the only relatively clear attempt to work out some specific account of them is in modern structural linguistics, which has attempted to elaborate a system of inductive analytic procedures of segmentation and classification that can be applied to data to determine a grammar. It is conceivable that these methods might be somehow refined to the point where they can provide the surface structures of many utterances. It is quite inconceivable that they can be developed to the point where they can provide deep structures or the abstract principles that generate deep structures and relate them to surface structures. This is not a matter of further refinement, but of an entirely different approach to the question. Similarly, it is difficult to imagine how the vague suggestions about conditioning and associative nets that one finds in philosophical and psychological speculations of an empiricist cast might be refined or elaborated so as to provide for attested competence. A system of rules for generating deep structures and relating them to surface structures, in the manner characteristic of natural language, simply does not have the properties of an associative net or a habit family; hence no elaboration of principles for developing such structures can be appropriate to the problem of designing a language acquisition device.

I have said nothing explicit so far about the doctrine that there are innate ideas and innate principles of various kinds that determine the character of what can be known in what may be a rather restricted and highly organized way. In the traditional view a condition for these innate mechanisms to become activated is that appropriate stimulation must be presented. This stimulation provides the occasion for the mind to apply certain innate interpretive principles, certain concepts that proceed from "the power of understanding" itself, from the faculty of thinking rather than from external objects. To take a typical example from Descartes (Reply to Objections, V): ". . . When first in infancy we see a triangular figure depicted on paper, this figure cannot show us how a real triangle ought to be conceived, in the way in which geometricians consider it, because the true triangle is contained in this figure, just as the statue of Mercury is contained in a rough block of wood. But because we already possess within us the idea of a true triangle, and it can be more easily conceived by our mind than the more complex figure of the triangle drawn on paper, we, therefore, when we see the composite figure, apprehend not it itself, but rather the authentic triangle" (Haldane and Ross, vol. II, p. 227). In this sense, the idea of triangle is innate. For Leibniz what is innate is certain principles (in general, unconscious), that "enter into our thoughts, of which they form the soul and the connection." "Ideas and truths are for us innate as inclinations, dispositions, habits, or natural potentialities." Experience serves to elicit, not to form, these innate structures. Similar views are elaborated at length in rationalist speculative psychology.

It seems to me that the conclusions regarding the nature of language acquisition, discussed above, are fully in accord with the doctrine of innate ideas, so understood, and can be regarded as providing a kind of substantiation and further development of this doctrine. Of course, such a proposal raises nontrivial questions of historical interpretation.

What does seem to me fairly clear is that the present situation with regard to the study of language learning, and other aspects of human intellectual achievement of comparable intricacy, is essentially this. We have a certain amount of evidence about the grammars that must be the output of an acquisition model. This evidence shows clearly that knowledge of language cannot arise by application of step-by-step inductive operations (segmentation, classification, substitution procedures, "analogy," association, conditioning, and so on) of any sort that have been developed or discussed within linguistics, psychology, or philosophy. Further empiricist speculations contribute nothing that even faintly suggests a way of overcoming the intrinsic limitations of the methods that have so far been proposed and elaborated. Furthermore, there are no other grounds for pursuing these empiricist speculations, and avoiding what would be the normal assumption, unprejudiced by doctrine, that one would formulate if confronted with empirical evidence of the sort sketched above. There is, in particular, nothing known in psychology or physiology that suggests that the empiricist approach is well-motivated, or that gives any grounds for skepticism concerning the rationalist alternative sketched above.

For further discussion of the question of historical interpretation, see Chomsky, *Aspects of the Theory of Syntax* (1965), ch. 1, and *Cartesian*

Linguistics (1966). For further discussion of matters touched on here, see also Chomsky, 'Explanatory Models in Linguistics,' in *Logic, Methodology and Philosophy of Science,* ed. by E. Nagel, P. Suppes, and A. Tarski (1962); J. Katz, *The Philosophy of Language* (1966); P. M. Postal, Review of A. Martinet, *Elements of General Linguistics* (forthcoming); and the selections in section VI of *The Structure of Language, Readings in the Philosophy of Language,* ed. by J. Fodor and J. Katz (1964).

SOCIAL CONCEPTS DIMENSION

Democracy and Education / RICHARD S. PETERS

That education should be "democratic" no one in a democracy would seriously dispute. This would be the equivalent of announcing in the Middle Ages that all education should be Christian. But what such an announcement would commit anyone to is far from clear. This is partly because of the vagueness which all such general terms of commendation must have if they are to fulfil their function of reminding a people of their ultimate valuations. It is also because of different interpretations which it is possible to give of the predication of "democratic" to "education."

This could mean, first of all, that the educational system of a community should be democratically distributed and organized, whatever interpretation is given to "democratic." A system, for instance, which neglected the education of half the population or about whose organization "the people" had no say would commonly be thought to be "undemocratic." Alternatively it might suggest that the organization of schools themselves should be "democratic." In other words a plea might be being made for the rights of the inmates, staff and pupils alike, to some say in the running of their institution. An English public school, run on highly autocratic lines, might be said to be "undemocratic" in this respect. Alternatively the announcement might be drawing attention to the desirability of the content of education being democratic. The school's part in training citizens in the skills and attitudes appropriate for membership in a democratic community might be being stressed. Needless to say a school system might be "democratic" in one or two of these ways but not in all. In dealing, therefore, with democracy and education it is necessary to treat separately at least these three possible interpretations. . . .

The Justification of Democracy

. . . It is often said that democracy is an impracticable form of government because it demands of the ordinary citizen qualities which only the few can possess. It must, in the end, represent the views of the twenty per cent who understand what twenty per cent means. This is particularly true nowadays, when estimates of government policy depend upon an understanding of economics which is beyond the reach of most, and of military and diplomatic secrets that no responsible government would ever divulge in public. If democracies appear to work it is only because the élite are not too much hampered by having to make concessions to uninformed prejudices.

There is something in this criticism, but not much. To start with, it rests upon a naïve view of what is required by the procedures of consultation and public accountability. In a representative system of government there is a tendency to interpret these procedures in terms of some fiction involving a substantive interpretation of notions such as "the will of the people." Those who are put in authority, be they members of Parliament or civil servants, are appointed to rule in the public interest; they are not necessarily delegates expressing either a sectional interest or "the people's will." . . .

Anyone in authority knows perfectly well that the opinion of the ordinary man about the balance of payments or about the advisability of retaining some remote naval base is not worth much. He knows, too, that he himself has to rely on experts to advise him about all sorts of aspects of policy. His task is not simply to follow public opinion but also to help create it; he must use his authority in support of proposals put forward by people who know what they are talking about. And the public can generally judge the wisdom of policies when they are confronted with their actual outcome. As, however, the stuff of political decisions is the adjustment of interests, a ruler will be very foolish not to consult the major interests affected by any proposals. But concern for the public interest also requires that the interests of individuals and minorities, who cannot exert strong pressure, should not be disregarded. There are issues, too, like those connected with sexual morality and crime, where public policy must be determined more by general moral considerations rather than by expert knowledge. On these matters the conscience of the "ordinary man" is often as sensitive as that of the ruler. One of the distressing features of modern democratic government is that rulers themselves are, perhaps, too much victims of the presuppositions of this criticism. The wide acceptance of the view that a government must have a "mandate," and the fear of being thrown out at the next election, often cripple government at a time when political parties are evenly matched. Many much needed reforms are not tackled either because there are no votes to be won by making them, or because votes will be lost if any government dares to tackle them. Present examples in England are the divorce laws and the anomalies connected with religious instruction in state schools.

Underlying this criticism, too, is perhaps the strange view that there could be some ideal government in which abstract notions of justice and of the consideration of interests are perfectly realized. This is a Utopian dream. To start with, as has been argued before, the very notion of government itself, implying the placing of some man in authority over others, is prima facie an affront to a rational man. It cannot, by its nature, be an ideal state of affairs; it is at best a necessary expedient. Given that there must be government the realistic question to ask is not whether democracy matches up to some fanciful ideal, but to consider soberly which state of affairs would be worst for a rational man. He must surely think, with Locke, that the worst state of affairs possible is "to be subject to the inconstant, uncertain, unknown, arbitrary will of another man." Starting with despotism he can work upwards through the possible forms of government and consider them soberly in terms of the potentialities for oppression and misery which they harbor. When he eventually comes to democracy he may be only too well aware of its frustrations, failings, and hypocrisies; but at least it need not represent such a threat to the individual as other forms of government. It may veer in that direction, if it becomes equated with majority rule, as de Tocqueville so clearly saw. But it need not. It has the supreme virtue that if particular occupants of office turn out to be even worse than expected—and why should it be thought that those who are anxious for office are likely to be angelic beings?—then at least they can be removed without a revolution.

A rational man can reflect, too, that a democracy in which authority is rationalized and in which consultation, safeguards on discussion and assembly, and public accountability are embedded in the practices of a people, represents the only form of political life which is consistent with the fundamental principles of morality. He may even come to enjoy some aspects of the public life which democracy makes possible. His feeling of fraternity may be focused on the striving for the public interest; he may even feel that doing what he can to preserve this thin crust of rationality is even more worth-while than pursuing some more private interest. It would be impossible for him to feel in relation to the state as the Athenians felt about their πολις ; but at least in the life of some institution of a democratic sort he might feel some joy in participation. He might feel kinship with other rational beings, both living and dead, in tackling problems rather than parading prejudices. He will know, of course, that any thought of a final solution to them is absurd. Indeed he may realize that the very expedients which are adopted to cure present ills open up dimensions of difficulty undreamed of by his predecessors.

But the point is to perpetuate the procedures for tackling problems, not to expect final solutions. The joy consists in traveling with others, not in arriving. Indeed what would count as arriving?

What implications for education are there in this somewhat pedestrian and piecemeal account of democracy? As was pointed out, "democratic" can be predicated of education in at least three ways. These must now be briefly explored.

The Democratization of Education

To say that education is not democratic may, first of all, be to condemn it for falling short of the general moral demands made on an educational system by those committed to the democratic way of life. Without education an individual in a modern industrial society is unlikely to be able to proceed very far in developing the particular aspect of a worthwhile form of life to which he is suited; also an educational system acts selectively in equipping citizens with skills and knowledge that are essential to the community's viability and development. From the point of view, therefore, both of the community and of the individual, a democrat would insist that education should be made available for all and that it should be fairly distributed. He would also demand, as a rational being committed to liberty, as well as to fairness and the consideration of interests, that as much freedom of choice should be given to parents and to children as is consistent with the pursuit of objectives falling under the other two fundamental principles, and that all these principles should be implemented with respect for persons. As was made clear earlier the enunciation of such general principles is much more likely to command universal assent than proposals for their implementation in concrete circumstances. In this respect they resemble the pronouncements of Rousseau's General Will. But there is no need at this juncture to retrace the ground covered previously.

Another highly debatable question is what institutional devices are appropriate for assuring procedures of consultation and public accountability which, it was argued, are necessary for making the democratic way of life a reality? No one would dispute that as education involves a vast expenditure of public money, those who are responsible for manning educational institutions should have to consult with those for whom they are run, and that they should be accountable to "the public" for the way in which they discharge their responsibilities. But the question is at what level this should take place, and what degree of autonomy should be accorded to the teaching profession. In England, for instance, though universities are financed largely by the state, the universities themselves, through the device of the Universities Grant Committee, which acts as a buffer between the universities and the Department of Education and

Science (formerly between the universities and the Treasury), enjoy a remarkable degree of autonomy. Colleges of education, on the other hand, are financially and administratively responsible to the local education authorities, or, if they are voluntary colleges, are largely responsible to the Department of Education and Science, and are constantly jibbing at the restrictions placed on them. From this point of view, however, their life is idyllic when compared with that of an American high school which comes under the jurisdiction of a local school board.

There is very little of a general sort that can be said about this matter. Decisions must depend on at least three major factors in respect of which countries differ greatly. There is first of all the general pattern of democratic procedures prevalent in a country, which will obviously influence the way in which education is administered. It is very difficult, for instance, to compare the English system of accountability with that of America, in view of the fact that England is about the size of New York State, which obviously affects very much the issue of central as distinct from local responsibility. Also, as has already been pointed out, the attitudes towards government in the two countries differ markedly. Both these considerations will affect the willingness of parents to hand over their children to a state educational system without insisting on the right. to a close scrutiny at a local level of what is being done.

Secondly, different educational institutions require different forms of control. Universities, with their emphasis on research, are very different from nursery schools and local technical colleges. Thirdly, there is the important difference of the variable status accorded to the teacher in different countries. Is he thought of mainly as an authority on the ultimate values of a community? Or is he regarded mainly as a person "hired" by the community to train citizens in useful skills and to select them efficiently for necessary occupations?

Obviously these three variables make it almost impossible for anything of a general nature to be said about the form and level of public accountability. Discussion would have to be detailed and concrete within the context of an established set of institutions. It is no good demanding a centrally organized and controlled system, e.g., the French system, in the U.S.A. where the size of the country and the democratic traditions are so different. A philosopher could add his contribution to such a discussion, but enough has been said to show that no substantive "solutions" can be deduced from philosophical considerations alone.

One general point, however, would follow from the stress placed on the concept of the teacher as "an authority," as the custodian of the quality of life of a community. That is that under modern conditions of democracy, which some have even gone so far as to class as "the rule of groups" rather than "the rule of the people," teachers must make themselves much more effective as an organized pressure group on matters of general educational importance. At the moment the public is aware of its collective pressure only in the matter of salary negotiations.

It is often said that this means that teachers should make themselves more effectively into a "profession" [1]—but what is meant by this? To the ordinary man being a member of a "profession" means little more than earning a salary rather than a wage. But there surely must be more than this tenuous type of similarity between a doctor, a dentist, and a barrister. Presumably members of professions are united also in having tasks which require specialist knowledge and a lengthy period of training. They must, too, have common standards of an ethical sort which are specific to their station and duties. They can be guilty of "unprofessional conduct." It is one thing for a university teacher to have an affair with his colleague's wife, but it is quite another thing for him to seduce one of his students. Members of a profession must therefore keep in active touch with the centers of teaching and research from which their specialist knowledge emanates, and they must have effective machinery at both the local and the central level for keeping in touch with each other and for making and implementing their collective decisions. In regard to the first requirement teachers have a dual obligation. On the one hand they have to keep in touch with developments in the "subjects" which they teach; on the other hand they have also to be *au fait* with developments in the "methodological" aspects of their task, e.g., in educational philosophy, psychology, and sociology. The role-reversal involved in putting themselves from time to time into the situation of pupils once more should also increase their insight into problems of teaching. In regard to the second requirement they should meet in their local associations to discuss matters of common concern. . . .

The School as a Democratic Institution

There has been a lot of talk since the time of John Dewey about the school as a democratic institution, but one suspects that few schools deserve such a title in any full-blown sense. And why should they? To start with, in England at any rate, the headmaster is appointed to do a job with very wide terms of reference and it is up to him how much of his authority he delegates. He is also responsible for the organization of a community of predominantly immature people. There are some matters, e.g., the curriculum and the competence of his staff, about which it would be quite inappropriate for him to consult pupils, let alone give them any powers of decision. It is important, therefore, that any discus-

---

[1] See M. Lieberman, *Education as a Profession* (Englewood Cliffs, N.J.: Prentice-Hall, 1956).

sion of democracy within the school should be prefaced by a realistic appraisal of what the formal position of the headmaster is.

Disillusionment with democracy is only too likely to develop if lip service is paid to procedures such as consultation and public accountability, while at the same time those taking part in them know full well that the headmaster is really making the important decisions. It is perfectly right and proper that he should be doing this on certain issues; that, after all, is implied by his being in authority. But in such cases the terms on which others are being consulted should be made clear. This applies in dealings both with staff and with pupils. Is this a situation where a meeting is summoned so that the headmaster may seek advice which perhaps he will not take? Or is it a meeting at which what is decided is what is going to be done? Those who have spent hours attending meetings in schools, colleges, and universities are only too familiar with the cynicism that can be bred if there is ambiguity on this cardinal point. Rationality requires not a haphazard summoning of retainers for "advice and consent" but a structured situation in which people know where they stand.

Once this general point has been made, the form and content of decision procedures becomes a very contingent matter. It depends very much on the age of the pupils, the substance of the decision to be made, and the tradition of the school. Any democratically minded headmaster will consult his staff about most things and provide as much scope as he can for corporate decision. He will encourage children to organize activities themselves, with or without staff participation, depending on the nature of the activity and the age of the children.[2] He may institute a school council or parliament, depending on how worth-while and effective he judges such a body can be, whose spheres of competence are necessarily bound to be very limited on crucial issues of school policy.

Education for Democracy

Nothing that goes on in a school can be looked at purely from the point of view of whether it is or is not consistent with the general principles of the adults who are responsible for it; there is also the question of its effect on children and the encouragement offered for the development of a way of life. Any school in a democratic society must therefore consider realistically what it can do to develop democratically minded citizens. The character of such citizens was outlined in the section on the Presuppositions of the Democrat, where it was explained how the democratic way of life, with its emphasis on discussion and the

---

[2] For further details of the various possibilities see A. K. C. Ottaway, *Education and Society*, 3rd ed. (London: Kegan Paul, 1962), Chapter IX.

use of reason, developed out of practices which were gradually established.

The fundamental principles were implicit in these practices. They were gradually made explicit and defended in a more abstract way as the new tradition of rationalism took root with its demand that nothing should be accepted simply because it is traditional. This did not mean necessarily a change in practices; it meant a different backing or "ground of legitimacy," to revert to Weber's way of making this point. Most British works in ethics and political philosophy since the time of Hobbes have been attempts to produce a rationale of this way of life. Critics of such works often make the derisory comment that they are rather like shadow boxing; for the philosophers do not doubt that people ought to act justly, be tolerant, consider the interests of others, keep promises, and tell the truth any more than they doubt that, in some sense, government ought to be by the consent of the people. What they argue about is how these principles can be justified. But on the view put forward in this book this is just what one would expect. For a democratic system can only work if there is a massive consensus at the level of fundamental principles.

It may be argued that the writings of Hegel, Marx, and the Existentialists are only explicable in the light of the *breakdown* of such a consensus. Hence the relativistic account of moral principles as merely reflections of historical or economic conditions, and the stress by Existentialists on individual decision. This may be true of Germany and France and might be a very important factor in explaining the failure of liberalism in these countries; but it certainly is not true of England and America. Of course there are acute disagreements about issues such as gambling, abortion, and extra-marital sex relationships. But it is precisely because there is agreement about the procedural principles of fairness, tolerance, and the consideration of interests, which provide a framework for such issues to be discussed, that we can afford to differ about lower-level matters where fundamental principles conflict. Such a consensus does not, of course, make these principles valid; that has not been argued. But it is necessary for making democracy more than a formal façade.

How then can schools contribute to initiating each fresh generation into this way of life? This is a vast topic comprising as it does the main substance of moral and political education. It would require a separate monograph to deal with it, and most of the issues would be psychological rather than philosophical. All that can be done in a brief space is to make one or two general remarks which will serve to link this topic with what has been touched upon before in this book.

The underlying idea of all such education must surely be that children should recapitulate in a brief span the more gradual development of their ancestors. They should be initiated into traditions in which the fundamental principles of reason are implicit. At first they will learn to act from others who know how to act, without understanding the reasons. Gradually they will come to grasp the principles underlying their actions, which make reasons relevant, and will be able to act with understanding and to adapt their practice to novel situations. They may also come to challenge some practices as being no longer rationally defensible.

In following this historical paradigm they will be doing, psychologically speaking, all that they can do in learning to live in a reasonable way. For in all education we are confronted by what I have elsewhere called the paradox of moral education.[3] The palace of reason has to be entered by the courtyard of habit. Even in a society where children are encouraged to develop as autonomous beings, it is not till about the age of seven or eight that the notion begins to dawn that rules are not transcendentally given as part of the social order but that there are reasons for them. They therefore have first to acquire a firm foundation of basic rules in a manner which does not incapacitate them for rational rule-following at a later stage. How they learn to do this is a comparatively unexplored psychological question. But obviously their relationships with parents, teachers, and other authority figures have much to do with it. For, like most difficult things in life, moral conduct is probably acquired by some process of apprenticeship. If all goes well they will gradually come to grasp in a more explicit way the fundamental principles which provide the backing for the rules which have become almost second nature to them. There are, it has been argued, certain fundamental attitudes underlying this way of life—an overall concern for truth, respect for persons, and a feeling of fraternity for others as persons. The contrast between reason and feeling is out of place; for feelings cannot exist without a cognitive core, and the reasonable man must have the appropriate attitudes to sustain him in his manner of life. There may well be a "natural" basis for such rational attitudes in curiosity and in sympathy for others, but how these become marked out as being of overriding importance, and how they become transformed by built-in standards, such as those of relevance, consistency, and impartiality, is an unexplored problem in moral development. Piaget makes much of the fact of the development from the transcendental to the autonomous stage in moral development.[4] But the explanation of the fact, especially in relation to the motivational aspect of such development, is not forthcoming.

Many have argued that peer-group experience is as critical in learning to grasp fundamental principles, such as those of fairness, tolerance, and the consideration of interests, as is the relationship with authority figures

[3] See R. S. Peters, "The Paradox of Moral Education," in *Moral Education in a Changing Society* W. R. Niblett (ed.) (London: Faber, 1963).
[4] See J. Piaget, *The Moral Judgment of the Child* (London: Kegan Paul, 1932).

in acquiring a firm foundation of basic rules. This may well be so. But those in authority can contribute much if they provide paradigm examples of reasonable behavior and if they help adolescents to accomplish one of the most difficult things of all—the development of a rational attitude towards authority. Any adolescent who has grown up in a fairly normal way must have an attitude towards authority which is to a certain extent ambivalent. On the one hand his attitude must be tinged with feelings of dependence, submissiveness, and perhaps admiration, which are precipitates of his early relationship with his parents; on the other hand there is also that hostility towards such figures which was first roused when they thwarted infantile desires for gratification and which is kindled afresh when they stand in the way of the assertion of independence in adolescence. This spark of hostility is often fanned into a flame by a combination of peer-group pressure and parental intransigence or feebleness.

Teachers are therefore very often the focus of attitudes towards authority which they themselves have done little to deserve. They have to learn, therefore, to develop a reasonably detached and uninvolved attitude towards hostile or clinging reactions towards themselves; for the reactions may be more towards what they represent than towards what they are. They must appreciate, too, that patterns of social control are different in families occupying different places in the socio-economic continuum. "Middle-class" families tend to be much more prone to employ persuasion and to adapt their discipline to individuals; it is person-oriented rather than status-oriented. "Working-class" families, on the other hand, tend to employ a much more status-oriented, all-or-nothing method of control in which commands and blows alternate with gusty expressions of affection. Teachers, who nowadays are predominantly recruited from a "lower middle-class" background, may more often encounter problems with discipline if they teach children from a predominantly working-class area.

The point was stressed that the teacher has to accept the fact that children may identify with him and that he must turn them outwards from an interest in him to an interest in what he is trying to teach. So, too, in the sphere of attitude training, the teacher must accept the fact that he may be regarded as a traditional status holder towards whom either total deference or defiance is due. He has to start from this attitude towards himself and work gradually towards developing a more rational attitude towards an office which he happens to occupy. He has to get children to grasp the point of having people in authority, and to learn to detach this from their like or dislike of the particular people whom they happen to find there.

About training in the manning of democratic institutions there is little to say that has not already been intimated. Much can be done by

instruction, by the study of institutions and of their historical development, by visits to Parliament and to council meetings; but practical
experience is of far more importance. People sometimes have the naïve
illusion that others have a natural flair for contributing to discussions or
fulfilling the responsibilities of an office; but of no activities is Aristotle's
contention that the things we have to learn to do we learn to do by doing
more true than of political acitivity. Administration requires judgment
above all things—judgment of people and judgment of priorities. This
can only be learned by practical experience, preferably under the tutelage of somebody who already has it. There is no way of formalizing it or
reducing it to recipes. It is imparted on the job rather than learned in
lectures. A beginning can be made with this at school if some members
of staff have the wisdom and the patience to act in an advisory capacity
on various committees and in connection with responsibilities undertaken by the pupils.

The willingness of children to participate in such democratic procedures and to take on responsibilities depends mainly on those intangible
factors often referred to as the "tone" or "the social climate of the
school." [5] It depends also very much on the emergence of leaders. There
are some, such as Sir Karl Popper, who argue that democrats should not
be preoccupied with the problem of training leaders; for they will
emerge all right. The proper preoccupation of the democrat should
rather be to devise institutions to protect ourselves against them should
they turn out to be too tyrannical.[6] This type of reaction is understandable in the light of the Nazi background against which Popper was
writing. It was strengthened, too, by revelations by psychologists about
"the authoritarian personality" and about the unsavory motives that
many leaders seem to harbor. Given, too, the assumption that power
tends to corrupt, a half-truth that many find impressive, the build-up
against training leaders in a democracy begins to look pretty impressive.

This reaction, however, is really too undiscriminating. It fails, for a
start, to distinguish different types of authority and to indicate the sort of
rational leadership that is appropriate in a democracy. There can surely
not be anything particularly objectionable about a reasonable, competent
man, with a sense of public responsibility and a desire to work with
others on some common task, being prepared to take office for a period, if
he is appointed by properly constituted procedures with a clearly defined
sphere of competence. Of course he may harbor strange motives for
doing what he does. He may have a repressed desire to dominate or a
yearning to demonstrate his virility. But what if he has? Any teacher may
well have such hidden motives too, as well as latent homosexual tenden-

[5] See A. K. C. Ottaway, *op. cit.*, Chapter IX, pp. 176–185.
[6] See K. R. Popper, *The Open Society and Its Enemies* (London: Routledge, 1945),
Vol I, Chapter VII.

cies or a reluctance to face a life among adults. The question is whether such motives distort or disrupt the discharge of his palpable duties. People can be judged only for their conscious intentions and for the competence and decency with which they discharge their duties. If we were all assessed by the state of our innermost souls very few of us indeed would participate in public life.

There is also the point that experience has shown that one of the main things that can be done in this sphere of training is to transform the concept which a person has of his task. There is not much at such a late stage than can be done about people's innermost motives. Judgment they can only pick up on the job, together with various tricks of the trade, if they work in the company of more experienced people. But attitudes to the discharge of duties can be altered by a combination of experience and group discussion. This is surely one of the main values of supervised teaching practice for teachers. Much along similar lines can be done with older students at school towards developing a rational attitude towards the exercise of authority.

A rational attitude towards authority is not conveyed purely by the way in which an individual teacher handles disciplinary problems with a class. It is conveyed more subtly in much more intangible ways. What chance, for instance, has an assistant master in encouraging such an attitude if he himself is treated in an authoritarian manner by the headmaster, often in front of the boys? If members of staff show little respect for persons in dealing with each other, there is little likelihood of children being so contra-suggestible that they will develop it. This "social climate" of a school is probably much influenced also by rituals; for rituals are one of the most effective ways for intimating what is of ultimate value without explicitly stating it. In a school the ritualistic aspect of committees, councils, and perfect systems may be as important as the actual training which is provided in carrying out concrete respon- sibilities. The point has often been made in this book that both in the sphere of education generally, and in that of moral education, children have to be initiated into forms of thought and behavior, the rationale of which they cannot at first properly understand. And they have to be got on the inside of these forms of thought and behavior before they can properly understand them. Rituals, as well as the use of authority, are a method by means of which the importance of a practice can be marked out and children made to feel that it is something in which they should participate. It is surely better than bribing them or goading them.

Rationalists often attack rituals because they lack instrumental value; they do little to promote any palpable purpose. This, of course, is just the point about them. If a practice has an obvious instrumental value, e.g., taking a train to work, there is no need for it to be ritualized. If, however, the point of a practice is difficult to discern because, perhaps, it is largely

internal to it, then ritual both serves as a lure for those who are outside
and also helps to revive and sustain the belief in it by those who are
inside.[7] There are many whose cynicism about the actual working of
Parliament has been tempered by participating in some of the majesty of
its rituals, most of which are steeped in historical significance. Such
rituals help to unite the past with the future and to convey the sense of
participation in a shared form of life. They do something to mitigate the
feeling any rational being must have about the triviality and transience
of his life upon earth. They do much, too, to develop that feeling of
fraternity which is the lifeblood of any effective institution.

Democracy is an extremely difficult way of life to sustain. The fundamental moral principles on which it rests—those of fairness, liberty, and
the consideration of interests—are principles which are imposed on
strong and primitive tendencies. Its emotional underpinning in respect
for persons and a feeling of fraternity for others as persons is accessible
only to rational men. It requires knowledge about and interest in public
affairs on the part of its citizens and a widespread willingness to work its
institutions. It needs, as is often said, constant vigilance to prevent
encroachments on the liberties of the individual, as well as institutional
safeguards through which such vigilance can find expression. Men do not
spring up like mushrooms to run its institutions; they have to be trained.
But what more fitting focus could there be for the feeling of fraternity
than that of contributing to such a form of life and training others to
perpetuate it?

[7] For further discussion of the importance of rituals see B. B. Bernstein, R. S.
Peters, and H. L. Elvin, "The Role of Ritual in Education," in Philosophical
transactions of Royal Society, Series B, "Ritualization of Behavior in Animals and
Man," 1967.

SPECIAL READING

Teaching and Training   / GILBERT RYLE

I have no teaching tricks or pedagogic maxims to impart to you, and I
should not impart them to you if I had any. What I want to do is to sort
out and locate a notion which is cardinal to the notions of teaching,
training, education, etc. about which too little is ordinarily said. This
notion is that of *teaching oneself* which goes hand in glove with the
notion of *thinking for oneself.* You will all agree, I think, that teaching

fails, that is, either the teacher is a failure or the pupil is a failure, if the pupil does not sooner or later become able and apt to arrive at his own solutions to problems. But how, in logic, can anyone be taught to do untaught things? I repeat, how, in logic, can anyone be taught to do untaught things?

To clear the air, let me begin by quickly putting on one side an unimportant but familiar notion, that of the self-taught man. Normally when we describe someone as a self-taught man we think of a man who having been deprived of tuition from other teachers tries to make himself an historian, say, or a linguist or an astronomer, without criticism, advice or stimulation from anyone else, save from the authors of such textbooks, encyclopaedia articles and linguaphone records as he may happen to hit on. He hits on these, of course, randomly, without having anyone or anything to tell him whether they are good ones, silly ones, old-fashioned ones or cranky ones. We admire the devotion with which he studies, but, save for the rare exception, we pity him for having been the devoted pupil only of that solitary and untrained teacher, himself. However, I am not interested in him.

What I am interested in is this. Take the case of an ordinary unbrilliant, unstupid boy who is learning to read. He has learned to spell and read monosyllables like "bat," "bad," "at," "ring," "sing" etc. and some two-syllable words like "running," "dagger" and a few others. We have never taught him, say, the word "batting." Yet we find him quite soon reading and spelling unhesitantly the word "batting." We ask him who taught him this word and, if he remembers, he says that he had found it out for himself. He has learned from himself how the word "batting" looks in print, how to write it down on paper and how to spell it out aloud, so in a sense he has taught himself this word—taught it to himself without yet knowing it. How can this be? How can a boy who does not know what "b-a-t-t-i-n-g" spells teach himself what it spells?

In real life we are not a bit puzzled. It is just what we expect of a not totally stupid child. Yet there is the semblance of a conceptual paradox here, for we seem to be describing him as at a certain stage being able to teach himself something new, which *ipso facto* was not yet in his repertoire to teach. Here his teacher was as ignorant as the pupil, for they were the same boy. So how can the one learn something from the other?

What should we say? Well, clearly we want to say that the prior things that we *had* taught him, namely words like "bat," "bad," "rat" and longer words like "butter," "running" etc. enabled him and perhaps encouraged him to make a new bit of independent, uncoached progress on his own. We had taught him *how* to read some monosyllables, *how* to run some of them together in dissyllables, and so on. We had taught him a way or some ways of coping with combinations of printed letters, though not in their particular application to this new word "batting." He had made this particular application himself. So to speak, we had previously from the deck shown him the ropes and now he climbs one of them with his own hands and feet; that is to say, not being totally stupid, he was able and ready to employ this slightly general knowledge that we had given to him on a new concrete and particular problem that we had not solved for him. We had given him the wherewithal with which to think it out for himself—and this thinking out was his doing and not ours. I could just as well have taken an example from the much more sophisticated stratum where a brilliant undergraduate makes a good philosophical move that no one else has ever taught him, and maybe no one else has ever made.

Naturally, most often the boy or the undergraduate, if asked Who taught you that? would reply not that he had taught it to himself or that he had learned it from himself, but rather that he had found it out or thought it out or worked it out for himself. Just this brings out a big part of what interests me, namely, that though in one way it is obviously impossible for one person's own discovery, whether trivial or important, to be simply what someone else had previously taught him—since it would then not be his discovery—, yet in another way it is and ought to be one main business of a teacher precisely to get his pupils to advance beyond their instructions and to discover new things for themselves, that is, to get them to think things out for themselves. I teach Tommy to read a few words like "bat," "run" and "running" in order that he may then, of his own motion, find out how to read lots and lots of other words, like "batting," that we have not taught to him. Indeed we do not deem him really able to spell or read until he can spell and read things that he has not been introduced to. Nor, to leave the schoolroom for the moment, do I think that Tommy has learned to bicycle until he can do things on his bicycle far more elaborate, speedy, tricky and delicate than the things I drilled him in on the first morning. I taught him the few elements on the first morning just in order that he might then find out for himself how to cope with hosts of non-elementary tasks. I gave him a few stereotyped exercises, and, as I had hoped and expected, in a couple of days he had developed for himself on this basis a fair wealth of boyish skills and dexterities, though he acquired these while I was away in London.

However, there remains a slight feeling of a puzzle or paradox here, and it comes, I think, from this source. A familiar and indispensable part or sort of teaching consists in teaching by rote lists of truths or facts, for example the proposition that 7×7 is 49, etc., the proposition that Waterloo was fought in 1815, etc., and the proposition that Madrid is the capital of Spain, etc. That the pupil has learned a lesson of this propositional sort is shown, in the first instance, by his being able and reasonably ready to reproduce word-perfectly these pieces of information. He gets them by heart, and he can come out with them on demand. Now every teacher knows that only a vanishingly small fraction of his teaching-day really consists in simply reciting lists of such snippets of information to pupils, but very unfortunately, it happens to be the solitary part which unschooled parents, Sergeant Majors, some silly publicists and some educationalists always think of when they think of teaching and learning. They think or half-think that the request "Recite what you have learned in school today, Tommy" is a natural and proper one, as if all that Tommy could or should have learned is a number of memorizable propositions; or as if to have learned anything consisted simply in being able to echo it, like a gramophone. As you all know, most teaching has nothing whatsoever in common with this crude, semi-surgical picture of teaching as the forcible insertion into the pupil's memory of strings of officially approved propositions; and I hope to show before long that even that small and of course indispensable part of instruction which is the imparting of factual information is grossly mis-pictured when pictured as literal cramming. Yet, bad as the picture is, it has a powerful hold over people's general theorizings about teaching and learning. Even Tommy's father, after spending the morning in teaching Tommy to swim, to dribble the football or to diagnose and repair what is wrong with the kitchen clock, in the afternoon cheerfully writes to the newspapers letters which take it for granted that all lessons are strings of memorizable propositions. His practice is perfectly sensible, yet still his theory is as silly as it could be.

Perhaps the prevalence of this very thin and partial notion of teaching and learning inherits something from the teaching and learning that are done in the nursery, where things such as "Hickory Dickory Dock" and simple tunes are learned by heart from that mere vocal repetition which enables the parrot to pick them up too.

Well, in opposition to this shibboleth, I want to switch the centre of gravity of the whole topic on to the notions of Teaching-to so and so, and Learning-to so and so, that is, on to the notion of the development of abilities and competences. Let us forget for a while the memorization of truths, and, of course, of rhymes and tunes, and attend, instead, to the acquisition of skills, knacks and efficiencies. Consider, for example, lessons in drawing, arithmetic and cricket—and, if you like, in philosophy. These lessons cannot consist of and cannot even contain much of dictated propositions. However many true propositions the child has got by heart, he has not begun to learn to draw or play cricket until he has been given a pencil or a bat and a ball and has practised doing things with them; and even if he progresses magnificently in these arts, he will have little or nothing to reply to his parents if they ask him in the evening to recite to them the propositions that he has learned. He can *exhibit* what he has begun to master, but he cannot *quote* it. To avoid the ambiguity between "teach" in the sense of "teach that" and "teach" in the sense of "teach to" or "teach how to," I shall now sometimes use the word "train." The drawing-master, the language-teacher or the cricket-coach *trains* his pupils in drawing or in French pronunciation or in batting or bowling, and this training incorporates only a few items of quotable information. The same is true of philosophy.

Part, but only part of this notion of training is the notion of drilling, i.e. putting the pupil through stereotyped exercises which he masters by sheer repetition. Thus the recruit learns to slope arms just by going through the same sequence of motions time after time, until he can, so to speak, perform them in his sleep. Circus-dogs and circus-seals are trained in the same way. At the start piano-playing, counting and gear-changing are also taught by simple habituation. But disciplines do not reduce to such sheer drills. Sheer drill, though it is the indispensable beginning of training, is, for most abilities, only their very beginning. Having become able to do certain low-level things automatically and without thinking, the pupil is expected to advance beyond this point and to employ his inculcated automatisms in higher level tasks which are not automatic, and cannot be done without thinking. Skills, tastes and scruples are more than mere habits, and the disciplines and the self-disciplines which develop them are more than mere rote-exercises.

His translators and commentators have been very unjust to Aristotle on this matter. Though he was the first thinker and is still the best, systematically to study the notions of ability, skill, training, character, learning, discipline, self-discipline, etc. the translators of his works nearly always render his key-ideas by such terms as "habit" and "habituation"—as if, for example, a person who has been trained and self-trained to play the violin, or to behave scrupulously in his dealings with other people acts from sheer habit, in the way in which I do tie up my shoelaces quite automatically and without thinking what I am doing or how to do it. Of course Aristotle knew better than this, and the Greek words that he used are quite grossly mistranslated when rendered merely by such words as "habit" and "habituation." The well-disciplined soldier, who does indeed slope arms automatically, does not also shoot automatically or scout by blind habit or read maps like a marionette.

Nor is Tommy's control of his bicycle merely a rote-performance, though he cannot begin to control his bicycle until he has got some movements by rote. Having learned through sheer habit-formation to keep his balance on his bicycle with both hands on the handlebars, Tommy can now try to ride with one hand off, and later still with both hands in his pockets and his feet off the pedals. He now progresses by experimentation. Or, having got by heart the run of the alphabet from ABC through to XYZ, he can now, but not without thinking, tell you what three letters run *backwards* from RQP, though he has never learned by heart this reversed sequence.

I suggest that our initial seeming paradox, that a learner can some-times of himself, after a bit of instruction, better his instructions, is beginning to seem less formidable. The possibility of it is of the same pattern as the familiar fact that the toddler who has this morning taken a few aided steps, tries this afternoon with or without success to take some unaided steps. The swimmer who can now keep himself up in salt water, comes by himself, at first with a bit of extra splashing, to keep himself up in fresh water. How do any formerly difficult things change into now easy things? Or any once untried things into now feasible ones? The answer is just in terms of the familiar notions of the development of abilities by practice, that is trying and failing and then trying again and not failing so often or so badly, and so on.

Notoriously a very few pupils are, over some tasks, so stupid, idle, scared, hostile, bored or defective, that they make no efforts of their own beyond those imposed on them as drill by their trainer. But to be non-stupid, vigorous and interested *is* to be inclined to make, if only as a game, moves beyond the drilled moves, and to practise of oneself, e.g. to multiply beyond 12×12, to run through the alphabet backwards, to bicycle with one hand off the handlebar, or to slope arms in the dark with a walking-stick when no drill-sergeant is there. As Aristotle says "the things that we have got to do when we have learned to do them, we learn to do by doing them." What I can do today I could not do easily or well or successfully yesterday; and the day before I could not even try to do them; and if I had not tried unsuccessfully yesterday, I should not be succeeding today.

Before returning to go further into some of these key notions of ability, practice, trying, learning to, teaching to, and so on, I want to look back for a moment to the two over-influential notions of teaching *that* so and so, i.e. telling or informing, and of learning *that* so and so, i.e. the old notion of propositional cramming. In a number of nursery, school and university subjects, there are necessarily some or many true propositions to be accumulated by the student. He must, for example, learn that Oslo is the capital of Norway, Stockholm is the capital of Sweden and Copen-hagen is the capital of Denmark. Or he must learn that the Battle of Trafalgar was fought in 1805 and that of Waterloo in 1815. Or that $7 + 5 = 12, 7 + 6 = 13, 7 + 7 = 14$, etc.

At the very start, maybe, the child just memorizes these strings of propositions as he memorizes "Hickory Dickory Dock," the alphabet or "Thirty days hath September." But so long as parroting is all he can do, he does not yet know the geographical fact, say, that Stockholm is the capital of Sweden, since if you ask him what Stockholm is the capital of, or whether Madrid is the capital of Sweden, he has no idea how to move. He can repeat, but he cannot yet use the memorized dictum. All he can do is to go through the memorized sequence of European capitals from start through to the required one. He does not qualify as knowing that Stockholm is the capital of Sweden until he can detach this proposition from the memorized rigmarole; and can, for example, answer new-type questions like "of which country out of the three, Italy, Spain and Sweden is Stockholm the capital?" or "Here is Stockholm on the globe—whereabouts is Sweden?" and so on. To know the geographical fact requires having taken it in, i.e. being able and ready to operate with it, from it, around it and upon it. To possess a piece of information is to be able to mobilize it apart from its rote-neighbours and out of its rote-formulation in unhackneyed and *ad hoc* tasks. Nor does the pupil know that $7 + 7 = 14$ while this is for him only a still undetachable bit of a memorized sing-song, but only when, for example, he can find fault with someone's assertion that $7 + 8 = 14$, or can answer the new-type question. How many 7s are there in 14?, or the new-type question "If there are seven boys and seven girls in a room, how many children are in the room?" etc. Only then has he taken it in.

In other words, even to have learned the piece of information *that something is so* is more than merely to be able to parrot the original telling of it—somewhat as to have digested a biscuit is more than merely to have had it popped into one's mouth. Can he or can he not infer from the information that Madrid is the capital of Spain that Madrid is not in Sweden? Can he or can he not tell us what sea-battle occurred ten years before Waterloo?

Notice that I am not in the least deprecating the inculcation of rotes like the alphabet, the figures of the syllogism, "Hickory Dickory Dock," the dates of the Kings of England, or sloping arms. A person who has not acquired such rotes cannot progress from and beyond them. All that I am arguing is that he does not qualify as knowing even that Waterloo was fought in 1815 if all that he can do is to sing out this sentence inside the sing-song of a memorized string of such sentences. If he can only echo the syllables that he has heard, he has not yet taken in the information meant to be conveyed by them. He has not grasped it if he cannot handle it. But if he could not even echo things told to him, *a fortiori* he could not operate with, from or upon their informative content. One cannot digest a biscuit unless it is first popped into one's mouth. So we see that even to have learned a true proposition is to have learned *to do* things other than repeating the words in which the truth had been dictated. To have learned even a simple geographical fact is to have become able to cope with some unhabitual geographical tasks, however elementary.

We must now come back to our central question: How is it possible that a person should learn from himself something which he previously did not know, and had not, e.g., been taught by someone else? This question is or embodies the apparently perplexing question: How can one person teach another person to think things out for himself, since if he gives him, say, the new arithmetical thoughts, then they are not the pupil's own thoughts; or if they are his own thoughts, then he did not get them from his teacher? Having led the horse to the water, how can we make him drink? But I have, I hope, shifted the centre of gravity of this seeming puzzle, by making the notions of *learning-to* and *teaching-to* the primary notions. In its new form the question is: How, on the basis of some tuition, can a person today get himself to do something which he had not been able to do yesterday or last year? How can competences, abilities and skills develop? How can trying ever succeed? We are so familiar, in practice, with the fact that abilities do develop, and that tryings can succeed that we find little to puzzle us in the idea that they do.

Looked at from the end of the teacher the question is: How can the teacher get his pupil to make independent moves of his own? If this question is tortured into the shape: How can the teacher make or force his pupil to do things which he is not made or forced to do? i.e. How can the teacher be the initiator of the pupil's initiatives? the answer is obvious. He cannot. I cannot compel the horse to drink thirstily. I cannot coerce Tommy into doing spontaneous things. Either he is not coerced, or they are not spontaneous.

As every teacher, like every drill-sergeant or animal trainer knows in his practice, teaching and training have virtually not yet begun, so long as the pupil is too young, too stupid, too scared or too sulky to respond —and to respond is not just to yield. Where there is a modicum of alacrity, interest or anyhow docility in the pupil, where he tries, however faintheartedly, to get things right rather than wrong, fast rather than slow, neat rather than awkward, where, even, he registers even a slight contempt for the poor performances of others or chagrin at his own, pleasure at his own successes and envy of those of others, then he is, in however slight a degree, cooperating and so self-moving. He is doing something, though very likely not much, and is not merely having things done to him. He is, however unambitiously and however desultorily, attempting the still difficult. He has at least a little impetus of his own. A corner, however small a corner of his heart is now in the task. The eager pupil is, of course, the one who, when taught, say, to read or spell a few words like "at," "bat" and "mat" travels home on the bus trying out, just for fun, all the other monosyllables that rhyme with "at," to see which of them are words. When taught to read and spell a dissyllable or two, he tries his hand, just for fun and often but not always unsuccessfully, on the polysyllables on the advertisement-hoardings; and just for fun he challenges his father to spell long words when he gets home. He does this for fun; but like much play it is spontaneous self-practising. When he returns to school after the holidays, although his spelling and reading are now far-in-advance of their peak of last term, he will stoutly deny that he has done any work during the holidays. It has not been work, it has been absorption in a new hobby, like exercising a new limb.

His over-modest teacher may say that he has taught this boy next to nothing—nor has he, save for the very beginnings of everything.

However, we should remember that although a total absence of eagerness or even willingness spells total unteachability, the presence of energy, adventurousness and self-motion is not by itself enough. The wild guesser and the haphazard plunger have freedom of movement of a sort, but not of the best sort. Learning how to do new and therefore more or less difficult things does indeed require trying things out for oneself, but if this trying-out is not controlled by any testing or making sure, then its adventurousness is recklessness and not enterprise. He is like the gambler, not like the investor. The moves made, though spontaneous, are irresponsible and they yield no dividends. Nothing can be learned by him from their unsuccesses or from their occasional fortuitous successes. He shoots away, but learns nothing from his misses—or from his fluke hits.

It is just here, with the notion of taking care when taking risks, that there enters on the scenes the cardinal notion of *method,* i.e. of techniques, *modi operandi,* rules, canons, procedures, knacks, and even tricks of the trade. In doing a thing that he has never done before, a person may, but need not, operate according to a method, sometimes, even according to a sheer drill that he has adhered to before. If he does, then his action is still an innovation, although the pattern of his action is a familiar and inculcated one. The poet composes a sonnet, taking care to adhere to the regulation 14 lines, to the regulation rhyming scheme, to the regulation metrical pattern, or else perhaps to one of the several permitted patterns—yet, nonetheless, his sonnet is a new one. No one has ever composed *it* before. His teacher who taught him how to compose sonnets had not and could not have made him compose this sonnet, else it would be the teacher's and not the pupil's sonnet. Teaching people how to do things just *is* teaching them methods or *modi operandi;* and it is just because it is one thing to have learned a method and another thing to essay a new application of it that we can say without paradox that the learner's new move is his own move and yet that he may have learned the *how* of making it from someone else. The cook's pudding is a new one and piping hot, but its recipe was known to Mrs. Beeton in the days of Queen Victoria.

Well, then, what sort of a thing is a method? First for what it is not. Despite what many folk would say, a method is not a stereotyped sequence-pattern or routine of actions, inculcatable by pure rote, like sloping arms or going through the alphabet. The parrot that can run through "Hickory Dickory Dock" has not learned how to do anything or therefore how not to do it. There is nothing that he takes care not to do.

A method is a learnable way of doing something, where the word "way" connotes more than mere rote or routine. A way of doing something, or a *modus operandi*, is something general, and general in at least two dimensions. First, the way in which you do a thing, say mount your bicycle, can be the way or a way in which some other people or perhaps most other people mount or try to mount their bicycles. Even if you happen to be the only person who yet does something in a certain way, it is possible that others should in future learn from you or find out for themselves the very same way of doing it. *Modi operandi* are, in principle, public property, though a particular action performed in this way is my action and not yours, or else it is your action and not mine. We mount our bicycles in the same way, but my bicycle-mounting is my action and not yours. You do not make my mincepies, even though we both follow the same Victorian recipe.

The second way in which a method is something general is the obvious one, that there is no limit to the number of actions that may be done in that way. The method is, roughly, applicable anywhere and anywhen, as well as by anyone. For however many people are known by me to have mounted their bicycles in a certain way, I know that there could have been and there could be going to be any number of other bicycle-mountings performed by myself and others in the same way.

Next, methods can be helpfully, if apparently cynically, thought of as systems of avoidances or as patterns of "don'ts." The rules, say, of English grammar do not tell us positively what to say or write; they tell us negatively not to say or write such things as "A dog *are* . . ." and "Those dogs *is* . . . ," and learning the art of rock-climbing or tree-climbing is, among hundreds of other things, learning never, or hardly ever, to trust one's whole weight to an untried projection or to a branch that is leafless in summer time.

People sometimes grumble at the Ten Commandments on the score that most of them are prohibitions, and not positive injunctions. They have not realized that the notice "Keep off the grass" licenses us to walk anywhere else we choose; where the notice "Keep to the gravel" leaves us with almost no freedom of movement. Similarly to have learned a method is to have learned to take care against certain specified kinds of risk, muddle, blind alley, waste, etc. But carefully keeping away from this cliff and from that morass leaves the rest of the countryside open for us to walk lightheartedly in. If I teach you even twenty kinds of things that would make your sonnet a bad sonnet or your argument a bad argument, I have still left you an indefinite amount of elbow-room within which you can construct your own sonnet or argument, and this sonnet or argument of yours, whether brilliant or ordinary or weak, will at least be free of faults of those twenty kinds.

There exists in some quarters the sentimental idea that the teacher who teaches his pupils how to do things is hindering them, as if his apron-strings coerced their leg-movements. We should think of the inculcation of methods rather as training the pupils to avoid specified muddles, blockages, sidetracks and thin ice by training them to recognize these for what they are. Enabling them to avoid troubles, disasters, nuisances and wasted efforts is helping them to move where they want to move. Road signs are not, for the most part, impediments to the flow of traffic. They are preventives of impediments to the flow of traffic.

Of course we can easily think of silly ways of doing things which continue to be taught by grown-ups to children and adhered to by the grown-ups themselves. Not all methods are good methods, or all recipes good recipes. For example, the traditional ban on splitting the infinitive was a silly rule. But the gratuitous though trivial bother of conforming to this particular veto was negligible compared with the handicap that would be suffered by the child who had never been taught or picked up for himself any of the procedures for composing or construing sentences. He would have been kept back at the level of total infancy. He could not say or follow anything at all if, for example, he had not mastered conjunctions, or even verbs, and mastering them involves learning how *not* to make hashes of them.

How does one teach methods or ways of doing things? Well, there is no simple answer to this. Different arts and crafts require different kinds of disciplines; and in some one particular field, say drawing, one teacher works very differently from another. Sometimes a little, sometimes a lot can be told; there is much that cannot be told, but can be shown by example, by caricature and so on. But one thing is indispensable. The pupil himself must, whether under pressure or from interest or ambition or conscientiousness, practise doing what he is learning how to do. Whether in his exercises in the art he religiously models his strokes after Bradman, or whether he tries to win the praise or avoid the strictures or sarcasms of a feared, respected or loved coach, he learns by performing and improves by trying to better his own and his fellows' previous performances by eradicating their faults. The methods of operating taught to him become his personal methods of operating by his own criticized and self-criticized practice. Whether in spelling, in Latin grammar, fencing, arithmetic or philosophy, he learns the ropes, not much by gazing at them or hearing about them, but by trying to climb them—and by trying to climb them less awkwardly, slowly and riskily today than he did yesterday.

So far I have been, for simplicity, dividing the contributions of the teacher and the pupil by saying that the teacher in teaching how to so and so is teaching a method or way of operating, while the pupil keeps his initiative by making his own at the start somewhat arduous, because new applications of that method. The teacher introduces the pupil to the ropes, but it is for the pupil to try to climb them.

But now we should pay some attention to the fact that pretty soon the pupil has become familiar with the quite general fact that for lots and lots of widely different kinds of operations—spelling, say, skating and bowling at cricket—there exist different *modi operandi*. There are spelling-mistakes and there are bowling-faults, and neither spelling nor bowling can go right unless these faults are systematically avoided. So now, when he undertakes an altogether new kind of operation, canoeing, say, he from the start expects there to be *modi operandi* here too. This too will be a thing that he will have to learn how to do, partly by learning how not to do it. But this time, it may be, there is no one to teach him, and not even any other canoeist to imitate. He has got to find out for himself the way, or anyhow a way, of balancing, propelling and steering his canoe. Well, at first he tries a lot of random things, and nearly all of them end in immersion or collision; but he does after a time find out some ways of managing his craft. He may not achieve elegance or speed, but he does find out how not to topple over and how not to run into obstacles. He is trained, this time purely self-trained, regularly to avoid some kinds of faulty watermanship. But it is because he had previously learned by practice, coaching and imitation the "hows" of lots of other things such as tree-climbing, spelling and skating, that he now takes it for granted that canoeing has its "hows" as well, which similarly can be learned by practice, trial and error, and looking for ways of avoiding the repetition of errors. Here, as elsewhere, he has to study in order to improve; but this time he has nothing to study save his own unsuccesses and successes.

His more reckless and impatient brother, though full of go, just makes a dash at it, and then another quite different dash at it, and learns nothing or almost nothing from the failures which generally result, or even from the successes which sometimes just happen to result. He is not a self-trainer.

The third brother is uninterested, slow in the uptake, scared or idle. He never chances his arm. He tries nothing, and so initiates nothing either successfully or unsuccessfully. So he never learns to canoe; never, perhaps, even regrets not having learned it or envies those who have. There is no question of his training himself in this particular art, or even, if he is a very bad case, of his being trained by anyone else; just as there was fifty years ago no real question of me training myself or of my being trained by anyone else in the arts of cricket or music.

The supreme reward of the teacher is to turn out from time to time the student who comes to be not merely abreast of his teacher but ahead of him, the student, namely, who advances his subject or his craft not just by adding to it further applications of the established ways of operating, but by discovering new methods or procedures of types which no one could have taught to him. He has given to his subject or his craft a new idea or a battery of new ideas. He is original. He himself, if of a grateful nature, will say that his original idea just grew of itself out of what he had learned from his teachers, his competitors and his colleagues; while they, if of a grateful nature, will say that the new idea was his discovery. Both will be right. His new idea is the fruit of a tree that others had planted and pruned. It is really his own fruit and he is really their tree.

We started off with the apparent paradox that though the teacher in teaching is doing something to his pupil, yet the pupil has learned virtually nothing unless he becomes able and ready to do things of his own motion other than what the teacher exported to him. We asked: How in logic can the teacher dragoon his pupil into thinking for himself, impose initiative upon him, drive him into self-motion, conscript him into volunteering, enforce originality upon him, or make him operate spontaneously? The answer is that he cannot—and the reason why we half felt that he must do so was that we were unwittingly enslaved by the crude, semi-hydraulic idea that in essence to teach is to pump propositions, like "Waterloo, 1815" into the pupils' ears, until they regurgitate them automatically.

When we switched from the notion of "hydraulic injection" to the notion of "teaching to" or "teaching how to," the paradox began to disappear. I can introduce you to a way or the way of doing something, and still your actual essays in the exercise of this craft or competence are yours and not mine. I do not literally make you do them, but I do enable you to do them. I give you the *modus operandi,* but your operatings or tryings to operate according to this *modus* are your own doings and not my inflictings and the practising by which you master the method is your exertion and not mine. I have given you some equipment against failing, *if* you try. But that you try is not something that I can coerce. Teaching is not gate-shutting but gate-opening, yet still the dull or the scared or the lame calf does not walk out into the open field. All this does not imply the popular sentimental corollary that teachers should never be strict, demanding, peremptory or uncondoning. It is often the hard taskmaster who alone succeeds in instilling mistrust of primrose paths. The father may enlarge the child's freedom of movement by refusing to hold his hand, and the boxing-instructor or the philosophy-tutor may enlarge his pupil's powers of defence and attack by hitting him hard and often. It is not the chocolates and the sponge-cakes that strengthen the child's jaw-muscles. They have other virtues, but not this one.

THE AUTHORS

Israel Scheffler (1923–   ). The leading figure of analysis in education in the United States; made Harvard a primary center of analytical philosophy and education; specialist in epistemology; provided the primary foundation for epistemological considerations in education. Born in New York City. Graduated from Brooklyn College (1945); M.A. in psychology, Brooklyn College (1948); M.H.L., Jewish Theological Seminary (1949); Ph.D. in philosophy, University of Pennsylvania (1952); honorary M.S., Harvard (1960). Instructor, Harvard Graduate School of Education (1952–1954); assistant professor and lecturer on education, Harvard (1954–1959); associate professor, Harvard (1959–1960); professor of education, Harvard (1961–1962); professor of education and philosophy, Harvard (1962–   ). Awarded Ford Foundation Fellowship (1951–1952); Guggenheim Fellowship (1958–1959). Major publications: editor, *Philosophy and Education* (1958); *The Language of Education* (1960); *The Anatomy of Inquiry, Philosophical Studies in the Theory of Science* (1963); *Conditions of Knowledge: An Introduction to Epistemology and Education* (1965); *Science and Subjectivity* (1968).

William Klaas Frankena (1908–   ). A leading contemporary American philosopher; professor of philosophy at the University of Michigan; specialist in recent developments in moral philosophy; particular interest and study in analysis and reason as related to moral education. Born Manhattan, Montana. Graduated from Calvin College (1930); M. A., University of Michigan (1931); Ph.D. in philosophy, Harvard University, (1937). Instructor in philosophy, University of Michigan (1937–1940); assistant professor, Michigan (1940–1946); associate professor, Michigan (1946–1947); professor of philosophy, chairman of the department, Michigan (1947–1961); professor of philosophy, Michigan (1961–   ); visiting professor at Columbia University, University of Tokyo, Harvard, Princeton. Chairman of the Board of Officers, American Philosophical Association. Major publications: *Ethics* (1963); *Three Historical Philosophies of Education* (1965); *Philosophy of Education* (1965).

Noam Chomsky (1928–   ). Proponent of mentalistic linguistics; the most distinguished leader and scholar in the field of transformational or generative grammar; indicates the consistent logical order of natural language; defines language competence and the requirements necessary for its acquisition by children. Born in Philadelphia. Graduated from the University of Pennsylvania (1949); M.A., University of Pennsylvania (1951); Ph.D., University of Pennsylvania (1955). Assistant professor of linguistics, Massachusetts Institute of Technology (1955–1958); associate professor, Massachusetts Institute of Technology (1958–1962); professor of linguistics, Massachusetts Institute of Technology (1962–   ). Ferrari Ward Professor of Modern Languages and Linguistics (1966–   ). Major publications: *Syntactic Structures* (1957); *Current Issues in Linguistic Theory* (1964); *Aspects of the Theory of Syntax* (1965); *Cartesian Linguistics: A Chapter in the History of Rationalist Thought* (1966); co-author with M. Halle, *Sound Patterns of English* (1968); *Language and Mind* (1968).

Richard Stanley Peters (1919–   ). Britain's most noted philosopher of education in the language analysis tradition; specialist in moral philosophy and reason; applied the analytical techniques to the principles and institutions of society and democracy. Born in England. Educated at Clifton College, Bristol; Queens College, Oxford; Birkbeck College, University of London; Ph.D., University of London (1949). Friends Ambulance Unit and Relief Service, London (1940–1944); classics master, Sidcot School, Somerset (1944–1946); part-time lecturer in philosophy and psychology, University of London (1946–1949); lecturer in philosophy and psychology, Birkbeck College, University of London (1949–1958); reader in philosophy, University of London (1958–1962); Professor of Philosophy of Education, University of London Institute of Education (1962–   ); visiting professor of Harvard Graduate School of Education (1961). Major publications: revised *Brett's History of Psychology* (1953); editor, *The Concept of Education* (1966); co-authored with S. I. Benn, *Principles of Political Thought* (*Social Principles and the Democratic State*) (1959); *Hobbes* (1956); *The Concept of Motivation* (1958); *Authority, Responsibility and Education* (1960); *Ethics and Education* (1966).

Gilbert Ryle (1900–   ). Leader of the Oxford analysts in philosophy; broke new ground in the epistemological studies of the nature of knowledge; clarified knowledge as related to dispositions and mental acts; related education to epistemological considerations giving great emphasis to "knowing how" and performance in educational achievements. Born in England. Educated at Brighton College and Queen's College, University of Oxford. Classical Scholar, Queen's College, Oxford; lecturer, Christ Church, Oxford (1925–1939); sometime junior and senior censor of Christ Church and junior proctor of the university (1926–1939); commissioned Welsh guard, ending as a major (1939–1945); Wayneflote Professor of Metaphysical Philosophy, University of Oxford (1945–1968); retired (1968–   ); Honorary Fellow of Queen's College, Oxford; Honorary member of American Academy of Arts and Sciences (1968). Major publications: *The Concept of Mind* (1949); *Dilemmas* (1954); *Plato's Progress* (1966); editor of the periodical *Mind*.

THREE Emphasis Upon Values (Perennialism)

Humanism

GENERIC NOTIONS AND BASIC THEMES

Several intellectual systems are labeled "Humanism," the term automatically denoting respect and acceptance. However, only one of these systems, which holds the enduring tenets of the dignity of man and the values stemming from Western tradition, can be recognized as the Humanist thought pattern. In terms of the Humanist thought pattern, man is an end, not a means; free, not a slave. These tenets are the standards upon which Western society has traditionally rested and education must preserve for the future. These tenets are not derived from experimental social science nor from mathematical statistics, but from the heritage of the great minds in Western history.

Two important generic notions characterize the Humanist thought pattern. The first is that the values held by a people affect history. When a people's values are of the highest quality, beneficence ensues, while decadence and barbarism are checked. Historically, the great war is the conflict between civilized man and barbaric man—the latter representing undisciplined behavior, crude tastes and manners, false romantic freedom, mass journalistic beliefs, and societies without permanent and enduring standards. Whether civilization rises or falls depends on how it uses the wisdom of the past, and how it puts into practice the moral values of civilized life. This notion implies another theme—that history itself is cyclical, that it consists of the rise and fall of civilizations, and that any particular fall is due to the decline in moral and aesthetic standards and values.

A second generic notion, which relates to the first, is that values are not relative but absolute, eternal, and unchanging. Values are not mere intellectual abstractions but fundamental measures of human experience. They are always pertinent to historical circumstances. This idea implies that human nature does not change and that the problems of history are not unique to particular persons or individual cultures. Human problems are value problems, and since human nature and values never change, the problems are as old as history itself. Thus, any serious issue that faces contemporary man has already been faced by ancient and medieval man. Wise men of the past are the best sources for teaching us the solutions to modern problems. It is up to modern man to use history's lessons if he is to overcome the conflicts of his own time.

The Humanist emphasis on literature relates to the two generic notions of history and eternal values. Great literature focuses on values, and it focuses upon them in a concrete way. That is, the great writings of

literature portray man in his historical circumstances, reaping the consequences from moral decisions and humanistic or barbaric behavior. In
this context, literary masterpieces are rudimentary philosophies of history. They indicate the great humanistic concerns, and reflect values
related to historical causation.

The emphasis on literature provides a clue to a peculiar mode of
Humanism; namely, that the values themselves (outside the initial
suggestion that man has dignity) are inexpressible in the usual sense.
The values are indeed absolute and eternal, prevalent in history, and
wholly reasonable in accordance with nature. But they cannot be stated
in verbal propositions. The only way they can be illuminated is in styles
of literary episodes.

By studying the history of literary writings, Humanists contend that it
is possible to identify some of the related factors in these inexpressible
values. They note two factors in particular. The first is the factor of
reason, not the reason of formal logic or ordinary language analysis, but
reason in agreement with nature. Nature carries within itself universally
the eternal laws of truth, right, and justice. Reason perceives these laws
by envisioning the connection between things in nature, marking natural
causes and effects, linking the future with the past, and identifying
nature's analogies. Reason seeks conformity to nature's laws, and thus
summons man to values and indicates wrongdoings in terms of nature's
prohibitions. An excellent example is the educational classic *Aesop's
Fables*. This work pictures reason in accord with nature indicating to
man right, justice, and truth.

Humanists identify as the second important factor concerning values
conformity to the core of Western intellectual heritage. Because the
values are eternal and reasonable, they have already been identified
indirectly in the outstanding writings of Western intellectuals. The crucial significance of these writings is not the exact content of the expositions, but rather the fact that each treatise rests on the eternal truths.
Inividual Western authors may differ in emphasis and particulars, but all
have in common the eternal core of truth and the acceptance of a
common heritage that makes possible the great conversation of Western
intellectuals. Recognizing the existence of a core that is more basic than
mere cognitive analysis is a factor in the illumination of the inexpressible
values.

Several ramifications follow from the concept of a core. One is that
scholars can use it to identify nontruth. Nontruth is, in reality, off-centeredness, that which does not conform to the core. Those who propose
it do not ground their notions in the eternal values. Nontruth is characterized as "going too far" or "going to extreme," a dangerous malady of
intellectualism. Wherever absolute values are absent, there smolders the

potential spark of extremism. Extremism is dangerous because historically it has led to fanaticism, emotionalism, and sometimes ruthlessness. Humanistic scholarship shows the unreasonableness and danger of off-centeredness by portraying the falseness and evil consequences of extremism.

A second aspect of the concept of a core is that the core reflects the social character of Western heritage and scholarship. Humanism as a philosophy is social in origin and development. An individual contributes to the whole of the core when he affiliates his writings with the truth and with tradition. Personal popularity is an anathema to Humanists. The great scholar seeks only to add to the core, either by producing a work of merit or by clarifying the works of others with a commentary or a gloss.

The role of education in Humanism closely follows the generic notions and themes in the thought pattern. Primarily, education must preserve civilization's concern for absolute values, the intellectual core, and the social character of Western tradition. Thus, the educational program for the young must teach respect for the standards, the heritage of ideas, and the values of Western civilization. Humanists have suggested that this respect must be taught in three main areas.

First, children must be taught to respect language, not the fluctuating language of common usage, but the fixed language of correct forms and absolute order stemming initially from the heritage of Greek and Latin. Civilized man has developed a sense of language perfection, and this sense must not be vulgarized by crude usage. Therefore, education must teach a respect for word etymology and a regard for the eternal order of correct grammar, and it must oppose any journalistic aberrations that occur in the speech and writings of uncultured man.

Respect for ancient Greek culture must also be fostered, because it is in this culture that Western man finds the origin of his Humanistic background. It is the Greeks who first pursued the study of man and the laws of human nature; it is they who created the ideal of a universally valid humanity. Through their genius, they gave to Western society a sense for the permanence of truth and goodness that cannot be dismissed. The young must learn to appreciate the contributions of the Greeks, and to honor their aims of harmony, reason, and the pursuit of ideals.

Children must also be trained to be mindful of the importance of the modern literary pole of academic intelligence. The literary scholars of today must be accorded respect because they have a very important function in society, that of cultural criticism. It is they who must judge the merits and goals of society, for only they have the knowledge of the standards by which the judgment can be made. They must judge music, literature, religion, and education. Society must learn to respect the wisdom of these scholars, and it must come to realize that literary scholarship is on a higher intellectual plain than scientific scholarship because it relates to the more important field of human values.

The educational practices of Humanism reflect the major interests of the movement. Humanists believe that the manner of education must reflect the central concern, respect for traditional Western intellectual values. As a rule, little consideration is given to educational techniques since educational gimmicks and easy methods cannot produce respect. In fact, many educational methods are so foreign to the aims of Humanism that most scholars of this thought pattern consider them detrimental to education. Certain practices, however, are implied by nature of Humanistic aims. The teaching of literature quite naturally is the central focus of Humanistic education. Not only must literature be the most important subject in the curriculum, but it must also be taught more carefully than any other subject. Thus the teacher who reads aloud and discusses with the students the content and values of the great masterpieces of literature has a central role. The teacher must be well trained in the humanities in order to display truth and to enhance the humanizing effect of literature on students. Because of this highly important function, the teacher must always be superior to the students in intelligence and background, and he must always be in a position of authority.

PEDAGOGICAL ORIENTATION— HUMANISTIC FOUNDATION

A Meaning for "Humanism" / JOSEPH W. KRUTCH

"Humanism" has been used to mean too many things to be a very satisfactory term. Nevertheless, and in the absence of a better word, I shall use it here to stand for the complex of attitudes which this discussion has undertaken to defend.

In this sense a humanist is anyone who rejects the attempt to describe or account for man wholly on the basis of physics, chemistry, and animal behavior. He is anyone who believes that will, reason, and purpose are real and significant; that value and justice are aspects of a reality called good and evil and rest upon some foundation other than custom; that consciousness is so far from being a mere epiphenomenon that it is the most tremendous of actualities; that the unmeasurable may be significant; or, to sum it all up, that those human realities which sometimes seem to exist only in the human mind are the perceptions, rather than merely the creations, of that mind. He is, in other words, anyone who says that there are more things in heaven and earth than are dreamed of in the positivist philosophy.

Originally, to be sure, the term humanist meant simply anyone who made the study of ancient literature his chief concern. Obviously it means, as I use it, very much more. But there remains nevertheless a certain connection between the aboriginal meaning and that which I am attempting to give it, because those whom I describe as humanists usually recognize that literature and the arts have been pretty consistently "on their side" and because it is often to literature that they turn to renew their faith in the whole class of truths which the modern world has so consistently tended to dismiss as the mere figments of a wishfully thinking imagination.

In so far as this modern world gives less and less attention to its literary past, in so far as it dismisses that past as something outgrown and to be discarded much as the imperfect technology contemporary with it has been discarded, just to that extent does it facilitate the surrender of humanism to technology. In literature is to be found, directly expressed or, more often, indirectly implied, the most effective correction to the views now most prevalent among the thinking and unthinking alike.

The great imaginative writers present a picture of human nature and of human life which carries conviction and thus gives the lie to all attempts to reduce man to a mechanism. Novels, and poems, and dramas are so persistently concerned with the values which relativism rejects that one might even define literature as the attempt to pass value judgments upon representations of human life. More often than not those of its imagined persons who fail to achieve power and wealth are more successful than those who do not—by standards which the imaginative writer persuades us to accept as valid. And because we do recognize in their re-creations our own sense of what life is like but do not recognize it in the best documented accounts of most biologists, sociologists, political scientists, or psychologists, those of us who are humanists believe the accounts of the poets, novelists, and playwrights to be truer. Literature has been chiefly concerned with the good life as something not identical with the high standard of living and with man as the maker of his destiny rather than as a creature wholly made rather than making. Literature, more than anything else, has kept alive whatever resistance still exists to the various dismal sciences which have come so near to complete triumph everywhere else.

It is no doubt because many people dimly recognize this fact that some "defense of the humanities" has become an expected part of the college commencement address and other formal discussions of the state of the world. But it is because the recognition is wavering and dim that such defenses are commonly so weak and so often take the form of a mere parenthetical remark likely to come down to something like this: "And of course the humanities are important too but I have not time to say more on that subject now." Most of even those who undertake to "defend the humanities" at some length seem often embarrassed by what strikes them as the weakness of their case and to be expressing a sentimental nostalgia for a lost cause rather than faith in a living reality.

What they most usually seem to be saying is that though, of course, it is by science and technology that men *live,* the arts can be expected to furnish certain graces and to provide an opportunity for refined relaxation. Letters and the other arts are, therefore, merely the ornaments of civilized life. But are they not rather, for an age which has little contact with either theology or philosophy, almost the only preservers of what Mr. Oppenheimer calls man's "humanity"?

Listen for a moment to a voice from another age:

"The truth is that knowledge of external nature, and the sciences which that knowledge requires or includes, are not the great or the frequent business of the human mind. Whether we provide for action or conversation, whether we wish to be useful or pleasing, the first requisite is the religious and moral knowledge of right and wrong, the next is an acquaintance with the history of mankind, and with those examples which may be said to embody truth, and prove by events the reasonableness of opinions. Prudence and Justice are virtues and excellences of all times and of all places; we are perpetually moralists, but we are geometricians only by chance."

When Samuel Johnson wrote that passage he was defending what was already beginning to look like a lost cause. To a certain small number of his contemporaries it was, perhaps, still only a powerfully clear statement of an obvious truth. To many others it was a reminder of something men were beginning to forget. But I doubt if there were any to whom it seemed the mere paradox it has by now become. Today the vast majority of thinking men assume without argument that "knowledge of external nature" *is* the great, the frequent, and almost the only legitimate business of men. It is, they think, upon such knowledge of external nature that both our safety and that prosperity by which we set so much store depend. We are not perpetually moralists, and geometricians only by chance. We have become geometricians perpetually and moralists only by chance—if at all.

Moreover, to have become geometricians perpetually we have been led to deny most of Johnson's other fundamental assertions. We may, to be sure, occasionally remember that an acquaintance with the history of mankind is sometimes useful. But even that is useful chiefly to remind us of the follies we should avoid. And even partial agreement stops there.

The dominant schools of psychology and sociology are so far from believing that Prudence and Justice are virtues of all times and of all places that they call upon the dominant school of anthropology to support their contention that *nothing* is true of all times and all places and that Prudence and Justice are so far from being the same everywhere that they do not exist except as abstractions derived from the local and temporary customs prevailing at some time and place. Morals are merely mores. There are cultures but no such thing as culture. There are justices, but no such thing as Justice. We are not merely geometers; we are non-Euclidean geometers to whom one premise is as valid as another and there is no truth except what is logically deducible from one arbitrary premise or another.

The most obvious result of the decision made some two centuries or more ago to consider the knowledge of external nature the greatest, the most frequent, and perhaps the exclusive business of the human mind is the physical world in which we live. Had we not made that decision, we should not produce such an abundance of goods, travel so fast, be able to speak across so many miles to such vast hordes of listeners, or, of course, be in a position to destroy so quickly and so easily whole cities full of our fellow human beings.

The second most obvious result is that loss of which I have just spoken, the loss of confidence in any criteria by which the right and the wrong or even the ugly and the beautiful may be distinguished. That we are the better for this loss of what they insist was a misplaced confidence, many positivists are ready to assert. But it is not certain that a good many of the perplexities, the uncertainties, the anxieties, and the dangers which do perplex this present world—despite the fact that it is so much more abundant and powerful than any previous world—are not related to just this loss.

If man has no true nature as distinguished from what his condition at a given time creates; if no persisting needs, tastes, preferences, and capacities are either met or frustrated by that condition; then there is no reason why he should not be as contentedly "adjusted" to the condition of what Johnson calls a "geometrician" exclusively. But if there *is* such a thing as human nature, and if both man's history and his literature give some clue as to what that nature is; if, indeed, they reveal it more surely than all the polls, questionnaires and tests which "geometry" has been able to devise; then Johnson may be right when he suggests that it is in man's nature to be moral and, perhaps, even religious; that it is, as a matter of fact, in accord with his nature to be a moralist perpetually and a geometer only by chance. And if you do believe this to be true, then it may also seem that the deepest cause of the anxiety which has given its name to our age; that the deepest cause of the fact that man is not so secure, so happy, and so content in his age of power and abundance as it would seem that he should be; that he is, indeed, so frequently forced to seek the aid of psychiatrists or those who can minister to a mind diseased that we are told it is impossible to train as many such ministers as are now needed—if all this is true then, it may be, I say, that the deepest reason is simply this: Man's condition as geometer and as the child of geometry is not harmonious with his nature.

However that may be, we are at least coming to realize more and more vividly something which the earliest proponents of salvation by geometry never suspected, namely, that science is not only the solver of problems but also, at the same time, the creator of other problems. That this is to some extent true, we began to realize a long time ago. We realized, for instance, that the invention of the steam engine created the problem of child slavery in factories. We are also beginning to realize that science creates both abundance and the new problem created by the necessity for endlessly increasing consumption—indeed, for increasing sheer waste —if we are not to be buried and smothered under the load of abundance. And, of course, no other such realization ever came with the dramatic suddenness and the terrifying urgency of the realization that when the secret of atomic fission was discovered we were faced with a problem incomparably more threatening than any which science or technology had previously created.

How is that problem to be solved or even to be approached? The usual answer to such a question when it is asked of relatively minor problems has been: With a hair of the dog that bit you. The answer to the problems created by science is more science.

But does past history suggest that this is how the problems have been solved—when they have been solved at all? In so far as, say, the problem of child slavery was solved, it was not solved by science but by the conscience of mankind. It was man the moralist, not man the geometer, who solved it. It seems indubitably evident that the problem created by atomic fission cannot be solved by more knowledge of the kind which makes atomic fission possible. We come up against the fact, so often asserted and so often unconvincingly denied, that science can tell us *how to do* many different things but not whether any specific thing which *can be done, ought to be done.* It can tell us how to make a uranium bomb and how to make a hydrogen bomb. It can tell how a city full of people may most efficiently, and even most cheaply, be destroyed. But it cannot tell us what city, if any, *ought* to be so destroyed.

Some answer to that question will have to be given. It was given once, more than a decade ago, over Hiroshima. It seems likely enough that we shall have to give an answer again in the possibly not distant future. Whether we did and whether we will again answer it wisely, I will not attempt to say. But one thing is certain. The answer we did give and the answer we will give is not a scientific answer. It was and it will be an answer which depends, not on how man is functioning as a geometer, but on how he is functioning as a moralist.

If morals are nothing but mores, then the answer we will give will depend simply on what deductions are made from the prevailing mores and it will be wise or foolish only to the extent that it is logically consistent with those prevailing mores. But if morals are more than mores; if they are, as Johnson assumed, permanent; and if good morals are defined in terms of what is harmonious with something enduring in man's nature—then the wisdom or folly, the righteousness or the wickedness of the answer will depend upon the extent to which we have a true understanding of man's nature and upon our ability and willingness to act in accordance with it.

Most of even those relativists who are quite convinced that morals are, indeed, nothing but mores, that there is no justice but only conceptions of justice, are ready to grant that the songs and sayings, the folkways and the literature of any people are among the great crystallizers and transmitters of mores and of conceptions of justice. In other words and to be quite specific, it is not science but humanism which will give the answer to the question, "Upon whom and under what conditions shall a city full of human beings be wiped out?"

Probably those who finally formulate and implement the decision will be dimly if at all aware of the ultimate determinants of that decision. Consciously they may well be geometers only, but unconsciously they will be moralists also, because though men may philosophize and moralize well or ill, consciously or unconsciously, philosophize and moralize they must and do. In a civilization like ours, in which only geometry is much regarded, in which the answers that every man must give to moral and aesthetic and metaphysical questions are usually given thoughtlessly and impromptu, most people philosophize badly.

Under these circumstances it is exceedingly odd that those who set out at college commencements and elsewhere to "defend the humanities" should so often seem hard put to find anything very convincing to say; are so prone to speak of mere graces, and to speak in such merely nostalgic—sometimes indeed merely sentimental—terms. "The humanities" are *not* the ornaments of civilization; they are its salvation—if indeed it is to be saved. They are the best embodiments of the most important aspect of that history of mankind which, as Johnson proclaimed, provides us with "those examples which may be said to embody truth and prove by events the reasonableness of opinions." And even if there is no Truth, no Right, no Wrong, and no Justice, then, at least, arts and letters are in any society the principal source of those illusions concerning Truth, Right, Wrong, and Justice which guide its conduct.

Is there any sign, any hope that we will realize in time that we are perpetually compelled to make moral choices as well as to perform certain acts, and that neither technology nor the relativist philosophy can help us to make those choices except at random and without realizing that they are inescapable?

Many of our leading scientists are saying that we are devoting too little time to "fundamental research." We are, they say, using up in technological development our present stock of potentially useful knowledge and are not learning ·enough of that pure science which is pursued for its own sake though it so often turns out to be unexpectedly useful. No doubt they are right. But we ought to be doing more "fundamental thinking" as well as more fundamental research, devoting more time to those large general questions which the boastfully practical generally regard as mere cobweb spinning. In the long run nothing which any pure scientist can add to our knowledge of the atom might have as much effect upon our future as what some philosopher or even some poet may say. We have used up or cast aside our fundamental thinking.

The delusion of power is like the delusion of wealth. The individual thinks that if only he had more money, all would be well. Nations—indeed, mankind as a whole—believe that they lack nothing except more power. If we could only travel faster, build larger machines, and create more destructive explosions we should achieve an even higher standard of living—and no other good is definable. Throughout the ages moralists have—with little effect, however—attempted at least to expose the delusions associated with the desire for individual wealth. Even today some continue to do so. But few are aware that the pursuit of power is also a kind of folly, and many hail even the atom bomb as merely an unfortunate preliminary to those "peaceful uses of atomic power" which will, at last, usher in that Golden Age which none of our other assumptions of power were quite sufficient to create.

In Samuel Johnson's *Rasselas* the inventor of a flying machine refuses to demonstrate his invention because, so he says, men should not be allowed to fly until they have become virtuous. However unassailable his logic may seem, it is hardly worthwhile to suggest that we should simply agree not to develop any new instruments of power until we know just how good use could be made of them. Neither scientists nor inventors would be likely to accept any such general principle. Neither can mere laws or "plans" bring technology under control. If anything could control it, that would be some change in man himself, who will continue to pursue power rather than wisdom just so long as it is in power that he takes the greatest pride. If his heart were elsewhere then he might—just possibly—accomplish things more worth accomplishing than those with which he is now so busy. He might then follow the logic of his own evolving nature rather than the logic of evolving technology. The tail might then stop wagging the dog.

In a recent book, J. Robert Oppenheimer said: "In some sort of crude sense which no vulgarity, no humor, no overstatement can quite extinguish the physicists have known sin; and this is a knowledge thay cannot lose." But what is this sin? Most of those who acknowledge it would answer correctly enough that it has something to do with the invention of the bomb and its use. But is it obviously wrong to beat to the draw an enemy who is trying to destroy you? Only the most uncompromising preachers of nonresistance as an unqualified obligation will say so.

Even more assuredly it is no sin to be a physicist. But if there is a sin of which the physicists were guilty, it was a sin they share with all who follow the faith of our times. It is the sin of believing that *the nature of the atom* is more important than *the nature of man;* that knowledge of matter is more useful, more important, and more significant than knowledge of another kind; that the most valid of injunctions is not "Know thyself" but "Know the Not-Self"; that the key to wisdom is not self-mastery but the mastery of the powers which lie outside of man.

We cannot now "control the machine" because we are hypnotized by it; because we do not really want to control it. And we do not want to control it because in our hearts we believe it more interesting, more wonderful, more admirable, and more rich in potentialities than we ourselves are. We cannot break the hypnosis, cannot wake from our submissive dream, without retracing one by one the steps which brought us more and more completely under its spell.

Those steps were not taken yesterday and they cannot be retraced unless we are both willing and able to reassess the values which the hypnosis has imposed upon us. That would involve a willingness to ask how many of the "advantages" which power has conferred upon us really are advantageous. It would mean also getting rid of all our love of the machine for its own sake, of our delight in the small gadget as well as in the great. But if we did do all that these things imply, then we might begin to recover from our hypnosis.

If there are any signs of such an awakening they are faint and dubious. The main current tends to run in the long-familiar direction. To the average citizen knowledge means science, science means technology, and (a last debasement) the meaning of technology is reduced to "know-how." It took a Russian satellite in the sky to shake our complacency and it was shaken only because it suggested that the Russians had more "know-how" than we. And the lesson most commonly drawn has been that education should put even greater stress upon the development of such know-how, leaving even less time for "fundamental thinking."

Someday we may again discover that "the humanities" are something more than ornaments and graces. Sociology and psychology may again find man's consciousness more interesting than the mechanically determined aspects of his behavior and we may again be more concerned with what man *is* than with *what he has* and *what he can do.* We might again take more pride in his intellect than in his tools; might again think of him as pre-eminently *Homo sapiens* rather than *Homo faber*—man the thinker rather than man the maker. We might—at some distant day—come to realize again that the proper study of mankind is man.

But that time is certainly not yet. We have forgotten that know-how is a dubious endowment unless it is accompanied by other "knows"—by "know what," "know why," and—most important of all at the present moment—"know whether." Quite blandly and as a matter of course we still ask what are the needs of industry, not what are the needs of man.

In the Sanskrit Panchatantra, that collection of romantic tales written down in an early century A.D., there is a fable which might have been devised for today. Three great magicians who have been friends since boyhood have continued to admit to their fellowship a simple fellow who was also a companion of their youth. When the three set out on a journey to demonstrate to a wider world the greatness of their art they reluctantly permit their humble friend to accompany them, and before they have gone very far, they come upon a pile of bones under a tree. Upon this opportunity to practice their art they eagerly seize. "I," says the first, "can cause these dead bones to reassemble themselves into a skeleton." And at his command they do so. "I," says the second, "can clothe that skeleton with flesh." And his miracle, also, is performed. Then, "I," says the third, "can now endow the whole with life."

At this moment the simpleton interposes. "Don't you realize," he asks, "that this is a tiger?" But the wise men are scornful. Their science is "pure"; it has no concern with such vulgar facts. "Well then," says the simpleton, "wait a moment." And he climbs a tree. A few moments later the tiger is indeed brought to life. He devours the three wise men and departs. Thereupon the simpleton comes down from his tree and goes home.

There is no more perfect parable to illustrate what happens when know-how becomes more important than common sense—and common sense is at least the beginning of wisdom.

The ancients had a wise motto: *"Quo Urania ducit"*—Wherever Wisdom leads. We have somehow mistranslated or perverted it. Our motto has become *"Quo Uranium ducit."* And that, of course, is the antithesis of humanism.

The Classics and National Life [1] / SIR RICHARD LIVINGSTONE

The title of my paper is vague and I must define its subject more precisely. The classics include Latin and Greek; am I dealing with both or emphasizing one? They may be regarded as fields of scholarship, as instruments of education, or as influences on the mind and the character; which aspect have I in mind? Let me take the second question first and say that these three aspects are a trinity which cannot be divided. Classical scholarship is the earth from which our studies grow and on whose condition they ultimately depend; not all the products of either the earth or of scholarship are fit for ordinary human consumption and most of them need treatment and transformation before they reach the family table, but as humanity would perish if the earth was destroyed, so the classics would vanish if scholarship disappeared. Classical teaching in schools and universities brings the products of scholarship to digestions with very various powers of assimilation, and needs perpetual thought and revision so that the maximum quantity of food may be healthily absorbed and so that the technique of teaching may not become mechanical routine. But there is another aspect of the classics besides scholarship and teaching. Such names as Goethe, Shelley, Mill, Matthew Arnold, Robert Bridges can hardly fail to suggest the classics, which were a chief formative influence on their minds, but they suggest neither classical scholarship nor classical teaching. They remind us of a further aspect of the classics, apparently unknown to many critics of a classical education and certainly often forgotten in controversy on the subject—the influence of Greek and Latin on the national mind, partly through poets and thinkers whose view of life has been moulded by them, partly through men of action whose early education was predominantly classical. It is with this aspect of the classics and this argument for their study that my address deals. It is the root and centre of the controversy about Greek and Latin, for the question that we discuss when we argue as to the place of the classics in education is whether we wish this influence to persist in national life or whether we feel that it can be dispensed with and discarded; whether their disappearance from our educational system would make little difference or whether it would be a disaster.

[1] Presidential Address to the Classical Association, London, 1941.

"The Classics and National Life" is reprinted from *The Rainbow Bridge and Other Essays on Education* by Sir Richard Livingstone. The Pall Mall Press, London; Clarke, Irwin & Company Limited, Toronto. Used by permission. Deletions have been made by the editor in the interest of brevity.

Approaching the classics from this angle I must talk chiefly of Greek. That is not to underestimate Latin. There are many arguments for its retention as a staple subject in secondary education, but there is one overwhelming reason. The majority of English words are Latin in origin, and without some knowledge of Latin no Englishman has an educated man's grasp of English. Even if a pupil takes Latin only to School Certificate standard, he can get some idea of the fineness and depth of tone in his own language and learn to strike some of its notes more accurately. And, linguistics apart, what intellectual stimulus he can get from being shown the descent of words like "civilization," "liberal," "urbanity," "society." Still, though Latin is indispensable to higher education, Greek is more important in the formation of the mind.

In a world of flux and mortality Greek seems to be one of the few imperishable things; humanity apparently cannot afford to let it die. Latin has survived for historical and practical reasons; it has been in continuous use from the Roman Empire to the present day, first as the *lingua franca* of educated men, then as the international tongue of scholars, and throughout in the services of the Roman Catholic Church; without it no scholarly study of European law and history, of the Romance languages, or even of English and Irish, is possible. But there are no such reasons to keep Greek alive, and it has had no such steady and continuous existence. The stream of Latin has been perennial, unbroken. Greek, like one of the rivers of its own land that vanish in seasons of drought, almost wholly disappeared in western Europe for hundreds of years, till human thirst drew its waters again from their deep cisterns.

There have been three Greek revivals in European history. The first came when Greece lay prostrate in the ruins of its lost independence, and Rome, though mistress of the world, turned to her to learn literature, thought, civilization; a paradox which no one felt more keenly than the Roman who wrote:

Graecia capta ferum victorem cepit.

Then the language, the outlook, and most of the influence were lost in western Europe and a new organization and new ideals took its place. Yet the Middle Ages found these insufficient for its life and turned to the Greeks as if they were the possessors of a great secret, who perhaps could not by themselves save the world but without whom it could not be saved. And this second Renaissance involved something which is unique in history—the revival in western Europe of a language which in those lands was to all intents and purposes dead. There is no more arduous task than to revive a dead language and men will only undertake and succeed in it when they feel a great need, a great hunger. It is characteristic of More's Utopians, who had so little to learn from Europe, that "when they heard me speak of Greek literature and learning (for in Latin there was nothing except the historians and poets that they seemed likely strongly to approve) it was wonderful how enthusiastically they urged me to allow them to learn it under my instruction. So I began to teach them, at first more because I did not wish to seem to refuse the labour than for any results that I hoped from it. But when we had advanced a little, their diligence at once convinced me that mine would not be given in vain . . ." [2] Sixteenth-century Europe did in fact what More imagined his Utopians doing.

The third revival of Greek, less recognized but no less real, began with the opening of the last century and may, and should, continue and increase. I shall say something of it and of some of its leading figures later. It is not comparable with the Renaissance, for its makers had not to revive a lost language, and turned to Greece not for actual knowledge, with which they were better provided already, but for something rarer —wisdom. Their need was spiritual (it is essentially a spiritual need that has caused all these three Greek revivals), and they saw that this two-thousand-year-old literature possessed something indispensable to human life, and wanting in the civilization of their day. They felt, long before the world felt it, the barrenness of the civilization created by the Industrial Revolution, and the need for a life which would embody the virtues for which the Greeks cared most—truth, beauty, and justice. The need is not dead nor the movement. Nothing is more remarkable than the interest in Greek and the appetite for it shown in this country by persons of all types and classes who know no Greek but happen to have come across Greek thought in translation. It is further evidence of the indispensability of Hellenism to a full human life, so that men will not let it die.

A study of these returns to a civilization apparently dead and gone would reveal much of the deeper needs of human nature, which continually deserts the path of its peace but is never permanently contented in error. In each of these Greek revivals there is a search for, and recovery of, some element without which spiritual health is impossible, a quickening and enriching of life. Glance for instance at the influence of Hellenism on the nineteenth century. What would you have expected England to become when the Industrial Revolution transformed it into a manufacturing nation and the Reform Bill of 1832 put the middle classes into power? You would have expected it to become the modern Carthage, all its thoughts given to industry and commerce, its motto

rem facias, rem,
Si possis recte, si non quocunque modo rem.[3]

[2] II, 6.
[3] Horace, *Epistles,* 1, 1, 65.

("Make money, money; honestly if you can, if not, by any
means, money.")

How easily wealth, or the less ignoble but equally immoral ideal of
power, might have become the ruling principle of the nation! And there
is that element in the history of nineteenth-century England. But manu-
facturers and markets are not the only words on its lips. Britain is a great
mercantile power and a great imperial power. But she is something more,
and that is due to two forces in the age which were hostile to materialism
in English life and politics. One was Christianity, the other was Hellenism, both equally hostile to the rule of Mammon or of the Miltonic Satan.
The former, which was much the stronger in the Victorian Age, is obvious
in Shaftesbury, Bright, and Kingsley, the latter in J. S. Mill, Matthew
Arnold and Walter Pater. The two combine in Gladstone and Ruskin.
Christianity and Hellenism were and are the bases of our national
culture, so far as we have one. If a nation possesses a culture, its life
flows on through deeps and shallows, past obstacles, eddies and backwa-
ters, in a steady current. Such a flow English life has so far maintained,
though at the moment this current of our culture is in danger, for the two
streams which form it, Hellenism and Christianity, are both weaker than
they were. In the nineteenth century they flowed strongly. Christianity
was far the most effective and influential, for it touched and coloured the
whole nation, while Hellenism only affected an *élite*. But it was a very
important *élite*. For, with certain exceptions, it was the educated classes
of the country.

I doubt if everyone realizes how important an influence Hellenism had
on nineteenth-century England, or how much of what we admire in it is
due to Greek, which counteracted its besetting sins. Without that element its pattern would have been broken, its texture threadbare and
mean. Take only the field of political and social thought, and consider
some men of the age whose minds and outlook were largely formed by
Greek influence; utilitarians like Mill and Grote, idealists like T. H.
Green, Matthew Arnold and Ruskin, and lesser but influential men like
John Morley, L. T. Hobhouse, Graham Wallas, Henry Sidgwick, Lowes
Dickinson, C. E. Montague, R. H. Tawney, Arnold Toynbee. Innumerable living names will occur to my audience; I will only mention two
eminent present-day representatives of poetry and thought—T. S. Eliot
and Professor Whitehead. Take from these men what Greece taught
them, and how completely they would have been changed! Take them
out of the last century and how you would have impoverished the
thought and action of England! [4]

For one thing English Liberalism would have lost its chief source and

[4] See also R. W. Livingstone, "The Position and Function of Classical Studies in
English Education" in *The Rainbow Bridge and Other Essays on Education* (London: Pall Mall Press, 1959).

most enduring quality. The influence of Greece is not confined to the Liberals. It is as powerful in Newman who hated their creed, in Ruskin who mistrusted it, in Pater who was wholly uninterested in it, in Bridges who was a poet and not a politician. Yet Greece is one of the chief makers of English Liberalism, if we are thinking not of that thin wine associated with the names of Cobden and Bright, but of the rich cordial, which, far back in English thought, is found in More and Milton, who also learnt it from Greece, and of which the grapes were pressed in a brighter land and in days when Manchester was an uninhabited swamp. I am thinking of the Liberalism of Mill and T. H. Green and Gladstone and Morley. It is clearly no accident that they and so many of the most characteristic Liberals of the age were brought up on the classics and drank deeply of the springs of Greece. One of the most famous of them has traced his creed to its origin. "Oxford," said Gladstone, "laid the foundations of my Liberalism. In the region of philosophy she had initiated if not inured me to the pursuit of truth . . . The splendid integrity of Aristotle . . . conferred upon me an inestimable service."

Certain Greek beliefs reappear in the best English Liberalism: the acceptance of reason as a guiding light in human conduct and affairs; the belief that truth is not a ready-made article, retailed by governments or even by churches, but something to be pursued and painfully won; the conviction that liberty is neither a privilege nor a luxury but a necessity in whose absence the human spirit contracts, withers, and finally dies.

But Hellenism is something more than a belief in reason and liberty. These words do not exhaust the contribution of Mill to English political thought, or of Gladstone to English political action, or of Greece to the ideal of human life. They are only part of a wider creed. Gladstone's statement of it is the more interesting, because he was an ardent Christian and churchman and because in him the two spiritual forces of the age, Christianity and Hellenism, combined. His address at Edinburgh University "On the Place of Ancient Greece in the Providential Order" may sometimes be old-fashioned in phrasing but its general conception is sound. He argues that Hebraism teaches the relations of man to God, but he sees clearly that it is not enough; it did not supply "the Christian ages with laws and institutions, arts and sciences, with the chief models of greatness in genius or in character." That was the function of the Greeks who created the ideal of civilization, "a thing distinct from religion but destined to combine with it." "Christianity meant for him a tradition of art, letters and politics, chiefly Greek and Roman in achievement and experiment, illuminated by the Christian revelation and itself contributing to its power." [5]

Hellenism by its influence on the educated class and through it on the

[5] These quotations are from *Gladstone and the Irish Nation* by J. L. Hammond, pp. 54 f.

national life, did much to save the soul of the nineteenth century. What of its uses to our own age?

Anyone who studies it has the inspiration of supreme achievements in art, architecture, literature, thought, politics, human character, and life, and of living with the men who created these and also created, in a world where they did not exist, science and philosophy and, something even more important, the scientific spirit. Further, he has seen most of the fundamental problems of life, not in the complicated forms which they assume in modern society and thought, but in their simplest shape. Take Plato for instance. Each age discovers some new attitude to life: how often Plato has been before it! We have conceived the idea of a planned society. Plato, living in free Athens, drew the first sketch of such a society. In his philosopher-king he anticipated Masaryk and Smuts; and —less happily—in the Nocturnal Council of the *Laws*, the purpose and methods of the Inquisition, if not of the Cheka. The early twentieth century saw the emancipation of women; Plato, in a world where women had neither liberty nor education, argued that they should have the same education and the same spheres of work as men. Hitler has taught and practised the gospel that might is right. In the *Gorgias* Callicles expounds the same doctrine and is answered by Socrates. In the *Laws* the materialist asserts that matter alone is real, and that religion, morals, law, and art are mere human inventions without a basis in nature; and Plato's retort is still the best summary reply to his view.[6]

But to study Greek is to see more than permanent problems and elements of human life. It is to see them fitted into a coherent design. There is nothing more characteristic of the Greek mind than their use (to which we have no equivalent) of two common and recurrent words, κόσμος and ἁρμονία "order" and "harmony" or "fitting-together." Those words reveal the Greek passion for an "ordered," harmonious" existence, in which all the elements and possibilities of human nature are "fitted together," find their place, and work without jar or clash. It is the artistic instinct, applied not to words or stone or marble but to life; a salutary correction to the English temperament which thinks in particulars and not in wholes, and to our age, in which there is so little order, so little "fitting together." The Greeks called the universe κόσμος—a far profounder word for it than "universe"—and they sought to make human existence a κόσμος inside the κόσμος which is its theatre.

Hence to study Greek is to study a great picture of human life; a picture which is not complete, but is the most nearly complete yet painted; which is essentially modern, for reason directs and controls its design; which is human, for its subject is man in his relation to the material universe, to religion, to knowledge and art, to politics and

[6] 889 f.

society. A man brought up on Greek is more likely to know clearly what he thinks, because he has lived with men who knew what they thought, and who formed a clear and consistent view of life. At least he will feel the need for such a view and be uncomfortable without it. Because he has seen this Greek picture of life, he will have a pattern with which to compare his own time, a standard by which to judge it. And he will have seen the world not as an Englishman or a Frenchman or a German or a Russian but as a human being. For Hellenism is a universal and supernational culture which each nation can adapt and modify as its own genius and tradition may suggest, but which, like Christianity, remains a common bond between all its children.

I am not of course suggesting that the Greeks spoke the last word about life—no view could be more untrue to their forward-looking spirit, eager, even in their decadence, "either to tell or to hear some new thing" [8]—or that the study of Hellenism is a complete equipment for the modern world. But it is an unrivalled base from which to go forward: partly because the Greeks were so great, partly because they were so simple, partly because they saw life as a whole and within their limits saw it completely. Greek is no substitute for modern studies, but it is a correction and assistance to them. An American scholar, brought up in his own country on sociology, once told me that he never realized what it was all about till he read Plato. The world of modern studies is so vast and complicated that the student almost inevitably fails to orientate himself in it. He is like a man who begins his study of a continent on a six-inch-to-the-mile map—intimate with details, never fitting them into a whole, unaware even that there is a whole. That perhaps is why Professor Whitehead wrote: "I will disclose one private conviction . . . that, as a training in political imagination, the Harvard School of Politics and Government cannot hold a candle to the old-fashioned English classical education of half a century ago." [9] And in this place I may add another testimonial. "The Oxford School of *Literae Humaniores* seems to my mature judgment the best scheme of education that I have ever heard of. . . . The subjects discussed are the eternal problems of thought, of conduct and of social organization. These are discussed, not by means of contemporary catchwords but by translating them back into another world and another language.[10]

These and other reasons explain the place which Greek has taken in education and its fascination for very different men and ages. But it has a special value and importance for us. In 1914, there was a tendency to look to science for salvation. Science is obviously one of the most powerful forces in the modern world and an indispensable element in

---

[8] *Acts of the Apostles,* XVII, 21.
[9] *Atlantic Monthly* (August 1926)
[10] Logan Pearsall Smith, *Unforgotten Years,* p. 159.

higher education, but few people today would argue that by itself it can make or save a civilization. In 1941 that rôle is assigned to economics or sociology. They too are indispensable to the health of the body of civilization, but they are not concerned with its soul, and have no answer to our deepest problem. As Plato said in the *Charmides*, "It is not the life of knowledge, not even if it includes all the sciences, which creates happiness and well-being, but a single branch of knowledge—the science of good and evil. If you exclude this from the other branches, medicine will be equally able to give us health, and shoemaking shoes, and weaving clothes. Seamanship will still save life at sea, and strategy win battles. But without the knowledge of good and evil, the use and excellence of these sciences will be found to have failed us." Of the truth of these prophetic words we are becoming aware. Our science has not created for us "happiness and well-being." It fulfils its function and bears its amazing fruits, but their "use and excellence" is "found to have failed us" and even to turn to our destruction, because our age, so strong in other ways, is weakest in that "science of good and evil" of which Plato speaks, and which we call a sense of values. Eric Gill, writing of English intellectual and artistic circles years ago, said: "The thing that strikes me most is the absence of any clear leading or sense of direction. R. himself, in the middle of his intellectual salon, sat profoundly on the fence, and all the other people seemed to be balancing themselves nicely in the same way . . . They all believed in beauty, were interested in truth, and had doubts about the good." [11] Fifty years have not made this description less applicable to us.

Ours is a very good age on the technical side; there is nothing wrong with its physics and chemistry, its biology, its mining and metallurgy; its political administration, considering human nature, is not bad. But it lacks that clear purpose which in prosperity guides men to use their resources and opportunities nobly, and in adversity keeps them steadfast and undismayed on their course and sustains them with the certainty of a better day which, if not they, their posterity will see. We live in a world clear, efficient, and creative in the realm of means, but almost wholly at sea about its ends. And our education suffers from and aggravates this weakness. At the best it teaches admirably isolated subjects, mathematics, languages, science, history, literature, technology; but they remain isolated. No common purpose informs and directs its processes. It provides its pupils with the means of living but leaves them in the dark about ends. That is the modern form of putting the cart before the horse: what wonder that the cart jolts so much and progresses so little!

We cannot have too much science, technology, economics, but they lose their usefulness unless we see clearly the ends for which we intend

[11] Eric Gill, *Autobiography*, p. 172.

to use them, and unless those ends are worthy of man. They deal with means and not with ends, and the more we have of them the more we need to strengthen, in both education and life, those studies whose subject is the "knowledge of good and evil." Education, we are often told, should be related to a social background. But a social background includes a spiritual element as well as economics, technology, and political machinery; and these exist for the sake of the spiritual element and not for their own. To ignore that element is to make life material and mechanical, and—what is not always realized—to deprive the machine of its chief motive power. In the modern world it is too often ignored; and part of the greatness of Plato and Aristotle as political and social thinkers is that they never forgot it. There are truths of economics and science: but there are even more important truths in which the mind needs to be dipped so deeply that it never wholly loses the dye—such, for instance, as Aristotle's words, "The state originates for the sake of life; it continues in existence for the sake of the good life." [12] "The chief task of politics is to produce a certain character in the citizens and to make them good and capable of noble actions." [13] "Man, when perfected, is the best of animals, but when divorced from justice he is the worst of all . . . Justice is the principle which brings order into political societies." [14] "The study of what man should be and what he should pursue is the noblest of all studies." [15] It is also the most important. That study fascinated the Greeks and pervades their thought on politics and life. Their success in it may be judged from Goethe's saying that of all men they have dreamed the dream of life best. Their literature is the record of that dream. That is why the world has continually recurred to it, and that, for any age and above all for our own, is the greatest argument for reading it.

· · ·

How incomplete is any serious study of literature without a knowledge of Greek liteature—not because of specific debts which later writers may owe it, but because it is the greatest European literature except perhaps our own, and because it is so unlike our own! To study literature seriously, yet remain ignorant of Greek literature, is like studying religion and remaining ignorant of Christianity. But, however successful our efforts, only a small minority in this or any country will learn Greek. Must the great mass of educated persons remain untouched by Greek thought? The answer is "Yes, unless they study it in translation."

Those who object to translations for such purposes have a case on paper; but only on paper. The Old Testament in the English version is not the Hebrew Scripture; yet we read it with profit. English translations

[12] *Politics*, 1, 2, section 8.
[13] *Ethics*, 1, 9, section 8.
[14] *Politics*, 1, 2, section 15.
[15] Plato, *Gorgias*, 487.

of *War and Peace* and *Peer Gynt* are far from what Tolstoy and Ibsen wrote; yet are we deterred from reading them? Plato in our language is not the same as Plato in his own; yet undeniably the thought and even the eloquence of Plato do stir the reader in a translation. It is of course absurd to go to the opposite extreme and say that nothing is gained by reading the original, if we have a good translation. That is untrue for good prose; it is still more untrue for poetry. It is untrue for modern languages; it is much more untrue for Greek. Those who care for great poetry, great prose, great thought, will always wish to learn the Greek language so that they can read the actual words written by Homer and Aeschylus and Plato and many others. If the Greekless reader missed nothing else, he would miss the most lovely and subtle instument of expression ever devised. But there is such a thing as a ὑδετερος πλοῦς; and sensible people do not refuse to be saved from shipwreck in a cargo boat, on the ground that they never travel in anything less than a liner. No sane person who can read great literature in the original prefers a translation. But our choice is not between the great majority reading Greek literature in the original and their reading it in translation. It is between their reading it in translation or not reading it at all. Who can hesitate between these alternatives?

Assuming that we prefer a knowledge of Greek thought in translation to entire ignorance of it, I would like to make three suggestions. First, the attention should be directed to Greek authors rather than to books about them. No discourse on the Greek ideal of liberal democracy will make the same impression as the statement of it in the second book of Thucydides, any more than a sermon on the Beatitudes can equal the words of St. Matthew. So begin with the Funeral Speech of Pericles, with the speech of the Laws in the *Crito*, with Plato's *Republic* and Aristotle's *Politics*, and go on to Zimmern's *Greek Commonwealth* or Barker's *Political Thought of Plato and Aristotle*. Bring the reader at once face to face with genius itself, and do not let us repeat without any justification a defect of some school teaching of the classics, in which the pupil spends two or three years in preparing to read two great literatures, but never gets a glimpse of them; like a man who goes lion-hunting through a jungle, and instead of lions sees only tangled vegetation in which the lions are supposed to live.

(May I suggest, in passing, a method of avoiding this defect of school teaching? It is worth putting on a blackboard once or twice a week something memorable in the language studied; a phrase from Horace or Tacitus or the Vulgate, a Latin epitaph ancient or modern, a Greek epigram, a line from a tragedy, a sentence from Plato. The class has something to look at in its moments of boredom, is reminded that its labours have a goal, and perhaps stores in memory something to delight and inspire.)

The Greeks then, before books about the Greeks. But if an English reader is thrown straight into Plato or Aristotle or even into Thucydides, unsupported and unhelped, he may crawl to the bank as quickly as he can and avoid the water in the future. This has been the cause of many failures to interest people in Greek. Even more than those who read the classics in the original, the Greekless reader needs an introduction and brief notes. Jowett did a great service by his translation of Plato, but it would have been greater if there had been explanatory notes and rather different introductions. The notes and introductions to Professor Murray's translations of Greek plays are models of what is needed. So are many volumes in the Budé series, especially those of Plato. The Clarendon Press, which has already published the *Apology, Crito,* and *Phaedo* [16] and Aristotle's *Poetics,* in translation, with notes and an introduction for English readers, has published a similar edition of the *Republic* by Professor Cornford. One feature of this edition is the brilliance of Professor Cornford's translation. This takes me to my third point. For our purpose good translations are essential, and by good I mean translations into good English. Most of our readers will know nothing of Greek literature or Greek thought and will come to it with uncertain if not suspicious minds. They will not get far with these new studies if their first impression of Plato (for example) is of a writer without imagination or style who, had he been English, would have used words like "wherefore" and addressed a jury as "O my judges" and a friend as "O my blessed Simmias." The ideal translation of the *Republic* would sound as if Plato had composed it in English, writing somewhat as Newman wrote; certainly it must not appear to be the work of an Englishman unfamiliar with English idiom. Such translations give a far more erroneous impression of Plato than actual errors in interpretation. Some scholars have perhaps too much knowledge and too many scruples to be good translators for our purpose; with a little more ignorance or lack of conscience they would do better.

I would put translators roughly into five classes. Some have done the work so well, that it need never be done again: for instance, Bigg's *Confessions* of Augustine, or Phillimore's Philostratus done into brilliant English, yet reproducing exquisitely the manner of the original. After these I should put such renderings as Rice Holmes's Caesar, Jackson's Marcus Aurelius, A. E. Taylor's *Laws* of Plato, Rackham's Aristotle's *Ethics* [17] and Butler's Quintilian, which on the whole read like original English. (There are of course many others.) Then close behind come a number of translations that will do till we get something better; Jowett's Plato for example. It has many errors, it shows genius in avoiding

[16] Under the title of *Portrait of Socrates.*
[17] Since this lecture was written, a still better version of the *Ethics,* by J. A. K. Thompson, has been published (Allen and Unwin).

difficulties, it is uneven—clearly much less pains were taken with the *Laws* than with the *Republic*—and it only resembles Plato as champagne which has been standing for some hours in a glass resembles champagne. Yet it was a great attempt: it has introduced innumerable people to Plato; and it is far better to read Plato in Jowett than not to read him at all. But Plato still awaits his translator. The late Professor Phillimore suggested Mr. Compton Mackenzie for the task. I suspect that so far as the *Republic* is concerned, Professor Cornford will be found to have done it. In a fourth class I put translations, like North's Plutarch, which are works of literature but reflect the translator rather than the author. Plutarch was not an Elizabethan; he was an enlightened Victorian with the outlook of Dr. Hammond or Professor Trevelyan, and North's English gives a wholly false idea of him. In the fifth class I put translations which have no reason at all for existing—but think it wiser not to give examples.

So far I have spoken only of prose. Poetry is a more difficult problem, for a Greek play in translation must read not only as if it had been written in English but as if it was poetry. Except for Shelley's *Cyclops*, how many Greekless readers had any reason to suppose that Euripides was a poet till Professor Murray translated him? It is arguable that poetry cannot be translated. Yet even here there are degrees of approximation to the original. I should put the *Agamemnon* of Mr. McNeice and Mr. Day Lewis's translation of the *Georgics* very high. The *Oxford Book of Greek Verse in Translation*, which covers the whole field of Greek poetry, shows what can be done in this kind. Prose translations of poetry are not so suitable for our purpose, but Dr. Mackail's renderings from the Greek Anthology show how effective they can be; and though Lang, Leaf and Myers is open to criticism, I have heard a good judge of literature, who is not at all impressionable, say that the death of Hector in their translation was too moving to read aloud.

There are two fields in which this study of Greek in translation can be developed. The first is the school. Shortly before the war a syllabus was drawn up for an optional subject in Group I of the General School Certificate, including Greek Literature and History in Translation, and was submitted to the Matriculation Council of London University.[18] Such a subject would not only enable pupils to learn something about Greek, but also give those teachers up and down the country, who at present teach no classics except School Certificate Latin, opportunities in a different and perhaps more interesting field. It is to be hoped that the project may be revived. But subjects can be studies apart from examina-

---

[18] The study of the classics in translation is now possible at the school stage in the G.C.E. and in university examinations. At Oxford passages in translation are induced in the Greek subject in Responsions and in the Intermediate Examination for Honours in English Literature.

tions and some masterpieces of Greek literature in English should normally be read in the highest forms of schools, so that it may be impossible for any boy or girl, who is capable of interest in such things, to leave school in total ignorance of what are probably the greatest intellectual and literary achievements of European man. Some acquaintance with them is an essential element in a liberal education. Equally important, the necessary books should be in the library of every secondary school. A subject can be encouraged by its inclusion in the curriculum; but also by its appearance on library shelves. Translations from, and books about, the classics should be included in the books recommended in schools for private reading. This is especially important in the lists for higher forms.

But outside the schools there is an equally important and even more neglected field for the study of Greek thought through translations. There are, I am sure, an immense number of persons who have never learnt anything of Greek or Greek thought in early life but who, if they came across it later would find it "a possession for ever." Let me give two instances. A scholarship in Greek was recently founded at an Oxford College by a lady who in middle life became an invalid, learnt Greek in her enforced leisure, and finding in its literature strength and solace in illness, left her fortune to promote its study. My second instance is contained in an extract from a letter written last Christmas by a lieutenant in the Navy to a relation who had sent him a volume of selections from Plato. "I must confess when I opened your parcel I was considerably shaken when I saw the title of the book. But I settled down after dinner last night and for about three hours I was fascinated. I had always held the view that a classical education was out of date and that a scientific education was of more practical use to the schoolboy in after life . . . Well, after reading quite a portion of this little book, which only professes to be a small selection from one man's work, I find it so very true to life nowadays and so very much to the point, that I feel I have missed something. Thank you so much for this present which has opened new fields for me." It would be easy to multiply instances.

I happen sometimes to broadcast to schools about Greek, and I am struck by the number of letters I get from adult listeners who ask where they can read more about Greek thought. Such adults have an advantage over school and university students just because they are adults, and bring to their studies that knowledge of men and affairs without which literature never comes fully to life. The student gets much from reading history and great literature at school and university; but, limited by his lack of first-hand experience of its theme—life and men—he sees its vision of them in a glass darkly. Fuller comprehension comes later, when, having learnt from living what life and its problems are, we read or re-read the masterpieces of poetry and thought.

Here surely is a fertile and untilled field for this Association which was founded "to promote the development and maintain the well-being of classical studies"—a chance to carry out these objects by bringing some knowledge of Greek and Latin in translation to educated persons who have never learnt the languages. It can be done by the private enterprise of members, and, where these exist, by branches of the Association. These are apt perhaps to confine themselves too exclusively to the reading of papers, and might organize play-reading and circles for reading and study, designed for the unconverted as well as for the elect. I believe that this will add in the next generation to those who wish to learn the classical languages. Show the parents what they have missed and they will be more anxious for their children not to miss it. But in this generation it will have results perhaps even more important. It will bring classical thought into channels which otherwise it could never reach. The more successful such efforts are, the more influence the classics will have in moulding the national mind. And that is the real issue. For, as I said earlier, in discussing the place of Greek in education, we are discussing the future of English thought, and perhaps of western civilization. We have a missionary task, deserving missionary fervour. And, as with all missions, it is a task for the individual as well as for the society.

PSYCHOLOGICAL DIMENSION

Literature and the Nature of Man   /
THEODORE SPENCER

. . . If we think of it as a whole (Shakespeare's picture of man's nature), we can see that his work embodies, more completely than that of any other artist, the primarily artistic vision. To see it as a whole is essential. As T. S. Eliot remarks, "the standard set by Shakespeare is that of a continuous development from first to last, a development in which the choice both of theme and of dramatic and verse technique in each play seems to be determined by Shakespeare's state of feeling, by the particular stage of his emotional maturity at the time. What is 'the whole man' is not simply his greatest or maturest achievement, but the whole pattern formed by the sequence of plays; so that we may say confidently that the full meaning of any one of his plays is not in itself alone, but in that play in the order in which it was written, in its relation to all of Shakespeare's other plays, earlier and later: we must know all of Shakespeare's work in order to know any of it." [1]

[1] T. S. Eliot, *Selected Essays* (New York, 1932), p. 170.

And as we look at all of Shakespeare's work, and try to derive from it his view of the nature of man, two facts emerge. In the first place there is the "continuous development" of which Eliot speaks, the development that begins with a period of experimentation—what we might call Shakespeare's "external" period—a development that continues with an enormous increase in dramatic scope and that presents the evil in man's nature with tragic force, a development that ends with acceptance, with regeneration, with a vision that sees human life as it is and sees it redeemed.

The second fact that emerges from our picture of Shakespeare's work as a whole—and this is something at which I have previously only hinted —is that though he drew very largely on what he inherited of the conventional concepts of man, and though his picture of man's nature would have been very different without them, nevertheless Shakespeare's vision of human life transcends anything given him by his time. The inherited concepts represent, of course, one particular codification of what is permanently true about humanity, and when a civilization lacks such codification, that civilization is in danger. But Shakespaere's presentation of Hamlet, of Lear, of Cleopatra, of Imogen and Miranda goes deeper than any codification: it is the individual human life, the thing itself underlying codification that Shakespeare gives us, and which makes him, in Ben Jonson's familiar phrase, "not of an age but for all time."

If we keep these two aspects of Shakespeare's vision of man in mind we may perhaps be able to accomplish the last of the three aims with which this discussion began. We have so far tried to see Shakespeare in relation to his time, and we have tried to see how his craftsmanship enabled him to use what his time gave him. The final problem remains: we must try to judge Shakespeare's work in relation to what we believe to be true of human experience as a whole. For the conflict between order and chaos, in the world, the state and the individual, the difference between appearance and truth, the search for what is most natural to man—these are the central problems of human thought; they were as pressing in the age of Aeschylus as they were in the age of Shakespeare and as they are today. The greatest writers have, directly or indirectly, always been concerned with them, and though these problems may take on different forms in different periods, it is only their accidents that change; the essence remains the same.

Since art, as Aristotle says, is an imitation of life, the individual artist is necessarily compelled to imitate the life of his own period, and it is clear enough that certain periods are more favorable to good art than others. It is also clear that there are different kinds of imitation, even in the same period, and that a writer like Ben Jonson, who is concerned with the surface of experience, who describes social vice rather than spiritual evil, whose characters, unlike Shakespeare's, never look inward or experience an inner division—it is clear that a writer like Jonson will give us a different picture of his period from that of a man who probes more deeply and resolves more conflicts. It is not with Ben Jonson, or others like him—admirable in their own sphere though they may be—that Shakespeare should be compared. He should rather be compared with those writers, and they are not many, who used the views of their time to see human nature in its broadest terms, and whose imitation of life is an imitation not only of man in relation to society, but also in relation to himself and to the larger forces by which he feels himself controlled.

The periods in which the greatest writers have flourished have been those which, like Shakespeare's, have enabled the writer to use all three relationships; and this means that they have been periods when the writer's medium has been close to the life of the people. In such periods the artistic form has been traditional in the sense that it has been taken for granted, as the drama was taken for granted in the time of Aeschylus and Shakespeare, the allegorical vision in the time of Dante, and the novel in the nineteenth century. And in each of these periods there seems to have been a heightened consciousness of the precarious balance in human affairs between order and chaos, with varying emphasis on religion, the state and the individual.

The *Oresteia* of Aeschylus, more than any other dramatic unity, represents a completely fused relationship between literature and society. As Professor Thomson has recently shown,[2] it was produced at a time when the drama had an intimate connection with religious and with social forms, and hence we find in its magnificent conception an interweaving, a fusion, of the three realms of man's being, the religious, the social and the individual; in the *Oresteia* an essential problem of man's nature is solved in relation to the gods, to the state and to himself. Orestes, the central figure of the trilogy, has killed his mother Clytemnestra because she had previously killed his father Agamemnon, and the moral problem he faces is whether or not he should be punished for having tried to avenge one crime by committing another. The situation is similar in many respects to that of Hamlet,[3] but it is treated very differently. The play of *Hamlet* is equivalent, as far as the action is concerned, only to the second part of the trilogy of Aeschylus, and if Shakespeare had wanted to treat Hamlet's story as Aeschylus treated that of Orestes, he would have had to write an introductory play about the murder of Hamlet's

[2] George Thomson, *Aeschylus and Athens* (London, 1941). Mr. Thomson writes (p. 297): "The great plays of Shakespeare were not immediately and consciously related to the social movement of his time; in the *Oresteia* the citizens of Athens witnessed the history of their civilization, culminating in a festival in which all of them annually took part."

[3] See Gilbert Murray, *The Classical Tradition in Poetry* (Cambridge Mass., 1930), pp. 205 ff.

father and a concluding one which would have assumed that Hamlet's revenge had been successful, but that he was now himself on trial before a court of supernatural powers. We can imagine the first play easily enough, but the last one is inconceivable in terms of Elizabethan drama. In the *Oresteia* of Aeschylus, on the other hand, the last play, the *Eumenides,* is the essential culmination of the whole story. When Athena solves the problem of Orestes' individual guilt she at the same time solves the problem of man's relation to the supernatural by appeasing the Furies, and she solves the problem of justice in the state by establishing the court of the Areopagus. The three realms of ethics, religion and government are all brought together in one solution, in one reconciliation. The intimate relation between drama and the life of the people in fifth-century Athens, combined with his own extraordinary genius, enabled Aeschylus to create a work which fused into a single unity the three essential aspects of the nature of man.

The other Greek dramatists accomplished nothing so grand as this. Yet if we think of the plays of Sophocles in chronological order—though general speculation about them, since only a small percentage of them has survived, cannot be very securely based—we can see that the view of human life which they present also ends in a reconciliation, like the end of the *Oresteia* and like the last plays of Shakespeare. *Oedipus at Colonus,* the play of Sophocles' old age, shows us Oedipus after his terrible ordeal, exiled and blind, stern and awe-inspiring, but no longer the proud and self-willed man whom Fate had so dreadfully punished. His death is miraculously calm:

> It was a messenger from heaven, or else
> Some gentle, painless cleaving of earth's base;
> For without wailing or disease or pain
> He passed away—and end most marvelous.[4]

His death also is surrounded by wider implications, for it is heralded by a thunderstorm sent by Zeus, and, because he dies on Athenian soil, Athens will be forever preserved from her enemies. The death of the individual hero is related to the gods and to the state.

The use of the *deus ex machina* by Sophocles in the *Philoctetes* and by Euripides in nearly all his plays may be seen as another method of giving universality to the individual action, and of relating human concerns to the supernatural powers that control them. But in the hands of Euripides this device becomes only too often merely a mechanical trick, and we feel that Euripides, here as elsewhere, is unscrupulously manipulating his plot in order to give his audience a false satisfaction that has no basic relation to a view of human experience in general; he is striving for

[4] Ll. 1661 ff., trans. F. Storr, Loeb Classics.

results that will surprise his audience rather than fulfill their expectations. There is a great difference between the Athena of Aeschylus, who solves the moral problem of Orestes with such rich social and religious connotations, and the Castor and Pollux of Euripides who appear at the end of Euripides' version of the story. The *dei ex machina* of Euripides merely describe what will happen to Orestes as a result of the murder, there is no weight of social implication; the effect, as usual with Euripides, is not an effect of grandeur but of pathos, and we think chiefly of Orestes himself, not of a world restored to order.

There is a striking parallel between Euripides and the dramatists, such as Webster, and—on a lower level—Fletcher, who immediately followed Shakespeare. In each case we find a kind of irresponsibility, an emphasis on the unusual, a fondness for solving the problems of plot by some external means, like a *deus ex machina*—all of them characteristics which may be immediately successful on the stage, but which illustrate a view of man's nature that tends to disintegration, to a divorce between literature and the essential concerns of man. In each case we feel that individualism is glorified, instead of being made, as it is in Shakespeare, one of the attributes of villainy, and when this happens in the thought and literature of an age, that age is on the road to decadence. For it means that one of the three realms in which man lives is being emphasized at the expense of the others, and that the proper balance between the individual, the state and the forces behind Nature has been lost. The part—and the same thing is true of all romantic literature—becomes more important than the whole, as it never does in Aeschylus, Sophocles or Shakespeare.

Nor does it, of course, in Dante. *The Divine Comedy* is the most perfectly ordered poem ever written, and the chief element in its order is Dante's use of the medieval view of life to present man in relation to the three realms of his being. In fact it would be possible to use the poem as an illustration, perhaps the best illustration, of the orderly view of the cosmos, the state and the individual which I described in the first chapter as so important a part of Shakespeare's intellectual and emotional inheritance. In *The Divine Comedy* the spheres of the Ptolemaic heavens correspond to various states of intellectual being and of moral purity; they control everything on earth, and, in Dante's words, "direct every seed to some end according as the stars are its companions" (*Purgatorio* xxx). To Dante man's worst sins are those by which his special faculty of reason has been corrupted, and throughout the poem man's function as a citizen receives equal emphasis with his function as a rational animal; his duty to the state is as much a part of his nature as his duty to God. And after Dante has described the whole orderly universe, disordered only by man's wrong use of his free will (and even that disorder is taken care of by the ordered punishments of Hell and Purgatory), at the end of the poem he finds beneath the order the unity that is its soul, and in the final vision he sees all the individual accidents and substances which are scattered in leaves through the universe "bound up by love in one volume."

In its final emphasis nothing could be more different from Shakespeare than this; though to Dante man's behavior in time may determine his place in eternity, Dante is primarily concerned with the eternal rather than the temporal world. His subject matter is as different from Shakespeare's as the form of the allegorical vision is different from the form of the drama. Yet though Dante may describe order and the life that begins with death, while Shakespeare in his tragedies describes chaos and the life that *ends* with death, nevertheless Dante and Shakespeare have one thing in common, for both use the same views of man's nature for their very different purposes, and like the greatest of the Greek dramatists, see man's situation in relation to the three realms in which his thought and action move.

The greatest novelists treat human experience in the same way; we have only to think of Tolstoi's *War and Peace* to realize that if the nature of man is to be fully presented in literature, the same fundamental relationships must inevitably be included. Tolstoi's account of Prince Andrew and of Pierre, of their relation to peace and war, includes a description of their relation to the external forces that move them and to the society in which they live, as well as a description of the various ways in which they try to find a moral basis for action. It is because *War and Peace* contains all these things, these central relationships in which man sees himself, that it is a touchstone by which other fiction can be judged. By its side the work of Dickens, even the work of Flaubert, takes on a smaller dimension, for Dickens and Flaubert do not describe so *much* of what we believe to be true of human nature. In the long run the criterion of literary greatness must be not only qualitative but quantitative as well; quantity, or scope, as far as the vision of human life is concerned, being itself the final quality.

Tolstoi's description of man's nature differs, however, from those of Aeschylus, of Dante and of Shakespeare. For in the earlier periods of human history it was much easier than it was in the nineteenth century to take a positive attitude toward man's primary relationships; in fifth-century Athens, in the Middle Ages and in the Renaissance, thought on the subject was far more clearly formulated than in Tolstoi's day. The earlier periods gave the writer a set of beliefs, the nineteenth century gave him a set of questions, and in no respect does Tolstoi more clearly reflect his time than in the way he presents Pierre Bezukhof, his main character, as *seeking* for answers to the meaning of life. Aeschylus, to be sure, is more original, more a creator of his own belief, than either Dante or Shakespeare, but Aeschylus could rely much more firmly than Tolstoi was able to do on a community of belief, just as he could relate his dramas much more closely to the social concerns of his audience, grouped together in a theater, than Tolstoi could relate his novels to his nineteenth-century readers, miles away from each other, scattered in a thousand arm-chairs.

Yet Tolstoi's questioning, so far as *War and Peace* is concerned, does produce an answer; an answer that is closer to Shakespeare's, perhaps, than those of Aeschylus and Dante. He also comes back to the individual experience, to the simplicity of the facts, to the marriage of Pierre and Natasha, to their life in their children, to that which is. The end of *War and Peace* lacks the exaltation of Shakespeare's last plays, because the medium is not poetry, but the meaning is the same. It is richer than the conclusion of Voltaire's *Candide,* whose hero shrivels into the restricted conviction that the only thing to do is to cultivate one's garden; it has a warmer human truth than the end of Goethe's *Faust,* whose hero self-consciously reclaims a swamp for the impersonal benefit of mankind.

When we think of the literature of the past in such general terms as those which I have been using, and which are universally applicable both to the life of action and to the art which interprets it, we are bound to have in our minds the thought of our own literature and our own lives. What strikes us at first is the contrast between the past and ourselves.

At the height of the Italian Renaissance, when, toward the end of the fifteenth century, the tradition of humanism was being felt with a new vigor and man's crucial position in the world of created nature was being re-stated with new force, Pico della Mirandola summed up the traditional thought of his time in his famous *Oration on the Dignity of Man.* To Pico, as to his contemporaries, man was in the center of things, since by the right use of his reason and his will, he could choose whether he would live the life of the angelic intellect or the life of the brutish senses. Heaven and hell were on either side of him, and, as the chief inhabitant of an ordered universe, his responsibility was to see that he played a conscious and rational part in the marvelous structure which the divine architect had created for him, so that he could praise the God who made him. Out of that view, that dramatic tension of responsibility, grew the drama of Shakespeare.

What has our own time to say that would be as typical of the twentieth-century view of man's nature as Pico's view was typical of the Renaissance? What can we say of the dignity of man?

At first sight it would seem that we could say very little. We see ourselves today as living on a minute satellite of a tiny solar system that is of an almost infinitesimal size compared to the hugeness of the galaxy to which it belongs, a galaxy that is itself only a small part of the material universe. We can comprehend our universe only in terms of mathematical formulae, we cannot see it. And our existence on this unthinkably small planet seems to have come about by accident. A set of apparently chance events started the peculiar biological process called life of which we are the temporary products. Both the space and the time which have produced us are incomprehensibly huge. And, to shift the focus, we owe what we are, not to our wills, but to a set of predetermined forces, the accidents of birth and environment, which decide what sort of beings we will be long before we are conscious of being. Our unconscious desires turn us this way and that, like weathervanes, and if we are to be happy, we are told, we must let the wind blow us where it pleases. "I think I could turn and live with animals," says Walt Whitman, "they do not make me sick discussing their duty to God." We pay a kind of lip-service to reason, but we trust our instincts more than we do our brains. We have lost any real belief in the capacity of intellect to dictate our actions, and our prevalent theory of education persuades us to adopt as our principle of behavior the motto which Rabelais put over the entrance to his Abbey of Thélème, "Fais ce que voudras"—Do what you please—without any of the Stoic principles of order which Rabelais had assumed the inmates of his Abbey to possess before they went there.

Believing ourselves to have no necessary relation to the cosmos, and to be at the mercy of our unconscious impulses, and hence finding ourselves in an unsatisfactory relation to two of the three aspects of our situation as human beings, we are in danger of over-emphasizing the importance of the third aspect, and of seeking in our relation to the state a compensation for the impersonality of the universe and the impotence of our wills. In some countries this over-emphasis has already gone almost as far as it can go, and the countries that remain are being forced into temporary imitation in order to destroy their rivals so that the balance may be restored.

In other words, as we look today at man's relation to the three aspects of his world, we seem to be facing a depressing and belittling situation, and our concept of the insignificant nature of man seems unlikely to produce any permanent expression of human life, in literature or elsewhere, that can compare with the expressions of the past.

And yet, if we consider more deeply, and take into account the possibilities of the future, this gloomy picture, which was given in such different terms at the beginning of the seventeenth century,[5] represents only a partial truth. Though some aspects of science—which bears the same relation to the thought of our day as religion did to the thought of the sixteenth century—seem to make man hopelessly insignificant, other aspects present him as occupying a more favorable and important position. From one point of view contemporary scientific thought about man

[5] For example the early seventeenth century, as represented by Godfrey Goodman (above, p. 26), thought of the decay of Nature as caused by original sin; we describe it by the second law of thermo-dynamics.

is even parallel to the religious thought of Shakespeare's day. For example Mr. Julian Huxley, in his essay on "The Uniqueness of Man," after discussing the differences that science observes between man and animals, remarks that "biology . . . reinstates man in a position analogous to that conferred on him as Lord of Creation by theology. There are, however, differences," he continues, "and differences of some importance for our general outlook. In the biological view, the other animals have not been created to serve man's needs, but man has evolved in such a way that he has been able to eliminate some competing types, to enslave others by domestication, and to modify physical and biological conditions over the larger part of the earth's area. The theological view was not true in detail or in many of its implications; but it had a solid biological basis." [6]

If man's importance can thus be formulated by the impersonal and long-range view of science, can we derive similar convictions by examining the more immediate and local situation? Biological science describes man in relation to Nature; is there any evidence at the present time that man's relation to his own consciousness and to the state promises anything more satisfactory than psychological or economic determinism would pessimistically describe?

If an awareness of the problem indicates the possibility of a more hopeful answer, we can, I believe, say "Yes." Of course it is far more difficult in our own time than it was in Shakespeare's to say that any one view is typical of the age or predominant in it, for variety of opinion is much greater with us, but there can be little question that serious thought about man's nature is at the present time moving away from determinism to a view that re-establishes some psychological hierarchy in man's structure. The old emphasis on reason and will, the division of man's mind into faculties, is not likely to be re-accepted, any more than what Mr. Huxley calls the theological view of man's relation to the other animals is likely to be re-accepted. But just as that theological view is recognized to have had "a solid biological basis," so the old concept of an element in man's nature which can know and can direct is recognized as having a solid psychological basis. "There is nothing in the intellect which was not first in the senses," said Locke. To which Leibniz replied, "Only the intellect itself." And modern psychology, returning to the central problems of man's nature, is trying to describe that "intellect" in terms consistent with scientific knowledge. "Mental life at its best," says one of the most distinguished of contemporary psychologists, "exhibits a consistency, a coherence, and a hierarchy of values." [7] And it is on this fact that emphasis is now being laid with increasing force; the higher,

[6] Julian Huxley, *The Uniqueness of Man* (London, 1941), p. 5.
[7] Wolfgang Köhler, *The Place of Value in a World of Facts* (New York, 1938), p. 411.

rather than the lower aspects of man's nature, are being re-examined and re-defined.[8] What is chiefly lacking (and it is a very large lack indeed) is an intellectual and emotional sanction—a conviction of truth like that which the Christian system gave in the sixteenth century—which will make the higher impulses of the mind seem the right ones to obey.

Certain people, as we know too well, have found a sanction in the state, but the sanction they have found is evidently not the kind that demands the use of man's highest faculties. And that is why, in government as in psychology and in science, fresh thought is being given to the old problems; necessity is forcing us to re-define our concept of the relation of the individual to the state. Here, as in natural science and in psychology, a change is taking place, and just as materialism and determinism have had to be abandoned because they do not fit the facts, so our unthinking acceptance of the nominal form of democracy, where the average citizen has had little or no relation or responsibility to the state —this also has had to be abandoned because it does not fit the facts. Upon the new order that may result, all our lives depend.

In other words the gloomy picture of man's present relation to the three aspects of his world, the picture which seems so easy to paint, need not, and, if our civilization is to survive, *must* not, be the right one. It gives only half the truth, just as the pessimism of the early seventeenth century gave only half the truth. And if we think of ourselves in relation to that period, and in relation to the two different views of man's nature which that period expressed, it would seem, as I suggested in the preface to this book, as if a three-hundred-year cycle were coming to a close. What brought about the essential conflict in Shakespeare's day was the fact that the old views of man were being broken by new discoveries which widened the split between what man should be and what he was, and which made the reality seem evil under the appearance of good. Order was breaking into chaos. And in the course of the three-hundred-odd years between that time and our own, the consequences of those new discoveries have been pushed, it appears, as far as they will go. Galileo's confirmation of Copernicus has become the cosmology of Einstein, Montaigne's comparison of man to animals has become a philosophy in which impulse and determinism are seen as the masters of behavior, Machiavelli has helped to produce what may be only the first of a series of Hitlers. Those once disruptive forces have almost created a new world of their own. But, as I have tried to indicate, their mastery is perhaps an appearance, and when the first half of the twentieth century

---

[8] I refer, not merely to the professional psychologists, but to those writers who are reconsidering the whole problem of man's nature. See W. Macneile Dixon, *The Human Situation* (New York, 1937); Sir Charles Sherrington, *Man on His Nature* (Cambridge, England, 1940); F. T. Stace, *The Destiny of Western Man* (New York, 1942).

is regarded three hundred years from now, as in this discussion we have regarded the early seventeenth century, our situation may perhaps be seen as the reverse of Shakespeare's, and our time may be described as a time when the new forces were not disruptive but collective, and when man's orderly relations to the three aspects of his world were not broken, but restored in a new shape.

If this is to happen—and enormous resources of thought and activity will have to be used to make it happen—literature will inevitably reflect the situation. Prophecy is, in such matters, rash, but we can safely say that if a first-class writer is to appear in our century he will have to present, in an artistic form that is taken for granted by his audience, the individual experiences of human beings in relation to themselves, to society, and to the larger forces that control them. The best writers of our generation have already recognized this responsibility, and any future historian of our time, in considering the work of Thomas Mann, of Proust, of Eliot, Yeats and Joyce (and there are others besides these), will see that each of them, in various ways, has been seeking for that ordered pattern of relationships which is the only true universality. Perhaps, for a complete expression of our age, we shall need a writer greater than any of these. Or we may, as seems likely, find that our time will be expressed in another form than that of the merely written word; the movies and the radio are closer to our lives than anything on a page. But whatever medium he may use, it is clear enough that the great interpreter of human life in our century, if he appears, will have to be in as intimate touch with the central problems of our thought and emotions as was the dramatic art of Shakespeare with the Renaissance conflict about man's nature.

But Shakespeare was in touch with something more than his age, and if we are to come back to our starting-point and try to arrive at a final view of his work as a whole, we must see it as a reflection of deeper truths than any that can be described by a local and temporary picture of the cosmos, of psychology, or of the state. Beneath any view of man's nature, at the very basis of human experience, are the elementary facts of birth, of life and of death. The rhythm of their sequence and renewal lies behind all our knowledge and emotions, and it is the rhythm that we share with all of living nature, with animals and grass. The earliest known religions are based on it, and so is the earliest literature. Birth, struggle, death, and that which is beyond death—these, as Gilbert Murray says, are the subjects of that primitive dance and song "which is the fountainhead of ancient classical poetry." [9] They have been the essential subjects of all great literature ever since, as they were the subject of the

[9] Murray, *op. cit.*, p. 51.

morality plays which were so important a part of Shakespeare's technical background. And if we think of Shakespeare's work in relation to this essential pattern, this fundamental rhythm, we shall have, perhaps, a view of the sequence of his plays that will both underlie and transcend any view that we can obtain by thinking of his work merely in relation to the ideas of his time. "Shakespeare," said Keats, "led a life of allegory; his works are the comment on it," and we may interpret this somewhat puzzling remark by remembering that Shakespeare's career was divided into three stages: a period of experiment and adaptation, a period of tragic vision, and a period of affirmation. Birth, struggle, death, and renewal; these are not only the themes of the individual final plays, they are the themes which describe the course of Shakespeare's work as a whole, from his earliest plays through *King Lear* to *The Tempest*. Such, we may say—as we think of art and life together, so that historical description and technical analysis merge into an understanding of the symbolism of all men's lives—such was the allegory of Shakespeare's life: to have illustrated in his own work more richly than any other writer, that rhythm, that sequence, that vision, which all human beings must recognize and accept as fundamental to the nature of man.

SOCIAL CONCEPTS DIMENSION

The Aims of Education / T. S. ELIOT

. . . In what I wrote about education several years ago, a critic finds an inconsistency. He says, "Mr. Eliot's chief complaint of other writers on education is that they seek to use the schools to achieve social purposes they have at heart. Then he falls into the pit he has digged for others: he wants to use the schools to advance social purposes of his own." Now, I do not think that anybody can think seriously about education who is devoid of social purposes of his own; and I am sure that these social purposes will guide him towards some of his conclusions about education. For anyone who denies that education should have a social purpose will be omitting something without which it is not education. But I think that anyone who considers education in relation to social purpose should try to be quite clear as to what social purposes guide his own theory of education; which are peculiar to himself, or to a group whose views are not shared by some other group; which he believes to apply to the society to which he and his sympathizers belong; and which, if any, apply to every society.

What I have been saying before, therefore, was intended to elicit the fact that the meaning of the term "social purpose" is subject to a good deal of variation. In a liberal democracy it should mean something discernible in the mind and temperament of the people as a whole, something arising out of its common ethos, which finds expression through a variety of intellectual leaders holding varied and sometimes conflicting opinions. In a totalitarian society, it may mean something formulated in the brains of a few persons in power, deduced from a particular political-social theory, and imposed by every means of compulsion and indoctrination, so that it may in time become integrated into the common ethos. This is a very different kind of social purpose. In a liberal society every writer on the subject will have some social purpose of his own; something he wishes to retain, restore, or introduce through the means of education. Therefore he should know himself how far his assumptions are his own, and how far he is justified in assuming that they are shared by all intelligent men of good will. He should, in short, examine his premises.

Now as education, it has been agreed, has several aims, the social purposes have to be guarded from interfering with the other aims; and also, we have to allow for the possibility that we may have several social purposes which have to be reconciled to each other. I remind you of the sage words of Gustave Thibon and Simone Weil, which I have already quoted. I shall take as an illustration "the ideal of equality of opportunity," because my previous reservations on the applicability of that ideal seem to have provoked especially strong dissent. This ideal certainly expresses a social purpose, and is equally applicable to other things than education: education is merely one of the benefits to which men and women should ideally have equal opportunity. This ideal has two very strong grounds of appeal, which must be distinguished. One is that ability is wasted, of which society has need, through our failing to recognize and train it. This is a utilitarian argument; it has force, but of a very different kind from the second. This is, that it is not just that any person should be prevented, by our failure to educate him, from the full development of his latent powers and faculties. The second seems to me the more universal and compelling, because it is a *moral* ground. Now on this ground at least, the assertion that every child should have equal opportunity for education is one which nobody will deny. The only difficulty comes when we proceed, from cherishing this ideal, to attempt to realize it; and when we give it priority, in our educational schemes, over other ideals of education.

If we pursued the ideal of equality of opportunity rigorously we should, it seems to me, have to see to it that no educational institution was superior to any other professing to supply the same grade of education. We should certainly have to see to it that no institution gave a better education simply because it could charge higher fees, and select its pupils for any other reason than intellectual promise. To what extent do the pupils at expensive private schools get a better education? What is it that their parents are paying for? I know that the motives from which affluent parents choose a school are often motives which have nothing to do with education. There is the desire that their children should mix with other children of the same economic status and social type; there is also the calculation that their children will make the sort of friends who will be "useful" to them in later life; there is also the simple snobbism attached to the name of a particular school or university. But there are better reasons than these: there is the attraction of a foundation with traditions, and a long list of distinguished alumni. And there is the best reason of all, especially for the private school—for it is in school days that this reason is the most cogent: the parents know that their child will be a member of a small group, that he will be taught in a class of fifteen or twenty instead of in a class of forty or fifty. Anyone who has ever tried to teach young children knows that the larger your class is, beyond fifteen or twenty, the less you can teach.

It is certainly desirable that every school in the country should have enough accommodation, and enough teachers, to be able to teach children in smaller groups. I thought, in 1944, that the Education Act of that year—an attempt, certainly, to improve state education—put the wrong things first. Instead of extending immediately the years of compulsory education, and thus adding to the number of pupils, we should in my opinion have aimed first at the supply of more teachers and accommodation for those already in the state-supported or -aided schools; and undertaken to give better teaching than we do, to those under fourteen. But when will we, in any country, provide the money for this reform? Again, before we train more teachers, we ought to consider whether we are paying our present teachers adequately. I have never worked in a coal mine, or a uranium mine, or in a herring trawler; but I know from experience that working in a bank from 9:15 to 5:30, and once in four weeks the whole of Saturday, with two weeks' holiday a year, was a rest cure compared to teaching in a school.

I am told that "no American advocate of equality of opportunity would argue that the rich should be forbidden to set up schools of their own, which might turn out to be superior to those supported by the State." This is advocacy of a limited equality, an equality qualified by a good deal of inequality. If the schools established by the rich for the rich turn out to be better schools (though I do not believe this is altogether true) then what becomes of equality of opportunity? And how can we limit our equality to an equal opportunity to get a good education? If one child has better opportunities in life than another, merely because his parents are richer, will not many people regard this situation as unjust? It would seem that inequality in education is merely a special instance of inequality in general, and if we affirm a principle in one area are we not driven to accept it in all? Certainly, some English advocates of equality in education would go much further than, as I am told, American advocates do: they would abolish the private school and the privately endowed institution, or bring them all into the state system.

The usefulness of the phrase "equality of opportunity" is confused by the various meanings which we attach to the word "opportunity"—it means different things to different people, and different things to the same people at different moments, often without our knowing it. That everyone should, as far as we can make it possible, be able to pursue the activity for which he is best fitted, is an aim which we can all applaud. One has sometimes observed the son of people in well-to-do circumstances, admirably qualified by talent and temperament to be a first-rate garage mechanic, yet never having the opportunity to become one. Pressure of family and environment, the acquirement of tastes incompatible with the occupation for which he is best fitted, and perhaps also a defective education, usually stand in his way. I am afraid that to most people at most times "opportunity" means a good many other things than the opportunity to develop the latent powers and capacities: it means opportunity to make money, to acquire a higher social status, to have power over others. For some young women, opportunity means opportunity to get a screen test; and only a small number of those who crave this opportunity deserve it. In short, opportunity is an empty term unless we can answer the question "opportunity for what?"

It would seem, then, that most of the time, when we talk of "equality of opportunity," we either do not know what we mean, or do not mean what we say, or else are driven to conclusions from which most people would shrink. It is avoiding the issue if we assume vaguely that "inequality" means only the injustice of overprivileged and underprivileged social classes. It may happen that a child at a state school finds a teacher who will elicit his aptitude for a particular subject, and that a child at an expensive private school has just the wrong teacher. But what about overprivileged and underprivileged areas in the same country? A poor state or country may not be able to provide such good equipment or teachers, such good libraries or laboratories, as a richer one. Should not that inequality be redressed also? Thus the claim of equality of opportunity, if pressed to its logical conclusion, seems to me to lead inescapably to a universal and exclusive state system of education, to the cost of which the richer parts of the country, like the richer individuals, will contribute proportionately, but from which they will derive only the same educational returns as their poorer neighbours. And next, is it just that the citizens of a wealthy or advanced nation should have greater opportunity for education than those of a backward one? Unless we maintain that some races or peoples are superior to others we seem to be forced toward the goal of a world system of education. And finally, if we are to have complete equality of opportunity in education, it seems to follow that we must have a uniform system for grading the intelligence of pupils, so that each shall receive just the kind and amount of education to which his gifts entitle him.

If, as I have suggested, the thoroughgoing application of the principle of equality of opportunity (reinforced by the other pressures of which I have spoken) tends towards increased control by the State, then the State will have something to say about opportunity. It will find itself limiting opportunity to those vocations which serve the ends of the State as conceived by those who happen to control the State. I am not suggesting that it would, in a Western democracy, reach the point of direction of labour; but by offering greater inducements and advantages and facilities in one direction rather than another, it might tend to limit education to the kinds of training which served the immediate purposes of the State.

The idea of equal opportunity, it would seem, has to be considered in relation to each of the three aims of education from which we started; and it might be that in this connection, also, one aim would be pursued in such a way as to interfere with another. The difficulty arises from the fact that we cannot, in practice, wholly separate one from another. There have been, no doubt, men who were animated by curiosity and the thirst for knowledge, to such a degree as to be able to pursue their studies quite apart from their actual calling in life. There have been Spinozas who, in order to be free to exercise a wholly unremunerative activity and one not regarded by the world as particularly useful, have been content to earn a modest livelihood by grinding lenses. There have been other men, in humble positions, in whom the speculative or contemplative motive has been so strong that they found happiness in this double life. On the other hand, there have been men so completely limited in interest to the duties of their occupation that they have seemed to be hardly more than machines. Most men escape from this only by way of recreations and hobbies, ordinarily of a rather trivial nature. The ideal is a life in which one's livelihood, one's function as a citizen, and one's self-development all fit into and enhance each other. For most of us, the full pursuit of any of these aims must interfere with another; and we are obliged, at best, to make almost day-to-day calculations and decisions between the several claims. We are all limited, by circumstances if not by capacities. To get anything you want you find you have to sacrifice something else that you want; and in getting it, you find that you have to accept other things that you do not want. Yet we must maintain that a man is not educated if he is merely trained to a trade or profession; that he has to play his part as a citizen; and that, as a citizen, to be something more than a voting machine, and, as a worker, to be something more than a working machine, he must be trained and developed to something more than citizenship and work. And we find that the principle of "equal opportunity" is meaningless—that is, susceptible of being interpreted by everybody in terms of what he *desires*, instead of what he ought to desire —unless we answer the question "opportunity for what?"

There are obviously some "opportunities" which ought to be available to everyone. Every man should have the opportunity of earning a livelihood in reasonable and decent conditions; of marrying and rearing a family who will also have the same opportunity; of rest and recreation, and so forth. You will observe that this sentence is made up of terms which will have different meanings in different social contexts: it is necessarily vague. But when we proceed beyond material necessities we get into a region of values. And so the assertion of "equal opportunity" leads us gradually to the point at which we must know what we mean by "the good life." The question "What is education?" or the question "What is the aim of education?" leads us to this point. Now it is unlikely that we shall all agree on an answer to the final question, "What is Man?" Therefore, what we mean in practice by "education" will be the highest common factor of what enough educated people mean by it. So you may say that "education" is likely to mean, in practice, a compromise between what different people mean by it.

I hope that it is by now clear that I do not complain of other writers that "they seek to use the schools to achieve social purposes which they have at heart." When we talk about education, we cannot stop at education as if it were a field which we could close off; an area in which we could come to agreement whatever our differences of philosophy. We must have a social purpose in education, and therefore, if we talk about education, we must be prepared to make clear to ourselves and to our hearers what our social purpose is. But the social purpose itself should not spring from a prejudice, an emotional bias in favour of equality or hierarchy, a bias in favour of freedom or of order. Nor is the social purpose in itself enough, for it does not take account of the whole nature of man.

We have seen that, just as we are led, the moment we begin to think seriously about education, to think about citizenship, so thinking about citizenship leads us to something beyond citizenship; for the good citizen in the end turns out to be the good man; and that leads wherever the whole problem of ethics is going to take us. Now a view of education such as Dr. Joad's, which suggests that training for citizenship and training for the development of one's latent powers and faculties can be carried on in separate departments, may seem clear enough about the discipline for citizenship, but offers no general prescription for the development, or we may say "the improvement" of man as man. As citizens, men must hold certain principles in common, and must agree on certain social habits; the fact of having to get on with other people imposes some discipline. But in the question of the development of latent powers, this view does not proceed to maintain that there are certain latent powers for good, and certain latent powers for evil, in man as man; it suggests rather, that each man has latent powers and faculties peculiar to himself, illustrated by the various ways in which men spend their leisure time. It is perfectly true that some men have an aptitude for and take enjoyment in doing their own repairs about the house; whereas others are much better advised to send for a plumber, a carpenter, or an electrician. I have no doubt that when Dr. Joad talks of latent powers and faculties, he is thinking of higher powers and faculties than those of the handy man. Nevertheless, he is leaving the area of latent powers and faculties uncontrolled. The danger of separation between the social and the private life—which has the corollary that the only criterion of morals is whether one's conduct is harmful to one's neighbours, and that every man should be free to do as he likes with *himself*—is that the social code, the code of citizenship, will become more and more constrictive, more and more exercising a pressure towards *conformity;* and that this public servitude to society will be compensated by extreme licence in whatever conduct is supposed to be none of society's business.

It is true that in a society organized on this principle the social may prove in the end to encroach more and more upon the private. In a society organized to carry out this principle, the rules of matrimony and sexual relations may be, at first, much relaxed. But then it may be found that this relaxation has undesirable social consequences—that it affects the birth rate unfavourably, in a nation which finds that it needs more workmen and soldiers; or that it has an unfortunate effect upon the children, who may begin to show psychological aberrations, or may grow up to be less desirable citizens than the government wants them to be: and then private life will be interfered with in the name of society. People may be ordered to have larger families, or to have no families at all, according to whether they are judged to be suitable breeders of future citizens. Thus the individual may find his privacy, his opportunity for exercising his moral freedom and responsibility gradually taken away from him in the name of society.

The restoration of a kind of order in people's private lives, however, when it is made in the name of a social purpose only, furthers the reduction of men to machines, and is the opposite from the development of their humanity. The assumption that you can have areas of control, and areas of complete freedom, must lead either to a suffocating uniformity of order, or to chaos. The actual degree of freedom or control may differ between one area and another. We are all more willing to submit to regulation of our public than of our private behaviour, and gradually, with the increasing complexity of modern civilization, we are prepared to submit to more and more regulations in the public interest. There are still people who object to being vaccinated, but few people now resent being isolated when they have typhoid fever. Most people recognize that the state of their drains is a matter in which they have a duty to their neighbours; though not everybody recognizes that he has the same duty in respect to the noise of his radio set. In a flat, one expects to have less freedom in many petty details of life than in a solitary cottage in the country. On the other hand, people in England since the war have objected, and they have my sympathy, to being forbidden to set up a tool shed in a country garden without a licence from the government, or being forced to employ a workman to do what they are capable of doing themselves. Fortunately, we do not yet submit to universal regulation in the public interest; and fortunately, we are still capable of being shocked by private behaviour, even when it does not appear to injure anyone but the culprit himself. And so long as we are capable of resenting control, and of being shocked by other people's private lives, we are still human. We are, at least, recognizing that man is something more than merely a social animal: that there should be limitations to social control. And by being shocked (when it is something more than a prejudice that is shocked) we are recognizing, however dimly, that there is some law of behaviour which is something more than a duty to the State.

What, then, should we mean by the development of the individual's latent powers and faculties, if we go further than Dr. Joad, and consider the individual, not as if he were a seed out of a packet with no name on it, which we plant and tend out of curiosity to see what it will become, and what sort of flower or fruit it will bear; but as a seed of a known plant which has been cultivated for many generations—a plant about which we know what its flower or fruit ought to be, if it receives the right nurture and grows to perfection? How are we to try to educate good men, seeing that the idea of the good citizen implies the good man? Are we to be content with a rough-and-ready description of the good citizen, leaving everybody to define goodness according to his own taste and fancy? As you may have feared, this question raises for me the final question, that of the relation of education to religion.

.   .   .

Unless we can get complete agreement about religious truth—that is, the ultimate truth about Man—we must not expect to be able to agree upon an ideal system of education which can be put into practice. Many situations in life have to be dealt with by compromise, and we must not repine over this misfortune of the human condition. But I think that it is very important, when we are forced by circumstances to stop short of the proper terminus of our speculations, to be aware of what we are doing; in respect to the present subject matter, not to pretend that a theory of education can be complete which excludes the ultimate religious problems—and I have said that "What is Man?" is one of these—and which attempts to delimit for the theory of education an area within which religion can be ignored.

I am now, I hope, in a position to remark that the inquiry into "the place of religious teaching in education" with which I have been occupying myself for some minutes is really unimportant for the purposes which I set myself in these discourses. Only, it is a problem which has to be inquired into first, before we can see how and why it is unimportant in this context. In my "aims of education" it is not the place of religion in education, but the place of education in religion, that is the vital issue.

.   .   .

So far, our aims have been for the individual: to train him to become the best that he is capable of becoming. We have been concerned only with the present, not with the past or the future. Now I suggest that one aim of education should be concerned with another obligation besides that towards the persons to be taught. If we consider only the latter, our curriculum may vary with every wind of doctrine; our notions of what is a good way of earning a living, of what is good citizenship, and of what is good individual development, may be at the mercy of the prevailing mood of one generation, or the caprice of individual educators. It should be an aim of education to maintain the continuity of our culture—and neither continuity, nor a respect for the past, implies standing still. More than ever, we should look to education today to preserve us from the error of pure contemporaneity. We look to institutions of education to maintain a knowledge and understanding of the past. And the past has to be reinterpreted for each generation, for each generation brings its own prejudices and fresh misunderstandings. All this may be comprehended in the term history; but history includes the study of the great dead languages and of the past of modern languages, including our own. Particularly, indeed, our own; for we need to understand the way in which our words have been used in the past, how they have developed and altered their meanings, in order to understand how we are using them ourselves. And to preserve the wisdom of the past, we need to value it for its own sake, not simply to defend it on the ground of its usefulness. To support religion on the ground of its usefulness is obvious error; for the question, of what use is man to God, is more important than the question, of what use is God to man; and there is an analogy—though I admit the danger of drawing such an analogy with temporal affairs—in our relation to our culture. For if we estimate the wisdom and experience and art of the past only in terms of its usefulness to us, we are in danger of limiting the meaning of "usefulness," and of limiting the meaning of "us" to those who are now alive. What I wish to maintain is a point of view from which it appears more important—if we have to choose, and perhaps we do have to choose—that a small number of people should be educated well, and others left with only a rudimentary education, than that everybody should receive a share of an inferior quality of education, whereby we delude ourselves into thinking that whatever there can be the most of, must be the best. And what I plead for is what Matthew Arnold spoke of as "the knowledge of the best that has been thought and said in the world" (and, I might add, the best that has been done in the world, and that has been created in the arts in the world); that this knowledge of history, in the widest sense, should not be reserved to a small body of experts—reserved to them and parcelled out among them —but that it should be the common possession of those who have passed through the higher grades of nonspecialized education; that it might well form, for most of them, the foundation for many of the more modern studies which now tend to be substituted for it. . . .

SPECIAL READING

Several Thousand Books / ALLEN TATE

. . . It has been frequently said that the mode of modern poetry is the mode of prophecy, a vision of the end of all things. This is obvious the moment we evoke the names of Rilke, Valéry, Montale, Yeats, Eliot. If the mode of modern poetry is prophecy, the rhetorical mode of prophecy itself is hyperbole. We foresee a future dominated and perhaps eventually destroyed by the evils, with no redemptive power of any good, of our own time.

I am therefore about to preach a sermon; and because I am not properly ordained for this office, I shall adopt not a holy but a secular text, which is as follows:

> *The price the man of today has paid for his increase in power is, it should seem, an appalling superficiality in dealing with the law of his own nature.*

This sentence was written by the late Irving Babbitt in 1919. I shall not refer to it again but rather offer you three characters modelled after Theophrastus, one living, the two others dead.

Every September, almost a century ago, Charles Eliot Norton greeted the first meeting of his classes at Harvard with a snobbish irony that we today might have to take literally. He is reported to have said: "I suppose that nobody in this room has ever seen a gentleman." The New England scholar, if rumor be reliable, has not been famous for humility. I surmise that Norton was inviting the students to look at one gentleman, perhaps the last, before the species became extinct. I intend no irony whatever when I say that nobody in this auditorium, either you out there or we up here, has ever seen an educated person. I may not be the oldest member of the faculty on this platform. Allow me the rhetorical privilege of believing that I am. So it is possible that I may have seen, some fifty to sixty years ago, one or two educated men. (At that time it was not necessary to consider whether there were educated women.) I have not seen an educated man since, and I fear that you will never see one.

As a small boy I knew a man who lived on a farm a few miles from a Kentucky county-seat, the population of which was about five hundred. I suppose he had been born about 1840; he had fought in the Confederate army and it was said that after 1865 he refused to recognize one of his brothers who had fought on the other side. He was a lawyer whose office was up a dingy flight of stairs above the feed store on the courthouse square. He had "read" law after the war in the office of an older lawyer; but before the war he had been graduated from a small sectarian college, a day's buggy-ride from the family farm; and while he was reading law for the state bar examinations he taught mathematics at his *alma mater*. (I once had his books on Conic Sections and the Integral Calculus.) I think I must have seen him last when I was about twelve or thirteen. It was summertime. He wore a shapeless, sweat-stained panama, black alpaca coat, unpressed broadcloth trousers, and string tie; he was very tall and very fat, with a smooth round face and unkempt white hair. I could not then have understood that he saw no difference between his vocation and his avocation, or that he did not know which was which. From early spring to early fall he spent most of his time on his farm. He sat under a tree in a far corner of the yard—which in England would have been called a park—reading Mommsen's *History of Rome,* or perhaps Lord Clarendon's *History of the Rebellion;* for he fancied himself a Jacobite. Back of his house stood an abandoned ice-house, down in the depths of which, on the sawdust floor, he had his laboratory apparatus with which he performed his chemical experiments—for what purpose and to what conclusions I do not know; and I doubt that he knew: he was only increasing his knowledge. He might have answered questions with obvious appeal to authority—"As Plato *says* in the *Phaidros*" —putting the verb in the present tense because Plato had lived only recently; or he might quote the *Georgics* and look hurt if the company kept an uncomprehending silence. He sat in a split-bottom rocking chair next to a big field of tobacco, a palmleaf fan in one hand, in the other his book, perhaps Cicero's *Letters to Atticus*. If the field-hands suckering the tobacco needed an order, he rose, placed the fan on the seat of the chair, his index finger between the pages of the book to mark the place; walked over to the fence, shouted his orders; and came back to his chair to resume his reading.

He was not a scholar; that is to say, he was not a professional scholar. He knew a little about many things—mathematics, science, the ancient classics, agronomy, the law; yet all of the little that he knew was alive in his daily life and was constantly brought to bear upon the human condition as he could know it in his place and time. Without being conscious of representing anything at all, he was an exemplar of the classical apothegm: Nothing too much. One would know that he would be as considerate of the plain people of his community as of Senator James or Justice McReynolds. He was, in short, an educated man.

The second figure that I evoke for this occasion was a generation younger than our lawyer-planter. He was not only a scholar; he was a great classical scholar. Our lawyer was a private person; our classicist was a public character, a professor of Greek; so I shall name him: Herbert Cushing Tolman. He was born in Massachusetts, educated in the classics by William Dwight Whitney at Yale; went to the German universities, as was the irresistible imperative of that era; came back to this country to teach, for more than thirty years, at a small Southern university. It was there that I became his student. I knew him nine months a year for four years. In bearing and in temper he was remarkably like his rural, non-academic counterpart in Kentucky. Yet he was a specialist. Besides his Latin and Greek, which he could speak better than our American professor of French could speak French, his Indo-European philology included Sanskrit and Ancient Persian; and he had mastered Babylonian cuneiform.

In his Greek classes he usually gave, towards the end of the period, a "prelection" of the assignment for the next day. On one occasion he recited a free translation of a Pindaric ode. When he had finished I raised my hand and asked: "Dr. Tolman, could we have read that translation somewhere?" "No, sir," he replied, "my reading is the way John Dryden might have rendered it into English prose." How he ever had time for English poetry we never knew. He had published a small book entitled *The Art of Translating*. He had time for everything that interested him because he was never in a hurry. One spring afternoon as I was passing his house I saw him lying in his hammock in the side yard. Some boyish impulse moved me to approach and speak to him. In my self-consciousness, and in a clumsy effort to impress him, I made up a Greek sentence to surprise him with. After he had risen and we had passed the time of day—which on my part included taking off my hat—I said: καῖρε, ἡ ἀταραξία τὸν φιλόσοφον ἔχει. He smiled. "No," he said, "not *has* me—*had* me from the beginning; I was born taking my ease. So your verb should be in the second aorist—not ἔχει, but ἔσχεν." He laughed and asked me to sit down in a garden chair, while he lay back in the hammock.

This man, a great scholar on the Renaissance model, no more than the Kentucky farmer-lawyer, knew the difference between vocation and avocation, between labor and leisure. These men were both in the strict sense amateurs, for what each did in his own way was done in the love of excellence. The competitive "advancement of knowledge"—produce or perish—the ostensible purpose of our university scholar, was incidental to the love of excellence. But love of anything is notoriously inept at getting one ahead in our world. When I try to revive the image of Tolman—the noble brow, the serene eyes, the benign mouth, all composed in an imponderable effect of innocence—I think of the great lines by W. B. Yeats:

> . . . all his Greek and Latin learning seemed
> A long blast upon the horn that brought
> A little nearer to his thought
> A measureless consummation that he dreamed.

Getting ahead in the world is now the purpose of education; and the university must therefore provide education for our time, not for all time; it must discover and then give to society what society thinks it wants and needs; and Government is now paying, perhaps bribing, the university to give the people what it, representing society, thinks that society ought to have. Society ought to have more and more technology, more and more specialization, more and more occultation of knowledge. I must linger a moment over the word occultation. I use it in the sense understood by the philosopher Scott Buchanan in a brilliant, forgotten book *The Doctrine of Signatures*. Occultation means turning the sciences into Black Arts, hidden arts, the purpose of which no single mind can comprehend. These are the applied sciences over which the true scientist, after the applications have been made, no longer has control. When the late Robert Oppenheimer tried to control the making of the hydrogen bomb, he was disqualified on pseudo-political grounds. Who—or what—disqualified him? The slowest member of the class could answer the question: Government disqualified him. Oppenheimer was satisfied with scientific knowledge; Government was bent upon power, upon the use of scientific knowledge as a Black Art for the control—and destruction is the ultimate control—of man and nature. For once the bomb is made, it has as its final cause, its end, which it may achieve through the agency of man, an explosion; but the agent being dehumanized is neutral, and has no responsibility for the consequences.

We have recently heard another version of the doctrine of means-as-end, this time from a humanist, our third character, who declares that the printed book is obsolete. The audio-visual *media* have replaced it. In a series of dizzy non-sequiturs, which remind one of Ralph Waldo Emerson, if Emerson were vulgarized and brought up to date, Mr. Marshall McLuhan assures us that the electronics *media* are their own subject-matter, or will eventually become so, when the rational, systematic thought, which developed after Gutenberg had invented movable type, has disappeared, as he promises it will speedily do. There will be less and less "content-analysis" and more and more identification of the auditor-spectator with the audio-visual medium. We shall give the television screen a catatonic stare. In this prelapsarian, illiterate Elysium it will no longer be necessary to learn how to read. All is sound and sight; the medium is its own message. This attractive chimera, which if universally followed would relieve us, as it has evidently relieved Mr. McLuhan, of the burden of thought, would, I make bold to conjecture, have pleased the late George Orwell. Yet I doubt that Orwell could be convinced that Marshall McLuhan exists; he would recognize him as one of his own fictional characters who had just stepped out of the pages of *1984* and changed his name to McLuhan. Satire is frequently a mode of prophecy. When "content-analysis" is forbidden or—what is the same thing—no longer "necessary," and the medium is its own "message," we may safely infer that the message will have been prepared by invisible Big Brother. Another name for Big Brother is Government; another, Society; still another may possibly be the University itself. The University, still proud, may try to disguise itself as Big Brother, with an even Bigger Brother, named Brother State, back of him. Will the University then agree to give Society what it thinks it wants, not what it is the responsibility of the University to tell Society that it needs?

As I approach the conclusion of these meditations I must remind you that the rhetorical mode of satire is hyperbole. I have been assuming that the abstraction Society never knows what it needs, but only what it wants, or what it is told that it wants by distant persons whose interest lies in the frustration of the human being. In those departments of the American University which self-interest has led me to observe, we are told—and we tell others—that what we need is more scholarly research; a more and more rapid advancement of knowledge (by which is meant inert information); more and more "research" for more and more dissertations which nobody will read but the authors of previous dissertations who will be as bored as the persons who wrote them. This reciprocal boredom is enthusiastically perpetuated because it leads to power: power in an *occulted* world of Black Art. What is occulted is the true purpose of literary studies. That true purpose is not to produce more studies of Coleridge and Hawthorne, but more Hawthornes and more

Coleridges. The name of this Black Art is Research, a term and a procedure borrowed from the natural sciences at a low level; that is, at the level of the applied sciences, which are, of course, the genuine and efficient Black Arts. One wonders where the laboratory for literary research is located. It is located, invisibly, in the heads of scholars who use the study of literature to maintain an academic power *élite*. I suggest that it would be better to try to *be* Coleridge than to *use* him, even if as pusillanimous Coleridges we fell flat on our noses and made fools of ourselves. Coleridge never did any research; he never even had a course in English literature. He had merely read, in six languages, by the time he died at the age of sixty-two, several thousand books.

Thus far, a secular gospel, or a vision of the end of all things.

THE AUTHORS

Joseph Wood Krutch (1893–1970). Distinguished American critic of drama and literature; varied career in the world of letters from theater critic to professor of dramatic literature; best known for his critical volumes on the modern temper and man's foolish enthusiasm for the social and natural sciences that threatens the ideal of the dignity of man. Born in Knoxville, Tennessee. Graduated from the University of Tennessee (1915); M.A., Columbia University (1916); Ph.D., Columbia (1924). Assistant professor, Brooklyn Polytechnic Institute (1921–1924); drama critic and later associate editor of *The Nation* (1924–1937); associate professor, Columbia University School of Journalism (1932–1935); professor of English, Columbia (1937–1943); Brander Mathews Professor of Dramatic Literature (1943–1952); retired (1952–1970). National Book Award for nonfiction (1954); Rockefeller Institute Ettinger Award (1954). Major publications: *The Modern Temper* (1929); *Experience and Art* (1930); *Five Masters* (1932); *American Drama Since 1918* (1939); *Samuel Johnson* (1944); *Henry David Thoreau* (1948); *Comedy and Conscience After Restoration* (1949); *Modernism in American Drama* (1953); *The Measure of Man* (1954); *Human Nature and the Human Condition* (1959).

Sir Richard Livingstone (1880–1960). Leading Greek scholar in Britain in the 1920's; became an authority on the theory of education as administrator of British colleges; accepted the classical approach to education for modern times; explained the ultimate aim and essence of education as the training of character. Born in England. Graduated with an M.A., New College, Oxford University (1900); honorary LL.D., St. Andrews, Dublin; honorary D. Litt., Cambridge, Belfast, Toronto, Durham, Manchester, London, Columbia, Yale. Temporary assistant Master at Eton College (1917–1918); vice-chancellor of Queens College, Belfast, Northern Ireland (1924–1932); president of Corpus Christi College, Oxford University (1932–1950); late Fellow, Corpus Christi College, Oxford (1950–1960). Arnold Essay Prize (1905). Major publications: *The*

Greek Genius and Its Meaning to Us (1915); *A Defense of Classical Education* (1917); *The Mission of Greece* (1928); *Greek Ideals and Modern Life,* (1935); *Portrait of Socrates* (1938); *The Future in Education* (1941); *On Education* (1944); *Plato and Modern Education* (1944); *Some Tasks of Education* (1947); *Education and the Spirit of the Age* (1952); *The Rainbow Bridge* (1959).

Theodore Spencer (1902–1949). Noted professor of English at Harvard; poet and writer of prose; authority on Shakespeare and the Elizabethans; indicated that the nature of man can only be viewed in the light of great literature. Born in Villanova, Pennsylvania; descendant of William Spencer. Attended Haverford, graduated from Princeton (1923); A.B., Cambridge University (1925); Ph.D. in English, Harvard University (1928). Instructor in English, Harvard (1927–1933); assistant professor, Harvard (1933–1939); appointed lecturer in English Literature, Cambridge University (1939); associate professor, Harvard (1940–1946); Boylston Professor of Rhetoric and Oratory, Harvard (1946–1949). Phi Beta Kappa poet, College of William and Mary (1942); Phi Beta Kappa poet, Tufts College and Harvard University (1943). Major publications: edited, *A Garland for John Donne* (1931); edited, *Joyce's Stephen Hero* (1944); co-authored with Mark Van Doren, *Studies in Metaphysical Poetry* (1939); *Death and Elizabethan Tragedy* (1936); *The Paradox in the Circle* (1941); *Shakespeare and the Nature of Man* (1942); *The World in Your Hand* (1942); *An Act of Life* (1944); *Poems 1940–1947* (1948).

Thomas Stearns Eliot (1888–1965). The most imposing poet of modern times; the virtual literary leader of the twentieth century; influenced by the Elizabethans and the symbolists in poetry; his own poetry is vividly modern yet rooted in the heritage of tradition; T. S. Eliot has emerged as the epitome of "the establishment"; once described himself as "an Anglo-Catholic in religion, a classicist in literature, and a royalist in politics." Born in St. Louis, Missouri. Graduated from Harvard (1909); M.A., Harvard (1910); attended The Sorbonne, University of Paris (1910–1911); Merton College, Oxford University (1914–1915). Teacher, Highgate School, London (1915–1917); clerk, Lloyds Bank Ltd., London (1917–1925); assistant editor, *The Egoist* (1917–1919); editor, *The Criterion* (1922–1939); literary editor, Faber & Faber, London (1925–1965); Clark lecturer, Trinity College, Cambridge University (1926); Charles Eliot Norton Professor of Poetry, Harvard University (1932–1933); Theodore Spencer Memorial Lecturer, Harvard. Awarded the Nobel Prize in Literature (1948); Order of Merit (1948); Commandeur Ordre des Ats et des Lettres; Officier, Legion d'Honneur; Order Pour le Merite; Hanseatic Goethe Prize; Dante Gold Medal. Major publications: *The Sacred Wood: Essays on Poetry and Criticism* (1920); *The Waste Land* (1922); *After Strange Gods: A Primer of Modern Heresy* (1934); *Murder in the Cathedral* (1935); *The Idea of Christian Society* (1939); *Notes Towards the Definition of Culture* (1949); *Christianity and Culture* (1960); *To Criticize the Critic* (1965).

Allen Tate (1899–   ). Literary critic of the modern school called New Criticism whose authors write in the tradition of I. A. Richards and T. S. Eliot;

because of personal associations and a similarity of outlook, John Crowe Ransom, Allen Tate, Robert Penn Warren, and Cleanth Brooks form a group within the New Criticism whose major theme has been that art completes man, restoring some of what has been taken from human nature by modern science and technology. Born in Winchester, Kentucky. Graduated from Vanderbilt University (1922); lecturer in English, Southwestern College, Memphis, Tennessee (1934–1936); professor of English, University of North Carolina Woman's College (1938–1939); poet-in-residence, Princeton University (1939–1942); chair of poetry, Library of Congress (1943–1944); editor, *Sewanee Review* (1944–1946); lecturer, New York University (1947–1951); professor of English, University of Minnesota (1951–1967). Awarded Bollingen Prize for Poetry (1956); Brandeis University Medal Award for Poetry (1961); Gold Medal from Dante Society (1962); Major works of prose: *Reactionary Essays on Poetry and Ideas* (1936); *America Through the Essay* (1938); *Reason in Madness: Critical Essays* (1941); *On the Limits of Poetry: Selected Essays* (1948); *The Forlorn Demon: Didactic and Critical Essays* (1953); *Man of Letters in the Modern World* (1955).

Natural Law
Philosophy

GENERIC NOTIONS AND BASIC THEMES

Although a number of historical systems of philosophy include concepts of natural law, only one contemporary thought pattern, which is logically designated Natural Law Philosophy, is dominated by this theme. The roots of this thought pattern extend back to Greek and Roman philosophy. However, because Thomas Aquinas wove together the ancient conceptual strands of natural law into a culminating system of philosophy, his systematized synthesis and redirection of natural law concepts is the primary intellectual foundation of Natural Law Philosophy.

The important generic notion of the thought pattern is that every movement must be grounded in something immobile. Natural Law philosophers contend that examination of natural bodies shows that everything that undergoes change must proceed from something that remains immovable. For example, to lift a weight with a lever one must use an immobile fulcrum. The issue of change and permanence was raised by the ancient Greek philosophers as they sought a rational explanation of reality. Some philosophers indicated that only permanence existed and viewed change as a mere illusion. Others accepted the fact of change, yet rested this mutability in some kind of order, Logos, or World Soul. Aristotle, however, with his careful analysis of the natural causes of change provided the most extensive explanation of it. Everything that is moved is moved by something. But there cannot be an infinite regress of such movers. Therefore, there must be an eternal first mover or first cause, a pure actuality that is not caused by something else.

According to the proponents of Natural Law Philosophy, "motion must be grounded in immobility" is a principle that is true of all forces in nature, both the physical world and the world of intellect. The immovable base of the intellect lies in certain self-evident principles; that is, deposits of unchanging knowledge. Motion is the process of reasoning, which can best be described as movement from general principles to more specific principles. There are two kinds of self-evident principles in the domain of intellect. Speculative reason flows from one kind of self-evident principles; practical reasoning, from the other kind. In both instances, these general principles are immediately known and dependent on sense perception. For example, speculative reason moves from a self-evident principle like "the whole is greater than its parts" to more specific knowledge about the world. On the other hand, "good is something which ought to be done" is an example of a self-evident principle from which practical reason moves to the more definite precepts of moral law.

A second generic notion in Natural Law Philosophy pertains to the degree of emphasis on the two kinds of reasoning and their relation to education. Although Natural Law philosophers consider speculative reason important and necessary in the program of acquiring knowledge about the world, they feel that reason pertaining to values and morality is more significant because it relates directly to the daily human life. They concede that speculative knowledge will indicate the value of God and order. For the most part, however, they feel that education should concentrate on practical knowledge, which affects the moral behavior of most individuals. However, in cases in which Natural Law Philosophy is in competition with other philosophies and its proponents feel they must emphasize the universal and scientific nature of the approach, speculative knowledge may be stressed.

In order to teach "doing the good and avoiding the evil" one must understand the nature of man, for the connection between the immobile truths of morality and human nature must be understood if man is to apply them. Educational philosophers of the Natural Law Philosophy thought pattern go to great lengths to define man's nature. Of primary importance in this endeavor is the clarification of man's place in the total scheme of things; that is, in the hierarchy of existences. Special attention is paid to the similarities and differences between man and the creatures below him, the lower animals, and those above him, the angels. Man resembles the lower animals in the biological functions, but he alone possesses an intellect. Brute animals do not comprehend knowledge or reason; they are guided instead by instincts. The intellect, on the other hand, is a characteristic man shares with the angels. Angels, however, are completely intellectual beings. They need not investigate, compare facts, or reason. Angels see everything in ultimate concreteness, all at once.

Man lacks both the instinct of animals and the angels' complete vision of concrete reality. Man knows only confusedly and in general. He must investigate through reason in order to concretize implicit knowledge. At one point, however, he shares the kind of sudden knowledge possessed by angelic nature; he does not require inquiry to experience the immediate and nondiscursive apprehension of the self-evident principles of speculative and practical knowledge. These principles are immediately known to man. However, they are not inborn, but arise out of minimal experience with reality as a result of sense-perception built up into memory.

Knowing the self-evident principles of practical knowledge means that there is an original, permanent, and unchanging standard of moral right, which every human has the capacity to know unmistakably. These self-evident principles are the primary precepts of natural law. Because every man has the capacity to know these precepts, we never err because we have failed to judge correctly the rightness and wrongness of these primary precepts, but only because we have willed not to adhere to them or failed to reflect upon them adequately in terms of particular actions and circumstances. Now the connection between the primary precepts of natural law and man's nature lies in man's natural inclinations. Just as other beings have inclinations toward their specific good, so man has inclinations toward his good, which consists of the achievements of certain ends related to his animal and rational nature. Man has a natural bent for self-preservation, sexual union, care and education of offspring, and living with others in society. Man also has an obligation to fulfill these natural desires. At the same time, man moves necessarily from these inclinations to the self-evident principles of natural law, for his natural inclinations are toward certain ends that he apprehends as good. Man is thus immediately aware of such precepts as "we ought to respect and preserve all human life," "sexual relationship needs some form of regulation and promiscuity ought to be avoided," "children must comply with parental rules," and "we ought to live together in society in obedience to certain rules."

Reason progresses from the general to the particular. Man tends to know the general principles of morality before he knows particular precepts. Some particular precepts, however, are so closely associated with the general or primary precepts that man knows them with a minimum of reflection, and even an uneducated person is aware of them. All people, except those whose conditions of life are very poor or those whose society follows depraved customs, know these precepts. These almost universally known precepts are proximate conclusions derived from primary precepts: for example, "do not murder," "do not steal what belongs to others," "do not commit adultery, fornication, or unnatural sexual acts," "do not drink too much," and "do not rear undisciplined children."

Natural law also includes tertiary precepts, which are as binding as the primary precepts and the proximate conclusions. However, these precepts are remote conclusions, for considerable reasoning ability is necessary to discover them. To know these tertiary precepts one must understand all the circumstances involved in a situation, and also possess a background of experience and education that can be brought to bear on the various points. Considerable reflection is necessary before one can see how these precepts follow from the self-evident principles. Therefore, although these precepts are derived from the primary precepts by natural reason, only the very wise have the reflective power to discern them. Topics involving such tertiary precepts are: "sex within marriage," "definite practices of child-rearing," "birth control practices," "divorce," "practices involving the political and economic life of a community."

In Natural Law Philosophy, education is perceived as fulfilling two kinds of functions. First, although the child's moral training is the responsibility of the parents, the school, as an objective institution, can assist the home in shaping the child's awakening conscience. Human beings are naturally aware of the basic precepts of natural law unless they are obstructed by bad conditions or society's depraved customs. Since these obstacles may easily be present, it is an educational duty to warn children of them and to prepare students to resist such influences in the future. Thus, a program aimed at warning children against those elements that conceal the precepts of natural law is one of the educational goals of the Natural Law Philosophy thought pattern.

Second, education must start children on the road to acquiring wisdom, the reflective power necessary for handling remote conclusions. Not everyone, however, will reach this final stage. Many, through lack of ability, time for scholarship, and/or commitment to learning, fail to attain it. Those who do not succeed are not, therefore, less worthy, but they require assistance in reaching their ends. Education must aim youth in the direction of becoming wise, and lay a foundation so that those who fail to acquire the necessary reflective power can accept the wisdom of others. Such training must emphasize reasoning, especially syllogistic reasoning, which starts from the general and arrives at the particular. However, age level must always be taken into account. What is expected of a college student is surely not the same as that expected of a six-year-old child. Because the reflective faculties of small children are not very advanced, they must be told what to do, and they must wait until they are older to see the reason for it. College students, on the other hand, because they are moving to the stage of wisdom can question, view other systems of thought, and use their reflective powers in regard to issues of speculative and practical reason.

The practices of the Natural Law Philosophy thought pattern are implied by the previously mentioned educational aims. Age level is viewed as a major factor in determining educational practices. Training the senses in an orderly manner (for example, as practiced in a Montessori school) in coordination with good discipline is desirable at the preschool level. Various educational methods relative to age development, and with emphasis on natural law and reason, are acceptable at the elementary and secondary levels. In higher education, however, students are approaching the stage of wisdom, and distinctive methods that are peculiar to the philosophy can be used; for example, the extended use of the syllogism, disputation, the method of commentary, and the method of the "Summa" (the Scholastic Method). In addition, the acquisition of natural and cultural knowledge are important at the higher levels of education.

Natural Law Philosophy's greatest influence on education is its emphasis on responsibility. Reflection on natural law, which indicates that children are the final aim of marriage, means that parents have the inviolable duty to educate their children. The state and the church may have a secondary responsibility to see that the parents fulfill their duty, but the primary obligation rests with the parents. On the other hand, parents in a complex society cannot possibly educate their children without assistance. Therefore, the institutions of state and church must aid the parents by providing schools and by giving the best professional and moral aid to their children's progress. The parents, however, have the right to decide what institution their children are to attend. The grounds for this right are moral, based on the principles of natural law.

PEDAGOGICAL ORIENTATION

Education and Values / LEO R. WARD

Education is a turning toward values. It is for values—it has to be. As soon as we delete values, we delete education. No values, no education; and where there is real education, there are genuine human values.

Each of those declarations says the same thing. The idea expressed may for a moment seem striking, but on second glance it is obvious and platitudinous. The idea does have points in its favor. First, it is absolutely true, and second, all philosophers, all educators and all citizens, when they come to think of it, are in perfect accord in accepting it. Besides, it summarizes chapters which went before. The idea that education is for values is a restatement of the chapter on end-seeking and of that on ends in education. Going for values is a going for ends, and, as a phenomenon to be contemplated or studied, this going for values falls within the teleological and end-seeking datum of all nature and all art. Lastly, education for values and as a turning toward values summarizes the chapters on the teacher and the student which said that education means bringing the child up, and the simple word "up" means nothing in the present context if not the child's development within himself and in and with society.

Education is education in and for values, or it is nothing defensible at

"Education and Values" is reprinted from Leo R. Ward, *Philosophy of Education*. Copyright, 1963 by Henry Regnery Company. Reprinted by permission of the publishers.

all. Try to think of a teacher who would be intent on indoctrinating the child in disvalues, in untruth and immorality, and on leading him into such a disvalue as ill health or imbecility. As I wrote these words, a professor was being dismissed from a neighboring state university on the charge that in public printed statements he had been misleading the student community and was anything but a light showing the students the way to truth and good. His presence at the university was a disvalue.

Socrates is the classic example of a teacher charged with misleading youths and showing them the way to radicalism, untruths and immorality. In his case, the charge was false, and eventually it was turned back on his accusers. The charge was the same in the two cases—a misleading of youth, an orientation toward evil and untruth. How then are we to know values from disvalues? David asks that question (Psalm 4) in these words: "Many say, 'Who will show us good things?'" And he gives a remarkable reply: "The light of thy countenance, O Lord, is signed upon us."

So far as God gives man direct light on human values, the issue does not arise. But schools operate on the theory that God does not ordinarily give this direct light. The question then remains, how are we to know human values, educational or other? How are we to know good things and to know good from evil? That basic question must be answered in general theory of values, and the answer must be such that it can be carried over without loss into the area of educational values. How are we to know good when we see it, and so mark it off from evil? How are we to draw the line between values and disvalues? Everybody is for value and against sin, but how are we to know the one from the other? Obviously this is a question in ethics and over-all theory of values, and a question of great relevance to philosophy of education.

What does it mean—to be "for value"? Before we can discern good from evil and value from disvalue, we must know the meaning of good or value. To say "for value" is to utter a tautology, since good or value is what all things are for. The classic designation of "good" in the first sentence of Aristotle's *Ethics* is that "good" is beautifully designated as that which all things are for, or at which all things aim. Aristotle's use of the idea "good" shows that his complete definition would read: Good is that at which all things *by nature* aim, no matter whether they are artificial rather than natural.

Two brief notes on the definition. First, does Aristotle mean "all"? Absolutely; as he says, every art and every science and every action and pursuit aims at some good; one by one they do it, and all of them do it; everything does, and all things do. Second, may the meaning of "good" be expressed in other terms, or is this thing "good" an irreducible—not capable of being reduced to some other idea—and is the word "good" irreplaceable? Reverting in part to our chapters on ends, we may say, as

Aristotle says, that "good" may be expressed as "end." The "good" at which all things aim is an end, and the highest good is the last end (assuming now that there is such an end not serving as means, but being simply *the* end). In short, "good" and "end" are convertible.

Is "the end" the only synonym for "good"? Man is aiming by nature at the end and at good, and so is everything else. Can end and good be otherwise expressed? They certainly can. Aristotle in effect says that man seeks to be man, and everything seeks to be itself; and St. Thomas carries the principle through when he says: "Everything desires to be, in its own mode of being." Its good and the end is being, and being of its own type. Man wants to be, and to be man—fundamentally and originally, that is his orientation and his good. So too for mosquito or rhinoceros or uranium or the English people; each wants to be, and its good is to be in its own type of being; the English not desiring to be mosquitos, or uranium to be the English. To be in its own type of being is its good and its end.

The basic good for anything is to be in its type. We add three complementary ideas. (1) A double negative from Aristotle: the then "proposed new order of society" would in reality mean the destruction of states, but the destruction of the state cannot be the good of the state; its good is that which preserves the state: thus Aristotle designates instrumental good as that which helps things to be (*Politics*, II, i-ii). (2) A double negative from Aquinas: With all its powers, everything resists disintegration, and thus declares for being. (3) Augustine is completed by Aquinas: The end-fulfillment for everything is that it be and fully be.

All tend to think of good or value primarily and almost exclusively in its extrinsic meaning: good or value is that which will help people to be, or help something to be. And people are right. X is good for Y if X will help Y to be and so far as it will help Y to be. However, intrinsic good or value is presupposed. Y's being is Y's intrinsic good. Brown's being is Brown's intrinsic good, and Brown is good in the intrinsic sense just so far as Brown is. When Brown was a child in the womb, Brown was good, and he was good just so far as he was. Once born, and growing and developing, Brown *was* somewhat farther than when he was in the womb; seeing, beginning to think and to talk and to walk, Brown, just so far, *was* somewhat more than Brown had been in the womb. Some day it is conceivable and desirable that Brown will be grown up—and that is exactly what the total job of education is aiming at. It is aiming at the grown-up Brown and the grown-up Smith and in general at the grown-up man.

Look at education as something that helps the child to grow into a man. Education is not something existing in a vacuum, but something strictly subordinate to the growth and development of man. So far as it helps man to grow and to be, it is—considered as a process and technique—an extrinsic or instrumental human value: it helps man to be, and it helps him just so far. In this sense, education is *good for* and is a value of an instrumental, contributory or extrinsic kind. Considered as a state of the child's or man's being, education is something inside man and is an intrinsic value. As an intrinsic value, education is primarily an end and not primarily a means. It is integral to the child and substantial with him. It is not good *for*, but good *in* and the good *of*. It is the *bonum honestum* and simply good; it is good with no strings attached; it does not have to serve any other end in order to be a good. It *is* an end, and it is as if *the* end. The idea of an end which is a good is easily grasped. Health is that kind of good; primarily a good, and not primarily good as a means. Health is integral to the child's being and substantial with it, and so is education.

Many goods are like that, primarily ends and not means, and they are intrinsic to the person. Aristotle notes (*Ethics*, Book 1) that some goods are only goods as means; tools and money; e.g., we want them only for use and to help us reach something beyond themselves. Some one end, he holds, has to be simply an end, sought only for itself. A third type—which includes many good things—is both good and good for; we would want it even if it did not lead any farther, though in fact it can lead to goods beyond itself; health is like that: anyone would want it even if it led no farther, and yet it does lead to many goods beyond itself. Pleasure is like that; it is a means to many goods, and yet in itself it is an end; and so is knowledge, and so is virtue, and so is appreciation, and sympathy, and a right love. Any of these is good and desirable in itself, and can assist us toward other goods. Each of them is both good and good for. We have therefore to accept the fact that human values naturally fall into classifications:

I. Intrinsic values, and extrinsic or contributory values
II. Values as ends only, and values as means only and values that are both means and ends

As a state of man's being, education is an inner development, and is both good and good for. It is something that man wants and something that nature wants, and in this sense is a value in a class with health or pleasure or virtue, and like these it can help toward additional good things such as friendship, or a good society in the family, the church or the state. In another of its common meanings, education is totally a means. When people speak of "education in Canada" or "education in Indiana" they are speaking of education as a means to help the child or to help society. They mean the whole education system in that place with its techniques and methods and apparatus. In this sense, education is a means and not at all an end or terminal value. We want it only as a means.

As a value, "education" is a bifurcated term. It is a means to many good things, and in an analogous sense, it is an end. It is an intrinsic and terminal good, and yet a remarkably good means, leading to many further goods. As intrinsic and terminal, it is the development and, so far, the perfection of the educated person, though not the end of the universe or of society or even of the human person. The human person is to be educated; not only society but nature demands it, and the person achieving an educated condition is achieving his good. The condition of being educated is a quasi autonomous end, just as man is a quasi autonomous being and as the state in its good condition and achievement is a quasi autonomous end or what Maritain calls an infra-valent end. The same holds of man in the good condition and achievement of being educated.

So much for the meaning of good. We must return to the problem of how man knows good things; the question asked by David. St. John of the Cross said that all values are mine if I just know how to manage myself. How can a man do that? Any man in any society is knee-deep in potential and actual good things, and his life is in the field of choice among values. How is a man to keep on the high road to truly human values?

Man's conscious philosophizing has been done historically on moral values, and there evidently is a problem of discerning the natural and philosophical grounds for allocating some actions and objects in the class of moral values, and some ruthlessly in the class of disvalues. Actions and objects are what they are, and granted to be good in themselves. By what legerdemain do they become humanly good?

Man is called to be fulfilled in his own type or species, and it would be odd to say the good of man is not to be. It is precisely this question —what is it to be man?—that all peoples are in practice engaged in trying to answer, and this is the value question that theorists are engaged in trying to answer. In practice, all are trying to be nothing better or worse than men. But it is a perpetual and inclusive job, and not a single soul, let alone any whole people, brings it off absolutely and once for all. Every man is truly a man, but no man expresses totally and fully what it is to be man. Any X expresses at once all that it is to be X. Man does not have that immediate success and never does have a perfect success.

Besides being good by nature, man is innately headed for all good, for all truth, virtue and beauty. To begin with, he is value-rich: he has his own being which is his initial intrinsic value. He will add to this, by increase in health and strength, by command and use of his powers, by built-in habits: a) of seeking truth, b) of knowing how to seek truth, c) of loving rightly and d) knowing how to love rightly, and e) of knowing how to give himself with prudence and a quasi infinite generosity to the kingdom of persons. Man is made to be and totally to be, but is not made to be any other being than man himself, and precisely this man. Many actions, objects and persons are helping him to be; that is the only way he can go on being and growing. In their relation to him, as helping him to be, they are good for him.

In reemphasizing both intrinsic and contributory human values, we are bringing to light the basic criterion of human values. At any moment the intrinsic values he has, i.e., his given being and his health and virtues, are humanly good precisely because they come up to the basic criterion "man"; any other criterion, in order to be valid, has to be secondary and reducible to this. Each intrinsic human value truly expresses "man" and "what it is to be man." Good health, e.g., does this, so far as it goes; and so do good habits of knowing and loving. Many things outside him help him to be; e.g., friends, houses, cars, tools of every kind, and money, though none of these is convertible into his being, or into *his* intrinsic values. They are nevertheless real human values because they help him to be. The measure of their human contributory value is the measure in which they help man to be. They cannot help man to be unless they fit "man" and come up to this radical criterion "man."

"Man" ideally taken is the measure of all human good things. What is destructive of the state cannot be the good of the state, and what is destructive of man cannot be his good. His good is thereby seen to be that which goes with his being.

It is difficult, sometimes, to know whether an object or an act does go with our being, and difficult to know whether object X is better than object Y. This difficulty need not shock us. Many things in the universe, including many things entering our lives and loves and hopes, are hard to know. It is hard to avoid mistakes in simple things like addition and subtraction. Man is a terribly complicated being, a) in his psychological make-up, b) in his physical make-up and c) in his social life with the total body politic and its parts and their multiple interrelations. He loves and hates, and is upset by many things. Even so, man does fairly well, and we hope that every teacher has the good sense to recognize that every primitive is truly man; we have not the slightest wish to belittle man or to go with those who do so. By three major modern events we have been taught to respect man—all over again, and almost more than ever. First, by psychological studies emphasizing the basic oneness as well as the struggle and anguish of all men. Second, by world political conditions which keep telling us that to survive we must know and respect all men. Third, by anthropology. Let us cite men who spent their lives studying primitive man. Alexander LeRoy spent twenty years living with and studying primitives, especially in east Africa, and then made his report. He said that he had gone to those peoples in 1877 with all the prejudices and phobias of his time, thinking them a degraded lot, "fetichist peoples, without religion or morality, with no family life, stupidly adoring animals, trees, and stones." After twenty years, he had arrived at quite a different view: "The savage! The primitive! He is you and I, almost. He is man, often an intelligent man; it is quite wrong to make his acquaintance and to judge him by the fantastic representations made of him by those who have never seen him." [1]

Even more famous as a student was Wilhelm Schmidt who went back to what we may call primeval man or primitive-primitive man. See what Schmidt finally thought of the primitive: [2]

"The prehistoric tools and weapons and those of the ethnologically oldest peoples of today are alone enough to show that he was a vigorous and daring man of action. To begin with, his mental powers made their way through nature and analyzed her phenomena; his synthetic activities mastered her by forming generalizing and classificatory ideas; he grasped the conception of cause and effect, and then adapted that to the relationship of means to end. His means, to effect the ends he desired, were his tools, which he invented and used."

The primitive is truly man and is trying to be more completely man. That is what we must say and all that we may say about any of us, whether the Englishman, the Chinaman or the aborigine in Australia. The perpetual struggle of man is to become man.

Therefore when we say that education is a turning toward values and is for values, the words are plainly tautological. Man is for values, and education is for man. And when people say that they want the child "to get science" or "to get art," they seem to suppose that the child could shake science or art out of a tree or squeeze it out of a tube; they seem to think getting an education is like getting a hat or a coat. In education, the getting is something far more intimate. It is an interior becoming, a growth in values, a relative leaving of our primeval stage, a putting off of that anterior and quasi empty stage of our being and a development within us of a relative fullness of manhood. Nature asks us to cooperate in developing the ideal and total man within every man.

Hence three important if simple truths—that education is inevitably for values and could never otherwise make any sense, that the value-growth possible in education is an interior growth and could never be an exterior growth, such as that in money or gadgets, and that schools are only one place where education can occur.

A child is not born with an appreciation of music or literature; he has to learn this kind of thing, and once he has achieved a sensitivity for good, this sensitivity is a built-in value, a part of his being, integral to him, and not something he puts on and off like his shoes. At first he had not intrinsic value, and afterward he actually has it. Nobody gives a course labelled "sensitivity for esthetic values." All the same, people

---

[1] Alexander LeRoy, *The Religion of the Primitives*. Newton Thompson (tr.). (New York: Macmillan, 1922) Preface and p. 175.

[2] Wilhelm Schmidt, *The Origin and Growth of Religion*. H. J. Rose (tr.). (New York: Dial Press, 1931) p. 136.

teach the sensitivity and a child can acquire it. If the child is blessed by being raised in a home whose members have sensitivity for good things, he will gradually begin to catch up with the family, without ever a thought on his part and without preaching on the others' part. If he is born into a community of families, neighbors and relatives with a sense for what is good, he will get a feel for good things. The best music and literature will begin to make sense to him, and nothing else will satisfy him. He then knows what is good and what is trash. Somehow he has achieved standards of taste; and he has taste. He was not born with it, but grew into it, and the corresponding good things developed within him. This kind of achievement comes on gradually; nobody sees it happening, and it is not subject to measurement. It is an incommensurable value, distinctively human, and it is both a terminal value and a means to other good things.

"Incommensurable" means a) that this acquired and built-in sensitivity could not be measured in arithmetical or mathematical terms, b) that it could not be measured by some secondary standard such as the mores and public opinion or the wishes of the state or the dictator, and c) that we could never learn how to make deals and trade this sensitivity value for some other value such as health, money, reputation or friendship. To say that it is "distinctively human" means that it fits man exactly and precisely as man, and much more intimately and properly than does his hat or some powder on his nose.

Consider ways in which this radically human value could be sidetracked and negated; for example, by radio and television programs, by movies and comics, by much of the teaching in homes and perhaps by some in schools. Because homes do a bad job of it, some teachers may, as if to make up the loss, become romantic and ecstatic about this value of sensitivity for esthetic values, and the last state of the child becomes worse than the first. We must emphasize nevertheless that education is for values, including this particular value.

We are ringing the changes on the "built-in" character of intrinsic values, and we need to do so. People are prone to think of education as plastered on from outside, especially when they see education in terms of hours spent in class and years spent in school and measure it in credits and top it off with a degree which itself is measured in terms of hours, years and credits. Education *is* a value and a very human value, and therefore can be measured only by the most human and elusive standard, namely by "man" himself taken as standard and measure.

Consider science as another example of human value in education. In what sense is science a human value, and does education exist for science as a value? In its first and basic existence and in its first and basic meaning, science is something that happens in a person, and not something that happens in a book or a test tube or a space ship, and thus it is primarily human and humanizing. Science first of all is something that comes to be in Newton's or Einstein's mind and is a perfection of that mind and sooner or later is the perfection of many minds. Mind is made to know. Now knowing is its imperfection and is a kind of non-existence of mind. By knowing, it is developed more and more, and exists more and more. Think of the dummy who does not know and perhaps cannot know. This "does not know" or "cannot know" is a gap in the man's being. Whitehead said that evil is "things at cross purposes." Not knowing the ordinary things available to be known is the evil of mind. Mind's orientation is to know, and not to remain in primal nescience.

Modern science is one of history's most remarkable instances of "knowing." Take what we know for generations about the structure and working of the cell. Aristotle, a great biologist, lacked this scientific knowledge, and anyone now having it has a perfection of being that Aristotle did not have. Having it is a human value, something fitting our nature and our being. Having this knowledge is both a terminal value and a means. Everyone knows that science as knowledge and as the perfection of human mind is an end, and everyone knows that it can help us toward other goods such as health and happiness. Within science-as-value is a particular meansvalue, since scientific knowledge can lead to further scientific knowledge. From this point of view, scientists speak of the heuristic value of science: once achieved, science helps to make additional discoveries. But we are interested in science in its most proper meaning, as a development and perfection of man. This intrinsic and spiritual value is possible, at least in an inchoate form, in school children.

That science cuts the roots from under subjectivism was a thesis held by Dewey as well as by Pope Pius XII. So far as scientific method dominates the layman's thinking, science has the additional value of helping us to square with things. Yet as everybody observes, some persons trained rigorously in scientific procedures such as mathematics or physics fail to respect evidence in other areas, are greenhorns on political problems, and fond of easy absolutes regarding persons and controversial social issues. In such instances, there is no transfer of abilities.

Let us return to the tautology, "education is for values." The task that each man and each society has in hand—naturally and perpetually—is to develop an over-all sensitivity for human values of all kinds. That is mankind's task and education's task. Subtly and inevitably, though as a rule unconsciously as well as inarticulately, man knows that his being is his good—see how he fights things thought to be destructive of his being. Why then does not every man and every society naturally and unfailingly grow to full stature? Many things get in the way. Serious among these evils or "things in the way" is a twin set of evils, one of which consists in taking means as ends: e.g., taking money or honor or pleasure as the end; and the other consists in taking a secondary standard of values as primary, or even of adopting a false standard.

Here we acclaim man "adequately and objectively taken" as the basic and inclusive standard of human values of all types, intrinsic and contributory, and cognitive, social, moral, esthetic, and health values. But man often substitutes some secondary standard for that primary one. Throughout a whole society he can at least act as if he took increase in wealth as the basic and all-inclusive standard and end; or act as if political power should have this ranking position. Again, the dictator tells people what to do, what to promote in arts and sciences, what to study in schools and to what extent; he takes himself as the law and measure of good in human life. The dictator as standard may even receive a conscious formulation, e.g., in Mussolini's axiom, "All in the state, nothing outside the state," or in Hobbes's teaching [3] that until the commonwealth took over, there was no good or evil, no merit or demerit, and no just or unjust. The king decides all questions of human values.

Positivism puts the right foot forward, wishing to find out what various groups do in fact value; it seeks a statistical report. But it errs when it holds that such a report is all we can know. It says that what people value, the people do value, and that is all there is to it. This opinion leads not only to the notion that good depends on what people take to be good, but leaves itself open to the dictator's power and whim. That a bare positivism in the field of values has no defense against dictatorship was a point made in the appendix to the final edition of his works by the distinguished German jurist, Gustav Radbruch, who had learned by bitter experience that mere positivism was capitulation to Hitler.[4]

Without knowing it, some persons turn democratic majorities into absolutes, and ask us to convert a possibly arbitrary standard of values into something radical and *ne plus ultra*. Democracy is thought or even said to generate standards of good and evil.[5]

A closely related problem is set by the mores, the customary ways of judging values and of acting. For the mores to become a law of action and a standard of values is routine practice and is sure to come about, above all among primitives. Much the same effect is reached by public opinion, say in an isolated village or when public opinion is stepped up by modern communications. People do not know what to do then except to line up and go along. Their neighbors act that way and perhaps their ancestors have acted that way. Hence for the educational and total good of society the importance of good and justified customs among primitives or others. But the mores, whether they are assumed or are repeated every hour on the hour, cannot justify themselves.

[3] Thomas Hobbes, *Leviathan*, Part One, ch. 13.

[4] Gustav Radbruch, *Rechtsphilosophie*. Fourth ed. (Stuttgart: 1950) pp. 352–355. Gustav Radbruch, "Die Erneuerung des Rechts," *Die Wandlung*, II (1947).

[5] Mrs. Agnes E. Meyer is one of those persons of good will, but confused mind, who try to convert democratic choices into absolutes. See Agnes E. Meyer, "Are our Public Schools doing their Job?" *Atlantic Monthly*, v. 182 (February, 1949), and cf. Leo R. Ward, *Religion in All the Schools*. (Notre Dame, Ind.: 1960), pp. 104–105.

The most nefarious of all standards that men attempt to apply to values is the Machiavellian. The prince was advised by Machiavelli [6] to seek his own advantage, no matter what. "And, therefore, he must have a mind disposed to adapt itself according to the wind, and as variations of fortune dictate, and, as I said before, not deviate from what is good, if possible, but be able to do evil if constrained . . . in the actions of men, and especially of princes, from which there is no appeal, the end justifies the means."

Throughout this book as well as in this chapter on education and values, we make the following assumptions. First, that in the educational and the general human realm, man is the central and core value; the top priority value is not science or art or history or the state itself, but man. Second, that man himself is the standard of human values, which means that, in order to be humanly good, things outside him and inside him have to measure up to him, and not he to them: they are not the standard and measure of human good; he is that standard and measure. Third, that an unacceptable standard, e.g., Machiavellian expediency, is seen to be unacceptable because it can never square with man: it attempts to turn things around and to sacrifice man to the advantage of some person or group. Fourth, at times men use secondary standards such as the mores and the voice of the people, and our assumption is that any such standard is defensible only so far as and because it lines up with the radical standard of human values.

The battlecries of modern times have been freedoms and rights. Men and whole societies act by these battlecries and guide their sacrifices by them. Men and societies so acting and so guiding their conduct, in education or elsewhere, are right. In education, in politics and in religion the "freedoms and rights of man" standards and the "dignity of man" standards are so close to the basic standard, "man," that they must be regarded as justified in themselves.

[6] Machiavelli, *The Prince;* c. 18.

PSYCHOLOGICAL DIMENSION

On Synderesis / MICHAEL CRONIN

Synderesis is the name given to the group of primary moral principles which belong naturally to the human mind. The Scholastics define it

"On Synderesis" is reprinted from Michael Cronin, "On Synderesis," *The Science of Ethics*, Vol I, General Ethics. Reprinted by permission of M. H. Gill and Son, Ltd. Dublin Ireland. Deletions have been made by the editor in the interest of brevity.

"habitus primorum principiorum." St. Damascene calls it a "naturale judicatorium."

Now, when we say that certain principles are natural we do not mean that they are innate, but only that without reasoning the mind comes quickly and easily to acquire them, and cannot help doing so. What these principles are we have already seen in our chapter on Intuitionism. Of these principles some we saw are intuitions in the strict sense—that is, the mind assents to them at once without reasoning. Certain other principles are, practically speaking, intuitions. For, though technically they are inferences and not intuitions, still so easily are they acquired and so necessarily, that they may be and are generally regarded as self-evident truths. The number of these primary self-evident principles it would be difficult to state, and the exact formula of each it would not be easy to determine. But we can say with certainty that all grown people who are capable of thinking at all believe in the goodness of honesty, and bravery, and kindness, and filial pity, and the care for offspring, and marriage, and in the evil of indiscriminate murder, &c. It is true, indeed, that many peoples did not regard virtues like honesty and piety as so strictly binding that they could not be set aside under certain exceptional circumstances. But Reason must recognise the *general* necessity of cultivating these virtues, and it is for moralists and those who are capable of judging of such things to say whether to any particular law there may in reality be an exception. In other words, it is for the moralist to determine scientifically the formula that will express the law truly and exactly. These self-evident moral principles constitute what Moralists speak of as Synderesis,[1] about which many interesting ques-

---

[1] Various attempts have been made by modern Ethicians to reduce all moral principles to a single principle inclusive of all the others. The more important amongst these principles may be divided into the following six classes, according as they are founded:—(1) On the conception of individual pleasure; (2) on the idea of individual liberty; (3) on the relation of the inner impulses to man; (4) on the idea of life; (5) on the idea of the common good; (6) on the idea of personality, whether individual or general.

(1) Under the first we have the principle of Hobbes—that the "good" is that which each man desires. This principle we have criticised in our chapter on The Good. (2) Under the second we have Fichte's principle, "Be free," Cousin's "Ens liberum maneat liberum," and similar principles of the Transcendental School, an examination of which will be found in the latter part of our chapter on Liberty, where it is shown that Liberty is not morality but only its pre-condition. (3) Under the third we have the principle "Never to choose a lower in the presence of a higher pleasure." This principle is examined in our chapter on Intuitionism. (4) Under the fourth we have the innumerable principles of Biological Ethics—*e.g.*, Thomasius' principle, "Do that which will make life long and happy"; Leslie Stephen's two principles, "Be prudent" and "Be virtuous," both ultimately grounded on the idea of life. Also Spencer's, "Seek the maximum of life," for which see chapter on Biological Evolution. (5) Under the fifth we have the several principles of Sociology—*v.g.*, "Seek the greatest good of society" (Mill), or "Homini quantum in ipso est colendam et servandam esse societatem" (Grote and Puffendorff), or "Neminen laede—suum

tions arise, some of which will be considered in the present chapter.

From the self-evident principles, taken in their strictest sense, it is possible, as we said, to derive certain proximate simple conclusions which all men must know. Other conclusions are not so evident, and to bring home their truth with unmistakable clearness to the ordinary mind we have to reason them out step after step, as we would a difficult proposition in geometry. These propositions are called remote conclusions. Though they are quite as true as the proximate, they are not, as we said, so evident, and consequently it is possible for minds to lose the consciousness of them or even never to come to a knowledge of them. But neither the first principles themselves nor the proximate and immediate conclusions from them can ever be lost to consciousness.

We now proceed to discuss two important questions on the primary Moral principles. The first—What is the origin of our general moral beliefs? or—How do we come as children to the understanding of general moral principles? The second is—Can belief in the moral principles decay, or, as it is usually put, can Conscience develop and decay?

On the Origin of a Child's Moral Beliefs

The expression "origin of our Moral beliefs" may mean either the logical *grounds on which educated men* maintain their beliefs; or the *original sources* whence *in past ages* men received their moral ideas; or, finally, it may mean the actual *beginnings of these beliefs* in the *child's mind* to-day. It is this last question that we are now to occupy ourselves with. What, we ask, is the source of a child's moral ideas? Do they come through the exercise of his own Reason without help from outside? Or are they gained by a process of reasoning helped on by instruction? Or are they wholly from tradition? [2]

At the outset we wish the reader to understand that this is mainly an historical question. We have nothing at present to do with the philosophy of duty or of the good—*i.e.,* with the question of the objective

---

cuique" (Leibnitz). All that we have said in the chapter on Utilitarianism applies here. (6) Under the heading of personality we have the three principles—(*a*) of individual personality (Kant), "Treat every man as person"; (*b*) of microcosmic personality (Dr. Lipps), "Realise the whole world in yourself"; (*c*) of universal personality (Hegel), "Realise the personality of Society." These principles are examined in the chapters on Universalism and on Rights.

The reader will have no difficulty in recognising from what has been said in the foregoing chapters that many of these principles are false, whilst others fail to include the whole moral law (and therefore are not to be regarded as primary principles in the sense intended by the Ethicians here mentioned) being principles only of certain departments of morals. Further criticism of these so-called primary principles, we think, will not be necessary at this point.

[2] The question of the possibility of inheriting these beliefs and of their origin in past ages has already been fully treated in our chapter on Evolutionist Ethics.

foundation of moral truths, or the reason why we ought to accept them. This we have fully explained in an earlier chapter. The question how a child comes in the first instance to believe that two sides of a triangle are greater than a third (we take it for granted that such a proposition has only to be put before the thinking child in order to command instantaneous acceptance) has nothing to do with the question—Why do you, a mathematician, accept it, or why ought you accept it? So, our present question is, not what is the right ground of our moral beliefs, but how do children generally come by their moral beliefs? Now, a child may accept mathematical truths on the word of his master; yet no one would, on that account, say that the proper ground of Mathematics is tradition. Why? Because mathematical propositions can be proved on mathematical grounds. So also with Morals. Once we have proved the reality of moral distinctions we have implicitly shown that the ground of our moral beliefs is not mere tradition, that Ethics is based upon Ethical grounds, as Mathematics is upon mathematical grounds. But our present enquiry has nothing to do with the question of the ultimate grounds of moral belief. It is a question of history only, but it is of great interest to the Ethician.

At first sight it would seem that the beliefs of children depend wholly on traditions—that is, on the teaching of parents and master. Children in civilised countries, long before they are able to reason or to express their thoughts with any clearness, have already been instructed in moral truths—that is, they have in the first instance accepted these truths on the ground of tradition only. Even savage children, from their very earliest years, are made familiar with the particular religious and moral persuasions of their tribe, so that from the beginning their moral beliefs are developed under pressure, if we might say so, of religious and political training.

Still, in spite of this fact, we maintain that the beliefs of chidren do not depend wholly on tradition. We claim that though a child begins with tradition, yet at the age of ten or twelve he has already come into possession of certain moral beliefs *which he holds with a strong intellectual conviction,* not on the strength of mere human testimony, but on account of their own intrinsic evidence. In other words, we take it for granted that at ten or twelve children no longer require the authority of their parents in the case of some moral principles, and that they adhere to these principles or propositions on account of the insight they now possess into the intrinsic truth of these propositions. These propositions may not be very many. But a boy of twelve (we say "Twelve," though we believe that the transition from tradition to belief on intrinsic grounds occurs at a much earlier period) believes on intrinsic evidence such truths as that he ought to honour his parents, that they should care for him, that he has rights against other men. Some beliefs he still holds on the ground of authority alone. If asked why he believes that America exists or that planets move, or that absolute monarchy is not good, he will answer "because so he has been told." But if asked why he believes that murder is bad, or, better still, if an argument be put forward in his presence to show that murder is good, it will be found that in answering he does not appeal to any authority for his belief, but will refer to some objective ground and argue the case out on its merits, thereby showing that he is conscious of the intrinsic unreasonableness of murder, and that he no longer believes on faith alone. The ground which he assigns may be far from satisfactory, but it is evident from his attitude that now he is believing on grounds intrinsic to the truth itself, although as yet he may not be able to express these grounds coherently. Thus, between his moral belief and his belief in facts into which he has as yet no personal insight, there is the very marked distinction that the one class of truth appeals to his own inner convictions from their inner evidence, the other only on the ground of an extraneous authority. The moral world, therefore, has begun to appeal to such a child for its own sake, and he will judge of it from what he feels and perceives, and will talk of it as a thing that he is familiar with, and will think for himself concerning the reasonableness of the moral laws, and will even question the judgment of other people about them, which shows that some at least of his judgments on moral matters are now received at first hand, and not on mere authority.

A child's judgments about remote conclusions may, many of them, be wrong. It would be strange if some were not. If a boy can form a wrong judgment about many simple truths of Physics it is impossible that he should not sometimes go wrong in Morals. But in general, on the broad moral principles, his judgment is perfectly trustworthy. No boy, for instance, could think that murder, and lying, and cruelty, and robbery are the right things, and ought to be done. Such a proposition he could not entertain for a moment, even if he tried. But his whole soul goes out to the thought of the goodness of truth, and of respect for parents, and of benevolence, and of honour. It goes out just as easily and as naturally as the flower opens up to the sunlight, from which fact we draw the conclusion that morality appeals to him to a large extent on the ground of its own objective evidence, and that, therefore, his assent to morals is not based on tradition alone.

We are led also to another conclusion—namely, that, since in the sphere of morals authority ceases at an early age to be necessary to a child's belief, and since the first principles of the moral law come so quickly to be believed on the ground of their own inner credibility, it seems evident that, even were no instruction given, the unaided Reason must succeed in time in constructing for itself a good deal of the moral law, although in an unsatisfactory way and in the rough, and at a comparatively late period in a man's career. To construct the natural moral law with any perfection needs experience and a ripened Reason. But granted a mind that can normally think, and granted that it has some experience, there is no doubt that even without instruction it must arrive at length at some rough idea of the moral system. What, therefore, is the effect of instruction on the young mind in the department of morals? Just this—aided by instruction the moral ideas come to it all the sooner, and aided by instruction they are necessarily cleaner cut and truer. Instruction in morality is like the plan of a city, which puts before us boldly and definitely at one glance the lie of every part, and its relation to the whole. In that one view we see the city as a whole, and also the direction of every passage and turn. Without such a plan we might, indeed, come some day to know the city, but only after much trying research and many failures—streets and roads often seeming to lead nowhere, and turns and passages to have no meaning. It is so with morals—with this *addendum,* that in morals the failures of research-time mean disaster to the individual. Instruction, therefore, is necessary even for the very life and welfare of the child. It is necessary also, and for another reason, to the world at large. For though it is true that unaided Reason will arrive after much thinking at some fair idea of the truths of Ethics, yet it is also true that our moral system could not develop, that the fabric of morals could not grow, did not each age hand down the results of its reasoning and its experience to the age that immediately succeeds it. Moral science is not more easily constructed than many branches of Physics, and if in the sphere of Physics each age did not build upon that which preceded it, the edifice of science could not be reared. In the same way instruction and tradition are necessary to moral science.

Having seen, now, that the moral beliefs of children are not dependent wholly upon tradition, it will be interesting to enquire, from what we know of the child mind, what would be the meaning of the conceptions "good" and "duty" if, these ideas being once supplied to the child, they were allowed to develop in his mind without further instruction. What, for instance, would a child understand by "good" and "duty" who was told that it was a good thing and a duty to be honourable and kind? That most children from the very beginning regard sin as directly and immediately an offence against God, and the moral law as His command, is only natural, since that is how they have been trained to think. That training is, we maintain, justifiable both on logical and on moral grounds. It is justifiable on logical grounds because, as we showed in the earlier chapters of this work, goodness and duty are in their last analysis founded upon God as supreme end, and, therefore, sin is truly a violation of God's will. Secondly, this religious interpretation of morality is morally necessary, because it is the conception of a personal relation of the child to a Supreme Being that appeals more than anything else to his mind and heart, and fires him with a love of the "good." But what now of the untrained child, or the child who has merely received the suggestion that certain acts are bad and others good? What in his mind will be the meaning of the two ideas "good" and "duty"? Naturally much will depend on the child himself. Some children never think. But some do think, and, granted that the child has come into the possession of a language—in other words, that he is normal and possesses the means of thinking—we maintain that his mind will, if allowed to develop, follow a very definite course. It will be found to pass through two distinct stages —(1) The stage at which evil is regarded as a violation of the law of nature,[3] and (2) the stage at which evil is regarded as breaking in upon the plans of Him who made nature what it is.

First—Badness to a child, who *has not yet been told* that it offends God, is simply this—that an order has been broken in on, and disorder has succeeded in its place. The child feels, when he has done certain acts, that there is something wrong with himself—that he is not what he should be. He steals, and he feels that there is a disturbance of the proper and natural distribution of things around him. A drunken man is to him a monster—something that falls short of the standard of nature. Disarrangement, deformity, disorder, have in these cases replaced arrangement, harmony, and design. Evil, therefore, is regarded as a violation of nature, and by nature a child means the original plan of things. This is the first step. Secondly, a child's mind, *particularly if it receives the least help in its work*, will very easily travel up to the thought of One who planned the world and made it. We say "particularly if, etc.," for even without help a child must soon begin to wonder what is the cause of the world, and even to assert that it must have a cause. But if once the idea of a first cause be suggested to him, the child's thought rises immediately to it, as to something that satisfies all the necessities of his mind, and when he accepts that belief in a First Cause, he accepts it, not indeed because it has been suggested, but because it is reasonable, because his whole being goes out to such a thought as giving everything around him meaning and completeness; in other words, the existence of a First Being explains everything that he can think. We are not now defending the logic of his thought. We maintain, indeed, that it is absolutely logical. But logical or not, a child's mind travels up to that thought of a first cause of the world as easily as it does to the thought of the maker of a watch or of a house. One of his first questions is how he himself came to be, and how his parents came to be, and how all things

[3] A child will not *formally* think of such a thing as *nature*. But, just as a psychologist experimenting upon the ordinary subject gets him to describe his experiences, and then makes use of these experiences, cataloguing them according to the methods and terminology of his science, so it will be found that the thoughts of the child have much in them of real scientific value, and that the prudent interrogator will be able to extract from them their genuine Ethical significance. In this sense we claim that a child regards evil-doing as unnatural.

come to be, and at the thought of a "First" who made all, his mind is at rest. And so he easily gets to the thought of sin. First, a bad act is a violation of nature—that is, it violates the original plan of the world; secondly, it is a disarrangement of *God's* plan, a disarrangement that can only be set right by God. How far that idea would carry a child we do not know. He might even think that to prevent a tree from flowering or to break down its branches (these things being in some sense against nature) was sin. We have no doubt that a child would at first get many erroneous ideas of his duty. But still we believe that his ideas will run in some direction such as that which we have indicated.[4]

Thus, even in the mind of the child, we find in some sense the rough outline of the whole philosophy of morals. Evil is to him a disarrangement of the original plan of things and a violation of *nature*, and consequently an offence against God. And, as we have seen, the philosophical account of evil is no other than this. Sin is a violation of the natural order. But it is also an offence against God, and it is as an offence against God that sin comes home to us most intensely, and this is the natural form that the idea of evil and of the violation of Duty assumes in the mind of a child.

With what rapidity, when once these ideas of goodness and duty are possessed, the proportions of the moral fabric begin to form will be readily understood. That lies and murder and disrespect of parents are unnatural can then be seen by the youngest mind. Particularly easy will be the formation of such judgments by those who are not left to their own resources, who have a few of the moral truths put ready-made before them for their acceptance. But when these judgments have been formed we still require the thought of the Higher Sanction and the Personal love of the first Creator if our love of the good is to be an actuating principle with us, and if the fabric of our moral beliefs is to have permanence and stability.

.   .   .

Can Conscience Develop and Decay?

"Can conscience develop?" is a question which we shall find no difficulty in answering. Since conscience is nothing more than the practical Reason[5] it can be educated and developed in two ways—(1) By the attainment of new truths, (2) by increase of power—*i.e.*, of energy and

---

[4] Parents might instruct a child to do certain things because such is their wish, but unless there was something in the natural relation of parent to child which appeals to the child's mind it could not know that is was its duty to pay heed to the word of its parents. The mere wish of the parent could not of itself generate a belief that that wish has the force of a law, and that it ought to be obeyed.

[5] More strictly, an act of the practical Reason.

acuteness—in the reasoning faculty itself. These things require no eluci-
dation; for the moral faculty is exactly on a par with the mathematical or
the commercial Reason, both of which can grow in the two ways mentioned—*i.e.*, objectively, by enlarging the sphere of knowledge, and
subjectively, by developing one's inner power of observation and
thought.

But a question of much more practical importance for Ethicians, and
of much greater difficulty as well, is the reverse of that just put—namely,
(1) Can Conscience decay, and if so (2) can it be lost altogether?—*i.e.*,
can Reason become partially blinded on moral matters, and if so can it
wholly lose sight of morality?

(1) We answer, first, that conscience can decay in two ways—(*a*) By
the weakening of the *general* faculty of Reason itself, (*b*) by loss of
perceptive power within the special sphere of morals. (*a*) Of the first
there is very little necessity to speak here. If the general faculty of
Reason becomes impaired our power of moral judgment, like that of the
mathematical judgment, must be to some extent adversely affected. We
can no more trust the judgment of a madman on moral matters than we
can trust his memory or his imagination on the facts of sense. But we
must speak more at length of the possibility of decay in Conscience itself,
or of Reason within the special department of morals. (*b*) May it happen
that whilst in every other department the Reason retains its strength and
balance, yet in the particular department of morals, of moral good and
evil, the Reason may become blurred and untrustworthy? That conscience does decay to some extent is a fact to which no observer of men
can close his eyes. There are men in whom the moral faculty has become
so irresponsive that they fail to see many truths that once were clear to
their minds, and obvious, and unmistakable. And this has come about,
not because of any explicit or formal process of reasoning that they have
gone through, but simply because conscience has lost its edge, because it
has been blunted by one or more of the thousand and one influences that
are wont to affect the practical Reason. The first of these influences is the
constant misuse of conscience; the second is the *influence of desire upon
thought.* By the misuse of conscience we mean the use of Conscience
against one's better judgment. We rarely do evil without excusing ourselves in some way, and making up our minds that what we do is lawful
—that it is well not to be too strict—that to err is human—that sin must
be condoned, &c. All this is against our better judgment. The still small
voice warns us that we are in the wrong. But the still small voice being
constantly unheeded soon goes below the threshold of our moral consciousness, and ceases to be heard. Then, secondly, there is the general
effect of desire on conscience and on the Reason generally. Prejudice and
desire are capable of warping the judgment not only in morals but in
every kind of belief. Scientists often err unconsciously in their account of

the laws of nature, because of some hobby or fancy for which they want to find support in the facts of nature. In politics, too, our views are influenced very much by our prejudices arising out of environment, or by the prevailing fashions of thought and speech. And just as our political and scientific views, so also our moral judgments are affected by our own desires or passions, and particularly by the views of that society in which we live. And we are affected in varying degrees according as our character is weaker or stronger, compromising or independent. Conscience, therefore, may decay, and even well-reasoned judgments be reversed through a variety of causes of which the cases just given are only a few prominent instances.

(2) But though conscience may decay there is still a limit to the reversibility or variability of our moral judgments. Our views on Political Philosophy may change, so far as to make us think that that particular system of taxation is the better one which suits our own business and requirements. But we cannot imagine a thinking man *genuinely* believing that there should be no such thing as government or "law and order" at all. So in morals, a man could never come to believe that indiscriminate murder and the complete neglect of children were lawful, or that the natural was the thing to be avoided, and the unnatural to be done. No, the first principles of Ethics and what has been called their proximate conclusions can never vanish from our minds, however much an evil life or prejudice or passion may affect us. We can imagine a man holding that in certain very exaggerated circumstances even murder would be lawful, though to the cold, unprejudiced, developed Reason it could never seem so. But no developed mind could ever believe that wanton murder was the good thing and to be done, and its opposite the bad thing and to be avoided. Hence, whilst the faculty of Conscience is quite capable of partial decadence it can never be wholly lost. A man can never despoil himself of his first principles or of a knowledge of his main duties, and as long as these remain they will not only keep up a claim on their own account, but will also act as an incentive in bringing back to his mind even those discarded truths which crime and passion have obliterated.

SOCIAL CONCEPTS DIMENSION

Education / AUSTIN FAGOTHEY, S. J.

That both the family and the state have an interest in education is admitted by all. The child is born and grows up as a member of the

"Education" is reprinted with permission from Austin Fagothey, S. J.: *Right and Reason*, 4th ed., St. Louis, 1967, The C. V. Mosby Co.

family that he may take his place later as a citizen of the state. Our question is: *Who has the primary right, the parents or the state?*

However educators may define education, we take it to mean any process of training the physical, mental, and moral powers of a human being to render him fit for the duties of life. Our question deals only with education during the formative period of a child's life and with education for the common duties of a human life. It does not deal with adult education, which is subsequent to the formative period, nor with vocational training, which is a requirement only for those pursuing that vocation. We are discussing the kind of education a child has a right to have and someone the duty to provide, a situation that sets up a special relation between teacher and pupil. Anyone who knows something has the right to teach it if he can get people to listen to him, but he cannot impose his teaching with authority. We are dealing here with education which the teacher has authority to impart and which the pupil has the duty to submit to respectfully, though his intellectual acceptance of what he is taught depends on his being convinced of its truth.

This main problem branches out into several others. We shall treat them as follows:

1) The primary right of the parents
2) The secondary rights of Church and state
3) The founding and conducting of schools
4) Academic freedom in the teachers

Parents' Primary Right

The right to educate their children belongs to the parents by the natural law, and is therefore a natural right. By the natural law parents have the *duty* to educate their children. The very reason why marriage exists as a natural institution is that both parents must provide for the long period of training necessary to raise a child. But one cannot have a duty without the right to fulfill that duty. Therefore by the natural law parents have the *right* to educate their children.

Since the parents are responsible for the child's existence, they are also responsible for all the child will need to live a decent and useful human life. They do not fulfill their duty simply by feeding, clothing, and sheltering the child; they must also see to it that the child, when grown, can take his place as a useful member of society, since society is natural to man. Therefore they must teach him the means of acquiring an independent livelihood, the means of communication with his fellow man, and the social virtues needed for life in common with others. More important still, the child is dependent on his parents for the formation of those good moral habits which the child will need for his own personal morality and for attaining his purpose in life. The parents can do this, and they can do it best. Hence they are picked out by nature for this work.

How much education is the child entitled to? At least the minimum essentials just described. Whether the child can expect more education than this depends on the child's ability, the circumstances of the family, the educational facilities available, and the prevalent level of culture. Parents should try to do the best they can for their children, but are not obliged to make extraordinary sacrifices. In this country one can hardly get along without knowing how to read and write, but this is not the case everywhere. The amount of education therefore depends on a combination of individual, family, and community requirements.

Rights of State and Church

The state has no right to interfere in what strictly belongs to the family. Education cannot belong to both family and state independently and on the same plane, for there would be a conflict of rights and duties. The family is prior to the state and had the obligation of educating the children before there was any state. The state is founded to supplement the family, not to destroy it, and hence cannot take away from the family its already existing right.

However, both Church and state have secondary rights in education, which by no means contravene the parents' primary right. Both Church and state have a right to all the means necessary for the fulfillment of their ends, and education comes within the scope of these means. The Church must have something to say about the education of her members, and the state of its citizens.

The Church has the right and the duty to oblige parents who are her members to give their children the proper religious education. But the Church has authority only over her members and uses no temporal sanctions to obtain her ends. Since the members belong to the Church voluntarily, they could hardly be good members unless they are willing to cooperate with the Church's educational program.

The state has the right and the duty to compel parents to fulfill their duty in educating their children. This is called a secondary right and duty, because it is valid only when the parents themselves fail in their duty. The state can compel parents to feed their children if they neglect to do so, but has no right to interfere when the parents discharge their obligation satisfactorily. The same is true in the matter of education. The state's right is not so much to *do* the work of education as to see that it is done. In this function it is only protecting the child.

Schools

Our discussion has been about education and not about schools, for schooling is only a means, and not always an absolutely necessary one, toward education. Parents had the duty of educating their children long before there were any schools, and the duty would remain were all schools abolished. Even today, if the parents have the ability and the leisure to give adequate instruction to their children at home, they have no moral obligation to send them to school at all. But few parents are qualified for this task today, and the home-educated child is handicapped by lacking the socializing influence of contact with those of his own age.

Ordinarily parents hand over the work of formal instruction and mental training to schools, but not entirely; the parents themselves must do the work of preschool education or hire someone to do it for them. This is the most important part of education and is best done by the parents themselves. Even when the child goes to school, the parents must continue their training out of school hours and must constantly watch the child's progress at school. The mere handing over of the child to others to educate does not absolve the parents of their responsibility. Parents must inform themselves on the character of the schools to which they send their children, and remove them if the influence threatens to prove harmful.

What are the rights of the Church regarding schools? The Church has the right to teach her own members their religion and for this purpose may open schools of religious instruction. Secular education does not directly belong to the Church's sphere of work, but, if it is either not being given at all or is being given in a way hostile to religious faith, there is no reason why the Church should not add a secular curriculum to the religious studies, and thus develop her schools (while preserving the denominational aspect) into ordinary private schools. The Church got into the work of secular education by historical accident, opening schools in the early Middle Ages, when there were no schools and no one else fit to start any. The Church has adjusted to the modern educational scene differently in different countries as circumstances seemed to warrant, either fitting her religious program into the state school system or continuing to conduct her own independent schools. At least, the Church's schools are legitimate private schools, and she has the right to continue those in existence and to establish others, if this seems expedient for safeguarding the faith of her members.

What are the rights of the state regarding schools? The state has the right to open and conduct schools when private initiative is insufficient for this work. The state must look after the common welfare and promote all works that are socially necessary. If private schools are too few and small, they must be supplemented by state schools, and where there are no private schools, the state must furnish all the facilities. But, if this work is already being done adequately by private schools, the state has no right to put them out of business by unfair tax-supported competition.

The state has not the right to monopolize education. Education is a legitimate form of private enterprise, subject indeed to a certain amount of government regulation, but there is nothing in its nature that makes it a public or state monopoly. The reason is that the primary right to educate their children belongs to the parents. In undertaking the work of education the state is simply supplying the parents with facilities to fulfill their duty. If the parents have other facilities at their command, they have no obligation to use those the state provides.

The state's right in education is entirely secondary and supplementary. The state may not make attendance at state schools compulsory, either by law or by undue favoritism. It may not force parents to send their children to one definite school, public or private, rather than another, though it may refuse to accept children from other tax-supported districts. It may not close private schools already operating, unless they have proved to be public menaces or frauds, nor may it refuse to allow the opening of new private schools. Even in its own public schools the state is acting under the authority delegated to it by the parents, who have the primary right; the state is only their agent and trustee. Therefore, the state must conduct these schools with a regard for the parents' wishes, and not force on the children a type of education the parents disapprove. This does not put on them the impossible task of listening to every parents' whim, but they must give the general type of education the parents as a group demand. This is not true of private schools where they are optional, but would be true of them if they carried the whole educational burden, for then they would be in a position like that of a privately owned public utility, which is obliged to put the common good before private interests.

The state has the right to regulate education within certain limits. As a measure of public protection, it may set reasonable standards to which schools, both public and private, must conform. It may set standards of qualification for teachers. It may prevent the teaching of injurious and subversive doctrines, just as it can forbid the sale of tainted food. It may prescribe courses in citizenship and see that a patriotic spirit prevails in the schools; but it has no right to dominate the whole curriculum. The proper integration of courses in a school and the methods of teaching to be adopted are the business of educators, not of politicians.

Has not the state, especially a democratic state, a particular interest in the education of its future citizens, so that this right transcends that of parents? The state has a right to a sufficiently educated citizenry, especially a democratic state that depends on an intelligent vote; hence, if the parents do not fulfill their duty, the state may force them to do so, not only for the child's sake but also for the state's sake. But this right is always secondary. The state has the right to see that parents educate their children into competent citizens but no direct right to take over this duty itself. Otherwise the state is encroaching on an essential right of the family, crowding the family out of its rights, and thus verging on totalitarianism.

Academic Freedom

Academic freedom is the name given to a teacher's privilege of teaching the doctrines and opinions he holds, without undue censorship by the state or even by the school that employs him. It is understood that academic freedom is expected chiefly at the university level, but it is extended somewhat to secondary and primary education.

The reasons for some degree of academic freedom are obvious. Advancement in science and culture is possible only where investigators are free to pursue truth wherever it leads. The teacher is supposed to be an expert in his field, and it is illogical to put him under the dictation of those who know less about the subject than he. He cannot be morally obliged to play the hypocrite and teach what he thinks false. He earns his living by teaching and should not be in constant fear of dismissal because his superiors adopt a change of view or policy, so that he would have to teach one year the contradictory of what he had taught the previous year. This last remark shows the connection between academic freedom and tenure.

But it cannot be maintained that academic freedom is absolute. First of all, it is subject to the same limitations as the right of free speech, and may not be defamatory, obscene, subversive, or otherwise malicious, since no one can acquire a right to immoral conduct. But academic freedom is subject to further restrictions because of the teacher's fourfold relation:

1) To his pupils
2) To their parents
3) To the school employing him
4) To the community

Even the university professor, except in graduate and professional schools, is dealing with immature minds, unable to compete with him on the same level, as yet untrained to give an exact appraisal of all he says or to argue with him from a rich background of experience. Speaking to these impressionable minds with the authority of his position, he must consider not only his own convictions and theories, but what effect these will have on the minds of the young. He is supposed to be forming and developing youth, not merely using them as a sounding board for any sort of idea he may get. If he feels that loyalty to his own convictions requires him to preach doctrines commonly regarded as inflammatory and subversive, let him give up teaching and enter the public arena to cross swords with his equals. It is one thing to present the students with an intellectual challenge, another to make it a policy to unsettle all the ideals and convictions the students have received at home and then leave them in this state of vacuity and disorientation. Such abusers of academic freedom are among the greatest enemies of youth.

The teacher is the agent and trustee of the parents. He has no independent authority over the child, must work in harmony with the parents, supplement the training of the home, and in general give the type of education the parents contract for. On the other hand, parents send their children to him because he is supposed to be an expert in his field, and he cannot adjust his teaching or the school's curriculum to meet every ignorant or meddlesome parent's demand. Here arises a conflict of rights and duties, in which the application of the ordinary principles may become quite difficult. The best solution seems to be the establishment of many schools with a wide variety of curricula and policies, among which parents may choose, so that parents can get the kind of education they want for their children and the teachers can teach what they believe.

The teacher has definite responsibilities to his employers and must fulfill the contract he makes with them. Before accepting the position he must inform himself on the ideals and policies of the school, for he has no right to take the position if he disagrees with them or intends to be disloyal to them. Academic freedom cannot be stretched to the point of allowing him publicly to oppose the policy of the school where he teaches; if he feels that he must, because of some change in his own views, he should seek other employment. The right of tenure may be invoked against arbitrary dismissal, but there can be no ethical ground for making it a reason why a school must tolerate treason in its own house. The school has a moral obligation to pupils and parents, and must be able to get rid of undesirable teachers as well as uncooperative pupils.

On the whole, we can consider the teacher in a threefold capacity: as a private individual expressing his personal opinions, as a scholar presenting the fruit of his research to the learned world, and precisely as a teacher in contact with his students. So far we have been discussing him in the last function. As a private individual, he may act as any other private person, so long as he makes clear that he is speaking for himself alone. As a scholar, he is somewhat in between; he is speaking to his equals and is open to their criticism on the same level, but he is under obligation to his school from which he derives his academic standing and on which his views may reflect; he cannot exempt himself entirely from their approval. This relation to his school puts some limitation on his academic freedom.

Let it be understood, however, that academic freedom certainly has its place, and a policy of overactive censorship, especially on the part of the state, would be most unwise. Any restriction of teaching should be done by the schools, which are capable of handling such matters, rather than by the state, which is capable of supplying the facilities for education but not of deciding what ought or ought not to be taught.

How far should the teacher be free to use his position to promote social progress? Should education be the creature of the existing social order, perpetuating the *status quo,* or the creator of a new social order, an active instrument for social reconstruction? Should the teacher fit his students to take their place in society as now organized or should he inspire them with the goal of building a better social order that will be the work of the younger generation? This battle between traditional and progressive education, involving as it does the whole relation of education to politics, is too extensive for full treatment here, but a few remarks are called for.

Since human society is never in a perfect condition, to strive for social betterment is not only a laudable aim but a moral obligation. The question regarding the teacher is twofold:

1) What sort of change is to be made in society?
2) Is the teacher the one to promote such change?

The building of a social order can be understood to mean either the carrying on of the present work to higher perfection on the same foundations or the altering of the present structure so drastically as to eventuate in a new one on different foundations. Education is one of the means that society relies on for its own further development, and all would agree that here at least it operates within its legitimate sphere. Whether it should be used for the purpose of remaking society, of creating what amounts to social revolution, depends on many factors, not the least of them being the kind of new social structure to be built. The first thing, then, that educational reconstructionists are obliged to do is to specify clearly and formulate exactly the social program they have in mind, so that they can submit it to the judgment of their fellow citizens.

Whether social reconstruction be justified or not, the question remains whether the *teacher* is the one to promote it. The form of government and the structure of society are political matters, to be decided by the ruling authority in the state; in a democracy this is the citizens, not the children in school nor their teachers precisely as teachers. If the latter judge that the citizens of today are so hopelessly conservative that the educators must take into their own hands the development of a new type of citizen for the future, they have ceased to be mere educators and have taken on themselves the role of legislators and governors. Who has given them such authority? They have the right, not as teachers but as citizens, to try to convince their fellow citizens of the worth of the changes they advocate, but they have not the right, as teachers, to introduce these changes surreptitiously by taking advantage of their pupils' innocence and disregarding the wishes of parents who may not want this kind of training for their children. It seems strange that they who make so much of the democratic method should constitute themselves into an autocratic elite, charged with the development of society and responsible to no one. To demand such a right under the guise of academic freedom is but a bid for political power.

Summary

By *education* we mean any process of training the physical, mental, and moral powers of a human being to render him fit for the duties of life. We deal with general and formative education only.

By the natural law the *parents have the primary right* to educate their children, for education belongs to the essential purpose of marriage, and where there is a duty there is a right to exercise that duty. The amount of education depends on the child's capacity, the family's resources, and the cultural level of the community.

Church and state have *secondary or supplementary rights* in education, each within its proper sphere. They are not to interfere when parents do the work adequately, but they have the right to see that it is done.

Schools are the ordinary means of education, but do not take the whole burden from the parents. The *Church* has the right to establish religious schools and to add to religious teaching a secular curriculum. The *state* should respect the rights of private schools, supply facilities when private initiative is inadequate, give the general type of education the parents approve, set minimum standards and make inspections if necessary, prohibit subversive teachings, and promote patriotism. The state must *not* monopolize education or dominate the whole curriculum.

Academic freedom, the teacher's privilege to teach what he believes without undue censorship, is a necessary part of the educator's life. But it has its limits. The teacher has special obligations to his *pupils,* because of their youth and inexperience, to the *parents,* whose agent and trustee he is, to the *school,* whose ideals and policies he is not allowed to subvert, and to the *community* of which he is a responsible and respected member. As a private individual he may say what he wishes, as a scholar he has some obligation to the school employing him, but precisely as a teacher he must form the minds of the young by continuing the child's home training according to the program of his school.

Moral Education / JACQUES MARITAIN

I do not pretend here to treat the question of Moral Education in a complete manner. I wish only to emphasize certain points that seem to me especially important from the philosophical angle.

There are four main points which I should like to discuss.

First: the nature and the limitations of the domain and function of the school with regard to moral education.

Second: the concrete, existential relationship between morality and religion.

Third: the basic role of the family in moral education.

Fourth: the moral teaching in the school.

The Role of the School in Moral Education

Before coming to my first point, I should like first of all to make it clear that a sharp distinction must be made between two essential parts of moral education, namely the *direct formation* of the will, or of the dynamism of human desires and freedom, and the *indirect moral formation* by means of the intellect's enlightenment. And the former depends basically not on the school and the university, but on the family—and on that spiritual family which is the Church.

At this point we may observe that in education broadly understood—I do not mean teaching—we may observe that educational training is in reality less an ethical art than a moral virtue implying a large part of art; it is in its very roots the practical wisdom (or, in Aristotelian terms, "prudence") of the head of the family. Because this particular ethical wisdom must necessarily involve a great deal of knowledge and a great deal of art and technical preparation as an essential ingredient, especially with regard to the intellectual formation of the child, it happened in antiquity that the father of the family shifted the responsibility of the art of teaching onto the *pedagogue,* who was a slave of the father of the family. From that time on, the pedagogue was to grow and develop in a singular manner, and to emancipate himself. Please do not believe I am suggesting that schools and colleges should be considered slaves of the *paterfamilias:* I mean that the historical development and freeing of the school, while assuming more and more importance, did not and could not annihilate the normal link which relates the school to the family, and that the part of the school in education concerns essentially knowledge and intellectual development.

"Moral Education" is reprinted from Jacques Maritain, "Moral Education," *A College Goes to School: Centennial Lectures.* Reprinted by permission of St. Mary's College, Indiana.

The school and the university constitute an educational sphere of their own, which is autonomous both with regard to the family and to the state—there takes place here that great humanistic privilege which is academic liberties, but in which the educational rights of the family and the educational rights of the political community have to be respected, and in actual fact intertwine. The school is not an organ either of the family or of the civil community; its position is free, not subservient, yet subordinated to superior and more primordial rights: subordinated, I should like to say, to the family's rights as regards primarily morality, to the state's rights as regards primarily intellectual equipment. Thus we understand the fact that in proportion as the child grows, the emphasis of this double subordination changes: the school, which at the beginning is more subordinated to the concerns of the family than to those of the political community, becomes finally, with university teaching, more subordinated to the concerns of the political community than to those of the family. Because the family refers primarily to man as a living being, to be born both to physical and to moral life, whereas the political community refers primarily to man as a rational being, therefore it is entitled to make special requirements with regard to the acquisition of knowledge, and to see to it that instruction be given to and received by all. I do not mean by making school and college education everywhere a part of the public services of the cities or the states; I mean by exerting control over it, and by helping or subsidizing privately endowed institutions. No doubt, the political community is interested too in the acquisition of moral virtues. But on the one hand it is here confronted with rights more fundamental than its own, namely, the rights of the family and those of the Church, which, by virtue of its mission spiritually to beget man for eternal life, possesses a full right to education—to be exercised in accordance with just civil laws. On the other hand, the very possibilities of the political community in matters of moral education are of no greater extent than those of the school, which has to do, by its very nature, with intellectual enlightenment more than with any direct formation of the will.

At this point I must stress the distinction between the will, practical reason, and speculative reason. Speculative reason deals with knowledge for the sake of knowledge alone; practical reason, with knowledge for the sake of action and good human conduct; the will, with action itself and human conduct itself. When I say that school and college education is primarily concerned with knowledge and intellectual enlightenment, I do in no wise mean that it is only concerned with speculative knowledge and speculative reason: on the contrary, I am convinced that our present school and college education is too much taken up by theoretical knowledge, and that the part of ethics and morality in it needs to be strongly developed and emphasized. What I mean is that this practical part does not essentially deal with the direct formation of the inner powers of desire and will, of conscience and freedom, but does essentially deal with the formation and enlightenment of practical reason: that is, with teaching about the nature and principles and the very science of morality, and with that immense part of human knowledge which bears on human manners and human conduct.

Morality and Religion

My second point deals with the concrete, existential relationship between morality and religion. Here a preliminary remark must be made. I just spoke of practical reason and moral teaching. As concerns now the will itself and the moral virtues, as having to be acquired and exercised by the individual person, ethical knowledge is indeed indispensable, yet, as a matter of fact, far from sufficient. For it is a question of right applications to and right judgment on particular cases; practical reason itself depends on the rectitude of the will and on the decisive trend of our very freedom. The melancholy saying of Aristotle, contrasting with the Socratic doctrine that virtue is only knowledge, is to be recalled in this connection. "To know," he said, "does little or even nothing for virtue." [1]

What does a great deal for virtue is love: 'because the root hindrance to moral life is basic egoism, and the chief yearning of moral life; liberation from oneself; and only love, being the gift of oneself, is able to remove this hindrance and to bring this yearning to fulfillment. But love is surrounded by our central egoism and in perpetual danger of becoming entangled in and recaptured by it, whether this egoism makes the ones we love a prey to our devouring self-love, or merges them in the ruthless self-love of the group, so as to exclude all other men from our love. Love does not regard ideas or abstractions or possibilities; love regards existing persons. God is the only Person whom human love can fly to and settle in, so as to embrace also all other persons and be freed from egotistic self-love. If a man actually loves another human being by that love which in some degree always consists in dying for the one loved, he actually loves God, and God first, at least in that manner in which all beings, even an atom or a grain of wheat, love God more than themselves. Yet the natural love of God cannot be stabilized in man so as to love God above everything in an efficacious fashion, and to love also all men, and in some manner all beings, unless it is perfected by love of charity.

At this point we may observe that a profound link exists between the sense of love and the sense of sin. For both love and sin are mysteries the

[1] *II Ethic*, Ch. 4, 1105b; cf. Saint Thomas Aquinas, *III Sent.*, dist. 35, ques. I, art. 3.9.2, a.s.

meaning of which is definitely seizable only with reference to God, and both depend on those depths of human personality and human freedom where man feels responsible for himself and is able to dispose of himself or give himself for some eternal pledge and through some irrevocable decision. In his book on *The Bourgeois Man,* Werner Sombart insists that man, in the rationalistic-capitalistic age, has become deprived of the sense of Being and the sense of Love. He became deprived, too, of the sense of Sin. Truly, we lost at the same time the sense of these three basic realities. Now to recover them is a matter of emergency for civilization. The sense of Love, the sense of Sin, the sense of Being, will be recovered at the same time, for they are intrinsically connected with each other. Or, rather, if we consider not the order of time, but the order of natural priorities, and if we remember that normally the curve of human achievements starts in the reason and ends in the will, we should say that the first to be recovered is the sense of Being, which primarily depends on the dynamism of speculative reason, then the sense of Sin, which primarily depends on the dynamism of conscience and practical reason, and then the sense of Love, which primarily depends on the dynamism of the will and inner tendential powers.

The previous considerations enlighten the question of the relationship between morality and religion. The core of morality is human reason, insofar as reason is the proximate rule of human actions. The core of religion is divine love, that is, indivisibly, love of God and brotherly love. Christianity fastens the moral to the supramoral—the moral order and the moral virtues to the theological order and the theological virtues, the greatest of which is charity. Christianity makes law appendant to love, and in this way it saves morality. For not only are reason and law, even the law of God, powerless to drag the heart of man to action if it is not quickened by love, but the very perfection of moral life and human life is suprahuman and supramoral, being perfection in love. We are wounded by sin indeed, and at the same time called upon to perfection, and there is no morality without striving toward self-perfection. If we aim at the moral ideal of the honest and sensible man, our average common behavior will drop down below morality. It will be lifted up to morality if the supramoral call and inspiration of the saints pass through our laborious and defective human life.

Thus we may understand the paradox that natural law exists, as the very basis of morality, and that nevertheless no effort of reason to establish among men a firm system of morality based only on natural law has ever been able to succeed; that moral philosophy is a fundamental and necessary requirement of culture and civilization, and that nevertheless moral philosophy is unable to ground good conduct of men if it is not backed up by faith. I am not pretending that a man who believes only in reason cannot have a genuine ethics of his own and a high standard of moral life. Nor am I pretending that a religious man cannot be morally perverted, or that religious men have always a standard of moral conduct worthy of their faith. That is nonsense! Religious men know they are sinners; but they also know that while staggering along we may climb the road to renascence and spiritualization. What I maintain is that with regard to the average behavior of mankind, morality without religion undermines morality, and is able to sustain human life for but a few generations.

Moral Education and the Family

In order to come to my third point, the basic role of the family in moral education, I should like to recall that nothing in human life is of greater importance than intuition and love, and neither intuition nor love is a matter of training or learning. Yet education must be primarily concerned with them. As for love, the question is above all to liberate the spiritual energies of the soul; those energies of goodness are badly repressed by the false realism and vulgarity of the wicked philosophy of life which is current today. Contrary to the precept of Descartes, who, in his provisory rules of Morals, decided to imitate the customs and doings of his fellow-men, we must first of all encourage personal conscience not to hesitate to disagree with collective behavior for the sake of truth, on the condition, of course, that it is certainly a question of truth. Such is the rule of the Gospel: "Do not ye after their works; for they say, and do not." [2] The first step to be taken by everyone who wishes to act morally, and to keep alive in himself the sources of love, is to make up his mind not to act according to the general customs and doings of his fellow-men.

Love, human love as well as divine love, is not a matter of training or learning, for it is a gift; the love of God is a gift of nature and of grace: that is why it can be the first precept. How could we be commanded to put into action a power which we have not received or may not first receive? Charity, or that love of God is communion in friendship, is a grace-given virtue, and grows, like other virtues, by its own acts. There are no human methods or techniques of getting or developing charity, no more than any kind of love. There is nevertheless education in this matter: an education which is provided by trial and suffering, and which primarily consists in removing impediments and obstacles to love, and first of all sin, and in developing moral virtues.

The help of educators is obviously needed here. As is the case with that which concerns in general the direct formation of the will, the educational sphere involved is first of all the family. Is not family love the primary pattern of any love uniting a community of men? Is not fraternal love the very name of that neighborly love which is but one with the love

[2] *Matt.* XXIII, 3.

of God? No matter what deficiencies the family group may present in certain particular cases; no matter what trouble and disintegration the economic and social conditions of our day have brought to family life, the nature cannot be changed. And it is an essential law of the nature of things both that the vitality and virtues of love develop first in the family and that moral and religious training is first at work in the family. Not only the examples of the parents, and the rules of conduct which they inculcate, and the religious habits and inspiration which they further, and the memories of their own lineage which they convey, in short the educational work which they directly perform, but also, in a more general way, the common experiences and common trials, efforts, sufferings and hopes, and the daily labor of family life, and the daily love which pushes forward in the midst of slaps and kisses, constitute the normal fabric where the feelings and the will as of the child are naturally shaped. The society made up by his parents, his brothers and sisters, is the primary human society and human environment in which, consciously and subconsciously, he becomes acquainted with love and from which he receives his ethical nourishment. Here both conflicts and harmonies have educational value; a boy who has experienced common life with his sisters, a girl who has done so with her brothers, have gained unawares invaluable and irreplaceable moral advance as regards the relationship between the sexes. Over and above all, family love and brotherly love create in the heart of the child that hidden recess of tenderness and repose the memory of which man so badly needs, and in which perhaps after years of bitterness, he will immerse himself anew each time a natural trend to goodness and peace awakens in him. Father's and mother's love is the natural fostering of the sources of love within the child. If they love God, the child will also know through them the very countenance of such a love, and never forget it.

I am aware that the examples of the parents are not always good, nor their educational work always well directed, nor their very love for their children always genuine, nor the life of the family group always heartening. We all know that the worst abuses and psychic deviations and unjust sufferings are possible in family life and education. French novelists, notably François Mauriac and Philippe Heriat, made clear what power of moral destruction a bourgeois family may display, and how the despotic love of some mothers may ruin the life of their sons. The history of the family, all through the centuries, is no prettier than any human history. What I maintain is that nature exists and nothing can get rid of nature. There are freaks in nature; then exceptional measures must be taken. But let us speak of what happens as a rule. Even at the most mediocre average level, nature at play in family life has its own spontaneous ways of compensating after a fashion for its own failures, its own spontaneous processes of self-regulation, which nothing can replace, and provides the child with a moral formation and an experience of mutual love, however deficient it may be, which nothing can replace. Many birds fall from the nest. It would be nonsense to undertake to destroy all the nests fairly well prepared by mother-birds, and to furnish the forests of the world with better-conditioned artificial nests, and improved cages.

It is not my purpose to speak now of the other educational sphere directly concerned with the mo al shaping of man, namely the Church, acting by means of its teaching precepts, sacraments, and liturgy, and its spiritual training and guidance, as well as by its manifold initiatives and undertakings, youth movements and organizations. Suffice it to say that here again we are confronted with the law of love proper to family, this time the very family of God, since grace causes men to be of the lineage of God, and, according to St. Paul, "fellow-citizens with the saints, and of the household of God." [3] To grow in the love of God, and, by the same token, of our fellow-men, is the serious business in this household. St. Paul also says: "He that loveth his neighbor hath fulfilled the law." [4] So that all the moral work by means of which Christianity endeavors to bring up the human person, is centered on the development, strengthening and purification of that brotherly love which actually enables us to become the neighbor of any man, by having pity on him and caring for his wounds.

As concerns finally the role of school and college education with regard to love as the very soul of moral life, two principles which I consider basically important find here a particular application. On the one hand, with regard to direct influence on the will, the role of the school amounts above all to that premoral training which depends not on teaching, but on humble policy, common life and discipline of the school: here the basic mood should be given in actual fact by constant attention to the requirements of the rules of justice in the school-community, and to the requirements of sincere fellowship and brotherly love. On the other hand, with regard to the indirect action on the will *by means of intellectual* enlightenment, the role of school and college education is momentous indeed, insofar as teaching of true or false knowledge has efficacy to liberate or hamper the spiritual energy of love within the soul. For it is by the fallacies of pseudo-science and false philosophy of life that love trying to find its way amidst the jumbled world of passions and instincts is often withered and killed. Nowhere is the vigilance and genuine information of the intellect of greater practical import. All errors which make fun of goodness, all those practical sophistries which keep moving in our atmosphere, and avail themselves of cheap Darwinism, cheap Machiavellianism or so called realism to make youth despair of the power of truth and love, should be thoroughly

[3] *Eph.* II, 19.
[4] *Rom.* XIII, 8.

discussed and accurately criticized. The existence and power of evil should be frankly criticized. The existence and power of evil should be frankly faced: and faced also the existence and power of God, which are greater. The true laws of being and of human existence, which are hidden to an empiricist gaze, but which reason and faith perceive, and which finally imply that evil is a bad payer and that love has the last word, should be contemplated without flinching and elucidated. A teaching which, not by empty idealistic words, but by dint of intellectual strength and exact disquisition of reality, inspires trust in goodness and generosity, is surely not enough to awaken the well-springs of love in the depths of human freedom, but it is efficacious to protect them, when they are present, and to set them free.

Moral Teaching in the School

At this point we may consider more closely the question of moral teaching in the school and the college. I pointed out a moment ago that as regards the actual acquisition of moral virtues, ethical knowledge is indeed indispensable, yet far from being sufficient. It is equally fair to reverse the statement, and to say: ethical knowledge is indeed far from being sufficient, but it is indispensable.

To know, if it is a question of speculative knowledge, does little for virtue: the little it does, nevertheless, is beyond question, because, on the average, knowledge—I mean knowledge which deals with objects "of most worth"—cleans and pacifies the mind; moreover speculative knowledge establishes the metaphysical principles concerning nature and the world which are the foundations of the ethical principles concerning human freedom and conduct. And to know these ethical truths, that is to possess practical and moral knowledge, to have practical reason enlightened and sound, does a great deal for virtue. I mean on the average. Virtue is not a by-product of knowledge, but true moral knowledge is a condition for virtue. As Father Gerald B. Phelan has remarked, "Human conduct is of its very nature reasonable and enlightened conduct, else it is not truly human." Thus the moral sciences are at the core of any true humanism. The education of man, therefore, necessarily involves a careful and extensive moral teaching. And since teaching is the proper job of the school and the college, obviously moral teaching concerning both personal and civic morals must be an essential part of the curriculum. The absence or poverty of such teaching in formal education is a great misfortune. Filling this gap will probably be one of the chief concerns of the reformation needed by our time. Moral teaching should be pursued all through formal education.

The trouble starts with the question of the nature and content of this teaching. Many efforts have been made in the last century, especially in

Europe, with hopes which proceeded from Kantian inspiration, to build in and for schools a morality of their own, disconnected from any religious creed and based on pure reason. The result was thoroughly disappointing. Sociologism and positivism were to nibble and consume the ethics of pure reason. Moreover, an ethics which, like that of Kant, ignores nature, good and the trend to happiness, and conceives of itself as merely law-giving by virtue of categorical imperatives, suffers from an incurable internal weakness.

There exists, nevertheless, a natural law. And there is a valid moral philosophy. Is it not possible to found on natural law and moral philosophy a consistent moral teaching in the school and the college? My answer is, yes and no. Natural law is unwritten and unsystematized law —too natural, so to speak, to become a subject of schoolteaching without losing its most human truth, inexpressible in the manner of a code. Moral philosophy is philosophy—too highly and delicately rationalized to become a subject of schoolteaching (except at the time when it is taught as philosophy) without losing its most valuable truth, which depends on all the principles and truths of philosophical reason. I would state, therefore, that in a good college curriculum moral philosophy should be taught—both through lectures and seminars—during the last two college years. But I think that during the years which precede philosophical training, no special teaching and courses should be given on morality abstractedly detached from its religious environment. Natural morality, however, natural law, and the great ethical ideas conveyed by civilization should be taught during these years. They are the very treasure of classical humanism; they must be communicated to the youth, not as a subject of special courses, but as embodied in the humanities and liberal arts, especially as an integral part of the teaching of literature, poetry, fine arts, and history. This teaching should be permeated with the feeling and concern of such values. The reading of Homer, Aeschylus, Sophocles, Herodotus, Thucydides, Demosthenes, Plutarch, Epictetus, Marcus Aurelius (better to read them carefully in translation than to learn their language and to read only bits), the reading of Virgil, Terence, Tacitus and Cicero, of Dante, Cervantes, Shakespeare, Milton, Pascal, Racine, Montesquieu, Goethe, Dostoevski, feeds the mind with the sense and knowledge of natural virtues, honor, pity, of the dignity of man and of the spirit, the greatness of human destiny, the entanglements of good and evil, the *caritas humani generis*, more than any course in natural ethics. It conveys to the youth the moral experience of mankind.

So much for *natural morality*. Another point deals with morality as backed up by faith and involving supernatural life. I previously discussed the unbreakable relationship which, in actual existence, links morality with religion. Truth to tell, merely natural or rational ethics, if it is taken as a complete system of morality, is abstract ethics, dealing with a possible man, not with man in his concrete and real existential status. Ethics is able really to constitute a full practical science only on the condition that it be a body of knowledge backed up by religion. Moral teaching, therefore, if it is to be a genuine enlightenment of practical reason, must not leave religion out of account; it must be given with a religious inspiration. This does not mean that moral rules should be presented only as dictated by religion. On the contrary, the reasons which make them necessary for human life should be ceaselessly stressed, as well as their natural foundations and suitabilities. Morality is steeped in intelligence, the goal is to awaken moral intelligence in the pupil. I think that the discussion of concrete instances, taken from ordinary life, and of particular *points of conscience* is better calculated to sharpen ethical awareness as well as to interest the child than mere emphasis on general principles. Discussions of this kind, relying upon the natural moral instinct of the youth, and asking his active participation, seem to me especially adapted for the first years of training in moral knowledge. Later on deeper and more general considerations would be embarked upon. Conformably to the chief importance of the matter, such moral teaching, both rationally developed and religiously inspired, should form the subject of special courses in the curriculum of schools and colleges.

It has moreover to remain distinct—I mean after the years of early formation—from religious training itself, which implies many other subject-matters than morality and must be more concerned with God than with man. I may run counter to the conventions of contemporary education, yet it is my own conviction that this religious training should not only be given in the family and the church-community, but should also be an integral part of the life of the school. I do not see how we can pretend that God has less right to have his place in the school than Euclid or Professor John Dewey. And it is the right of the child to be allowed to acquire through his formal education religious knowledge as well as any knowledge which plays an essential part in the life of man.

Such are the principles which dominate the question. They are, to my mind, grounded in the nature of things. If they are still disregarded by many, this is, in my opinion, mainly as a result of the difficulties involved in their application, and because of the interference of other principles, such as the lay or merely temporal character of the state.

Yet I am convinced that these difficulties may be overcome without the latter principle being denied or imperiled. With the denominational schools, colleges or universities, the problem of religious training and of moral teaching given in connection with religion is obviously solved from the very start. Even the whole structure of education should be inspired by the very philosophy of life and the fundamental outlook proper to the denomination of the school, which is a prominent advantage from the religious and spiritual point of view. The problem is rather to avoid youth's being ignorant or even distrustful of those who are educated in other lines and who will be their fellow-citizens, and to assure among all that mutual understanding which is required by civic friendship and co-operation in the temporal common good. This problem can be easily solved by establishing regular contacts between students of the diverse schools and colleges: either in youth-camps and youth-organizations, or during some periods of common work (for instance, educational visits or travels, common exercise in physical training, etc.), or, as concerns especially universities, by conferences or congresses of students.

Now, if it is a question of nondenominational schools, colleges, and universities, either privately endowed or founded by the city or the state, this time the problem of mutual acquaintance and understanding among youth belonging to different spiritual families is solved from the start. It is the problem of religious and religiously inspired moral teaching which makes difficulties. The general solution consists in having religious training and moral teaching given by diverse teachers, who belong to the different religious creeds in which the students share.

Conclusion

What I have discussed in all my previous remarks is what moral teaching should normally be. Now, before concluding, I must add that as regards moral education, we do not find ourselves in normal conditions. The modern world has met with a complete failure in moral education. As a result, the task of moral re-education is a matter of public emergency. Every serious observer recognizes the fact that children have not only to be trained in behavior, in manner, proper conduct, law observance and politeness, but that this very training remains deficient and precarious if genuine inner formation is not given. In order for teachers in public schools not to face discipline and violence, the theory that children must begin by letting loose and exhausting the instincts of the primitive man does a rather feeble good turn; frank recognition of the authority of teachers, and strong moral principles, that is, taught in utter trust in their truth, surely do more for school discipline than the eventual intervention of police force. I think therefore that, owing to circumstances, additional emphasis should be brought to the teaching of natural morality. The normal way of giving this teaching, which is, as I have pointed out, to have it embodied in the humanities, literature, and history, does not suffice in the face of the tremendous degradation of ethical reason which is today observable. For the moment the evil is still more in intelligence than in behavior, I mean in still civilized countries. Exhausted and bewildered by dint of false and dehumanized philosophy, reason confesses thorough impotence with regard to the justification of any ethical standard. The question is to recover natural and rational adherence of the mind to the most elementary values of human life, to justice, to pity, to freedom. To such a disease of human intelligence and conscience, special remedies should be given, not only by the badly needed revival of religious faith, but also by a revival of the moral power of reason. Accordingly, if teachers may be found whose reason is less sick than that of their students, special teaching should be provided, in schools and colleges, for the principles of natural morality.

At this point I should like to suggest that, according to the nature of things, the field in which natural morality feels most at home, and least deficient, is the field of our temporal activities, or of political, civic, and social morality: because the virtues at play in this field are essentially natural virtues, directed toward the good of civil life or of human civilization, even when they are strengthened by more divine ones; whereas, in the field of personal morality, natural virtues, and the whole trend of moral life, and the very impulse toward the ends of this life cannot be embraced by reason with regard to our real system of conduct in actual existence, unless divine love, which is charity, and the supratemporal destiny of the human person, and the Gospel's virtues, which are grace-given virtues, be also taken into account, and in the first place. As a result, the teaching of natural morality will be inclined, in virtue of its own object, to lay stress on what may be called the ethics of political life and of civilization. Which is all to the good (for here it enjoys its maximum strength and practical truth), on the condition that the teaching of natural morality resist the temptation of neglecting enlightenment about the very root of morality, which is personal morality, and above all the temptation of warping and perverting all its work by making itself a tool of the state and a mere shaping of youth according to the collective pattern supposedly needed by the price, greed or myths of the earthly community.

THE AUTHORS

Rev. Leo Richard Ward (1893–   ). American philosopher promoting natural law as the basis of philosophy, anthropology, and education; scholarly writer on Roman Catholic education in America; indicated the revival of Natural Law Philosophy among non-Catholics as well as Roman Catholics; finds the key to education in the values that lie in the nature of man and his relations to nature and final cause. Born in Melrose, Iowa. Graduated from the University of Notre Dame (1923); Ph.M., Catholic University of America (1927); Ph.D., Catholic University of America (1929); studied at Oxford University (1934–1935), and at Catholic University, Louvain Belgium (1935–

1936). Associate professor of philosophy, University of Notre Dame (1928–1940); professor of philosophy, University of Notre Dame (1940–   ). Major publications: *Blueprint for a Catholic University* (1949); *New Life in Catholic Schools* (1958); *The Living Parish* (1959); *Religion in All the Schools* (1960); *God and World Order* (1961); *Philosophy of Education* (1963); *All Over God's Irish Heaven* (1964); *Ethics: A College Text* (1965).

Rt. Rev. Mgr. Michael Cronin (1871–1943). Irish churchman and scholar; intellectual and pastoral leader in Dublin; published *The Science of Ethics*, an authoritative two-volume work on natural law and the practical problems of ethics in the cultural circumstances of modern industrial societies. Born in Dublin, Ireland. Educated at Clonliffe College, Dublin; Propaganda College, Rome; Universities of Berlin and Munich; B.A. and M.A., Royal University of Ireland; D.D. Rome (1895). Won junior fellowship in Royal University of Ireland (1904); professor of ethics and politics, University College, Dublin (1909–1925); Canon of Dublin Metropolitan Chapter and Parish Priest of Rathgar, Dublin (1925–1930); Vicar General Archdiocese of Dublin (1930–1943). Published: *The Science of Ethics* (1909); *Primer of the Principles of Social Science* (1927).

Austin Fagothey, S.J. (1901–   ). Long-time professor of philosophy at Santa Clara University whose text *Right and Reason* is one of the most widely used texts on ethics in Roman Catholic colleges; states the natural law position on education and applies it to the circumstances of family, church, and state. Born in San Francisco. Graduated from Gonzaga University (1923); M.A., Gonzaga University (1924); S.T.L., Weston College (1932); Ph.D., Gregorian University, Rome (1949). Instructor in philosophy, University of Santa Clara (1932–1934); professor and chairman of the department of philosophy, Santa Clara (1935–1936); professor of dogmatic theology, Alma College (1936–1938); professor and chairman of the department of philosophy, University of Santa Clara (1938–   ). Roman Catholic priest, member of the Society of Jesus. Published *Right and Reason: A Textbook in Ethics* (1953).

Jacques Maritain (1882–   ). The most prominent leader of Neo-Scholasticism in the modern world; early abandoned the philosophy of Begson for orthodox Neo-Thomism; member of the vanguard of the Catholic intellectual revival in France; authority on Saint Thomas Aquinas; numerous writings on the relation of reason—speculative and practical—to art, politics, history, and education. Born in Paris, France. Educated at the Sorbonne, University of Paris; Ph.D., in philosophy, University of Paris (1905); studied biological science, University of Heidelberg (1905–1908); staff, The Maison Hachette Publishers, studied Thomism under the Dominican Father Clerissac (1908–1913). Professor of philosophy, Institut Catholique in Paris (1913–1940); visiting professor of philosophy, Columbia University (1940–1944); Ambassador to the Vatican for France (1945–1948); visiting professor of philosophy, Princeton University (1948–1953); professor emeritus, Princeton (1953–   ); visiting professor of Medieval Studies at the Pontifical Institute of Toronto. Major publications: *La Philosophie Bergsonienne* (1914); *Éléments de Philosophie* (1920, 1924);

Antimoderne (1922); *Reflexions sur l'intelligence et sur savie propre* (1923); *Three Reformers: Luther, Descartes, Rousseau* (1925); *Art and Scholasticism* (1930); *The Degrees of Knowledge* (1937); *True Humanism* (1938); *Scholasticism and Politics* (1940); *Saint Thomas and the Problem of Evil* (1942); *Education at the Crossroads* (1943); *Christianity and Democracy* (1944); *Existence and Existent* (1948); *Man and the State* (1949); *The Philosophy of Nature* (1951); *The Range of Reason* (1952); *Creative Intuition in Art and Poetry* (1953); *On the Philosophy of History* (1957).

Existential
Phenomenology

GENERIC NOTIONS AND BASIC THEMES

Contemporary thinkers tend to avoid identification with any philosophical label. Philosophers of Existential Phenomenology are no exception. Indeed, they strongly suggest that they are as much opposed to the notion of "school" philosophy as are the linguistic philosophers. The reasons they give for their opposition are entirely consistent with their approach to philosophy. For Existential Phenomenology is a critique of the systems, institutions, and technologies that endeavor to destroy the essential human qualities and disrupt man's authentic relation to the world. Existential Phenomenology's fundamental tenet is the inherent value of the human being within phenomena. Anything that hinders man's existence must be rejected. Since "school" philosophy emphasizes systems at the expense of pure meaning and persons, Existential Phenomenology must oppose it.

Although Existential Phenomenology is not a school-oriented philosophy, it nevertheless is a distinct thought pattern. It is a cultural movement with generic notions, basic themes, and a peculiar philosophical methodology. Existential Phenomenologists can be identified by their common concerns, by the thinkers and philosophers to whom they give major consideration, by the professors under whom they studied. Thus, despite variations and differences, a common frame of reference can be discerned.

In a discussion of Existential Phenomenology, it is always valuable to refer to its two sources: Existentialism and Phenomenology. Existentialism is more particularly a literary movement with a basic concern for personal existence and the conduct of life, than a philosophical program. Soren Kierkegaard was the first to utilize the term "existential" and thus is known as the father of Existentialism, but parallels to his conceptions can also be found in the writings of Fyodor Dostoyevsky. Phenomenology, in contrast, is strictly a philosophical enterprise, interested in the profound problems of meaning and knowledge. Its founder was Edmund Husserl who developed a Transcendental Phenomenology in his search for essences. Modern Phenomenologists have rejected Husserl's Transcendental Phenomenology, but they remain indebted to him for his initiation of a new philosophical attitude and method.

In terms of its content, modern existential thinking focuses on the human person in a technological and scientific age. Many Existentialists are pessimistic about modern life and indicate that utopianism based on science is an illusion. They believe science and technology have brought human beings loneliness and alienation rather than peace and progress. The institutional organization of science, by and for the state, has dehumanized man. To be saved from complete nihilism, man must choose individual freedom in order to regain his human existence. This choice involves commitment to personal truth. Individual subjectivity must become paramount, not only in one's concern for himself, but also in his relations with others. Other human beings must not be treated as objects to be manipulated and used, but as subjects in person to person confrontation. Existential thinking focuses on the notions of paradox, despair, anxiety, absurdity, faith, hope, and love to indicate a man's personal relationships to the world, to others, and to himself.

Phenomenological thinking, on the other hand, is a spirit and method of philosophy. Its aim is to discover the roots of phenomena. Such thinking involves a deliberate attempt to put aside all scientific and metaphysical interpretations that obstruct considerations of phenomena in their bare simplicity. Scientism has been obsessed with reductionism and objectivity; metaphysics has been overly dependent on system and tradition. Philosophy must avoid the extremes that these systems engender and return to unadulterated phenomena and to an innocence in "first-viewing." Although the data Phenomenologists consider are phenomena pure and simple, this fact does not suggest phenomena are separate from the experiencer. The very act of phenomenological work is to enlarge and deepen the meaning of the knower. Intentionality is the characteristic feature of man's knowing. Human acts are intentional acts, which signifies, among other things, that the mental activity of human consciousness cannot be considered in causal terms. Because his acts are intentional, man can view phenomena purely. He can thus overcome Cartesian dualism of subject against object and accept the object as it is meant and intended. Furthermore, the principle of intentionality helps us understand that man himself cannot be objectified as a cause and effect entity. Instead, man is a free being without necessary connections between his past and immediate choice. An individual, in other words, can make a decision, one that contradicts anything he has done before. It is on this ground that Phenomenologists make explicit the meaning of human consciousness related to human existence.

Existential Phenomenology is an attempt to coordinate the existential condition of man (Existentialism) with the unity of phenomena (Phenomenology); that is, it seeks to view man participating in a world of things and events and encountering other men. The first key generic notion of this thought pattern deals with the uniqueness of man. Although Existential Phenomenologists emphasize man's place in the world, or man's relationship to Being in general, or even man's relationship to God, they still indicate that there is a certain uniqueness and mystery about the human person. This mystery is not a mysticism, for the phenomena of man is life as it is lived. It is rather an awareness of man's deep and complex meaning, a fact which cannot be grasped by science or rationalism.

The generic notion of the uniqueness and mystery of man implies that previous definitions of man have been wholly inadequate. The descriptive approach is inaccurate because it reduces man to either animality, rationality, or a poorly conceived amalgamation of both. Nor is definition by ends acceptable. Man can never be defined by certain ends, for it is the manner of his existence, not ultimate attainments, that make him what he is. Nor is it possible to define man by his nature, because he has no preformed nature. Man creates his own nature in the decisions and commitments of his own historical being. Thus, no strict definition of man is possible. Man must be accepted as he is, a unique creature whose dignity and status is different from all other living entities.

The uniqueness of man derives from the emotions, feelings, and the nonabstract qualities of perception and thinking. Existential Phenomenologists conceive these conditions differently, but all propose some emphasis of this kind. Martin Heidegger, for example, emphasizes a being that is not explicitly defineable but that possesses the abilities of meditative thinking; Martin Buber stresses the interacting subjectivity in dialogue; Maurice Merleau-Ponty speaks of the wholeness of perception founded in an ambiguous finite body; and Friedrich Nietzsche points to the necessary feeling of extremes in emotions and the will to power. All Existential Phenomenologists accept some form of human internalization, a type of feeling that lies deep within the core of human existence. So central is this second generic notion that it is the key to such existential and phenomenological concepts as love, hate, sex, hope, care, anxiety, and so on.

The difficulty in defining man and the recognition of the wholeness of his nonabstract qualities indicate that other than the strictly philosophical means are necessary for portraying him. Thus another generic notion of Existential Phenomenology is that literature and the arts can cooperate with philosophy in identifying man and teaching the world about him. Jean Paul Sartre is a playwright, Heidegger speaks of the poets as pathbreakers with special vision into the meaning of things, Nietzsche declares that the secrets of man are so emotional and unusual that they must be expressed by the special poetic form of the dithyramb, and Merleau-Ponty indicates that the mediums of painting, the novel, and the cinema are important for communicating man's existence.

These generic notions: (1) the uniqueness of man, (2) the sense of wholeness in emotion and nonabstract perception or thought, and (3) the coordination of the arts with philosophy, are proposed by the Existential Phenomenologists as the keys to education and educational practice. Although Existential Phenomenology distinctly resembles humanism in its focus on the human and on literature and art, differences exist in matters of focus and the kind of literature and art admired and utilized. The humanistic outlines for education are present in Existential Phenomenology, but the kinds of values are quite different from those of humanism per se.

The educational interest in Existential Phenomenology is the individual person, a living being of feelings and emotions who must come face to face with himself and others. One great educator of this persuasion was Johann Heinrich Pestalozzi. This is not the Pestalozzi of "object teaching" and sense perception as he is understood in America, but the Pestalozzi who stressed love and human concern, the sensitive teacher of humanness and mystery, the creator of the literary works *The Evening Hours of a Hermit* and *Leonard and Gertrude*. Pestalozzi's life represented existential commitment, tragedy and sorrow. Failing in almost everything he did, Pestalozzi saw beyond his problems to the true value of human life and human love. Pestalozzi inferred that love is the true basis of education, the foundation even of educational methodology. When love takes root in the teacher and the student, not only is personal worth created, but also the study of the basic elements of language, form, and number takes on new meaning.

Following the lead of Pestalozzi (and the example of many others) Existential Phenomenologists make the teacher the center of attention. Whereas in progressive education the teacher remains in the background principally as an observer or guide, in Existential Phenomenology the teacher is in the foreground. He initiates the act of education through his person, and influences the lives of his students with his own life. His relationship with students is not sentimental or permissive, but disciplined and often opposing. For this reason, a polarity exists between teacher and student, and often the relationship is one of risk. As Martin Buber indicates, the teacher selects a part of the effective world that is concentrated and manifested in his own being, and communicates with the students about it. Thus he does not impart mere objective knowledge, but knowledge related to his own subjectivity. Student resistance is often manifested in the process of instruction, but such resistance is natural and necessary in order that the student may retain his own being. The polarity seems rigid, for the distinction between teachers' and students' intentions calls forth the separation of roles. However, when achievements have been made and the student realizes that the teacher has loved him even in conflict and failure, the relationship ultimately bursts into one of friendship.

Other thought patterns contend that the final aim of education is public, cognitive knowledge, social adjustment, or allowing students to follow some inherent developmental plan. Existential Phenomenologists state that the final aim is the becoming of a human person, a person who lives and makes decisions about what he will do and be. "Knowing," in the sense of knowing oneself, social relationships, and biological development are all part of this becoming. But human existence, and the value related to it, is the primary factor in education. Man's reality is his being in the world—acting, feeling, and deciding. This reality is the key to education, the point of its origin, the final condition of its end.

Any subject in school (even extracurricular activities like athletics, music, and debating) can present existential situations for teaching and the development of personal beings. However, some subjects better reflect the meditative awareness of the existential condition than others. The two most prominent of these are literature and the arts. In these man's being is expressed concretely in existential moments, and students must study these expressions of human conditions and come to a self-realization of their own being through meditative thinking about them. This type of thinking, however, calls for a degree of maturity on the part of the students. For this reason, several Existential Phenomenologists insist that dramatic and literary presentation must wait until the students have passed into puberty and young adulthood and are aware of the existence of the various kinds of social intercourse.

Existential Phenomenology's whole approach to education and educational practice centers upon human persons. Humanness prescribes what must transpire between teacher and student. It indicates the teacher's role and activities, the subject matter to be studied, and the way this subject matter is to be approached by the students, as well as the reasons for all these. Humanness is antithetical to programs that emphasize mechanical teaching, groupings that may create loss of identity, or systems that aim for mere socialization or cognitive and analytical acquirements. The human self, relative to a dynamic world, is what is essential in becoming, and thus forms the key to education.

PEDAGOGICAL ORIENTATION— PHENOMENOLOGY

Thinking / MARTIN HEIDEGGER

Let us not fool ourselves. All of us, including those who think professionally, as it were, are often enough thought-poor; we all are far too easily

"Thinking" is reprinted from Martin Heidegger, "Memorial Address to Conradin Kreutzer" (Oct. 30, 1955), in *Discourse on Thinking*, John M. Anderson and E. Hans Freund (trans.), Harper & Row Publishers. *What is Called Thinking?* by Martin Heidegger, translated by Fred D. Wieck and J. Glenn Gray. Copyright © 1968 in the English translation by Harper & Row, Publishers, Incorporated; originally published in German under the title of *Was Heisst Denken?*, copyright 1954 by Max Niemeyer Verlage, Tuebingen. Reprinted by permission of Harper & Row, Publishers.

thought-less. Thoughtlessness is an uncanny visitor who comes and goes everywhere in today's world. For nowadays we take in everything in the quickest and cheapest way, only to forget it just as quickly, instantly. Thus one gathering follows on the heels of another. Commemorative celebrations grow poorer and poorer in thought. Commemoration and thoughtlessness are found side by side.

But even while we are thoughtless, we do not give up our capacity to think. We rather use this capacity implicitly, though strangely: that is, in thoughtlessness we let it lie fallow. Still only that can lie fallow which in itself is a ground for growth, such as a field. An expressway, where nothing grows, cannot be a fallow field. Just as we can grow deaf only because we hear, just as we can grow old only because we were young; so we can grow thought-poor or even thought-less only because man at the core of his being has the capacity to think; has "spirit and reason" and is destined to think. We can only lose or, as the phrase goes, get loose from that which we knowingly or unknowingly possess.

The growing thoughtlessness must, therefore, spring from some process that gnaws at the very marrow of man today: man today is in *flight from thinking*. This flight-from-thought is the ground of thoughtlessness. But part of this flight is that man will neither see nor admit it. Man today will even flatly deny this flight from thinking. He will assert the opposite. He will say—and quite rightly—that there were at no time such far-reaching plans, so many inquiries in so many areas, research carried on as passionately as today. Of course. And this display of ingenuity and deliberation has its own great usefulness. Such thought remains indispensable. But—it also remains true that it is thinking of a special kind.

Its peculiarity consists in the fact that whenever we plan, research, and organize, we always reckon with conditions that are given. We take them into account with the calculated intention of their serving specific purposes. Thus we can count on definite results. This calculation is the mark of all thinking that plans and investigates. Such thinking remains calculation even if it neither works with numbers nor uses an adding machine or computer. Calculative thinking computes. It computes ever new, ever more promising and at the same time more economical possibilities. Calculative thinking races from one prospect to the next. Calculative thinking never stops, never collects itself. Calculative thinking is not meditative thinking, not thinking which contemplates the meaning which reigns in everything that is.

There are, then, two kinds of thinking, each justified and needed in its own way: calculative thinking and meditative thinking.

This meditative thinking is what we have in mind when we say that contemporary man is in flight-from-thinking. Yet you may protest: mere meditative thinking finds itself floating unaware above reality. It loses touch. It is worthless for dealing with current business. It profits nothing in carrying out practical affairs.

Any you may say, finally, that mere meditative thinking, persevering meditation, is "above" the reach of ordinary understanding. In this excuse only this much is true, meditative thinking does not just happen by itself any more than does calculative thinking. At times it requires a greater effort. It demands more practice. It is in need of even more delicate care than any other genuine craft. But it must also be able to bide its time, to await as does the farmer, whether the seed will come up and ripen.

Yet anyone can follow the path of meditative thinking in his own manner and within his own limits. Why? Because man is a *thinking*, that is, a *meditating* being. Thus meditative thinking need by no means be "high-flown." It is enough if we dwell on what lies close and meditate on what is closest; upon that which concerns us, each one of us, here and now; here, on this patch of home ground; now, in the present hour of history.

What does this celebration suggest to us, in case we are ready to meditate? Then we notice that a work of art has flowered in the ground of our homeland. As we hold this simple fact in mind, we cannot help remembering at once that during the last two centuries great poets and thinkers have been brought forth from the Swabian land. Thinking about it further makes clear at once that Central Germany is likewise such a land, and so are East Prussia, Silesia, and Bohemia.

We grow thoughtful and ask: does not the flourishing of any genuine work depend upon its roots in a native soil? Johann Peter Hebel once wrote: "We are plants which—whether we like to admit it to ourselves or not—must with our roots rise out of the earth in order to bloom in the ether and to bear fruit." (*Works*, ed. Altwegg III, 314.)

The poet means to say: For a truly joyous and salutary human work to flourish, man must be able to mount from the depth of his home ground up into the ether. Ether here means the free air of the high heavens, the open realm of the spirit.

We grow more thoughtful and ask: does this claim of Johann Peter Hebel hold today? Does man still dwell calmly between heaven and earth? Does a meditative spirit still reign over the land? Is there still a life-giving homeland in whose ground man may stand rooted, that is, be autochthonic?

Many Germans have lost their homeland, have had to leave their villages and towns, have been driven from their native soil. Countless others whose homeland was saved, have yet wandered off. They have been caught up in the turmoil of the big cities, and have resettled in the wastelands of industrial districts. They are strangers now to their former homeland. And those who *have* stayed on in their homeland? Often they are still more homeless than those who have been driven from their homeland. Hourly and daily they are chained to radio and television. Week after week the movies carry them off into uncommon, but often merely common, realms of the imagination, and give the illusion of a world that is no world. Picture magazines are everywhere available. All that with which modern techniques of communication stimulate, assail, and drive man—all that is already much closer to man today than his fields around his farmstead, closer than the sky over the earth, closer than the change from night to day, closer than the conventions and customs of his village, than the tradition of his native world.

We grow more thoughtful and ask: What is happening here—with those driven from their homeland no less than with those who have remained? Answer: the *rootedness*, the *autochthony*, of man is threatened today at its core.[1] Even more: The loss of rootedness is caused not merely by circumstance and fortune, nor does it stem only from the negligence and the superficiality of man's way of life. The loss of autochthony springs from the spirit of the age into which all of us were born.

We grow still more thoughtful and ask: If this is so, can man, can man's work in the future still be expected to thrive in the fertile ground of a homeland and mount into the ether, into the far reaches of the heavens and the spirit? Or will everything now fall into the clutches of planning and calculation, of organization and automation?

If we reflect upon what our celebration today suggests, then we must observe the loss of man's autochthony with which our age is threatened. And we ask: What really is happening in our age? By what is it characterized?

The age that is now beginning has been called of late the atomic age. Its most conspicuous symbol is the atom bomb. But this symbolizes only the obvious; for it was recognized at once that atomic energy can be used also for peaceful purposes. Nuclear physicists everywhere are busy with vast plans to implement the peaceful uses of atomic energy. The great industrial corporations of the leading countries, first of all England, have figured out already that atomic energy can develop into a gigantic business. Through this atomic business a new era of happiness is envisioned. Nuclear science, too, does not stand idly by. It publicly proclaims this era of happiness. Thus in July of this year at Lake Constance, eighteen Nobel Prize winners stated in a proclamation: "Science (and that is modern natural science) is a road to a happier human life."

What is the sense of this statement? Does it spring from reflection? Does it ever ponder on the meaning of the atomic age? No! For if we rest

---

[1] The German *Bodenständigkeit* is translated *rootedness* or *autochthony* depending on a literal or a more figurative connotation. (Tr.)

content with this statement of science, we remain as far as possible from a reflective insight into our age. Why? Because we forget to ponder. Because we forget to ask: What is the ground that enabled modern technology to discover and set free new energies in nature?

This is due to a revolution in leading concepts which has been going on for the past several centuries, and by which man is placed in a different world. This radical revolution in outlook has come about in modern philosophy. From this arises a completely new relation of man to the world and his place in it. The world now appears as an object open to the attacks of calculative thought, attacks that nothing is believed able any longer to resist. Nature becomes a gigantic gasoline station, an energy source for modern technology and industry. This relation of man to the world as such, in principle a technical one, developed in the seventeenth century first and only in Europe. It long remained unknown in other continents, and it was altogether alien to former ages and histories.

The power concealed in modern technology determines the relation of man to that which exists. It rules the whole earth. Indeed, already man is beginning to advance beyond the earth into outer space. In not quite twenty years, such gigantic sources of power have become known through the discovery of atomic energy that in the foreseeable future the world's demands for energy of any kind will be ensured forever. Soon the procurement of the new energies will no longer be tied to certain countries and continents, as is the occurrence of coal, oil, and timber. In the foreseeable future it will be possible to build atomic power stations anywhere on earth.

Thus the decisive question of science and technology today is no longer: Where do we find sufficient quantities of fuel? The decisive question now runs: In what way can we tame and direct the unimaginably vast amounts of atomic energies, and so secure mankind against the danger that these gigantic energies suddenly—even without military actions—break out somewhere, "run away" and destroy everything?

If the taming of atomic energy is successful, and it will be successful, then a totally new era of technical development will begin. What we know now as the technology of film and television, of transportation and especially air transportation, of news reporting, and as medical and nutritional technology, is presumably only a crude start. No one can foresee the radical changes to come. But technological advance will move faster and faster and can never be stopped. In all areas of his existence, man will be encircled ever more tightly by the forces of technology. These forces, which everywhere and every minute claim, enchain, drag along, press and impose upon man under the form of some technical contrivance or other—these forces, since man has not made them, have moved long since beyond his will and have outgrown his capacity for decision.

But this too is characteristic of the new world of technology, that its accomplishments come most speedily to be known and publicly admired. Thus today everyone will be able to read what this talk says about technology in any competently managed picture magazine or hear it on the radio. But—it is one thing to have heard and read something, that is, merely to take notice; it is another thing to understand what we have heard and read, that is, to ponder.

The international meeting of Nobel Prize winners took place again in the summer of this year of 1955 in Lindau. There the American chemist, Stanley, had this to say: "The hour is near when life will be placed in the hands of the chemist who will be able to synthesize, split and change living substance at will." We take notice of such a statement. We even marvel at the daring of scientific research, without thinking about it. We do not stop to consider that an attack with technological means is being prepared upon the life and nature of man compared with which the explosion of the hydrogen bomb means little. For precisely if the hydrogen bombs do *not* explode and human life on earth is preserved, an uncanny change in the world moves upon us.

Yet it is not that the world is becoming entirely technical which is really uncanny. Far more uncanny is our being unprepared for this transformation, our inability to confront meditatively what is really dawning in this age.

No single man, no group of men, no commission of prominent statesmen, scientists, and technicians, no conference of leaders of commerce and industry, can brake or direct the progress of history in the atomic age. No merely human organization is capable of gaining dominion over it.

Is man, then, a defenseless and perplexed victim at the mercy of the irresistible superior power of technology? He would be if man today abandons any intention to pit meditative thinking decisively against merely calculative thinking. But once meditative thinking awakens, it must be at work unceasingly and on every last occasion—hence, also, here and now at this commemoration. For here we are considering what is threatened especially in the atomic age: the autochthony of the works of man.

Thus we ask now: even if the old rootedness is being lost in this age, may not a new ground and foundation be granted again to man, a foundation and ground out of which man's nature and all his works can flourish in a new way even in the atomic age?

What could the ground and foundation be for the new autochthony? Perhaps the answer we are looking for lies at hand; so near that we all too easily overlook it. For the way to what is near is always the longest and thus the hardest for us humans. This way is the way of meditative thinking. Meditative thinking demands of us not to cling one-sidedly to a single idea, nor to run down a one-track course of ideas. Meditative thinking demands of us that we engage ourselves with what first sight does not go together at all.

Let us give it a trial. For all of us, the arrangements, devices, and machinery of technology are to a greater or lesser extent indispensable. It would be foolish to attack technology blindly. It would be shortsighted to condemn it as the work of the devil. We depend on technical devices; they even challenge us to ever greater advances. But suddenly and unaware we find ourselves so firmly shackled to these technical devices that we fall into bondage to them.

Still we can act otherwise. We can use technical devices, and yet with proper use also keep ourselves so free of them, that we may let go of them any time. We can use technical devices as they ought to be used, and also let them alone as something which does not affect our inner and real core. We can affirm the unavoidable use of technical devices, and also deny them the right to dominate us, and so to warp, confuse, and lay waste our nature.

But will not saying both yes and no this way to technical devices make our relation to technology ambivalent and insecure? On the contrary! Our relation to technology will become wonderfully simple and relaxed. We let technical devices enter our daily life, and at the same time leave them outside, that is, let them alone, as things which are nothing absolute but remain dependent upon something higher. I would call this comportment toward technology which expresses "yes" and at the same time "no," by an old word, *releasement toward things*.[2]

Having this comportment we no longer view things only in a technical way. It gives us clear vision and we notice that while the production and use of machines demands of us another relation to things, it is not a meaningless relation. Farming and agriculture, for example, now have turned into a motorized food industry. Thus here, evidently, as elsewhere, a profound change is taking place in man's relation to nature and to the world. But the meaning that reigns in this change remains obscure.

There is then in all technical processes a meaning, not invented or made by us, which lays claim to what man does and leaves undone. We

---

[2] *Die Gelassenheit zu den Dingen. Gelassenheit,* although used today in German in the sense of "composure," "calmness," and "unconcern," also has older meanings, being used by early German mystics (as Meister Eckhart) in the sense of letting the world go and giving oneself to God. "Releasement" is not as old a word in English, but because it is rare and so free from too specific connotative meanings, it can carry with relative ease the very special and complex meanings which are implicit here and made explicit in the Conversation which follows. (Tr.)

do not know the significance of the uncanny increasing dominance of atomic technology. *The meaning pervading technology hides itself.* But if we explicitly and continuously heed the fact that such hidden meaning touches us everywhere in the world of technology, we stand at once within the realm of that which hides itself from us, and hides itself just in approaching us. That which shows itself and at the same time withdraws is the essential trait of what we call the mystery. I call the comportment which enables us to keep open to the meaning hidden in technology, *openness to the mystery.*

Releasement toward things and openness to the mystery belong together. They grant us the possibility of dwelling in the world in a totally different way. They promise us a new ground and foundation upon which we can stand and endure in the world of technology without being imperiled by it.

Releasement toward things and openness to the mystery give us a vision of a new autochthony which someday even might be fit to recapture the old and now rapidly disappearing autochthony in a changed form.

But for the time being—we do not know for how long—man finds himself in a perilous situation. Why? Just because a third world war might break out unexpectedly and bring about the complete annihilation of humanity and the destruction of the earth? No. In this dawning atomic age a far greater danger threatens—precisely when the danger of a third world war has been removed. A strange assertion! Strange indeed, but only as long as we do not meditate.

In what sense is the statement just made valid? This assertion is valid in the sense that the approaching tide of technological revolution in the atomic age could so captivate, bewitch, dazzle, and beguile man that calculative thinking may someday come to be accepted and practiced *as the only* way of thinking.

What great danger then might move upon us? Then there might go hand in hand with the greatest ingenuity in calculative planning and inventing indifference toward meditative thinking, total thoughtlessness. And then? Then man would have denied and thrown away his own special nature—that he is a meditative being. Therefore, the issue is the saving of man's essential nature. Therefore, the issue is keeping meditative thinking alive.

Yet releasement toward things and openness to the mystery never happen of themselves. They do not befall us accidentally. Both flourish only through persistent, courageous thinking.

Perhaps today's memorial celebration will prompt us toward this. If we respond to the prompting, we think of Conradin Kreutzer by thinking of the origin of his work, the life-giving powers of his Heuberg homeland. And it is *we* who *think* if we know ourselves here and now as the men who must find and prepare the way into the atomic age, through it and out of it.

If releasement toward things and openness to the mystery awaken within us, then we should arrive at a path that will lead to a new ground and foundation. In that ground the creativity which produces lasting works could strike new roots.

Thus in a different manner and in a changed age, the truth of what Johann Peter Hebel says should be renewed:

We are plants which—whether we like to admit it to ourselves or not—must with our roots rise out of the earth in order to bloom in the ether and to bear fruit.

What is Called Thinking?

By way of this series of lectures, we are attempting to learn thinking. The way is long. We dare take only a few steps. If all goes well, they will take us to the foothills of thought. But they will take us to places which we must explore to reach the point where only the leap will help further. The leap along takes us into the neighborhood where thinking resides. We therefore shall take a few practice leaps right at the start, though we won't notice it at once, nor need to.

In contrast to a steady progress, where we move unawares from one thing to the next and everything remains alike, the leap takes us abruptly to where everything is different, so different that it strikes us as strange. Abrupt means the sudden sheer descent or rise that marks the chasm's edge. Though we may not founder in such a leap, what the leap takes us to will confound us.

It is quite in order, then, that we receive notice from the very start of what will confound us. But all would not be well if the strangeness were due only to the fact that you, the listeners, are not yet listening closely enough. If that were the case, you would be bound to overlook completely the strangeness which lies in the matter itself. The matter of thinking is always confounding—all the more in proportion as we keep clear of prejudice. To keep clear of prejudice, we must be ready and willing to listen. Such readiness allows us to surmount the boundaries in which all customary views are confined, and to reach a more open territory. In order to encourage such readiness, I shall insert here some transitional remarks, which will also apply to all subsequent lectures.

In universities especially, the danger is still very great that we misunderstand what we hear of thinking, particularly if the immediate subject of the discussion is scientific. Is there any place compelling us more forcibly to rack our brains than the research and training institutions pursuing scientific labors? Now everyone admits unreservedly that the arts and the sciences are totally different from each other, though in official oratory they are still mentioned jointly. But if a distinction is made between thinking and the sciences, and the two are contrasted, that is immediately considered a disparagement of science. There is the fear even that thinking might open hostilities against the sciences, and becloud the seriousness and spoil the joy of scientific work.

But even if those fears were justified, which is emphatically not the case, it would still be both tactless and tasteless to take a stand against science upon the very rostrum that serves scientific education. Tact alone ought to prevent all polemics here. But there is another consideration as well. Any kind of polemics fails from the outset to assume the attitude of thinking. The opponent's role is not the thinking role. Thinking is thinking only when it pursues whatever speaks *for* a subject. Everything said here defensively is always intended exclusively to protect the subject. When we speak of the sciences as we pursue our way, we shall be speaking not against but for them, for clarity concerning their essential nature. This alone implies our conviction that the sciences are in themselves positively essential. However, their essence is frankly of a different sort from what our universities today still fondly imagine it to be. In any case, we still seem afraid of facing the exciting fact that today's sciences belong in the realm of the essence of modern technology, and nowhere else. Be it noted that I am saying "in the realm of the *essence* of technology," and not simply "in technology." A fog still surrounds the essence of modern science. That fog, however, is not produced by individual investigators and scholars in the sciences. It is not produced by man at all. It arises from the region of what is most thought-provoking—that we are still not thinking; none of us, including me who speaks to you, me first of all.

This is why we are here attempting to learn thinking. We are all on the way together, and are not reproving each other. To learn means to make everything we do answer to whatever essentials address themselves to us at a given time. Depending on the kind of essentials, depending on the realm from which they address us, the answer and with it the kind of learning differs.

A cabinetmaker's apprentice, someone who is learning to build cabinets and the like, will serve as an example. His learning is not mere practice, to gain facility in the use of tools. Nor does he merely gather knowledge about the customary forms of the things he is to build. If he is to become a true cabinetmaker, he makes himself answer and respond above all to the different kinds of wood and to the shapes slumbering within wood—to wood as it enters into man's dwelling with all the hidden riches of its nature. In fact, this relatedness to wood is what maintains the whole craft. Without that relatedness, the craft will never be anything but empty busywork, any occupation with it will be determined exclusively by business concerns. Every handicraft, all human dealings are constantly in that danger. The writing of poetry is no more exempt from it than is thinking.

Whether or not a cabinetmaker's apprentice, while he is learning, will come to respond to wood and wooden things, depends obviously on the presence of some teacher who can make the apprentice comprehend.

True. Teaching is even more difficult than learning. We know that; but we rarely think about it. And why is teaching more difficult than learning? Not because the teacher must have a larger store of information, and have it always ready. Teaching is more difficult than learning because what teaching calls for is this: to let learn. The real teacher, in fact, lets nothing else be learned than—learning. His conduct, therefore, often produces the impression that we properly learn nothing from him, if by "learning" we now suddenly understand merely the procurement of useful information. The teacher is ahead of his apprentices in this alone, that he has still far more to learn than they—he has to learn to let them learn. The teacher must be capable of being more teachable than the apprentices. The teacher is far less assured of his ground than those who learn are of theirs. If the relation between the teacher and the taught is genuine, therefore, there is never a place in it for the authority of the know-it-all or the authoritative sway of the official. It still is an exalted matter, then, to become a teacher—which is something else entirely than becoming a famous professor. That nobody wants any longer to become a teacher today, when all things are downgraded and graded from below (for instance, from business), is presumably because the matter is exalted, because of its altitude. And presumably this disinclination is linked to that most thought-provoking matter which gives us to think. We must keep our eyes fixed firmly on the true relation between teacher and taught—if indeed learning is to arise in the course of these lectures.

We are trying to learn thinking. Perhaps thinking, too, is just something like building a cabinet. At any rate, it is a craft, a "handicraft." "Craft" literally means the strength and skill in our hands. The hand is a peculiar thing. In the common view, the hand is part of our bodily organism. But the hand's essence can never be determined, or explained, by its being an organ which can grasp. Apes, too, have organs that can grasp, but they do not have hands. The hand is infinitely different from all grasping organs—paws, claws, or fangs—different by an abyss of essence. Only a being who can speak, that is, think, can have hands and can be handy in achieving works of handicraft.

But the craft of the hand is richer than we commonly imagine. The hand does not only grasp and catch, or push and pull. The hand reaches and extends, receives and welcomes—and not just things: the hand extends itself, and receives its own welcome in the hands of others. The hand holds. The hand carries. The hand designs and signs, presumably because man is a sign. Two hands fold into one, a gesture meant to carry man into the great oneness. The hand is all this, and this is the true handicraft. Everything is rooted here that is commonly known as handicraft, and commonly we go no further. But the hand's gestures run everywhere through language, in their most perfect purity precisely when man speaks by being silent. And only when man speaks, does he think—not the other way around, as metaphysics still believes. Every motion of the hand in every one of its works carries itself through the element of thinking, every bearing of the hand bears itself in that element. All the work of the hand is rooted in thinking. Therefore, thinking itself is man's simplest, and for that reason hardest, handiwork, if it would be accomplished at its proper time.

We must learn thinking because our being able to think, and even gifted for it, is still no guarantee that we are capable of thinking. To be capable, we must before all else incline toward what addresses itself to thought—and that is that which of itself gives food for thought. What gives us this gift, the gift of what must properly be thought about, is what we call most thought-provoking.

Our answer to the question what the most thought-provoking thing might be is the assertion: most thought-provoking for our thought-provoking time is that we are still not thinking.

The reason is never exclusively or primarily that we men do not sufficiently reach out and turn toward what properly gives food for thought; the reason is that this most thought-provoking thing turns away from us, in fact has long since turned away from man.

And what withdraws in such a manner, keeps and develops its own, incomparable nearness.

Once we are so related and drawn to what withdraws, we are drawing into what withdraws, into the enigmatic and therefore mutable nearness of its appeal. Whenever man is properly drawing that way, he is thinking —even though he may still be far away from what withdraws, even though the withdrawal may remain as veiled as ever. All through his life and right into his death, Socrates did nothing else than place himself into this draft, this current, and maintain himself in it. This is why he is the purest thinker of the West. This is why he. wrote nothing. For anyone who begins to write out of thoughtfulness must inevitably be like those people who run to seek refuge from any draft too strong for them. An as yet hidden history still keeps the secret why all great Western thinkers after Socrates, with all their greatness, had to be such fugitives. Thinking has entered into literature; and literature has decided the fate of Western science which, by way of the *doctrina* of the Middle Ages, became the *scientia* of modern times. In this form all the sciences have leapt from the womb of philosophy, in a twofold manner. The sciences come out of philosophy, because they have to part with her. And now that they are so apart they can never again, by their own power as sciences, make the leap back into the source from whence they have sprung. Henceforth they are remanded to a realm of being where only thinking can find them, provided thinking is capable of doing what is its own to do.

When man is drawing into what withdraws, he points into what withdraws. As we are drawing that way we are a sign, a pointer. But we are pointing then at something which has not, not yet, been transposed into the language of our speech. We are a sign that is not read.

In his draft for the hymn "Mnemosyne" (Memory), Hoelderlin says:

> "We are a sign that is not read,
> We feel no pain, we almost have
> Lost our tongue in foreign lands."

And so, on our way toward thinking, we hear a word of poesy. But the question to what end and with what right, upon what ground and within what limits, our attempt to think allows itself to get involved in a dialogue with poesy, let alone with the poetry of this poet—this question, which is inescapable, we can discuss only after we ourselves have taken the path of thinking.

PEDAGOGICAL ORIENTATION— EXISTENTIALISM

The Education of Character / MARTIN BUBER

Education worthy of the name is essentially education of character. For the genuine educator does not merely consider individual functions of his pupil, as one intending to teach him only to know or be capable of certain definite things; but his concern is always the person as a whole, both in the actuality in which he lives before you now and in his possibilities, what he can become. But in this way, as a whole in reality and potentiality, a man can be conceived either as personality, that is, as a unique spiritual-physical form with all the forces dormant in it, or as character, that is, as the link between what this individual is and the sequence of his actions and attitudes. Between these two modes of conceiving the pupil in his wholeness there is a fundamental difference. Personality is something which in its growth remains essentially outside

"The Education of Character" is reprinted from Martin Buber, "The Education of Character," An Address to the National Conference of Palestinian Teachers, Tel-Aviv, 1939, *Between Man and Man*. Reprinted with permission, Routledge & Kegan Paul, Ltd. and The Macmillan Company. Copyright © 1965 by the Macmillan Company.

the influence of the educator; but to assist in the moulding of character is his greatest task. Personality is a completion, only character is a task. One may cultivate and enhance personality, but in education one can and one must aim at character.

However—as I would like to point out straightaway—it is advisable not to over-estimate what the educator can even at best do to develop character. In this more than in any other branch of the science of teaching it is important to realize, at the very beginning of the discussion, the fundamental limits to conscious influence, even before asking what character is and how it is to be brought about.

If I have to teach algebra I can expect to succeed in giving my pupils an idea of quadratic equations with two unknown quantities. Even the slowest-witted child will understand it so well that he will amuse himself by solving equations at night when he cannot fall asleep. And even one with the most sluggish memory will not forget, in his old age, how to play with x and y. But if I am concerned with the education of character, everything becomes problematic. I try to explain to my pupils that envy is despicable, and at once I feel the secret resistance of those who are poorer than their comrades. I try to explain that it is wicked to bully the weak, and at once I see a suppressed smile on the lips of the strong. I try to explain that lying destroys life, and something frightful happens: the worst habitual liar of the class produces a brilliant essay on the destructive power of lying. I have made the fatal mistake of *giving instruction* in ethics, and what I said is accepted as current coin of knowledge; nothing of it is transformed into character-building substance.

But the difficulty lies still deeper. In all teaching of a subject I can announce my intention of teaching as openly as I please, and this does not interfere with the results. After all, pupils do want, for the most part, to learn something, even if not overmuch, so that a tacit agreement becomes possible. But as soon as my pupils notice that I want to educate their characters I am resisted precisely by those who show most signs of genuine independent character: they will not let themselves be educated, or rather, they do not like the idea that somebody wants to educate them. And those, too, who are seriously labouring over the question of good and evil, rebel when one dictates to them, as though it were some long established truth, what is good and what is bad; and they rebel just because they have experienced over and over again how hard it is to find the right way. Does it follow that one should keep silent about one's intention of educating character, and act by ruse and subterfuge? No; I have just said that the difficulty lies deeper. It is not enough to see that education of character is not introduced into a lesson in class; neither may one conceal it in cleverly arranged intervals. Education cannot tolerate such politic action. Even if the pupil does not notice the hidden motive it will have its negative effect on the actions of the teacher himself by depriving him of the directness which is his strength. Only in his whole being, in all his spontaneity can the educator truly affect the whole being of his pupil. For educating characters you do not need a moral genius, but you do need a man who is wholly alive and able to communicate himself directly to his fellow beings. His aliveness streams out to them and affects them most strongly and purely when he has no thought of affecting them.

The Greek word character means *impression*. The special link between man's being and his appearance, the special connexion between the unity of what he is and the sequence of his actions and attitudes is impressed on his still plastic substance. Who does the impressing? Everything does: nature and the social context, the house and the street, language and custom, the world of history and the world of daily news in the form of rumour, of broadcast and newspaper, music and technical science, play and dream—everything together. Many of these factors exert their influence by stimulating agreement, imitation, desire, effort; others by arousing questions, doubts, dislike, resistance. Character is formed by the interpenetration of all those multifarious, opposing influences. And yet, among this infinity of form-giving forces the educator is only one element among innumerable others, but distinct from them all by his *will* to take part in the stamping of character and by his *consciousness* that he represents in the eyes of the growing person a certain *selection* of what is, the selection of what is "right," of what *should* be. It is in this will and this consciousness that his vocation as an educator finds its fundamental expression. From this the genuine educator gains two things: first, humility, the feeling of being only one element amidst the fullness of life, only one single existence in the midst of all the tremendous inrush of reality on the pupil; but secondly, self-awareness, the feeling of being therein the only existence that *wants* to affect the whole person, and thus the feeling of responsibility for the selection of reality which he represents to the pupil. And a third thing emerges from all this, the recognition that in this realm of the education of character, of wholeness, there is only *one* access to the pupil: his *confidence*. For the adolescent who is frightened and disappointed by an unreliable world, confidence means the liberating insight that there is human truth, the truth of human existence. When the pupil's confidence has been won, his resistance against being educated gives way to a singular happening: he accepts the educator as a person. He feels he may trust this man, that this man is not making a business out of him, but is taking part in his life, accepting him before desiring to influence him. And so he learns to *ask*.

The teacher who is for the first time approached by a boy with somewhat defiant bearing, but with trembling hands, visibly opened-up and fired by a daring hope, who asks him what is the right thing in a certain situation—for instance, whether in learning that a friend has betrayed a secret entrusted to him one should call him to account or be content with entrusting no more secrets to him—the teacher to whom this happens realizes that this is the moment to make the first conscious step towards education of character; he has to answer, to answer under a responsibility, to give an answer which will probably lead beyond the alternatives of the question by showing a third possibility which is the right one. To dictate what is good and evil in general is not his business. His business is to answer a concrete question, to answer what is right and wrong in a given situation. This, as I have said, can only happen in an atmosphere of confidence. Confidence, of course, is not won by the strenuous endeavour to win it, but by direct and ingenuous participation in the life of the people one is dealing with—in this case in the life of one's pupils—and by assuming the responsibility which arises from such participation. It is not the educational intention but it is the meeting which is educationally fruitful. A soul suffering from the contradictions of the world of human society, and of its own physical existence, approaches me with a question. By trying to answer it to the best of my knowledge and conscience I help it to become a character that actively overcomes the contradictions.

If this is the teacher's standpoint towards his pupil, taking part in his life and conscious of responsibility, then everything that passes between them can, without any deliberate or politic intention, open a way to the education of character: lessons and games, a conversation about quarrels in the class, or about the problems of a world-war. Only, the teacher must not forget the limits of education; even when he enjoys confidence he cannot always expect agreement. Confidence implies a break-through from reserve, the bursting of the bonds which imprison an unquiet heart. But it does not imply unconditional agreement. The teacher must never forget that conflicts too, if only they are decided in a healthy atmosphere, have an educational value. A conflict with a pupil is the supreme test for the educator. He must use his own insight wholeheartedly; he must not blunt the piercing impact of his knowledge, but he must at the same time have in readiness the healing ointment for the heart pierced by it. Not for a moment may he conduct a dialectical manœuvre instead of the real battle for truth. But if he is the victor he has to help the vanquished to endure defeat; and if he cannot conquer the self-willed soul that faces him (for victories over souls are not so easily won), then he has to find the word of love which alone can help to overcome so difficult a situation.

So far I have referred to those personal difficulties in the education of character which arise from the relation between educator and pupil, while for the moment treating character itself, the object of education, as a simple concept of fixed content. But it is by no means that. In order to penetrate to the real difficulties in the education of character we have to examine critically the concept of character itself.

Kerschensteiner in his well-known essay on *The Concept and Education of Character* distinguished between "character in the most general sense," by which he means "a man's attitude to his human surroundings, which is constant and is expressed in his actions," and real "ethical character," which he defines as "a special attitude, and one which in action gives the preference before all others to absolute values." If we begin by accepting this distinction unreservedly—and undeniably there is some truth in it—we are faced with such heavy odds in all education of character in our time that the very possibility of it seems doubtful.

The "absolute values" which Kerschensteiner refers to cannot, of course, be meant to have only subjective validity for the person concerned. Don Juan finds absolute and subjective value in seducing the greatest possible number of women, and the dictator sees it in the greatest possible accumulation of power. "Absolute validity" can only relate to universal values and norms, the existence of which the person concerned recognizes and acknowledges. But to deny the presence of universal values and norms of absolute validity—that is the conspicuous tendency of our age. This tendency is not, as is, sometimes supposed, directed merely against the sanctioning of the norms by religion, but against their universal character and absolute validity, against their claim to be of a higher order than man and to govern the whole of mankind. In our age values and norms are not permitted to be anything but expressions of the life of a group which translates its own needs into the language of objective claims, until at last the group itself, for example a nation, is raised to an absolute value—and moreover to the only value. Then this splitting up into groups so pervades the whole of life that it is no longer possible to re-establish a sphere of values common to mankind, and a commandment to mankind is no longer observed. As this tendency grows the basis for the development of what Kerschensteiner means by moral character steadily diminishes. How, under these circumstances, can the task of educating character be completed?

At the time of the Arab terror in Palestine, when there were single Jewish acts of reprisal, there must have been many discussions between teacher and pupils on the question: Can there be any suspension of the Ten Commandments, i.e. can murder become a good deed if committed in the interest of one's own group? One such discussion was once repeated to me. The teacher asked: "When the commandment tells you 'Thou shalt not bear false witness against thy neighbour,' are we to interpret it with the condition, 'provided that it does not profit you?'" Thereupon one of the pupils said, "But it is not a question of my profit, but of the profit of my people." The teacher: "And how would you like it, then, if we put our condition this way: 'Provided that it does not profit your family?'" The pupil: "But family—that is still something more or less like myself; but the people—that is something quite different; there all question of *I* disappears." The teacher: "Then if you are thinking, 'we want victory,' don't you feel at the same time, 'I want victory?'" The pupil: "But the people, that is something infinitely more than just the people of to-day. It includes all past and future generations." At this point the teacher felt the moment had come to leave the narrow compass of the present and to invoke historical destiny. He said: "Yes; all past generations. But what was it that made those past generations of the Exile live? What made them outlive and overcome all their trials? Wasn't it that the cry 'Thou shalt not' never faded from their hearts and ears?" The pupil grew very pale. He was silent for a while, but it was the silence of one whose words threatened to stifle him. Then he burst out: "And what have we achieved that way? This!" And he banged his fist on the newspaper before him, which contained the report on the British White Paper. And again he burst out with "Live? Outlive? Do you call that life? We want to live!"

I have already said that the test of the educator lies in conflict with his pupil. He has to face this conflict and, whatever turn it may take, he has to find the way through it into life, into a life, I must add, where confidence continues unshaken—more, is even mysteriously strengthened. But the example I have just given shows the extreme difficulty of this task, which seems at times to have reached an impassable frontier. This is no longer merely a conflict between two generations, but between a world which for several millennia has believed in a truth superior to man, and an age which does not believe in it any longer—will not or cannot believe in it any longer.

But if we now ask, "How in this situation can there be any education of character?", something negative is immediately obvious: it is senseless to want to prove by any kind of argument that nevertheless the denied absoluteness of norms exists. That would be to assume that the denial is the result of reflection, and is open to argument, that is, to material for renewed reflection. But the denial is due to the disposition of a dominant human type of our age. We are justified in regarding this disposition as a sickness of the human race. But we must not deceive ourselves by believing that the disease can be cured by formulæ which assert that nothing is really as the sick person imagines. It is an idle undertaking to call out, to a mankind that has grown blind to eternity: "Look! the eternal values!" To-day host upon host of men have everywhere sunk into the slavery of collectives, and each collective is the supreme authority for its own slaves; there is no longer, superior to the collectives, any universal sovereignty in idea, faith, or spirit. Against the values, decrees and decisions of the collective no appeal is possible. This is true, not only for the totalitarian countries, but also for the parties and party-like groups in the so-called democracies. Men who have so lost themselves to the collective Moloch cannot be rescued from it by any reference, however eloquent, to the absolute whose kingdom the Moloch has usurped. One has to begin by pointing to that sphere where man himself, in the hours of utter solitude, occasionally becomes aware of the disease through sudden pain: by pointing to the relation of the individual to his own self. In order to enter into a personal relation with the absolute, it is first necessary to be a person again, to rescue one's real personal self from the fiery jaws of collectivism which devours all self-hood. The desire to do this is latent in the pain the individual suffers through his distorted relation to his own self. Again and again he dulls the pain with a subtle poison and thus suppresses the desire as well. To keep the pain awake, to waken the desire—that is the first task of everyone who regrets the obscuring of eternity. It is also the first task of the genuine educator in our time.

The man for whom absolute values in a universal sense do not exist cannot be made to adopt "an attitude which in action gives the preference over all others to absolute values." But what one can inculcate in him is the desire to attain once more to a real attitude, and that is, the desire to become a person following the only way that leads to this goal to-day.

But with this the concept of character formulated by Kerschensteiner and deriving, as we know, from Kant is recognized to be useless for the specifically modern task of the education of character. Another concept has to be found if this task is to be more precisely defined.

We cannot conceal from ourselves that we stand to-day on the ruins of the edifice whose towers were raised by Kant. It is not given to us living to-day to sketch the plan for a new building. But we can perhaps begin by laying the first foundations without a plan, with only a dawning image before our mind's eye.

According to Kerschensteiner's final definition character is "fundamentally nothing but voluntary obedience to the maxims which have been moulded in the individual by experience, teaching, and self-reflection, whether they have been adopted and then completely assimilated or have originated in the consciousness through self-legislation." This voluntary obedience "is, however, only a form of self-control." At first, love or fear of other people must have produced in man "the *habit* of self-conquest." Then, gradually, "this outer obedience must be transformed into inner obedience."

The concept of habit was then enlarged, especially by John Dewey in his book, *Human Nature and Conduct.* According to him character is "the interpenetration of habits." Without "the continued operation of all habits in every act" there would be no unified character, but only "a juxtaposition of disconnected reactions to separated situations."

With this concept of character as an organization of self-control by means of the accumulation of maxims, or as a system of interpenetrating habits, it is very easy to understand how powerless modern educational science is when faced by the sickness of man. But even apart from the special problems of the age, this concept can be no adequate basis for the construction of a genuine education of character. Not that the educator could dispense with employing useful maxims or furthering good habits. But in moments that come perhaps only seldom, a feeling of blessed achievement links him to the explorer, the inventor, the artist, a feeling of sharing in the revelation of what is hidden. In such moments he finds himself in a sphere very different from that of maxims and habits. Only on this, the highest plane of his activity, can he fix his real goal, the real concept of character which is his concern, even though he might not often reach it.

For the first time a young teacher enters a class independently, no longer sent by the training college to prove his efficiency. The class before him is like a mirror of mankind, so multiform, so full of contradictions, so inaccessible. He feels "These boys—I have not sought them out; I have been put here and have to accept them as they are—but not as they now are in this moment, no, as they *really* are, as they can become. But how can I find out what is in them and what can I do to make it take shape?" And the boys do not make things easy for him. They are noisy, they cause trouble, they stare at him with impudent curiosity. He is at once tempted to check this or that trouble-maker, to issue orders, to make compulsory the rules of decent behaviour, to say No, to say No to everything rising against him from beneath: he is at once tempted to start from beneath. And if one starts from beneath one perhaps never arrives above, but everything comes down. But then his eyes meet a face which strikes him. It is not a beautiful face nor particularly intelligent; but it is a real face, or rather, the chaos preceding the cosmos of a real face. On it he reads a question which is something different from the general curiosity: "Who are you? Do you know something that concerns me? Do you bring me something? What do you bring?"

In some such way he reads the question. And he, the young teacher, addresses this face. He says nothing very ponderous or important, he puts an ordinary introductory question: "What did you talk about last in geography? The Dead Sea? Well, what about the Dead Sea?" But there was obviously something not quite usual in the question, for the answer he gets is not the ordinary schoolboy answer; the boy begins to *tell a story*. Some months earlier he had stayed for a few hours on the shores of the Dead Sea and it is of this he tells. He adds: "And everything looked to me as if it had been created a day before the rest of creation." Quite unmistakably he had only in this moment made up his mind to talk about it. In the meantime his face has changed. It is no longer quite as chaotic as before. And the class has fallen silent. They all listen. The class, too, is no longer a chaos. Something has happened. The young teacher has started from above.

The educator's task can certainly not consist in educating great characters. He cannot select his pupils, but year by year the world, such as it is, is sent in the form of a school class to meet him on his life's way as his destiny; and in this destiny lies the very meaning of his life's work. He has to introduce discipline and order, he has to establish a law, and he can only strive and hope for the result that discipline and order will become more and more inward and autonomous, and that at last the law will be written in the heart of his pupils. But his real goal which, once he has well recognized it and well remembers it, will influence all his work, is the great character.

The great character can be conceived neither as a system of maxims nor as a system of habits. It is peculiar to him to act from the whole of his substance. That is, it is peculiar to him to react in accordance with the uniqueness of every situation which challenges him as an active person. Of course there are all sorts of similarities in different situations; one can construct types of situations, one can always find to what section the particular situation belongs, and draw what is appropriate from the hoard of established maxims and habits, apply the appropriate maxim, bring into operation the appropriate habit. But what is untypical in the particular situation remains unnoticed and unanswered. To me that seems the same as if, having ascertained the sex of a new-born child, one were immediately to establish its type as well, and put all the children of one type into a common cradle on which not the individual name but the name of the type was inscribed. In spite of all similarities every living situation has, like a newborn child a new face, that has never been before and will never come again. It demands of you a reaction which cannot be prepared beforehand. It demands nothing of what is past. It demands presence, responsibility; it demands you. I call a great character one who by his actions and attitudes satisfies the claim of situations out of deep readiness to respond with his whole life, and in such a way that the sum of his actions and attitudes expresses at the same time the unity of his being in its willingness to accept responsibility. As his being is unity, the unity of accepted responsibility, his active life, too, coheres into unity. And one might perhaps say that for him there rises a unity out of the situations he has responded to in responsibility, the indefinable unity of a moral destiny.

All this does not mean that the great character is beyond the acceptance of norms. No responsible person remains a stranger to norms. But the command inherent in a genuine norm never becomes a maxim and the fulfilment of it never a habit. Any command that a great character takes to himself in the course of his development does not act in him as part of his consciousness or as material for building up his exercises, but remains latent in a basic layer of his substance until it reveals itself to him in a concrete way. What it has to tell him is revealed whenever a situation arises which demands of him a solution of which till then he had perhaps no idea. Even the most universal norm will at times be recognized only in a very special situation. I know of a man whose heart was struck by the lightning flash of "Thou shalt not steal" in the very moment when he was moved by a very different desire from that of stealing, and whose heart was so struck by it that he not only abandoned doing what he wanted to do, but with the whole force of his passion did the very opposite. Good and evil are not each other's opposites like right and left. The evil approaches us as a whirlwind, the good as a direction. There is a direction, a "yes," a command, hidden even in a prohibition, which is revealed to us in moments like these. In moments like these the command addresses us really in the second person, and the Thou in it is no one else but one's own self. Maxims command only the third person, the each and the none.

One can say that it is the unconditioned nature of the address which distinguishes the command from the maxim. In an age which has become deaf to unconditioned address we cannot overcome the dilemma of the education of character from that angle. But insight into the structure of great character can help us to overcome it.

Of course, it may be asked whether the educator should really start "from above," whether, in fixing his goal, the hope of finding a great character, who is bound to be the exception, should be his starting-point; for in his methods of educating character he will always have to take into consideration the others, the many. To this I reply that the educator would not have the right to do so if a method inapplicable to these others were to result. In fact, however, his very insight into the structure of a great character helps him to find the way by which alone (as I have indicated) he can begin to influence also the victims of the collective Moloch, pointing out to them the sphere in which they themselves suffer —namely, their relation to their own selves. From this sphere he must elicit the values which he can make credible and desirable to his pupils. That is what insight into the structure of a great character helps him to do.

A section of the young is beginning to feel today that, because of their absorption by the collective, something important and irreplaceable is lost to them—personal responsibility for life and the world. These young people, it is true, do not yet realize that their blind devotion to the collective, e.g. to a party, was not a genuine act of their personal life;

they do not realize that it sprang, rather, from the fear of being left, in this age of confusion, to rely on themselves, on a self which no longer receives its direction from eternal values. Thus they do not yet realize that their devotion was fed on the unconscious desire to have responsibility removed from them by an authority in which they believe or want to believe. They do not yet realize that this devotion was an escape. I repeat, the young people I am speaking of do not yet realize this. But they are beginning to notice that he who no longer, with his whole being, decides what he does or does not, and assumes responsibility for it, becomes sterile in soul. And a sterile soul soon ceases to be a soul.

This is where the educator can begin and should begin. He can help the feeling that something is lacking to grow into the clarity of consciousness and into the force of desire. He can awaken in young people the courage to shoulder life again. He can bring before his pupils the image of a great character who denies no answer to life and the world, but accepts responsibility for everything essential that he meets. He can show his pupils this image without the fear that those among them who most of all need discipline and order will drift into a craving for aimless freedom: on the contrary, he can teach them in this way to recognize that discipline and order too are starting-points on the way towards self-responsibility. He can show that even the great character is not born perfect, that the unity of his being has first to mature before expressing itself in the sequence of his actions and attitudes. But unity itself, unity of the person, unity of the lived life, has to be emphasized again and again. The confusing contradictions cannot be remedied by the collectives, not one of which knows the taste of genuine unity and which if left to themselves would end up, like the scorpions imprisoned in a box, in the witty fable, by devouring one another. This mass of contradictions can be met and conquered only by the rebirth of personal unity, unity of being, unity of life, unity of action—unity of being, life and action together. This does not mean a static unity of the uniform, but the great dynamic unity of the multiform in which multiformity is formed into unity of character. Today the great characters are still "enemies of the people," they who love their society, yet wish not only to preserve it but to raise it to a higher level. To-morrow they will be the architects of a new unity of mankind. It is the longing for personal unity, from which must be born a unity of mankind, which the educator should lay hold of and strengthen in his pupils. Faith in this unity and the will to achieve it is not a "return" to individualism, but a step beyond all the dividedness of individualism and collectivism. A great and full relation between man and man can only exist between unified and responsible persons. That is why it is much more rarely found in the totalitarian collective than in any historically earlier form of society; much more rarely also in the

authoritarian party than in any earlier form of free association. Genuine
education of character is genuine education for community.

In a generation which has had this kind of upbringing the desire will
also be kindled to behold again the eternal values, to hear again the
language of the eternal norm. He who knows inner unity, the innermost
life of which is mystery, learns to honour the mystery in all its forms. In
an understandable reaction against the former domination of a false,
fictitious mystery, the present generations are obsessed with the desire to
rob life of all its mystery. The fictitious mystery will disappear, the
genuine one will rise again. A generation which honours the mystery in
all its forms will no longer be deserted by eternity. Its light seems
darkened only because the eye suffers from a cataract; the receiver has
been turned off, but the resounding ether has not ceased to vibrate.
To-day, indeed, in the hour of upheaval, the eternal is sifted from the
pseudo-eternal. That which flashed into the primal radiance and blurred
the primal sound will be extinguished and silenced, for it has failed
before the horror of the new confusion and the questioning soul has
unmasked its futility. Nothing remains but what rises above the abyss of
to-day's monstrous problems, as above every abyss of every time: the
wing-beat of the spirit and the creative word. But he who can see and
hear out of unity will also behold and discern again what can be beheld
and discerned eternally. The educator who helps to bring man back to
his own unity will help to put him again face to face with God.

PSYCHOLOGICAL DIMENSION

The Child's Relations with Others / MAURICE MERLEAU-PONTY

By way of introduction I should like to indicate to you, in this lecture
and the next, what place this year's subject occupies within the study of
child psychology in general.

You can easily see the relation between this year's proposed subject
and the subject we dealt with last year. Last year we attempted a study
of certain aspects of the child's relations with nature—for example, the
child's perception. These included the child's knowledge of external
natural facts, also his representation of external facts (e.g., in drawing),

"The Child's Relations with Others" is reprinted from Maurice Merleau-Ponty, "Les
relations avec autrui chez l'enfant," from the series Cours de Sorbonne given in Paris,
1960, translated by William Cobb, The Primacy of Perception and Other Essays.
Copyright © 1964 by Northwestern University Press, printed with permission. Deletions have been made by the editor in the interest of brevity.

ـe way his imagination makes use of perceptual experiences, his organi-
ـation of these experiences into causal relations, and, finally, what has
sometimes been called the child's conception of the world—that is, the
group of ideas (if such they can be called) that would permit the child
to have a view of the world.

The last paragraph brings us to the question of intelligence in the
child, and you can see that, regardless of the diversity of questions we
raised last year, they all involved not the relation between the child and
other living beings but rather the child's relations to nature.

This year, on the contrary, in discussing the child's relations with
others, we will be concerned with his relations with his parents, his
brothers and sisters, other children, and even, if there is time, with his
school environment, his social class, and, in general, his relation to
culture, to the civilization to which he belongs. It is quite likely that we
will not be able to treat these last questions this year, since to do so
would take us too far and we have enough to occupy ourselves in the
child's relations to parents, brothers and sisters, and other humans.

It might seem as though the question we shall treat this year is *more
special* than last year's question. It might seem that last year we studied
the "infrastructure" of the child's understanding, the collection of processes that enable him to feel, perceive, and understand; whereas this year
we are interested in a fairly narrow sector of this perception and understanding—the perception and understanding of others. It might seem
that last year we were concerned with the psychology of understanding
in the child, while this year we will concern ourselves with the much
more limited subject of affectivity.

This, however, is not the relation between the two kinds of question. I
do not at all believe that the question of relations with others is a
secondary and more particular problem, more strictly confined to affectivity than the problem with which we occupied ourselves last year.

The very results of last year's study prevent us from treating the
problems of relations with others as secondary and subordinate.

In speaking of the child's perception or of causal relations as grasped
by the child, what struck us was the fact that, in the case of the child's
perception, it is not a matter of a simple reflection of external phenomena
within the child or of a simple sorting of data resulting from the activity
of the senses. It seemed to us to be a question of an actual "informing"
[*Gestaltung*] of experience in the child. For example, in the case of
causal relations, which have traditionally been thought to have been
learned by an intellectual operation in the child, we have seen instead,
with Michotte, that such relations are anchored in the child's very
perception of external events and that perception in the child is not a
simple reflection nor the result of a process of sorting data. Rather, it is a

more profound operation whereby the child organizes his experience of external events—an operation which thus is properly neither a logical nor a predicative activity.

When we considered the child's imagination, it appeared likewise that we could not assimilate what is called the *image* in the child to a kind of degraded, weakened copy of preceding perceptions. What is called *imagination* is an emotional conduct. Consequently here again we found ourselves, as it were, *beneath* the relation of the knowing subject to the known object. We had to do with a primordial operation by which the child organizes the imaginary, just as he organizes the perceived.

When we examined the child's drawing, one of the faults we found with the famous book by Luquet was precisely this: The child's drawing is considered by Luquet to be an abortive adult drawing, and the development of the child, viewed through the stages of his drawing, appears as a series of frustrations of the attempt to represent the world as the adult does (at least the white, "civilized," Western adult)—that is, according to the laws of classical geometrical perspective. We tried to show, on the contrary, that the child's processes of expression could not be understood as simple breakdowns on the road to "visual realism" and that, instead, these processes testified to the presence in the child of a relation with things and with the sensible very different from the one that is expressed in the perspective projection of drawing in the classic style.

Finally, it appeared to us, following certain indications of Wallon, that there is perhaps no place for the question of the child's conception of the world. In order to be able to speak of a conception of the world, the child would actually have to totalize his experience under general concepts. But, as Wallon remarked, an entire sector of this experience is fragmentary [*lacunaire*] for the child; it contains what Wallon called "ultra things," i.e., entities of which the child has no direct experience, which are at the horizon of his perception—like the sun, the moon, etc. These entities remain for the child in a state of relative indetermination; he has, strictly speaking, no conception of them. With respect to nearby objects, the child often has a conception that is very close to that of the adult (Huang). The concepts of animism and of artificialism, employed a bit recklessly, are adult ways of expressing the child's confusion in the face of "ultra things"; they are the expedients sometimes used by the child in replying to the adult's questions and perhaps do not arise in his own experience.

All this, I believe, converged on the following idea: What classical academic psychology calls "functions of cognition"—intelligence, perception, imagination, etc.—when more closely examined, lead us back to an activity that is prior to cognition properly so called, a function of organizing experiences that imposes on certain totalities the configuration and the kind of equilibrium that are possible under the corporeal and social conditions of the child himself.

In another course, moreover, we examined the problem of the acquisition of language, and there again we reached the same kind of conclusion: The acquisition of language appeared to us to be the acquisition of an open system of expression. That is, such a system is capable of expressing, not some finite number of cognitions or ideas, but rather an indeterminate number of cognitions or ideas to come. The system that is speech is learned by the child, not at all by a genuine intellectual operation (as though by means of intelligence the child understood the principles of speech, its morphology, and its syntax). Rather, what is involved is a kind of *habituation*, a use of language as a tool or instrument. The employment of language, which is an effect and also one of the most active stimuli of intellectual development, does not appear to be founded on the exercise of pure intelligence but instead on a more obscure operation—namely, the child's assimilation of the linguistic system of his environment in a way that is comparable to the acquisition of any habit whatever: the learning of a structure of conduct.

These results lead us to think that between the functions of understanding we studied last year and affectivity itself there must be an altogether different relation than that of the simple subordination of the latter to the former.

However, I would like to show this more directly by means of two examples. First, recent studies have tended to show that even external perception of sense qualities and space—at first glance the most disinterested, least affective of all the functions—is profoundly modified by the personality and by the interpersonal relationships in which the child lives. The second example has to do with the learning of language. Certain authors show that there is a very close and profound relation between the development of language and the configuration of the human environment in which the child develops.

.   .   .

The Problem of the Child's Perception of Others: The Theoretical Problem

Before studying the different relations established between the child and his parents, his peers, other children, brothers, sisters, or strangers, before undertaking a description and analysis of these different relations, a question of principle arises: How and under what conditions does the child come into contact with others? What is the nature of the child's relations with others? How are such relations possible from the day of birth on?

Classical psychology approached this problem only with great difficulty. One might say that it was among the stumbling blocks of classical psychology because it is admittedly incapable of being solved if one confines oneself to the theoretical ideas that were elaborated by academic psychology.

How does such a problem arise for classical psychology? Given the presuppositions with which that psychology works, given the prejudices it adopted from the start without any kind of criticism, the relation with others becomes incomprehensible for it. What, in fact, is the psyche [*psychisme*]—mine or the other's—for classical psychology? All psychologists of the classical period are in tacit agreement on this point: the psyche, or the psychic, is *what is given to only one person*. It seems, in effect, that one might admit without further examination or discussion that what constitutes the psyche in me or in others is something incommunicable. I alone am able to grasp my psyche—for example, my sensations of green or of red. You will never know them as I know them; you will never experience them in my place. A consequence of this idea is that the psyche of another appears to me as radically inaccessible, at least in its own existence. I cannot reach other lives, other thought processes, since by hypothesis they are open only to inspection by a single individual: the one who owns them.

Since I cannot have direct access to the psyche of another, for the reasons just given, I must grant that I seize the other's psyche only indirectly, mediated by its bodily appearances. I see you in flesh and bone; you are there. I cannot know what you are thinking, but I can suppose it, guess at it from your facial expressions, your gestures, and your words—in short from a series of bodily appearances of which I am only the witness.

The question thus becomes this: How does it happen that, in the presence of this mannequin that resembles a man, in the presence of this body that gesticulates in a characteristic way, I come to believe that it is inhabited by a psyche?[1] How am I led to consider that this body before me encloses a psyche? Classical psychology's conception of the body and the consciousness we have of it is here a second obstacle in the way of a solution of the problem. Here one wants to speak of the notion of *cenesthesia,* meaning a mass of sensations that would express to the subject the state of his different organs and different bodily functions. Thus my body for me, and your body for you, could be reached, and be knowable, by means of a cenesthesic sense.

A mass of sensations, by hypothesis, is as *individual* as the psyche itself. That is to say, if in fact my body is knowable by me only through

---

[1] I use the vague term "psyche" on purpose, in order to aviod any theory of consciousness that might be implied by a more precise term.

the mass of sensations it gives me (a mass of sensations to which you obviously have no access and of which we have no concrete experience), then the consciousness I have of my body is impenetrable by you. You cannot represent yourself in the same way in which I feel my own body; it is likewise impossible for me to represent to myself the way in which you feel your body. How, then, can I suppose that, in back of this appearance before me, there is someone who experiences his body as I experience mine?

Only one recourse is left for classical psychology—that of supposing that, as a spectator of the gestures and utterances of the other's body before me, I consider the totality of signs thus given, the totality of facial expressions this body presents to me, as the occasion for a kind of decoding. Behind the body whose gestures and characteristic utterances I witness, I project, so to speak, what I myself feel of my own body. No matter whether it is a question of an actual association of ideas or, instead, a judgment whereby I interpret the appearances, I transfer to the other the intimate experience I have of my own body.

The problem of the experience of others poses itself, as it were, in a system of four terms: (1) myself, my "psyche"; (2) the image I have of my body by means of the sense of touch or of cenesthesia, which, to be brief, we shall call the "introceptive image" of my own body; (3) the body of the other as seen by me, which we shall call the "visual body"; and (4) a fourth (hypothetical) term which I must re-constitute and guess at—the "psyche" of the other, the other's feeling of his own existence—to the extent that I can imagine or suppose it across the appearances of the other through his visual body.

Posed thus, the problem raises all kinds of difficulties. First, there is the difficulty of relating my knowledge or experience of the other to an association, to a judgment by which I would project into him the data of my intimate experience. The perception of others comes relatively early in life. Naturally we do not at an early age come to know the exact *meaning* of each of the emotional expressions presented to us by others. This exact knowledge is, if you like, late in coming; what is much earlier is the very fact that I perceive an expression, even if I may be wrong about what it means exactly. At a very early age children are sensitive to facial expressions, e.g., the smile. How could that be possible if, in order to arrive at an understanding of the global meaning of the smile and to learn that the smile is a fair indication of a benevolent feeling, the child had to perform the complicated task I have just mentioned? How could it be possible if, beginning with the visual perception of another's smile, he had to compare that visual perception of the smile with the movement that he himself makes when he is happy or when he feels benevolent— projecting to the other a benevolence of which he would have had intimate experience but which could not be grasped directly in the other? This complicated process would seem to be incompatible with the relative precociousness of the perception of others.

Again, in order for projection to be possible and to take place, it would be necessary for me to begin from the analogy between the facial expressions offered me by others and the different facial gestures I execute myself. In the case of the smile, for me to interpret the visible smile of the other requires that there be a way of comparing the visible smile of the other with what we may call the "motor smile"—the smile as felt, in the case of the child, by the child himself. But in fact do we have the means of making this comparison between the body of the other, as it appears in visual perception, and our own body, as we feel it by means of introception and of cenesthesia? Have we the means of systematically comparing the body of the other as seen by me with my body as sensed by me? In order for this to be possible there would have to be a fairly regular correspondence between the two experiences. The child's visual experience of his own body is altogether insignificant in relation to the kinesthetic, cenesthesic, or tactile feeling he can have of it. There are numerous regions of this body that he does not see and some that he will never see or know except by means of the mirror (of which we will speak shortly). There is no point-for-point correspondence between the two images of the body. To understand how the child arrives at assimilating the one to the other, we must, rather, suppose that he has other reasons for doing it than reasons of simple detail. If he comes to identify as bodies, and as animated ones, the bodies of himself and the other, this can only be because he globally identifies them and not because he constructs a point-for-point correspondence between the visual image of the other and the introceptive image of his own body.

These two difficulties are particularly apparent when it comes to accounting for the phenomenon of imitation. To imitate is to perform a gesture in the image of another's gesture—like the child, for example, who smiles because someone smiles at him. According to the principles we have been entertaining, it would be necessary for me to translate my visual image of the other's smile into a motor language. The child would have to set his facial muscles in motion in such a way as to reproduce the visible expression that is called "the smile" in another. But how could he do it? Naturally he does not have the other's internal motor feeling of his face; as far as he is concerned, he does not even have an image of himself smiling. The result is that if we want to solve the problem of the transfer of the other's conduct to me, we can in no way rest on the supposed analogy between the other's face and that of the child.

On the contrary, the problem comes close to being solved only on condition that certain classical prejudices are renounced. We must abandon the fundamental prejudice according to which the psyche is that which is accessible only to myself and cannot be seen from outside. My "psyche" is not a series of "states of consciousness" that are rigorously closed in on themselves and inaccessible to anyone but me. My consciousness is turned primarily toward the world, turned toward things; it is above all a relation to the world. The other's consciousness as well is chiefly a certain way of comporting himself toward the world. Thus it is in his conduct, in the manner in which the other deals with the world, that I will be able to discover his consciousness.

If I am a consciousness turned toward things, I can meet in things the actions of another and find in them a meaning, because they are themes of possible activity for my own body. Guillaume, in his book *l'Imitation chez l'enfant*,[2] says that we do not at first imitate others but rather the actions of others, and that we find others at the point of origin of these actions. At first the child imitates not persons but conducts. And the problem of knowing how conduct can be transferred from another to me is infinitely less difficult to solve than the problem of knowing how I can represent to myself a psyche that is radically foreign to me. If, for example, I see another draw a figure, I can understand the drawing as an action because it speaks directly to my own unique motility. Of course, the other *qua* author of a drawing is not yet a whole person, and there are more revealing actions than drawing—for example, using language. What is essential, however, is to see that a perspective on the other is opened to me from the moment I define him and myself as "conducts" at work in the world, as ways of "grasping" the natural and cultural world surrounding us.

But this presupposes a reform not only of the notion of the "psyche" (which we will replace henceforth by that of "conduct") but also of the idea we have of our own body. If my body is to appropriate the conducts given to me visually and make them its own, it must itself be given to me not as a mass of utterly private sensations but instead by what has been called a "postural," or "corporeal, schema." This notion, introduced long ago by Henry Head, has been taken over and enriched by Wallon, by certain German psychologists, and has finally been the subject of a study in its own right by Professor Lhermitte in *L'Image de notre corps*.[3]

For these authors, my body is no agglomeration of sensations (visual, tactile, "tenesthetic," or "cenesthesic"). It is first and foremost a *system* whose different introceptive and extroceptive aspects express each other reciprocally, including even the roughest of relations with surrounding space and its principal directions. The consciousness I have of my body is not the consciousness of an isolated mass; it is a *postural schema*. It is the perfection of my body's position in relation to the vertical, the horizontal, and certain other axes of important coordinates of its environment.

[2] Paris, 1925.
[3] Paris, 1939.

In addition, the different sensory domains (sight, touch, and the sense of movement in the joints) which are involved in the perception of my body do not present themselves to me as so many absolutely distinct regions. Even if, in the child's first and second years, the translation of one into the language of others is imprecise and incomplete, they all have in common a *certain style* of action, a certain *gestural* meaning that makes of the collection an already organized totality. Understood in this way, the experience I have of my own body could be transferred to another much more easily than the cenesthesia of classical psychology, giving rise to what Wallon calls a "postural impregnation" of my own body by the conducts I witness.

I can perceive, across the visual image of the other, that the other is an organism, that that organism is inhabited by a "psyche," because the visual image of the other is interpreted by the notion I myself have of my own body and thus appears as the visible envelopment of another "corporeal schema." My perception of my body would, so to speak, be swallowed up in a cenesthesia if that cenesthesia were strictly individual. On the contrary, however, if we are dealing with a schema, or a system, such a system would be relatively transferrable from one sensory domain to the other in the case of my own body, just as it could be transferred to the domain of the other.

Thus in today's psychology we have one system with two terms (my behavior and the other's behavior) which functions as a whole. To the extent that I can elaborate and extend my corporeal schema, to the extent that I acquire a better organized experience of my own body, to that very extent will my consciousness of my own body cease being a chaos in which I am submerged and lend itself to a transfer of others. And since at the same time the other who is to be perceived is himself not a "psyche" closed in on himself but rather a conduct, a system of behavior that aims at the world, he offers himself to my motor intentions and to that "international transgression" (Husserl) by which I animate and pervade him. Husserl said that the perception of others is like a "phenomenon of coupling" [*accouplement*]. The term is anything but a metaphor. In perceiving the other, my body and his are coupled, resulting in a sort of action which pairs them [*action à deux*]. This conduct which I am able only to see, I live somehow from a distance. I make it mine; I recover [*reprendre*] it or comprehend it. Reciprocally I know that the gestures I make myself can be the objects of another's intention. It is this transfer of my intentions to the other's body and of his intentions to my own, my alienation of the others and his alienation of me, that makes possible the perception of others.

All these analyses presuppose that the perception of others cannot be accounted for if one begins by supposing an ego and another that are *absolutely* conscious of themselves, each of which lays claim, as a result, to an absolute originality in relation to the other that confronts it. On the contrary, the perception of others is made comprehensible if one supposes that psychogenesis begins in a state where the child is unaware of himself and the other as different beings. We cannot say that in such a state the child has a genuine communication with others. In order that there be communication, there must be a sharp distinction between the one who communicates and the one with whom he communicates. But there is initially a state of pre-communication (Max Scheler), wherein the other's intentions somehow play *across* my body while my intentions play across his.

How is this distinction made? I gradually become aware of my body, of what radically distinguishes it from the other's body, at the same time that I begin to live my intentions in the facial expressions of the other and likewise begin to live the other's volitions in my own gestures. The progress of the child's experience results in his seeing that his body is, after all, closed in on itself. In particular, the visual image he acquires of his own body (especially from the mirror) reveals to him a hitherto unsuspected isolation of two subjects who are facing each other. The objectification of his own body discloses to the child his difference, his "insularity," and, correlatively, that of others.

Thus the development has somewhat the following character: There is a first phase, which we call pre-communication, in which there is not one individual over against another but rather an anonymous collectivity, an undifferentiated group life [*vie à plusieurs*]. Next, on the basis of this initial community, both by the objectification of one's own body and the constitution of the other in his difference, there occurs a segregation, a distinction of individuals—a process which, moreover, as we shall see, is never completely finished.

This kind of conception is common to many trends in contemporary psychology. One finds it in Guillaume and Wallon; it occurs in Gestalt theorists, phenomenologists, and psychoanalysts alike.

Guillaume shows that we must neither treat the origin of consciousness as though it were conscious, in an explicit way, of itself nor treat it as though it were completely closed in on itself. The first *me* is, as he says, virtual or latent, i.e., unaware of itself in its absolute difference. Consciousness of oneself as a unique individual, whose place can be taken by no one else, comes later and is not primitive. Since the primordial *me* is virtual or latent, egocentrism is not at all the attitude of a *me* that expressly grasps itself (as the term "egocentrism" might lead us to believe). Rather, it is the attitude of a *me* which is unaware of itself and lives as easily in others as it does in itself—but which, being unaware of others in their own separateness as well, in truth is no more conscious of them than of itself.

Wallon introduces an analogous notion with what he calls "syncretic sociability." Syncretism here is the indistinction between me and the other, a confusion at the core of a situation that is common to us both. After that the objectification of the body intervenes to establish a sort of wall between me and the other: a partition. Henceforth it will prevent me from confusing myself with what the other thinks, and especially with what he thinks of me; just as I will no longer confuse him with my thoughts, and especially my thoughts about him. There is thus a correlative constitution of me and the other as two human beings among all others.

Thus at first the *me* is both entirely unaware of itself and at the same time all the more demanding for being unaware of its own limits. The adult *me*, on the contrary, is a *me* that knows its own limits yet possesses the power to cross them by a genuine sympathy that is at least *relatively* distinct from the initial form of sympathy. The initial sympathy rests on the ignorance of oneself rather than on the perception of others, while adult sympathy occurs between "other" and "other"; it does not abolish the differences between myself and the other.

SOCIAL CONCEPTS DIMENSION

The Future of Our Educational Institutions /
FRIEDRICH NIETZSCHE

. . . "You used to say no one would strive to attain to culture if he knew how incredibly small the number of really cultured people actually is, and can ever be. And even this number of really cultured people would not be possible if a prodigious multitude, from reasons opposed to their nature and only led on by an alluring delusion, did not devote themselves to education. It were therefore a mistake publicly to reveal the ridiculous disproportion between the number of really cultured people and the enormous magnitude of the educational apparatus. Here lies the whole secret of culture—namely, that an innumerable host of men struggle to achieve it and work hard to that end, ostensibly in their own interests, whereas at bottom it is only in order that it may be possible for the few to attain to it."

"That is the principle," said the philosopher,—"and yet you could so far forget as to believe that you are one of the few? This thought has

"The Future of our Educational Institutions" is reprinted from Friedrich Nietzsche, *The Future of Our Educational Institutions,* lectures delivered by Nietzsche as professor of Classical Philology, Basel University, 1872. Permission to reprint by George Allen and Unwin Ltd, London. Deletions have been made by the editor in the interest of brevity.

occurred to you—I can see. That, however, is the result of the worthless character of modern education. The rights of genius are being democratised in order that people may be relieved of the labour of acquiring culture, and their need of it. Every one wants if possible to recline in the shade of the tree planted by genius, and to escape the dreadful necessity of working for him, so that his procreation may be made possible. What? Are you too proud to be a teacher? Do you despise the thronging multitude of learners? Do you speak contemptuously of the teacher's calling? And, aping my mode of life, would you fain live in solitary seclusion, hostilely isolated from that multitude? Do you suppose that you can reach at one bound what I ultimately had to win for myself only after long and determined struggles, in order even to be able to live like a philosopher? And do you not fear that solitude will wreak its vengeance upon you? Just try living the life of a hermit of culture. One must be blessed with overflowing wealth in order to live for the good of all on one's own resources! Extraordinary youngsters! They felt it incumbent upon them to imitate what is precisely most difficult and most high,— what is possible only to the master, when they, above all, should know how difficult and dangerous this is, and how many excellent gifts may be ruined by attempting it!"

"I will conceal nothing from you, sir," the companion replied. "I have heard too much from your lips at odd times and have been too long in your company to be able to surrender myself entirely to our present system of education and instruction. I am too painfully conscious of the disastrous errors and abuses to which you used to call my attention— though I very well know that I am not strong enough to hope for any success were I to struggle ever so valiantly against them. I was overcome by a feeling of general discouragement; my recourse to solitude was the result neither of pride nor arrogance. I would fain describe to you what I take to be the nature of the educational questions now attracting such enormous and pressing attention. It seemed to me that I must recognise two main directions in the forces at work—two seemingly antagonistic tendencies, equally deleterious in their action, and ultimately combining to produce their results: a striving to achieve the greatest possible *expansion* of education on the one hand, and a tendency to *minimise and weaken* it on the other. The first-named would, for various reasons, spread learning among the greatest number of people; the second would compel education to renounce its highest, noblest and sublimest claims in order to subordinate itself to some other department of life—such as the service of the State.

"I believe I have already hinted at the quarter in which the cry for the greatest possible expansion of education is most loudly raised. This expansion belongs to the most beloved of the dogmas of modern political economy. As much knowledge and education as possible; therefore the greatest possible supply and demand—hence as much happiness as possible:—that is the formula. In this case utility is made the object and goal of education,—utility in the sense of gain—the greatest possible pecuniary gain. In the quarter now under consideration culture would be defined as that point of vantage which enables one to 'keep in the van of one's age,' from which one can see all the easiest and best roads to wealth, and with which one controls all the means of communication between men and nations. The purpose of education, according to this scheme, would be to rear the most 'current' men possible,—'current' being used here in the sense in which it is applied to the coins of the realm. The greater the number of such men, the happier a nation will be; and this precisely is the purpose of our modern educational institutions: to help every one, as far as his nature will allow, to become 'current'; to develop him so that his particular degree of knowledge and science may yield him the greatest possible amount of happiness and pecuniary gain. Every one must be able to form some sort of estimate of himself; he must know how much he may reasonably expect from life. The 'bond between intelligence and property' which this point of view postulates has almost the force of a moral principle. In this quarter all culture is loathed which isolates, which sets goals beyond gold and gain, and which requires time: it is customary to dispose of such eccentric tendencies in education as systems of 'Higher Egotism,' or of 'Immoral Culture—Epicureanism.' According to the morality reigning here, the demands are quite different; what is required above all is 'rapid education,' so that a money-earning creature may be produced with all speed; there is even a desire to make this education so thorough that a creature may be reared that will be able to earn a *great deal* of money. Men are allowed only the precise amount of culture which is compatible with the interests of gain; but that amount, at least, is expected from them. In short: mankind has a necessary right to happiness on earth—that is why culture is necessary—but on that account alone!"

"I must just say something here," said the philosopher. "In the case of the view you have described so clearly, there arises the great and awful danger that at some time or other the great masses may overleap the middle classes and spring headlong into this earthly bliss. That is what is now called 'the social question.' It might seem to these masses that education for the greatest number of men was only a means to the earthly bliss of the few: the 'greatest possible expansion of education' so enfeebles education that it can no longer confer privileges or inspire respect. The most general form of culture is simply barbarism. But I do not wish to interrupt your discussion."

The companion continued: "There are yet other reasons, besides this beloved economical dogma, for the expansion of education that is being striven after so valiantly everywhere. In some countries the fear of religious oppression is so general, and the dread of its results so marked, that people in all classes of society long for culture and eagerly absorb those elements of it which are supposed to scatter the religious instincts. Elsewhere the State, in its turn, strives here and there for its own preservation, after the greatest possible expansion of education, because it always feels strong enough to bring the most determined emancipation, resulting from culture, under its yoke, and readily approves of everything which tends to extend culture, provided that it be of service to its officials or soldiers, but in the main to itself, in its competition with other nations. In this case, the foundations of a State must be sufficiently broad and firm to constitute a fitting counterpart to the complicated arches of culture which it supports, just as in the first case the traces of some former religious tyranny must still be felt for a people to be driven to such desperate remedies. Thus, wherever I hear the masses raise the cry for an expansion of education, I am wont to ask myself whether it is stimulated by a greedy lust of gain and property, by the memory of a former religious persecution, or by the prudent egotism of the State itself.

"On the other hand, it seemed to me that there was yet another tendency, not so clamorous, perhaps, but quite as forcible, which, hailing from various quarters, was animated by a different desire,—the desire to minimise and weaken education.

"In all cultivated circles people are in the habit of whispering to one another words something after this style: that it is a general fact that, owing to the present frantic exploitation of the scholar in the service of his science, his *education* becomes every day more accidental and more uncertain. For the study of science has been extended to such interminable lengths that he who, though not exceptionally gifted, yet possesses fair abilities, will need to devote himself exclusively to one branch and ignore all others if he ever wish to achieve anything in his work. Should he then elevate himself above the herd by means of his speciality, he still remains one of them in regard to all else,—that is to say, in regard to all the most important things in life. Thus, a specialist in science gets to resemble nothing so much as a factory workman who spends his whole life in turning one particular screw or handle on a certain instrument or machine, at which occupation he acquires the most consummate skill. In Germany, where we know how to drape such painful facts with the glorious garments of fancy, this narrow specialisation on the part of our learned men is even admired, and their ever greater deviation from the path of true culture is regarded as a moral phenomenon. 'Fidelity in small things,' 'dogged faithfulness,' become expressions of highest eulogy, and the lack of culture outside the speciality is flaunted abroad as a sign of noble sufficiency.

"For centuries it has been an understood thing that one alluded to

scholars alone when one spoke of cultured men; but experience tells us
that it would be difficult to find any necessary relation between the two
classes to-day. For at present the exploitation of a man for the purpose of
science is accepted everywhere without the slightest scruple. Who still
ventures to ask, What may be the value of a science which consumes its
minions in this vampire fashion? The division of labour in science is
practically struggling towards the same goal which religions in certain
parts of the world are consciously striving after,—that is to say, towards
the decrease and even the destruction of learning. That, however, which,
in the case of certain religions, is a perfectly justifiable aim, both in
regard to their origin and their history, can only amount to self-immola-
tion when transferred to the realm of science. In all matters of a general
and serious nature, and above all, in regard to the highest philosophical
problems, we have now already reached a point at which the scientific
man, as such, is no longer allowed to speak. On the other hand, that
adhesive and tenacious stratum which has now filled up the interstices
between the sciences—Journalism—believes it has a mission to fulfil
here, and this it does, according to its own particular lights—that is to
say, as its name implies, after the fashion of a day-labourer.

"It is precisely in journalism that the two tendencies combine and
become one. The expansion and the diminution of education here join
hands. The newspaper actually steps into the place of culture, and he
who, even as a scholar, wishes to voice any claim for education, must
avail himself of this viscous stratum of communication which cements
the seams between all forms of life, all classes, all arts, and all sciences,
and which is as firm and reliable as news paper is, as a rule. In the
newspaper the peculiar educational aims of the present culminate, just as
the journalist, the servant of the moment, has stepped into the place of
the genius, of the leader for all time, of the deliverer from the tyranny of
the moment. Now, tell me, distinguished master, what hopes could I still
have in a struggle against the general topsy-turvification of all genuine
aims for education; with what courage can I, a single teacher, step
forward, when I know that the moment any seeds of real culture are
sown, they will be mercilessly crushed by the roller of this pseudo-cul-
ture? Imagine how useless the most energetic work on the part of the
individual teacher must be, who would fain lead a pupil back into the
distant and evasive Hellenic world and to the real home of culture, when
in less than an hour, that same pupil will have recourse to a newspaper,
the latest novel, or one of those learned books, the very style of which
already bears the revolting impress of modern barbaric culture—". . .

"Now, silence for a minute, my poor friend," he cried; "I can more
easily understand you now, and should not have lost my patience with
you. You are altogether right, save in your despair. I shall now proceed
to say a few words of comfort to you. How long do you suppose the state

of education in the schools of our time, which seems to weigh so heavily upon you, will last? I shall not conceal my views on this point from you: its time is over; its days are counted. The first who will dare to be quite straightforward in this respect will hear his honesty re-echoed back to him by thousands of courageous souls. For, at bottom, there is a tacit understanding between the more nobly gifted and more warmly disposed men of the present day. Every one of them knows what he has had to suffer from the condition of culture in schools; every one of them would fain protect his offspring from the need of enduring similar drawbacks, even though he himself was compelled to submit to them. If these feelings are never quite honestly expressed, however, it is owing to a sad want of spirit among modern pedagogues. These lack real initiative; there are too few practical men among them—that is to say, too few who happen to have good and new ideas, and who know that real genius and the real practical mind must necessarily come together in the same individuals, whilst the sober practical men have no ideas and therefore fall short in practice.

"Let any one examine the pedagogic literature of the present; he who is not shocked at its utter poverty of spirit and its ridiculously awkward antics is beyond being spoiled. Here our philosophy must not begin with wonder but with dread; he who feels no dread at this point must be asked not to meddle with pedagogic questions. The reverse, of course, has been the rule up to the present; those who were terrified ran away filled with embarrassment as you did, my poor friend, while the sober and fearless ones spread their heavy hands over the most delicate technique that has ever existed in art—over the technique of education. This, however, will not be possible much longer; at some time or other the upright man will appear, who will not only have the good ideas I speak of, but who in order to work at their realisation, will dare to break with all that exists at present: he may by means of a wonderful example achieve what the broad hands, hitherto active, could not even imitate— then people will everywhere begin to draw comparisons; then men will at least be able to perceive a contrast and will be in a position to reflect upon its causes, whereas, at present, so many still believe, in perfect good faith, that heavy hands are a necessary factor in pedagogic work."

"My dear master," said the younger man, "I wish you could point to one single example which would assist me in seeing the soundness of the hopes which you so heartily raise in me. We are both acquainted with public schools; do you think, for instance, that in respect of these institutions anything may be done by means of honesty and good and new ideas to abolish the tenacious and antiquated customs now extant? In this quarter, it seems to me, the battering-rams of an attacking party will have to meet with no solid wall, but with the most fatal of stolid and slippery principles. The leader of the assault has no visible and tangible opponent to crush, but rather a creature in disguise that can transform itself into a hundred different shapes and, in each of these, slip out of his grasp, only in order to reappear and to confound its enemy by cowardly surrenders and feigned retreats. It was precisely the public schools which drove me into despair and solitude, simply because I feel that if the struggle here leads to victory all other educational institutions must give in; but that, if the reformer be forced to abandon his cause here, he may as well give us all hope in regard to every other scholastic question. Therefore, dear master, enlighten me concerning the public schools; what can we hope for in the way of their abolition or reform?"

"I also hold the question of public schools to be as important as you do," the philosopher replied. "All other educational institutions must fix their aims in accordance with those of the public school system; whatever errors of judgment it may suffer from, they suffer from also, and if it were ever purified and rejuvenated, they would be purified and rejuvenated too. The universities can no longer lay claim to this importance as centres of influence, seeing that, as they now stand, they are at least, in one important aspect, only a kind of annex to the public school system, as I shall shortly point out to you. For the moment, let us consider, together, what to my mind constitutes the very hopeful struggle of the two possibilities: *either* that the motley and evasive spirit of public schools which has hitherto been fostered, will completely vanish, or that it will have to be completely purified and rejuvenated. And in order that I may not shock you with general propositions, let us first try to recall one of those public school experiences which we have all had, and from which we have all suffered. Under severe examination what, as a matter of fact, is the present *system of teaching German* in public schools?

"I shall first of all tell you what it should be. Everybody speaks and writes German as thoroughly badly as it is just possible to do so in an age of newspaper German: that is why the growing youth who happens to be both noble and gifted has to be taken by force and put under the glass shade of good taste and of severe linguistic discipline. If this is not possible, I would prefer in future that Latin be spoken; for I am ashamed of a language so bungled and vitiated.

"What would be the duty of a higher educational institution, in this respect, if not this—namely, with authority and dignified severity to put youths, neglected, as far as their own language is concerned, on the right path, and to cry to them: 'Take your own language seriously! He who does not regard this matter as a sacred duty does not possess even the germ of a higher culture. From your attitude in this matter, from your treatment of your mother-tongue, we can judge how highly or how lowly you esteem art, and to what extent you are related to it. If you notice no physical loathing in yourselves when you meet with certain words and tricks of speech in our journalistic jargon, cease from striving after culture; for here in your immediate vicinity, at every moment of your life, while you are either speaking or writing, you have a touchstone for testing how difficult, how stupendous, the task of the cultured man is, and how very improbable it must be that many of you will ever attain to culture.'

"In accordance with the spirit of this address, the teacher of German at a public school would be forced to call his pupil's attention to thousands of details, and with the absolute certainty of good taste, to forbid their using such words and expressions, for instance, as: '*beanspruchen*,' '*vereinnahmen*,' '*einer Sache Rechnung tragen*,' '*die Initiative ergreifen*,' '*selbstverständlich*,'[1] etc., *cum tædio in infinitum*. The same teacher would also have to take our classical authors and show, line for line, how carefully and with what precision every expression has to be chosen when a writer has the correct feeling in his heart and has before his eyes a perfect conception of all he is writing. He would necessarily urge his pupils, time and again, to express the same thought ever more happily; nor would he have to abate in rigour until the less gifted in his class had contracted an unholy fear of their language, and the others had developed great enthusiasm for it.

"Here then is a task for so-called 'formal' education [2] [the education tending to develop the mental faculties, as opposed to 'material' education,[3] which is intended to deal only with the acquisition of facts, *e.g.* history, mathematics, etc.], and one of the utmost value: but what do we find in the public school—that is to say, in the headquarters of formal education? He who understands how to apply what he has heard here will also know what to think of the modern public school as a so-called educational institution. He will discover, for instance, that the public school, according to its fundamental principles, does not educate for the purposes of culture, but for the purposes of scholarship; and, further, that of late it seems to have adopted a course which indicates rather that it has even discarded scholarship in favour of journalism as the object of its exertions. This can be clearly seen from the way in which German is taught.

"Instead of that purely practical method of instruction by which the teacher accustoms his pupils to severe self-discipline in their own language, we find everywhere the rudiments of a historico-scholastic method of teaching the mother-tongue: that is to say, people deal with it as if it were a dead language and as if the present and future were under no obligations to it whatsoever. The historical method has become so universal in our time, that even the living body of the language is

---

[1] It is not practicable to translate these German solecisms by similar instances of English solecisms. The reader who is interested in the subject will find plenty of material in a book like the Oxford *King's English*.

[2] German: *Formelle Bildung*.

[3] German: *Materielle Bildung*.

sacrificed for the sake of anatomical study. But this is precisely where culture begins—namely, in understanding how to treat the quick as something vital, and it is here too that the mission of the cultured teacher begins: in suppressing the urgent claims of 'historical interests' wherever it is above all necessary to *do* properly and not merely to *know* properly. Our mother-tongue, however, is a domain in which the pupil must learn how to *do* properly, and to this practical end, alone, the teaching of German is essential in our scholastic establishments. The historical method may certainly be a considerably easier and more comfortable one for the teacher; it also seems to be compatible with a much lower grade of ability and, in general, with a smaller display of energy and will on his part. But we shall find that this observation holds good in every department of pedagogic life: the simpler and more comfortable method always masquerades in the disguise of grand pretensions and stately titles; the really practical side, the *doing*, which should belong to culture and which, at bottom, is the more difficult side, meets only with disfavour and contempt. That is why the honest man must make himself and others quite clear concerning this *quid pro quo*.

"Now, apart from these learned incentives to a study of the language, what is there besides which the German teacher is wont to offer? How does he reconcile the spirit of his school with the spirit of the *few* that Germany can claim who are really cultured,—*i.e.* with the spirit of its classical poets and artists? This is a dark and thorny sphere, into which one cannot even bear a light without dread; but even here we shall conceal nothing from ourselves; for sooner or later the whole of it will have to be reformed. In the public school, the repulsive impress of our æsthetic journalism is stamped upon the still unformed minds of youths. Here, too, the teacher sows the seeds of that crude and wilful misinterpretation of the classics, which later on disports itself as art-criticism, and which is nothing but bumptious barbarity. Here the pupils learn to speak of our unique *Schiller* with the superciliousness of prigs; here they are taught to smile at the noblest and most German of his works—at the Marquis of Posa, at Max and Thekla—at these smiles German genius becomes incensed and a worthier posterity will blush.

"The last department in which the German teacher in a public school is at all active, which is often regarded as his sphere of highest activity, and is here and there even considered the pinnacle of public school education, is the so-called *German composition*. Owing to the very fact that in this department it is almost always the most gifted pupils who display the greatest eagerness, it ought to have been made clear how dangerously stimulating, precisely here, the task of the teacher must be. *German composition* makes an appeal to the individual, and the more strongly a pupil is conscious of his various qualities, the more personally will he do his *German composition*. This 'personal doing' is urged on

with yet an additional fillip in some public schools by the choice of the
subject, the strongest proof of which is, in my opinion, that even in the
lower classes the non-pedagogic subject is set, by means of which the
pupil is led to give a description of his life and of his development. Now,
one has only to read the titles of the compositions set in a large number
of public schools to be convinced that probably the large majority of
pupils have to suffer their whole lives, through no fault of their own,
owing to this premature demand for personal work—for the unripe
procreation of thoughts. And how often are not all a man's subsequent
literary performances but a sad result of this pedagogic original sin
against the intellect!

"Let us only think of what takes place at such an age in the production of such work. It is the first individual creation; the still undeveloped
powers tend for the first time to crystallise; the staggering sensation
produced by the demand for self-reliance imparts a seductive charm to
these early performances, which is not only quite new, but which never
returns. All the daring of nature is hauled out of its depths; all vanities
—no longer constrained by mighty barriers—are allowed for the first
time to assume a literary form: the young man, from that time forward,
feels as if he had reached his consummation as a being not only able, but
actually invited, to speak and to converse. The subject he selects obliges
him either to express his judgment upon certain poetical works, to class
historical persons together in a description of character, to discuss serious
ethical problems quite independently, or even to turn the searchlight
inwards, to throw its rays upon his own development and to make a
critical report of himself: in short, a whole world of reflection is spread
out before the astonished young man who, until then, had been almost
unconscious, and is delivered up to him to be judged.

"Now let us try to picture the teacher's usual attitude towards these
first highly influential examples of original composition. What does he
hold to be most reprehensible in this class of work? What does he call his
pupil's attention to?—To all excess in form or thought—that is to say, to
all that which, at their age, is essentially characteristic and individual.
Their really independent traits which, in response to this very premature
excitation, can manifest themselves only in awkwardness, crudeness, and
grotesque features,—in short, their individuality is reproved and rejected
by the teacher in favour of an unoriginal decent average. On the other
hand, uniform mediocrity gets peevish praise; for, as a rule, it is just the
class of work likely to bore the teacher thoroughly.

"There may still be men who recognise a most absurd and most
dangerous element of the public school curriculum in the whole farce of
this German composition. Originality is demanded here: but the only
shape in which it can manifest itself is rejected, and the 'formal' education that the system takes for granted is attained to only by a very
limited number of men who complete it at a ripe age. Here everybody

without exception is regarded as gifted for literature and considered as capable of holding opinions concerning the most important questions and people, whereas the one aim which proper education should most zealously strive to achieve would be the suppression of all ridiculous claims to independent judgment, and the inculcation upon young men of obedience to the sceptre of genius. Here a pompous form of diction is taught in an age when every spoken or written word is a piece of barbarism. Now let us consider, besides, the danger of arousing the self-complacency which is so easily awakened in youths; let us think how their vanity must be flattered when they see their literary reflection for the first time in the mirror. Who, having seen all these effects at *one* glance, could any longer doubt whether all the faults of our public, literary, and artistic life were not stamped upon every fresh generation by the system we are examining: hasty and vain production, the disgraceful manufacture of books; complete want of style; the crude, characterless, or sadly swaggering method of expression; the loss of every æsthetic canon; the voluptuousness of anarchy and chaos—in short, the literary peculiarities of both our journalism and our scholarship.

"None but the very fewest are aware that, among many thousands, perhaps only *one* is justified in describing himself as literary, and that all others who at their own risk try to be so deserve to be met with Homeric laughter by all competent men as a reward for every sentence they have ever had printed;—for it is truly a spectacle meet for the gods to see a literary Hephaistos limping forward who would pretend to help us to something. To educate men to earnest and inexorable habits and views, in this respect, should be the highest aim of all mental training, whereas the general *laisser aller* of the 'fine personality' can be nothing else than the hall-mark of barbarism. From what I have said, however, it must be clear that, at least in the teaching of German, no thought is given to culture; something quite different is in view,—namely, the production of the afore-mentioned 'free personality.' And so long as German public schools prepare the road for outrageous and irresponsible scribbling, so long as they do not regard the immediate and practical discipline of speaking and writing as their most holy duty, so long as they treat the mother-tongue as if it were only a necessary evil or a dead body, I shall not regard these institutions as belonging to real culture."

. . .

Both the philosopher and his companion sat silent, sunk in deep dejection: the peculiarly critical state of that important educational institution, the German public school, lay upon their souls like a heavy burden, which one single, well-meaning individual is not strong enough to remove, and the multitude, though strong, not well meaning enough.

Our solitary thinkers were perturbed by two facts: by clearly perceiving on the one hand that what might rightly be called "classical education" was now only a far-off ideal, a castle in the air, which could not

possibly be built as a reality on the foundations of our present educational system, and that, on the other hand, what was now, with customary and unopposed euphemism, pointed to as "classical education" could
only claim the value of a pretentious illusion, the best effect of which
was that the expression "classical education" still lived on and had not
yet lost its pathetic sound.

. . .

"Just think of the innumerable crowd of teachers, who, in all good faith,
have assimilated the system of education which has prevailed up to the
present, that they may cheerfully and without over-much deliberation
carry it further on. What do you think it will seem like to these men
when they hear of projects from which they are excluded *beneficio
naturæ;* of commands which their mediocre abilities are totally unable to
carry out; of hopes which find no echo in them; of battles the war-cries of
which they do not understand, and in the fighting of which they can take
part only as dull and obtuse rank and file? But, without exaggeration,
that must necessarily be the position of practically all the teachers in our
higher educational establishments: and indeed we cannot wonder at this
when we consider how such a teacher originates, how he *becomes* a
teacher of such high status. Such a large number of higher educational
establishments are now to be found everywhere that far more teachers
will continue to be required for them than the nature of even a highly-
gifted people can produce; and thus an inordinate stream of undesirables
flow into these institutions, who, however, by their preponderating
numbers and their instinct of 'similis simile gaudet' gradually come to
determine the nature of these institutions. There may be a few people,
hopelessly unfamiliar with pedagogical matters, who believe that our
present profusion of public schools and teachers, which is manifestly out
of all proportion, can be changed into a real profusion, an *ubertas
ingenii,* merely by a few rules and regulations, and without any reduction in the number of these institutions. But we may surely be unanimous
in recognising that by the very nature of things only an exceedingly
small number of people are destined for a true course of education, and
that a much smaller number of higher educational establishments would
suffice for their further development, but that, in view of the present
large numbers of educational institutions, those for whom in general
such institutions ought only to be established must feel themselves to be
the least facilitated in their progress.

"The same holds good in regard to teachers. It is precisely the best
teachers—those who, generally speaking, judged by a high standard, are
worthy of this honourable name—who are now perhaps the least fitted,
in view of the present standing of our public schools, for the education of
these unselected youths, huddled together in a confused heap; but who
must rather, to a certain extent, keep hidden from them the best they
could give: and, on the other hand, by far the larger number of these

teachers feel themselves quite at home in these institutions, as their moderate abilities stand in a kind of harmonious relationship to the dullness of their pupils. It is from this majority that we hear the ever-re-sounding call for the establishment of new public schools and higher educational institutions: we are living in an age which, by ringing the changes on its deafening and continual cry, would certainly give one the impression that there was an unprecedented thirst for culture which eagerly sought to be quenched. But it is just at this point that one should learn to hear aright: it is here, without being disconcerted by the thundering noise of the education-mongers, that we must confront those who talk so tirelessly about the educational necessities of their time. Then we should meet with a strange disillusionment, one which we, my good friend, have often met with: those blatant heralds of educational needs, when examined at close quarters, are suddenly seen to be trans-formed into zealous, yea, fanatical opponents of true culture, *i.e.* all those who hold fast to the aristocratic nature of the mind; for, at bottom, they regard as their goal the emancipation of the masses from the mastery of the great few; they seek to overthrow the most sacred hierarchy in the kingdom of the intellect—the servitude of the masses, their submissive obedience, their instinct of loyalty to the rule of genius.

"I have long accustomed myself to look with caution upon those who are ardent in the cause of the so-called 'education of the people' in the common meaning of the phrase; since for the most part they desire for themselves, consciously or unconsciously, absolutely unlimited freedom, which must inevitably degenerate into something resembling the satur-nalia of barbaric times, and which the sacred hierarchy of nature will never grant them. They were born to serve and to obey; and every moment in which their limping or crawling or broken-winded thoughts are at work shows us clearly out of which clay nature moulded them, and what trade mark she branded thereon. The education of the masses cannot, therefore, be our aim; but rather the education of a few picked men for great and lasting works. We well know that a just posterity judges the collective intellectual state of a time only by those few great and lonely figures of the period, and gives its decision in accordance with the manner in which they are recognised, encouraged, and honoured, or, on the other hand, in which they are snubbed, elbowed aside, and kept down. What is called the 'education of the masses' cannot be accom-plished except with difficulty; and even if a system of universal compul-sory education be applied, they can only be reached outwardly: those individual lower levels where, generally speaking, the masses come into contact with culture, where the people nourishes its religious instinct, where it poetises its mythological images, where it keeps up its faith in its customs, privileges, native soil, and language—all these levels can scarcely be reached by direct means, and in any case only by violent demolition. And, in serious matters of this kind, to hasten forward the progress of the education of the people means simply the postponement of this violent demolition, and the maintenance of that wholesome unconsciousness, that sound sleep, of the people, without which counter-action and remedy no culture, with the exhausting strain and excitement of its own actions, can make any headway.

"We know, however, what the aspiration is of those who would disturb the healthy slumber of the people, and continually call out to them: 'Keep your eyes open! Be sensible! Be wise!' we know the aim of those who profess to satisfy excessive educational requirements by means of an extraordinary increase in the number of educational institutions and the conceited tribe of teachers originated thereby. These very people, using these very means, are fighting against the natural hierarchy in the realm of the intellect, and destroying the roots of all those noble and sublime plastic forces which have their material origin in the unconsciousness of the people, and which fittingly terminate in the procreation of genius and its due guidance and proper training. It is only in the simile of the mother that we can grasp the meaning and the responsibility of the true education of the people in respect to genius: its real origin is not to be found in such education; it has, so to speak, only a metaphysical source, a metaphysical home. But for the genius to make his appearance; for him to emerge from among the people; to portray the reflected picture, as it were, the dazzling brilliancy of the peculiar colours of this people; to depict the noble destiny of a people in the similitude of an individual in a work which will last for all time, thereby making his nation itself eternal, and redeeming it from the ever-shifting element of transient things: all this is possible for the genius only when he has been brought up and come to maturity in the tender care of the culture of a people; whilst, on the other hand, without this sheltering home, the genius will not, generally speaking, be able to rise to the height of his eternal flight, but will at an early moment, like a stranger weather-driven upon a bleak, snow-covered desert, slink away from the inhospitable land."

SPECIAL READING

Risk and Failure in Education / OTTO F. BOLLNOW

Risk as a Characteristic Factor in the Field of Education

Finally, we have to pay attention to the last form in which the existential factor in education is noticed. Until now, we have been

"Risk and Failure in Education" is reprinted from Otto Friedrich Bollnow, "Wagnis und Scheitern in der Erziehung," *Existenzphilosophie und Pädagogik*, translated by John Paul Strain. Copyright © W. Kohlhammer Verlag GmbH., Stuttgart, Germany, 1959. Reprinted by permission.

concerned with investigating the existential events, or, more generally speaking, the unstable processes as they occur in the life of the person to be educated. In this connection, we have suggested that the proper behavior of the educator, whose function it is to consider these events, is to accept them with understanding when they arise, and even to induce them, if possible, within very small limits. There is, however, another sphere in which the existential factor in education is important, in the life of the educator himself. Crises arise in his own life that are due to the particular exposed position of his existence as a result of the unreserved engagement of his person that he is challenged to show. The responsible acceptance of the risk, coinciding with the possibility of failure, characterizes the unavoidable existential moment in every educator's life. Consequently, we will close the present study with a consideration of this aspect.

Every educator knows of situations in the daily practice of his profession when something goes wrong in education, when he does not reach the goal he has been striving so hard for, when his relation to children becomes more and more a conflict in which he is finally defeated, and when, in the end, he even fails in his whole engagement. That is the painful and shadowy side of his profession. He does not like to talk about it. It is understandable that theoretical thinking in the field of pedagogics does not concern itself with these things. They have been considered accidental instances that unfortunately might occur to us as imperfect human beings, but which, in principle, could have been avoided with a better and more skillful program of education. The possibility that failure has a far deeper foundation, that it is actually founded in the essence, even in the dignity of education itself, has never been thought of. In reality, however, risk will be an innermost essential characteristic of education as long as education is considered a form of association with free beings, who are basically unpredictable in their freedom because they do not act mechanically. For the pupil always has the chance to evade the intentions of the educator, to turn against these intentions and to thwart them for inscrutable reasons. Therefore, the possibility of failure has been a determinative factor in the act of education from the beginning. One has to accept it consciously if one wants to carry out education in its full sense.

This connection remained hidden so long as education was thought to be analogous to a kind of handicraft work. As a matter of fact, it is still viewed that way today even if it is not often admitted. Like the craftsman who produces what has been ordered from the material he has been given, or like the sculptor who wants to carve his sculpture out of rock, so the educator supposedly forms his "student material" according to the rules of psychological knowledge with a view toward the educational goals laid down for him. If he fails in this formation, the failure results

either from a mistake in practicing his craftsmanship, or from an inadequacy in the material, although he should have recognized this by virtue
of his knowledge and thus such an oversight also amounts to an error in
his craftsmanship. Basically, this should not have necessarily happened
to him. The success of educational activity depends solely on the
efficiency and carefulness by which the educational act is carried out.
Therefore, success lies primarily within the realm of conscious human
planning.

The same conclusion holds true, by the way, if one starts from the idea
of organic development. For in this case, education is restricted to
avoiding disruptions of the child's own unfolding according to his own
nature, something which cannot fail. If occasionally the educator does
not reach the goal he had expected, it is, according to this point of view,
either because he made the wrong conceptions about the available talent
or because he showed a lack of attention in efficiently preventing external disturbances. In both cases, the failure could have been avoided
because success, in this conception, lies basically in the realm of human
planning. However, an overwhelming disaster might intrude from the
outside; for example, a disease or accident might violently interrupt a
promising beginning in development. But in this case, the cause is an
outside factor that could not have been considered at the outset of the
student's education. The educator need not blame himself in this instance. It is a mishap, but no real failure. It has only affected the
educator in an external sense and has not struck a blow at his inner self.

Both positions can be applied within limits, and they can illuminate
certain aspects of the educational process significantly. However, the
initial approach of both positions already represents a misunderstanding
of the real nature of education, which is that here a free human being
encounters another individual in a demanding way, and that from the
beginning the educator in his educational approach has to consider the
pupils' freedom, which generally eludes all predetermination. Recognizing the freedom of the other human being, means, at the same time,
affirming the daring character of education, because in this recognition
lies the possibility that an attitude may arise from the freedom of the
other individual that may reject the teacher's educational attempt and
eventually destroy it. This is something totally different from a deficiency
in the material or an absence of ability on the part of the student. It is
also something different from a mishap coming from the outside. It is an
active resistance of the other's will to the intention of the educator. And
so, I always have to include the possibility of real failure if I am at all
willing to acknowledge the other human being in his freedom, a freedom
to move toward what appears to me evil in regard to my educational
goal. The pupil always has the possibility of thwarting the well-intentioned educational attempt. This is no longer just an educator's failure in

a practical task; it is a failure in his innermost self. But to attempt to abolish the so-caused condition of daringness in education, and in that way to avoid the danger of failure, necessarily degrades the other human being to a mere material for my manipulation and thus offends the dignity of this other person and the dignity of education itself.

The possibility of failure constitutes the difficulty, and often enough the tragedy, of the educational profession, because failure in this profession means something quite different from failure in any other. In the case of the latter, we mostly have failure in performing certain practical tasks. The concerned person may then turn to other tasks and remain unaffected by the failure in his inner self. The educator, on the other hand, fails in his innermost core because he collapses in a situation where he has identified himself existentially with all his strength. The educator not only has to overcome the passive resistance of the material day by day, he also has to break the active resistance of his reluctant pupils. It is in this circumstance that we find the reasons why teachers are worn out and get old before their time. To fail in the innermost core is the tragedy of the educational profession. It weighs so much heavier, for it will not be glorified with the hero's laurel, but mostly elapses in the curse of ridiculousness without glory. The real tragedy of the educator has not yet had its poetic presentation, and therefore, has seldom found sympathy from fellow-men.

Trial, Gamble, and Risk

We will first try to point out through conceptual clarification the nature of genuine educational risk by distinguishing it from two other phenomena that, in a similar way, are exposed to the possibility of failure but cannot be called a risk. These two are "trial" and "gamble." Both are data in the field of educational reality (a fact that cannot be denied) and frequently interfere with the idea of risk. We will first try in a more general sense to point out the nature of these concepts, and then we will investigate their importance for education.[1]

A person can try something. In this connection, one can say, perhaps more precisely, that he is testing something. This is already the case with each work of handicraft. The artisan tries something new because he considers the old method insufficient and wants to better it, or he wishes to find out whether he should not replace the usual material with something better and cheaper; or he tries a new knack or new method of

[1] I refer to G. Kudritzki, "Wagnis und Scheitern: Eine phänomenologische Erörterung in pädagogischem Hinblick" ("Risk and Failure: A Phenomenological Discussion under the Aspect of Education"), dissertation, University of Tübingen, 1959, in which the problem is approached from a different side and these ideas are pursued much further.

production, and so on. First, one tries it only because he does not know if the expected result will really materialize; in other words, whether it will work. One simply tries it. As an often-used proverb says, "The proof of the pudding lies in the eating," and this means that prior reflections are very limited and that one wants to see the results of the new experience. The results will then determine the correctness of the attempt. Also, the experiment may fail. Perhaps "fail" is too harsh a word, because if the experiment does not work, it will not be unusual and need not affect the person involved in his innermost feelings. He is sorry, of course, because he has spent time and effort. But an unsuccessful trial produces a result. It shows what will not work. One has simply to try something else, and man learns through the continuous testing of new things.

There have been trials of this kind since man's beginning. Modern science has developed the trial into a well-ordered method by making possible causal and systematic research through reproduction of the experimental conditions and variations of the factors involved. This happens in the experiment, which, in this special sense, is no longer just a groping trial, but a well-planned procedure that serves to enlarge knowledge systematically. In this context, we need not discuss it further.

Moreover, man may let the matter take its course by gambling on something. This leads us into another field, which cannot simply be compared with "trying" or "testing." One can sample the tightness of a rope by exposing it to a test before its use. But one can also do without a foregoing test and merely rely on its being all right without it. In an experimental situation, one wants to learn something, one is concerned with the discovery of noticeable principles. In gambling, one exposes himself to an unpredictable chance. In so doing, he remains passive, with no influence over the outcome of the event. He merely lets the matter take its course.

Sometimes, gambling cannot be avoided. The merchant, for example, necessarily gambles in his planning, for the outcome of his business depends on the market situation and other unpredictable factors, even though modern insurance represents an attempt to reduce the extent of the gamble. Another proverb says, "Nothing ventured, nothing gained" and this is exactly what we are referring to as gambling. At the beginning of a trip, one gambles as far as the weather is concerned, even if today insurance companies try to lessen this risk. Thus all of life is full of small and large gambles, and in planning one has to try to estimate correctly the extent of every gamble.

But to make an avoidable gamble is foolish and leads to punishment, for it derives no longer merely from external circumstances, but goes much deeper. Whoever gambles with his life, for example, acts without responsibility, for life should not be exposed to any kind of gambling. Gambling always refers to something that is at one's disposal. To gamble with life is to reduce it to something that is at one's disposal. On the other hand, one might risk one's life for something, but this differs from gambling with it, for one is consciously accepting danger because of a deeper responsibility. Unlike gambling, this case involves accepting a real risk.

The concept of true risk leads us to a totally new field. We can determine the difference best by saying: I always gamble something, but in the final analysis, I risk myself. Wherever I risk something, at the same time, I am charging myself with my own person. From an ethical point of view, a gamble may appear indifferent and often even hazardous, but a real risk always occurs because of genuine ethical responsibility. Thus the failure of a real risk weighs much heavier. When an experiment happens to fail, this will not affect man in his innermost self because it happens on an objective level. When something "goes wrong" in a gamble, it may be painful in a single case, but it too merely affects man from the outside. But when a real risk fails, then the person who dared it is hit by the failure in his innermost core. In this case, an unsuccessful risk always means genuine failure. Concealed in every risk as such is the possibility of failure.

Application to Education

Now all three forms reappear in the special field of educational activity. A teacher who wants to meet the changing requirements of his profession has to test many things. He tests a new teaching method, he watches how the students react to various new materials, and he tries hard to match their interests. A teacher only remains "alive" by always trying something new. Also, a trial can be carried out systematically as in a scientific experiment. But in that case we are already in the province of educational research and not in that of immediate education itself.

The educational trial can fail, and especially an experiment in teaching. For the educator, this does not generally mean anything else than the failure of an experiment. In a single case, he might regret this failure, but he will learn from it and it will lead him to new experiments. So trials are part of the educational practice, and they are important devices for the progress of education. But an unsuccessful experiment does not mean a failure at all.

Sometimes the educator has to gamble as well, especially when quick decisions have to be made and he has very little time to reflect on them thoroughly. Basically, such situations are no different from those that require gambling in general and are not really typical of the nature of the conduct of education. Therefore, we might skip them here.

The real risk, on the other hand, is connected with the conduct of education in a special way. Boys and youth have to be dared, says

Herbart in a well-known work; and by that he does not refer to just any gamble where the educator lets the development take its course and where failure might be accepted as a mishap.[2] But the very nature of educational necessity requires this risk. In order to become men, Herbart continues, the students must not be prevented from testing their youthful courage and perhaps their recklessness. In education for freedom and ethical independence, there is no way to avoid this risk, and exaggerated caution and fearfulness in the name of "protection" prevent the growing person from coming of age. The mother duck, cackling helplessly after her lively swimming ducklings, is an adequate image of the protective tendency of the helpless educator.

But here too the real risk must be sharply distinguished from mere adventurousness. The adventurer seeks danger and enjoys its special appeal. He risks everything for the fascination that danger brings, not for the goal he wishes to attain. An analogy exists in the case of the adventurous educators. Quite a few might be found among the leaders of the "youth movement." They are those who become intoxicated with the influence they exert over young people and who endanger the young by driving them into situations that they probably are not able to cope with. The genuine educational risk distinguishes itself from mere adventurousness to the extent that it is necessary and is carried out with the highest ethical sense of responsibility.

In any single case, this risk can be of various kinds. There can only be an attempt in a groping way to point out some typical possibilities in order to illuminate the common factor of the risk in each of them. The difficulty lies in the fact that we are moving in a field closely bordering on the unexpressible, and we have to be satisfied to gain some more definite features of a subject not easily determined, features that might become the basis for further illuminating attempts.

A Simple Example as a Starting Point

It may be easiest if I try to illustrate the daring engagement of the educator by means of an example that I am most familiar with in my own educational situation, even though it stands on the lowest level of the phenomena to be treated here—I mean the relation between the academic teacher and his doctoral candidate. When a candidate begins a research project under the conduct of his teacher, it is a joint enterprise in which not only the student but also the teacher may fail. It is already a risk to suggest a topic for a certain person to work on. Everybody needs "his" topic, and it is not foreseeable in the beginning how a particular

---

[2] J. F. Herbart, *Allgemeine Pädagogik*, Samtliche Werke, edited by K. Kehrbach (Langensalza, 1887), Vol. II, p. 19.

individual will get along with his topic. Today only a few students understand that one has first to find a topic, that one has to try and give up various projects until the topic to be investigated crystallizes slowly out of the vague compass of possibilities.

However, this idea will not be pursued further at this point, although the tensions that arise from the different perspectives in the matter will be indicated. The teacher, for example, who recognizes that it is important for the student to find his own way, yet sees the pupil on a false road, tries nevertheless to shorten the detour for him if he is afraid that too much time will be wasted and especially if the student's economic condition requires a quick completion of the work. Or if he sees his pupil laboring with tasks that exceed his abilities, he advises him to give up his favorite way. This too is not easy because the person in question is very much attached to the preliminary work that leads into the problems and cannot be dissuaded from it. And even more difficult are the cases in which the student is really on the wrong track and is caught in wrong thoughts. In such cases, the educator must interfere. One recognizes the whole delicacy of the educational risk in this kind of interference.

Everybody is fond of his own thoughts, or at least he stands close by them. As a result, he does not listen to causal explanations. One really has to make one's criticism direct and sometimes even harsh in order to make the other person listen. Sometimes, one even has to evoke a crisis in the work with a sharp reproof. Then the wrong path may be given up, and the work can proceed in a correct way. But the person in question may instead become frightened by the criticism and lured into contradiction with himself by his teacher. Then the success of the work is a question mark, and both the pupil and the teacher fail.

There is, in a manner of speaking, both a soft and a hard way in directing a work. To follow the soft way means that one encourages one's student, supports him, and refrains from speaking his own doubts, in the hope that everything will straighten out in the course of the later development of the work. However, as often happens, everything is not straightened out and then one has to use the hard way, using sharper criticism, revealing weaknesses unsparingly, and trying to manage a revision of the work. How far one can go and how far one must go, are exactly those matters that pertain to the question of risk. With helpful criticism, one might make possible a breakthrough. But one can also cause a termination of the whole work or make the pupil suspicious for a long time. Generally, one cannot foresee what will happen, but one must risk the interference nevertheless. Moreover, very often the teacher is thrust into situations without preparation. The fervor of discussions may develop things so fast that one must act on the moment without being able to measure the single consequence. Thus the honest intention to help often creates an irreversible disaster. Then not only has the pupil failed, but also the teacher, even though the public does not notice the failure because of the loneliness of educational responsibility.

In my position I have often painfully noticed such difficulties. But corresponding situations can be found in any educational field. One has to give orders, make decisions, and so on, in cases where the consequences are not foreseeable and immediate decisions must be made. This is not a scientific experiment carried out for the benefit of experience, in which one is interested only in the objective results that do not involve the individual who carries out the experiment. Sometimes, an educational situation of this type almost shades over into gambling when one runs a risk in the hope that the decision will be correct. But this situation is also a genuine risk because my whole person becomes involved in it and because I consciously accept responsibility for the outcome. Therefore, failure is not simply a pitiful mishap, but a real breakdown in which the person involved is hit in his innermost core.

Risk in the Practice of Authority

After this preparatory example, we must try to analyze some typical possibilities of risk and failure in education. One occasion of unavoidable risk can be found in the daily occurrence of a disciplinary difficulty for the individual since this, to a smaller and larger extent, belongs also to the nature of education. I am not practicing real education when I am able to force the child to obey me, either through physical superiority or through the enforcement of school regulations that are based on the general public order. Education begins when I order something whose fulfillment I cannot achieve by force and that I know I cannot force. I always get into situations in which I have to give orders if I want to reach my goal. On one side, I can give orders because I can depend on the child's own practical and ethical understanding to cause him to respond to the appeal of my order. But in this case, a moment of unavoidable uncertainty on my part is always involved, for I do not know whether or not the child has this insight and whether or not it will be effective in this case. To an extent, a gamble is surely involved. On the other hand, I cannot limit myself to cases in which my orders are certain to be followed, for in such cases, my orders would be merely carried out mechanically and would lack any educational value. In anticipation of this result, I have to give those orders that I cannot be sure will be carried out. From this uncertainty arises the real risk of giving orders, a risk that educational responsibility requires me to accept.

This fact leads us to the problem of the use of authority. Giving orders always makes me throw my authority on the scale. But the nature of authority is not to enforce things in a causal-mechanical way, but rather to turn to a free individual who submits himself to the authoritative demand. The voluntary quality of this submission, however, must be produced through the process of education. So the educator again and again comes to that border where he has to face resistance, or injustice, or mere disorder, with nothing behind him but the power of conviction that is derived from his ethical sincerity. If in the process he encounters the resistant child or youth, fully conscious of his own external powerlessness as a teacher, he accepts a risk to which he resolves with his strength—his existence as a human being. Only by taking this kind of risk can educational success be attained. And the more convincing an educator is in his whole personality, the more certain success will be. However, he can never be totally certain. He may assume the risk and fail, and then not only has he lost a gamble, but he has failed in his primary function. In everyday practice, the risk usually occurs in a trial of strength of the educator's position of authority after the authority itself has been called into question. In the rarest cases, the educator is able to restore the loss of authority by external means and then he really is defeated in the eyes of his pupils. After this defeat, he can never hope to rise to authority again. He really has failed.

The Risk of Trust

Another possible necessary risk that includes the possibility of educational failure lies in the trust that the educator must show toward the child. The idea that the healthy development of the human being can only take place in an atmosphere of trust has been discussed extensively elsewhere.[3] Any distrust that I show toward another person changes him. It makes him as stupid and lazy and perfidious as I expected him to be. Vice versa, every instance of trust changes him in a positive way into the better person he had been expected to be. One can make a person better by believing that he is better. As Nicholi Hartmann once said: "Moral strength coming from the one who trusts is an eminently educational power." He adds, "trust can transform man towards good as well as towards evil, be it whatever he believes."[4]

Trust shown toward the young is especially required in critical situations in which an individual student has been brought back from his wrong direction by educational interference, whether through exhortation or punishment, and in which he displays timid and vulnerable signs of new life. The steadfastness of any new resolution does not depend on

---

[3] Compare O. F. Bollnow, *Neue Geborgenheit* (Stuttgart, 1955), pp. 19 ff; *Wesen und Wandel der Tugenden* (Frankfurt on the Main, 1958), pp. 175 ff. A. Nitscheke, "Angst und Vertrauen," *Die Sammlung*, 7. Jahrg. 1952, pp. 175 ff; H. Haucke, "Die anthropologische Funktion des Vertrauens und seine Bedeutung für die Erziehung" (dissertation, Tübingen, 1956); R. Schottlaender, "Theorie des Vertrauens" (Berlin, 1957).

[4] N. Hartmann, *Ethik* (Berlin, 1926), pp. 429 f.

the student alone, but also upon the trust the educator shows in his resolution. For example, when a person, after any mistake, honestly promises to do better, the strength with which he makes this new commitment depends on the educator to whom he promises it. The educator trusts the student in question to keep his promise. Without the help of this trust, even the most solid resolution comes to naught. Indeed, nothing is colder and more discouraging than an educator's declaration in plain words that he cannot trust this promise after so many unkept promises, that he is convinced that the person involved will retrogress despite all good resolutions. This skepticism, no matter how much it is grounded in past experience, has a destructive effect because it deprives the person, despite all his honest intentions, of the strength to carry out his promises, which in turn, always depend on trust in the one to whom the promise is made. Therefore, in spite of all disappointments, the educator must constantly renew his strength for trusting.

But a difficulty arises in that this transforming power of trust (quite similar to the effect of authority), is not a type of mechanical effect. That is, trust does not necessarily achieve results. It too is based on a risk that the educator always has to initiate anew. In the same way, Hartmann points out: "All trust and all belief is a risk; it always requires a fraction of ethical courage and strength of soul to achieve it. It always happens with a certain engagement of the person." And further: "The one who trusts yields himself into the hands of the person he is trusting, he risks himself." [5] Therefore, the risk of trust shown to the child may succeed, and if so, then the educational involvement was worthwhile. But at the same time, there may also be failure, and then the educator appears as the one who had lacked necessary precaution, one who had acted with irresponsible credulity and stupidity. The educator then must bear ridicule as well as experience failure in his work.

A situation of this type occurred after 1918 when social welfare education (Bollnow refers to reformatories, ed.) did away with the customary bars and locked doors, and trusted that their pupils would not run away despite the lack of such external compulsions. It is known that great educational success has come from taking this risk. Such a trust, however, always remains a risk, and thus, as in the case of any other risk, we accept the possibility of failure. Therefore, success can only be achieved when the effort is backed by all the internal strength available to the teacher, and it will fail immediately as soon as this strength recedes and trusting becomes a matter of routine.

Trust always means exposing oneself without reservation to something that is unprovable and unenforceable because it depends upon the unpredictable free will of another human being. Therefore, the one who

[5] N. Hartmann, *op. cit.*, 426 f.

trusts must always become involved with his whole human strength, and in this way expose himself to possible failure. Because his whole personality is involved, he is hit most deeply when there is a lack of success. In this case, the lack of success means a genuine failure through which the educator is somehow destroyed. So not only has the reputation of the educator been deeply hurt through this failure, and thus his prospects of succeeding in other instances with the one who has let him down have been injured, but he has also failed with all the other students.

One must always remember, however, that the educator does not fail because he may have made a mistake that could have been avoided through better understanding. The consequences of a failure are found in quite a different area. The educator may fail even when he has done everything correctly. The possibility that trust can bring disappointment is one of the factors that is in the nature of risk, factors that are basically unpredictable because they are not evoked by any cause. In this possibility lies an element of fate, which here breaks into education and destroys everything that can be reached by careful human planning.

Now the educator might try to avoid the gamble of trust simply by telling the child (or any human being) that he trusts him, since he knows that the child needs this trust as a backing for his development. But the educator may not identify himself completely with this trust, but rather use his "realistic" knowledge of human weakness to construct limitations and reservations so that from the very beginning he takes into account certain possibilities of disappointment. An approach like this may be very realistic, and the educator involved may know how to protect himself. But from the educational point of view, it has no value. For educational reasons, it is not sufficient that the educator merely pretends to trust. He must honestly convince himself of his own trust. He has to get involved wholly in this trust of his, or he will not appear trustworthy to the child (or to the other person). Again, this does not mean that he may yield himself carelessly and credulously to cheap illusions. No, he needs all his skeptical-realistic knowledge. In his own soul, however, he must have faced the conflict of this knowledge and the risk of trusting irrespective of how it may look to the outsider. Despite all his knowledge about the danger of disappointment, he must trust honestly if his trust is to have meaning for the other person.

Above all, these demands of trusting indicate the special difficulty of the educator. It necessarily lies in the destiny of his profession that he may be disappointed in his trust. The trust may backfire, and the danger of becoming resigned or becoming bitter is always present. There is no way to avoid the fact that many educators are given over to bitterness and practice their profession as a mere external routine. The educator's function, however, is always to rescue himself from resignation, and renew the strength of trust in spite of all disappointments. This effort almost exceeds human strength, and one may say that the educator continuously asks too much of himself in the face of the demands of this trust. These excessive demands may be the ultimate reason why so many educators grow old before their time. By the same token, however, the opposite may be true, and the vitality of this trust causes them to remain inwardly young.

The Risk of Uncovered Openness

Another form of educational risk lies in the fact that the teacher may not only expect from the child that which he is capable of doing without much difficulty at his particular level of development, but also something in excess of that requirement. The teacher talks with the small child, for example, not at the level of speech that the child himself uses at that age, but rather in the form of the next higher level of speaking in order to challenge him toward further development. That is, the teacher creates a "tide of development" that pulls the child forward. At the same time, a risk is also run when too much tension has been created, and so the child fails under this tension and becomes discouraged. The teacher, at least for a certain length of time, has to expect things from the child that approach the limits of the child's strength, not only in the intellectual field but also in the ethical requirements of self-sacrifice or demands against oneself.

This process leads to a special extending of the risk. In this case, the area concerned is not so much practical skill and knowledge, but things that appeal to a human being in his emotional sphere and that somehow touch the realm of what is "sacred" to man. Such things can be found in the great figures of literature or in questions of human culture. Children have to be given more than they are prepared for or are capable of receiving at their respective level of development. But there is always the danger that children may not acquire these things and that they may develop negative judgments that will become ingrained and bar them later from an adequate access to life or that they may simply fight against these things in a momentary attitude of defiance. In assuming this type of risk, the teacher exposes his own innermost self, for there is always the danger that he will become suspect or even ridiculous from the students' point of view in terms of those things that concern him most.

This leads us to a decisive point. The teacher always has to fight for the spiritual values that he seeks to convey; and because of this, he must not exclude his students from the innermost sphere of feelings and convictions that man usually hides as the most vulnerable core of his soul. The teacher must open, so to speak, the intimate part of his soul to the not-yet-mature person because this is the only way to introduce this sphere to another human being. Everyone has the right to protect the sphere of things that concern him most deeply from the observation of others. He has, one might say, the right to have a mask behind which he may hide his most sacred feelings, revealing them only in rare moments to another trusted person. Only the teacher is forced again and again to talk about the most sacred and most fragile matters to persons who will accept them in a manner that he cannot predict. The poet is in a much more favorable situation because he can write down his innermost feelings in the loneliness of his room and need not defend them before any audience. Only the teacher—and in a similar way the minister—finds himself in a situation where he has to talk about the things that concern him most deeply. Do not misunderstand, this does not mean that he has to talk about himself and his emotional life. Such action would be perfidious indeed and contrary to the detachment that is always necessary.[6] But by talking about things with sincerity and without an ironic overlay, he reveals his own feelings because his feelings are so much connected with his inner self. The educator simply cannot avoid this. It is the price he must always pay to achieve the risk of openness. There arises the danger, of course, that these inner things will become for him simply teaching materials that he presents to others without inner inhibition, perhaps even with a feeling of satisfaction. Then he can easily take an unctuous and sentimental tone that only embarrasses the listeners, for the good audience experiences the same shy reticence as the good speaker. A good audience is moved only when the speaker's reticence is noticed, and this is necessary in order to speak of these delicate matters in public.

Thus, the inwardly vivid teacher always constantly struggles against his natural desire to protect himself, a desire that he has to overcome in order to speak of the things that are so important to him. Only then will he succeed in conveying these lasting values. And like Orpheus, who forced the wild beasts to be quiet through the strength of his singing, so the teacher—through the sacrifice of his uncovered openness—brings things within reach of his students that they never would have gained by themselves. He may succeed in this endeavor. But it always remains a risk. At the same time, there is always the danger that communication with the other person is not achieved or is interrupted, and that he will appear strange and may even gain nothing but ridicule from the students at that point which affects him in his innermost self. The teacher, we may say, has to show his soul openly although everybody else may hide it behind protective covers. Because of this risk in openness, something that he has to achieve anew each time, the teacher's fate, in a very special way, lies in the hands of his students.

[6] Compare E. Meinberg, "Das distanzlose Kind" (dissertation, University of Tübingen, 1959).

The Failure

Another feature can be clarified with an example that does not quite belong to the sphere of real failure but that leads into it. An amazing impression is left in the minds of school boys, even after decades, by the proper apology of a teacher to his student because of the teacher's mistake, or because of a suspicion he had held that proved to be unfounded, or because of a thoughtless scolding. A mishap of this kind is far from a failure. The teacher has apologized for the mistake, and the apology has had a far greater effect than any flawless educational experience could have had. So we ask, what is the basis for the unexpected positive result and the unproportionate effect? The reason might well lie in the fact that the teacher has left the throne of perfection, and by this act, he has acknowledged an ultimate equality with students, removing the usual teacher-student relationship. The student feels himself elevated by this acknowledgment and the teacher has lost nothing in the eyes of his student. Furthermore, the teacher has gained something, for by deciding to overcome himself, he has gained greater respect from all his students.

But one can go a step further and point out other cases where teachers and educators have failed in the real sense of the term because student resistance broke the teacher down in human despair. With this defeat, it happens (not always, but quite frequently) that the teacher's failure and his despairing breakdown (one cannot say any longer that this is educational), has an extraordinary effect on the young persons. They experience something as a consequence of their unexpected success in making the teacher fail, and they are affected by this in their innermost self. Through their chance experience of succeeding recklessly with their own power, they appear to recognize the senselessness of this power and the superiority of the teacher's high form of existence. They find these conclusions obvious because of the teacher's inability to protect himself against raw force, which reveals the inner superiority of his ethical position. Such is the striking experience of a regretful conscience that never intended the situation to go so far. Put even more bluntly, the one who arouses respect radiates all his purity because of his vulnerability and his inability to protect himself against treachery. An experience of this sort apparently cannot be gained by merely observing others, but only by going through the shameful experience of having offended respectability.[7]

In this manner the defenseless failure of an educator can become

[7] Concerning the connection between respect and shamefulness in general see O. F. Bollnow, *Die Ehrfurcht* (Frankfurt on the Main, 1958).

obvious in a singularly shocking experience of boys breaking down a teacher, which need not always happen. When it does, the failure of many educators is final. It will occur, however, mostly to those whose quality already has become obvious in another context. And therefore, successful teaching in this instance, if it occurs, cannot be realized as conscious planning but as an excusable mistake. Whoever wants to provoke such an experience consciously would degrade the seriousness of the process to a mere spectacle whose inner dishonesty would soon be recognized. On the other hand, at the border of conscious planning and of education itself as such, this fear of failure arises that really moves man in his depths and will purge him in the manner of a genuine crisis. Here we have the experience of a genuine borderline situation in a person's life. Something as absolute as fate has broken into everyday routine.

At the same time, this is a borderline case and one must not overemphasize the observation, as if these things belonged to the daily life of education. Although one must note that the danger of failing is a constant threat, one has to be careful not to exaggerate it. Certainly, failure of this type is terrible for the educator. Fortunately, however, such events do not occur in the regular everyday life of the educational profession, but are very rare. Not the failure, but rather the possibility of failure, must be considered in the educational behavior at any moment of the risk of trust. Fortunately, failure is still the exception; it is an exception that does not stem from an external accident but something that existed in the nature of education from the beginning. But below the level that is marked by the danger of failure, the life of planned education goes on at its regular pace. The necessity for careful planning and for thwarting disturbances, of course, remains uncontested.

This leads us back to the more general context. As we pointed out in the beginning, we are not concerned with trying to replace the traditional "classical" education of steady processing in life and education with a new "existential" education of unsteady forms. That would present too simple a picture and it would mean exchanging one bias for another. We rather have to understand existential events as exceptions that structure the educational events as a whole and from which one discovers a whole new educational understanding. The correlation between these two spheres, between unsteady and steady proceedings, has to be pursued and must be the object of further intensive research.

I will stop here. These thoughts represent only a beginning. I am painfully aware of their provisional and fragmentary value. But it seems to me—and here I ask for understanding if this hope should seem unrealistic—that this start will lead us from the narrowness of present educational problems into a free level of fertile new questions.

SPECIAL READING

The Role of Love in Education / EDUARD SPRANGER

Genuine education can only subsist in the element of love. It creates an ambience of affection. This is an old idea which has the support of Plato just as much as Pestalozzi. It cannot be assumed, however, that the idea has always been taken for granted. Looking back over history it would seem as if affection has sometimes been completely and utterly suppressed by severity. There is also another reason why the idea that affection is necessary to education needs close examination: Whoever claims the support both of Plato and of Pestalozzi has produced two such different witnesses that it is far from clear exactly what they are called upon to establish.

The obvious train of thought arising from all this is based on our observation of "life" in the simplest sense of the word. The higher animals show a care for their young which appears to have the same ultimate root as human motherly love. However, this animal care for the welfare of the young both before and after birth is so "instigated" by creative nature that it completely stops when it is no longer "necessary." This urge, limited in duration, and very subtle in make-up, is called an instinct. It has nevertheless enough in common with intelligence to be a guiding power transcending yet working through the individual. The human child's need for help and care lasts much longer than any animal's, although it must be conceded that this measurement is made abstractly and mathematically, i. e. not in terms of proportion of life span, and is in consequence biologically false. The comparison implies, however, that the inescapable connection of all upbringing with the medium of love may be traced to a simple root basic to life itself. Whenever affection appears in human education, it will then only be a sublimation of a completely basic biological drive, implanted in man by nature, i. e. an instinct.

What then do we understand by the place of affection in education? In what sense is it the medium, the atmosphere which protects the upbringing of young life? Perhaps we could say it is that which gives the educator his impulse, both to struggle upwards and to persevere in his efforts to educate.

1. It is the most fundamental meaning we have anticipated here: parental love seems to be the archetype of all upbringing and education. The bloodstream itself governs its functioning. There is nothing to equal the self-sacrifice of motherly love and the father's genuine care for the

"The Role of Love in Education" is reprinted from Eduard Spranger "The Role of Love in Education," *Universitas*, A German Review of the Arts and Sciences Quarterly, English Language Edition, Vol. 2, 1958, No. 3. Permission granted by Wissenschaftliche Verlagsgesellschaft M. B. H. Stuttgart, West Germany.

growing child. Even if this fundamental order is frequently perverted by guilt or fate, it nevertheless remains obvious that genuine education is born in the family. It is equally obvious that those engaged in education should take parental care as their guiding pattern, indeed, they should carry it within them as an urge given to them as a part of human nature.

If one were to count the places where parental care is appealed to by Pestalozzi, that outstanding embodiment of the living power of love in education, one would never come to an end. Yet the thought is not so obvious as it has become through the words of the Bible and the challenging statements of Pestalozzi. Protection and care, the daily provision of food, the aids to development provided in social life, these are presupposed in every orderly family. Instinct and tradition both take care of this. But is this really that deliberate development of educational growth, which we mean by genuine education? This development is often given a very poor chance. The notion that it is generally better in so-called "educated" families than it is in simple families of limited means is only partly correct. The former have more "wealth" at their disposal, yet he who has this wealth may nonetheless still be in the dark about how to use it, about standards, aims and the right means to achieve them. A mother cannot draw on her instincts for all that is necessary for this development. Pestalozzi himself finally realized this. Otherwise he would not have spent so much trouble in trying to imbue mothers with the right spirit for their task. Fathers often blunder astonishingly when they attempt to educate. In short, the capacity to educate does not automatically come with motherhood or fatherhood, despite all the love contained in these relationships. It must be considered as something which may, but does not necessarily, come of its own accord. Were this otherwise, parents would not so often seek advice from some accessible "born educator." The love felt by a mother or father is not that love which we consider essential to genuine education. Parental love is the gift of nature. Education presupposes a mind grown fully conscious of itself.

The half-truth, however, that affection in education has its archetype in the love of parents for their children stems from historical causes. The ethical principles of which we have spoken have made education in the family sacred. The religions make it the moral duty of the parents to give their children more than merely physical care.

In simpler cultures there are usually no educators beside the members of the family. Later on other institutions take over for religion and war—for music and gymnastics, as the ancient Greeks said. But the general and cultural heritage of the tribe or nation is stored up, handed on and added to by the family. For each culture a common tradition of education is built up. Thus, while instinct is the ultimate foundation of education, and while it provides the element of affection, it is nevertheless not from this but from tradition that the parents draw the accumulated wisdom they need to educate their children.

In civilizations influenced by Christianity the parents' duties are prescribed by religion. All the particulars are moulded by religion. It is precisely here that elements of a spiritual nature come into play as well as natural instinct. Education in the full sense has already begun. We take over an infinite amount from the richness of tradition. It is a precious possession of the family which should be preserved with respect.

But tradition alone is not sufficient. Everything which goes under the name of tradition has become weakened in our modern world. Moreover a positive change has occurred; new conditions have developed for which new forms of education must be created. The basic requirements nevertheless remain unchanged. The new forms of education must be developed just as were the old in their time. In this development affection or love must play a part, and the affection required is a very special kind of intellectual love. Here the "born" educator, i. e. one matured and imbued with the spirit of education, must be called upon. He is much more than the so-called educational "expert."

So we must arrive at the conclusion that fatherhood and motherhood alone can perform no educational miracles. Nevertheless, we should not deny that the feeling "It is blood of my blood for which I care" can strengthen the impulse towards education, just as it increases the duty to educate. Such natural factors always remain necessary conditions for all life, including the life of the intellect. Human nature is shared by us all and we all call ourselves "human beings." Yet he who brings with him nothing more than this kind of humanity has not yet been given the call to educate. Of necessity the educator must have worked earnestly on himself. Neither the mere instinct to educate nor natural parental love are adequate. In adolescence, when far more is demanded than mere "protective warmth," children themselves begin to grow aware of this.

2. The root of affection in education as Plato understands it is something completely different. He makes an attempt to struggle against the paederastic abuses of his Greek contemporaries in so far as he gives them a deep spiritual significance. Here too, a natural sensual inclination is presupposed. Originally the educator loves the youthful beauty of his pupil. This it is which attracts him, even in a fortunate instance inspires him. In the "Symposium" Plato tries to explain their passion to those possessed by the homosexual eros. This passion bears the traces of the mystery which plays around the demi-god of this name.

Following Plato many educators have developed the concept of an educational Eros, which need not remain homosexual, and made it a type and fundamental characteristic of human nature. The Renaissance in particular cultivated it. Later on it gained new life in the circles of the

new humanism through Winkelmann's enthusiasm for beauty, and it
became woven into the general cult of Greece. The underlying aesthetic
strand is unmistakable. But one cannot overlook the dangers of the
compelling power of such an ideal. Apart from the uncommittedness of
the aesthetic enthusiasm, severely attacked by Kierkegaard, the idea of
educational eros carries with it a sexual undertone. The drive contained
in it cannot always be mastered. The moment the supremacy of the pure
ideal is in doubt, the "educational" trembles on the verge of vice.
Creative as is the enthusiasm which arises from the erotic, the educator
must combine it with the strictest asceticism. We cannot therefore hide
from ourselves the fact that we have once more failed to find the
phenomenon we are seeking. Affection, if it is to fulfil its true function in
education, must be rooted in purity of mind. Aristocratic onesidedness
also diminishes the value of the conception. Neither beauty of youthful
appearance, nor even beauty of soul, should be the thing which draws
forth the passion to educate. Both are gifts of fortune. Their connection
with strict morality is dubious. "Strikingness" has its value, but this is
very far from the highest kind of value.

We can only admit the true eros of the soul as an element which is
occasionally helpful. But if one byepasses guilt and sorrow, need and
death, and thinks of the soul's purpose as merely to blossom in its
greatest beauty, then this is no longer a conception of life deepened
through the school of Christianity. Even if this beauty is made to signify
everything that deserves the name of divine, the whole tendency of the
line of thought is in the opposite direction. We are thus led back again to
Pestalozzi's ideas, but this time to that element in his conception of
affection in education which is of Christian origin.

3. It is precisely the aid of the shrunken and suffering soul which is the
message of Christian love. Seen from this religious standpoint the place
of affection in education is often understood as if affection were only
necessary because of the negative sides of man, as if it only had to
struggle against these. There is certainly no lack of evidence in human
life that this negative aspect exists. Man is subject to limitation and
exposed to manifold physical threats. The fact that he is at the mercy of
time is the source of innumerable spiritual sufferings. If we measure him
by the image of what he was in the original order of creation according
to Christian teaching, then he is depraved and a prey to original sin. The
reality of sin thus occupies the centre of our being. If one also takes into
account the consideration that all frailties must be particularly great in
the period of immaturity (there is a school of depth psychology which
speaks of the natural inferiority complex of children and young people)
then it follows automatically that one can only treat children with pity
and compassion and also with a regret for their sinful condition.

Those children deserve our special help who are in need and in moral danger through the inadequacies of society. In the early stages of capitalism it is notorious that there was enormous misery among children and young people. Industrial and technical society has always placed great difficulties in the way of the integration of young people. It is therefore natural that warm-hearted educators took special care of suffering children. In consequence of their specialised experience they were inclined wholly to identify affection in education with the desire to give relief. Some simply acted out of pity. Others were activated by the high moral ideal which conceives help for others, love of one's neighbour, the alleviation of suffering and the salvation of souls as the centre of moral action.

This is not the place to go into the subtle interpretations which can make this fundamental attitude understandable and applicable today. The Roman *caritas* had already advanced beyond the Greek *agape*. Yet further developments were brought about by the Christian socialist movement of the 19th century; it was precisely in the realm of education that this movement did most good.

However worthy of respect the Christian conception of love may be, however highly it and its manifold manifestations may rank in the moral world, it would nevertheless be a mistake to equate it simply with that special type of affection required in education. It may appear connected with *agape*, with *caritas*, or with Christian social welfare work, and the personalities in whom this connection has been explicit are among the greatest in the history of education. But none of these things fulfil the particular task of education. Education has its own fundamental purpose which would still be valid if sin and economic distress and mental suffering were not regarded as the central realities of human life.

The things we are here concerned with should only be considered from a philosophical standpoint. We cannot here take into account points of view of religious origin; this would go beyond the limits we have consciously set ourselves. Revealed religions are not open to criticism. Simple facts, however, may be established.

If affection in education appears in the context of cultural life in intimate connection with other forms of intellectual love, the degree to which they are compatible with one another will vary. Wherever the belief in the original depravity of man is predominant (even if the inheriting of sin is understood purely spiritually) there education towards integrity of thought, feeling and action becomes doubly necessary. At the same time, however, it becomes an almost hopeless undertaking, especially since the educator himself is a prey to the common overriding fate. Nobody is going to deny that man stands between good and evil, just as he belongs by nature to two worlds. The true educator will be filled with the confidence that his honest endeavours are not predestined to futility. The more honestly he considers the diagnosis, the more he believes in his heart in better alternatives. He wants to use his modest powers to help this dual natured creature, this wanderer between two worlds, a little further on its ascent. If he is filled with a fundamental pessimism, even though it be deeply founded in religion, then the educationalist in him will nevertheless be crippled by it.

Rousseau confesses with courage his conviction that man was good "by nature." Strictly speaking there is neither good nor bad "by nature." There is also no such thing as pure optimism. For if there were no strong cause for pessimism, optimism would lack purpose and force. The same is true vice versa. It is therefore only a question of laying greater emphasis on one side or the other. The educator must believe that the good will triumph. In saying this we have already pointed to an essential element in that type of affection which is a genuine part of education.

This line of argument must here, however, remain fragmentary. It is certain that every higher form of love ennobles those who respond to it with understanding. It also ennobles the one who loves. All pure love ennobles. Nevertheless neither the eros of the soul nor caritas is completely identical with the affection which manifests itself in education. This type of affection can be linked with both of them as an important part of their make-up, and this close association is traceable historically as a powerful force in spiritual life. Yet the essentials of education have received varying interpretations at different times. This shows that the affection underlying education must be a thing in its own right. If we first investigate the nature of this affection we shall be in a better position to understand its component elements.

4. Personal love in its general sense appears under two forms. It is first of all the mental disposition of a person who inclines towards his beloved in her totality. His love at the same time surrounds the beloved and draws out the beloved's personality. If only something specific in the beloved is loved, then love in its full sense is absent. Love is secondly a union of two personalities whose spirituality has been awakened, provided the inclination is mutual. Love between three is only possible when each stands to each in a fundamental love relationship of this kind. That sympathy which unites several people and leads to the creation of a "circle of friends" is still far distant from personal love. For this a really self-transcending relationship is necessary. As soon as the beloved also truly loves the relationship becomes mutual and a genuine union springs into existence. This does not always happen. It is precisely love as found in education which can remain one-sided. It will always be so when directed towards a being as yet spiritually unawakened to whom the true significance of this love is therefore entirely incomprehensible.

Affection in education is necessarily directed towards an individual. Language usage, indeed, gives rise to expressions like, we love the Italians or the young or brunettes. But these pallid meanings do not concern us here. Certainly I can say that I "love" my sixth form pupils for I like them and care for them. This is something entirely different from the love which is by its very nature the heart of education. This love belongs to that higher stage: the one individuality mingles with the other. At this point the question immediately arises whether it is possible for one individual to have this kind of relationship with a large number of others at the same time. One certainly has to admit that to do this in the fullest sense is impossible. We have been accustomed with Pestalozzi to emphasize that education presupposes a medium of love. But perhaps one has not considered thoroughly enough what is meant by this. The medium of love indicates a climate, an atmosphere in which men live with one another. Personal love makes too great a demand on the whole man for it to be divided among any number of people. This is also true of love in education. In what follows, therefore we are only able to develop a theoretical ideal. Just as the picture of the true educator which we are projecting is primarily an ideal creation, so also love in education is described in its highest perfection. It can only be expected that each genuine educator should embody something of this ideal attitude. The general medium or the climate of affection is something far less extreme. That I should like the young may properly be demanded of me if I have chosen teaching as my profession. I will only become a true educator when at least a spark of that higher personal love, the heart of education, becomes alive in me. We should now describe this more exactly.

Every kind of personal love, although directed towards the whole man, has dominant and distinguishing characteristics. The love which is fundamental to education is one such specialized form. It is characteristic of it that it should attempt to develop its object. The first noteworthy consequence is that this is an affection which makes demands on its object. True love is on the whole unselfish. It demands nothing but hopes and also gives everything. This love is equally unselfish. It tries to help the beloved's development for his own sake. It thereby assumes that the form towards which he is expected to develop will enhance his worth and that thus he will grow worthy of love. This concern can only be justified on metaphysical grounds, viz. by the belief in the universal value of that which is here demanded. Where this belief is absent there can be no genuine educational relationship whatsoever. Mere official position is utterly inadequate. It can neither create a genuinely educational relationship nor can it achieve that deeper transmutation of the beloved's nature. Not merely official position, but a spiritual passion is needed to achieve this. It is this spiritual passion which I consider to be the heart of education.

Since the pupil cannot possess the qualities which the educator, half unnoticed, demands of him it must be for something else that the pupil is loved. This is a second characteristic of the type of affection peculiar to education. It is the potentialities of the growing man which are loved. In the light of affection these potentialities become visible for the first time. This affection makes it possible to perceive from the as yet undeveloped pupil what will subsequently be the spontaneous direction of his growth. The potentialities drawn out by the educator are in part such as are general to the intellectual make-up of man and the higher aspects of his nature, and in part such as can only be glimpsed in this unique individuality. "Thus you must be, for thus I understand you." The more he takes this individuality into account, the greater becomes the force of his love since he thinks he perceives something of genuine worth. His love is thereby open to greater risks. But there is no love without risk.

No education is thinkable that does not require exertion and achievement. Even the greatest of geniuses cannot achieve anything in contravention of the laws governing human life. On the contrary, genius consists in a sensing of the interconnection between eternal laws. It is the object of affection in education to prevent future disappointments. It must be stern today so that fate will not in the future overwhelm the unsuspecting. It makes demands and is prepared to accept the fact that the extent of the love underlying these demands will go unrecognized. Even very sincere teachers have now and then failed to understand this. An impartial observer has to judge consequently they could not have had the "true" affection. The third characteristic appertaining to it is the gentle leading towards the recognition of those laws, quite distinct from one another, to which all natural and intellectual life is subject. Only on this basis can "true" freedom grow. Genuine love aspires to make the beloved free.

The nature of the affection underlying education therefore leads to the creation of communities of a very special kind. Their shaping cannot be left to chance. Nor can they be so constituted that from the very beginning the highest possible degree of love can be awakened in response. Here the educator must make demands on his pupils. Caritas bent on other objects can in certain instances make many renunciations and sacrifices. There may be reasons which make this comprehensible. But the affectionate guidance of youth requires a consideration not only of the present but also of the future. Even if the teacher and his wards share common aims in cheerful friendship the laws involved in the relationship and the moral law remain valid. Affection cannot ignore these laws. Jesus, too, did not deny the law but wished to fulfil it, namely with the spirit of a free inner consent. In the last resort education also depends on the spirit. The whole educational art culminates in writing the behest "love your duties" into the hearts of the young, so that they will more and more perceive that these demands are made on them by love. The fourth characteristic of affection in education is therefore that love begets love. This is done by genuine devotion, not by negligent complaisance or careless "laissez faire."

If it happens that the pupil returns the affection of the teacher, then a wonderful power is awakened. The pupil perceives maturity and, divining its nature, grows with the perception. In this process, too, idealization occurs. The educator is not seen simply as a particular person with all his idiosyncracies and faults, but as an ideal. The nature of intellect is such that it is precisely the growing who possess the greatest power to idealize people. This ennoblement through an inner ideal is part of the mystery of the process of mental growth. An identification should only take place with real worth and not with all the accidentals to be found in the personality of the educator. Genuine love and not uncritical imitation must become active on the part of the maturing person. The psychology of the subconscious often overlooks the fact that a youth's drive to experiment in identifying himself with adults is not in itself specifically educational.

Thus a mutual development of the two personalities can occur. This relationship is one of the most beautiful possible in human life. It is not without reason that poets have celebrated it as much as the meeting of men and women in that love which leads to a union creative both physically and spiritually.

It is the natural result of the conditions of human life that affection in education is normally directed from the older towards the younger. Spiritual as it is, it is nevertheless based on the relationship between the generations. The young need the loving help of the older generation and the mature bear the responsibility of seeing that the young find the path into intellectual maturity which is the right one for them. The possibility of a genuine educative affection being directed towards someone older than oneself is by its very nature practically ruled out. Affection in education always stems from pleasure in young life. Something akin to the spiritual passion we have described can, however, occur between people of the same age. It is not uncommon for young people who are friends with one another to have the purpose of mutual development. This is even an essential characteristic of friendship based on intellectual affinity. Both commit themselves to striving for a common ideal which is envisaged by each in his own particular way. Nevertheless, however beautiful such a communion may be, it does not fall within the scope of this article.

Perhaps I should add that the affection we have described is compatible with the various types of education discussed in my book "Educational Perspectives" (Paedagogische Perspektiven, 4th edition, Heidelberg 1956 p. 93 ff.). I do not want to go over the same ground again in detail. It is an error to think that only the so-called free type of education is compatible with affection. Affection can also operate in authoritative (committed) types of education, for the committal to authority springs from a vision of a man as he ought to be. Just as it is more difficult to educate in freedom, since the essentially educational relationship may thereby easily be lost, so also the strict and authoritative type of education is not necessarily repressive. The old educational tradition in Germany, based as it is on religion, even prefers rigid forms, because it knows the future risks of human life and wants to guard against misguided action.

Here, however, it must be emphasized that one should not change impulsively from one method to the other. The true educator has a natural feeling for method. Either his affection permits freedom, in which case he must try to apply restraint, or he naturally inclines towards sternness, and then he must know the point where it becomes his duty to begin to allow freedom. Responsible freedom is the goal of man. He who only knows half of this truth has a mistaken idea of human nature, and is therefore not fitted to be an educator.

Many do not know that there can be a wrathful love, a love which pities, a love which waits in expectation, a love which may even be withdrawn for a time. But this love will always remain helpful and never reject; otherwise it would not be worthy of its name. If it is difficult to describe the right attitude for an educator, then it is very difficult indeed to apply this attitude in practice. Unlike other forms of love this affection cannot simply well up and stream out. It is necessarily bound up with thought and is indeed more painful than any other type of affection.

Theoretical analysis is made difficult by the fact that the affection which has been the centre of our discussion often occurs interwoven with other forms of love. It is precisely for this reason that we had first to consider it by itself. Now it should be possible to trace clearly that which is specifically educative in a parent's love for his children, and also what the necessary conditions are if a spiritual affection is to have a genuinely educative purpose. Thus it becomes apparent that the maintenance of waifs and strays as such is not necessarily educative. There must be something more than a concern for public welfare. Even a religious concern for the salvation of the soul must take a special turn if it is to become really capable of encouraging mental and spiritual growth. Naturally the earlier proposition, that all really deep and genuine love is ultimately rooted in religion, still stands.

On the other hand it has become clear that there is no point in using the social context to define that ideal type of human mentality which is centred in love. Such a definition places too exclusive an emphasis on the mere intercourse between men or on the forces moulding society. Personal love, of which the love found in education is distinguished as a particular species, arises from a metaphysical basis only weakly manifest in modern society. A "spiritual passion" is more than a social force.

For Pestalozzi the love felt for a poor waif child is the central type for the love specific to education. It cannot be doubted that in his case this love really grew from a spiritual root. We should not, however, pretend that such a spiritual passion burns in every school room where children are treated kindly. Genuinely educative love is a very high, and therefore a very rare, phenomenon. Certainly an educator should centre his work and being in such a consuming passion. But we do not mean to imply that everyone who is somewhat fond of children is already possessed of this spirit. Rather we are here describing an ideal which one should set before one's mind if one claims to educate. We mean this in the sense of the Bible when it says, "Not that I possess it already, rather I hunger after it that I may seize it." After all, there are no "born" educators, but one must gradually strive to meet the demands of this vocation.

There is another error to be avoided and we must warn against it before we close. Perhaps it is superfluous to stress this particular point. Love alone is not sufficient. All love needs, although in many different senses, some goal. If one were to believe that a sincere interest were sufficient to make youth "better," then this would be equivalent to having a sail but no ship and no wind. There would be no progress. One must be something before one can become an ideal for the pupil, one must have something in order to give, one must oneself have expended energy in order to be able to arouse energy. No illustration is needed to show what this means in practice. As I have already said, the capacity to educate is proportionate to the care one has taken to educate oneself. The true educator has an inner fulness of life which flows over and fertilizes his neighbour's field. He has an aspiring energy within him which carries others along with it. But these are only images for something real, something inexhaustible in its multiplicity. He who has not succeeded in achieving something with his own potentialities and environment, something able to stand firm in present day life, cannot hope to lend a helping hand to others. Nevertheless there is a mystery in this of which many are not aware. The genuine educator always feels a dissatisfaction within himself, a dissatisfaction especially within the ethical centre of his being. You have not achieved what you could and should have achieved, help this hopeful youth that he may succeed better. This must be your substitute for what you have tried to achieve in vain.

So we are once again before the deep wisdom of the Socratic and Platonic conception of education, to whose temple every educator must make his pilgrimage. He draws his strength from the resources of the ideal and from the painful awareness of humanity's need. In giving, he himself receives inner riches. But he never attains that moment in which he can say, "It is fulfilled." He is always on the way accompanied by enduring and silent hope.

THE AUTHORS

Martin Heidegger (1889–   ). The most distinguished German philosopher of contemporary times; leader of Existential Phenomenology; protégé of Edmund Husserl until he developed his own Phenomenological system; strongly influenced by Nietzsche in his early period; unproductive period of fifteen years prior to and during World War II; after the war his return to writing showed a new emphasis, and the concept "Being" took the place of the concept "Nothing"; refers to himself not as an Existentialist but as a "Denker" (Thinker). Born in Messkirch in Baden, Germany. Jesuit priest, studied Catholic theology at the University of Freiburg; studied natural science and philosophy, coming under the influence of Edmund Husserl; Ph.D., University of Freiburg (1914). Leader of Husserl's philosophy seminar (1918–1923); professor ordinarius, University of Marburg (1923–1928); succeeded Husserl as professor of philosophy, Freiburg (1928–1933); rector of the university, Freiburg (1933–1934); professor of philosophy, Freiburg (1934–1945); retirement, forbidden to teach by French occupying powers (1945–1949); semi-retired lecturer in philosophy (1949–   ). Major publications: *Die Lehre vom Urteil im Psychologismus* (1912); *Die Kategorien und Bedeutungslehre des Duns Scotus* (1914); *Being and Time* (1927); *Kant and the Problem of Metaphysics* (1929); *What Is Metaphysics?* (1930); *Vom Wesen Des Grundes* (1931); *Die Selbsthauptung der Deutschen Universität* (1933); *Vom Wesen der Wahrheit* (1943); *An Introduction to Metaphysics* (1953); *Aus der Erfahrung des Denkens* (1954); *Vorträge und Aufsätze* (1954); *What is Called Thinking* (1954); *Discourse on Thinking* (1959); *Die Frage nach dem Ding,* (1962).

Martin Buber (1878–1965). Philosopher of the Existential Dialogue; student of Wilhelm Dilthey (his bridge to Existential Philosophy); strongly influenced by Friedrich Nietzsche, Soren Kierkegaard, and Fyodor Dostoyevsky; philosophical emphasis on "the between" of things and persons rather than the individual; clarifies this relationship relative to teacher and pupil. Born in Vienna, Austria; youth spent in the home of his grandfather, a famous rabbinic scholar; educated at the universities of Vienna, Leipzig, Berlin, and Zurich; intensive study of the teachings of Hasidism; active in the Zionist movement, editorial director of Der Jude (1897–1923); professor of Jewish philosophy, University of Frankfurt (1923–1933); teacher in Jewish secondary schools, Germany (1933–1938); professor of social philosophy, Hebrew University, Jerusalem (1938–1951). Major publications: *Daniel: Dialogues on Realization* (1913); *Die Jüdische Bewegung, Gesammelte Aufsätze und Ansprachen* Vol. I & II (1916, 1921); *I and Thou* (1923); *Rede über das Erzieherische* (1926); *Moses* (1949); *Between Man and Man* (1947); *Dialogisches Leben: Gesammelte philosophische und pädagogische Schriften* (1947); *Das Problem des Menschen* (1948); *Two Types of Faith* (1951); *Good and Evil: Two Interpretations* (1953), *Pointing the Way* (1957).

Maurice Merleau-Ponty (1909–1961). Professor of pedagogy, psychology, and philosophy at the University of Paris; allied with the Existentialists but more precisely a phenomenologist with intellectual roots in the philosophy of Edmund Husserl; considered the study of the child and his psychology important for any philosophical attempt to understand individuality and inter-subjective existence; lectured to his classes on pedagogy at the Sorbonne, notes collected and published by his students. Born at Rochefort-sur-Mer, France. Graduated from Ecole Normale Supérieure, the most outstanding of France's "grandes écoles" (1927–1934). Teacher in French lycée, continuing studies in psychology and philosophy .(1934–1941); French resistance (1941–1943); founded and edited with Jean Paul Sartre *Les Temps modernes* (1945–1953); professor of philosophy, psychology, and pedagogy, Sorbonne, Collége de France (1949–1961); acceded to the chair of philosophy once held by Henri Bergson (1952–1961). Major publications: *The Structure of Behavior* (1942); *Phenomenology of Perception* (1945); *Sense and Non-Sense* (1948); *Langage et communication* (1948); *In Praise of Philosophy* (1953); *Signs* (1960); *The Primacy of Perception and Other Essays* (1964).

Friedrich Nietzsche (1844–1909). Philosopher of the transvaluation of values and the ideal human personality of physical strength and mental energy; sought to unmask hypocrisy and the emptiness of institutions; critical of the state and its schools because they are grounded in "the slave morality," aiming only for mediocrity and utility. Born Röcken, Germany. Educated at the universities of Bonn and Leipzig; influenced intellectually by Hellenism, Schopenhauer's philosophy, and personal correspondence with Richard Wagner (1864–1867); military service (1867–1868); Ph.D., without thesis or examination, University of Leipzig (1869); professor of classical philology, University of Basel (1869–1879); retirement and writing, various European health resorts (1879–1889); illness (1889–1909). Major publications: *The Birth of Tragedy out of the Spirit of Music* (1872); *Philosophy in the Tragic Age of Greece* (1876); *Human, All-Too-Human* (1878); *Thus Spake Zarathustra* (1885); *Beyond Good and Evil* (1886); *The Genealogy of Morals* (1887); *The Antichrist* (1888); *Twilight of the Idols* (1889); *Nietzsche Contra Wagner* (1889); *Ecce Homo* (1889); *The Will to Power* (1895); *The Future of Our Educational Institutions* (first published 1909).

Otto Friedrich Bollnow (1903–   ). Germany's most famous contemporary philosopher of education; voluminous writer on education and educational problems; attempts to relate education to German philosophy; leading representative of the Existential point of view in philosophy of education. Born Stettin, Germany. Educated at the Universities of Berlin, Greifswald, and Göttingen; Ph.D., University of Göttingen (1925); lecturer on philosophy and pedagogy, The Peagogical Institute of the University of Göttingen (1931–1939); professor of psychology and pedagogy, University of Giessen (1939–1946); professor of philosophy, psychology, and pedagogy, University of Mainz (1946–1953); professor of philosophy, psychology, and pedagogy, University of Tübingen (1953–   ). Major publications: *Wilhelm Dilthey: Einführung in seine Philosophie* (1936); *Das Wesen der Stimmungen* (1941); *Existenzphilosophie* (1943); *Einfache Sittlichkeit* (1947); *Rilke* (1951); *Die Pädagogik Der Deutschen Romantik* (1952); *Neue Geborgenheit: Das Problem einer Überwindung des Existenzialismus* (1955); *Die Lebensphilosophie* (1958); *Existenzphilosophie und Pädagogik* (1959); *Mass und Vermessenheit* *des Menschen* (1962); *Mensch und Raum* (1963); *Die Pädagogische Atmos-phäre* (1964); *Französischer Existentialismus* (1965); *Krise und neuer Anfang* (1966); *Sprache und Erziehung* (1966).

Eduard Franz Ernst Spranger (1882–1963). One of the famous personalities of German culture and educational life; six honorary doctor's degrees conferred upon him in Europe and Asia; emphasized in all his writings the dominant value of the individual, but the development of this theme can be traced through three distinct periods: (1) pre-World War I, preservation of tradition rooted in German Classicism, (2) Weimar Republic, psychological studies and the German educational and ethical-cultural system, and (3) post-World War II, German Existential Phenomenology; most famous for his psychological studies in the second period, but contributed greatly to the newer German philosophy as related to education. Born in Berlin, Germany. Educated at the University of Berlin in philosophy, history, and German studies; Ph.D., University of Berlin (1909). Lecturer in philosophy and pedagogy, University of Berlin (1909–1911); professor of philosophy and pedagogy, University of Leipzig (1912–1920); professor of philosophy and pedagogy, University of Berlin (1920–1945); professor of philosophy, Tübingen University (1945–1953); retirement (1953–1963). Awards: Pour le Mérite Order, Pestalozzi World Prize; Hanseatic Goethe Prize, Italian Cortina Prize. Major publications: *Wilhelm von Humboldt und die Humanitätsidee* (1909); *Wilhelm von Humboldt und die Reform des Bildungswesens* (1910); *Types of Men* (1921); *Psychologie des Jugendalters* (1924); *Der Bildungswert der Heimatkunde* (1923); *Pestalozzis Denkformen* (1947); *Die Magie der Seele* (1947); *Der Unbekannte Gott* (1951); *Zur Geschichte der Deutschen Volksschule* (1951); *Aus Friedrich Fröbels Gedankenwelt* (1951); *Pädagogische Perspektiven* (1951); *Kulturfragen der Gegenwart* (1953); *Der Eigengeist der Volksschule* (1955); *Der geborene Erzieher* (1957); *Das Gesetz der ungewollten Nebenwirkungen in der Erziehung* (1962); *Vom metaphysishen Leid* (1963).

Index

Index

Index